WHO'S WHO IN THE COSMIC ZOO?

AN END TIMES GUIDE TO ETs, ALIENS, GODS & ANGELS

BOOK FOUR

COVENANTS

Ella LeBain

COVENANTS

Book Four: An End Times Guide to ETs, Aliens, Gods & Angels

Copyright © 2018 Ella LeBain
All rights reserved.
ISBN-13: 9780692988633
ISBN-10: 0692988637

No part of this publication may be reproduced, stored in a retrieval system or transmitted in any way by any means, electronic, mechanical, photocopy, recording or otherwise without the prior permission of the author except as provided by USA copyright law.

Published by Skypath Books, LLC
3051 W. 105th Ave., #351961 | Westminster, Colorado 30035
USA 1.720.977.9110 | www.skypathbooks.com
Where the Sky Is the Limit!
"The Heavens Declare the Glory of God." (Psalm 19:1)

Book Design Copyright © 2018 Skypath Books,
All Rights Reserved.
Cover Art Illustration by Lori Garcia, www.TLCUnlimited.com
Editing Contributions by Colleen Vaughn Henderson

Published in the United States of America ISBN:
1. Social Sciences / Sociology of Religion
Religion / Ancient Mysteries/ Eschatology

CONTENTS

DEDICATION

This book is dedicated to the Lord of the Cosmos, the Creator of Heaven and Earth, without whose Loving Support, Grace, Guidance and Protection, this manuscript would not have been possible, for which I am eternally grateful.

In addition to, I am dedicating this book to all those wounded by religion, all those whose fire has gone cold, to all those who have left the church, been excommunicated, lost their tribes, agnostics and especially to those who consider themselves religious. May you all find something useful within the pages of this book to restore your soul back to its Creator.

ACKNOWLEDGEMENTS

My deepest gratitude goes to my loving and devoted husband and daughter, without whose love and support, this manuscript would not have been possible. They have stuck with me through all the spiritual battles and never stopped believing in my vision and goal. They are my true loves and soul mates whom I am blessed to be journeying with through this earth experience.

INTRODUCTION

Everything in the Universe is subject to change,
and everything is right on schedule.
~ Anonymous

One of the hallmarks of our history on planet earth is that, at one time or another, all races and tribes have been enslaved. From all the research we can conclude that this pattern arises from extraterrestrials and aliens who view the oppression and enslavement of humans as their natural right and privilege. Talk about entitlement mentality!

The promises of God illuminate this historical darkness of enslavement in one form or another, highlighted in the words of the Lord here, who states why He came to earth, and what His intentions are, to set captives free.

> "The Spirit of the Sovereign LORD is on me, because the LORD has anointed me to proclaim good news to the poor. He has sent me to bind up the brokenhearted, to proclaim freedom for the captives and release from darkness for the prisoners,"
>
> (Isaiah 61:1; Luke 4:18)

Disclosure and the Church

In the body of Christ, it is the sheep who hear and know His voice. (John 10:27) They will not be moved through fear but will receive a new anointing from the Spirit of the Lord to understand and discern this new movement of His Spirit in these last days.

Those who are fooled into following the religious spirit will have the hardest time accepting new information into their existing religious views. Many will fall away because of feeling betrayed by God, doubting their faith and not being able to reconcile how this expanded worldview can really be true. Others will use their fundamentalist mindset to create a new type of spiritual bigotry by insisting all aliens are demons, by closing their eyes to the fact that God made extraterrestrials to serve Him too.

While it may be true that all demons are aliens, not all aliens are demonic evil spirits. There's a difference between demons and evil spirits. While all demons inhabit evil spirits, demons are entities, not spirit. Demons are intelligent entities filled with evil spirits. There are entities alien to human life which are parasitic, using humans as hosts, slaves, or as genetic material to create hybrid bodies. They're soul-less beings looking to steal soul energy from humans, because God created us, not they, in His image.

Aliens are a different life form from humans, and not all aliens are filled with demonic entities. The four living creatures of Ezekiel and Revelation are not human, nor angelic, but are alien life forms that serve the Lord. This is the discernment that the church must incorporate into its teachings and theology to end this incessant fundamental dogma that creates fear and galactic bigotry.

The disclosure of the alien presence and extraterrestrial life here on earth need not shatter anyone's faith in the Creator God, on the contrary it should expand and strengthen it.

Jesus was clear that He had to go and bring together another sheep fold, so when He returns we can all be one-fold under One Shephard. (John 10:16) This is proof that He is the Savior and Kinsman-Redeemer of all human life, including extraterrestrial, intra-terrestrial, and interdimensional humans, who are also victims of Lucifer's rebellion and its subsequent curse in the universe. Why else would He promise to create a new heavens and earth? The present one has been infected by a curse and under a dark spell from the fallen angels, which has permeated and spread like a cancer.

The good news is that the fallen angels are outnumbered two to one, as only one third of Heaven's angels followed Lucifer in his rebellion whereas two thirds remained faithful to the Creator. The root cause of racism and antisemitism on earth comes from the genetic wars between aliens and the Elohim who are the ETs and sons of God.

It's not as important to understand our genetic roots as it is to accept the solution through Christ *who* breaks the power of the darkness over our DNA and has come to set the captives free. That would be us. We must remember we are all saved behind enemy lines, and we were bought with a price, which is the Divine Blood of Christ that has the power to break down strongholds, dissolve curses, heal brokenness, and transform lives. This is the supernatural Grace that is the foundation of faith in God.

The acceptance of others who are made differently than we, yet are human nonetheless, who are brought into unity through common faith in *who* Christ is and what He's done for us, is the key feature of our common unity. Aligning with Him heals the divisions, the misunderstandings that are rooted in racism and antisemitism. Racism and antisemitism are cancers in the body of Christ. It's the antithesis of the Great Commission which is to go out into the whole world and take the gospel of truth and good news of grace to all peoples of the earth, that *includes* the humans living *inside* the planet, ETs and aliens from other worlds.

> "He said to them, "Go into all the world and preach the gospel to all creation."
> (Mark 16:15)

My background as a researcher, paralegal, legal assistant to New York and Denver law firms of twenty-five years showed me the need for this book, *Covenants.* The idea of spirits and demons having the power to foul up our lives, make us hurt, attack our happiness on earth, is not foreign to us, but the fact that they stand upon legal ground to do so may be a real surprise. That we have recourse against them and their dirty tricks, curses, alien implants, and harmful side effects, is seldom even mentioned by churches or psychologists. How to apply that recourse, which is vital to our world and our lives now, is almost never explained to us.

As I pointed out in Books One and Two of my book series, that there is such a thing as *spiritual legal ground,* and too many people are confused between the Almighty God's authority and satan's authority, who is the god of this world. So much so, that many confuse the god of this world, who is satan, with the Lord of all Creation. Herein, we will continue to discern and unpack this human condition. This Series of *Guidebooks to ETs, Aliens, Gods and Angels,* began as one book, but has been divided into five. Therefore, I tend to think of it as one long discussion, that is compartmentalized. For those who have been following this book series, I connect the dots in Book Four to what you've previously read, to expound on the discussion, and for all those who haven't read the previous books, I provide you with the Chapters and page numbers in discussion within the Notes, for further study, which is for the purpose of coherence.

Further in this Book Four of *Who's Who in the Cosmic Zoo?* we will lance the boils of racism and anti-Semitism on our planet and address the root cause of our inability to live in peace and cooperation with each other. I expose the *alien agenda* for what it is, and how it all fits into the ancient End Times Prophecies written down over two and half thousand years ago.

A covenant (cov·e·nant, kəvənənt/noun) is an agreement, or contract, undertaken between two or more individuals, with each understanding the terms. We have forgotten some of the terms under which we covenant with our Creator while living on earth. This Earth is where Heaven and Hell meet, sandwiched between two kingdoms with clashing ideologies, the middle ground of an extraterrestrial and spiritual war. We can see evidence of this clash of two kingdoms through human behavior, thoughts, and spirits. It is our destiny to exercise our free will as to which kingdom we belong, which ideology we identify as our own: The Draconian Kingdom of Darkness and Enslavement, or the Kingdom of Heaven of Light, Love and Grace.

In making that decision, we first must investigate all the facts as they are, and not as we think they are, or how they have been presented to us in the past by others. Our own personal fate and that of the entire world is far too important to be made haphazardly or left to someone else, who may have very different ideas and aims than we do ourselves.

Many people suffer from depression, and hopelessness about the meaning of life. There are approximately 3 billion Christians in the world, and most of them have been put under a powerful spell through the Church of Rome's indoctrination, not to question anything. It's time to question everything and discern truth from lies within the Hebrew Scriptures. Too many people have suffered unnecessarily because of the denial of these truths.

The truths I am about to disclose to you, is a journey through history, ancient scriptures, exopolitics and whistleblowers, that will prove to you, that the roots of racism, prejudice, and social injustices began with aliens in an ancient battle of genetic warfare over humankind. I will also point you into the direction of the solution, a solution that is offered to all of humankind at this time, and is therefore, without prejudice, but is waiting for you to discover.

I invite you to continue with this journey of books, as I will make sure you will leave with more knowledge, deeper understanding and hopefully a renewed compassion for each other and the world we live in.

Let's get down to business with that now!

CHAPTER ONE

The End Times Disclosure of Alien Life

KNOWLEDGE EMPOWERS. Ignorance endangers.
(Hosea 4:6)

"There is nothing concealed that will not be revealed,
or hidden that will not be known."
(Matthew 10:46)

We are living in the Information Age! Apparent to almost overload, TMI, (Too Much Information) and the Age of Disclosure. There is a difference, though, between soft and hard disclosure.

Soft disclosure is like soft selling; it is all about innuendo and hint, *what-if* and *wouldn't- it-be-nice*? There may be mysterious leaks of information about alien presences to archaeologists, researchers, or linguists, which inspire media producers to focus on exopolitical themes. Hard disclosure, on the other hand, is an official recognition of what most of us already know. . . we're not alone.

Hard disclosure first occurred on May 11, 2004, when the Mexican Air Force released a film of 11 UFOs flying over Campeche, Mexico.[1] There has been a flurry of videos-no-longer-available and cover up since then, which some think for good reasons others find frustrating in the extreme. The Truth Movement sees the withholding of facts and information as a Truth Embargo. The conglomeration known as the Disclosure Movement, run by diverse groups, really want the truth, no matter how it tastes. There are others among us who only want a piece of it, and to use that piece to support a diabolical agenda, one that leads to the End Time Mass Deception. Their idea is to create the New World Order through alien technology, and a One World Religion to maintain control of the cosmos.

And lastly, there are the aliens themselves, who are split down the middle about Disclosure, yet most lean towards continuing as they have been all along, operating incognito, keeping their movements concealed, and more importantly protecting their motives, intentions and manipulations of humankind.

The issues of national security, public safety, and advanced exotic technology are pivotal points of the restraint of information on hard disclosure, yet it is inevitable.

There are as many opinions amongst national leaders regarding disclosure as there are amongst the aliens themselves! Some ETs shy toward secrecy, as disclosure doesn't serve their best interests, while others, for e.g., the human ETs that live inside the Earth, who are at war with draconian forces, want disclosure to humans, because they need our help. Some people see our planet and its population for what it is, a prize for competing aliens and intraterrestrials. This is a cosmic dilemma for those who know, and whose jobs are to protect the security and national interests of the world.

Soft disclosure began in the mid-1970s, when a cabal of secret societies, the Illuminati, ET-Alien-Human Alliance, began to test public reaction to contact with alien life, by deliberately and intentionally giving facts about spacecraft, extraterrestrials, and aliens to the entertainment industry. We see evidence of this as Steven Spielberg worked with the world's leading Ufologist, Jacques Valle` on *Close Encounters of the Third Kind.*[2] Spielberg also made *ET,*[3] a title word which was changed from the original *EBE*, whose appearance was based on one of the actual aliens retrieved from one of the many UFO crashes. EBE stands for Extraterrestrial Biological Entity, in this case a short grey with big black buggy eyes. Spielberg made EBE look human by giving him big human blue eyes and cute enough to hide among the children's cuddly stuff toys.

Close Encounters of the Third Kind is an epic compilation of many true stories of abduction, contact, and government collusion, presented as science fantasy. The Truth is indeed Stranger than Fiction!

All of this, and more, is part of the process of preparing the public for the news that we already know, that we are not alone, that we in fact have never been alone, and that our government has long had evidence of extraterrestrial and alien life. Disclosure is such old news, the Sumerians talked about it in cuneiform! There are some who point to Harry Truman as the first US President to have had to deal with an exopolitical situation, that was passed on to President Dwight Eisenhower, who then in turn passed that baton to President John F. Kennedy, who allegedly wanted disclosure, but was assassinated before he had the chance.

As Americans, as human beings, we hold so many diverse opinions about how and why the world should be run. This same gulf separates those who have been dealing with the alien presence for decades. We must carefully sound this gulf, through spiritual discernment of the motivations of all involved, and how they coincidentally fit into the End Times Prophesies Timeline laid out in the ancient Scriptures, if we are going to navigate the cosmos successfully.

Racism and Aliens

According to the Oxford Dictionary, "the definition of *racism,* in English: 1. Prejudice, discrimination, or antagonism directed against someone of a different race based on the belief that one's own race is superior. 2. The belief that all members of each race possess characteristics, abilities, or qualities specific to that race, especially to distinguish it as inferior or superior to another race or races."

Racism, however, is not the disagreement of political ideologies, which many today, who happen to disagree with a political group, nation, or religious belief, have in the past decade or so, begun to call that *racism.* However, irrational hatred of any racial group, for the sake of *who* they are, not what they believe, or where they live, is *racism.*

Racism is the number one social problem on Planet Earth, which seems to span the annals of time. What are the spiritual root causes for what has become a systemic problem? Could it be something more than a spirit of hate that fans the fires of racist thoughtforms? In this book, I'm going to prove through multiple historical timelines, that earth's racism is rooted in a cosmic and genetic war between competing extraterrestrial-alien gods.

Let's move forward in this discernment by adding that Anti-Semitism is racism too, in fact one of the first and foremost instances of it in history found in the ancient scriptures, that includes racial bigotry, racial hatred, and racial jealousy in all its forms!

There is a difference between the Jewish race and the Jewish religion. Anyone can convert to a religion, but the Jewish race, is within the DNA, passed down through the bloodlines, it's tribal. Arabs are a race of Semitic peoples originating from the Middle East, along with Jews. However, in the past century, the word, *Anti-Semitism* has been associated predominately with hatred of the Jewish peoples.

Arabs can be both Muslim, Christian, Zoroastrian, Buddhist, New Ager and Atheist. To be against any of these religious beliefs, is not racism. There are both black and white Arabs. To malign Arabs for their skin color or racial characteristics, is *racism.* To hate anyone based on their skin color, or external characteristics is racial bigotry. This is an important discernment, because many today have perverted the meaning of the word, *racism.* It has unfortunately, become a politically charged word, that gets thrown at people who disagree politically. Disagreeing with a nation's policies is not racist. Nationalism is not necessarily racism, it may be seen as tribalism, but as the history of planet earth proves, nations are typically made up of multiple races. For e.g., the United States of America is made up of just about every race of peoples on planet Earth. Yet, American are a nation of peoples, not a race.

Islam is a political ideology run by a theocracy based on Sharia Law, which is a lifestyle that includes religious beliefs. People who follow Islam are called Muslims.

Muslims can come from any race. There are both white Caucasians who become Muslim, black Africans, Asians, Indians, Arabs, who may follow Islam. People who disagree with the political ideologies of Islam are not racist, because Islam is a not a race, it's a totalitarian, patriarchal, expansionist political system masked as a religion.

Regardless of whether it's the political policies or religious beliefs, again, to disagree with any aspect of Islam, is not by definition, racism. The word, Islam comes from the Arabic root, 'salema' meaning submission. The basic tenet of Islam is that all non-Muslims must submit to Muslims, and all women must submit to men. Again, this is not about race, but about the implantation of totalitarian, political and religious beliefs.

In Book Two, *Who is God?* we discerned the history of the gods and their religions. Herein, we are going to discern the historical roots of racism based on the competing implantations from ETs, Aliens, gods and Angels, and what are the remedies and solutions for healing racism on Earth. As we move forward through this Age of Disclosure, a lot of information from the past is surfacing, that may alter the way people view their respective traditional religions. The word, *apocalypse,* is Greek for Revelation. We are in the age of Knowledge and Revelation, causing an awakening on planet Earth. For some, it will be the light that heals, for others, the light will expose and destroy centuries of lies. Either way, it's a time that calls for courage. The courage to face truths about our history, no matter how uncomfortable that may feel at first. For, the Truth will eventually set us free.

NOTES:

1. Lloyd Vries, Mexican A.F. Pilots Film UFOs, https://www.cbsnews.com/news/mexican-af-pilots-film-ufos/, May 12, 2004
2. Stephen Spielberg, Director - Screenplay, *Close Encounters of the Third Kind,* 1977
3. Stephen Spielberg, Director, Melissa Mathison, Screenplay, *ET,* 1982.

CHAPTER TWO

How Disclosure of ETs Impacts Religion

"I saw that the woman was drunk with the blood of God's holy
people, the blood of those who bore testimony to Jesus.
When I saw her, I was greatly astonished. Then the angel said to me:
"Why are you astonished? I will explain to you the mystery of the
woman and of the beast she rides, which has the seven heads and ten
horns. The beast, which you saw, once was, now is not, and yet *will
come up out of the Abyss* and go to its destruction. The inhabitants
of the earth whose names have not been written in the book of life
from the creation of the world will be astonished when they see the
beast, because it *once was, now is not, and yet will come.*
"This calls for a mind with wisdom.
The seven heads are seven hills on which the woman sits."
(Revelation 17:6-9)

Revelation 17 is the prophecy of the last days of the End Times that points to the Whore of Babylon, which the Church of Rome adopted, and became none other than the Roman Catholic Church, also known as the Sovereign State of Vatican City, a city that sits on the seven hills of Rome, Italy, and is a government within the nation of Italy, that answers to no one but itself. It even has its own bank and police force. The prophetic words, specifically tell of a beast who emerges out of the Abyss, which is located *inside* the Earth.

The word, *Vatican,* literally means, "Divining Serpent." It is derived from the Latin words, *Vatis,* which means "Diviner" and *Can,* meaning "Serpent." Vatican City and St. Peter's Basilica were built on the ancient pagan site, known in Latin, *vaticanus mons,* or *vaticanus collis,* which means a hill or mountain of prophecy. This ancient religion of the Roman Empire, was a form of dark magic, that worshipped the Serpent, who is Lucifer/Satan, the Reptilian Alien Beast inside the earth. All those priests, bishops, pastors, and church leaders that promulgate it, are warlocks and wizards casting spells on church goers. The Religious Spirit is the Counterfeit Spirit, that holds millions hostage, in bondage to alien agendas.

The agenda of the coming antichrist is to foster the idea of unity, that we are one united, on one planet, a One World worldview, with a religion that is inclusive, assuring us that we are all the same. It sounds so exalted, innocent, and human!

A document in book form espousing this view, extoling the virtues of unity, will be presented to the world, which must challenge the traditional religious ethos. The long-expected antichrist may be compared to a composited reincarnation of Apollo, Osiris, and Nimrod. He will be someone of power, persuasion, substance, who can unite all the world's religious views and traditions into one. Such a task is humanly impossible, given the enormous differences between various religious beliefs and the people who hold them!

In the Christian faith alone, are hundreds of denominations, along with non-denominational churches, with a fair share of cults, all of whom despise all others and reject any notion of union or of compromise. In fact, the rifts between some churches are so deep as to be called gulfs, unbridgeable and irreparable, which only God the Messiah can heal. The Antichrist, who is the counterfeit messiah, manages to pull it all together for a very short time due to supernatural help.

According to End Times Prophesies, the Lord of Heaven and Earth, lets him attempt this, as a social experiment to see who His true believers are, and who are not in the end, will follow the Anti-Messiah i.e., Antichrist. Due to the divisions and strife within the Church, the Anti-Messiah definitely gets a foothold on unity because, so many have been wounded by Church division, ex-communications and persecutions over their petty differences, giving spiritual legal ground over to the antichrist. However, only one quarter of the world, end up following him, the rest war against him or are succumbed by him.[1]

In Genesis 11:6 we see that God knows very well that a united humanity will find nothing impossible. He had to confuse our languages back in the day to keep earth humans from storming heaven with the Tower of Babel which many believe was a city that was built as an airport base with a space tower that supported space travel into the heavens. However, in the succeeding verses, v.7, it implies that the Lord was not acting alone, but in plurality with other gods, who were opposed to humans having the ability to penetrate space in the heavens. So, they, the plurality who are the Elohim, chose to confound their language, which was one at the time, into many, and scatter them all throughout the earth, which created differences. The Lord Yahuah, did not object, and this act of ET intervention, according to Genesis 11, appears that they most definitely acted together in plurality.

We can draw a great deal of insight from this intervention, and we may conclude that the divisions and disharmony amongst men, even amongst the most devout of Christians, is a brokenness born of our separation from Him, which nothing but

Christ can heal. The One who can truly satisfy the human heart is the One who made it. While what unites us is far greater than what divides us, that being Christ Jesus, in Whom we are all one body, the mission here is one of kindness and charity, not building towers or ruling the world by force. It is the real Messiah who will unite the body of both Jews, Gentiles and Extraterrestrials under the auspices of His Heavenly Kingdom coming to Earth! *The Truth is Stranger than Fiction*!

Cognitive dissonance is a psychological term that describes a mental state reacting to new information that does not fit into old models. The alien presence is such a phenomenon that provokes cognitive dissonance. People have literally made up their minds before even learning of the evidence.

Modern Christians, who are university educated and secularly minded, tend to think that they already know everything there is to know, and measure their faith by absolutes. Once saved, always saved; all aliens are demonic fallen angels; conversely, charismatics and New Agers believe all aliens are benevolent space brothers here to help us. We all know that even the hard evidence of photos, videos, physical signs and evidence, are phenomenon that simply doesn't fit into our reality.

If, however, we start from the premise that its reality, which is a given, here's where we need to go next.

Let's examine the words of Jesus, about the *spirit* of unbelief which blinds, deafens and mutes the *spirit,* (Mark 9:24,25; Matthew 12:22; Luke 11:14; Zechariah 3:2; Isaiah 35:5,6). The *spirit* of unbelief is not limited to a belief in God or Jesus, but is the very spirit that operates in cover-ups of all kinds. This includes the veneer of sophistication cast over countless Christians, Jews, and Muslims, that Satan is just some made up mythological being which represents the combined shadow of humanity, fear and terror and paranoia. Not so at all! It is exactly the Satan who causes the shadow, the fear and the sorrow, not the other way around! It is his modus operandi to work behind the scenes, in the darkness, with the cockroaches, to confuse us so much so, that we don't see his influence behind our own personal problems, or the problems of this world. If the boogie man isn't real, then people can all just relax and stop imagining things. But the truth of the matter is that he is real, very real, and people who have been told that the devil is just an excuse are operating under his influence!

The spirit of unbelief causes spiritual blindness, deafness and even a muteness. The physical symptoms which correspond to this spiritual condition include attention deficit disorders, especially in adults, Epstein-Barr, chronic fatigue, tinnitus, deafness, blindness, and muteness. When these demon spirits are finally rebuked and cast out of people, they literally came back to life, woke up, hear, see, and speak. The spirit of unbelief, the Bible says, is rooted in haughtiness and pride.

It is true that many aliens are in fact demonic entities that use humans like cattle. The Bible also reveals that the aliens are outnumbered two to one, that the Lord of Hosts commands legions upon legions of extraterrestrial mighty warrior angels. These are not fluffy light beings, but warrior beings that serve the Kingdom of Heaven. This is the liberating truth, gained through discernment, that I am teaching in my book series.

As a Messianic Jew, I will share freely the knowledge passed down to me by my ancestors, though that body of knowledge was dissected, altered almost beyond recognition by the Church of Rome. The Church and its satellites are frequently the oppressors of the truth, the facts, and of the Jewish People and Israel itself. It is for this very reason that many Jews today reject Jesus is the Messiah out of hand, because Jesus is so misrepresented by people who use Him to oppress others. This is not just limited to Jews, but to scientists, and to true believers. I have seen the light, both spiritually and scripturally, that Yeshua Jesus is indeed the Jewish Messiah as prophesied by the Old Testament, who came in the flesh and was resurrected. The spirit of unbelief has blinded the eyes of those who read scripture from seeing this. Only the Holy Spirit can reveal the truth behind scriptures. I share these truths in my book series.

It is a great joy that many Jews are waking up to the fact that Yeshua Jesus is the Messiah, which is the fulfillment of end times Bible prophesies. I am a remnant and a witness to that fact. Just as many Gentiles are completing the times of the Gentiles, as the Lord promised in Luke 21:24, the number of Messianic Jews has grown in the world and in Israel. We have been living in these End Times since He ascended again into heaven. The mass deception that Matthew 24:24 predicted is to come upon us all, and sadly the Church has not prepared us for it, because it is not prepared itself through lack of knowledge and discernment.

The Religious Spirit

When the Jews reject Yeshua it has, unfortunately given *spiritual legal ground* to the enemy to inhabit them. The enemy is not just a spirit but entities that rule this world, who are lizard beings, aka the Serpent Race. That's why Jews are often attacked as being serpents. This is like when Christians reject the Holy Spirit, they end up with the occupancy of the Religious Spirit instead of the indwelling Holy Spirit. In the Spiritual Realms, the Religious Spirit wars against the Holy Spirit. It's a counterfeit spirit. This was played out, when the High Priests, the Jewish Sanhedrin and Pharisees, conspired to crucify Christ, because they were threatened by His Supernatural Power, to resurrect the dead, heal the sick and diseased and cast demons out of people.

It was the Religious Spirit, which was expressed as the Spiritual Pride, and Jealousy of Yeshua's Power, along with Fear of losing their authority and position of power in the temple, that created the conditions that lead to His Death. But they failed, because Death had no power of Him. He rose again out of His Grave three days later and walked the planet for an additional forty days, before He ascended into a *cloud*, which took Him into Heaven. The same *cloudship* He will return in, according to the Angels (ETs) who were there to witness this and help the disciples transition into this new era. See, Acts 1:9.

The disastrous combination of ignorance and arrogance of humanity lies in the spirit of religion. From the Gospel of Thomas, v102 Jesus said, "Damn the Pharisees! They are like a dog sleeping in the cattle manger: the dog neither eats nor [lets] the cattle eat."

Jesus said in Matthew, "Woe to you, scribes and Pharisees, hypocrites! For you are like whitewashed tombs which on the outside appear beautiful, but inside they are full of dead men's bones and all uncleanness." (Matthew 23:27-28 - NASB)

The Religious Spirit- Contains - Confines - Complains - Criticizes - Controls - Compromises – Condemns. However, the work of the Spiritual Path in Christ is to Break it off! To be liberated from its limitations and bondages by breaking free through entering into Sonship with Poppa God through Christ. The very experience of becoming into 'right relationship' with the Lord Almighty, transforms your spirit which effects every other part of your life. Jesus overcame the Religious Spirit, and therefore so can you, because for those who have invited Christ into their hearts, this spiritual legal ground truth holds true: "Greater is he who lives within me, than he who lives in the world." (1 John 4:4)

The Religious Spirit is a particularly malicious demon that creates discord and strife inside the church. It partners with Leviathan, a python-like spirit, the presence of which squeezes the life force out of Christians through strife, misunderstandings and confusion, the twisting of words. The religious spirit is a lying spirit, the one illuminated by the Church Thyatira, which often points fingers of accusation at those who are actually speaking and teaching Truth. Think of Jezebel in relation to Elijah in 1 Kings, whose tactics are like those of Saul Alinsky, to discredit the truth speaker while preventing her own evil works from being exposed. Some call this narcissistic projection. Jezebel represents all the false prophets, so numerous in our world, which is a mass of confusion, cover-ups and a rejection of truth, facts and knowledge.

Half-Truths are Still Lies

For example, most Christians just don't believe in aliens; others do believe in such beings, but think that the aliens are all demons or display demonic tricks. They don't believe there are any good aliens.

There is some truth to some statements made by the Accuser, however, *half-truths are still lies*. The truth of the matter is that the Church of Rome has covered up a great deal of history and distorted our notions of reality since it took upon itself the power to edit and canonize the Bible in 325 A.D. Christians who think, Constantine was acting on behalf of the Holy Spirit, must read Constantine's Creed, which was blatantly, antichrist, anti-Semitic and anti the God of Israel, who is Yahuah.

One really needs to question, 'why?'

Claiming all aliens are demons is not true, and not the fruit of discernment. It is the continuation of ignorance. Looking at the evidence and comparing it to Scripture develops discernment. You can't discern the counterfeit from the truth unless you first know the original very well. Unfortunately, the Church of Rome has been in sole and total possession of the knowledge and means necessary for discernment, and for whatever reason, has kept it all to themselves, to the point of forbidding us to even read the Word for ourselves. The Roman Catholic Church has been instrumental in keeping us all under the spell of aliens, demons, power hungry humans, via the conclaves, councils, and creeds. The Roman Catholic Church will use its power to activate its own End Time agenda, to be the final authority of god on earth. The question that should be on all our lips is, "which god?" In Book Two, *Who is God?* I spend over 560 pages describing the different gods and that of the God of gods, and how to discern between them.[2]

This is a subject multi-layered and multi-faceted, which requires not just intellectual and spiritual discernment but the courage to face the truth and the backbone to accept it.

Jesus said, "I have not given you a spirit of fear, but of power, love and sound mind." (2Timothy 1:7)

In 2015, NASA's Astrobiology Program gave a $1.108 million grant to the Center for Theological Inquiry, because they wanted to know how the *disclosure* of alien of extraterrestrial life could impact Christianity. As a UFO investigator and ET/Alien researcher, an experiencer of the supernatural, and an avid Facebooker, I can tell you that this project is not going very well. We can all discern this for free, without a million-dollar donation. There is a religious belief that has spread like a contagion among tech-savvy Christians that there are indeed aliens, but they are all demons.[3]

Announcing the NASA grant, CTI's director William Storrar said, "The aim of this inquiry is to foster theology's dialogue with astrobiology on its societal implications, enriched by the contribution of scholars in the humanities and social sciences. We are grateful to the NASA Astrobiology Program for making this pioneering conversation possible."

The decision to donate over a million dollars to a religious group to see what they thought about extraterrestrial life was controversial to say the least. *The Freedom from Religion Foundation* wants NASA to revoke the grant, but NASA gave no answer to their contacts.

Most Christians struggle with the idea that aliens and extraterrestrials are frequently mentioned in the Bible scriptures, even as ancient history. My books prove these references to be factual and authentic, with hundreds of scriptures from the Jewish scriptures corroborating these historical facts, most of which were covered up and some outright rejected from the Bible Canon by the Church of Rome. The church may have had the best of intentions at the time, but our society has grown up, and it's time for this Truth to be told. We need the Church to reveal the knowledge that can save us from the mass deception, by expanding our understanding of the Creator God whom we all serve.

The reason NASA had to create a study that was funded by a grant is that the Establishment Clause of the First Amendment prohibits any 'sponsorship, financial support, and active involvement of the sovereign in religious activity.' FFRF Staff Attorney Andrew Seidel writes to NASA officials that "Specifically, the government may not fund religious projects, as various courts have ruled over the years."[4]

Scientists and secularists opposed this endeavor, seeing it as a waste of time and misuse of taxpayer dollars. They stated that it was inappropriate for NASA to fund this religious study, because religion deals in matters of faith, not fact, and faith-based arguments inevitably boil down to arguments that cannot be settled by appeal to empirical evidence. Secondly, history shows that religion does one of two things when presented with scientific discovery: denial, or incorporation of the fact as "evidence" or "proof."

The John Templeton Foundation, known for funding projects that promote an overlap between religion and science (much to the indignation of many high-profile atheists) is co-sponsoring this project. They feel that if the Templeton Foundation wishes to fund religious research, it can use its $3 billion to do so, whereas, the U.S. government may not. The scientists and atheists feel this project is a colossal waste of money for an organization that's already underfunded. It's much harder to make that case that NASA needs a greater slice of our federal budget when it's spending that money on something that wouldn't advance our knowledge in any meaningful way. Therefore, we can all conclude that cognitive dissonance works not just in religious people, but also in the scientific communities.

Scientists just can't see the connection between God and science. As I've presented as my first thesis in Book One of *Who's Who in The Cosmic Zoo,* science is the very *mind* of God. Many scientists who are capable of faith understand this connection, just as all the scientists of the Renaissance Era relied on their faith in God for the solutions to their experiments.[5] Albert Einstein, arguably one of the best scientific minds of our time, held an agnostic belief. He was raised Jewish, attended Catholic schools, and was fascinated by the presence of Jesus of Nazareth. He never espoused a particular religion but was far from an atheist. Deeply intuitive and by nature a spiritual man, he relied on an inner faith that he was not alone in the universe.

The character of the world today is such that scientists are not encouraged to make such connections, to keep science and God as separate, sometimes contradictory, subjects. Einstein didn't think so, so why should they? After all, he will always be remembered for his theory of relativity which can be taken both ways, not just in the mathematical sense of physics, but also between the realms of spirit and science. It's all relative to the original point, that science is the mind of God. The more science discovers, the closer we come to the Creator.

There is a very good reason why NASA is funding such a controversial study, which may have to do with official disclosure. The government wishes to know which churches will stay intact during the apocalypse and which churches will fall apart through cognitive dissonance.

Contrary to what most Christians have been taught, the *apocalypse* is not the end of the world, but is the Greek word for *unveiling,* or, *Revelation.* The final book of the Bible is the book of Revelation, which includes information on the End of Days. Much of it is written in a cryptic language that can identify aliens as being in the spotlight during the last days of this Age. I have discerned their identity throughout this book series. Book One is an A-Z Compendium on *who* they are, *where* they come from, and *who* they were in the ancient scriptures.

"There's nothing new under the sun."
~ King Solomon (Ecclesiastes 1:9)

I strongly suggest that Christians read our Word from a different perspective. There is no excuse in 2018 not to look up the true meanings of the Hebrew words. These words reveal a whole dimension of gods, aliens, angels and extraterrestrials, in vivid color and character. And, knowing the difference between singularity and plurality gives insight and discernment of the Word, when the Lord is acting on His own, or there is the intervention of his Council of gods, the Elohim. These beings have been there in black and white in our Books all the time, but simply covered up and lost in poor translations. This new *revelation* will help Christians to discern the real meaning of the End Times apocalypse. This long-lost light will awaken us to *who* these beings are and were in ancient times, as well as explaining the *alien presence* on Planet Earth.

A great place to start would be *Who's Who in The Cosmic Zoo?* which was written to illuminate both Christians, Jews, New Agers, atheists, and all those in denial about this very real dilemma.

Grace is not a teaching, it's a person named Jesus Christ.
The law condemns the best of us, but Grace saves the worst of us.

Freedom

There is nothing more precious than our freedom. Some people say that love is the noblest emotion, and while this is true, we know that love must be freely given to be of any value. There are so many people who have become wounded and bitter, who can no longer give or receive love. Christ heals that very issue, if you allow Him, as His whole life was spent loving us to the point of setting us free.

The whole reason for the Messiah's life and death was to redeem the human race from the captivity and enslavement to alien masters who have usurped this earth and turned it into a prison planet. Is it any wonder that people live in hell on earth?

All the miracle technologies being *discovered* today, like antigravity, acoustic levitation, time travel and teleportation, were written about as having existed and used extensively in antiquity. The cycle has come full circle, and ancient tech is being redeveloped again. Reverse engineering crashed crafts are only part of the story.

There have been over 100 documented cases of people being born with tails, and scaly skin like a reptile. Our story takes on a tinge of the sinister.

"A man must be big enough to admit his mistakes,
smart enough to profit from them, and strong enough to correct them."
~ John C. Maxwell

"Do not correct a fool, or he will hate you;
correct a wise man, and he will love you."
(Proverbs 9:8)

Notes:

1. Joel Richardson, *Mideast Beast* (New York: WND Books, 2012). p. 39
2. Ella LeBain, *Who is God?* Book Two, Skypath Books, 2015.
3. http://ancientufo.org/2016/06/nasa-granted-1-1million-study-alien-life-impact-christianity/
4. http://helenastales.weebly.com/blogue/why-did-nasa-issue-a-11million-grant-to-study-how-alien-life-could-impact-christianity
5. Ella LeBain, *Who's Who in The Cosmic Zoo?* Book One, *A Spiritual Guide to ETs, Aliens, Gods and Angels,* Tate. 2013, http://www.whoswhointhecosmic-zoo.com

CHAPTER THREE

How Prepared are the World's Religions for ET?

"Two possibilities exist: either we are alone in the Universe or we are not.
Both are equally terrifying."
~ Arthur C. Clarke

World renowned physicist Albert Einstein was asked his opinion about the possibility of extraterrestrial life in the universe. His response was, "Other beings, perhaps, but not men," he answered. Then he was asked whether science and religion conflict. "Not really, though it depends, of course, on your religious views."

Hinduism records literally millions of gods from outer space, who fought wars over the earth in flying cities called *Vimanas* and used nuclear weapons over and upon earth. These accounts are found in the Vedic Scriptures of the *Mahabharata, Upanishads, The Bhagavad Gita, the Vedas,* and other Hindu texts. So many New Age and Christian cults are saturated with Eastern thought and viewpoint that we need real discernment here as to how these groups are going to differentiate between a counterfeit alien savior and the real thing.

David Weintraub, the Professor of Astronomy and Physics within Vanderbilt University in his 2014 book, *Religions and Extraterrestrial Life – How Will We Deal With It,*[1] goes into detail well worth researching. He predicts our reaction to the scientific discovery of life on other worlds based on our religious beliefs, as did Einstein. Weintraub said, "When I did a library search, I found only half a dozen books and they were all written about the question of extraterrestrial life and Christianity, and mostly about Roman Catholicism, so I decided to take a broader look."

His book documents the viewpoints of multiple religious leaders and theologians and what they think about extraterrestrial life, spanning more than two dozen major religious sects. He stated that some of the Asian religions already have this concept of extraterrestrial life built into their belief systems through their scriptures, while others will need an adjustment when full disclosure occurs.

Contrary to popular belief, the Judeo-Christian faith does in fact have ETs and aliens embedded within their scriptures, and this is graphically illustrated in Book Two: *Who Is God?* wherein I prove that the historical interventions of extraterrestrial life have always been there, but were lost in the various translations. I proved this all through revealing the original Hebrew meanings of the words that the long history of ET and aliens exist within the books of the Bible, including the New Testament. This brings us back full circle to the End Times Prophesies, and how these are being fulfilled, which doesn't only *include* the mass deception of the alien presence on Earth, but points to a final battle between ETs, aliens, gods, and angels.[2]

The Discovery of Life on Exoplanets

In the past two decades both professional and amateur astronomers have made remarkable progress in discovering hundreds of exoplanets, some within close proximity to our solar system, as well as some intersecting our solar system. (Please see my Chapters on Nibiru/Nemesis in Book Three, *Who Are the Angels?* [3] and Book Five, *The Heavens*). That number has grown to more than 1,000. By 2045, there could be more than one million exoplanets identified in our local universe.

> "If even one exoplanet shows signs of biological activity – and those signs should not be hard to detect, if living things are present – then we will know Earth is not the only place in the universe where life exists," Weintraub[1] points out. "Although it is impossible to prove a negative, if we have not found any signs of life after a million exoplanets have been studied, then we will know that life in the universe is, at best, exceedingly rare." [sic]

Here is what is widely circulated about the Nibiru system: it belongs to a solar system of six independent objects; its sun, Nemesis, is a brown dwarf star, also known as our sun's evil twin, because of a dark reddish-brown color that is causing sunrise and sunsets to have pink and red tints. It is also referred to as the dark star or black sun. Then there are planets Helion, Arboda, and the two moons, Harrington and Ferrada, and Nibiru which has four moons in orbit. Nibiru itself will not hit the earth but its passing will cause major earth changes. One of its comets, which the book of Revelation calls *Wormwood*, will hit the earth, causing a third of the waters to go bitter. The word *Wormwood* means bitterness. This is part of God's judgment, the Bowls of Wrath in the last days as predicted in Revelation.

Because of its sheer mass, the presence of the giant planet careening through our solar system produces profound changes on every planet and moon including our sun. Our earth will be substantially affected by Nibiru's presence. It is the cause of climate change on earth, as it is attracting coronal mass ejection in its direction, which in turn cause seismic activity, tidal waves and monster storms. Earth is currently in the midst of a pole shift, which will be completed after the passing of Nibiru. Nibiru is expected to pass earth twice, once on its way towards our Sun, with its second passing, expected to be the worse for earth, as it will pick up speed from being catapulted around the sun, causing the earth's axis and poles to turn upside down again.

We are told by the prophet Isaiah to expect a pole shift during God's judgment on the Earth that precedes the return of the Lord.

> "Behold, the LORD makes the earth empty, and makes it waste, ***and turns it upside down,*** and scatters abroad the inhabitants thereof. . . .The land shall be utterly emptied, and utterly spoiled: for the LORD hath spoken this word. The earth mourns and fades away, the world languishes and fades away, the haughty people of the earth do languish. The earth also is defiled under the inhabitants thereof; because they have transgressed the laws, changed the ordinance, broken the everlasting covenant. Therefore, hath the curse devoured the earth, and they that dwell therein are desolate: therefore, the inhabitants of the earth are burned, and few men left."
>
> (Isaiah 24:1, 3-6)

These signs in the heavens are from the LORD and from Him alone, regardless of how they are interpreted or what causes them to occur. They are ordered by the Creator, who created all things, both visible, and invisible.

This is why the LORD promises to recreate the Heavens and the Earth, because the cyclical order of these two systems intersect and collide with one another every 3,600 years, wreaking havoc on earth and our solar system.

> "See, I will create new heavens and a new earth. The former things will not be remembered, nor will they come to mind." (Isaiah 65:17)

> "Then I saw a new heaven and a new earth, for the first heaven and earth had passed away, and the sea was no more." (Revelation 21:1)

> "What has been is what will be again, and what has been done is what will be done again, and there is nothing new under the sun."
> (Ecclesiastes 1:9)

We must be ready for lifeforms that come with the presence of these exoplanets intersecting with our solar system. We are not alone here, as our ancient history, biblical scriptures, stone tablets and architectural relics point repeatedly to the fact that other life forms have visited us before, and have promised to visit again. The promised return of the gods comes from the prophesies left behind from their last visit, which was approximately 3,600 years ago. They are returning for a Divine Appointment, to harvest their seed on earth.

Weintraub reported that public opinion polling indicated close to one third of Americans believe extraterrestrials exist. However, American beliefs vary considerably due to religious affiliation.[4]

Belief in extraterrestrials varies by religion:

- 55 percent of Atheists
- 44 percent of Muslims
- 37 percent of Jews
- 36 percent of Hindus
- 32 percent of Christians

Of the Christians, more than one third of the Eastern Orthodox faithful (41 percent), Roman Catholics (37 percent), Methodists (37 percent), and Lutherans (35 percent) professed belief in extraterrestrial life. Only the Baptists (29 percent) fell below the one-third threshold.

Weintraub concluded that the Asian religions would likely accept the discovery of extraterrestrial life much easier than the Judeo-Christian religions. Some Hindus speculate that humans may have reincarnated on earth as aliens, and vice versa, in addition to the Buddhist cosmology, that includes thousands of inhabited worlds.

While Weintraub quotes passages in the Quran that he thinks appears to support the idea of spiritual beings on other planets, he does mention that these beings may not practice Islam as it is practiced on Earth. "Islam, like other faiths, has fundamentalist and conservative traditions. All Muslims, however, likely would agree that the prophetically revealed religion of Islam is a set of practices designed only for humans on earth." [sic]

Despite the fact, that the religion of Islam was founded on the belief that their beloved prophet and warrior Mohammed was visited by the alleged angel Gavril, who I proposed in Book Three: *Who Are the Angels?* [3] is an extraterrestrial that came to earth to counterfeit the Judeo-Christian Archangels. This fallen angel Gavril did not bear witness to the sovereignty of the savior Yeshua Jesus, but influenced Mohammed to compete with the Judeo-Christian faiths through warfare.

It's also important to note that Mohammed allegedly ascended into heaven through a cloud. Book Two: *Who is God?*[2] has a rather extensive chapter detailing all the cloud-ships mentioned in the Jewish Bible. As the Quran is essentially a twisted and distorted copy of the both the Old and New Testaments, we can expect the occasional similarity.

With respect to the existence of extraterrestrial life in Judaic scriptures or rabbinical writings, Weintraub concluded that there are few Talmudic and Kabbalistic commentaries that assert that as space is infinite, containing immeasurable worlds, the existence of extraterrestrial intelligence cannot be denied. He also added that Jews generally think that the discovery or disclosure of extraterrestrial life would certainly affect them and alter the foundation of their religion.

As I've said multiple times in this book series, most Jews do not actually know, let alone understand their own scriptures, as they depend on their Rabbis to read it and interpret it for them. Likewise, most Catholics don't read the bible, and depend on their Priests and Popes to read and interpret it for them, as finally, in similitude, most Muslims do not read or understand their Quran, but depend on their Imams, Mullahs and Muftis to interpret it to them.

Therefore, it's understandable that most religious people are in the dark about ETs and aliens validated by their own bibles. By not reading The Word for ourselves, we miss the fact that much of the ancient texts are mangled, the true meanings having been lost in translations and drowned out in various theologies. It's no wonder that Christians and Muslims would have the hardest time accepting ET, let alone discerning between good and evil extraterrestrials and aliens.

The Christian Debate on ETs and Aliens

As I've been trying to present for 38 years, there is a real need for the ancient knowledge to re-emerge regarding the basic truths and teachings of ETs and aliens within the tenets of Christianity, which after all is *grafted into* the *Covenants* of the Judaic Tree and its scriptures. This is the whole reason I put my heart and soul into this five-book series. The truth must be told!

In Book Two: *Who is God?* I catalog hundreds of scriptures, in both Testaments and in the many rejected Jewish texts, which prove that there are both good and evil in every manifestation of intelligence: in aliens, in extra-terrestrials, gods, and angels. My second great commission is to teach *discernment* between the two, as this book series is a Spiritual Guide to ETs, aliens, gods and angels. It's not limited to *spiritual* discernment either, as I've reiterated in *Who is God? discernment* includes learning how to *discern* the Word of God properly, fully, and correctly, despite the many layers of translations, pronunciations, and linguistical complexities of the original Hebrew and Aramaic languages.[2] In this realm, the *Truth* lies within the details.

Weintraub concluded that within the Christian fold, only the Roman Catholics have seriously pondered the possibility of life on other worlds. In fact, the Roman Catholic Church has had theological debates on extraterrestrial and alien life that have gone on for a thousand years. To the Catholic mind, the crux of the matter is original sin. The struggle is with the question that if intelligent aliens are not descended from Adam and Eve, do they suffer from original sin? Do they need to be saved? If they do, then did Christ visit them and was He crucified and resurrected on other planets? He summarizes, "From a Roman Catholic perspective, if sentient extraterrestrials exist, some but perhaps not all such species may suffer original sin and will require redemption."

In fact, the Vatican owns two of the world's most sophisticated telescopes, named LUCIFER. One is situated in the Vatican Observatory and the other in the middle of the Arizona desert. The Vatican Astronomers and Research Scientific Staff, Br. Guy Consolmagno and Fr. Paul Mueller, are two Jesuit Priests who co-authored, *Would You Baptize an Extraterrestrial? and Other Questions from the Astronomers' In-box at the Vatican Observatory.* In it they discuss the interconnectedness between science and faith and how the Catholic Church intends on dealing with ET. They plan on baptizing them and leading them to Christ.[5]

When asked by Guy Consolmagno, Vatican Astronomer, "Would *you* baptize an extraterrestrial?" Paul Mueller, the Jesuit astronomer, replied, "First, some disclaimers. When I'm representing and acting on behalf of the Catholic Church, in my role as a priest, it's not up to me to decide who can or cannot be baptized. It's up to the Church to decide that. So, my first and simplest answer to your question would be this: I'll be ready and willing to baptize an extraterrestrial if and when the Church decides it's OK to do so."[6]

"Well, one thing you notice is this: The religious believer tends to say that the existence of extraterrestrials would support their religious faith, and the nonbelievers tend to say just the opposite – that the existence of extraterrestrials would invalidate religious faith. So, both believers and non-believers tend to see the existence of ET as supporting their respective positions!

"Nineteenth-century believers such as the German theologian Joseph Pohle or the English astronomer John Herschel argued that because God is so overabundant in His creativity, He must have filled the universe with intelligent beings, not just us. On the other hand, Thomas Paine (the guy who wrote *Common Sense* and *The Age of Reason* during the American Revolutionary War) mocked Christianity for insisting that either, of all the worlds in the universe, God chose to be incarnated only in ours just because "one man and one woman had eaten an apple"; or else that "the person who is irreverently called the Son of God . . . would have nothing else to do that to travel from world to world, in an endless succession of death, with scarcely a momentary interval of life."

"In other words, there's nothing on this topic that has been suggested in recent times that hasn't already been discussed, ad nauseam, for hundreds of years. There's nothing new about wondering about aliens and how they fit into our religion. After all, we've been telling stories about alien races and nonhuman creatures since storytelling began. Just look at all the monsters in the *Odyssey* and other Greek legends!

"Even the Bible talks about nonhuman intelligent beings. Besides the angels, there's that odd passage at the beginning of Genesis, chapter 6, that refers to some creatures called the Nephilim and describes these "sons of God" taking human wives. And the Psalms and the books of the prophets are full of references to the "holy ones," those "in the sky," the "morning stars . . . and heavenly beings" who sing praise to their Creator.

"Back when we were talking about the Big Bang and reviewing ancient cosmologies, we described all those "planetary intelligences" and "daemons" that the ancients assumed existed in the spaces between the planets. That was the worldview of the people who wrote the Bible; they were perfectly happy accepting the existence of other intelligent beings besides humans."[7] [sic]

Disturbingly, they go on to discuss at length that many people are hungry for ET contact, wanting to believe that ETs exists, as the ETs must be a race of beings more advanced than us, who could lead us through our problems, guide us into the future, even *save* us. The two priests discussed how people want a savior, and how they will look to aliens to be that savior.

A facet of insight is shared by Guy, about the sci-fi movie, *The Day the Earth Stood Still,* when the alien comes to Earth to help humankind called himself, "Mr. Carpenter," in case the parallel isn't obvious enough.

The conclusion to this conversation is that "before we talk about whether or not to baptize ET, we need to acknowledge that history. Baptism can be offered as a gift, but it should never be imposed by force or done under pressure. That goes for the Jews, Muslims, Hindus, Native Americans, and others who have been confronted with forced baptism in the past. And that goes for any ETs we may encounter in the future." [8]

Weintraub found that diversity amongst Protestant denominations, where individuals are encouraged to interpret scripture independently, leads to many conflicting approaches to the question of extraterrestrial intelligence. Weintraub focused on the views of Lutheran Theologian Paul Tillich, who argued that God must be everywhere, therefore the need for salvation is universal and the saving power of God must be everywhere. At the same time, he also maintained the viewpoint that God's plan for human life is not necessarily the same as his plan for the aliens. [9]

As I concluded in Book One of *Who's Who in the Cosmic Zoo?*, the transforming power of indwelling Holy Spirit through Jesus Christ, that literally saves lives, minds, bodies, relationships, and of course souls, is being observed by a group of Watchers, extraterrestrial researchers, tracking our progress and taking back data to their own planets. I also state that the Lord of Heaven and Earth is in fact the Cosmic Christ, whose story was written into the very stars and constellations long before there were scriptures on Earth. His plan of Salvation extends out to all the Universe, and that includes life on other worlds, planets, star systems, and galaxies. Proof of this is found in the very words of Jesus Christ Himself in the scripture, as Jesus told His disciples in John 10:16, "And I have other sheep that are not of this fold. I must bring them also, and they will listen to my voice. So, there will be one flock, one shepherd."[10]

Some theologians have surmised this, to refer to the Gentiles, but I say that the Gentiles are just other people, human, and earthly. They would not be described as 'not of this fold', which suggests a whole different genetic make-up.

In Book Five, *The Heavens*, I draw out all the star pictures, and clarify the very names of the stars themselves, which illustrate a Divine Plan of Salvation that was written first into the starry hosts before writing was invented on Earth. This proves that there is a Cosmic Christ who brings all of creation under His sovereign reign, that His Kingdom of Heaven is universal in every sense of the word.

Fundamental and Evangelical Christians, Weintraub concluded, are most likely to have the hardest time accepting the discovery and disclosure of extraterrestrial life. The very word, *funda-mental* implies a type of mind bent inward on itself, that the *mentalism* is based on dogma rather than truth. This indicates a bondage to *religious spirits* that are against the Holy Spirit, *Who* is the giver and revealer of all Truths. The Holy Spirit witnesses to the Word of God, and if the Word of God is not read properly, or translated correctly and thereby misinterpreted, then funda-*mentalism* could take hold, due to ignorance and misunderstanding. This can become a spiritual stronghold of the *religious spirit,* that blinds, deafens and mutes the Christian into believing a lie, and denying the Truth.

The astronomer's research indicated "...most evangelical and fundamentalist Christian leaders argue quite forcefully that the Bible makes clear that extraterrestrial life does not exist. From this perspective, the only living, God-worshipping beings in the entire universe are humans, created by God, who live on Earth." Southern Baptist evangelist Billy Graham was a prominent exception who stated that he firmly believes "there are intelligent beings like us far away in space who worship God."[5] [sic]

In addition, Professor Weintraub identified two religions – Mormonism and Seventh-day Adventism – whose very theology embraces extraterrestrials. In Mormonism, God helps exalt lesser souls, so they can achieve immortality and live as gods on other worlds. Mormons believe that if they are faithful on Earth, they will get their own planet in the next life to rule over. Ellen White, who co-founded Seventh-Day Adventism, wrote that God had given her a view of other worlds where the people are "noble, majestic and lovely" because they live in strict obedience to God's commandments, suggesting that other worlds believe in God and Jesus too.[4]

Weintraub concludes, "While some of us claim to be ready, a great many of us probably are not… very few among us have spent much time thinking hard about what actual knowledge about extraterrestrial life, whether viruses or single-celled creatures or bipeds piloting intergalactic spaceships, might mean for our personal beliefs [and] our relationships with the divine." [11]

Religious Leaders and Disclosure of Extraterrestrial Life

It seems ironic that disclosure of extraterrestrial contact would come through religious leaders and not government officials. We live in such extraordinary times, and the unexpected is becoming norm.

Allegedly, Pope Francis was contacted by a Nordic extraterrestrial from inside the earth, who then reached out to the Dalai Lama, suggesting a panel of religious leaders unite in faiths and common-unity, to be friends with each other and work towards merging all the earth religions into one inter-faith. This concept is nothing new, as there are many New Age Churches on the rise in the past several decades that consider themselves inter-faith churches, where they accept all faiths, all religions as One, and believe that despite their differences, they all worship one God.

For those who have read Book Two in this series, *Who is God?* I proved that this is not the case at all. The major religions do not, in fact, worship the same god. This is the spiritual and scriptural discernment I expound, proving just *who* these gods were in ancient history, and how two of the main religions, the Judeo-Christian and the Muslim, absolutely do not worship the same god. I prove through linguistics and history that these two gods are actually ancient enemies, and cannot, nor have they ever been, 'One'.

In addition, other religions have over a hundred gods in their pantheon. The pagans, Hindus, New Agers, are not even monotheists, making it impossible for them to agree on, much less worship one god.

The main mission of the Antichrist, who will rule the New World Order through a One World Religion, will attempt to unite the religious leaders of the world. Herewith, I present real documented evidence that steps toward establishing a One World Religion have already begun, and not just through a group of religious world leaders getting together and agreeing to be friends and support each other despite their differences. More importantly, through the interventions and contact through Nordic Human Extraterrestrials from *inside* the earth, contacting the Pope and the Dalai Lama to gain their support of said ET's world agenda to unite under one religion, the religion of the final antichrist, the Counterfeit Messiah.

Pope Francis received the 2016 Charlemagne prize, an award only given to those who help to create unity in the world. Interestingly, this prize is named after the first world ruler of the Roman Empire, who was given complete political and religious authority by Pope Leo III who crowned Charlemagne on Christmas day, 800 A.D. Pope Francis said himself that he is only going to serve as Pope for a few years, and then he will relocate.

Coincidentally, a Nostradamus prophecy that appears to point to Pope Francis states he will "change territory" when a second sun appears in the sky. That second sun is the Nemesis-Nibiru system that is being photographed all around the world during sunrises and sunsets, and is seen more clearly in the southern hemisphere. It's unclear if Nostradamus was referring to the appearance of Planet X or Nibiru, but his prophecy is ominous for the Pope. Similarly, according to the St. Malachy prophecies, there is reference to the 'Pope of the double sun'.

It's no secret that Pope Francis' mission is to unify the world under one religion. Since he was elected Pope he has worked aggressively towards influencing the world toward the religion of the Antichrist, a one world religion. He's gone so far as to say outlandish, heretical statements deny the authority and Lordship of Jesus Christ, while promoting Luciferianism.

His published work *The Joy of Love* reiterates that his mission is for the world to accept a common religion, which he calls love. Though he does not change church doctrine, he does dismiss the authority of God's Word in exchange for what he calls the 'freedom of conscience', a Protestant view. This blasphemous and dangerous document proves just how far down the rabbit hole Pope Francis has taken Roman Catholics to brush aside the authority of the Word of God in both the Old and New Testaments and the sovereignty of the Lord. He is most definitely one of the false prophets that have emerged to prepare the world for the Antichrist religion.

I remember growing up in New York City in the 1960s and 70s, and there was a common phrase we would use to prove something true or false. When someone would doubt our story about something, we would say, 'Is the Pope Catholic? Is the sky blue?' Well, the sky is still blue, but this Pope is no longer Catholic. In fact, Pope Francis is the first Jesuit Priest ever to become Pope.

Some popular threads on the net point to Pope Francis as the last pope, the fabled Peter the Roman. However, Pope Francis himself, in his own words, reveals this is not the case, as there is another that comes after him, for whom he is preparing the way. Presently he is being accused of protecting the ring that traffics human children to be used as child prostitutes for the elite and other pedophiles.

An alarming, almost prophetic work is the novel called *Lord of the World.* This is a fictitious story about a character named Father Francis, who leaves the Roman Catholic Church to join the new world religion of the Antichrist. Father Francis leads a procession of worship to the antichrist who is a U.S. Senator named Julian Felsenburgh, a very Jewish name. As my readers may remember, that I wrote in Book Two that the Antichrist was going to be a Jew, not a Muslim. At the end of the second part of *Lord of the World,* Rome is destroyed, and the new pontiff relocates to Nazareth.

Lord of the World was written in 1907, by a Catholic Monsignor, Robert Hugh Benson, chillingly stands up to the test of time in its presentation of ideas about the future. This novel truly falls into the category of *The Truth is Stranger than Fiction,* because it accurately predicts a future world that includes legalized euthanasia, one-party states, and weapons of mass destruction.[13]

Lord of the World is prophetic on multiple levels, as Benson envisions affluence leading to apathy, atheism and a loss of faith by many Catholics. Set in England with occasional forays to Rome and Jerusalem, Monsignor Benson focuses his attention solely on Catholic Christians. This was necessary for flow, also to illustrate the variety of responses amongst Catholics, who can be seen representing all believers in Jesus Christ. There were those tried by adversity who immediately fell away; those who like the seed among the rocks and thorns, died from lack of root; and finally, those who persisted, grew stronger because of struggle. The point being, that the Grace of God and response to that Grace determined if a soul remains committed. Theological training and denominational affiliation were not at issue. There were, however, many apostate priests.

I include the mention of *Lord of the World* because of its prophetic significance, with respect to its illustration of the Antichrist and his rise during the End Times and how he was preceded by a Catholic Priest, named Father Francis who sought out to unify the world through one religion, the religion of the Antichrist.

In January of 2016, Pope Francis published a commercial for his one world religion agenda, titled, *The Pope Video -Inter-Religious Dialogue,* which can be found on the Pope's YouTube channel and on his One World Religion website.[14]

This is what he said translated from Italian to English, and what he put together as his prayer to be disseminated around the world:

> "Most of the planets' inhabitants declare themselves believers. This should lead to dialogue among religions." Richen Kandro, a Buddhist Lama said, "I have confidence in Buddha." Daniel Goldman, a Jewish Rabbi said, "I believe in God." Guillermo Marco`, a Catholic Priest said, "I believe in Jesus Christ." Omar Abboud, an Islamic leader said, "I believe in God, Allah." Then Pope Francis says, "Many think differently, feel differently, seeking God or meeting God in different ways. In this crowd, in this range of religious, there is only one certainty we have for all: We are all children of God." [sic]

Then they all say individually, one at a time, "I believe in love." It ends with the Pope's final remarks, "I hope you will spread my prayer request this month, that sincere dialogue among men and women of different faiths may produce the fruits of peace and justice. I have confidence in your prayers." [sic]

Ironically, despite the Pope's words to enter into an inter-faith dialogue, all comments were disabled on his Pope Video Channel. At least he's consistent with his hypocrisy.

On June 14, 2017, at The Hague in the Netherlands, Pope Francis joined the Dalai Lama and other global religious leaders in a joint interfaith statement promoting friendship and unity between different faiths with the hopes that it will foster understanding and ease tensions around the world.

This 3-minute video, posted all over the internet, available in 16 languages on their own 'Make Friends' YouTube channel, include religious leaders from Christian, Muslim, Jewish and multiple other faiths, joined the leadership of Pope Francis and Dalai Lama, in their appeal for friendship amidst diversity in the most religious countries.

The press release stated:

> Each of the leaders contributed a personal statement for the exclusive purpose of creating this joint appeal. Ayatollah Al-Milani advises people to make friends with followers of all religions. Patriarch Bartholomew calls on the world to "recognize the beauty of God in every living human being". Pope Francis and Rabbi Abraham Skorka demonstrate how their religious experiences have been enriched by their interfaith friendship. Grand Mufti of Egypt Shawki Allam stresses not to focus on differences between religious groups. The Dalai Lama calls for a deepening of spiritual friendship. Rabbi Jonathan Sacks says "One of the wonderful things about spending time with people completely unlike you is that you discover how much you have in common. The same fears, hopes and concerns." Archbishop of the Church of Sweden Antje Jackelén stresses the importance for society: "This should start a process that will take prejudices away and where new insights and hope is born." The Archbishop of Canterbury adds that "It's not complicated, start with sharing what we all share, which is the pleasure of conversation."

The Dalai Lama said, "we can exchange a deeper level of experience" through personal contacts and friendships.

Rabbi Dr. Alon Goshen-Gottstein, director of the Elijah Interfaith Institute who helped organize the joint statement, called the appeal "a significant novelty from a theological perspective."

The Archbishop of Canterbury Justin Welby said in a video message that "friendships across faiths are the key to beginning to work out how we deal with difference. We don't deal with differences by pretending it doesn't exist. We deal with it by building relationships."

In the video, Muslim cleric Ayatollah Sayyid Fadhel Al-Milani said: "Our advice is to make friends to followers of all religions," while Pope Francis and Rabbi Abraham Skorka say that their religious experiences have been enriched by friends from other faiths.

"We cannot deny that in the books of many religions you can find texts that are not very open, even hostile, to people of other faiths," he said. "Therefore, when the world's most important leaders call for friendship, they are in fact affirming a particular way of practicing religion and rejecting another."[14]

Coincidentally, the joint statement at The Hague, seemed to emerge around the same time as rumors were circulating that the Pope was involved in a secret initiative with two other religious leaders to disclose the existence of human looking extraterrestrials.[15]

Dr. Michael Salla, the pioneer of Exopolitics, has been the messenger of the reports and claims of Secret Space Program insider and MILAB whistleblower, Corey Goode. Goode claims he receives briefings from multiple reliable sources, including a representative ET from the Inner Earth's Civilization, named, Ka Aree, that the Pope and two other religious leaders were planning to appear together publicly alongside a human looking Nordic extraterrestrial. At the time of the publication of this manuscript (2018) to date, this has not happened yet.[15]

Goode was told that Ka Aree gave him two versions of how open contact with extraterrestrials will happen:

1. Three religious leaders come out and introduce an angelic ET race who bring us a book and a new "esoteric/New Age" type religion based on "Oneness".
2. was almost the same except it was only the Pope standing next to a Nordic announcing the same thing.

Dr. Salla concluded that if Goode's information is accurate, it will be the religious community which officially announces the existence of extraterrestrial life. Salla believes that the result would cause national governments to quickly release any information they wanted to publicly disclose about their relations with the visitors. Knowing how tightly these secrets are held by my own government, I find this scenario doubtful, at best, because the military industrialized complex is hierarchical in nature, with the Navy at the helm of the Secret Space

Program, which was exposed as being called, *Solar Warden*, by UK hacker Gary McKinnon. *Solar Warden* is a deep space fleet of space ships similar to *Star Trek* and *Star Wars*.

The contact between extraterrestrials and aliens with our government goes far and deep, at least seventy years of legal agreements between our several government agencies and groups of aliens from the inner earth. As our government still denies the very existence of Area 51, we can expect little in the way of disclosure, as it would open up a can of worms. In the interest of National Security, this simply would not be allowed to happen. Even in the event of a space-based war, our government would have to disclose only that we see weather balloons and the moon in the sky, as the whole story would be covered up to protect their own self-interests and secrets. This rabbit hole runs very deep inside the earth.[15]

Even a rumor of disclosure is enough to be manipulated into another religion, as a covert agenda to mentally, spiritually and even physically control the masses through fear, uncertainty, panic, secret technologies and implants. See, my chapter on *Implants and Spiritual Limitation Devices.*

Salla believes there is an opportunity for the US government to disclose its historic association with whom he calls 'visitors', which he claims was found in a leaked 1989 Defense Intelligence Agency document. This document's authenticity is disputed, though much of it may be factually accurate. Therefore, Salla wrote in his October 8, 2017 Article on Exopolitics.org, that there is good reason to believe that the Vatican and the DIA are covertly cooperating in preparing the public for disclosure of the friendly human-looking extraterrestrial visitors.[15]

Back in the 1990s, there were documents released from various whistleblowers through a series of books titled the Matrix, penned by an ex defense contractor, under the pseudonym, Valdemar Valerian, who was identified as John Gray. In it, he published documents released by CIA agents proving that the CIA and the Vatican were in fact in bed together for decades working on a joint covert project called, *Operation Holy See.*[16] [See, Matrix III]

Therefore, I would have to substantiate by connecting the dots to what Salla reported that the Vatican and the DIA are working together as well, as something credible and plausible.

While Goode did not disclose *who* the other two religious leaders were in the planned disclosure initiative, Salla postulates that one was the Dalai Lama, due to a 2013 lecture during which he strongly hinted that he would play a prominent role in such an announcement.[17] On May 9, 2013, at the University of Portland, Oregon, the Dalai Lama spoke on "Universal Responsibility and the Inner Environment" he made the following comment:

> Eventually, if we receive some visitor from another galaxy come, Look: same human being. Maybe a little different sort of shapes, but basically the same. Furthermore [it is the] same sentient being. Respect them. Look at them. It's the same sentient being. We can immediately shake hands[s] if they have some sort of similar hand there, then we can shake hand[s]. If we put too much emphasis [on] "We are human being[s] on this planet", then someone from the outside comes, a stranger. Always watch for [?]. That creates anxiety, more fear.

Salla discerned that the Dalai Lama's emphasis on "sameness" or "oneness" was significant as it revealed the role he would play in shaping world opinion on visiting extraterrestrial life.[17]

The only problem I have with calling the ETs *visitors*, is, as I've stated in Book One of *Who's Who in the Cosmic Zoo?*[18] that this is deceptive, because 90% of ETs and aliens are not visiting at all, but are living with us, inside the earth! Before we can get to 'yes' with ET, we need to understand what exactly has been going on inside our planet, and the important role it plays in the fulfillment and revelation of End Times Prophecy. Specifically, the awakening of sleeping giants, and the emergence of imprisoned fallen angels to the surface of the earth. Those are fallen extraterrestrials held captive inside the earth since the last galactic war between the angels. Angels are all extraterrestrials, and the fallen ones, who fell out of heaven, lost their first estate, which was their original position in God's Celestial Armies. This ties into the widely prophesied End Time space war called, Armageddon, which takes place over the ancient space portal of Jerusalem, Israel.

Salla goes on to say that if the scenario described to Goode by the inner earth representative is accurate, then the Pope, alongside the Dalai Lama, and a third religious leader who Salla hypothesizes to be a prominent Muslim leader such as Shawki Allam, the Grand Mufti of Egypt (who also participated in the *Make Friends with Unity* and Friendship statement), could be the threesome, to very well disclose to the world the existence of human looking extraterrestrial life.

The fact that they are calling three religious leaders of different faiths to deliver disclosure should make everyone's hair stand on end. The agenda here being played is to get the world to accept not only a one world religion, and all I have to say, is good luck with that one, but more importantly, to lay the foundation for the world to accept the Antichrist, who is also going to be known as the alien savior.

I understand how much people want to know the truth about ETs and aliens, and how so many people have risked so much, put their careers on the line, to investigate and research extraterrestrials, the alien presence, and UFOs. However, but after all these years, will we really just swallow their spin, hook line and sinker? What about science? Do you think the atheists, the secularists and the scientific community will just come right along, no questions asked? I think not! As if what this world needs right now is another alien religion? But, from the viewpoint of End Times Bible Prophesies, that's exactly how things will go down.

Let me just reiterate that according to Bible Prophesy only twenty-five percent of the world will in the end whole-heartedly follow the Antichrist. The other seventy-five percent becomes part of the resistance, and victim to his horrific torment inflicted on both Jews and Christians during the Great Tribulation. Contrary to popular belief, and the New World Order Agenda, the antichrist does not get the *whole world in his hands*, since the last three and a half years of his reign erupts in warfare.

This is what will begin the real *war of the worlds*, which is why disclosure of alien life has been kept secret for all these years. We humans can't get along and tolerate our own differences, so how blind do these religious leaders have to be? Until humans are transformed by God Himself, we're also not going to get along with the ETs or the aliens either. The only edge they have on us is advanced technology, which has been traded with our governments in exchange for permission to take genetic samples taken from abductees all these years.

And here's the open secret; the aliens who have been doing the abductions, collecting biological materials from humans are using it to create a hybrid race of human-aliens that will *replace* earth humans in the future. This is the plan revealed to abductees, who are now called *experiencers*, because dare we tell the truth about being victimized by aliens. However, I am telling you the truth here, that this is not what they want you to think. Cover-ups need to be unmasked, not glossed over, to get to the truth, and the fact that they are planning on using three different religious leaders to tell the world about ETs and aliens, wreaks of ulterior motives and deep state political agendas. Let the reader beware.

Salla reported on the motivations of the human looking (Nordic) extraterrestrial visitors, who plan to make an announcement to the religious community, and what Goode had to say in response to many questions Salla asked him regarding his information on them, on June 26, 2017. Goode's inner Earth Nordic Human representative, Ka Aree stated:[17]

> "that the Nordics have worked with Humanity for a very long time. They have mostly worked quietly in the background, but do pop up in historical documents referenced as "Angels". They would directly interact with certain groups within the Military and Government (including the founding fathers of the United States) as well as with various religious leaders. They have been heavily involved in developing Humanity in a number of ways." [sic]

Salla concluded that the June 2017 statement on friendship and unity across religious diversity, along with the Dalai Lama's 2013 comments on respect and friendship for aliens, would be extended to visiting extraterrestrial life.[17]

Again, words matter here, and I want my readers to connect the dots with the fact that these beings live inside the earth. We essentially share our planet with them. So how can we accurately call them, *visitors*? They may be aliens to us, they may even be extraterrestrials who originated from another place in the cosmos, but if they live inside our planet, and according to Goode, have been working with humanity throughout our known history, then they are no longer visitors, who perhaps have overstayed their welcome.

There are cover-ups within cover-ups going on here, with some whistle-blowers being actual agents of disinformation. Some act the double game unaware of what they are doing, as they are implanted, skewed and influenced by a prior belief. We must keep this in mind while researching.

In an article written by Dr. Michael Salla, on June 22, 2017, titled, *World Religions Unite as Prelude to Extraterrestrial Disclosure,* he reported that there are four [extraterrestrial] groups who would no longer abide by the M [Muhammad] Accords, but instead begin a gradual process of contacting people via dreams. A Nordic looking group is said to be leading this effort.[17] Let the reader beware, the Nordic ETs, the Blonds, the Aryans, were also the ones who contacted Hitler, and shared their technology with him. They claim to be in competition with the Dracos, the Reptilian Lizard-like Group, also residents of *inner earth.*

It should be noted that the Muhammed Accords do not directly relate to the prophet Muhammed, but were reached during the period when Islam was first established by him. Corey Goode described the Muhammad Accords as an extraterrestrial treaty negotiated around the seventh century A.D., whereby all alien groups agreed to stop openly revealing themselves to humanity and to only work in the background to secretly influence global elites.

Salla concludes that Goode was reporting that four groups of inner earth ETs were committed to having open contact with surface dwellers, and claim to have started the process to make it a reality. He claims further that world religious leaders have already been contacted as intermediaries to introduce humanity to the extraterrestrials, and in particular, the Nordic race.[17]

When we examine the real history of WWII as a war between science and magic, we realize that the contacts between Hitler and his supermen, his master race, we end up with exactly the same race of human ETs, the Nordic race of blond, blue eyed, white skinned proto humans who dwell inside the earth. Are you connecting the dots here yet?

When Salla asked Goode about the motives of the Nordic race leading this initiative, he said that the extraterrestrials inside the earth see themselves as Brothers and Sisters of the Confederation of Planets, an alliance of mainly human-looking extraterrestrials with whom inner-Earth civilizations closely work according to the Law of One book series.[17] In Book One of *Who's Who in the Cosmic Zoo?* I included a two-page chart of all the ETs and alien races that have been in contact with terrestrial humans to date, and included in the middle of the chart, the category of the Alliance Confederation, of which was given to me intuitively in 1998, that included the following races of ETs/Aliens:[19]

- Reptilian Humanoids from Capella that iridescent, luminous;
- Large Lizard-like beings who now want peace;
- Blonds, Nordics, from Nibiru, Janos;
- Beings from Orion, Aldebaran; Pleiades; Sirius, Arcturus; Sol System; Cassiopeans; Zeta Reticuli; Human Zeta Hybrids: "Essassanis" and Ashtarians (Fallen Angels);
- Red-Haired human; possibly clones (Eva-Borgs);
- Genetically altered, Red-haired Human-Reptilian Hybrids w/soul matrix.[19]

Salla remarks on how meaningful it is that the Vatican has been playing a leading role by encouraging its church to begin to view extraterrestrials as potential brothers in Christ.[17] We have the two Jesuit astronomers Consolmagno and Mueller, who have an ongoing discussion on how to handle ETs, as well as the marketing campaign of UNICEF, encouraging tolerance of extraterrestrial children.[5]

Goode reports on his YouTube channel that an announcement of the disclosure of ETs is forthcoming, but told Salla that this might still be a few years away. He mentioned that in 2008 the Vatican Chief Astronomer Gabriel Funes discussed extraterrestrials in an interview titled: *The Alien is my Brother.*

Goode told Salla that Nordic extraterrestrials were involved in a contact initiative with major religious groups, which was communicated to him via two pilots working with a US Air Force controlled secret space program. He found it more than a coincidence that the June 13 leak of an alleged Majestic-12 document authored by the Defense Intelligence Agency, standing was given to human-looking extraterrestrials guiding diplomatic relations with human terrestrials. This is what the alleged document said:[17]

> "There are several variations more-or-less like ourselves. The majority of these are friendly and are the bulk of our EBE contacts. Most have a high degree of psychic ability and all use science and engineering of an advanced nature."

Prominent researchers such as Dr. Robert Wood and Stanton Friedman believe the document shows no sign of forgery and is worth serious investigation. According to Salla's research of the document, there is enough in it consistent with historical records, providing an important overview of recent human interaction with extra-terrestrials dating back to Nikola Tesla's radio experiments in the late 1800's. Salla concludes that the document contains genuine information.[17]

Notes:

1. David Weintraub, Professor of Astronomy and Physics, Vanderbilt University, *Religions and Extraterrestrial Life – How Will We Deal With It?* Springer International Publishing, 2014.
2. Ella LeBain, *Who Is God?,* Book Two, Skypath Books, 2015.
3. Ella LeBain, *Who Are the Angels?,* Book Three, Skypath Books, 2016.
4. David Weintraub, Ph.D., Professor of Astronomy and Physics, Vanderbilt University, *Religions and Extraterrestrial Life – How Will We Deal With It?* Springer International Publishing, 2014.
5. Guy Consolmagno and Fr. Paul Mueller, *Would You Baptize an Extraterrestrial? and Other Questions from the Astronomers' In-box at the Vatican Observatory,* Image, Random House, New York, 2014. [p. 252, 254-257]
6. Ibid., p.252
7. Ibid., p. 255-256
8. Ibid., p. 256-257
9. David Weintraub, Ph.D., *Religions and Extraterrestrial Life – How Will We Deal With It?* Springer International Publishing, 2014.
10. Ella LeBain, *Who's Who in the Cosmic Zoo?,* Book One-Third Edition, *A Spiritual Guide to ETs, Aliens, gods and Angels,* See, Concluding Words, Tate, 2013, http://www.whoswhointhecosmiczoo.com
11. David Weintraub, Ph.D., Professor of Astronomy and Physics, Vanderbilt University, *Religions and Extraterrestrial Life – How Will We Deal With It?* Springer International Publishing, 2014.
12. David Salisbury, Are the world's religions ready for E.T.? https://news.vanderbilt.edu/2014/09/29/religion-ready-for-et/ September 29, 2014
13. Robert Hugh Benson, Catholic Monsignor, *Lord of the World,* Dodd, Meade & Co., 1907
14. Pope Francis, *The Pope Video -Inter-Religious Dialogue,* www.popesprayer.net; www.thepopevideo.org

15. Michael E. Salla, Ph.D., *Will Dalai Lama Join Pope Francis in Disclosing Extraterrestrial Life?,* http://exopolitics.org/will-dalai-lama-join-pope-francis-in-disclosing-extraterrestrial-life/, October 8, 2017
16. Valdemar Valerian, *Matrix III, The Bio-Chemical, Neurological and Electronic Mind Control of the Masses,* Leading Edge Research Group, 1991.
17. Michael E. Salla, Ph.D., *World Religions Unite as Prelude to Extraterrestrial Disclosure,* http://exopolitics.org/world-religions-unite-as-prelude-to-extraterrestrial-disclosure/ June 22, 2017
18. Ella LeBain, *Who's Who in the Cosmic Zoo?* Book One – Third Edition, Chapter One: *Discerning Categories,* p. 25-42, Tate, 2013.
19. Ibid., p.90-91, WWCZ-B1-3ed

CHAPTER FOUR

Contracts and Agreements

"As above, so below."
~Hermetic Law

Think of it: every time you log on to anything on the Net, you automatically agree to abide by the rules of that entity. Our world is so full of all kinds of contracts and agreements that we frequently don't bother to read the fine print. That old Hermetic law of, "as above so below", based on the philosophy of our world being but a microcosm of a much larger macrocosm of the cosmos, still operates effectively. This includes contracts and agreements, the origins of which lie in the cosmic drama of spiritual warfare.

Every human being on earth is involved in this drama, a fierce fight over the soul, the mind, the body, to the destiny of the entire race. And as the old western saying goes, 'the devil's in the details', which we ignore to our own peril. I was a legal assistant and paralegal for twenty-five years, and as a Jewish-Christian I prefer to say, 'the *Truth* is in the details'. This is the basis of discernment. Discernment begins with the ability to recognize truth from lies. Before you can identify the counterfeit, you must first know the original, a recurring theme in this five-book series.

A Faustian contract or bargain is a deal or pact with the Devil, best remembered in the legend of Faust and the figure of Mephistopheles, but elemental to many Christian folktales as 'the devil's contract'. This has become a cultural norm in the west, which we frequently use to describe our current set of work circumstances.

Christian teaching asserts that all acts of witchcraft, both white and black magic, from voodoo to Wicca, are pacts between the contracting person and the satanic hierarchy, or demons. We may call it Santeria or freedom of expression, but what is really happening is an exchange of soul substance for earthly substance, the human essence for transitory gratification of the flesh or desire nature. We do this knowingly, most of time, but not always; we humans are so easily deceived and manipulated, and in New Age circles, where the wounded wander without benefit of the truth, disaster can overtake the unwitting.

The favors that we seek vary by the situation and circumstance, but most often include preserving our youth, gaining forbidden knowledge, wealth, power, or revenge on our enemies. Such bargains are dangerous regardless, as the price of all demonic service is the person's soul. The whole situation leads to a demoralizing end, with the steady draining of life force, daily interference in normal activities, deprivation of sleep, and strange illnesses and symptoms, to the eventual eternal damnation for the foolhardy adventurer. This is called spiritual trafficking, because the soul energy is stolen, and the human is vampirized, to be used for whatever demonic purpose.

Just as human trafficking debases women and children into sex slaves, vampirizing their souls through abuse, so witchcraft acts the same spiritually, vampirizing the spiritual purity and power of humanity. This often begins as extreme fatigue and flu-like symptoms, that increases as an effect of the spell. What I'm going to distinguish for you, my readers, in this book, is how to discern the differences, energetically speaking, and what steps you can take towards liberation and salvation from spiritual trafficking. Being drained, spiritually, mentally, and physically, can happen through both black and white magic, because it's all being done from the same source, demonic intelligences, aliens and dark spirits.

The fortunate souls who awaken out of this cosmic stupor in time to read between the lines and notice the devil's details realize that their only chance of deliverance from spiritual bondage and slavery is by turning towards the only One in the Cosmos who has the power to break these Faustian contracts. That One is Jesus the Christ.

Too many times these hidden contracts are being made through simple, innocent-sounding verbal agreements. New Agers confess semi-truths, and speak aloud invocations to who they are led to believe may be ancient gods, goddesses, ascended masters, and extraterrestrials, when in spiritual reality, these beings are demons and fallen angels in detailed masquerade. This puts the unthinking, undiscerning New Ager into a Faustian contract. They are deceived into thinking that they are in contact with highly developed beings, as demons have the power to appear, to shape shift, to glamour, into anyone or anything that the person wants them to be, thereby pulling off an illusion, just as a well-crafted actor does on the silver screen. These fallen angel demons have the power to speak, to create visions, and even to create miracles in the life of us earth humans, to hook us into the deception even further.

New Agers and researchers of the paranormal seek proof that the supernatural is real. Of course, it is real, but it is not all good. In my opinion, these investigators need to be more skeptical, more knowledgeable of human weaknesses, and equipped with powers of discernment so as not to fall into the many deceptive traps that the supernatural demons and aliens have set for them.

What is sorely lacking here is the ability to *discern,* to see and distinguish, to differentiate between these beings. We must begin by measuring every being by the cosmic litmus test, which is where they stand with the Creator God and the One who has been given power and authority over all the heavens and the earth, and that is the Lord Jesus Christ. I know that there are many people that do not want to hear this Truth. It sounds too Christian. It is. But not to do so is to throw the baby out with the bathwater, so to speak.

The dogma of religion, and its attendant religious spirits, along with many other satanic strongholds on the churches, have turned many people away from Christianity and from imperfect, human Christians. This is the number one cause of people to doubt the power of Christ. Doubt and un-belief is the work of Lucifer and his fallen angels, which has been going on for millennia. It is so important to reveal the true spirit behind the disenchantment with the church, and its' falling away in apostacy. The satanic agencies work day and night, roaming the earth, pulling people away from the truth, preventing us from seeing it by literally attaching deaf, blind and dumb spirits to us earth humans so that we become spiritually deaf, spiritually blind and spiritually mute. This is not the work of God, but the work of the demonic realms.

It's also important to distinguish and discern between those who follow a religion, and are in bondage to religious spirits, and those who follow closely in a dynamic living relationship with Jesus Christ and His Holy Spirit. The religious are void of true spiritual power, while those who really imitate Christ are therefore empowered in the spirit realm to cast out demons, heal the sick and raise the dead. These powers come from the anointing of the Holy Spirit to those who place their faith in Christ. It is only from Christ's Holy Spirit that one can obtain the powers of discernment of spirits and can see spiritually into the supernatural realms and can tell good from evil. The deceptions are fast and thick, and like trying to read fine print in a dark room, we can't see everything. Remember the devil and the Truth are in the details! This is how so many people get snookered and bamboozled, by missing the subtleties.

Think of how you feel when you watch a favorite movie, or one which you have been waiting to see. You get totally immersed in the story, following closely, identifying with your favorite character, until you don't see the actor portraying him anymore, you see the illusion he is portraying. It's exactly the same with the alien fallen angels and demonic realms. We get involved and identify with the story. We want to believe, and they invent some story to help us believe in something done supernaturally, or through technology that may be more advanced than ours. It is basically a trick, and we think we were privy to a miracle, or some kind of other worldly event.

We understand today that the visions of Fatima were all done by holographic technology, yet so many believers fell for this trick, hook, line, and sinker. They believed it was the Virgin Mary crying and bleeding for them. This was nothing more than a circus of smoke and mirrors to divert peoples' attention from the truth of

Christ, however, religious the imagery. Let's face it, the Virgin Mary does not have all the power in heaven and earth and inside the earth, as does her son, Jesus Christ. She is not the ultimate authority, as she herself told forevermore in John, chapter 2, verse 5. Mary His mother told us 'whatsoever He says to you, do it.' How much clearer can it get? But she has become idolized, against her express wishes and statements. She has essentially been given the place of the pagan goddesses that were worshipped prior to Christianity.

Worshipping angels, anything in the heavens or on earth, or under the earth, or in the sea, the sun, moon, stars, planets, ascended master, saints, extraterrestrials, aliens, ancient gods or goddesses, anyone or anything other than God, are all forms of idolatry, according to Scripture. The demonic realm knows this well, and they find it easy to trick and fool us earth humans into putting all these other beings ahead of our Creator. Doing so holds that soul in bondage. However, the soul doesn't discern that it's in bondage, instead often thinking we are being spiritual and religious and are receiving protection from all these deities. We set up altars and light candles and burn incense and give all kinds of offerings to created beings just like us. The beings that do our bidding or answer our prayers are the fallen angel demons whose job it is to keep us earth humans from knowing, seeing, and hearing the truth of Christ.

I've been saying throughout this book series that Jesus Christ does not belong to any one religion. He was assigned to be the Savior of the Universe, and welcomes all races and all religious backgrounds to put their faith in His salvation. When people hear the word salvation, one automatically thinks salvation from Hell. While this is certainly included for the afterlife, the salvation that Christ offers is in the here and now! It offers salvation from the lies, deception, and bondage of the satanic realms, fallen angels and demonic strongholds.

There's an old saying, that a lie will travel half way around the whole world before the truth gets its boots on. Think about how many lies people readily accept as truth, before even investigating. Think about how many myths that have become philosophies, which begin as lies spun out into all kinds of forms, that have in fact become whole belief systems, which are merely lies sandwiched between truths? As a race, we seem to be susceptible to falsehoods! The power of suggestion, as in hypnosis, is likened to being put under a spell. When we think about it, it is in fact essentially what hypnosis is, a spell, a form of surrendering our own discernment to another. Satan can create not only an implanted thoughtform in our own mind, but a collective thoughtform, a programming that if ever questioned or deviated from, can mean rejection from society and our peers because they too have believed the lie. This is certainly not a new phenomenon, it's been done over and repeatedly throughout the centuries. It's the old hypnotic truth which Hitler once used to destroy the civilized world, that a lie told often enough becomes the truth.

The Celestial Mafia

We all know how the mafia works: if we are in trouble, in debt, in a crisis beyond our capacity, we can always go to the mafia for help. The mafia will buy your debt or solve the crisis and ease the troubles, and then you will be owned by the mafia. This is a type of spiritual contract and agreement, because when you sell your soul to the mafia, you sell your soul to the demons and evil spirits that are behind it. When people call out and ask for help, frequently in desperate situations, they will just cry out, 'help me, somebody, help me!' And someone will answer, but it isn't necessarily God. Other times people cry out to God in a test case circumstance, and say, 'God, if you're real, please help me now.'

These prayers get answered too, not by the Most High, but by the 'god of this world', whom Jesus Himself identified, as Lucifer, or Satan and his hierarchy of fallen angels and demons. They are the celestial mafia. They will shape-shift into any god you want to see, and so subtle and so cunning is their deception, you won't know with whom you're really dealing. So, it has been for millennia, as many who have been offered kingdoms by the god of this world have entered into contracts and agreements with Lucifer, who has the power and authority to grant them. Earth has been Lucifer's kingdom since before the Evadamic era (Adam and Eve and the garden of Eden), till now, even though Satan, the earth, and Adam and Eve were cursed. Lucifer the fallen was allowed to test the pair of humans in the garden and when they failed the test, Lucifers' kingdom remained in his hands. We can read in Genesis 3:15 the prophesy of the One who will crush his authority, and that was none other than Yeshua HaMashiach, Jesus Christ.

The final temptation of Christ in the desert by Lucifer the Satan was the ultimate; he tempted Jesus by offering Him the Faustian Contract that if Jesus would fall down and worship him, Satan would give Him authority and power over the kingdoms of the earth. "And the devil, taking Him up into a high mountain, showed to Him all the kingdoms of the world in a moment of time. And the devil said to Him, 'all this power will I give you, and the glory of them: for that is delivered to me; and to whomsoever I will I give it. If you therefore will worship me, all shall be yours.' We read this one in Luke 4:4-7, which chimes perfectly with Mark 1:13 and Matthew 4: 1-11. Who was Satan to make such an offer, but the one who is known as the god of this world, the prince of the powers of the air of UFOs! This earth was and still is Lucifer's kingdom. Yet, Jesus responded, by saying, "Get you behind me, Satan: for it is written, you shall worship the Lord your God, and Him only shall you serve." (Luke 4:8)

While Christ resisted Lucifers' Satanic offer, many others have not been so strong. This is why the history of planet earth is one of the rise and fall of empire after empire, kingdom after kingdom. Even the ancient alien astronauts of the earths' distant past who erected monolithic structures, temples, pyramids, and ruled kingdoms here got no free pass for setting up their domains. They all had to have entered into some kind of contract and agreement with the god of this world, who is Lucifer the Satan.

The proof, as they say, is in the pudding. Take the symbolism of the snake, seen in virtually every culture both ancient and modern, in fact it is even on the emblems of British royalty. Where do we first encounter the snake, and whom does he turn out to be in disguise? The evidence is seen throughout history in just about every major religion, established alongside the kingdoms and gods it served. They had to include the worship of Lucifer, along with the pantheon of his fallen extraterrestrial angels, who all had god complexes. Their symbolism is rife throughout human history, proving to be his mark on those contracts which set up religions and kingdoms in every name.

The dragon is also seen throughout the world in temples, and considered to be a lucky emblem, particularly by the Chinese. The symbols of stars, planets, winged beings, winged cherubim, is found throughout the ancient world. The worship of a multitude of gods, goddesses, ancient kings and queens, and hosts of statutes made of stone, metals, and clay, may all give the appearance of freedom and diversity of religions, but in essence, these are all the same idolatry. These are creatures of the Creator God. They are, however, the mark of Lucifers' kingdom, echoed by the extraterrestrial and alien beings that have entered into Faustian contracts with him to establish their strongholds on earth.

Jesus said, "By their fruits you shall know them," (Matthew 7:16). So, what are the fruits of Lucifers' kingdoms? Bondage, slavery, disease, conflict, war, sorrow, suffering, oppression, injustice, immorality, curses, death. When a kingdom is blessed by the Creator God, it is radiant with peace, freedom, victory, liberation, health, healing, light, and love. Granted, it's been a mixed bag on earth, but each and every one of the kingdoms of old have all fallen and perished, no matter how great they once were. Why? Because they all had Faustian contracts with Lucifer and his fallen angels in one form or another and all ended up betraying and rebelling against the Creator God and his creation.

When the Annunaki of the ancient Sumerian tablets genetically engineered humans in the first known in-vitro fertilization program, for producing a human slave race, they entered into an agreement first with Lucifer the Satan. This became the template for all future kingdoms, which was the master-slave relationship, and holding us earth humans in bondage. In fact, several researchers have postulated today that the return of the Annunaki coincides with the final battle that is to be fought in the heavens between the forces of darkness and Jesus Christ and His heavenly hosts. Jesus will defeat Lucifer and his Satanic kingdoms once and for all and establish His Kingdom of Heaven on Earth to reign for a thousand years.

In my opinion, not only are these Annunaki gods in a Faustian contract with Lucifer, but so are several other alien groups, like the gods behind the Mayan calendar, the Nephilim Lord Pacal, the gray aliens, several groups from Orion, Aldebaran, Ursa Major, the ancient gods from Sirius and the reptilian/Draconian forces from Draco.

All these ancient civilizations were given authority and power from Lucifer through agreements with him. They were eventually brought down by the Creator God and punished by Yahuah for their sin of rebellion. Further outrage was brought down on them for mating with earth human women, and the sexual immorality that they spread by mating with both humans and animals, the awful offspring that were created, and their lust for human flesh. The earth itself was cleansed of them not once but twice.

Interestingly, modern Nephilim are not gigantic at all, but hardly noticeable alien-human hybrids that have been created artificially. Most of the abductions of us earth humans and the harvesting of human ova and sperm and other genetic materials goes into hybridization. These hybrids are being released onto earth to surface in societies and blend in with the natural earth human population. These hybrids have special qualities, like the Borg in *Star Trek the Next Generation*, they are implanted with programs from *inside* the earth, to carry out the agenda of Lucifer the Satan and his fallen angels. Most earth humans are unable to tell them apart from other natural earth humans, and would refrain from being so politically incorrect.

Genetic engineering is nothing new. The racism it spawned is the legacy of the various extraterrestrial and alien gods that set up their kingdoms on Earth. The scriptures are rich with blessings and curses throughout the Old and New Testaments, the Hebrew and the Greek Scriptures. In fact, the scriptures are clear that curses are attached to bloodlines up to and even exceeding ten generations. Racism has caused genocide several times in history, so we know that these beings do not adhere to the Creators guidelines that all men were created equal. These beings that push the agenda of genocide are at war with the Creator, a perfect example of which is the fallen angelic alien beings which inspired Nazi ideology. Those possessed, attempted to wipe all traces of prior Judaic genetics and DNA off the face of the earth.

The God of the Judaic genetics put His DNA into this group of humans as His experiment and chose them to be a light to others by expressing Him through them, through intelligence, compassion and morality. That's what his group was originally 'chosen' for. When they rebelled, and grew disobedient through idolatry and immorality, He punished them, by allowing the god of this world, to have his way with them, but because of His Covenant with them, He never allowed the god of this world to successfully wipe them out. He always saved a 'remnant' to fulfill 'His' original purposes. This God has been at war with the god of this world.

The god of this world, takes out his animas towards the God of the Jews on the Jews and Israel and because Jesus was a Jew, and Christians follow His teachings, they too are targets of the wrath of the god of this world because the God of the Jews gave His Spirit to the Gentiles as an addendum to His original experiment, with the intention that by putting 'His Spirit of Purity' into the people that were outside of His genetic experiment, who are known as Gentiles or the Nations, then they would carry out His purposes, He thought that would make His own people jealous, with the hopes that they would turn back to Him in repentance in heart and lifestyle. Some did, but sadly many did not, as they were misled and hypnotized by the god of this world, who tempted them with various types of lusts, perversions and even outright atheism in their own God by luring them to follow various idols and pseudo gods, who are alien fallen angels that are in legion with Lucifer's Rebellion.

An important discernment is one of the chief characteristics of the God of Israel, who is Yahuah, is a deep sense of morality and moral code. Whereas the god of this world, is just the opposite and maintains an immoral, perverted nature on purpose in his age long rebellion against Yahuah. As I connected theses dots in Book Two, *Who Is God?* to the Sumerian myth of Enki and Enlil, two gods who fought over humankind. For those familiar with this myth, Yahuah would be compared to Enki and Lucifer/Satan would be Enlil.

As I've mentioned before, the Jewish people were created by Yahuah as His people, and it is through their bloodline, the bloodline of King David through His mother's side, that Jesus Christ was born. Christ came not only to save the Jews, but all races, all nations, and all religions of the earth. For each race and each nation is but a microcosm of the greater macrocosm representing the races and nations of the cosmos. This is why I am asserting throughout this book series that Jesus is the Cosmic Christ, who came to save all races and nations from the bondages of the Dark Lord, who has brought nothing but curses upon whole star clusters and stars with planets throughout the cosmos. Why else would the Creator promise to recreate the heavens and earth, if not for the fact that they have become corrupted and have entered into accursed states through the rebellion of Lucifer and his fallen extraterrestrials?

Salvation through the grace of Christ is not only offered to humankind but to ALL creation, which includes animals, aliens and extraterrestrials, even the extra-dimensionals, which is evidenced in scriptures. His goal and covenant promise has been, "I have come to set the captives free." (Isaiah 61:1; Luke 4:18) Free from the bondages and slaveries of the god of this world.

THE DESTINY OF GLORY

> "I consider that the sufferings of this present time are as nothing compared with the glory to be revealed for us. For <u>all of creation</u> awaits with eager expectation the revelation of the children of God; for creation was made subject to futility, not of its own accord but because of the one who subjected it, in hope that creation itself would be set free from slavery to corruption and share in the glorious freedom of the children of God. We know that <u>all</u>

creation is groaning in labor pains even until now; and not only that, but we ourselves, who have the first fruits of the Spirit, we also groan within ourselves as we wait for adoption, the redemption of our bodies."

(Romans 8:18-23-(NABRE)

As above, so below. The entire universe is ordered through contracts, agreements, and treaties. It is the basis of all political theory including exopolitics. Let's not forget that when Lucifer rebelled, he persuaded one third of the heavenly stars, or extraterrestrial angels, to follow him. The other two thirds remained faithful to the Creator and continue to be to this day. They too have struggled with the forces of darkness in their own worlds, their own star systems and planetary spheres, and have aligned with the Office of Christ in the heavens to defeat the forces of darkness. They wish to eradicate the Satanic influences from their worlds. It takes power, it takes authority and it takes a lot of organization. Jesus Christ was given authority over the heavens, the earth, and all things *inside* the earth. The earth is a representative of the cosmos.

All the races on the earth are representatives of many of the root races in the cosmos. Of course, there must be races in the cosmos that are not represented on earth, and these are most likely those races that are not involved in the rebellion. The extraterrestrial races not involved in the rebellion make up two thirds of heaven's 'angels' who are the faithful extraterrestrials to the Creator God, and never rebelled. They remain in service to the Kingdom of Heaven, and at the Second Coming of Yeshua/Jesus, He will order them from all four corners of the heavens to join Him in His Long-awaited Return to Earth as He ends the final battle of Armageddon with His breath and a Word. Jesus said, in the Gospel of Thomas[1], v103, "Congratulations to those who know where the rebels are going to attack. [They] can get going, collect their imperial resources, and be prepared before the rebels arrive." We are in space war between ETs/ fallen angels, rebellious ETs, aliens, and those ET races who uphold the image, likeness and moral code of the Creator. *Star Wars* is real to a large extent, and this planet is the stage for it and its gene wars, which explains why racism is the number one social problem on planet earth.

Understanding this, we can see that earth has been used throughout time as a testing ground for human souls. This is what is termed 'The Grand Experiment'. Earth has always been a battlefield, locked in the bondage of duality. It may appear imbalanced most of the time, as it seems that the forces of darkness win in this realm; but what we see here is illusionary, and what the Creator sees is the human heart and human spirit, and how it chooses to respond to all the injustice in this world. The Creator discerns whether or not our soul seeks to have a relationship with the Living God, and not with the dead idols or with those who have fallen out of heaven. The one thing that the Creator is testing is our loyalty, to make sure that those who are allowed entrance into the upper heavens are worthy, and that He and the heavenly hosts do not get another Lucifer clone on their hands.

"I am the gate; whoever enters through me will be saved.
He will come in and go out, and find pasture. ~ Jesus"
(John 10:9)

Karmic Contracts

Karmic contracts are between souls who have unfinished business here on earth or with others. They can also be bestowed upon souls who need to learn certain spiritual lessons, such as forgiveness, compassion, tolerance, patience, and endurance. These contracts are set up in the heavens for the perfection of souls. If for instance a soul desires to learn forgiveness, it can contract with another soul to play the dark role during a life, so that they can express the quality so dear to Christs' own heart. If another soul wants to express compassion, it can contract with another soul that wants the experience of being rescued and aided, even handicapped in some way, so these are bound in this relationship to practice their perfections. All karmic contracts feel like bondage of some kind, but it is an illusion, remember. These can be within families, marriages, and even between employer and employee.

Jesus spoke about this several times when He said, "For I have come to turn a man against his father, a daughter against her mother, a daughter-in-law against her mother-in-law, a man's enemies will be the members of his own household" (Matthew 10:36).

The following is a revealing scripture written in the Gospel of Thomas[2], a book that was not discovered until very recently. It is compatible with the scripture from Matthew. Jesus said, "People think, perhaps, that I have come to throw peace upon the world. They don't know that I have come to throw disagreement upon the world, and fire, and sword, and struggle. For there will be five in one house. Three will oppose two. Two will oppose three. The father will oppose his son and the son oppose his father. And they will stand up and they will be alone." (Thomas 16a, 16b)[2].

These are karmic contracts. They test and try the soul. They are difficult relationships. A person may even have a karmic contract with a soul mate, people who love each other intensely yet battle continuously. We all know first-hand couples who may love each other, but are not able to be in the same room for too long. They endure trouble and struggle with each other, yet they are bound to each other. This is a love bond, but it's still a karmic contract. Some karmic contracts are more difficult than others. Whenever a person in your life becomes a nemesis you know it's some kind of karmic contract that is calling you to stretch the love, compassion, forgiveness, tolerance, patience, and long-suffering in your soul to the limit.

Let's connect the dot to our sun's twin star, *Nemesis*, and how it's intersection and overlapping orbit of one of its most rebellious planets, *Nibiru, aka Planet X, Hercolubus, the Red Dragon, Phoenix,* has a whole mythology attached to it, that connects it to the Sumerian myth between two Extraterrestrial brothers, Enki and Enlil, who are believed to be Yahuah and Lucifer/Satan. When you extrapolate it out to a battle between these two gods, you get what these types of 'karmic' contracts are, considering that the big showdown between them is a Divine Appointment on Earth for a final battle over dominion of Earth, this solar system and perhaps even this entire sector of this galaxy and of course, us humans.

Lucifer/Satan's Kingdom and Personality

There is a tried and true observation of hierarchical structures, that it all rolls downhill. Whatever attitude and behavior exhibited by those at the top of an organization will trickle down to the rest of its members, subjects, servants, employees, and community. This works for heads of families, heads of state, national leaders, church leaders, corporations, and all political and social structures. Being that this earth is headed by Lucifer, his domain and his kingdom, it is his personality which pervades the planet. Not one single human being is immune from its effects. Lucifers' kingdom consists of Powers, Principalities and demons. Satan's Principalities have a pecking order. There are stronger ruling demons and lesser demons that answer to, serve, and protect each principality. These demons form the front rank of the army of the Satanic hierarchy.

Lucifers' Satanic Personality = Lucifers' Satanic Kingdom:

Rejection, Hatred, Violence, Bondage, Slavery, Jealousy & Envy, Condemnation, Shame, Pride, Guilt, Lying, Greed, Covetousness, Revenge, Retaliation, slander, Critical Spirit, Fear, Terror, Unforgiveness, Unmerciful, Self-Pity, Gossip, Self-Centered, Narcissistic.

The Nature and Spirit of God = God's Kingdom:

Love, Joy, Peace, Freedom, Liberation, Gentleness, Goodness, Faith, Longsuffering, Virtue, Purity, Wisdom, Justice, Honesty, Fairness, Sincerity, Knowledge, Understanding, Grace, Mercy, Excellence, Forgiveness, Compassion, Devotion, Truth.

"A double-minded man is unstable in all his ways."
(James 1:8)

Every one of us on earth as human beings wrestle with this spiritual duality every day of our lives. This is the free will zone we live in, and all of our testing comes through the decisions and agreements we make. Each day, we can choose to serve Lucifer in Satan's kingdom, or the Lord in God's Kingdom. We can choose to be loving, or choose to allow the negativity to take over our personalities and souls. We can choose light or darkness, but the choice remains ours.

> "For our struggle is not against flesh and blood, but against the principalities, against the powers and authorities, and against the rulers of the darkness of this world, against the spiritual forces of evil in the heavenly realms." (Ephesians 6:12)

Lucifer's Satanic personality comes through his seven major principalities, or princedoms, which are ruled by Archdemons (Archons) who are then in charge of lesser demons. These represent attributes of the Satanic personality by creating strongholds and armors to establish the seven principalities in the lives of all of us humans on earth.[3] These are:

1) Accusing Spirits: these nasty entities keep people in the blame game. They rule over our desire to criticize, and our fear of being criticized ourselves. They inspire prejudices, fear of others. They are the spirits of judgment which prey upon our vanity and our self-esteem, who whisper in our minds the lie of inequality ('she is prettier than I am, so others will like her more!') which gives rise to suspicion mistrust, condemnation, defensiveness, worry, depression. Accusations are frequently disguised as harmless gossip, the raised eye brow of innuendo, which we believe makes us look wise and sophisticated, but is so un-Christ-like. When we start keeping a record of wrongs, make plans to get even or even the score with others, we are hosting Accusing Spirits. These demons make sure that people on earth do not get along and accept each other. They are unloving spirits. The Religious Spirit comes out of this Principality which blocks the Spirit to God's Grace and Love.

From the Gospel of Thomas, v102 Jesus said, "Damn the Pharisees! They are like a dog sleeping in the cattle manger: the dog neither eats nor [lets] the cattle eat."[4] This corresponds to the Words of Jesus in Matthew 24:23-24, "Woe to you, scribes and Pharisees, you hypocrites! You pay tithes of mint, dill, and cumin, but you have disregarded the weightier matters of the Law: justice, mercy, and faithfulness. You should have practiced the latter, without neglecting the former. You blind guides! You strain out a gnat but swallow a camel.

2) Spirits of Bitterness: this is a major stronghold against which everyone on earth must guard, as this principality personifies Lucifer most perfectly. He is bitter as hell at his treatment by the Most High, and he wants to be sure it spreads. He

inspires us to hold on to resentment, by holding grudges, and withhold our forgiveness when we are wronged. He rages, stirs up anger, inciting hatred and in his own image, even murder. Jesus called him in this spirit, *The Manslayer*, a murderer from the beginning. Just as Enlil wanted to wipe out humankind, Enki had compassion and wanted to save humans, so today, this spiritual battle ensues between Christ and Satan, Jesus and Lucifer. Our deep dark thoughts, murderous envy, desire for revenge, for retaliation, for getting even, are inspired by these Unloving Bitter Spirits. They go further with inciting us to slander, to speak cruel truths or untruths, ignite our own fury when such malice is directed against us.

Those who practice any form of sadism are hosting spirits of bitterness, who wish others to hurt as much as they do themselves. Even the minor spirits of spitefulness, the door slammers, the key jammers, the button pushers in the next cubicle, eventually grow, when fed upon our hearts, into treachery, power-over, dominance. Jesus expressly forbids us to engage in any hierarchy in aspect of our lives through Peter, first book, chapter 5. The minor spirits which breed impatience eventually sprout into agitation, discontent, antagonism, then open contempt for authority, which translates into anarchy. The fruits of these spirits are enmity and the contention which erupts into confrontation, open fighting, unconcealed hostility, violence, terrorism. The ultimate aim is murder.

When we give in to even mild irritation, a spate of temper, video violence, a wrathful wish, the desire to cause strife by a seemingly innocent, we are hosting bitter spirits. The annoying bickering and discord of quarreling which will follow, the sarcastic rejoinder, the self-pitying tone of defense, are all music to the ears of bitter spirits. Using our words to cast aspersions on others, back stabbing and wishing them ill will, is a type of dark witchcraft, which these bitter spirits serve. Then the host is in bondage and their spirit and soul becomes consumed by their grudges and inner rage, they become in *covenant* with satan through bitterness.

Metaphysically speaking, spirits of bitterness cause cancer in the physical body. The spirit is an implant in the form of a cancer virus. They often manifest as other types of viruses, parasites and bacteria that cause the body infection and disease. All of which can be cast out through Jesus, who restores both body and soul.

3) The Spirits of Self-Bitterness go hand in claw with the spirits of bitterness, as both are the heart of the Unloving Spirit. Satan has his throne in the kingdom of self, and the principality of self-bitterness which is protected by strong armor. This spirit induces shame, misplaces feelings of guilt, of internalized hatred and condemnation. We frequently accuse ourselves of worthlessness, heaping abuse on ourselves which we would never visit on another person. In the end, we can sabotage our best efforts and plans, just by giving in to these bitter spirits of abasement and denial. We can let them direct our thoughts to the exclusion of all interests and concerns except those

which benefit us, as in narcissists. We can revel in false humility while trumpeting to the world how noble and exalter we are while we secretly steal from the collection box. The most obvious sign of these spirits is self-mutilation, as in piercings, tattoos, elective implants; the aim is ultimate self-destruction, as in murder and suicide.

4)The spirits of Jealousy & Envy: we all know how destructive these spirits can be! When unleashed, this one iniquity destroyed the peace of the universe, as Lucifer became jealous of God and desired His place on the heavenly throne. The feeling which God Himself describes to us as His jealousy of our love, our adoration and our worship, is quite distinguishable from the jealousy of the enemy of us! Satanic spirits counterfeit love, and these evil spirits form this principality. The two principalities of jealousy and envy, and the principality of bitterness and rejection network together to bring sorrow, wrath, and destruction to all of us. The Satanic principality is built on envy, resentment, suspicion, or as Webster defines it, 'discontent or ill will directed towards another's good fortune because one wishes it had been his.'

We recall the first recorded murder of Abel by Cain was inspired by pure, sheer jealousy. To this day, we know that jealous rages often results in the brutal murder of those we love the most. In both the Hebrew and Greek the words for jealousy and envy are interchangeable in Scripture, both describing covetousness. To covet is to idolize. Idolatry is rooted in jealousy. The Creator God has warned us repeatedly throughout the entire Bible, to put no other gods before Him. The true force of God is not jealousy but zeal, or 'to be zealous.' God is jealous or zealous over us, and the focus of His jealousy is our love, as He wants us to love Him for Himself, of our own free will, on our own accord. Not because we can cajole favors from Him or use Him as a cosmic vending machine, but because we want to love Him for His goodness.

5) The unloving spirits of Rejection form their own principality, and all its armor can cause the human heart to reject God, reject love, reject good in life, by pushing it away. When we push others away we also reject Christ. These wicked spirits also create rejection for us by causing others to reject us when we do reach out to them, and this can hurt deeply.

There are four levels of this spirit of rejection; the fear of rejection; self-rejection; rejection of others; and the desire of rejection. This demonic principality and all its armor holds a person in spiritual, mental, and psychological bondage, creating isolation and loneliness, because the person stops reaching out for relationships for fear of rejection. The spirit of rejection tells people that they will never belong, and makes them feel like misfits. However, the truth is, there are no misfits in God's Heavenly Kingdom. Beings are accepted through Christ for *who* they are, not always what they are. This is why this spirit inspired racism, antisemitism, and rules over all kinds of bigotry, which is essentially the rejection of others who aren't like yourself.

Rejection is a supporting assertion of Satanic lies; he says you are not worth the chemicals you are made from, but Jesus thinks you are to die for. Rejection causes a person to turn away, withdraw from good company, to hide human needs and withhold worthy contributions to conversations and company. Rejection causes us to look for love in all the wrong places, which perpetuates this cycle of rejection. Rejection blocks all possibility for reconciliation, which networks with the principality of bitterness. Rejection creates loneliness, despair, and suicide. Jesus Christ was acquainted with the spirits of rejection, but He did not accept them, He instead counseled them on their sins and suggested they follow a different path, not allowing them to impede His mission. We who follow Christ will confidently expect similar tests and challenges in our lives for our belief. Our value doesn't decrease based on someone's inability to see our worth. I am worthy because God says I am!

6) The principality of Fear is a major stronghold on planet earth. We are all well acquainted with fear, which comes in many forms and armors. They range from minor phobias of cats to the number 13 to the sheer terror of 9/11. When we are pursued by the spirit of fear, we experience the 'flight or fight' syndrome, sudden intense rushes of adrenaline and cortisol, floods through our bloodstreams, which can increase our strength for running like a rabbit or fighting like a bear. Too much, too often, too repeatedly, this syndrome will result in PTSD, hosts of immune breakdowns, general dis-ease, and eventually heart failure. Our hearts were not made to host fear!

Denial is a form of fear, a fear of facing the truth and its consequences. Denial is a major armor of fear.

Fear has a strong connection to punishment. Lucifer is being punished by being cast out of his lofty spot in heaven and brought down to earth. His final punishment will be destruction in the lake of fire, 'and never shalt he be anymore'. So, he is full of fear.

"For God has not given us a spirit of fear; but of power, and of love and of a sound mind" (2 Timothy 1:7). Imagine living in a world without fear! Without the spirit of fear, without the need to fear anything? That is the Kingdom of God! "There is no fear in love. But perfect love drives out fear, because fear has to do with punishment. The one who fears is not made perfect in love" (1 John 4:18). The antidote for fear is faith in God. It takes faith to have courage even when the circumstances say otherwise. Courage is feeling the fear but moving forward with faith anyway, even when facing extreme dangers.

7) Occultism, Pharmacia & Sorcery: This is a major problem principality for planet earth, as it has held entire nations in bondage for millennia. Occultism is any hidden practice or belief that opposes the law of God. The word occult means that

which is hidden or secret. The lure of secret knowledge is a chief method of Lucifer the Satan in seducing us humans into a state of pseudo-enlightenment. Remember, Lucifer was once the Angel of Light, and as the god of this world, he is the god of its wisdom and enlightenment. This lure charms many into that network of principalities, along with self-bitterness, narcissism, and self-pride, so that we of earth really believe his lie that we too can be gods and goddesses. This was the cause of Lucifer's downfall, his pride in himself, and his belief that he could be higher than the God that created him.

Occult practice is used to gain favor with Lucifer and his demonic hierarchy in the form of Faustian contracts, to receive and maintain power, fame and wealth on earth, in exchange for a human soul. Most people who enter into this contract do not fully realize the implications in the fine print, as their present life circumstances and their need for power and control overshadows any thought of the condition and future of their soul in the afterlife. This type of power contract is so alluring, it has recruited high officials in both military and political arenas to achieve and maintain their status of power and control. As I've stated previously, not only are we on earth vulnerable to this siren song, but also extraterrestrials who seek power on earth.

Recently, America's Morning News correspondent Robert M. Stanley authored a book, *Covert Encounters in Washington, D.C.* a revealing work about unethical extraterrestrial and inter-dimensional entities which manipulate terrestrial elite swamp-dwellers. These seek control of the human population in finance, politics, media, religion, and in governmental and public events in Washington, D.C., and other world capitals. Robert Stanley states, "We are dealing with a shape-shifting ET that is apparently known to the U.S. government."[5]

Stanley's work further reveals how the Masonic layout of the District of Columbia's architecture and infrastructure is used as a dimensional mind control panel by unethical inter-dimensional lower-order extraterrestrials. They manipulate the worldwide permanent war economy and arms industry by maintaining control of the decision-making processes in the national Congress. He notes the prevalence of the Annunaki extraterrestrials and interdimensional entities interacting in the power establishment and their interconnection with Satanic networks within the U.S. Armed Forces.[6]

In the conclusion of his book *Covert Encounters in Washington, DC,* Robert Stanley writes: "For some reason, the U.S. military has a publicly-admitted, open-door policy for practicing Satanists and Luciferians. For example, there is the case of Satanist Lieutenant Colonel Michael Aquino who trained at the Defense Intelligence College at Bolling Air Force Base in Washington, D.C. News reports indicate he was a prime suspect in a series of pedophile scandals involving the sexual abuse of hundreds of children, including the children of military personnel. But even as Aquino was being investigated by Army Criminal Investigation Division officers for his involvement in the pedophile cases, he retained the highest-level security clearances and was involved in pioneering work in "military psychological operations".

"The Pentagon also gave its blessings to Aquino's long-standing public association with the Church of Satan and his successor church the Temple of Set. This, despite the fact that Aquino's Satanic activities involved overt support for neo-Nazi movements in the United States and Europe.

"In April 1978, the U.S. Army published A Handbook for Chaplains to "facilitate the provision of religious activities." Both the Church of Satan and the Temple of Set were listed among the other religions to be tolerated inside the U.S. military. A section of the handbook dealing with Satanism stated, often confused with witchcraft, Satanism is the worship of Satan (also known as Baphomet or Lucifer). Classical Satanism, often involving black masses, human sacrifices, and other sacrilegious or illegal acts, is now rare.'"

"Regarding his work in psychological operations, Colonel Aquino stated, "Mindwar is a permanent state of strategic, psychological warfare against the populations of friend and foe nations alike. In its strategic context, mind-war must reach out to friends, enemies, and neutrals alike across the globe through the electronic media possessed by the United States which have the capabilities to reach virtually all people on the face of the Earth.

"State of the art developments in satellite communication, video recording techniques, and laser and optical transmission of broadcasts make possible a penetration of the minds of the world in ways that would have been inconceivable just a few years ago."[7] [sic]

Occult involvement is not always this deep. As Robert Stanley wrote, there may be a difference between witchcraft and Satanism, but witchcraft is still an occult practice ruled by this same principality of demons. Each time anyone dabbles in the practices of witchcraft, a demonic entity/spirit is attached to the person. Even though spells are cast to invoke goddesses, demons answer the call, and it is they who are the ones making the spell work for the spell caster. Remember all Faustian Contracts are designed to deceive the practitioner into focusing on life here on earth, all the while their soul is being claimed for the Satanic kingdom. The sin of witchcraft is a serious offense to the Creator God and the Lord will judge all those who practice it. The Lord so loves a sincere penitent, even of this dark crime! Yes, this includes the so- called white magic of Wiccan. It is all witchcraft, all rebellion against God.

According to the Bible there are three major branches of occult activity:

1. The witchcraft or power branch includes: hypnosis, mind control, parakinesis, voodoo, telekinesis, touch healing, table tipping, astral projection, levitation, witchcraft, any martial arts which require the meditation on strange gods.
2. The divination or knowledge branch includes: astrology, automatic writing, channeling, crystal balls, ESP, clairvoyance, color therapy, pendulum divining, handwriting analysis, kabala, horoscopes, iridology, mediums, mind reading, omens, séances, numerology, palm reading, phrenology, telepathy, tarot cards, tea leaf reading, false religions, occult books, water witching.
3. Sorcery using physical objects can include: amulets, ankhs, charms, crystals, hallucinogenic drugs, hex signs, lucky symbols, Ouija boards, pagan fetishes, religious artifacts, and zodiac charms talismans.

While many believe that these activities are innocent and harmless, they are all gateways and access points for spiritual legal ground for demonic activity. It was for these very practices that the original inhabitants of Canaan were ejected.

> "When you enter the land the Lord your God is giving you, do not learn to imitate the detestable ways of the nations there. There shall not be found among you anyone who makes his son or his daughter pass through the fire, (human sacrifice) one who uses divination, one who practices witchcraft, or one who interprets omens, or a sorcerer, cast spells, ask ghosts or spirits for help, or consults the dead. Anyone who does these things is detestable to the Lord, and because of these detestable practices the Lord your God will drive out those nations before you."
>
> (Deuteronomy 18:9-12)

> "But cowards, unbelievers, the corrupt, murderers, the immoral, <u>those who practice witchcraft</u> (the magic arts, sorcerers), idol worshipers, and all liars--their fate is in the fiery lake of burning sulfur. This is the second death."
>
> (Revelation 21:8)

> "Seers will be put to shame. <u>Those who practice witchcraft will be disgraced</u>. All of them will cover their faces, because God won't answer them."
>
> (Micah 3:7)

"The light of a lamp will never shine in you again. The voice of bridegroom and bride will never be heard in you again. Your merchants were the world's great men. By your magic spell all the nations were led astray."

(Revelation 18:23)

"In that day," declares the Lord, "I will destroy your witchcraft and you will no longer cast spells and there will be no more fortunetellers."

(Micah 5:10, 12)

"Outside are the dogs, those who practice magic arts, (witchcraft, occult, human sacrifices) the sexually immoral, the murderers, the idolaters and everyone who loves and practices falsehood."

(Revelation 22:15)

"The rest of mankind that were not killed by these plagues still did not repent of the work of their hands; they did not stop worshiping demons, and idols of gold, silver, bronze, stone and wood--idols that cannot see or hear or walk. And they did not repent of their murders or their witchcraft or their sexual immorality or their thefts."

(Revelation 9:21)

"For rebellion is as the sin of witchcraft, and stubbornness is as iniquity and idolatry. Because you have rejected the word of the LORD, he has also rejected you from being king."

(1 Samuel 15:23)

"He sacrificed his own son in the fire, practiced sorcery and divination, and consulted mediums and spiritists. He did much evil in the eyes of the LORD, provoking him to anger."

(2 Kings 21:6)

"The nations you will dispossess listen to those who practice sorcery or divination. But as for you, the LORD your God has not permitted you to do so."

(Deuteronomy 18:14)

"Do not eat meat that has not been drained of its blood. "Do not practice fortune-telling or witchcraft." (Leviticus 19:26); "None of you may eat blood, nor may an alien living among you eat blood."

(Leviticus 17:12)

It is very clear that the Lord hates the hidden occult practices because these are the tools, strongholds, and principalities of Satan. This presents a huge dilemma to those in new age circles who innocently dabble in Wicca, white magic, divination, and fortune telling. While we may believe in the light and the power of love, our souls are still bound to unclean and deceiving demons of the Luciferian hierarchy. Dabbling in, engaging with, or outright practicing of all forms of idolatry are the worship of Lucifer. The demons, the stars, the planets, ancient gods, goddesses, are all legitimate gateways for demons to infiltrate, oppress, and torment the life, spirit and soul of any of us humans on earth.

When we repent, which means to turn back from the mistake or sin, to feel regret and contrition, the Lord is faithful and quick to forgive, cleanse and deliver that person from bondage to Satan. If a person dies in these spiritual errors or sins, there is little hope for them, as it is the legal authority of the god of this world, Satan, to claim ownership of that soul. It is only while there is still breath and life in the body that one has the opportunity to repent from all involvements in the occult, so that the soul may be saved from the clutches of Satan.

These contracts and agreements are legal and binding, all the way into the spiritual dimensions of our world. Along with all the favors asked, the demonic has legal authority to oppress, torment, deceive, blind, and block the human spirit, mind, and body and that includes the host's descendants in the form of generational curses and assignments on the bloodline. While some people appear to be blessed and have it all, with fame, wealth and power, their inner lives are tormented, because they do not have the true peace that only God can give. How many rich and famous people do you know who are plagued with all kinds of afflictions, like scandals, heartache, and illness? While their Faustian contracts may have paid off by giving them the fame, wealth, and power they desired, their spiritual lives are anything but free and clear.

There are those among us who exemplify that 'ignorance is bliss'. They have no idea what they've dabbled in, they believe the lies as truth, they stubbornly cling to the false belief that they are the creators of their own reality, or that they themselves are gods and goddesses awaiting ascension, when all the while they are being duped, hooked into by vampires, implanted with the doctrines of demons, who masquerade as angels of light.

Another stronghold and armor of this seventh principality is the Pharmacia. This is the realm of pharmaceuticals and the numbing and dumbing down of the natural spirit in the human body, so as not to perceive the truth from the Creator and His Holy Spirit. All spiritual conditions which are diagnosed as psychological and medical disorders, are treated with pharmaceuticals, which drags the soul deeper into bondage. While the individual condition and dis-ease, and how they all correspond to the bondage to these seven principalities, is beyond the scope of this book, we can suffice to say that health, healing, homeostasis, and well-being are achieved and maintained through an active living relationship with the Creator God and the Lord Jesus Christ. It is He who came to heal of all our dis-eases, providing we repent and turn to Him, along with the practice of following His good example of proper nutrition and healthful living.

As a nutritionist and certified wellness educator, and I can tell you that most diseases can be prevented through the deliverance out of the kingdom of darkness into the kingdom of God, followed by proper nutrition and right living. It may not happen overnight, but the process is tried and true. Healing dis-eases and the deliverance of the spiritual conditions from darkness is the subject matter of my next book. So, stay tuned. In the meantime, please refer to the wonderful work of Art Mathias, at www.akwellspring.com, for the path of liberation from the seven principalities. His works include *Biblical Foundations of Freedom-Destroying Satan's Lies with God's Truth,* and for the spiritual causes behind every mental and physical dis-ease, *In His Own Image-We Are Wonderfully Made.*[8]

It's important to remember that there are legal rules of engagement when it comes to spiritual warfare. One is to know that Christ has been given all the power and authority in heaven, on earth and *inside* the earth. "All power is given unto Me in heaven and in earth," Matthew 28:18. "That at the name of Jesus every knee should bow, of things in heaven, and things in earth, and things under the earth; And that every tongue should confess that Jesus Christ is Lord, to the glory of God the Father," Philippians 2:10, 11. This means that He is the Commander in Chief of the Heavens, He is The Captain, Jesus Christ.

> "The message of the cross is foolish to those who are headed for destruction! But we who are being saved know it is the very power of God."
>
> (1 Corinthians 1: 18)

> "In the same way, even though God has the right to show his anger and his power, he is very patient with those on whom his anger falls, who are destined for destruction."
>
> (Romans 9: 22)

Breaking Contracts and Agreements

We can break all contracts and agreements with Satan just as easily as seeking divorce from an abusive spouse. However, we must be discerning! Here is another subtle deception that requires our full attention and understanding, as many new age folks are of the belief that they can break and rescind contracts and agreements with the dark forces when they no longer serve them. They call in 'The Light', the ascended masters, and invoke things like the violet flame or other colors of the rainbow, and believe these prayers and invocations are enough to do the trick and free them from their previous agreements, vows, implants, imprints, people, places, and things that no longer serve them. This is spiritual fraud.

Remember, Lucifer *is* 'The Light' they summon. What they are essentially doing is calling on fallen angels to rescue them from other fallen angels! Demons masquerade as angels of light, as we know from the second letter to the Corinthians, chapter 11 verse 14. And that is exactly what happens, they are simply transferred over to a different group of demons, who placate them into the false belief that they will be safe and free with their belief in them and their affirmation of 'The Light.'

These people are never free, they may experience some 'feel good' butterflies behind their neck, which are the fallen angelic demons who are now in charge of their spirits. They may even experience a few months of peace, but all they really have done is resold their debt to another group within the Celestial Mafia. By following the doctrines of demons, however subtle, however loving and illuminating the appearance, these seductive beings all work for the same boss, Lucifer the Satan, the Devil himself.

The solution? Please take it from one who has been there. I have spent 25 years in new age circles, done all the prayers, only to find myself deep under the spells of witchcraft which nearly drained my life away. I turned to every known god and goddess who promised protection and to break the powers of darkness. They all failed to liberate me, and the only God who was able to save my life, was none other than the Lord Jesus Christ. He is the only one who has the authority and power to break curses, and to deliver us earth humans from the powers and principalities of darkness, by breaking their contracts, and agreements, and breaking down the strongholds of the seven major principalities of Lucifer the Satan. The peace and freedom that comes from Him is real and eternal.

I will address in more detail this process along with sharing the necessary prayers that will create breakthroughs in the heavenly realms in a companion workbook to this book, titled, *Finding Freedom.*

"No one can receive anything unless God gives it from heaven."

(John 3:27)

NOTES:

1. The Text of the *Gospel of Thomas* from the Scholars Version translation published in *The Complete Gospels*, verse 103, https://selfdefinition.org/christian/Gospel-of-Thomas-Scholars-Version-15-pages-1961.pdf
2. Ibid., verse 16a, 16b
3. Art Matthias, *Biblical Foundations of Freedom,* Wellspring Ministries 2000, p. 59
4. *Gospel of Thomas,* Ibid, verse 102
5. Robert M. Stanley, *Covert Encounters in Washington, D.C.,* CreateSpace, April 18, 2011
6. Alfred Labremont Webre, JD, MEd., Exopolitics Blog: *Secret U.S. Mars program & Life on Mars,* http://wxopolitics.blogs.com/exopolitics/2011
7. Ibid., Stanley, 2011
8. Art Mathias, *Biblical Foundations of Freedom-Destroying Satan's Lies with God's Truth, In His Own Image-We Are Wonderfully Made,* Wellspring Publishing, 2000, 2010, www.akwellspring.com

CHAPTER FIVE
Agreements with God

"It is a terrible (fearful) thing to fall into the hands of the living God."
(Hebrews 10:31)

"...work out your own salvation with fear and trembling."
(Philippians 2:12)

"Notice how God is both kind and severe.
He is severe toward those who disobeyed,
but kind to you if you continue to trust in his kindness.
But if you stop trusting, you also will be cut off."
(Romans 11: 22)

When we turn to the Lord, we are turning away entirely from the kingdom of darkness and trusting the power of God to translate us into His kingdom. While we may experience all kinds of miracles in the process, the responsibility is ours to turn away from all known sin, error, mistake, involvement in Lucifers' Satanic kingdom. The earth is a battlefield, as we have already established, and turning to the Living God, who is victorious over all the evil schemes of Lucifer/Satan, is no exception. The kingdom of darkness does not let go of a soul easily, and they will fight and torment us and do everything in their power to create doubt in the life of the believer. This is all used as testing, to strengthen the soul of the believer, by God.

> "All things work together for good for those who love God and are called according to His purpose."
>
> (Romans 8:28)

The Lord does not leave us exposed, as He promises to be our refuge, our shield, and our protector in times of troubles, He promises to hide us under the shadow of His almighty wing, and to defend us in all our battles. He also equips us with His own armor, the armor of God:

> "Put on the whole armor of God that you may be able to stand against the wiles of the devil. For we wrestle not against flesh and blood, but against principalities, against powers, against the rulers of the darkness of this world, against spiritual wickedness in high [places]. Therefore, put on the full armor of God, so that when the day of evil comes, you may be able to stand your ground, and after you have done everything, to stand. Stand therefore, having girded your loins with truth, and having put on the breastplate of righteousness, and your feet shod with the preparation of the gospel of peace; In all circumstances take up the shield of faith, with which you can extinguish all the flaming darts of the evil one; Put on salvation as your helmet, and take the sword of the Spirit, which is the word of God. Praying always with all prayer and supplication in the Spirit, by staying alert with all perseverance and supplication for all God's people."
>
> (Ephesians 6:11-18)

God's Covenants

The word *testamentum* is the Latin word often used to express the Hebrew word which signifies *covenant*; so, the titles, Old and New Testaments, are used to denote the old and new covenants.

In the Bible, the Hebrew word *brit* (pronounced *breet*) means covenant, a binding agreement or arrangement between two parties, whether unilaterally or bilaterally, involving obligations, responsibilities or obedience. A covenant can be a promise, oath, pledge, vow, pact, treaty, as in 2 Chronicles 16:3, an alliance, compact, contract, arrangement, agreement, and more. Throughout history men have entered into agreements and made covenants in the attempt to ensure that the other party would follow through on his part of their agreement. These covenants were often sealed in blood, and later they became written documents, as we have today in our present legal arenas. In fact, the word British is actually a Hebrew word, which translates to the people of the covenant. *brit* - covenant; *ish* - people.

The New Covenant is all about Grace. To God, Grace is the covenant that He has with us earth humans. "For by grace you have been saved through faith" (Ephesians 2:8, 9) The Blood Covenant that God has with man is through Jesus Christ. Before Christ, the priests of Israel sacrificed the blood of goats and lambs upon the altars, for the propitiation of man's sins. Jesus Christ became the ultimate Lamb of God, and truly was the final blood sacrifice in Israel, as this practice ended after the crucifixion of Jesus Christ.

The sacrifice of Jesus Christ is the greatest love story known to man. Jesus said, "No one takes My life, but I gladly lay it down on My own initiative..." in John 10:18.

There were many instances related in the Gospels of the Pharisees when other religious and political leaders tried to take Jesus' life, but they could not. There is proof in Luke 4:28-30 when the angry crowd tried to throw Jesus off a cliff, but it says, "He passed through their midst." According to the Buddhist Scriptures, the Hindu Brahman conspired and plotted to have Jesus killed for rebuking them, but they did not succeed either. Jesus took refuge in the Buddhist temples until He was ready to travel back to Judea and begin His three years of preaching, teaching, healing, and casting out demons in the land before his death and resurrection.

Jesus willingly gave His life at the exact time that God intended. Revelation 13:8 says, "The Lamb of God was slain before the foundation of the world." In other words, before God created the world and all it contains, He knew He would send His Son to save His creation from sin. Genesis 3:15 was the first of 653 prophesies in the Old Testament about the Lamb of God.

Jesus did not make the ultimate sacrifice, Jesus was the ultimate sacrifice. In Exodus 12, God promised the children of Israel that Moses would lead them out of Egypt into the Promised Land. They were instructed to take an unblemished lamb, slaughter it, put its blood over the doorposts, and eat what was left as the Passover lamb. The lamb's blood caused the plague of death to 'pass over' them, to heal them and feed them. Exodus 12 truly represented the foreshadowing of the blood covenant with the world.

Life is in the blood. "For the life of the flesh is in the blood: and I have given it to you on the altar to make an atonement for your souls: for it is the blood that makes an atonement for the soul." (Leviticus 17:11) Consequently, Christ had to suffer and die because sin had to be paid for with innocent blood, an unblemished lamb. He paid the price for humanity. The Blood Covenant is for our deliverance and freedom from the bondage from the kingdom of darkness, Lucifer's kingdom.

In the Old Testament, whenever two people or two groups wanted to make peace, share their wealth and blessings with each other, they would make a covenant. Often it was called a blood covenant. This practice still exists in many parts of the world. In many African nations, tribal chiefs make a blood covenant with a rival tribe by offering gifts and drinking each other's blood. As a result, the threats of harm or attack were quelled. The practice of cutting each other's wrist and then rubbing dust into the wound, producing a scar as proof of the covenant they had made, would stave off any enemy or cannibal.

This is why Jesus Christ said in John 6:53, "Unless you eat My flesh, and drink My blood, you have no part in Me." He was not encouraging cannibalism. What He was saying, 'When you receive My death and put your faith in My blood, then you have a blood covenant with Me. Your enemies will now be My enemies. Your battles will now be My battles. Your problems will now be My problems. I will fight them, win them, and solve them! I am now your partner for life. I will defend you and protect you and cover you because you honor My covenant by honoring My blood.'

In a Hebrew or African covenant between two people, agreements were made, gifts were exchanged, and blood was shed to ratify the covenant. Everything that belonged to one person, now belonged to the other as well, just as in a marriage. This was, and is, the most powerful form of contract that exists in the world. When Jesus went to the cross, He became the gift, the sacrifice and the blood that now brings us into covenant with God. This is the power of a covenant. An exchange is made. Gifts are given. Agreements are made and sworn to be kept, by the shedding of blood.

Through His blood, God adopts us as his sons, daughters, and heirs to His Kingdom. He says, "All that is Mine is now yours and all that is yours is now Mine. Everything we have belongs to God, and everything He has belongs to us. But what do we have to offer? Gods says, "Bring Me your sin, and I will bring you My righteousness. Bring Me your sickness, and I will bring you My health. Bring Me your lack, and I will bring your My provision. Bring Me your confusion, and I will bring you My peace. Bring Me your depression, and I will bring you My joy."

This is why Jesus so willingly laid down His life. He knew that He had to be the final animal sacrifice that would bring us into covenant with God. No other sacrifice would do. No greater love could be possible. No clearer proof that God would back up His promises. Now all the promises of God in the Bible are available to us, not because we are a good or bad person; but because God backs up His promises with His very own blood. Blood is the guarantee. Blood is the proof. We are only asked to receive this gift of Grace through faith.

MY REFUGE AND MY FORTRESS

God's Covenant with you is expressed in Psalm 91 which is all about the promise made to all those who put their trust in the Lord and love Him. That's the covenant. If you trust Him, He will protect you and command His angels to guard you in all your ways. (v. 11). In fact, it is a type of marriage contract because it promises God's protection and salvation comes to those who love the Lord. If you love Him, you will receive His salvation and deliverance, long life and blessings. That's the agreement. It works both ways. There is, however, one condition, the key word is that illustrates in the end its your choice, is "if". If you put your faith in Him, all these benefits will be bestowed upon you.

This psalm is a promise to all those who exercise faith in the Lord, are the ones who get His Protection, His Angels, His Freedom from Disease, His Peace during the storms and battles of life. This is one Psalm, that many on the Spiritual Path, along with many who are new to walking with Christ, focus on, oftentimes exclusively, until a sense of mastery of confidence in the Lord is reached, along with all His benefits that come with being in Covenant with the Lord through faith.

Psalm 91 is read when people need protection, when they feel fear, or in need of covering. When you read the Psalms out loud, it's essentially putting God's Word into your own mouth and being. For Healing and Deliverance issues, we use Psalm 91 before all deliverance sessions. We *personalize* the psalm, which applies the Word into ourselves, in a way that it essentially washes us with His Word, which breaks off lots of negativity. Here is the Psalm, personalized, of course you must refer to yourself when you read the Lord's words, as he or she respectively. Otherwise, the word for you, becomes I and me. This really helps clear the air before bedtime too, when people are anxious, nervous about something, or in fear of the night.

To be read out loud:

I choose to dwell in the secret place of the Most High God, and I will rest and abide under the under the shadow of the Almighty, El Shaddai.

I will say of the LORD, He is my refuge and my fortress: my God; in Him will I trust.

Surely, he will deliver and save me from the snare of the fowler, and from the deadly pestilence.

He will cover me with his feathers, and under his wings I find refuge and trust: his truth shall be my shield and buckler.

I will not be afraid for the terror by night; nor for the arrow that flies by day;

Nor for the pestilence that walks in darkness; nor for the destruction that wastes at noonday.

A thousand shall fall at my side, and ten thousand at my right hand; but it shall not come near me.

Only with my eyes shall I witness and see the reward of the wicked.

Because I have made the LORD, my refuge, even the Most High God, my habitation;

There, no evil shall befall me, neither shall any plague come nigh (near) my dwelling.

For He shall give His Angels charge over me, to keep me in all of my ways.

They shall bear me up in their hands, lest I dash my foot against a stone.

I shall tread upon the lion and serpent: the young lion and the dragon I shall trample under feet.

The Words and Promises of God:

> "Because he/she has set his/her love upon me, therefore will I deliver him/her: I will set him/her on high, because he/she knows my name.
>
> When he/she shall call upon me, I will answer him/her: I will be with him/her in trouble; I will deliver him/her, and honor him/her.
>
> With long life will I satisfy him/her, and show him/her my salvation."
>
> (Psalm 91:1-16)

God's Covenant with Israel

> "Because he loves me," says the Lord, "I will rescue him; I will protect him, for he acknowledges my name. He will call upon me, and I will answer him; I will be with him in trouble, I will deliver him and honor him. With long life will I satisfy him and show him my salvation."
>
> (Psalm 91:14-16)

There is a scripture in Genesis in which the Lord speaks a covenant, a promise that everyone who blesses the nation that God gave to Abraham, and its citizens, He would in turn bless them. That nation became modern Israel, the citizens now Jews from the tribe of Judah. Consider for a moment that the nation of Abraham was conquered, and its citizens dispersed into exile for 1,878 years, after which the Jews were given back their homeland in 1948.

> "The Lord had said to Abram, "Leave your country, your people and your father's household and go to the land I will show you. "I will make you into a great nation and I will bless you; I will make your name great, and you will be a blessing. I will bless those who bless you, and whoever curses you I will curse; and all peoples on earth will be blessed through you."
>
> (Genesis 12:1-3)

As with all marriage contracts and covenants go, the love bond goes both ways. There are consequences for breaking any contract, especially one that involves love, a broken heart! One thing we know from the scriptures is that the Lord Yahuah is a being of integrity. He keeps His Word. He says what He means, and He means what He says. Many have asked both Jew and Gentile, why did God choose this stiff-necked stubborn group of people? My short answer, is because this subset of human beings was seeded with His DNA from the twelve sons of Jacob, whose name was later changed by God Himself to 'Israel'. As family dramas go, some keep the faith, and others stray. That's the history of the Israelites.

The Jews came out of the tribe of Judah. Before that time, there were no Jews. The Israelites were dispersed all over the globe. Some scholars believe that one of the lost tribes, that of Manasseh and Ephraim, ended up in India. Today there is a group in India who maintain the old traditions of ancient Israel, including circumcision. Ethiopia has a group of Jews who also come from one of these lost tribes of Israel. We know, from the Word of the God, that His covenant comes from His heart, but at the same time it is a legal contract, binding in Heaven and on Earth. The Lord is passionate over His Bride. This oath to the Israelites is spelled out in the Torah, the book of Deuteronomy:

> "For you are a people holy to the Lord your God. The Lord your God has chosen you out of all the peoples on the face of the earth to be his people, <u>his treasured possession</u>. The Lord did not set his affection on you and choose you because you were more numerous than other peoples, for you were the fewest of all peoples. <u>But it was because the Lord loved you and kept the oath he swore to your forefathers</u> that he brought you out with a mighty hand and <u>redeemed you from the land of slavery</u>, from the power of Pharaoh king of Egypt. Know therefore that the Lord your God is God; <u>he is the faithful God, keeping his covenant of love to a thousand generations of those who love him and keep his commands</u>. But those who hate him he will repay to their face by destruction; he will not be slow to repay to their face those who hate him."
>
> (Deuteronomy 7:6-10)

The following verse explains that God's covenant with Israel is still in effect today:

> "Brothers, let me take an example from everyday life. Just as no one can set aside or add to a human covenant that has been duly established, so it is in this case. The promises were spoken to Abraham and to his seed. The Scripture does not say "and to seeds," meaning many people, but "and to your seed," meaning one person, who is Christ. What I mean is this: The law, introduced 430 years later, does not set aside the covenant previously established by God and thus do away with the promise. For if the inheritance depends on the law, then it no longer depends on a promise; but God in his grace gave it to Abraham through a promise."
>
> (Galatians 3:15-17)

Another interesting piece is that the Lord Yahuah is the one to determine the boundaries of the nation of Israel, not the United Nations, not even the President of the United States. This is His *covenant* with Israel as written in Deuteronomy:

> "When the Most High gave the nations their inheritance, when he divided all mankind, he set up boundaries for the peoples according to the number of the sons of Israel. For the Lord's portion is his people, Jacob his allotted inheritance. In a desert land he found him, in a barren and howling waste. He shielded him and cared for him; he guarded him as the apple of his eye, like an eagle that stirs up its nest and hovers over its young, that spreads its wings to catch them and carries them on its pinions. The Lord alone led him; no foreign god was with him."
>
> (Deuteronomy 32:8-12)

This means that the boundaries of the nation of Israel is based on a percentage of the number people descended from the twelve tribes of Israel. That includes all the lost tribes. His people are called the 'apple of his eye', and this metaphor represents the 'lens' of the eye. The lens of the eye is what He sees through. Israel is the lens by which the Lord gauges the world. He looks at the world through the lens of Israel. He renders judgment and blessing based on the treatment of His people. Nations are blessed or cursed based on their treatment of Israel.

> "For this is what the Lord Almighty says: "After he has honored me and has sent me against the nations that have plundered you—for whoever touches you touches the apple of his eye—I will surely raise my hand against them so that their slaves will plunder them. Then you will know that the Lord Almighty has sent me."
>
> (Zechariah 2:8, 9)

Israel is the most contentious piece of real estate on planet earth. Yet it is the Lord who determines the boundaries of Israel. After all, it all ends there, at Mount Megiddo, at the battle of Armageddon. The New Jerusalem will be downloaded out of the heavens and overlaid on the old Jerusalem and the Lord Yahuah's son, Yeshua, the Lord Jesus Christ, will assume the ancient throne of David and reign from the New Jerusalem. Israel is the Lord's portal. Therefore, it is the site of so many spiritual battles between the forces of Heaven and Satan, who is the god of this world. They are fighting over the power of that portal and the land. Yet, the Lord's eyes are continually on His land, every year, up until the end of our present timeline when He returns.

> "Observe therefore all the commands I am giving you today, so that you may have the strength to go in and take over the land that you are crossing the Jordan to possess, and so that you may live long in the land that the Lord swore to your forefathers to give to them and their descendants, a land flowing with milk and honey. The land you are entering to take over is not like the land of Egypt, from which you have come, where you planted your seed and irrigated it by foot as in a vegetable garden. But the land you are crossing the Jordan to take possession of is a land of mountains and valleys that drinks rain from heaven. It is a land the Lord your God cares for; the eyes of the Lord your God are continually on it from the beginning of the year to its end."
>
> (Deuteronomy 11:8-12)

The Israelites lost the land for 1,878 years, because they turned away from the Lord, and did not accept and recognize their Messiah when He was sent. The Israelites have a long history of being disobedient to the Lord, being seduced by foreign gods and engaging in idolatry. All breaches of contract have their consequences, and this was definitely one of them! The Lord dried up their land, and scattered His people into the hands of their enemies and other nations. The land of Israel was in a drought for over 1850 years. It only started to rain and become restored as the 'land of milk and honey' in the early twentieth century, when His prophecy and promise was fulfilled.

> "Be careful, or you will be enticed to turn away and worship other gods and bow down to them. Then the Lord's anger will burn against you, and he will shut the heavens so that it will not rain, and the ground will yield no produce, and you will soon perish from the good land the Lord is giving you."
>
> (Deuteronomy 11:16-17)

Jerusalem is the home of the Lord's heart. When King Solomon built his glorious first temple and dedicated it to the Lord, this is what the Lord said:

> "The LORD said to him: "I have heard the prayer and plea you have made before me; I have consecrated this temple, which you have built, by putting my Name there forever. My eyes and my heart will always be there."
>
> (1 Kings 9:3)

Many of you know the history, that the temple was destroyed, not once but twice. But to the Lord, it still lives in His heart, spiritually, in heaven. After the final blood sacrifice was shed through Yeshua, there was no longer any blood sacrifice made in Israel or any other place by the Israelites. The New Covenant was then made, which includes our bodies as the 'temple of the Living God'. Yet, the prophecy also tells us that the temple in Jerusalem will be built a third time, where the desolation of abomination will take place.

Foreshadowed by the slaughter of a pig by Antiochus the Fourth, the being known as the Antichrist will deceive Israel into accepting him as their Messiah as Jews begin blood sacrifices again. The antichrist then starts persecuting all those who refuse to worship him. Yet, despite these cosmic wars, the Word of the Lord tells us that His heart and His eyes will always be in Jerusalem. These battles are divine appointments allowed by the Lord, to weed out the wheat from the chaff, the faithful from the rebels.

The Promise of a "New Covenant"

There are multiple scriptures citing the promise from the Lord of a new covenant. This New Covenant is also called The Blood Covenant which came through the finished work of Yeshua on the Cross, who took on the sins of humanity and become a curse, so that all can be delivered from the curse of the law. It is also known as the *Covenant of Grace*. The prophets of the Old Testament all wrote about it and foresaw it.

> "As for you, because of the *blood of my covenant* with you, I will free your prisoners from the waterless pit."
>
> (Zechariah 13:11)

> "I will make an *everlasting covenant* with you"
>
> (Isaiah 55:3 - cf. 42:6; 49:6-8; 59:21; 61:8)

> "I will make a *new covenant* with the house of Israel and with the house of Judah"
>
> (Jeremiah 31:31-34 - cf. 23:5; 32:40; 50:5)

> "I will make a *covenant of peace* with them; it will be an everlasting covenant"
>
> (Ezekiel 37:26 - cf. 16:60,62; 34:23,25)

In Ezekiel chapter 37, the prophet is given a vision of a valley of dry bones, which is Israel, and these bones come back to life, are reborn, or reincarnated. He promised to give the land of Israel back to His people, and that promise, and prophesy was fulfilled. After 1,878 years, Israel became a nation in one day, May 14, 1948.

Ezekiel's Vision of the Dry Bones

> "I was carried off in the Merkavah, and I was then set down in the middle of the valley which was full of bones, and I walked around and around and there were many bones and they were very dry. The Lord said to me, "son of man, can these bones live?" and I answered, then he said to me: "Son of man, these bones are the people of Israel. They say, 'Our bones are dried up and our hope is gone; we are cut off.' Therefore, prophesy and say to them: 'This is what the Sovereign LORD says: My people, I am going to open your graves and bring you up from them; I will bring you back to the land of Israel."
>
> (Ezekiel 37:11-12)

This is another scripture in the Bible that was not deleted by the first ecumenical council of Nicaea in 325 A.D., which decreed reincarnation as heresy. The Lord Himself promised to open up the grave and bring new life, which is another way of explaining reincarnation. Being true to His word, He did it! All those souls who settled in Israel from 1948 till this present day all lived there before in ancient times. Their physical bodies were decayed, but the Lord preserved their souls and gave them new lives.

> "And I will settle you in your own land. I will take the Israelites out of the nations where they have gone. I will gather them from all around and bring them back into their own land. And they and their children and their children's children will live there forever."
>
> (Ezekiel 37:21, 25)

Only the Lord has the power put new flesh on old bones, and give the soul the breath of life to live again. No matter how you want to explain it or what you call it, He alone controls the process of reincarnation, putting the soul back into a body to live again. This is a covenant, a promise that He made nearly three thousand years ago.

> "He led me back and forth among them, and I saw a great many bones on the floor of the valley, bones that were very dry. He asked me, "Son of man, can these bones live?" I said, "Sovereign LORD, you alone know." Then he said to me, "Prophesy to these bones and say to them, 'Dry bones, hear the word of the LORD! This is what the Sovereign LORD says to these bones: I will make breath enter you, and you will come to life. I will attach tendons to you and make flesh come upon you and cover you with skin; I will put breath in you, and you will come to life. Then you will know that I am the LORD.'" So, I prophesied as I was commanded. And as I was prophesying, there was a noise, a rattling sound, and the bones came together, bone to bone. I looked, and tendons and flesh appeared on them and skin covered them, but there was no breath in them. Then he said to me, "Prophesy to the breath; prophesy, son of man, and say to it, 'this is what the Sovereign LORD says: Come, breath, from the four winds and breathe into these slain, that they may live.'" So, I prophesied as he commanded me, and breath entered them; they came to life and stood up on their feet—a vast army. ......Then you, my people, will know that I am the LORD, when I open your graves and bring you up from them. I will put my Spirit in you and you will live, and I will settle you in your own land. Then you will know that I the LORD have spoken, and I have done it, declares the LORD.'"
>
> (Ezekiel 37)

While there are many scriptures that relate to Israel, this was a *covenant* promise from the Lord Yahuah, that Israel was going to be reborn, which indeed did happen in 1948. His-story begins and ends with and in Israel, as that is where the final battle of Armageddon takes place. This battle happens on a mount south of Jerusalem, known as Har Megiddo which in Hebrew translates as *the field of blood,* an ancient battlefield portal, where the Jewish Messiah, Yeshua HaMashiach, Jesus the Christ, returns in full glory with all the hosts of Heaven, fleets of spaceships, and ends the battle with His Word. He binds the enemies of Israel, and has an angel cast Lucifer/ Satan, and his antichrist in the lake of fire. He reclaims the throne of David in Jerusalem and sets up His Kingdom on the Earth, where He will reign triumphantly for a millennium.

Notes:

All Bible quotes from biblehub.com

CHAPTER SIX
Aliens and Religion

"Those who say religion has nothing to do with politics,
do not know what religion is."
~ Mahatma Gandhi

Racism was created by the fallen angels, those alien gods that came to earth, through a series of genetic manipulations of human beings. The separation of the human race, to divide and conquer, was the goal. So too was the reason for their setting up of differing religions, along with the implementation of spiritual limitation devices, to keep us humans from seeing the truth. Many of these alien gods, fallen angels, had a god complex. They are in open rebellion against our Creator Father God, and they want to be worshipped themselves. They attack God by trying to hurt, enslave and kill God's children. It is their motis operandi to mislead humans away from their Creator God, with whom they compete for human attention, even worship. They used men to channel their agenda and create a form of worship of themselves! Remember, the fallen angels come as angels of light, but their agenda is to steal as many souls as they can from the Creator God. All the prophets were divinely guided and channeled the angels and the lords, but not all those angels and lords were of the light.

Religion has always been a means of experimentation by the gods. The early dynasties of ancient Egypt demonstrate this with real drama! Consider the reign of Akhenaton, the pharaoh with the elongated egg head, who came from a planet within the Sirius star system, who ruled Egypt for seventeen years during the eighteenth dynasty, died in 1336 B.C. His mission was to introduce monotheism into human consciousness, during a time when polytheism was the only tradition in Egypt. This notion of worshipping one god, the sun god as the sole Creator, was so radical that he was anathematized after his death. Egypt fell back into polytheism, idolatry, and slavery, which later proved its undoing. In fact, in the Bible, the Hebrew word for Egypt, which is Mizraim, means bondage. According to the Kabbalists, *Egypt* is used as a code word for the human ego, for our incessantly reactive, self-seeking nature. Any aspect of our nature that controls us is *Egypt*. It's the oldest master-slave relationship in Creation.

These early experiments of religion and religious movements elucidate how easily we humans can be swayed. Frederich Engles and Karl Marx,[1] authors of *The Communist Manifesto,* 1948, well known as the founders of modern communism, rightly observed that "religion is the sign of the oppressed creature", and "religion is the opiate of the masses." Radical ideas for their time, particularly since humanity has been steeped in religion for millennia. They also said, "religion is the impotence of the human mind to deal with occurrences it cannot understand." These observations demonstrate that religion itself is a kind of crutch that humans cling to… but why? Clearly, religion is *not* the same as spirituality, or following the spiritual path, or having a personal relationship with the living God. Let's examine and define our language, as religion has been difficult to define. One standard model of religion, used in religious studies courses, was proposed by Clifford Geertz, who simply called it a "cultural system". [2] A critique of Geertz's model by Talal Asad categorized religion as "an anthropological category." [3]

According to Wikipedia, r*eligion* is a cultural system that creates powerful and long-lasting meaning, by establishing symbols that relate humanity to truths and values. Many religions have narratives, symbols, traditions, and sacred histories that are intended to give meaning to life or to explain the origin of life or the universe. They tend to derive morality, ethics, religious laws, or a preferred lifestyle from their ideas about the cosmos and human nature. The word *religion* is sometimes used interchangeably with *faith* or *belief system*, but religion differs from private belief in that it has a public aspect. Most religions have organized behaviors, including clerical hierarchies, a definition of what constitutes adherence or membership, congregations of laity, regular meetings, or services for the purposes of veneration of a deity or for prayer, holy places (either natural or architectural), and/or scriptures. The development of religion has taken different forms in different cultures. Some religions place an emphasis on belief, while others emphasize practice.

According to popular authors, Erich von Däniken, Zecharia Sitchin, Robert K. G. Temple, intelligent extraterrestrial beings called *ancient astronauts* or *ancient aliens* visited Earth in the past and this contact is connected with the origins or development of human cultures, technologies, and religions. They propose that the deities themselves from all the religions are actually extraterrestrials, and the subsequent miracles they performed were in fact evidence of their advanced technologies and, were taken as proof of their divine status, establishing their 'god' status in the minds of ancient humans.

The apocryphal *Book of Enoch* tells of flying objects and beings called "the Watchers" who have mutinied against heaven and descended to earth. His book goes further as Enoch is taken on journeys to various corners of the Earth in the flying object and at one point even travels to the heavens in a spaceship he called a 'fiery chariot'. His two scrolls, 1 and 2 Enoch, describe in great detail the events on earth, the timeline of the end of days, the coming of the Son of Man and the portals of the stars of heaven. See my Chapter on the *Fallen Angels and Watchers*, in *Who Are the Angels?* Book Three.[4]

Proponents of the ancient astronaut theory argue that the evidence for prehistoric interaction with alien beings comes from gaps in archaeological records and the missing link in our jump from Neanderthal to Homo Sapiens.[5]

The Book of Genesis states that "When men began to multiply on the face of the ground, and daughters were born to them, the sons of God saw that the daughters of men were fair; and they took to wife such of them as they chose... The Nephilim were on the earth in those days, and afterwards, when the sons of God came in to the daughters of men, and they bore children to them." In the King James version, they are identified as giants (Genesis 6:1-4).[6] See my chapter on *Giants* in Book One of *Who's Who in the Cosmic Zoo?*

Chuck Missler and Mark Eastman argue in their book, *Alien Encounters: The Secret Behind the UFO Phenomenon* that UFOs carry the fallen angels, or offspring of fallen angels, the Nephilim of Genesis, who have now returned.[7] They believe it was this interbreeding between the angels and humans that led to what they call the gene pool problem. Noah was perfect in his generations, that is in his genealogy, which was not tarnished by the intrusion of fallen angels. It seems that this adulteration of the human gene pool was a major problem on the planet earth.

Erich von Däniken[8] saw an extraterrestrial connection in this passage, and suggests that here "we have the sons of God, who interbred with human beings." Von Däniken also suggests that the two angels who visited Lot in Genesis 19 were not angels, but ancient astronauts who used atomic weapons to destroy the city of Sodom. They came to warn of the impending disaster, as there was a timetable to the destruction and were sent to save the righteous. Von Däniken questioned why God would work on a timetable and why an "infinitely good Father" would give "preference to 'favorite children,' such as Lot's family, over countless others." This is because of the bloodline of Noah's genealogy, which was untarnished, while the countless others who were offspring from the children of the Nephilim which were causing all the problems, had to be stopped.[8]

Ancient artifacts and painting illustrate representations of flying saucers in medieval and renaissance art. This supports the ancient astronaut theory, and suggests that the modifiers of humanity return to check up on their creation throughout time, and can still intervene in human affairs. Paleolithic cave paintings, Wondjina in Australia and Val Camonica in Italy bear a resemblance to present day astronauts. All those in support of the ancient astronaut theory claim that similarities, such as dome shaped heads, are interpretations of beings wearing space helmets, and prove that early man was visited by a space faring race.

The ancient alien astronaut theory proposes that the gods were extraterrestrials whom our ancestors misinterpreted as gods, because they were so superior as to appear supernatural. Von Däniken says all the ancient texts are descriptions of ET beings, and that our ancestors made them out to be gods to be worshipped. However, I am asserting to the ancient alien astronaut theory, that many of these ET gods did in fact have a god complex, and were responsible for setting up religions to safeguard their power over us.

Homer's Iliad of 8 B.C. tells the story of a great war between jealous gods. In 3800 B.C., the Sumerians wrote in their stone tablets of the Annunaki, which Archeoastronomer Zecharia Sitchin translates as meaning, 'those who from heaven come to Earth'. The Bible talks about the Anakim, who were giant beings, just like the Sumerian Annunaki. Could the Anakim of the Jewish Bible be in fact the Sumerian Annunaki, just in a slightly different language? For more info, see my Chapter on the *Annunaki* in Book One of *Who's Who in The Cosmic Zoo?* [9]

Mount Olympus was the residence of the Greek God Zeus. The ancient texts describe a 'rumbling' to the point that, 'the entire top of the mountain lifted off.' The mountain top did not lift off, but mountain tops were a popular landing place for ancient space craft. What was being described was the ET Zeus en route from Mt. Olympus as he lifted off in a spacecraft.

Zeus was also known for wielding a lightning bolt that was destructive and was used in wrath. Poseidon used a trident to create tidal waves. Both were actual technological devices and weapons that directed forceful energy. Apollo was the son of Zeus and Leto, really a demigod, because his mother was human. Apollo rode in a Chariot of Fire, taught astronomy, and how to build roads and architecture. Apollo also had the power to bring illness and plague. These Greek gods were the same which the Romans recognized during their heydays, they only changed their names, and named the planets after them. Zeus became Jupiter, Poseidon became Neptune. Apollo was worshipped by the Romans and seen as the Sun God or Helios. The Greek God Heracles, who later became Hercules to the Romans, was the son of Zeus (Jupiter) and the mortal woman Alcmena. The demigod Hercules was famous for his super strength. All these matings between the 'gods' and mortal women, were the first accounts of what we call today, UFO abduction stories.

> "There were giants in the earth in those days; and also after that, when the sons of God came in unto the daughters of men, and they bore children to them, the same became mighty men which were of old, men of renown."
>
> (Genesis 6:4)

These mighty men of renown became the gods and demigods of Greek and Roman mythology.

These extra-terrestrials were part of the group of the sons of God and fallen angels that rebelled against the Creator. They all had god complexes. The ancient alien astronaut theorists believe all of these gods were extraterrestrials who arrived here on spacecraft. Morally, spiritually and ethically, I am asserting that not all of them were benevolent towards humankind. Because they mated with earth women, they tend to fall into the category of the rebels who begat the Nephilim.

In the Hindu texts, there are similar stories of gods mating with mortal women. Queen Kunti was given a secret mantra to summon any god and have a child with him. Kunti conceived a son Karna through the god Surya. She couldn't believe it, so she abandoned her baby in a basket in a river, who was later adopted by a chariot driver and was named Karna who became one of the central characters in the cosmic drama, 'Mahabharata.' Then she received a son Yudishtira from the god Dharma, then Bhima from the god Vayu, and Arjuna, from the god Indra. Kunti revealed the mantra to Madri, who bore twin sons Nakula and Sahadeva from the twin gods the Asvins. The five sons became known as the Pandavas. These demigods later fought a great war in the epic Mahabharata. Arjuna then defeated his distant half-brother Karna. The Mahabharata tells of vimanas, space craft, which orbited the earth and threw fire at one another. It describes gigantic cities that surrounded the earth, called mansions, a perfect description of mother ships. Battles raged over the earth against the forces of evil monsters that wanted to devour humankind.

What is consistent in all these ancient texts are the stories of ET gods mating with earth women, producing all kinds of demigods, star children, giants and monstrosities.

The ancient Nazca Lines, hundreds of enormous ground drawings etched into the high desert landscape of Peru, over 190 square miles long, that can only be seen from the air. These consist primarily of geometric shapes, but include depictions of a variety of animals and one human figure. The Nazca lines are hard evidence of ancient astronauts, as these figures can only be seen from above, yet were drawn on the ground. These are most likely mileposts to extra-terrestrial landing sites. These simple drawings etched into the desert plains could have been done by the people of Peru, who still do not yet have the technology to design and view from space. These lines were formed by extra-terrestrials, for who else would have such capacity in 500 B.C.?

The fact that there are such inconsistencies, gaps, incomplete explanations of historical and archaeological data, point to the existence of ancient astronauts. The level of technological sophistication necessary for constructing so many ancient monuments, temples, buildings, and stone circles, is not within our grasp today! The enormous amount of anachronistic evidence, sometimes referred to as 'out-of-place artifacts', as well as the vast amount of artwork and written accounts on stone tablets, can only be interpreted as close and continued contact with extraterrestrials and their technologies.

As I've been saying throughout this book, the greatest evidence of extraterrestrial contact we have is written in our Bible, both the Old and New Testaments. Ancient scriptures of Vedic literature, the Mahabharata, and the Apocrypha, the Books of Enoch, tell the same stories with different names. All point to ancient contact with extra-terrestrials, alien gods, who played out dramas with each other, both on the earth and over the earth. These ancient scriptures tell a very detailed story of the battles fought over earth, humans and human cultures, along with the insistence from these various gods that they be worshipped in a form known as *religion.*

Who Created Racism?

"But the one who hates his brother is in the
darkness and walks in the darkness,
and does not know where he is going, because
the darkness has blinded his eyes."
(1 John 2:11)

There is evidence, corroborating testimony from whistleblowers and investigative researchers, that two competing extraterrestrial/alien races from *inside* the earth, who are known as the Nordic Aliens aka Blonds aka Aryans, and the Reptilians aka Dracos aka Draconians[10] (See, Book One of *Who's Who in The Cosmic Zoo?*), are two groups that helped the Nazis, achieve antigravity technology. According to Dr. Michael Salla[11] in his 2015 book, *Insiders Reveal Secret Space Program and Extraterrestrial Alliance,* in accordance with the late whistleblower William Tompkins[12] in his 2015 book, *Selected by Extraterrestrials,* who worked as a spy for the US Navy during WW2, claims that the Nazis had thirty different space crafts that were witnessed in Nazi Germany during the late 1930s and early 1940s. Some of these crafts were weaponized. There was corroborating documentation to prove Tompkins claims.[11, 12]

Furthermore, Tompkins revealed that fourteen of the thirty spacecrafts were actually 'given' to the Nazis by the Reptilians, the rest of the sixteen crafts were developed by the Nordics working with the German Rocket Scientists.[12] This means that both competing alien groups gave spacecraft to the Nazis. One must question, why? And while we know that the Reptilians hate the God of Israel, so they take out their hatred on God's children, the Jews and born-again Christians, why would a seemingly beautiful human looking race of extraterrestrials help Hitler to achieve his goal of complete genocide of the Jewish Race?

It's certainly no coincidence that this group of Nordic ETs, who are platinum blonds, very white skinned, with blue eyes agreed to work with a megalomaniac who was inspired to create a pure 'white Aryan Race'. While both competing races may be competing for power over the earth and *who* runs the world, they both seemed to be on the same side of history, backing a man who was inspired by aliens to commit genocide on a group of humans based on their genetic identities as Jews.

During the Holocaust, it wasn't only Jews who were rounded up and sent into the death camps, but so were others who seemed to have been one quarter or one eighth Jewish in them, who didn't even identify as Jews, because they did not follow the Jewish religion, yet because of their genetics they were starved to death and burned in gas chambers. Blacks, gypsies and homosexuals were also rounded up for experimentation. A total of 11 Million people died under the Nazis, approximately 6 Million of them were Jews. The disclosure from Tompkins and Goode, revealed that the Nazis had human slaves working for them in underground facilities during the war. Many of whom were Jews and Blacks that were harvested from the concentration camps. The genocide of what amounted to two-thirds of Europe's Jews, happened while these two groups of competing alien races fed Hitler with flying saucers some of which had weapons.

Perhaps these two seemingly competing groups of aliens are not so different after all? Why would these human ETs, help Hitler towards the genocide of the Jewish race? Perpetuate and continue using humans as slaves and fodder for their various alien-hybrid experiments? Could it be that they are in rebellion to the God of Israel? One thing both Jews and Blacks share, is a common history of slavery and racism. Many Israelites were dark skinned coming out of Africa. Egypt is in Africa. As I've written about this before that slavery began by the Ancient Sumerians, who genetically manipulated humans to use as slaves. African Blacks were in bondage to African Muslims who began the slave trade to Europeans. This rabbit hole goes deep with its roots beginning with the Annunaki, a race of giant alien lizard men, who experienced mutiny and family conflict amongst themselves, which has inevitably played out on Earth.

The Nazis used human slaves to help engineer their space crafts in underground caves. The Holocaust was a perfect cover for what amounted to the abduction of millions of humans, who were missing in Germany and throughout Europe, which included Jews, Black and others considered, 'undesirables' by the Nazi White Supremacists, who were working together with these White skinned aliens and lizard men. Got the picture? There's nothing new under the sun.

So, ask yourself this question, *who* created racism? Why is it after years of evolution and development of the human mind, psyche, and cultural integration, particularly in one of the grandest social experiments in the world, the United States of America, have resorted to racism being used a political calling card, when others don't agree with their policy, they're branded racist. Why can't people just disagree based on policy? Why does their motive always have to be under suspicion of racism? Whatever happened to being able to disagree, agreeably? Could it be, these politicians are actually 'projecting' their own racism into the mix, by instigating the flames of racism, anti-Semitism, by stirring the pot of the past, despite decades of improvement in race relations?

One should really ask oneself, *who* is behind the degradation of those who have worked all their lives to improve race relations in America and transcend beyond racial divisions, only to have been regressed by those in positions of political powers to use the 'race card' against them? Doesn't that tell you, that no matter what the human race does to accept and integrate all races, that it's never good enough for the archons of this world whose sole purpose is to keep humans divided over race?

It's time we look at the alien implants of racism, anti-Semitism and hatreds over having different genetics, by alien races who share this planet that are obviously threatened by the human race That maybe, racism is not something that humans should be constantly guilt tripped and manipulated over, but just perhaps, there is an alien presence on earth, whose very agenda is to control the earth for themselves, who are very much racist in and of themselves, who project their own racial superiority over the human race? Maybe they are 'inspiring' racial motives, racial projections, even where it doesn't exist just to keep humans divided over it?

Americans witnessed on multiple occasions during the Obama Administration, where accusations of racisms flew out of the White House almost daily, just because people who happened to be both black, white, brown, and yellow simply didn't agree with the President's policies and agenda, were all branded as racist for not agreeing with him because he was black. For the record, President Obama was not 100% black. He was Mulatto, Obama was biracial, he was half white and half black. His mother was white, and his father was black. As a result, there were some black people who never fully accepted him as black, yet the record shows, that 52% of white Americans voted for Obama during the 2008 Presidential elections. So how could they all be racist if they voted in the first Black and White President?

Yet despite his unprecedented victory, racism was still used as a political tactic to shame those who disagreed with his policies, not because he was black or white, but simply because they were not in the best interests of Americans. Unfortunately, shaming and blaming others who didn't agree with him by calling them racists, inevitably caused America to regress racial relations back to pre-Civil Rights Movement, birthing today's Black Lives Matter movement, which is countered with all lives matter.

Suffice it to say, that black people can be racist and prejudice against whites, just as much as they project it visa-versa. Again, who is to benefit from all these accusations, some of which are false and used to manipulate political winds of change? And more importantly, I want my readers to consider *who* is influencing those who point the fingers of racism at those who simply don't agree with their ideas, and *who* is benefitting by stirring the pot and thereby widening the racial divide?

There are beings that live inside this planet that do take sides, and want invisible control of human affairs, who see humans the way most humans see cattle, as a commodity to be used as a resource in multiple ways. Just like cattle, who can produce more milk alive, than dead, so can humans produce more *soul energy* when they are distressed, threatened and suffering through divisions, war and conflicts, than if we're dead. Think about it, no matter how hard people try to accept each other for what and *who* we are, someone is always pointing fingers and keeping the fires of the racial division alive. Why is that? Is it all our fault, like they want us to believe we are responsible for global warming, when climate change has absolutely nothing to do with human action, but forces beyond human control, like the cycles of the sun and the presence of multiple exoplanets intersecting within our solar system creating climate change on all the planets in our solar neighborhood. This suggests that humans are not the cause of warming or climate change, despite being blamed for it.[13]

Therefore, I am asserting, that humans are being played like a tune, by the archons of this present world, to keep racial divisions alive, front and center, even though those being fingered as racist are just the opposite. This is not to suggest, that racism, anti-Semitism and prejudice doesn't exist in people, it does, but being falsely accused for it, when it's not there, by not accepting differences as natural disagreements, which has absolutely nothing to do with the color of one's skin or genetics, is not racially motivated disagreement. To suggest it is, is the presence of a spirit and/or entity whose very agenda is to keep people divided over racial differences, religious differences and political differences because it feeds them with human soul essence and energy, and keeps humans distracted from realizing their full potential and God given purpose which is to express God's love through them to all of humankind. *The principal ingredient of life is love.*

"God is love. Therefore love,
without distinction, without calculation,
without procrastination, love."
~ Henry Drummond

According to whistleblower Corey Goode, these Nordic Alien Blond Humans have been in contact with the Vatican, the United States and Russia. I can't help but remember the movie, 'V', where a group of good looking humans, landed in spaceships pretending to be all friendly and benevolent, who were really lizards underneath a human exterior. Could these Nordic Blond Aryan Human ETs, actually be part of the Draconian Empire that they claim they are competing with? Why else would they both help the same side in WW2? A side that was *hell bent* on committing genocide on an entire race of people, and using others considered to be undesirables as slaves to an experiment, and thereby establishing a superior *all white* Aryan race? The fact that the Nazis were assisted by aliens which was covered up for decades that is being revealed now through the spiritual guts of whistleblowers like Goode and Tompkins, leaves us to connect the dots to their obvious motives and agenda to divide humanity. Challenging humans to now have to collectively *spiritually discern* which god they serve?

Just because these beings are technologically more advanced than humans, doesn't necessarily mean they are more evolved spiritually, nor does their gifting of spacecraft to the Nazis, make them benevolent beings, on the contrary, their motives must be scrutinized and put to the test. For my readers who remember the lesson in Book One of *Who's Who in The Cosmic Zoo?* that just because an extraterrestrial or extradimensional appears *human* doesn't necessarily mean they are benevolent to earth humans. As many, on the contrary have proven to be *controllers* and *manipulators* of planet earth, beginning with the historical record of the Annunaki by the ancient Sumerians in the Enuma Elish.

I also want to connect one more dot here for my readers consideration, and that is the historical and spiritual similarities between blacks and Jews. Both have a history of enslavement; the Israelites were in bondage to Egyptian Slave Masters for 400 years. The blacks were in bondage first to Muslim Slave Traders, who in turn were bought by white Europeans and then traded to the early Americans. Over 28 Million Africans have been enslaved in the Muslim world during the past 14 centuries while much has been written concerning the Transatlantic slave trade, surprisingly little attention has been given to the Islamic slave trade across the Sahara, the Red Sea and the Indian Ocean.

While the European involvement in the Transatlantic slave trade to the Americas lasted for just over three centuries, the Arab involvement in the slave trade has lasted fourteen centuries, and in some parts of the Muslim world, it continues to this day. A comparison of the Muslim slave trade to the American slave trade reveals some interesting contrasts.

While two out of every three slaves shipped across the Atlantic were men, the proportions were reversed in the Muslim slave trade. Two women for every man were enslaved by the Muslims.

There is ever growing evidence that the same force/entity/influence behind the persecution of blacks is the same entity behind the persecution of Jews. It is no coincidence that in the language of Astrology, both blacks and Jews are ruled by the planet Saturn. The planet of hardships, limitation and oppression. I must add, that on a personal note, I have found great comfort amongst my black brothers and sisters in Black Charismatic Churches from America to South Africa. I am accepted as a sister, regardless of my skin color and my Jewish heritage. On a soul level, there is great similitude and empathy for our shared histories.[14]

As you read through this book, you will discover the unmasking of *who* and *what* is behind the racism and antisemitism on this planet.

UFO Religions

"The final test of all Religions, is not Religiousness, but Love.
The only way to judge a religion, is to see how much it Loves.
Love is the only true religion."
- Henry Drummond

All the religions set up on planet earth were established by different extraterrestrial gods. Some of these gods were fallen sons of heaven and fallen extraterrestrial angels who had god complexes and demanded worship from us earth humans, along with various sacrifices to appease their lustful appetites. These gods have had an ongoing conflict with the Almighty Creator Lord, which began when Lucifer rebelled and persuaded one third of heaven's angels (extraterrestrials) to follow him. Since then they have been playing out their cosmic dramas and rebellion on earth and battling over the control of us earth humans. See Book Two: *Who is Gods?* for further elucidation.[15]

Yahuah, the God of Israel, the one who gave Moses the ten commandments on Mount Sinai, established the basis for morality and righteousness for all faiths. After the law was received, the Abrahamic faiths were corrupted in various ways by the god of this world, who is Lucifer the Satan and his fallen angels. Today there are many versions of Judeo-Christian philosophy, many churches and temples, some of which have become infiltrated by fallen angel dogma and adhere to a variety of doctrines from demons. Some of these religions were later set up by aliens, the fallen angel demons, and can be seen as UFO religions or cults. Let's discern.

The varied UFO religions, which include Nation of Islam, Theosophy, Scientology, The Urantia Book, and Heaven's Gate, can be differentiated by the dogmatic acceptance of ancient and present-day contact with extraterrestrial intelligence as a matter of faith. Many of these faiths rely on the reinterpretation of a mixture of ancient scriptures with new revelations, which have all been channeled to them by their prophets, who are fallen angels in masquerade. All of these are associated with fantastically advanced technology, spacecraft, and superior, intelligent aliens. All of these religions are cults with an agenda. By sandwiching truth and scientific data between falsehoods and lies, many have been misguided into gross immorality, such as murder, self-murder, and sexual perversions, all because they believe some being from the sky or inside the earth appeared to them and told them so. These are the hallmarks of the influence of fallen angels.

Islam was formed by a man named Mohammed, who considered himself a prophet. All the prophets of the Bible made lasting prophecies, yet Mohammed is one of so many prophets without a proven prophetic legacy. Many scholars debate his prophesies or predictions, which were all short term in nature, predicting the conquering of neighboring towns. Many people don't realize that Mohammed himself was promiscuous, which the Abrahamic faith considers grossly immoral. Muhammad had sex with just about anyone he pleased, thanks to Allah's extraordinary interest in his personal sex life, as depicted in the Qur'an.

Although the Qur'an doesn't appear to have enough space for topics like universal love and brotherhood, which Muslims sometimes insist are there, but aren't, the list of sexual partners that Muhammad felt himself entitled to enjoin is detailed more than once, sometimes in categories and sometimes in reference to specific persons, like Zaynab & Mary. The Hadith records the historical account of Mohammed's intense sexual appetites in great detail.

Muhammad was married to thirteen women, including eleven at one time. He relegated them to either consecutive days or, according to some accounts, all in one night. He married a prepubescent 9-year-old girl and even his adopted son's wife. On top of that, Muhammad had a multitude of slave girls and concubines with whom he had sex - sometimes on the very days when they had watched their husbands and fathers die at the hands of his army.

So, by any realistic measure, the creator of the world's most sexually restrictive religion was one of the most sexually indulgent characters in history.

It appears that Allah managed to hand down quite a few "revelations" that sanctioned Muhammad's personal pursuit of sex to the doubters around him. Interestingly they have become part of the eternal, infallible word of the Qur'an, to be memorized by generations of Muslims for whom they have no possible relevance.

There are numerous passages in the Qur'an that justify sex with young prepubescent girls, all types of pedophilia, other men's wives conquered through battle, slave girls, slave women, and as Mohammed exemplified polygamy, he married thirteen women at the same time, including a nine-year old girl.

Qur'an (33:50) - *"O Prophet! surely We have made lawful to you your wives whom you have given their dowries, and those whom your right hand possesses out of those whom Allah has given to you as prisoners of war, and the daughters of your paternal uncles and the daughters of your paternal aunts, and the daughters of your maternal uncles and the daughters of your maternal aunts who fled with you; and a believing woman if she gave herself to the Prophet, if the Prophet desired to marry her-- specially for you, not for the (rest of) believers; We know what We have ordained for them concerning their wives and those whom their right hands possess in order that no blame may attach to you;"*

This is a special command that Muhammad handed down to himself that allows virtually unlimited sex, divinely sanctioned by Allah. One assumes that this "revelation" was meant to assuage some sort of disgruntlement in the community over Muhammad's hedonism.

Qur'an (66:1-5) - "O Prophet! Why ban thou that which Allah hath made lawful for thee, seeking to please thy wives?..." Another remarkable verse of sexual convenience concerns an episode in which Muhammad's wives were jealous of the attention that he was giving to a Christian slave girl. But, as he pointed out to them, to neglect the sexual availability of his slaves was against Allah's will for him!

Qur'an (4:24) - "And all married women (are forbidden unto you) save those (captives) whom your right hands possess." Allah even permitted Muhammad and his men to have sex with married slaves, such as those captured in battle.

From the Hadith:

Muslim (8:3309) - Muhammad consummated his marriage to Aisha when she was only nine.

Bukhari (62:18) - Aisha's father, Abu Bakr, wasn't on board at first, but Muhammad explained how the rules of their religion made it possible. This is similar to the way that present-day cult leaders manipulate their followers into similar concessions.

Muslim (8:3311) - The girl took her dolls with her to Muhammad's house (something to play with when the "prophet" was not having sex with her).

Bukhari (6:298) - Muhammad would take a bath with the little girl and fondle her.

Muslim (8:3460) - "Why didn't you marry a young girl so that you could sport with her and she sport with you, or you could amuse with her and she could amuse with you?" Muhammad posed this question to one of his followers who had married an "older woman" instead of opting to fondle a child.

Bukhari (4:232) - Muhammad's wives would wash semen stains out of his clothes, which were still wet from the spot-cleaning even when he went to the mosque for prayers. Between copulation and prayer, it's a wonder he found the time to slay pagans.

Bukhari (6:300) - Muhammad's wives had to be available for the prophet's fondling even when they were having their menstrual period.

Bukhari (93:639) - The Prophet of Islam would recite the 'Holy Qur'an' with his head in Aisha's lap, when she was menstruating.

Bukhari (62:6) - "The Prophet used to go round (have sexual relations with) all his wives in one night, and he had nine wives." Muhammad also said that it was impossible to treat all wives equally - and it isn't hard to guess why.

Bukhari (5:268) - "The Prophet used to visit all his wives in a round, during the day and night and they were eleven in number." I asked Anas, 'Had the Prophet the strength for it?' Anas replied, 'We used to say that the Prophet was given the strength of thirty men.'"

Bukhari (60:311) - "I feel that your Lord hastens in fulfilling your wishes and desires." These words were spoken by Aisha within the context of her husband having been given 'Allah's permission' to fulfill his sexual desires with a large number of women in whatever order he chooses. (It has been suggested that Aisha may have been speaking somewhat wryly).

Tabari IX:137 - "Allah granted Rayhana of the Qurayza to Muhammad as booty." Muhammad considered the women that he captured and enslaved to be God's gift to him.

Tabari VIII:117 - "Dihyah had asked the Messenger for Safiyah when the Prophet chose her for himself... the Apostle traded for Safiyah by giving Dihyah her two cousins. The women of Khaybar were distributed among the Muslims." He sometimes pulled rank to reserve the most beautiful captured women for himself.

Tubari IX:139 - "You are a self-respecting girl, but the prophet is a womanizer." Words spoken by the disappointed parents of a girl who had 'offered' herself to Muhammad.

Thanks to Muhammad's extremely poor judgment (at best) and explicit approval of pedophilia, sex with children became deeply ingrained in the Islamic tradition. For many centuries, Muslim armies would purge Christian and Hindu peasant villages of their menfolk and send the women and children to harems and to the thriving child sex slave markets deep in the Islamic world. The Ayatollah Khomeini, who married a 12-year-old girl, even gave his consent to using infants for sexual pleasure (although warning against full penetration until the baby is a few years older). In April 2010, a 13-year-old Yemeni girl died from injuries suffered to her womb during intercourse.

Some clerics show relative mercy on underage girls by advocating a process known as "thighing", which is known in the West as child molestation. According to a recent fatwa (known as 23672): *"My parents married me to a young girl who hasn't yet reached puberty. How can I enjoy her sexually?"*, the Imam answers that he may, *"hug her, kiss her, and ejaculate between her legs."*

So controversial was Muhammad's desire to marry his adopted son's wife that he had to justify it with a stern pronouncement from Allah on the very institution of adoption, which has had tragic consequences to this day. Verses 33:4-5 of the Qur'an are widely interpreted to imply that Islam is against adoption, meaning that an untold number of children in the Islamic world have been needlessly orphaned - all because Muhammad's lustful desires for a married woman went beyond even what the other six wives that he possessed at the time and a multitude of slaves could satisfy.

Muhammad forbade his ten widows from remarrying, even making sure that this "divine" order was forever preserved in the eternal word of Allah - Qur'an (33:53). To add insult to injury, they were all summarily disinherited from Muhammad's estate by his successor, courtesy of another divine order given to Abu Bakr from Allah.

Muhammad's sexual antics are an embarrassment to those Muslims who are aware of them. In particular, their prophet's marriage to Aisha when she was 9-years-old! The thought of a 52-year-old man sleeping and bathing with a young girl is intensely unpleasant and it reflects the disgusting character of a sexual glutton rather than a holy man. Critics even allege that Muhammad was a pedophile. Some

Muslims respond by denying the Hadith itself, which is a mistake. The accounts of Muhammad sleeping with a 9-year-old are no less reliable than those on which the five pillars of Islam are based. They have been an accepted part of tradition and did not become controversial until social mores began to change with the modern age.

In summary, Islam's holiest texts portray Muhammad not as a perfect man, but as a complete hedonist. Not only did he exhibit gluttony, he grew ever more lustful as he aged. On top of it all, his personal 'revelations' from Allah seem to pointedly justify his debauchery. The gullible masses continue to venerate and memorize these verbal assaults on credibility as if they are the holiest of utterances.[16]

Sharia law states that a woman who claims that she has been raped by a man needs to have four men as witnesses, otherwise she is subject to be stoned for committing adultery. It is apparent that these laws were written by men, for men, and only men. If four men are dispassionately watching a rape take place, isn't that a gang rape? If they were going to take the part of the woman, wouldn't they have tried to prevent or interrupt the act while it was taking place? What kind of men are these?

The following is a true story, sadly one of many. While many Americans continue to deny any danger in Sharia, every week more women and children are persecuted under Islamic law all over the world. The only way to find out about these tragic stories is through international papers or blogs like NRB. We have heard stories of death for adultery in the past, but this was a case so beyond the pale that even some mainstream media picked up on it.[17] Posted by Rhonda Robinson on News Real Blog, February 5, 2011:

> "Late in the night last Sunday, in a village in Bangladesh, a 40-year-old married man (Mahbub) abducted his 14- year-old cousin and raped her. While being dragged and then raped, the girl (Hena) cried out for help from the village. But instead of punishing the rapist, Muslim leaders accused her of adultery. She was reportedly beaten by Mahbub's family and then forced to face a Sharia court the next day. That court sentenced a fatwa proclaiming little Hena must face 100 lashes from a bamboo cane and the rapist was only given a financial penalty for his part (though the local authorities would later claim he was supposed to be whipped too).
>
> Hena was given no chance to appeal. The same day the fatwa (recently fatwas were made illegal in Bangladesh) was issued, it was carried out. Hena was forced to take strike after strike after strike of that cane. Somewhere between 70-80 lashes she collapsed. The girl was then taken to the hospital where she then died from the wounds inflicted by the Sharia court."[17] [sic]

How can this be called the Religion of Peace? When there is sexual violence openly and legally perpetrated upon women and children, we are in the realm of the Satanic and Demonic. One thing we know for sure is that when children are abused by their family members, a curse is released on the family, opening the door for demons and evil spirits to take over completely. This is true for all kinds of abuse, physical, emotional, mental, and sexual, regardless of religion. Race, religion, sexual orientation, or nationality regardless, this is a spiritual law and child abuse gives Satan all the legal authority he needs over the abusers and, sadly, even the children, to torment them with post-traumatic stress, low self-esteem, and victim consciousness.

The following story in the Bible reveals why the Muslim religion and all Muslim practitioners are under a generational curse from the Creator God. The bastard curse is a Satanic tool to control bloodlines, families, and yes, even nations. The bastard curse originated with the Nephilim, as our God destroyed them with the flood, to kill the bastard offspring. The next stop in keeping the bastard curse in the bloodline of God's people occurred with Abraham. God had covenanted with Abraham, declaring that he would be the father of many nations. Abraham and Sarah faithlessly preempted God by taking Hagar and producing the bastard son Ishmael. Ishmael was cursed. He was never in the Divine plan. Ishmael was the result of Abraham's personal decision to do his will his own way, instead of God's way.

> "Then the angel of the Lord (extraterrestrial messenger) told her, o back to your mistress and submit to her. The angel added, I will increase your descendants so much that they will be too numerous to count. The angel of the Lord (extraterrestrial messenger) also said to her (Hagar): You are now pregnant, and you will give birth to a son. You shall name him Ishmael, for the Lord has heard of your misery. <u>He will be a wild donkey of a man; his hand will be against everyone and everyone's hand against him, and he will live in hostility toward all his brothers</u>."
>
> (Genesis 16:9-12) (emphasis and comments mine)

Ishmael would be unable to live peaceably with any man. The bastard curse prevents people from having fellowship with God and with others. The curse lasts for at least 400 years or 10 generations. Naturally Satan doesn't stop fostering this curse simply because the time runs out, but endeavors to keep it running continually with subsequent generations as well. It can only be broken by Jesus Christ, who took on all the curses of humankind on the cross. Ishmael, and all his progeny, are under this curse. The Muslims of today are the spiritual descendants of Ishmael, who claim Abraham as their father. This curse is still in effect. This explains why Islam has been at war with the world in general, but especially with the religious practitioners of Judaism, Christianity, Hinduism, and Buddhism.

We scoffed en masse at the gurus of the 1960s, who were selling little more than recruitments to women to have sex with them. They were mocked, condemned, and toppled from their status as 'holy men.' Yet there are 1.9 billion Muslims in the world that hang on every word that Mohammed said as gospel truth, and consider him to be a holy man. The hypocrisy is so blatantly obvious! But to those who *choose* to believe a lie, spiritual illumination eludes them, and they are in bondage to it. This is the evidence of a false prophet, and the hallmark of fallen angels masquerading around as 'holy men.'

The realm of the demonic is vast with all kinds of deceptive spirits, especially those known as *religious spirits* which are not from god, but are evil spirits. *Religious spirits* like to mentor others and attempt to mold them into their own respectable images. The problem with that is the image of a *religious spirit* deceitfully appears righteous. *Religious spirits* use image as camouflage. They are full of hypocrisy, pride, false humility, self-righteousness, criticism, legalism, and rebellion. The purpose of the *religious spirit* is to stand in the way of God's work. *Religious spirits* are all about appearances, form, carnality, and have no genuine spiritual substance. Self-righteousness and dead religious works are the fruit of *religious spirits. Religious spirits* try to burden us with a form of godliness while denying the power thereof to make us ineffective in accomplishing God's Divine plan for our lives.

This is the modus operandi of the fallen angels in their war with the Creator God over us, to interfere with God's Divine plan for the human race. *Religious spirits* taking over religious practice while denying the spiritual power thereof has been an effective way to keep the practitioners blindsided and in spiritual bondage, to keep us off the true spiritual path of discernment. *Religious spirits* cause fundamentalism, a condition that is pervasive across the board in *all* religions.

According to the latest estimated accounts on Wikipedia, based on the population of 6.8 billion people in the world, the four largest religions consist of Christianity, Islam, Buddhism, and Hinduism. The breakdown is as follows: Christianity is the world's largest religion with 2.7 billion; (40%); Islam is between 1.3 - 1.57 billion (19-21%), Buddhism with 500 million - 1.5 billion (7-21%); Hinduism with 950 million - 1 billion (14-15%). Judaism is practiced by about 13 million people with about 40% living in Israel and roughly 40% living in the United States.

In 2005, author Jim Rutz wrote a book entitled, *Megashift,* and coined a new phrase to define the fastest growing segment of the population. He calls them *core apostolics* – or "the new saints who are at the heart of the mushrooming kingdom of God." Rutz makes the point that Christianity is overlooked as the fastest-growing faith in the world because most surveys look at the traditional Protestant denominations and the Roman Catholic Church while ignoring Christian believers who have no part of either. He says there are over 707 million "switched-on disciples" who fit into this new category and that this churchless body is exploding in growth. "The growing core of Christianity crosses theological lines and includes 707 million born-again people who are increasing by 8 percent a year," he says. So fast is this group growing that, under current trends, according to Rutz, the entire world will be composed of such believers by the year 2032.[18]

At the time of the writing of this chapter (2017), I researched the internet and asked how many Christians are in the world today? Between 2010 – 2050, 31.4% of the world's population will be Christian. There are now as of the last consensus in 2015, 2.92 Billion Christians.[19]

This is the answer I got from WikiAnswers:

> 'Many sources mention 2.92 billion Christians in the world (about one third of the total population of the planet), but estimating numbers is fraught with difficulties. What is included among the definition of 'Christian' is not agreed upon by many of the groups involved.
>
> The term 'Christian' in its simplest definition refers to one who believes in Jesus Christ (as God). Drawing the line between 'Christian' and those who belong to 'sects' is problematic. Add to this the fact that no-one can really tell if a person is a Christian at heart, or if they are just paying lip-service to the name. This is impossible for any but God who sees the heart to judge. The numbers can be taken, then, as a best estimate of how many identify with Christianity in some way.
>
> However, it is now impossible to say with any certainty, as, while practicing Christians have been in decline in some Western countries, there has been a recent surge in 'membership' in parts of the West, and in the East the numbers who are becoming new Christians daily is astronomical.
>
> There are estimated now nearly 110 *million* Christians in China (compared with just 5,000 in the 1960s) and in South Korea, churches regularly have tens of thousands of members each. In one church, the Yoido Full Gospel Church in Seoul, there are over 800,000 members who meet each Sunday in several sittings in a vast hall. So, whilst it is difficult to give a definite answer to the actual number of Christians in the world (estimates range from 2 - 3 billion), Christianity remains the most dominant of the world, and is still growing at an astonishing rate.'[20]

The point is that it is hard to define a Christian, because of the status of 'religion.' There are so many denominations and sects as WikiAnswers mentioned, and many who do not disclose their personal faiths for fear of persecution. But God knows who they are, and His numbers are accurate, and that's all that matters.

In 2011, I attended a seminar that was demonstrating the healing power of God's Word and His Spirit, there was a woman who was suffering from muscle pain. The leaders prayed over her, yet she still did not feel relief, so I pulled out a cold laser, which is used effectively to relieve muscle pain. I talked to her about the laser, and she was interested in trying it. She shared with me that she had been taking over-the-counter pain meds. A laser is drug free, the wonderful technology of light waves. While in the middle of applying a treatment on her painful muscles, I was quickly rebuked by one of the church leaders, to 'put that thing away, we are only healing with the Holy Spirit today.' Even though I immediately complied, I later reminded them that one of the nine gifts of the Holy Spirit *is* the gift of knowledge.

Light technology is the fruit of knowledge. Yet they were so threatened by this. They insisted, on only healing through the Holy Spirit. But if the Holy Spirit imparts knowledge, then that **is** healing through the Holy Spirit! This is particularly ironic, after the minister had taught how important it is to listen to the voice of the Holy Spirit for each individual healing, as He may tell you to do things that are odd, as Jesus did, by using his spit on several occasions, so the important thing is to be obedient to His Spirit when it comes to healing others. I heard the voice of the Lord very clearly in my heart to share the laser with this woman in pain, because it works. I was obedient to the Lord, yet I was rebuked for bringing something 'odd' or new to the healing process. What spirit rebuked me? It certainly wasn't the Lord, but the *religious spirit* operating in this particular church leader, who just couldn't reconcile in her mind that laser technology could be from God.

Another example would be someone coming for healing who has a headache. After questioning them a bit, and finding out that they hadn't eaten or drank anything for days, perhaps ministering them some bread and water? Or soup may be the hands of the Holy Spirit? More illnesses are borne of dehydration and low blood sugar levels from hunger, than demons could muster up. While it's always good to pray for people who are ill, sometimes, it's as simple as offering them nourishment in the way of food and drink? This is why listening to the Holy Spirit during healing, is more than just spiritual ministry, the gift of knowledge is *knowing* what to do to minister to someone in need. It could range from the simple offerings of a glass of water to giving them warmth to knowing when other types of practical needs are required.

"Be not forgetful to entertain strangers:
for thereby some have entertained angels unawares."
(Hebrews 13:12)

There is a pointed lesson in the tale of the devout Christian man caught in the sinking of a ship on which he was traveling. As he struggled in the waters, drowning, he called out to the Lord to save him. The Lord immediately sent a lifeboat, whose crew tried to grab him from the waves. "No," shouted the man, "Jesus will save me!" They threw him a life ring, with line attached, that he could grab on to, but he flung it away, saying, "The Lord will save me!" They finally grabbed him by the shirt and hauled him up kicking and fighting into the small craft, and he promptly jumped back out, saying, "Go away!! The Lord is going to save me!" We can fill in the sad ending to many incidents in life we have witnessed with this attitude!

Most people who have a demonic stronghold in their lives have opened to it through their own unresolved issues, mostly unconfessed sin for which they are trying to compensate. The woman who rebuked me for sharing a cold laser to relieve another woman of muscle pain, was a major church leader, and was obese. Each time I would see her, she had grown. The spirit of gluttony cannot be hidden, because it creates obesity. Yet hardly anyone in church circles addresses this addiction and disorder. In this seminar, they talked about drug addictions, even alcoholism, but never do they mention food addictions, which are caused by the spirit of gluttony. These very people will come forward to cast out demons in others, but their own human temples are defiled by demon spirits. The *religious spirit* rides on people like this, because they have a foothold.

> "You hypocrite, first take the plank out of your own eye, and then you will see clearly to remove the speck from your brother's eye."
>
> (Matthew 7:5)

The way to freedom is through confession, repentance, and renouncing these sins through Christ, who is faithful and just, to forgive and offer deliverance. But the spiritual stronghold too often is pride, guilt, and shame, which all belong to Satan, giving him power and authority over them. Do you see how subtle it is? Yet like the proverbial elephant in the living room, most Christians turn a blind eye for fear of offending anyone because, let's face it, most people in America today are overweight or obese. Yet these very same Christians do not think twice about judging another for a sinful lifestyle when in denial of their own bondages. Hypocrisy is a fruit of the *religious spirit.* As 2Timothy 3:5 said, having an outward form of godliness (religion) but denying its true power. Does that mean that these types of Christians are not saved? Not necessarily, as only the Lord is the final judge of that, but it does mean that their journey with the Lord is thwarted, and they are losing power to Satan. 1 Corinthians 5:5, even says, to give their flesh to Satan for destruction of his flesh, so that their soul may be saved by God on the day of the Lord.

The *religious spirit* causes a judgmental attitude, and creates religious fundamentalism. Some people within the church are so heavily steeped in judgment that they miss the freedom that Christ offers. Remember He said, "I have come to set the captives free." Just because a person is cloaked with the outward appearance of religion, he can still fall for and fervently believe many of the false teachings that the *religious spirit* has managed to infiltrate within the churches. What secures our salvation is listening to the Lord, and living out His will in our lives. This is what I believe Jesus is referring to, when separating His church into sheep and goats:

> "And before him shall be gathered all nations: and he shall separate them one from another, as <u>a shepherd divides his sheep from the goats</u>: And he shall set <u>the sheep on his right hand, but the goats on the left</u>. Then shall the King say unto them on his right hand, Come, ye blessed of my Father, inherit the kingdom prepared for you from the foundation of the world: For I was and hungered, and you gave me meat: I was thirsty, and you gave me drink: I was a stranger, and you took me in: Naked, and you clothed me: I was sick, and you visited me: I was in prison, and you came to me. Then shall the righteous answer him, saying, Lord, when saw we you and hungered, and fed you? or thirsty, and gave you drink? When saw we you a stranger, and took you in? or naked, and clothed you? Or when saw we you sick, or in prison, and came to you?
>
> And the King shall answer and say to them, Truly I say to you, in as much as you have done it to one of the least of these my brothers, you have done it to me. Then shall he say also to them on the left hand, depart from me, you cursed, into everlasting fire, prepared for the devil and his angels: For I was an hungered, and you gave me no meat: I was thirsty, and you gave me no drink: I was a stranger, and you took me not in: naked, and you clothed me not: sick, and in prison, and you visited me not. Then shall they also answer him, saying, Lord, when saw we you and hungered, or thirsty, or a stranger, or naked, or sick, or in prison, and did not minister to you? Then shall he answer them, saying, Truly I say to you, inasmuch as you did it not to one of the least of these, you did it not to me. And these shall go away into everlasting punishment: but the righteous into life eternal."
>
> (Matthew 25:32-46)

The criteria Jesus is using here to separate His true sheep from the goats, are *the actions* his believers are expected to take towards the brethren. Did they nurture those who were in need? Did they tend to those who needed help? While Jesus gives five examples of tending to those in need, we know, there are all kinds of needs. What about someone being thirsty for comfort, love friendship or light? or for medicine? or for knowledge?

What about someone who comes to you for healing, and the Holy Spirit reveals through the gifts of discerning of spirits, what spirits are causing their illness, and through the gift of knowledge what they need to do in their lives to correct their lifestyles from preventing those demons from returning? While this is the subject matter of my next book, *Finding Freedom,* devoted to healing, suffice it to say now, that there are so many Christians who are so focused on the belief that all they need to do is believe in Jesus and they will be instantly healed, that they miss the doctor He sends to them in the flesh. The fruits of their lives show they are constantly dealing with one form of illness after another.

Sadly, when the word of Knowledge is given to them, to change their diet and their lifestyle, and break generational curses, there is nothing but resistance. These are demonic strongholds that cause the believer to fervently believe that they do not need nutritional advice, nor do they need to change their lifestyle to attain healing, or bring some unconfessed sin to the throne of Grace. They fall back into the mantra that if it's God's will for them to be healed, they will be healed. The whole truth is that God requires changes in both attitude and lifestyle to release His power to heal and deliver, and many studies have shown this time and again. Faith and belief definitely go ahead of these changes, but not when false beliefs, pride and ego are blocking the believer from having the truth. This may hurt pride and egos, but doesn't Christ tell us, to pick up our cross and carry it daily? What is that cross? It is our ego.

Religious Spirits are No Respecter of Persons

As I mentioned earlier, there are many Christians who are Christian in name only. If they are not living by Christ's precepts and following His teachings, then according to the words of Jesus Christ Himself, they will not enter into the Kingdom of Heaven. This is the province that the *religious spirit* is present, which takes over their lives, giving them a false sense of security. The *religious spirit* attacks all religions, including New Agers, which contains many agnostics. Spiritually speaking, the *religious spirit* battles with the Holy Spirit, which is the spirit of Christ. The Holy Spirit wants to fill believers with the mind of Christ, but when a believer chooses to be taken over by *religious spirits* and infiltrated with other demonic spirits, the power of the Holy Spirit is suppressed in their lives. This is the core and heart of the spiritual warfare over each and every soul, including believers, on planet Earth.

As far as religion goes, Jesus was Jewish, He is the Messiah of Israel, even though many of His own people did not recognize Him as their Redeemer. There are many Jews who ***do*** recognize Yeshua as their Saviour and are considered to be Completed, or Messianic Jews. Jesus said He came to do the will of the Father, His Father being the Almighty Lord Yahuah, who the Jews continue to worship to this day. Yahuah has an everlasting covenant with His people, and with Israel. He promises to save them in the end, and give them every opportunity to realize their salvation through Yeshua HaMashiach (Jesus Christ).

Jesus is no respecter of persons, and has come to save all peoples from all religions and from all nations. Jesus Christ is the only spiritual power that overcomes and breaks the bondages imposed on us humans by Lucifer the Satan, his fallen angels, and the rogue extra-terrestrial aliens. It is my assertion, which I prove throughout this book, that Christ is the Saviour of both earthly and extra-terrestrial civilizations, which have been overtaken by the Luciferian rebellion. This is why Christ came to Earth, to become the final sacrifice for all sins and to break all curses by defeating spiritual evil.

Let's not forget that the Christian movement was initiated by Jews. New religious sects branched out of early Christianity, which then became that major political stronghold known as Catholicism. Catholicism is a mixture of the new religion, Christianity, and pagan Mithraism, as concocted by the Roman Emperors Constantine, Justin and Justinian.

Following the destruction of Jerusalem in 70 A.D. the followers of Jesus, who were Jews, spread out through the known world. These people studied and prayed and sought God, according to their ability. Some of these people supposed that merging their identity with that of Rome would lessen the persecution of Christianity, and gain official recognition by the Empire. Others accepted this position in a lukewarm manner, out of lack of knowledge. They were Romans and they knew these teachings, but were ignorant of Jewish scripture and doctrine. In the New Testament Paul and others warned that pagan and other heretical views were being introduced into the Church. It can be argued that these Romanized teachings were included in these warnings.

Other people sought a more mystical approach, such as the Gnostics. As time went by many minor Christian sects sprang into being. There has never been just one united Christendom, as the incredibly diverse teachings, doctrines, views, and beliefs attest. Once Constantine the Great embraced the young religion, favoring Christians and granting political power and recognition, the Catholic Church was born, and began a long process of distilling and canonizing its beliefs into an authorized, orthodox hierarchy. This form is what we today refer to as Roman Catholicism.

Other branches of Christianity continued but were forced underground by increasingly severe persecution by the Roman orthodoxy. Sects like the Albigensian, Cathars, Arians, Anabaptists, and the Coptic Church, which maintain that their teachings are the true Christian faith, were forced into secrecy or decimated. At this point it is impossible to identify any as being truly apostolic, or as the direct teachings of the Apostles. Though most other forms and sects were either absorbed or destroyed by the Church Catholic, it never quite rubbed away all traces of original Christianity.

Many scholars believe the founding of the Roman Catholic Church was in 312 A.D. when Emperor Constantine proclaimed he had a vision from heaven to conquer the enemies of Rome with a special sign – the sign of the cross. He went on to unite the Roman Empire under this sign and under this religion, a universal or Catholic Church. Others point to earlier dates pertaining to certain Church fathers. Still others prefer later dates of councils, such as that of Nicaea, or other ecumenical councils. In my opinion, the Catholic Church began on February 27, 380 A.D. when Emperor Theodosius issued his edict, *De Fide Catolica*, in Thessalonica, published in Constantinople, declaring Catholic Christianity as the state religion of the Roman Empire.

During the 2nd and 3rd centuries, the Christian movement spread throughout the Roman Empire like wildfire. In order to keep up with the socio-political mores of the time, Christian tenets and catchwords were blended into Mithraism, which eventually gave way to a bastard hybrid church form which we know today as the Roman Catholic Church. Jesus Christ stands in the place of Mithras, all the Roman ceremonies remained as sacraments, like the Eucharist, the religious hierarchy of the priesthood, and the pagan gods and goddesses were exchanged for prayers to Christian saints. Mother Mary is venerated instead of the Roman Goddesses, which became a main ploy to encourage both Christians and pagans to join the church. Mother Mary actually represents Semiramis, who was the Mother of Tammuz and the consort of Nimrod, the Goddess of the original Assyrian-Babylonian religion that later became known as Mithraism to the early Romans after the conquest of Assyria in 7 B.C. and Babylon in 6 B.C., then Mithras became known as the Sun god, in keeping the same Mother-Son-Sun Worshipping religion. See, *Who is God?* Book Two: Chapter Twenty-Three: *Babylonian History, Where it All Began,* subsection: *Who is Semiramis?*[21] p.371-373

The visions of Emperor Constantine and his victory sign, which gave him the upper hand, linger in Christian history. Whether it was a cross of fire or a Chi Rho (Christogram), he did win the war, and instigated secular and spiritual orthodoxy in his empire. Adopting some of the Old Testament into the pantheonic religion of Rome, he added varied excerpts from an errant church, which resulted in the political socio-religious organization of today. The principal early Christian sects are generally recalled today as Catholic Orthodox Christianity and Gnosticism, although other groups existed unremarked and unadopted.

As the Roman Empire eventually fell, the Roman Catholic Church split into two distinct forms, the Eastern Orthodox and the Western Roman Catholic Church, each claiming to be the original. Later, Christianity devolved into Protestantism, as the Church of England left the Roman Church and became known as the Anglican, and Martin Luther spurred the Protestant Reformation. Each of these groups claims to be the restoration of the One True Church revealed by the Master Yeshua; however, none of these reflect the original Messianic Church, which began by all Jews, prior to the Paulian era, who's task was to take the gospel to the Gentiles. The original Messianic Church is how it will end when the 144,000 believers from the twelve tribes of Israel gather in Israel in the last days, who all hold the mark of God, as stated in Revelation 7. This final remnant will most likely be the closest to the original Messianic Church.

Martin Luther was corrupted by Replacement Theology, which inspired Hitler's Jewish genocide, which was a total bastardization and perversion of the original Messianic Church that brings both Jew and Gentile together under one God. Luther's distorted viewpoint was to replace the Jews with Gentiles, this has never been God's plan.

In 1954, the Jesuits were formed as the militant arm of the Roman Catholic Church to kill off the Protestant Reformation. They weren't any better, because they were protecting the Roman Catholic Church which is based on the Paganism of Babylon, which was a far cry from the original Messianic Church as well. Let's not forget the history, that it was the Church of Rome that oppressed both Jews and ruled over ancient Israel with an iron hand. However, the unseen hand influencing these groups to war against each other, is as nefarious and demonic as these murderous religions are. It's the Alien Draconian Reptilian Agenda to keep humanity divided, especially divided over who God is, because that's what threatens them to their very core, humanity being empowered through one God, who is the only God that can take them down, and that is Yeshua HaMashiach, the Lord and Master Jesus Christ.

Under Constantine and later emperors, Roman state patronage of the Catholic Orthodox Church ensured that it was able to expropriate the property of other churches and their adherents. This militant arm of the church provided a cover for persecution and absorption, until there was only one Christian Church left in the Roman Empire. And so, will it be in the last days, when the last Vatican Pope is used to usher in the era of the Antichrist who is the Counterfeit Messiah. See, Revelation 13.

While Catholicism became a socio-political stronghold, true Christians follow the Living Christ, who had resurrected and ascended to the Father. Christians are filled with the Holy Spirit, while Catholics worship the crucified Christ on the cross, pray to saints and to Mother Mary for intercession, which according to scripture creates a false religion through idolatry, a sin considered rebellion and equal with the sin of witchcraft in the Bible. This is the reason, so many offshoots and sects of

Christianity abound. Note well that the Catholic priesthood usurps the power from the believers, as it is written in Matthew 23:9: 'And do not call anyone on earth 'father,' for you have one Father, and He is in heaven.' The Catholic church has been taken over by the *religious spirit*. This is why, so many recovering Catholics fall away and turn to New Age beliefs and philosophies, because they feel suffocated by the *religious spirit* which is void of true spiritual power.

Since so many offshoots of Catholicism were formed into what amounts to today's mainstream Christianity made up of multiple denominations and even non-denominational churches, most of whom have never repented from the evils and falsehoods of Constantine's Creed, becomes the spiritual legal ground the Draconian Satans need to infiltrate Christian churches with the demon known as the *religious spirit*, keeping 'Churchianity' disempowered or handicap to say the least.

So many people end up throwing out the baby with the bathwater! By leaving the church, they abandon their faith completely, citing all the contradictions within the Church, the strictness with the laws, the hypocrisy, the piling on of the guilt and the shame, the long history of child sexual abuse covered up and tolerated by the institution. While it is easy for a believer to blame God for allowing this, one really needs to question, 'which god?' The disordered state of the Christian church is due to the infiltration of Lucifer the Satan, the Draconian Reptilian Lord of Darkness, who has been in the driver's seat for millennia, through secret occult practices, wars, finances, and the murders in the name of Christ of any who don't comply or tow the company line.

The Character of the Religious Spirit

The following information comes from the *Wellspring School of Ministry*,[22] and identifies the character of the *religious spirit* we have been examining. It is being used here with their kind permission with emphasis and commentary by me.

<u>This spirit wants to hold people in one place mentally, tied to the traditions of men</u>. It wants people to hold on to "something" rather than trusting and holding onto God. People get comfortable in their traditions and rituals, the things that all people are "used to" and have "always known" and have "always done" which can provide a false sense of security. It can replace having an intimate spiritual relationship with the Creator. It makes people think that all they need is to "do", to "perform" and that is enough to satisfy their religion.

In Matthew 17, Peter saw Jesus talking to Moses and Elijah. He then wanted to build three tabernacles as their home. Men are inclined to want to build things, instead of seeking the deep spiritual truths that were being revealed, or enjoying their relationship with God.

The *religious spirit* wants us to be afraid of what is new or different from our experience or worldview. Everyone is affected by this spirit in some way or another regardless of where one is on the religious spectrum. That includes those in New Age, Metaphysical and Occult circles. Every church develops its own traditions and ways of doing things. Every church, in doing this, runs the risk of putting its traditions ahead of God. This is called idolatry.

The *religious spirit* desires to make our relationship with God one of obligation and duty instead of passion. Religion can be used to control. If people do what they are told to do and go through the external motions of the church, then they think they will be okay. The outward appearance becomes all that matters, not what is on the inside. Folks pray because they are *supposed* to pray. People go to meetings, because they are *supposed* to go to meetings. People feel like they are right with God because they have done what was required.

The *religious spirit* focuses on the letter of the law. When we become focused on the letter of the law, then love, unity, peace, kindness and charily disappear. All that matters is, filling the block and completing the requirement. The healing, miracle or blessing is gone. Instead we focus on whether or not they violated a scripture. "God doesn't work that way." "This can't be of God, He didn't do that for me." "I have never experienced it, so it cannot be of God." Remember how the Pharisees accused of Jesus of blasphemy when He healed someone on the Sabbath? The letter of the law kills, but the spirit brings life. (2 Corinthians 3:6)

Yeshua was defending his law called a *kal v'chomer,* which means 'light and heavy' argument, known in philosophy as reasoning *a fortiori*, "from greater strength". It implies the phrase of 'how much more'![23] Which is what Yeshua meant when He said, "You permit breaking the Sabbath in order to observe the *mitzvah* of circumcision; how much more important it is to heal a person's whole body, so you should permit breaking *Shabbat* for that!" (John 7:23)

The *religious spirit* says we must look good. We can stay in bitterness, jealousy and envy, fear and rejection as long as we are doing what looks good on the outside. We can stay in our fear, anxiety and worry instead of being at peace with God, because it is hidden on the inside. We focus on the outward and we cut off our soul from God. He tells us that it is what is inside of us that defiles us. We focus on the outward sins of smoking and drinking and drugs and not the inward sins of judging, hypocrisy, lying bitterness, unforgiveness and all the other little dark things that are inside of us. The religious spirit tells us that our sins of anger and jealousy cannot be seen so they are not as bad as the outward sins.

The *religious spirit* keeps us from the things of the spirit. It tells us the gifts of the Holy Spirit in 1 Corinthians 12 cannot operate or function. It keeps us from the power of God. It keeps people focused on the word and the letter of the law. It tells us that we cannot have feelings. We end up disregarding feelings and looking down on those that express emotions. The letter of law becomes the deciding factor. The letter of the law does not care about people. It shows no love, unity or charity. Thus, we end up walking by sight and not by faith.

The Word and the Spirit are one, but the religious spirit puts everything on the word or law. This kind of thinking gets us so shut off from anything to do with feelings that we miss out on the moving and the leading of the Holy Spirit. We miss out on hearing the Holy Spirit speak to us. We miss out on that close relationship and fellowship.

The *religious spirit* says, 'You have to.' It says that you must get up early every day and pray. Is this passion or obligation? It says you must tithe. We should want to tithe and give donations because of our love for God and for others. It says that we must bless our meals. It says that have to dress a certain way. It says that we must have an outward appearance. It says that we must be in the church every time the doors are open. It says that we have to be at every meeting.

The *religious spirit* makes people doctrinally obsessed. This spirit creates *fundamentalism, an extreme* which crosses the board in all religions. It causes people to lose charity with other believers, creates denominations or other cliques. It blots out the character of Christ by speaking against other believers who see the issues differently. It causes people to distil the teachings of men into doctrines of Christianity, just as the Pharisees did in Matthew 15, then the Word of God has no effect. Jesus said, "You shall know them by their love for one another." (John 13:35)

The *religious spirit* breeds confusion. This spirit creates confusion between the words of men and the Word of God. 1 Thessalonians 5:21 says to test and prove everything. There are three tests: first, does the Word of God forbid or contradict a practice, teaching or doctrine? Second, does the practice, teaching or doctrine bear good fruit, or does it harm people? If something is harming people, it cannot be of God. Third, it is important to study the history of the church to see if the practice, teaching or doctrine has been taught or practiced before. 'There is nothing new under the sun.' (Ecclesiastes 1:9). The practice or doctrine may be new to you, but if it is not of God, it will not be new in history. The Lord says, "I change not." (Malachi 3:6).

The *religious spirit* breeds rebellion. The religious spirit comes and says, "you have to" and we say, "no way." This results in a bad attitude towards others. It says in the Bible, 'rebellion is as the sin of witchcraft.' (1 Samuel 15:23).

It is important to remember, our enemy is not each other, or ourselves. "For we do not wrestle against flesh and blood, but against principalities, powers, the rulers of the darkness of this world, and against the cosmic powers and spiritual forces of evil in the heavenly places." (Ephesians 6:12)

The *religious spirit* breeds unforgiveness and judgment. When we have refuse to have fellowship, when we have looked down our noses at others because they sing differently, worship differently, express emotion, fall the floor, laugh, cry, shake, speak in tongues, believe that God is healing, or do not cry, do not fall on the floor, do not express emotion, do not laugh, do not speak in tongues, we have judged them as different from us. God is the Father of all of us, and Jesus came to save us all.

The *religious spirit* wants us to judge others and ourselves. We need to *discern* that the demonic realm is responsible for most of the sorrow and corruption in the world, and not blame God for it.

The *religious spirit* does not care about mercy. It doesn't care about people, because it comes from the Satanic forces whose job it is to block us from having a relationship with the Living God. This spirit doesn't care about love. It cares about the letter of the law even if all of humanity suffers for it.[24]

By their Fruits You Shall Know them

I am sure anyone reading would agree with me, that this demonic principality called the *religious spirit* has caused more wars, more division and more heartache and suffering on this planet than can be calculated. It is this *religious spirit* that causes people to become disenchanted with God, to become agnostics or even atheists. John Lennon's famous song, *Imagine,* has a line in it, "imagine no religion," which atheistic groups use as their bumper sticker. The *Freedom from Religion Foundation* states that all the world's problems are caused by religion.[25] There would have been no 9/11, no Spanish Inquisition, no Taliban, no Crusades, no human sacrifices to various and sundry gods. Religious wars would be conspicuously absent from world history and nobody would follow cult leaders in sipping down toxic Kool-Aid.

As Dr. Chuck Missler rightly points out in his article, *Religion is Just a Patsy,* "while Religion is a convenient scapegoat for the atheist, who wants to justify himself in a world of believers (sic). The atheist has a serious problem in blaming the evils of the world on religion, though (sic). For every complaint against religious people, there are plenty of complaints to be made against the faithless. Have people been slaughtered in the name of religion? Certainly. Yet, the Crusades are a drop in the bucket compared to the massive death toll caused by atheistic regimes. The leaders of the French Revolution shoved God out of their social justice crusade (sic), and the result was a blood bath. Stalin is responsible for the deaths of at least 20 million of his own people, and Mao Zedong's death toll runs upwards of 40-70 million (sic). From Pol Pot in Cambodia to the Kims in North Korea, governments freed of "religion" – those utopias of atheistic communism - have murdered millions upon millions of people. People of various religions continue to fight all around the world, but, anti-God governments *streamline* human death. Any time people get starry-eyed about imagining "no religion too" they need a little history lesson."[26]

Trying to resist this *religious spirit* intellectually, politically, or in one's own flesh is futile. As I've mentioned, this is a principality and stronghold of the lords of darkness of the alien presence on earth, just as the spirit of unbelief is. "We fight not against flesh and blood, but against powers [archons], principalities [demonic princes and their personalities], rulers of the darkness and spiritual wickedness in the heavens [aliens and fallen angels]." (Ephesians 6:12) The *religious spirit*, as wicked as it is, must be brought down by the only force in the universe which has the spiritual power to dissolve it and crush its stronghold, and that power is the presence of Jesus Christ. The same goes for the spirit of unbelief.

Atheists have a point about the *religious spirit* being the cause of so much murder, discontent and chaos in the world, but sadly they are throwing the baby out with the bathwater. While religion has its demonic strongholds, we can easily bypass them by finding the Spirit of God within, the prize, the treasured jewel. For every human soul who finds it and walks with His Spirit is well equipped to defeating the *religious spirit* while maintaining salvation. Atheists trade the fruits of the *religious spirit* for those of the spirit of unbelief and the spirit of narcissism. The atheist makes it all about him, he does not need God or any religious path, he just needs secularism, science and to believe in himself. He will not be controlled by the demonic religious spirit! But he is so obviously being controlled and spiritually blinded by the god of this world, who is Lucifer the Satan, because there is no neutral ground in the universe, you're either owned by God or possessed by Satan.

Every human is a vessel for a higher power. Those who are deceived into various forms of narcissism, that's it's all about them, whether they are atheist who just believe in themselves, is a self-deluded lie they tell themselves because they don't know their Creator. Most atheists have estranged or emotionally absent parents, causing them their first psychic soul wound, making it hard for them to believe in a loving God, while others have parents who experienced that and pass it on to their children. However, because the *evidence* of the Creator is in the creation, and being that they are created beings, who house a soul, that soul comes from the Creator. Therefore, there is no such thing as a true atheist, because all soul-matrixed beings were given a soul, matrixed by their Creator with the Creator's imprint within. Being made in the image and likeness of the Elohim gods, means being imprinted with the spark of the Creator God within. This is often misunderstood as oneself, but one's soul, is one's God spark, which is their lifeforce within it.

Then there is another delusion of a different type of atheistic-agnostic thought-forms, and that is the New Age Cult of Spiritual Narcissism, which states that, 'you are God' or 'I am God'. This diminishes the authority, lordship and kingship of the

King of the Kingdom of Heaven who is the Lord Yeshua. It essentially says, I don't need to respect him, because I'm God, and therefore equal or greater than Christ. This is the lie of Satan, who was ousted out of the Kingdom of Heaven and allowed to war over souls on earth, for a time, until the end of this age, when the final day of reckoning comes, and the Messiah-King returns to separate His sheep from the goats.

'I am God', is not an accurate statement, and is used as spiritual legal ground for the demons of idolatry and rebellion to the Lord. The *Truth* is in the *details*. We are made in the *image* and *likeness* of God and the gods (Elohim), making us *God Sparks*, not necessarily little gods being used to perpetuate the ancient wars between the gods. We are made to be vessels of the Creator God, to play our *part* in His Divine Plan. That doesn't make us god over the plan, it does make us willing servants and participants in His Grand Plan, but it doesn't make us the God of gods. That's the discernment and understanding many New Agers are missing. There is a God of gods, who has power over all the gods.[27] See, Book Two, *Who Is God?* Chapter Eight – *Who Are the Gods?* pp. 129-136

While Satan's alien presence on earth can possess souls, he can't create them. He can mimic them, counterfeit souls by stealing people's memories, and making a composite of soul-like qualities, which are nothing more than computer generated implants known as screen memories in psychology. This is how many people who are implanted at a young age grow up believing they are something other than what the Creator God of all Spirits and Souls made them for. This is the true meaning of *lost souls*, which is someone who no longer knows *who* they are, and have lost their original identity. Many lost souls, including atheists are under Satan's spell of mind control through alien implantation. They are implanted to disbelieve in the core essence of *who* they truly are, which is their soul and the Creator of their soul. Even an atheist who believes the deception that alien Annunaki ET gods created humankind, questions *who* created the gods?

Dr. Chuck Missler writes: "Atheists and humanists are quite capable of morality and moral decision making. Yet, in rejecting the one true God, atheists and humanists make themselves their own gods. Because they have no greater yardstick to measure by, it often happens that they reject one evil only to turn around and embrace something far worse."[26]

<u>Religion cannot save you</u>. Salvation is found through a personal, intimate, one-on-one relationship with the Almighty Creator and His Savior Jesus Christ. Depending on the religion, it may offer people the path to finding God, but religion in and of itself is not God, and belonging to any particular religion, church, temple, circle or mosque does not guarantee the salvation of the human soul. Religion cannot cause the inner transformation of the heart and mind, only the Spirit of God can do so. There is a vast difference between religion and spirituality. To live spiritually means to follow the Spirit of God, which does not always fit into a box. It does not

do things religiously, to impress others, but moves with the spirit of wisdom, knowledge, discernment, and love. Religion does not heal; the Spirit of God heals. While some religions condone and even promote violence, this does not represent the Spirit of God. I have been asked, can you have God without religion? Absolutely! One is not obligated to belong to any religion in order to have a personal intimate one on one relationship with the Living God. There is freedom in God. Jesus said,

"I have come to set the captives free."
(Isaiah 61:1; Luke 4:18)

To think that a church, temple, or mosque is where god lives, and you must stay loyal to it above all else is a form of idolatry. Anything that comes between you and your relationship with the Almighty is idolatry. If you worship churches, statutes, stupas, traditions, angels, or any other spirit, then it is a false religious path.

The answer is not in religion, the answer is in the personhood of Jesus Christ. Unfortunately, the god of this world, Lucifer the Adversary and his fallen ET angels and false gods, are enemies of Christ. They have infiltrated all the religions, including Christianity. This is a book about discernment, so it's important to discern between the satanic strongholds and the *Spirit* of God. Christ is the only force in this world that can set a person free from the powers of darkness. That's the spiritual reality. The *Spirit* of God is changing lives every day on this planet, without religion, without even Bibles, in countries which outlaw both. "It is not by might, not by power, but by my *Spirit,* says the Lord Almighty." (Zechariah 4:6)

> "But the fruit of the *Spirit* is love, joy, peace, longsuffering, patience, gentleness, goodness, faithfulness, temperance and self-control: against such there is no law."
>
> (Galatians 5:22)

Hinduism and Alien Gods

Hinduism is based on the caste system. If you read my section on the Draconian Reptilians[28] in Book One of *Who's Who in the Cosmic Zoo,* [p.154-177] you will see that they base their entire hierarchy on a caste system, which is almost identical to Hinduism.

Hinduism differs from Christianity and other monotheistic religions in an almost entire negation: it does *not* have a single founder, a specific theological system, a single concept of deity, a single holy text, a single system of morality, a central religious authority, or the concept of a prophet, despite being bound in legalism.

Hinduism is more like an all-encompassing way of life, much as is Native American spirituality. Hinduism has been generally regarded as the world's oldest organized religion. It consists of "*thousands of different religious groups that have evolved in India since 1500 BCE* (sic)." Because of the wide variety of Hindu traditions, freedom of belief and practice are notable features of Hinduism. Most forms of Hinduism are henotheistic religions, meaning they recognize a single deity, and view other Gods and Goddesses as manifestations or aspects of that supreme God. Most of the Hindu gods and goddesses are Nephilim, those living results of *transhuman* experiments, mating fallen extraterrestrial angels or sons of God with us and animals. This is why, many of the Hindu gods and goddesses have multiple arms, animal heads, exhibit supernatural powers, and are gigantic in size or shape.

Henotheistic and polytheistic religions have been recognized as the world's most tolerant faiths, in the same fashion of polytheistic ancient Egypt. Hinduism is a form of polytheism, which is what brought down ancient Egypt. However, there are incredible parallels between Hinduism and Christianity. Christianity shares some of its best beliefs with Hinduism; the future reward in heaven or punishment in Hell; the concept of Purgatory; a day of judgment; resurrection after death; the need for repentance for sin; salvation that requires faith in the Savior; a belief in angels and evil spirits; a belief that disease and sickness are caused by evil spirits; a past war in heaven between good and bad angels; free will; that God is considered the *Word of Logos*; common religious texts referring to '*the blind leading the blind*', '*a new heaven and a new earth, "living water," "all scripture is given by the inspiration of God," "all scripture is profitable for doctrine," "to die is great gain,"*; prayer and fasting; being born again.

Krishna, the hero and savior of the Mahabharata and the Bhagavad-Gita, is a type of Christ figure, whose life bears striking similarities to the life of Yeshua HaMashiach, or Jesus the Christ. According to the scriptures, both were crucified, resurrected, and ascended to heaven. Only Hinduism condones the worship of a pantheon of gods and goddesses, which Yahuah, the God of the Judeo-Christians considers idolatry.[29] See, *Who is God?* Book Two: Chapter: Twenty-Six: *The Office of Christ,* sub-section: *Will the Real Savior Please Step Up,* p.432-440.

The Mahabharata, also known as the Vedas, are the Hindu scriptures that tell the detailed stories of blue skinned gods who flew in their *Vimana* spacecraft around the earth and fought off evil monsters that wanted to devour humankind. Their great bravery and courage elevated many of the key figures to the status of deities, gods and goddesses. See, my section on the Vegans[30] Book One of *Who's Who in the Cosmic Zoo?* pp. 411-412, that includes more information on the blue-skinned humans who later became known as the Hindu gods, heroes, and goddesses of India.

Notes:

1. Frederich Engles and Karl Marx, *The Communist Manifesto,* 1948.
2. Clifford Geertz, *Religion as a Cultural System*, 1973.
3. Talal Asad, *The Construction of Religion as an Anthropological Category*, 1982.
4. Ella LeBain, *Who Are the Angels?* Book Three, Chapter Six: *Fallen Angels and Watchers*, p. 127-132, Skypath Books, 2016.
5. Zecharia Sitchin, *Genesis Revisited, Earth Chronicles,* Mass Market, 1990.
6. Ella LeBain, *Who's Who in the Cosmic Zoo?* Book One – Third Edition, Chapter on Giants, p. 208, Tate, 2013.
7. Chuck Missler and Mark Eastman, *Alien Encounters: The Secret Behind the UFO Phenomenon,* Koinonia House Inc; Revised edition (October 31, 2003).
8. Erich von Däniken, *Chariots of the Gods: Unsolved Mysteries of the Past,* BANTAM; Reprint edition (1972).
9. Ella LeBain, *Who's Who in the Cosmic Zoo?* Book One – Third Edition, *Annunaki,* p. 110-118, Tate, 2013
10. *Who's Who in the Cosmic Zoo?* Book One – Third Edition, *Draconians,* pp.154-181
11. Dr. Michael Salla, *Insiders Reveal Secret Space Program and Extraterrestrial Alliance,* Exopolitics Consultants, Hawaii, 2015
12. William Mills Tompkins, *Selected by Extraterrestrials: My life in the Top-Secret World of UFOs, Think-Tanks and Nordic Secretaries,* CreateSpace, 2010; 2ed. 2016.
13. Kate Ravilious, *Mars Melt Hints at Solar, Not Human, Cause for Warming, Scientist Says,* National Geographic News, February 28, 2007, http://news.nationalgeographic.com/news/2007/02/070228-mars-warming.html
14. Dr. Marcus Garvey Jr., *The Arab Muslim Slave Trade Of Africans, The Untold Story,* November 15, 2012, http://originalpeople.org/the-arab-muslim-slave-trade-of-africans-the-untold-story/
15. Ella LeBain, *Who is God?* Book Two, Skypath Books, 2015.
16. Used with Permission from *The Religion of Peace*, www.thereligionofpeace.com/Quran/025-Muhammads-sex-life.htm
17. Rhonda Robinson, News Real Blog, February 5, 2011
18. Jim Rutz, *Megashift,* Empowerment Press (CO), 2005.
19. http://www.pewforum.org/files/2015/03/PF_15.04.02_ProjectionsFullReport.pdf
20. Wiki Answers: https://en.wikipedia.org/wiki/Christian_population_growth#cite_note-PewProjections-2

21. Ella LeBain, *Who is God?* Book Two: Chapter Twenty-Three: *Babylonian History, Where it All Began,* subsection: *Who is Semiramis?* Skypath Books, 2015. p.371-373
22. Art Mathias, *Wellspring School of Ministry,* https://akwellspring.com/
23. David H. Stern, Ph.D., *Restoring the Jewishness of the Gospel: A Message for Christians*, Messianic Jewish Publishers, Clarksville, MD., 1998.
24. Art Mathias, *Wellspring School of Ministry Workbook,* p.47, Wellspring Publishing, 2010, https://akwellspring.com/
25. Freedom from Religion Foundation, https://ffrf.org/
26. Dr. Chuck Missler, *Religion is Just a Patsy,* http://www.khouse.org/articles_cat/
27. Ella LeBain, *Who Is God?* Book Two, Chapter Eight – *Who Are the Gods?* pp. 129-136, Skypath Books, 2015.
28. Ella LeBain, *Who's Who in the Cosmic Zoo?* Book One – Third Edition, Chapter-Five: Draconian-Reptilians, p.154-177, Tate, 2013.
29. Ibid., *Who is God?* Book Two: Chapter: Twenty-Six: *The Office of Christ,* sub-section: *Will the Real Savior Please Step Up,* p.432-440.
30. Ibid., *Who's Who in the Cosmic Zoo?* Book One, Ibid., pp. 411-412

CHAPTER SEVEN

Who Created Religions? God or ETs?

"How can we, without absurd arrogance, believe ourselves to have been uniquely favoured? If humans did find alien animal life, they would need to determine if these alien beings were rational, have "spiritual sense," and are fallen like humans are. If all three were present in these extraterrestrial life forms, and if we discovered that no form of redemption had reached them, then the human task might be to evangelize them. Redemption, starting with us, is to work from us and through us to the extraterrestrial beings.
Those who are, or can become His sons,
are our real brothers even if they have shells or tusks.
It is spiritual, not biological, kinship that counts."
(C.S. Lewis, *Religion and Rockets, 2002*)

In approximately 500 A.D., Mohammed was visited by an angel, who was an extra-terrestrial messenger, and was given the Qur'an. He formed a new religion to compete with Christianity and Judaism. Could this being whom Mohammed encountered, who was used to channel the Qur'an, have been, in reality, one of the fallen angels? Is it possible that this being was already in a cosmic conflict with the Christ and the Lord of Israel? Even though the Qur'an repeats and acknowledges the history of the Judeo-Christian Bible, to many scholars, it's more like the plagiarism and the perversion of both Old and New Testaments.

It includes the visit of Gabriel to Mary by affirming the virgin birth of Jesus Christ, however, the Qur'an points to a different future 'Mahdi' that will come as a saviour to Muslims that wars against Christians, Jews New Agers, Atheists, Secularists and even some Muslims who don't believe as they do, branding them as infidels. It includes many blatant anti-Christian and anti-Semitic statements, anti-Other decrees, and justifications for having sex with young boys and underage girls, all of which are contradictory to the laws of God and considered perversions of morality.

History shows that since the formation of Islam, it has been at war with both Christians, Jews, Hindus, and Buddhists, all the world's major religions. Doesn't that reveal something about its true nature? While it claims to be a religion of peace, the actions of the past 1500 years contradict that claim. Perhaps Allah and Mohammed are being guided by a different spirit and more importantly different god than the Christians, Jews, and Hindus? We must consider this point, as that same kind of conflict doesn't exist between Christians, Jews, and Hindus, who all seem tolerant of one another. Most Christians accept other religions, as do Jews, and Hindus are at peace with the rest of the world, so if Islam was really the peaceful religion it claims to be, then why is it always at war with the rest? This is precisely why many have pointed towards Islam for the appearance of the antichrist.

Hinduism and Judaism have many parallels: both have in their ancient manuscripts a belief in reincarnation, both adhere to legalism, aestheticism, and both have similar creation stories about giants, monster hybrids and cosmic battles with evil aliens who want to devour humankind. Both point to saviours, the Hindus have Krishna, the Jews have Yeshua, aka Jesus Christ despite many Jews who still don't believe that He is in fact their Messiah-King that they pray to and wait for.

> "Behold, He is coming with the clouds, and ***every eye will see Him--even those who pierced Him. And all the tribes of the earth will mourn because of Him***. So, shall it be! Amen."
>
> (Revelation 1:7)

The main difference between Hinduism and Judaism is polytheism versus monotheism. The Jews believe in one God, the Hindus believe in a pantheon of gods and goddesses. To the Jews this is idolatry, yet both believe in a saviour or Messiah figure to save them. What if Krishna was one of the incarnations of Jesus Christ? What if they were one soul just inserted into different times and places on the timeline and different cultures/races? How much different were the East Indians from the race of Israelites and Semites? While they may have been two distinctly different races, they seemed to co-exist parallel on the earth at around the same time. In fact, many believe that the East Indians were one of the lost tribes of Israel, who simply migrated away from the land of Israel. The research I am presenting within this book, certainly seems to prove that, which would make a whole lot of sense, especially considering today's Christian communities within India and Pakistan, who recognize the Kingship and Lordship of Jesus the Christ.

Just as Buddhism came from Hinduism, which was a shift from the legalism and aestheticism to freedom of spirit, so it was that out of Judaism came Christianity, through Jesus Christ who said, "I've come to set the captives free." (Isaiah 61; Luke

4). One thing that Buddhism and Christianity do have in common is the shift from the bondage of having to live up to the 'letter of the law', to living by the 'spirit of the law.' (Matthew 5:20-44; Romans 2:28-29) Both lead to the paths of the heart, the focus is on the inner man, not the physical man.

Still, Buddhism was created by one of the fallen angels as a rebellion from Hinduism and as a deterrent from the Divine Plan of Salvation. The fact that there is no saviour in Buddhism indicates that that there is an element of deception and denial that was inserted by one of the satans to obscure the true path. The onerous task of saving oneself from the wheel of karma lies on the individual alone, who must achieve the path of enlightenment by his own efforts. We know that this is a false path, because we are saved by grace through faith, so no man can boast. As we've already discussed, Lucifer is the god of this world, and he is known as the god of enlightenment. He comes as an angel of light.

Buddhism denies the path of a saviour, which is a subtle implant of spiritual limitation, inserted into this belief system to obscure the truth of the Divine Plan of Salvation. "*We are the change we've been waiting for*" is nothing more than a narcissistic implant deceiving its host in thinking it's a god. The truth is, no amount of meditation or chanting can save someone from the bondage of the alien fallen angels, who continues to seek and keep us humans enslaved. If they were truly gods, then where's their power to deliver from demonic oppression? Satan cannot cast out satan. Jesus said,

> "So, if Satan could cast out Satan, then he is divided against himself; then how shall his kingdom stand?"
>
> (Matthew 12:26)

Likewise, Buddhists who think they're god, do not have the power to raise the dead, or cure the incurable, or authorize miracles, signs and wonders, only the God of gods can do that.

The biggest difference is that Buddhism does not believe in a Saviour as does Hinduism and Christianity. Buddhism believes we can save ourselves by cleansing our minds through meditation and following the eightfold path. But what happens during their so called 'cleansing process' an unknown, unexpected agent enters the wash? The mind is like a sponge, and not everybody is in control of their own thoughts, those who are, are the ten percent of the population that are resistant to hypnosis because of a strong mind.

This is where the rubber meets the road in Buddhism which is weak in the face of demonic influences, proving through a mere quieting of the mind making it inept, and insufficient for delivering it. Thereby needing a much stronger medicine, and that's the presence of the Living Word, Jesus Christ through the intervention of the

Holy Spirit. Just speak to the thousands of so called Buddhists who have turned their focus on a living breathing relationship with the Living Christ. They will tell you that it's only through inviting the Holy Spirit in, that they now have the supernatural peace that keeps their hearts and minds through Christ.

There are many sects of Buddhism, all with different approaches to the religion, all striving for liberation through chanting and mediation, yet some worship Buddha, well idols of Buddha in the form of Buddha statutes, after all, there were many Buddhas. This is inspired by *religious spirits* which holds the worshippers in bondage to the god of this world. This is idolatry and considered spiritual legal ground for the assignment of demons on one's mind, body and spirit through etheric implants. One of the many names for Lucifer is Buddha, or 'the enlightened one'. As we've discussed in this book series several times, we humans are not capable of saving ourselves from the cosmic evil, which consists of a hierarchy of principalities, powers, rulers of the darkness and cosmic evil in heavenly places that are alien to us on earth and to all humanity. The Divine Plan of Salvation was written in the stars before the beginning of time for the entire universe to see and to witness, not just us on earth. See, Book Five: *The Heavens*, my Chapter: *The Divine Plan of Salvation as Written in the Stars.*

Counterfeit Angels and their Prophets

So, Mohammed claims to have been visited by the archangel Gav'ril, which has been interpreted as Gabriel... but could this have been Gav'ril the fallen *counterfeit* angel, not God's Holy Archangel Gabriel? The Hadith, which details the historical account of the life of Mohammed, tells of his lustful sexual appetites with multiple wives and young girls, including prepubescent girls and how he particularly enjoyed them. His life reflects sexual immorality, yet he founded one of the most sexually restrictive and repressive religions on the face of the earth. This reveals not only the fruit of hypocrisy, but that the basis of the belief system is more likely false, as the angel who visited him and inspired Islam is more likely than not a fallen angel, whose motives were to inspire a new cult to overshadow Christianity, take the focus away from God, to take our eyes off the Lord.

Why would the Creator Father in Heaven send an angel, an extra-terrestrial messenger, to inspire a new religion when He had just finished and accepted the one perfect sacrifice, and begun the work of salvation? Why would a new prophet be necessary when we have already been saved by God Himself? Why would we of earth start off a new religion with the persecution of one of God's people? This was one of the interventions of the satans, the enemies of God, who established Islam to offset the growth of Christianity, Judaism, and Hinduism. Think about it, historically speaking, from its inception, Islam has been not just at war but in a Holy 'Jihad'

War against the entire world. Islam is the only religion *hell-bent* on warring with all the religions of the world, and against God's people, for dominance. This is the work of the *alien gods*, the fallen angels, the rebellious extra-terrestrials, who are at war with the Creator God and His Divine Plan for us humans.

The fact that Islam was created by the fallen angels to compete against Christianity, Judaism, and Hinduism, can be gleaned from within the Qur'an, where there are passages and beliefs that the 'Mahdi' will come to save them. The alarming revelations of *The Islamic Antichrist,* in which author Joel Richardson documents the similarities between the Antichrist of the Bible, and the Mahdi of the Qur'an, postulates they are one and the same person and spirit.[1]

He also cited the Islamic teachings used by some Muslims, like then-President Mahmoud Ahmadinejad, believed that they can speed the coming of the Mahdi, their end-times savior, by creating chaos, from which they expect him to emerge.

Richardson's book presents his analysis of the Biblical account of the end times and that of the Quran, offering his conclusion about the Antichrist, who is described by the Bible as the ultimate enemy of God and His people, the Jews and Christians. The Mahdi, in Islam, is forecast to be someone who comes to establish a worldwide Islamic caliphate.

> "You have the bad guy of the Bible, he primarily persecutes God's people, Jews and Christians," Richardson said. Meanwhile the "12th Imam," or Islam's 'Mahdi,' "causes Jews and Christians to submit to Islam or be killed."

Both prophecies determine that for 7 years, a leader in the world will make peace in the Middle East, then break the accord to try to invade Israel while killing non-believers and setting up a seat of government on the Temple Mount which the bible calls, *the abomination of desolation.* (Daniel 9:27, Matthew 24:15)

While the biblical Antichrist is evil personified, the culmination of antagonism to God and His word, Richardson describes the Islamic perspective:

> "The Mahdi is Islam's primary messiah figure Muslims believe will come at the end of the age to lead Islam to global dominance. Much popular discussion of Mahdism in recent years has inaccurately expressed that belief in the Mahdi as merely a Shia phenomenon. While variances in the details do exist between Sunni and Shia Muslims on this issue, belief in the Mahdi is nevertheless not reserved to one group or the other. Numerous renowned Muslim scholars, Sunni, Sufi and Shia affirm the orthodoxy of belief in the coming of the Mahdi."
>
> Richardson said, "In both stories, Jesus returns. On the biblical side, Jesus returns to deliver his people from being persecuted. On the Islamic side, a

'Muslim Jesus' tells the Christians of the world, 'You've had it wrong all along. I never said God was my father. I never died on the cross.'" [sic]

Richardson also noted in a recent article, when Iran launched a surface-to-surface missile, it had the words "Ya Mahdi" emblazoned on its body – the equivalent of "Go Mahdi." He noted Muslims believe their savior's return can happen only when "bloodshed and chaos" are worldwide. "What circumstance," he questioned, would bring that about more quickly "than using nuclear weapons against the nation of Israel?"[2]

Richardson's book also takes on the popular assumption among Christians that the Antichrist will come from a revived Roman Empire, which many have assumed is associated with the Roman Catholic Church and the European Union. Today's Europe is ripe for a new leader to rise up and lead them out of the godlessness of Europe, which began as Christian countries. Germany for example, has long abandoned Christ today, that if the Rapture happened today, no one in Germany would even know about it. Europe has absorbed the Muslim invasion due to political correctness or incorrectness as many with a moral compass tend to believe. They have yielded to the god of Islam and traded their history of Christianity, so their women and children can be raped at will by invading Muslims. Europe is ripe for the Antichrist to emerge.

> "The Bible abounds with proofs that the Antichrist's empire will consist only of nations that are, today, Islamic," Richardson explains. "Despite the numerous prevailing arguments for the emergence of a revived European Roman empire as the Antichrist's power base, the specific nations the Bible identifies as comprising his empire are today all Muslim."[1]

In Europe today, both England, France and Germany have 'no go zones' that are strictly Muslim neighborhoods. Germany has literally bent over backwards to absorb thousands of Muslims. The British Empire, which was once an example of the Church of England, the break-away kingdom from the Roman Empire and the first Protestant Church to break away from the Roman Catholic Church, has now succumbed to the Muslim invasion.

As of 2017, the Mayor of London is Muslim, the Mayor or Birmingham is Muslim, the Mayor of Leeds is Muslim, the Mayor of Blackburn is Muslim, the Mayor of Sheffield is Muslim, the Mayor of Oxford is Muslim, the Mayor of Luton is Muslim, the Mayor Oldham is Muslim, the Mayor of Rochdale also is a Muslim. All of which was achieved by just 4 million Muslims out of a population of 66 million Brits. There are now over 3,000 Muslim Mosques, over 130 Muslim Sharia Courts, over 50 Million Sharia Councils, along with Muslims only no-go zones across the

UK. 78% of Muslim women don't work and depend on welfare, free benefits and housing, along with 63% of Muslim men who are unemployed and are also enjoying free benefits and housing. And this was the nation that helped push back the Nazis.

Germany's Nazis have now been replaced by Islamists who live by Sharia Law. See, Book Two: *Who Is God?* for Chapter Twenty-Four: *What is Islam?* Sub-section: *What is Sharia Law?*[3] pp. 397-399. Women have absolutely no rights under Sharia Law. This is the antithesis of all western countries. There's no question about it, the Muslim invasion has spread throughout Europe making Europe ripe for the rise of the Antichrist or Islamic Mahdi.

Richardson believes the key error of many previous prophecy scholars involves the misinterpretation of a prediction by Daniel to Babylonian King Nebuchadnezzar in the Book of Daniel Chapter 2. Daniel describes the rise and fall of empires of the future, leading to the end times. Western Christians have viewed one of those empires as Rome, when, claims Richardson, Rome never actually conquered Babylon and was thus disqualified as a possibility. It had to be another empire that rose and fell and rose again that would lead to rule of this "man of sin," described in the Bible. That empire, he says, is the Islamic Empire, which did conquer Babylon and, in fact, rules over it even today. Turkey, Iran have now been taken over by Islamic clerics. The Ottoman Empire once ruled Israel and will attempt to do so again in the last days.

Jesus, Hindus, Buddhists & Zoroastrians

One of the great mysteries of the New Testament Bible involves the activities and whereabouts of Jesus during His teens and twenties. There is a huge gap in the chronology from Jesus' Bar Mitzva to when He began preaching. Most people say that He just worked as a carpenter or hung out in the desert, yet there is no record of any miracles, healings, or sermons being given during this seventeen-year period. Many people believe Jesus travelled to India to reconnect with one of the lost tribes of Israel which ended up there. There were well-established trade routes from the time of Alexander the Great, from Israel to India. There are intriguing records in India which suggest that Jesus used this route to travel to India, along with where He stayed, what He did, and what He said. Surely these reports are worth pursuing!

In 1890, a Russian by the name of Nicolas Notovich, published a travelogue of a journey he took through India, Kashmir, Ladakh and Tibet. Notovich ended up in a Tibetan Temple of Buddhists where he was recovering from a broken leg while one of the Lamas tells him that Jesus is revered as a Bodhisattva who was called *Issa* and that He trekked to India to study the Vedas and Buddhism. The Lama shared with Notovich, a manuscript in the possession of the Tibetan Buddhists for centuries, which tells of Jesus stirring up a caste war against the Brahmins that caused Him to have to leave India. Sounds just like our Jesus to leave a mark wherever He went! The manuscript includes all the sermons He preached in India, and how on His way back home to Israel, He stopped off in Persia where He preached against Zoroastrianism. This manuscript is known as *The Buddhist Scriptures*[4], and Notovich published most of them in his travelogue called, *The Unknown Life of Jesus Christ.*[5]

The Buddhist Scriptures records Jesus travelled to India between the ages of 13 and 30 and includes the accounts of his travels back to Israel. The story of His preaching to the Israelites, His crucifixion, and the resurrection were added after His death. This manuscript includes accounts of His rebukes of the Hindu Brahman Priests, in which He reprimanded them for exalting themselves, along with the issue of idolatry, the worship of idols and false gods. He scolded them for their human sacrifices, about which He says, 'that which is sacrificed to idols is dead works, and the idols don't hear you anyway, worship the Lord your God only, the Creator of Heaven and Earth.' The Brahman Priests did not like that, and, the accounts say, they had plotted to have Jesus killed. Jesus spent a lot of time in Buddhist temples in refuge hiding, and eventually left India to journey to Persia, where He rebuked the Zoroastrians in the same fashion for their idolatry and falsehood.

In India and Tibet Jesus was called *Issa*, and it is interesting to note that this is the name used for Him in the Qur'an.

In, *The Unknown Life of Jesus Christ*, He said,[5] "All the things done without God are only gross errors, illusions and seductions, serving but to show how much the heart of the doer is full of presumption, falsehood and impurity.[5] 'Put not your faith in oracles. God alone knows the future. He who has recourse to the diviners soils the temple of this heart and shows his lack of faith in his Creator.[4]. 'Belief in the diviners and their miracles destroys the innate simplicity of man and his childlike purity. An infernal power takes hold of him who so errs, and forces him to commit various sins and give himself to the worship of idols. 'But the Lord our God, to whom none can be equaled, is one omnipotent, omniscient and omnipresent; He alone possesses all wisdom and all light."[5]

Jesus sojourned six years among the Buddhists, where He found the principle of monotheism still pure. Arrived at the age of twenty-six years, He remembered His homeland, which was then oppressed by a foreign yoke. On His way homeward, He preached against idol-worship, human sacrifice, and other errors of faith, admonishing the people to recognize and adore God, the Father of all beings, to whom all are alike, the master as well as the slave; for they all are His children, to whom He has given this beautiful universe for a common heritage. The sermons of Jesus made a profound impression upon the peoples who heard Him, which exposed Him to all sorts of dangers provoked by the clergy. Yet He was saved by the very idolaters who, only the preceding day, had offered their children as sacrifices to their idols!

While passing through Persia, today's Iran, Jesus almost caused a revolution among the worshippers of Zoroaster's doctrine. The priests refrained from killing him only out of fear of the peoples' vengeance. They resorted to artifice, and led Him out of town at night, with the hope that He might be devoured by wild beasts. Jesus escaped this period and arrived safe and sound in the land of Israel.

According to Luke, Jesus was about thirty years old when He began preaching to the Israelites. According to the Buddhist chroniclers, Jesus' teachings in Judea began in his twenty-ninth year. All of His sermons are not mentioned by the Evangelists, but have been preserved by the Buddhists, and are remarkable for their character and divine grandeur.

Luke 1:80 says, 'And the child grew, and waxed strong in spirit, and was in the deserts till the day of his showing unto Israel.' The Apostle says that Jesus was in the deserts, however, the Buddhists explain this version of the Gospel doesn't specifically say which deserts? According to them He crossed the Sind, a name which signifies 'the Indus River.'

The Sanskrit language was transformed when words were passed into the Persian language, which caused letters and sounds to shift slightly, yet the meanings remain the same.

A cult known as Jainism flourishes on the peninsula of Hindustan, a link between Buddhism and Brahmanism. Its devotees teach the destruction of all other beliefs, which they declare are contaminated with falsehood. It dates as far back as the seventh century, B.C. Its name originates from Djain, or conqueror, which is assumed is the symbol of its triumph over its rivals.

I remember listening to a sermon by a charismatic pastor who once said, 'I wish there more accounts of what Jesus did, I would imagine that not all of his work was written down in the Gospels, it seems that everywhere he went his very presence caused people to shift, from those who only had to touch the hem of his robe, to those who believed all he had to do was give the word, and people from a distance were healed, to all the miracles, healing and deliverance he did that was recorded.' Well, the Buddhist scriptures do tell much of those missing pieces.

One thing to keep in mind is that the Buddhist scriptures have never been sold or fully published, but are kept under lock and key by Tibetan Monks in their library of hundreds of ancient scriptures. Lay people are not allowed access to these scriptures, but only the Llamas. They have been shared with only with certain individuals, and Notovich was one of them. In my opinion, this adds to the authenticity and credibility of these scriptures, as the Tibetan Llamas had no hidden agenda to create fraud by publishing these scriptures. It also appears from the amount of information that is available that there is more than one manuscript, more than one scroll of Buddhist scriptures.

In 1920, Levi H. Dowling wrote *The Aquarian Gospel of Jesus The Christ*, which became very popular in the 1960s. It was responsible for the Jesus Freak movement, as nearly every hippie had a copy of it. It is said to have inspired the song by the Fifth Dimension, *The Age of Aquarius* as well. The book is approximately 470 pages and includes the Life and Works of Jesus in Tibet, Western India, Persia, Assyria, Greece and Egypt. These scriptures, kept hidden over the centuries, would have shed much needed light on the missing years and work of Jesus Christ, but were deliberately kept out of the canonized bible.[6]

Knowing what we do know about the unique mission of Jesus Christ, it is understandable that His journey through India and the Middle East would align with who He was, and what He was here to teach, which was to become the bridge for the Living God and man, through restoring the broken relationship with the Creator Father. One of the biggest issues that has consistently grieved the heart of the Creator was idolatry, human and animal sacrifices to false gods, which have proved to be fruitless over the ages, feeding Draconian Reptilian Blood Lusty alien gods that live inside the earth aka Lucifer/Satan. This was a large part of the teachings of Jesus Christ throughout his journeys through Tibet, India, and the Middle East.

Christian Churches and their Denominations

Unfortunately, modern day Christianity is at the mercy of the *religious spirits* who dictated the religion of Christianity through their decrees by the Council of Nicaea in 325 A.D. During this council, men decided what scriptures were to be canonized into the Bible, known as the Holy Scriptures. These church Fathers created the mock up for what Christians believe today as the unadulterated *Word of God*. Yes, the Bible is true, and it is also one of the historical accounts of the interaction of extraterrestrials and men, of the many interventions of whom the Bible calls Malachim, or Angels, which is the Hebrew word for 'messengers'. While the accounts of the words of God are relatively still intact, it is however unfortunate and perplexing that so many of the Words of God are missing from the Bible. These are recorded in the many books that did not make it into the compilation of the canon by the Council of Nicaea.

This loss is due to the many *spiritual battles* fought over us earth humans, some of which were won, some obviously lost, today creating a gap in our understanding, as many believers are unfortunately left in the dark about many subjects, such as reincarnation, fallen angels, and the lost years of Jesus Christ. That gap is filled by the *spirit of religion*. The *Books of Enoch* are invaluable as an aid to understanding the cosmic drama between all the celestial beings, those who fell from heaven, those who rebelled against the Creator, what they did, and how this situation in which we on earth find ourselves today is all related, as well as the vast amount of astronomical knowledge that Enoch imparts to us about the universe, the stars, the dimensions, portals and the planets. The *Book of Enoch* also coined the phrase *the Son of God,* and was one of the first texts to predict the coming of Jesus Christ. In fact, Jesus Himself as well as His disciples quoted the *Book of Enoch* so many times, the *Book of Enoch* was sacred scriptures to the early church.

The Catholic Church rejected Enoch's scriptures in 325 A.D. thereby casting doubt on its credibility for centuries in Christian circles. Yet two millennia later, as we are living in the age of knowledge, even the Bible says that in the last days, knowledge will increase. We know that the earth has been and continues to be a battlefield between the kingdoms of darkness and the kingdom of light. We also know that just because a religion authorizes or rejects some issue, doesn't necessarily make it so. The forces of darkness, the fallen angels and the satans, have interfered with the dissemination of knowledge and revelation to the masses, because it is easier for them to manipulate and control people when they are ignorant.

So, it is with the Buddhist scriptures which also contains the Word of God as spoken by Jesus Christ, or *St. Issa* as He was called in India. Imagine if the Buddhist scriptures and the Books of Enoch were canonized into the Bible, it would be a whole different world, and religions as we know them today would have been altered forever. But perhaps that is precisely the reason that the Church fathers in Nicaea chose to reject these scriptures, because of the political state of affairs at that time, and the church's agenda to be upheld as the ultimate power on earth.

"God has paid us the intolerable compliment of loving us,
in the deepest, most tragic, most inexorable sense."
C.S. Lewis ~ *The Problem of Pain*

Demons in the Church

Satan's works 24/7 to keep us from truth, salvation, and liberation from his dark kingdom of powers, principalities, and his network of rulers of the darkness. He certainly does not stop at the doorway of the church or at the boundaries of our imagination. Most of us do not understand the gravity or the subtlety of this spiritual battle when we come to Christ and become a *saved* Christian. Sadly, there are many churches that won't even say the 'D' word, and discuss the demonic, let alone accept the fact their church is infested with demons. This explains why many in their congregation are not free. I have personally spoken to pastors who are afraid to discuss how the demonic works, for fear of causing post-traumatic stress in their congregation.

They continue to deny demonic interference even though Jesus Christ commanded all His followers to "Heal the sick, raise the dead, cleanse the lepers, cast out demons: freely ye received, freely give." (Matthew 10:8). They think the commandments of Christ are debatable. As it is the duty of a demon to instill doubt, we know who is doing all the talking here! These are churches without power. When asked if they performed deliverance, the other 'D' word, they responded, 'deliverance, what's that?' Jesus said, "I tell you the truth, anyone who believes in me will do the same works I have done, and even greater works, because I am going to be with the Father." (John 14:12)

Is it any wonder that Satan would be working overtime in the body of those who profess their belief in Jesus Christ? They believe they are saved. But here is how subtle Satan's lies and denials can be: he blinds their eyes, covers up their ears and literally causes them to be spiritually dumb and mute to what goes on in the spirit realm. This can only flourish in an atmosphere of denials and unbelief. This kind of demon-spirit is pervasive in the churches who refuse to hear about deliverance, and are therefore blinded into thinking that demons don't exist in a person who has already accepted Jesus Christ. Well I've got news for you, this couldn't be further from the truth.

Deliverance, and all that it entails, is an uncomfortable subject for anyone in denial or immersed in secular humanism, and many of today's churches only want to preach, teach, and hear *feel good* theology. The apostate churches are afraid that if it is brought out into the open that many people are bound by demons because they have not fully repented from sins, from generational sins and curses, they would feel condemned instead of feeling loved. Well, ask yourself, what's more important, being free or having some temporary discomfort to one's ego?

Freedom comes with a price. Jesus paid the price, but many mistakenly believe that their freedom and deliverance is automatic. It is not. He said, He came to call sinners to repentance. This is a process. Many have become Christians in name only. They are filled with the *religious spirit*, not the Holy Spirit. This is why Christians can be demon possessed, contrary to popular Christian belief. Many may repent of their outer sins, like drinking and smoking, but never follow through with all their inner sins, sins of the heart, relationship and family sins, sins of their ancestors, and this is exactly what keeps them in legal bondage to the demonic realm.

Sadly, there are many churches today who practice cheap grace. They teach grace without the power of the cross, and they teach forgiveness without repentance. They also merge all kinds of universalism into their doctrines and allow false teachings to pervade the church. These all give legal authority to Satan's realm which causes demons to infiltrate and hold believers in bondage. They fail to discern the spirits, and are therefore mislead by the counterfeit spirit, which keeps church members in demonic strongholds.

This kind of Christianity is lukewarm, that is so despicable by the Lord's standards:

> "So then because you are *lukewarm*, and neither cold nor hot, I will spew you out of my mouth."
>
> (Revelation 3:16)

They also pretend to be religious, but deny the power of the Holy Spirit, and do not know the power of the blood of Christ. They have never fully repented from Satanic power and authority. This is what the scripture says about them:

> "Having a form of godliness, <u>but denying the power thereof</u>**: from such turn away.**"
>
> (2 Timothy 3:5)

The Shadow of the Church

The scriptures tell us that we war not against flesh and blood, but against principalities, powers, rulers of the darkness and spiritual hosts of wickedness in the heavens. (Ephesians 6:12). There are seven major principalities which hold most people in bondage. These include bitterness, self-bitterness, jealousy and envy, fear, accusatory spirits, rejection, and the occult. There are many layers and armors to these principalities, which cover every negative emotional, mental, and spiritual condition known to humankind.

They reflect the essential personalities of the satans, who inhabit the realm of the fallen angels and their demons. These areas must be surrendered to the Lord Jesus Christ, one by one, through confession and repentance. Then, having covered all spiritual legal ground, Satanic power and authority are ejected from the life of the believer, this is true deliverance from the Holy Spirit. This takes away satan's foothold.

When we display the personality traits of the demonic, like ego, pride, narcissism, stubbornness, unforgiveness, vengeance, anger, greed, we can see that part of our personality belongs to the satans, and his demons have legal authority to oppress our life in a variety of ways. Many Christians, who believe in the Lord, do not recognize this blind spot, and wonder why they are constantly being attacked, or why they struggle with health issues and problems.

Because of these blind spots and denials, a shadow-self springs into being, that hidden part of us that is wounded and held in bondage through fear, bitterness, jealousy. Many believers are unaware of this phenomenon, and how it not only affects our lives, but the lives of those we attempt to pray for and lay our hands on for healing. When a person lays hands on another, energy transference occurs. If the Christian truly has the anointing of the Holy Spirit, then they are transferring the power of the Holy Spirit to heal and to deliver through their hands. Jesus Christ said all those who believe in Him are given the authority to heal the sick, cast out demons and raise the dead. However, not all Christians are free and clear from their own sinfulness, which dulls and compromises their anointing. When they lay hands on others, they are transferring their own spirits, and their unresolved and unrepentant sins which have become their shadow.

It is this shadow, this lingering sin, where demons legally attach and unbeknownst to the blind and ignorant believer, they are being used as vessels for Satan. Their touch feels heavy, instead of healing, thereby lowering the vibration of the person they have just laid hands on, often leaving pain, confusion, and disappointment instead of freedom and relief. This arises from a reservoir of unrepentant self-hate, guilt, shame, anger, are all the strongholds of bitterness and self-bitterness. There are many more examples, but I'll leave them for my next book on healing, *Finding Freedom,* as to what blocks miracles from happening.

The same type of shadow dancing is common with those who work in the fields of Energy Healing in New Age circles and Metaphysical Churches. If the practitioners are not clear themselves, then they are open to being used by the demonic realm to steal energy from those they work on, always unbeknownst to them. This happens through the attachment of entities, which are all demonic. Even lightworkers are operating through demons, who all masquerade as angels of light.

It's important to discern that not everyone who calls himself Christian is living his life filled with the Holy Spirit, and exercising his God given-authority to heal the sick and cast out demons through the power of the Holy Spirit and the Word of God. As I've mentioned before, many are Christian in name only. There are so many denominations of Christian churches which disagree with one another on doctrine, and discord always gives Satan a foothold.

Catholicism is by definition, the world's largest cult. A cult is an organization that is run by one man, in this case the Pope. While the Catholic laity has many redeeming qualities, such as being charitable to the poor of the world, the Catholic church as an institution and corporation is one of the richest in history. However, the church as an institution doesn't pay tax and is not required to answer questions as to its holdings, we must rest on assumptions. This church is the restructuring of several pagan cults, Mithraism blended with the worship of Mother Mary and a crucified Christ on the cross.

I certainly do not need to remind my readers of the many instances of pedophilia and sexual abuse scandals involving the Catholic church. Numerous Catholic priests were involved over decades, whose crimes were covered up by the Church, which then transferred the unrepentant criminals to unsuspecting parishes. All influenced by the demonic realms! Major lawsuits emerged in 2001 claiming that priests had sexually abused minors. Some priests resigned, others were defrocked and jailed, and there were financial settlements with many victims. The United States Conference of Catholic Bishops commissioned a comprehensive study that found that four percent of all priests who served in the US from 1950 to 2002 had faced some sort of accusation of sexual misconduct.[7]

So many things are scripturally off with respect to Catholicism. The fact that the Bible says, "And do not call anyone on earth 'father,' for you have one Father, and he is in heaven." (Matthew 23:9). The entire Catholic church is based on a hierarchy called the priesthood, whose members wield worldly power and are all called, 'father'. "Jesus became a priest, not by meeting the physical requirement of belonging to the tribe of Levi, but by the power of a life that cannot be destroyed." (Hebrews 7:16)

Christ rose from the dead. He walked among His disciples for forty days before ascending into the *cloud* that took him to Heaven. This is the basis of the Christian faith. The power, the proof, and the life of Christianity lies in the resurrection. Yet Catholics worship a crucified Christ. In place of the resurrection comes the dogma of a Church and the real Christ is replaced by an image, an idol if you will. Even the teachings of Jesus Christ became twisted and falsified. In every Catholic Church, a dead Jesus hangs on a cross with nails in hands and feet, with thorns in His head and with a wound in His side. This is a real voodoo-technique for blocking His power, as if! The subconscious message to everyone who sits in a Catholic church, is: "Jesus is dead! He is dead and no longer has any power. He was victimized and so are you!" Not only is this a lie, it opens the door to the demonic realm to keep believers in bondage, in suffering. It marginalizes the living power of the overcoming, resurrected Christ that His Holy Spirit promises to empower every believer.

Back in 313 A.D., the struggles of the early church were lessened by the recognition of Christianity by the Emperor, Constantine I. By 380 A.D., Christianity became the state religion of the Roman Empire, which promptly began its fall in 376 A.D. Catholic orthodoxy persisted in the Eastern Roman Empire until the Fall of Constantinople. There were seven ecumenical councils, beginning in 325 A.D., beginning with the Council of Nicaea through the Council of Trent in 1563, which collectively decided which books were to be canonized into the Holy Bible, and which books were to be rejected for a variety of reasons. These councils also decided upon various interpretations of doctrine, and how they were going to define their church as a power structure.

It was an empirical goal of Constantine as emperor to unify his subjects, to get everyone on the same page, loyal to one state, obeying one set of laws, following one version of Christianity, which is why the councils were formed. This was the political agenda of Rome. In order to include everyone and every belief, they combined ancient pagan rituals with Mithraism and called it Catholicism. They replaced Mithras with Jesus, yet all the rituals stayed the same, the Eucharist, the incense, the hierarchy of the priesthood. The pagan goddesses were replaced by Mary, the Mother of Jesus, who was venerated as the Mother of God, and the councils declared it heresy if anyone would deny that. The variety of worship of the pagan gods and goddesses was replaced by petitioning the saints, those whom the council and papacy deemed worthy of sainthood. Of course, all the disciples were made into saints, St. Peter, St. Paul, St. Thomas, ad infinitum. This is how the Romans got into Catholicism.

In 1929 the Lateran Council formed the Vatican we know today, which is a government in and of itself. Vatican City is actually an independent state, spoken of as a new creation, not as a vestige of the much larger Papal States (756–1870 A.D.) which had previously encompassed much of central Italy. Today the Vatican dictates church policy and sees itself as having the authority of Christ on Earth. The pope considers himself the Vicar of Christ. If this were not as close to blasphemy as one can get, there is so much going on within the walls of the Vatican City it could fuel a series of Dan Brown novels.

It is chilling to know that a Jesuit priest, Malachi Martin, died for exposing the pedophilic Satanism among a group of false cardinals and other priests that were in league with a secret Masonic diabolicus that began following the "enthronement of the fallen Archangel Lucifer" in the Roman Catholic citadel on June 29, 1963.[8]

There have been several priests who have come forward as whistleblowers to expose the Vatican's sinister plan toward an anti-Christian New World Order, while preparing for the coming of the Antichrist. According to Thomas Horn in his book, *Apollyon Rising 2012*, there were a number of Catholic priests who came forward to expose how the changes were taking place within the ranks of the Vatican. Father John F. O'Connor presented a two-hour presentation on DVD, *The Reign of the Antichrist,* and outlined the catalyst for this scheme unfolding because of Masonic conspirators within the organization called *Alta Vendetta* which essentially takes control of the papacy in order to help the False Prophet deceive the world's faithful, including Catholics, into worshiping the Antichrist when he arrives.[8]

Of course, most Catholics are unaware of these infiltrations within the Vatican and the church hierarchy. Catholic believers are judged according to their faith, not because they belong to a corrupted church. There are many loving and charitable Catholics with a deep faith in the Lord who, despite their affiliation to the Catholic Church, will be saved. Naturally, it is all about our personal relationship and faith in Jesus Christ. Anyone within any church who has sold out to Satan have already sealed his fate.

I want to encourage my readers to do their own research with respect to the compromises and hidden agendas of the Vatican and the Catholic Church.

Malachi Martin wrote in his expose`, *The Keys of This Blood*:

> "Most frighteningly for John Paul, he had come up against the irremovable presence of a malign strength in his own Vatican and in certain bishops' chanceries. It was what knowledgeable Churchmen called the "superforce." Rumors, always difficult to verify, tied to the installation to the beginning of Pope Paul VI's reign in 1963. Indeed, Paul had alluded somberly to "the smoke of Satan which has entered the Sanctuary". . . an oblique reference to an enthronement ceremony by Satanists in the Vatican."[9]

Martin revealed more detail of the "Luciferic enthronement ceremonies by Satanists within the Vatican" in his book, *Windswept House:*

> "The Enthronement of the Fallen Archangel Lucifer was effected within the Roman Catholic Citadel on June 29, 1963; a fitting date for the historic promise about to be fulfilled. As the principal agents of this ceremonial well knew, Satanist tradition had long predicted that the Time of the Prince would be ushered in at the moment when a Pope would take the name of the Apostle Paul [Pope Paul VI]. That requirement - the signal that the Availing Time had begun - had been accomplished just eight days before with the election of the latest Peter-in-the-Line."[10]

Horn reports that in 1965, Pope Paul VI granted Martin a dispensation from his Jesuit and priestly duties, in a move to New York. As a member of the Second Vatican Council and personal secretary to renowned Jesuit Cardinal Augustine Bea, Martin was privy to privileged information pertaining to the secretive church and world issues, including the Third Secret of Fatima, which Martin hinted spelled out parts of the plan to formerly install the dreaded False Prophet during a "Final Conclave." Through this, Martin claimed that an Illuminati-Masonic group made up of Western plutocrats called "The Assembly" or the "Superforce" had infiltrated the highest levels of Vatican administration and were working to bring about a New World Order, may have led to involvement by operatives of the same group concerning his untimely, some say "suspicious" death in 1999.[8]

Revelation 17:9 relates the fate of the whore of Babylon, who sits on seven hills. Rome sits on seven hills. Many Biblical scholars believe that Babylon is an allegory of Rome, because it relates to the characteristics of Roman rule, its brutality, greed, paganism. Rome has been the seat of power of the old world for millennia. Some believe it still is today, spiritually. Revelation 17:18 talks about it ruling and having dominion over all the kings of the earth, possibly through the final Antichrist who is supposed to emerge out of the ancient Roman empire.

In both the books of 4 Ezra, 2 Baruch and the Sibylline oracles, Babylon is a cryptic name for Rome. Elsewhere in the New Testament, in 1 Peter 5:13; Babylon is used to refer to Rome. Revelation 17:9 says, "This calls for a mind with wisdom. The seven heads are seven hills on which the woman sits." Most scholars typically understand this as the seven hills of Rome. A Roman coin minted under the Emperor Vespasian circa 70 A.D. depicts Rome as a woman sitting on seven hills.[11]

According to the *International Standard Bible Encyclopedia*, "The characteristics ascribed to this Babylon apply to Rome rather than to any other city of that age: (1) as ruling over the kings of the earth (Revelation 17:18); (2) as sitting on seven mountains (Revelation 17:9); (3) as the center of the world's merchandise (Revelation 18:3, 11–13); (4) as the corrupter of the nations (Revelation 17:2; 18:3; 19:2); (5) as the persecutor of the saints (Revelation 17:6)."[12]

No doubt Rome and the Vatican state are playing a role in the end times game.[13] See *Book Two: Who Is God?* chapter: *Who Are the Gods?*

Witchcraft in the Church

Witchcraft is often portrayed as innocent, yet it is strictly forbidden by the Word of God (Deuteronomy 18:9-14, Leviticus 19:31, 20:6; Isaiah 8:19). "I will render your witchcraft powerless, and mediums will no longer exist among you." (Micah 5:12-ISV) Any type of witchcraft uses spirits to carry out its message, and these spirits work within the hierarchy of Lucifer the Satan. Spiritually speaking, for discernment purposes, the Kingdom of Heaven does not employ witches, nor does it use sorcery or spirits. Even the seemingly innocent white magic, goddess worship, and earth magic, invoke spirits which are not from the Holy Spirit.

We must remember that we are engaged in spiritual warfare, which is designed to take us out, steal our joy, and prevent our entrance into the Kingdom of Heaven. It is the Creator's plan that we will be redeemed and allowed into the Kingdom of Heaven, *if* we accept the atonement for our sins through the blood of Christ. Lucifer the Satan and his fallen angels lost that place in heaven and out of jealousy, spitefulness, malevolence, they want us to lose, too. The kingdom of darkness knows how to masquerade as light because Lucifer once was an angel of light and son of heaven, this is why he is now the great counterfeiter and deceiver.

There is an entire hierarchy of spirits that work in the realms of witchcraft. Witchcraft itself is a 'controlling spirit'. This spirit came through the enemies of God in the Old Testament, through the pagan gods of Ashtoreth/Astarte that controlled the evil Queen Jezebel and the fallen King Ahab. (See, 1Kings 16-22) They were all destroyed by the power of God, yet their spirits continue to torment us on earth. As I've pointed in Book Two: *Who Is God?* see, Chapter Seven: *Discernment of Gods, Angels and Demons,* sub section: *The Divine Feminine and the False Goddess,*[14] [p. 108-112] that the demon known today as the *Jezebel Spirit,* is not a woman's spirit, it is a demon spirit, and all demons are male by nature. This demon was around long before the evil Queen Jezebel was born, it simply attached itself to her and possessed her and used her to carry out it it's evil plans to take down the Kingdom of Israel through her worship of the fallen angels Astarte/Ishtar/Lilith.

Satan uses spirits of divination, python spirits along with the spirit of Astarte, Ishtar or Lilith who disguises herself as the earth goddess, Mother Mary, and a host of other seemingly friendly goddesses. Her goal is to get followers to worship her, sacrifice to her, and become bound by demons of darkness for believing in lies and false paths. 'There is a way that seems right to a man but the end of that road leads to destruction.' (Proverbs 14:12, 16:25) Let me add for further discernment, that demons of darkness often masquerade as lightworkers, that angels of light can be spirits of error. People are often *blinded* by their false light. They also keep the goddess worshippers in bondage through spirits of self-righteousness, guilt, and a spirit of religion, the *religious spirit,* causing the goddess worship experience to be a masquerade of love, light and deception.

Besides the seemingly innocent white magic, there is black magic, uncloaked outright wickedness which seeks to destroy, to assume power, as well as the outright worship of Lucifer the Satan, who is the Dragon, Lizard King. There is yet another form of witchcraft which is not easily discerned, and hides itself inside religious organizations, even Christian churches, Jewish and Islamic temples. Remember witchcraft is all about *control.* So, think of all the controlling churches and temples you have ever experienced, and you have encountered the spirit of religious witchcraft.

There is another subtle form of witchcraft which comes from the flesh. In Greek, the word for flesh is 'sarx.' "Now the works of the flesh (sarx) are manifest, which are these; adultery, fornication, uncleanness, lasciviousness (unbridled lust), idolatry, witchcraft, hatred, variance (contention), emulations (jealous rivalry), wrath, strife, seditions, heresies, envyings, murders, drunkenness, revellings (evil carousing), and such like: of the which I tell you before, as I have also told you in time past, that they which do such things shall not inherit the kingdom of God" (Galatians 5:19-21).

Witchcraft is considered to be one of the works of the flesh. The works of the flesh are temper tantrums, bad attitudes, negative body language, stubbornness, negative words, and negative confessions. All of these are workings of witchcraft. 'Life and death are in the power of the tongue.' (Proverbs 18:21) 'The tongue also is a fire, a world of evil among the parts of the body. It corrupts the whole person, sets the whole course of his life on fire, and is itself set on fire by hell.' (James 3:6). We all have the power to possess what we confess. Spells are cast through words. Many people throw word curses around without realizing it, through backstabbing, gossip, complaining and having a bad attitude. These are all forms of control, hence of witchcraft.

Spiritual or astral trafficking is also witchcraft. The practice of having the spirit leave the body to astral travel to that of another for the purpose of controlling thoughts, reading a life, or stealing energy, is astral trafficking. If you've ever felt disoriented or confused for no reason, emotionally and physically drained without having made effort, suddenly clumsy, or just generally debilitated, without having the flu, it is an attack of spirit trafficking and witchcraft. Satan wants to cloud your vision and stop you from reaching your destiny in God. When an individual is under assault through witchcraft, he/she cannot connect with their true spiritual vision, as motivation is either gone or lacking. Those who have been targeted by curses will feel emotionally drained and carry a dark cloud in their countenance. The back of the neck becomes tight, a band of oppression around the head manifests as a headache. We may assume that we are sick, but it is not the flu, it is witchcraft.

Often when one is the object of curses, witchcraft, or trafficking, many inordinate fears will plague the mind, dark images will flash and disturb sleep. When curses are aimed at a whole congregation, this can manifest as problems within personal relationships, causing discord, disputes, and quarrels. Irritation is easily triggered, tolerance is low and patience even lower, and people complain about one another, increasing the spirit of gossip and backbiting. Rebellion against church leaders seems justified and the temptation to withdraw from that church is strong. This is all done to distract the body of Christ from its primary focus and calling.

Religious witchcraft can ruin churches, performed on church members. These are the ones who want to 'lord it' over your life. They may speak in tongues, uttering filthy oaths and epitaphs in ancient forgotten languages none can understand but the demons who inspire them. They may lay on hands in prayers for healing, but those on the receiving end, only get worse, not better. This is because what they are doing is transferring their demon spirits onto the person whom they are touching! Not everyone who heals in Jesus name is anointed by the Holy Spirit. There are so many Christians who have not completely repented of their inner sins, which blocks their anointing, yet the god of this world is all too ready to jump in and counterfeit a false healing, a temporary stoppage. All the while both parties are totally unaware that they are being used by demons. You may think, how can that be?

The number one reason is that of legal spiritual ground. This is when a sincere believer does not release or repent of all their sins, both known, unknown and generational. This is what makes deliverance necessary in our churches, which, peculiarly, many churches do not even teach or preach it, let alone allow anyone to even say the 'D' word. (Demons, demonic, devils, and Deliverance). I once spoke to a Pastor of a church inquiring about his service, and asked if he had a deliverance ministry? He was dumbfounded, and dumbstruck. Do we need further proof? Many will say they are healing in the name of Jesus, but do not have a clue that true healing comes from deliverance of the demonic. If we examine the Scriptures for the facts, we note that all the miraculous healings which Jesus performed involved kicking out demons, evil spirits and devils from people. People were healed, the dead were resuscitated from the dead, the blind saw, the deaf heard and the mute spoke.

The spirit of witchcraft seeks to block the power of the Holy Spirit, controlling and thwarting the life of every one of us, believer and nonbeliever alike. This spiritual warfare can be indiscernible to us in our busy, daily life. Whenever religious activities are motivated by *religious spirits* and the fleshly desires of being noticed, we are being beguiled by a form of witchcraft. "Having a form of godliness but denying the power thereof: from such turn away" (2 Timothy 3:5). Religion and religiosity relays on the spirit of witchcraft when we intentionally avoid the ministry of the Holy Spirit.

There are many religious denominations which claim to be Christian yet attack the ministry of the Holy Spirit. They challenge the work and expression of the Holy Spirit, it's miracles, healing, deliverance, prophecy, it's Gifts and its baptism. Instead, they uphold vain traditions and worldly programs designed by men. Religion is nothing but witchcraft when it is governed by the flesh rather than the Spirit of God. The elements of religion are a lack of spiritual sensitivity, insensitivity to others' true needs, fundamentalism, legalism and debate, hypocrisy, self-righteousness, and a form of piousness that denies the power of the Holy Spirit.

The kind of witchcraft which emanates from our flesh can be a bigger battle for us to fight than the Harry Potter style. Through the blood of Christ, we are empowered to crucify the works of the flesh and its old nature. "You were taught, with regard to your former way of life, to put off your old self, which is being corrupted by its deceitful desires; to be made new in the attitude (spirit) of your minds", (Ephesians 4:22).

Witchcraft is essentially a type of *mind control* 'spell' that is implanted onto people. It can make you believe that up is down and black is white, etc. It can take a lie and purport it as truth. The following are the *six key lies* taught in 'Churchianity', which is found in the various Christian religions and cults. Many who believe in these lies, do so, because this is what they are taught in seminary school. Others, because their church teaches and reinforces them.

Like all lies, these are major stumbling blocks to understanding the truth about the End Times Prophesies, which act as blinders on modern day Christians. These lies just keep getting passed down, stemming from Constantine's Creed, which was antichrist, anti-Semitic and anti the God of Israel. These lies are primarily in the New Testament, which do not match the truths embedded within the Jewish Bible. They are therefore, 'rogue' scriptures, as they do not represent the God of Israel, who sent Jesus. However, some of these lies stem from a misunderstanding due to mis-translations and mistransliterations from the Old Testament. These lies were covered up by the Church of Rome and have since trickled down through the many offshoot Christian denominations that were accepted as truth, until now.

1. There is no reincarnation based on one scripture, where there are like two dozen scriptures that prove otherwise. See, *Who is God?* pp. 455-484
2. Women are not equal and shouldn't teach men, inconsistent with the Book of Judges. See, *Who is God?* pp.485-500
3. All aliens are demons. Inconsistent with the Books of Ezekiel and Revelation. See, *Who is God?* pp. 71-88
4. There are no Extraterrestrials, just fallen angel demons. See, *Who is God?* pp.71-88; *Who Are the Angels?* Chapters Two, Three, Four, Five, Conclusion
5. There are no good Extraterrestrials in the Bible. See, *Who is God?* pp.71-88; *Who Are the Angels?* Chapters Two, Three, Four, Five, Conclusion
6. Christians replace unbelieving Jews and Israel. See, my next Chapter: Replacement Theology.

Notes:

1. Joel Richardson, *The Islamic Antichrist,* WND, March 3, 2015
2. Bob Unruh, *Islamic Antichrist? 'What do you say we go start slaughtering people so Jesus will come back'*, http://www.wnd.com/2011/02/264985/#0hWdu5xVw1bvLWW0.99http://www.wnd.com/2011/02/264985/, February 18, 2011
3. Ella LeBain, *Who Is God?* Book Two - Chapter Twenty-Four: *What is Islam?* Sub-section: *What is Sharia Law?* pp. 397-399, Skypath Books, 2015.
4. Virchand Raghavji Gandhi, Nicolas Notovitch, *The Unknown Life of Jesus Christ: From an Ancient Manuscript Recently Discovered In A Buddhist Monastery,* translated from French, 1887. http://www.tubetoptelevision.com/the/the-unknown-life-of-jesus-christ-from-an-ancient-manuscript-recently-discovered-in-a-buddhist-english.pdf
5. Nicholas Notovich, *The Unknown Life of Jesus Christ,* Wilder Publications, December 18, 2008.

6. Levi H. Dowling, *The Aquarian Gospel of Jesus The Christ,* 1920, http://www.sacred-texts.com/chr/agjc/
7. John Jay Report, *The Nature and Scope of Sexual Abuse of Minors by Catholic Priests and Deacons in the United States* 195O-2OO2. United States Conference of Catholic Bishops, Washington, D.C., 2004, Bruni, p. 336
8. Tom Horn, *Apollyon Rising 2012,* Defender Publishing, Craine, MO. 2009. p. 328-329.
9. Malachi Martin, *Keys of this Blood: Pope John Paul II Versus Russian and the West for Control of the New World Order,* Simon and Schuster, New York, 1991. p. 63
10. Malachi Martin, *Windswept House,* Doubleday, New York, 1996. p. 7
11. *The Whore of Babylon,* Wikipedia, https://en.wikipedia.org/wiki/Whore_of_Babylon
12. James Orr, *International Standard Bible Encyclopedia,* Wm. B. Eerdmans Publishing Co.,1939. http://www.internationalstandardbible.com/
13. Ella LeBain, *Who Is God?* Book Two – Chapter Eight: *Who Are the Gods?* p. 129-136, Skypath Books, 2015.
14. Ibid., *Who is God?* Chapter Seven: *Discernment of Gods, Angels and Demons,* sub section: *The Divine Feminine and the False Goddess,* p. 108-112.

CHAPTER EIGHT
Replacement Theology

"All who hate Zion will be confounded and put to shame."
(Psalm 129:5)

Approximately 60% of Christian churches and cults believe in and teach a doctrine known as *replacement theology*, the belief that God broke His covenant with the Jews and converted it to a covenant with the Gentiles instead. Replacement Theology is a grievous error, one which only breeds anti-Semitism in the church, and has brought down many innocent lives for religious reasons. For He promised Abraham and all his descendants,

> "I will bless those who bless you, and whoever curses you I will curse; and all peoples on earth will be blessed through you."
>
> (Genesis 12:3)

Replacement theology is the view that Israel, having failed God, has been replaced by the Church. The Church is now seen as spiritual Israel and spiritual Jerusalem. This teaching claims that all the promises and blessings, in fact Israel's entire inheritance, now belongs to the Church. However, all is not lost for Israel; it gets to keep all the curses.

Dispensational theology, according to nearly all pre-tribulation theory, teaches that God has separate strategies for dealing with the Church and with the Jews. When you consider the change in focus during the tribulation, from the Church to Israel, the belief in a pre-tribulation rapture provides a good example for this transfer of attention.

To say that the people of Israel are no longer God's chosen people is really playing with fire because the Antichrist will likely be saying the same thing when he tries to destroy the Jews *again* during the tribulation. Those in the church who uphold replacement theology will be in the cheering section when the Beast goes on his Jew-killing campaign. Replacement theology is rooted in anti-Semitism.

"The Lord will not reject his people; he will never forsake his inheritance."
(Psalm 94:14)

"This is what the Lord says, he who appoints the sun to shine by day, who decrees the moon and stars to shine by night, who stirs up the sea so that its waves roar - the Lord Almighty is his name: 'Only if these decrees vanish from my sight,' declares the Lord, 'will the descendants of Israel ever cease to be a nation before me.'"
(Jeremiah 31:35-36)

The false teaching of demonically-influenced replacement theology comes from a lying spirit, from the antichrist spirit, who inspired the misinterpretation and misunderstanding of the following scriptures:

"I want you to understand this mystery, dear brothers and sisters, so that you will not be conceited. Some of the people of Israel have hardened their hearts, but this will last only until the full number of Gentiles comes to Christ."
(Romans 11:25)

"Once, you Gentiles were rebels against God, but when the people of Israel rebelled against Him, God was merciful to you instead. Now they are the rebels, and God's mercy has come to you so that they, too, will share in God's mercy."
(Romans 11:30-31)

Romans 11 teaches that the Gentile believer called the *wild branch,* is grafted into Israel. Romans 11 also clearly teaches that *the natural branches* will be grafted in again because the Lord did not send the Jewish people away forever. Romans 11 clearly teaches that *all Israel* will be saved and warns against pride in the *wild branches*, who are the Gentiles, that they too could be cut off. He rebukes them, calling them, "you wild branches, who do not support the root, the root which supports you."

The truth is that the Gentile believers are grafted into Israel. Gentiles become part of Israel, they do not replace Israel or the Jewish people. All Christians must remember that their faith is in the God of Israel, and every single book of the Bible, both the Old and New Testaments were all penned by Jews, and of course the obvious, that their Messiah, the Lord Yeshua Jesus Christ, is Jewish. Repeat, **is** Jewish. Jesus lives, He is not dead, and He is Jewish, He is not Christian. He, a Jew, is Christianity personified.

> "And the scripture, foreseeing that God would justify the Gentiles through faith, preached before the gospel to Abraham, saying, in you shall all nations be blessed."
>
> (Galatians 3:8)

> "Before you Gentiles knew God, you were slaves to so-called gods that do not even exist. So now that you know God (or should I say, now that God knows you), why do you want to go back again and become slaves once more to the weak and useless spiritual principles of this world?"
>
> (Galatians 4:8)

The Jews in Jesus' day were looking for a triumphant Messiah to deliver Israel from the power of Rome. Jesus set them straight regarding Jerusalem in Luke 21:24, in respect to what the prophet Daniel revealed regarding the *times of the Gentiles.* It is an important bit of information given to us by Christ because it tells us that ultimate peace will not occur in Jerusalem until specific *times* has been fulfilled.

> "Woe to those who are with child and to those who nurse babes in those days; for there will be great distress upon the land, and wrath to this people, and they will fall by the edge of the sword, and will be led captive into all the nations; and Jerusalem will be trampled underfoot by the Gentiles until the times of the Gentiles be fulfilled."
>
> (Luke 21:23-24)

What Are the Times of the Gentiles?

Based on Scriptural revelation *the times of the Gentiles* began when national Israel, because of her relentless idolatry and disobedience, was sent into exile by God, to Babylon. This caused Israel to no longer be the head, but the tail, as Moses worded it in Deuteronomy 28:1,10,13-15 (vss. 43-44).

> "Now it shall be, if you will diligently obey the Lord your God, being careful to do all His commandments which I command you today, the Lord your God will set you high above all the nations of the earth."
>
> (Deuteronomy 28:1)

> "So, all the people of the earth shall see that you are called by the name of the Lord and they shall be afraid of you."
>
> (Deuteronomy 28:10)

> "And the Lord shall make you the head and not the tail, and you only shall be above, and you shall not be underneath, if you will listen to the commandments of the Lord your God, which I charge you today, to observe them carefully, and do not turn aside from any of the words which I command you today, to the right or to the left, to go after other gods to serve them.
>
> (Deuteronomy 28:13-14)

But God also warned Israel that if she failed to obey the Lord and go after other gods:

> "The alien who is among you shall rise above you higher and higher, but you shall go down lower and lower. He shall lend to you, but you shall not lend to him; he shall be the head, and you shall be the tail."
>
> (Deuteronomy 28:43-44)

The times of the Gentiles mentioned in Luke 21:24 should not be confused with the *fullness of the Gentiles* revealed in Romans 11:25, which have to do with Gentiles being graciously grafted into the olive tree, the *blessings of Abraham* through faith, during this Church age. With respect to *the times of the Gentiles*, it does not matter if the Jews have control over Jerusalem, or even if they rebuild their temple on the Temple Mount, Jerusalem will be trampled underfoot until Daniel's prophecies regarding Gentile political dominion is completely fulfilled. Jerusalem was trampled underfoot by Babylon, Persia, Greece and ancient Rome; she will again be trampled underfoot by the Antichrist when he comes to power during the time of Jacob's troubles, otherwise known as the seven-year tribulation period.

The Lord has a covenant with Israel that is ancient. "I will remember my covenant with Jacob and my covenant with Isaac and my covenant with Abraham, and I will remember the land." (Leviticus 26:42) Despite the fact that He was disappointed and angry at them for their many stubborn and rebellious ways, in spite of the fact that He punished them severely by allowing them to be scattered all around the globe and given over to their enemies, He still kept His promise to return them to their homeland, as prophesied through Ezekiel:

> "Then he said to me: "Son of man, these bones are the whole house of Israel. They say, 'Our bones are dried up and our hope is gone; we are cut off.' Therefore, prophesy and say to them: 'This is what the Sovereign Lord says: O my people, **I am going to open your graves and bring you up from them**; (reincarnation) **I will bring you back to the land of Israel**. Then you, my people, will know that I am the Lord, when **I open your graves and**

> **bring you up from them**. (reincarnation/rebirth) **I will put my Spirit in you and you will live, and I will settle you in your own land**. Then you will know that I the Lord have spoken, and I have done it, declares the Lord.'"
> (Ezekiel 37:11-14)

Today's Israel is a sovereign state, and even now its people are not without struggle, for the very word, *Israel,* means he who struggles with God. The Lord has a covenant with Israel and promises to return to save the people at the bitter end. It is His will that every Jew should recognize his Messiah in Yeshua. Perhaps, if they did, there would be fewer problems in Israel, but the truth of the matter is that this is where it all ends up and the final battle, *the war of the worlds,* culminates in and around Jerusalem, on the ancient battlefield known as Har Meggido. The Lord promises to return to this spot to save Israel, and all those who believe on Him.

It is God's will that every Jew recognize and have a personal encounter with his Messiah. In many respects, all the suffering of the Jewish people has been caused by their rejection of Him both before the times of Christ through their idolatries and their rebellion, and after the time of Christ by rejecting their fellow Jews who did recognize *who* He was at the time. Remember, Christianity began by and through Jews.

The Twelve Jewish Disciples of Yeshua, along with all those who recognized him as the Messiah of Israel during his ministry were all Jews. The historical record reports that thousands throughout the land of ancient Israel knew Him, as they witnessed His miracles of healing, resurrections of the dead, demonic deliverances and of course his miraculous feeding of the multitudes with just one loaf of bread and one fish. So, for today's Christians to suggest that *all Jews* rejected the Messiah, this is simply not true. Jews began Christianity, those who were blinded by the *religious spirit* that was on the Pharisees and Sanhedrin, did reject him. However, *all* those who return to the Lord will be saved, both Jew and Gentile and all those in between.

Anti-Semitism

The spirit of anti-Semitism is spread throughout the world, despite many Christian churches, through the ministry of demons. Lucifer the Satan has hated God's people since the beginning, because he hates God, and his hatred of all of God's creation continues to today. Satan attacks God's people in his pursuit of rebellion, and will do anything to drive the people out of the land that the Lord gave them. Satan influences the leaders of nations to go against Israel, because he knows it is the Lord who loves, protects, and sustains Israel and its people.

The Jews were hated for killing Jesus. Let's not forget, Jesus was crucified by the Romans. If all the Jewish people had recognized Him as their Messiah, then someone else would have given the kill order, because Jesus came with a specific mission, to die for our sins. This was necessary to deal with the problem of sin once and for all, which causes separation from God.

We learn from the Buddhist scriptures that the Brahmin Priests wanted Jesus killed because He rebuked them for exalting themselves and for their idolatry. He managed to dodge those attempts on His life because His appointed time to die was in Jerusalem, not in India. My point is that if it weren't for the Jews, someone else would have had to have Him killed, because that was His mission, to lay down His life as the final sacrificial Lamb of God, and to take back the keys of Death and Hades from Satan. *Who* killed Jesus? It was you and I and everyone born to humankind. Jesus said,

> "The reason my Father loves me is that I lay down my life, only to take it up again. No one takes it from me, but I lay it down of my own accord. I have authority to lay it down and authority to take it up again. This command I received from my Father."
>
> (John 10:17,18)

> "And one shall say to him, 'What are these wounds in your hands?' Then he shall answer, 'Those, with which I was wounded in the house of my friends.'"
>
> (Zechariah 13:6)

The Jews have become the universal scapegoat. They are blamed for everything that goes wrong in the world, from the plague, to the world's economic problems to the problems in the churches. The truth is that Yeshua Jesus was the final scapegoat for humanity's sins, errors, problems. For all the Jews to continually be hated and persecuted on the account of the ones who didn't believe, is highly suspect. This is more than throwing the baby out with the bathwater. The truth of the matter remains that Yeshua Jesus has hundreds of thousands of Jewish followers, He chose Jews as His disciples, His church was started by Jews, and He remains a Jew from that day to this. These facts must be remembered particularly in the Christian churches who claim the name of Jesus, but deny the Jews and Israel.

Why Do Jews Reject Their Messiah?

Most Jews will tell you that they don't reject their Messiah; it's just that he hasn't arrived yet. The truth is that they didn't recognize Him when He came to be the final blood sacrifice for their sins. Yeshua (Jesus) was prophesied from the book of Genesis through the prophets of the Old Testament and specifically identified in the

Books of Enoch, as the one who first suffered and is then elevated to sit at the right hand of the Almighty and rule the Kingdom of God.

This is a book about spiritual discernment, so let's look at the Jews rejection of Yeshua from a spiritual perspective. According to the Old Testament, the Jewish people have a long history of rebellion, disobedience towards the Lord of Israel (Yahuah). They were punished severely several times for worshipping pseudo gods and idols, to the point where the Lord took His protection away from them, and gave them up to their enemies to be punished. They were scattered around the world, lost their land, were persecuted, taken into slavery, and lived under oppressive empires. But despite all that, the Lord still wanted to save them. He sent Yeshua, the One (the Shaliach-the Sent One) who was promised and prophesied throughout the Word of God, both in the scriptures and in the star pictures of old. See Book Five: *The Heavens,* my chapter, *The Word of God in the Stars.*

It was an ancient Jewish belief that one sign of the Messiah would be that his saliva would have healing properties. Jewish tradition taught that in matters of dispute with respect to inheritance, God had a test which would supernaturally reveal who the legitimate son was; heir to the leadership birthright, and family property inheritance. The people of the second temple period were well aware of a tradition of the Sages which proclaimed that the saliva of a legitimate first-born heir, would have healing properties against injury or disease.[1]

Yeshua healed a deaf and mute man by delivering him from the deaf and dumb spirit,

> "After he took him aside, away from the crowds, Jesus put his finger into the man's ears. Then <u>He spit</u> and touched the man's tongue. He looked up to heaven and with a deep sigh, said to him, "Ephphatha!" (which means, "Be opened!"). At his, the man's ears were opened, his tongue was loosened, and he began to speak plainly."
>
> (Mark 7:33-35)

Yeshua healed a blind man,

> "Jesus said, "While I am in the world, I am the light of the world." Having said this, <u>He spit</u> on the ground, made some mud with <u>his saliva</u>, and put it on the man's eyes. "Go," he told him, "wash in the Pool of Siloam" (which means 'sent'). So, the man went and washed, and came home seeing."
>
> (John 9:5-7)

Again, Yeshua healed a blind man, "He took the blind man by the hand and led him outside the village. When <u>he had spit on the man's eyes</u> and put his

> hands on him, Jesus asked, "Do you see anything?" He looked up and said, "I see people, they look like trees walking around." Once more Jesus put his hands on the man's eyes. Then his eyes were opened, his sight was restored, and he saw everything clearly."
>
> (Mark 8:23-25)

The spirit of unbelief blocks miracles from happening. This is why, Jesus took the man away from the crowd because of their unbelief. It was the spirit of unbelief that prevented Him from doing miracles in His home town. (Matthew 13:57). The spirit of unbelief creates the deaf and dumb spirit, literally causing a demon spirit stronghold to block one's spiritual ears and cause spiritual deafness, so the afflicted can no longer hear the voice of the Spirit of God. In time, this can turn into physical deafness, or tinnitus. This same kind of demon spirit creates spiritual muteness, where the soul is blocked from having any spiritual understanding of God's plan whatsoever. Unbelief is a huge stronghold used by Satan. It also comes under the judgment of God.

> "But the cowardly, <u>the unbelieving</u>, the vile, the murderers, the sexually immoral, those who practice magic arts, the idolaters and all liars--their place will be in the fiery lake of burning sulfur. This is the second death."
>
> (Revelation 21:8)

Jesus rebuked their unbelief:

> "<u>O unbelieving and perverse generation</u>," Jesus replied, "how long shall I stay with you? How long shall I put up with you?"
>
> (Matthew 17:17)

Unbelief debunks miracles, clouds understanding and eventually blocks entrance into the Kingdom of God. The spirit of unbelief causes a person's spiritual eyes to be closed, so they cannot see the light and truth of God. The spirit of unbelief causes the soul to have a spiritual breakdown causing separation from God, it's very Source and Creator. To compensate for these spiritual deficiencies, the *religious spirit* takes over, along with the armor of pride, bitterness, arrogance, intellectualism, and legalism. This was the spiritual condition of the Pharisees, scribes and Sanhedrin whom Yeshua faced in ancient Israel.

Pharisees were separatists, the word itself meaning *separated.* Initially devout and well-motivated, this sect became more and more rigid and legalistic. The central issue for the Pharisees was the preservation of the Sabbath. The Pharisees succeeded in turning the Sabbath rest into a burden, rather than a blessing. Today's Orthodox

Jews and Hasidim continue in the footsteps of the ancient Pharisees, confusing and turning many off their religion because of their strict and unreasonable obsessions for not lifting a finger to do anything on the Sabbath, not even allowing one to take a photograph, which is not considered work, but a hobby or pleasurable pursuit by many, but this and other types of touching technology or even sweeping your floor, or washing your dirty dishes is strictly forbidden on the Sabbath.

For many in this day and age, living like this is a burdensome bondage, which is lost in the anal retentiveness of the *letter of the law,* while sorely lacking in the *spirit of the law,* which is to rest in the Lord on the Sabbath for the purpose of restoration, not create another hardship. There are many places on earth, where leaving dirty dishes would attract insects within hours, just because it's the Sabbath, doesn't mean people shouldn't live cleanly and pay attention to hygiene, which ironically is a central theme in Judaism, but is sadly filled with hypocrisies.

"In 167 B.C. Antiochus' army put a stop to the Jew's sacrifices. The people of Jerusalem, under the leadership of Matthias, revolted and then fled to the desert. Their hiding place was soon discovered, and the pursuing soldiers demanded that they repent and surrender. The Jews refused to give in, but they also refused to fight because it was the Sabbath. They would not block the entrances to their caves or fight in any way. Approximately 1000 men, women and children died without resistance, because they considered the Sabbath sacred."[2]

The death of 1,000 people resulted from the sincere conviction that the Sabbath should not be violated. Then in John chapter 9, Yeshua was criticized by the Jews for healing a blind man on the Sabbath. Yet, was not the Sabbath for resting? Why not from the burden of illness and disease? Healing is Restoration, the very word *rest* comes from *restoration*, which is the heart of the Sabbath.

> "And He has qualified us as *ministers of a new covenant*, not of the letter but of the Spirit; for the letter kills, *but the Spirit gives life*."
>
> (2 Corinthians 3:6)

The Pharisees took upon themselves the task of keeping Judaism pure of foreign and pagan influence. Yet, their legalism caused them to be oppressed by the *religious spirit* which blinded their spiritual eyes and ears to the "spirit of the law." It was the Pharisees who eventually gave the order to have their promised, longed-for, long-awaited Messiah crucified.

They seemed to be more concerned with losing their position and status as priests and scribes then allowing the Spirit of God to teach them and reveal His plan of Salvation for them. Their bondage to the *religious spirit* and the spirit of unbelief caused them to lynch their own Messiah. Because of this, a curse was put upon them and all their generations, known as the High Priest Curse, which affects all those who are born Jews since 30 AD. However, for those Jews who realize Yeshua, and repent on behalf of their ancestors, this generational curse is broken through the applied blood of Christ, which takes away all sin and breaks all curses.

> "While Pilate was sitting on the judge's seat, his wife sent him this message: "Don't have anything to do with that innocent man, for I have suffered a great deal today in a dream because of him." But the chief priests and the elders persuaded the crowd to ask for Barabbas and to have Jesus executed. "Which of the two do you want me to release to you?" asked the governor. "Barabbas," they answered. "What shall I do, then, with Jesus who is called Christ?" Pilate asked. They all answered, "Crucify him!" "Why? What crime has he committed?" asked Pilate. But they shouted all the louder, "Crucify him!" When Pilate saw that he was getting nowhere, but that instead an uproar was starting, he took water and washed his hands in front of the crowd. "I am innocent of this man's blood," he said. "It is your responsibility!" All the people answered, "**<u>Let his blood be on us and on our children</u>**!"
>
> (Matthew 27:19-25)

The irony and beauty of the story is that Yeshua came to break the curse of the law. He came to set everyone free from all curses. They only need turn to Him, accept and repent.

> "Christ redeemed us from the curse of the law by becoming a curse for us, for it is written: "Cursed is everyone who is hung on a tree."
>
> (Galatians 3:13)

He used His Divine Blood as the final blood sacrifice so that all could have atonement with God. One could argue that if the priests and scribes hadn't insisted that the crowd have Jesus executed, then how could Messiah have become the Lamb of God? This simplistic argument is easily demolished by the fact that He had so many other enemies, someone would have had Him murdered. Just imagine what our world would be like right now if it hadn't been the Jews who gave the nod? Be that as it may, that is all His-story now which was all the will of God as prophesied by the Old Testament Prophet Isaiah in Chapter 53.

Rabbis today may claim that they are followers of Moses. But is this true? In the books of Moses, the Lord God required the blood of select beasts to atone for sin. Without blood, there is no atonement. "For the life of the flesh is in the blood: and I have given it to you upon the altar to make an atonement for your souls: <u>for it is the</u>

blood that makes an atonement for the soul." (Leviticus 17:11) It is God's will for His Divine Blood to be upon all His children.

What have the rabbis been doing for the souls of the Jewish people for almost 2000 years? One thing is for sure--they have not been making atonement for their souls based on the law of Moses. The rabbis have not been shedding blood for the souls of their people. God's prescription for atonement was not fasting one day a year, giving good advice, saying prayers which most Jews don't understand, going to Hebrew school, donating money, or having a kind look on your face. It was the blood of specific beasts, shed in a prescribed manner by specially selected persons, the Levitical priesthood, as outlined in the books of Moses.

For almost 2000 years, this atonement has not occurred, nor should it. The Jewish temple in Jerusalem was destroyed in 70 A.D., not long after the death, burial, and resurrection of the Lord Jesus Christ, the Lamb of God who was sacrificed for the sins of the world that all humankind might receive remission. "In fact, according to the law of Moses, nearly everything was purified with blood. For without the shedding of blood, there is no forgiveness." (Hebrews 9:22).

The destruction of the temple also ended the sacrificial system of Moses. Israel was forced to stop shedding blood. You would think if the Pharisees were such sticklers about the law, then why didn't they designate another place to offer blood sacrifices? What an interesting historical coincidence, that after Yeshua bled to death on the cross of Calvary, the priests stopped doing animal sacrifices. Because Yeshua was the final Lamb of God!

After the great work was accomplished on the cross of Calvary by Messiah Jesus, the blood of bulls, lambs and goats were no longer needed nor accepted by the Lord Yahuah. Now God only accepts the blood of Jesus that was shed on Calvary's cross. That is why the rabbis have no temple and no blood. God is pleased with the blood of Jesus. While the Lord Jesus Christ was on the earth, God the Father testified, "This is my beloved Son, in whom I am well pleased." (Matthew 3:17; 17:5). That perfect, one-time sacrifice pleased Him and satisfied the law, and redemption was accomplished. Now it was--and is--time for the people to believe in the Son of God, the Lord Jesus Christ, the Son of David, the Messiah, the Lion of the tribe of Judea, the King of Israel.

The blood of bulls and of goats could never take away sins (Hebrews 10:11) – which is why the Levitical priesthood had to keep on offering them repeatedly. When the Son of God offered Himself to the Father Yahuah, it was the supreme sacrifice, the perfect life for perfection, a once in history act. Before He died, the Lord Jesus Christ said, "It is finished." Three days later He rose from the dead, "God has raised him up, having loosed the pains of death: because it was not possible that he should be held of it. (Acts 2:24). He arose and is now seated on the right hand of God and lives to make intercession as the High Priest in the order of the Melchizedek for His people.

The Lord God gave Israel the blood of Yeshua/Jesus. That is why the temple was destroyed in 70 A.D., never to rise again in the same old way. The Old exchange of animal blood for atonement was no longer necessary. The blood of Jesus has power over the old covenant and any covenant with the devil, because His blood is incorruptible, He is the Son of God who became the Son of Man, His blood came from God, it is Divine.

> "So, shall they fear the name of the LORD from the west, and his glory from the rising of the sun. When the enemy shall come in like a flood, the Spirit of the LORD shall lift up a standard against him."
>
> (Isaiah 59:19)

That standard was the atoning work of the Lord Jesus Christ, "the blood of his cross" (Colossians 1:20); God "hath set forth [Christ] to be a propitiation through faith in his blood" (Romans 3:25); Believers are "justified by his blood" (Romans 5:9); we have "redemption through his blood, the forgiveness of sins" (Ephesians 1:7; Colossians 1:14; 1 Peter 1:17-18); Gentile believers "who sometimes were afar off are made nigh by the blood of Christ" (Ephesians 2:13); the blood of Christ "purges the conscience" of the child of God (Hebrews 9:14); we "have boldness to enter into the holiest by the blood of Jesus" (Hebrews 10:19); we were "sanctified with the blood of the covenant" (Hebrews 10:29); we are "sprinkled" (1 Peter 1:2), "cleansed" (1 John 1:7) and "washed" (Revelation 1:5) by that same blood.

> "And they overcame him (Satan) by the blood of the Lamb, and by the word of their testimony;
>
> (Revelation 12:11)

But what have the rabbis and elders been doing all these years? Instead of pointing the way to the Messiah, it seems that the rabbis have used all their power to keep their own people from knowing Yeshua, the Lamb of God, the Son of David, the Messiah, who was slain for the sins of the world. They have zealously followed the same policy, the spirit of unbelief and hindrance that the Pharisees, Sadducees, Herodians, scribes, and lawyers followed:

> "Woe to you lawyers! For you have taken away the key of knowledge. You did not enter yourselves, and you hindered those who were entering."
>
> (Luke 11:52)

In my opinion, it is the void in knowledge of modern day Jews, who believe they are saved by the Law and not by grace, that will accomplish the building of the third temple. The man who will be known as the final Antichrist will manage to deceive the Jews in Israel to worship him in their newly rebuilt third Temple. They will reinstate animal blood sacrifices in that newly rebuilt temple, which the prophet Daniel calls, the 'abomination of desolation'. They will be sacrificing the blood of animals to their God, and the prophecy says that the Antichrist will stop it.

Antichrist leads the New World Order and will establish a One World Religion and he will end animal sacrifices because of the overwhelming protest against it by animal rights activists. He will claim to be god and the Messiah King of Israel. He will be the Great Pretender, pretending to be the long-awaited Messiah, stopping the killing of innocent animals, while demanding the blood of Jews and all those who refuse to follow him, worship him, and take his mark to be able to buy and sell under his One World Digitalized Currency. Jews will be heavily persecuted by him, becoming what the book of Revelation calls, *the saints of the tribulation.*

It is shocking to learn that some Christians believe that there will be sacrifices required in the Kingdom of God when it comes to earth. The King of the Kingdom is Yeshua Jesus, whose final sacrifice was perfect in the eyes of God. Scripture says that no flesh can enter into the Kingdom of God. The reason some Christians mistakenly believe that further sacrifices are necessary is through misinterpretation of the prophesies in Daniel 7, who is prophesying of the time when the Antichrist sets himself up in the third rebuilt temple in Jerusalem when animal sacrifices are reinstated. However, what many Christians are ignorant to, is that animal sacrifices during Passover have already been reinstated at the Temple site in Jerusalem, that began on Passover of 2008.[3] They put it on YouTube that shows the video of a young goat's blood being poured on the spot as their future altar for the rebuilt Temple.

The Jewish Orthodoxy will already have animal sacrifices in place at the Temple before Antichrist takes over. He shockingly ends it, which throws them all for a loop. After all, why would a God of Love necessitate the shedding of innocent blood? The Levitical scriptures that state, there is no remission of sins without the shedding of blood, that Christ fulfilled, was *not* inspired by the Heavenly Father, but the Earthly one, who is the god of this world, the original legalist and blood lusty carnivorous Reptilian Alien known as Lucifer/Satan, the Beast.

This is where knowledge of the original Hebrew comes in. There are many laws within the law books, that were transmitted from the Elohim, *who* are not *Yahuah.* They may have served Yahuah's experiment, but clearly, when you see the word 'Elohim' in the Hebrew Bible, it is always translated as 'God' in the English Bibles, which confuses people as to which god is at play. As I pointed out and proved in Book Two, *Who is God?* that one of the most famous Bible stories, which birthed two of the world's major religions, when Abraham was tested to sacrifice his miracle baby Isaac, was not being tested by the Lord Yahuah, but by Satan and the Elohim.

Remember, it's the reptilian gods who demand blood sacrifices, not the God of Love who resides in Heaven. This is a big discernment, when sorting out *who is who* in the cast of characters of Biblical gods.

When Jesus paid the ultimate price with His blood sacrifice, it was to end all blood sacrifices, as well as to pay the god of this world with His blood to be the *ransom* for the release of all the souls past, present and future that satan held in bondage. This is why Jesus now holds the keys of both Death and Hades (Revelation 1:12), because he paid for it, with his own blood. Whom did he pay? The god of this world, who was Enlil, Baal, Allah, Lucifer/Satan.

The Old Testament scriptures were messed with by the kingdom of darkness to make sure they got their blood. Look at all the ancient religions and their gods who could only be appeased through the blood sacrifices, all were reptilian alien gods (feathered serpents) who literally vampirized the life force within the blood. See, Book Two: *Who Is God? The Lifeforce is in the Blood,*[4] p. 262. The spiritual discernment is, that the Creator, the God of gods, does not require blood, He requires faith, obedience and an open heart to serve His Divine Will.

God rebuked the rulers of Jerusalem in Isaiah 28:14-19, and prophesied of His precious corner stone that was going to come to the earth and rescue it from Death.

> "Why hear the word of the LORD, you scornful men, that rule this people which is in Jerusalem. Because you have said, we have made a covenant with death, and with hell are we at agreement; when the overflowing whip shall pass through, it shall not come to us: for we have made lies our refuge, and under falsehood have we hid ourselves: Therefore, thus said the Lord GOD, <u>Behold, I lay in Zion for a foundation a stone, a tried stone, a precious corner stone, a sure foundation: he that believes shall not make haste</u>. Judgment also will I lay to the line, and righteousness to the plummet: and the hail shall sweep away the refuge of lies, and the waters shall overflow the hiding place. <u>And your covenant with death shall be disannulled, and your agreement with hell shall not stand; when the overflowing whip shall pass through, then you shall be trodden down by it. From the time that it goes forth it shall take you: for morning by morning shall it pass over, by day and by night: and it shall be a vexation only to understand the report</u>."
>
> (Isaiah 28:14-19)

Even King David knew the Lord:

<u>The LORD (Yahuah) says to my Lord (Yeshua)</u>: "Sit at my right hand until I make your enemies a footstool for your feet." (Psalm 110:1)

In the original Hebrew, the first LORD is substituted for the name Yahuah (YHVH) who is the Father, the second Lord is the word *adonai,* which is just *lord.* It is clear, that King David was relating to Yeshua who did make several appearances in the Old Testament (Christophanies) before coming in the flesh as the Son of God and Son of Man.

> "The stone which the builders refused is become the head stone of the corner. This is the LORD'S doing; it is marvelous in our eyes."
>
> (Psalms 118:22, 23)

That cornerstone was Yeshua HaMashiach, Christ Jesus, who will return as the King of Glory. Today's rabbis offer no blood for the nation of Israel. Judaism is clearly not the religion of Moses, it is something else entirely. It is essentially the tradition of the elders that the Lord Jesus Christ condemned (Matthew 15:3-9; Mark 7:5-13)!

> "Satan, who is the god of this world, has blinded the minds of those who don't believe. They are unable to see the glorious light of the Good News. They don't understand this message about the glory of Christ, who is the exact likeness of God."
>
> (2 Corinthians 4:4)

Remember, the Lord Yahuah has a covenant with Israel and the Jewish people. He promised to restore them to their land, (Ezekiel 37) which He has done. He also promises to redeem them (Zechariah 10:6), which He has done through sending the Lamb of God, Yeshua. The history of the turbulent relationship between the Lord and His people is like an ongoing family drama – a love-hate relationship. What the Lord repeatedly demands is repentance from their unbelief; stubbornness, pride, and rebellion, which is the historical relationship He has with them. He made it very clear to the forefathers and to Israel's past kings that He would reject them for their sins:

> "But they did not listen to me or pay attention. They were stiff-necked (stubborn) and did more evil than their forefathers.'"
>
> (Jeremiah 7:26)

> "For the LORD had said to Moses, "Tell the Israelites, 'You are a stiff-necked people. If I were to go with you even for a moment, I might destroy you. Now take off your ornaments and I will decide what to do with you.'"
>
> (Exodus 33:5)

> "You stiff-necked (stubborn) people, with uncircumcised hearts and ears! You are just like your fathers: You always resist the Holy Spirit!"
>
> (Acts 7:51)

This was what the Lord Yahuah said to King Saul, after He chose David to be the King of Israel:

> "For rebellion is as the sin of witchcraft, and stubbornness is as iniquity and idolatry. Because you have rejected the word of the LORD, he has also rejected you from being king."
>
> (1 Samuel 15:23)

It is because of these generational sins that He is allowing the whole drama in Israel to play itself out. The person who will be known as the final antichrist will deceive Israel and the Jewish people. They will accept him as their Messiah and then they will be persecuted by him, worse than any other persecution that has happened to date, known as the time of Jacob's troubles (Jacob was later renamed Israel, which literally means in Hebrew, 'he who struggles with God'.) This is part of the Lord's plan because He literally wants to bring Israel to her knees, so she will acknowledge His name 'Yeshua' as savior.

As we established in Book Two, *Who is God?* the God of Israel's name is Yahuah and Yahushua aka Yeshua is His Son.[5] The Son is the manifestation of Yahuah in the flesh, which is why He said, "I and the Father are One." (John 10:30) Yeshua means in Hebrew, Yahuah is our Salvation/Savior. This is a mystery to all those blinded by the spirit of unbelief and bitterness, but for those whose eyes have been opened, it is as clear as day, just *who* Yeshua was and is to come.

Sadly, because the Jews have turned their hearts against God in unbelief, they will accept the coming antichrist as their messiah, and be deceived by his initial masquerade until he starts persecuting and killing them. Then they will realize that they have missed their true Messiah. The Bible tells us that the prophet Elijah will return with Moses and preach the good news of Grace to Israel one last time, which will be its final window of Grace. The prophesy tells us that they will not recognize their own prophets but kill them and allow them to lie dead in the streets until they are miraculously resurrected.

We are told that the Lord will save one third of His people during the tribulation period the time of Jacob's troubles. Because Satan, the god of this world, has blinded them from the truth, instead of following their Lord and Creator, they end up following the spirit of Belial, the spirit of lies and denial. This is why all battles finally converge upon Israel. All the Lord wants from Israel is for them to acknowledge His

Name and accept His final blood sacrifice for sins, transgression, and iniquities. They will know who their real Savior is in the end, who is coming to reward His faithful and punish the wicked.

> "Look, your house is left to you desolate. For I tell you, you will not see me again until you say, 'Blessed is he who comes *in the name of the Lord*.'"
>
> (Matthew 23:39)

> "Blessed is the one who comes *in the name of the LORD*; We have blessed you from the house of the LORD."
>
> (Psalm 118:26)

The Holocaust was a precursor, one of the worse punishments for the Jewish people, which saw the persecution and murder of one third of the Jewish population on the earth at that time. But the time of Jacob's troubles, scripture tells us, will be far worse than we can imagine. During the seven-year reign of the antichrist, the last three and half years will be brutal, and two thirds of the Jewish people will perish, leaving only a one third remnant which will be saved in the end.

> "In the whole land," declares the LORD, "two-thirds will be struck down and perish; yet one-third will be left in it. This third I will bring into the fire; I will refine them like silver and test them like gold. They will call on my name and I will answer them; I will say, 'They are my people,' and they will say, 'The LORD is our God.'"
>
> (Zechariah 13:8,9)

The Lord wants Israel to recognize His name. He allows this cosmic family drama to play itself out before everlasting peace can come to show once and for all, that Israel needs Him, too. In the meantime, the Jews, God's chosen people, are still waiting to meet their Messiah. Yet, the irony is, that the very thing they pray for is the very thing they fear, a personal close encounter with Yeshua, because whenever that happens for a Jew, they weep in sorrow and repentance. But His is the sacrifice that is pleasing to the Lord, a contrite heart and humble spirit, (Psalm 51:17) does the Lord require, which in turns causes Him to pour out His Grace and Mercy on all who repent to Him. This is the blood of Covenant through Yeshua.

The lack of recognition of *who* Yeshua is by his own people, the Jews, is nevertheless being utilized by God in a Grand Divine Plan (Romans 11:25-27) that allows *everyone else* to be saved (Joel 2:32; Romans 10:13). The Bible clearly states that "those who are first will be last, and those who are last shall be first" (Matthew 19:30 and

20:16, Mark 10:31, and Luke 13:30). The Jews were the first of God's people, but many are kept unaware of their own Messiah until everyone on the earth hears about Jesus Christ. This is the meaning of, 'until the time of the gentiles is fulfilled'. Once that happens, the remaining followers of Judaism will realize that Yeshua Jesus was the Messiah.

> "And I will pour on the house of David, and on the inhabitants of Jerusalem, the spirit of grace and of supplications: ***and they shall look on me whom they have pierced, and they shall mourn for him***, as one mourns for his only son, and shall be in bitterness for him, as one that is in bitterness for his firstborn."
>
> (Zechariah 12:10)

> "Behold, he cometh <u>with the clouds</u>; ***and every eye shall see him, and they that pierced him***; ***and all the tribes of the earth shall mourn over him***."
>
> (Revelation 1:7)

By that time, Jesus will have returned to the earth, to save Israel from the persecutions of the Antichrist and end the war of Armageddon. Those who do not accept Him will face God in judgment and be cast into the lake of fire (hell).

"Even after Jesus had done all these miraculous signs in their presence, they still would not believe in him. This was to fulfill the word of Isaiah the prophet: "Lord, who has believed our message and to whom has the arm of the Lord been revealed?" (Isaiah 53:1) For this reason they could not believe, because, as Isaiah says elsewhere: "<u>He has blinded their eyes and deadened their hearts, so they can neither see with their eyes, nor understand with their hearts,</u> nor turn—and I would heal them." (Isaiah 6:10) Isaiah said this because he saw Yeshua's glory and spoke about him." (John 12:37-41)

Yeshua came from the bloodline of King David. When He returns He will take over the throne of David in the New Jerusalem. King David was very close to the Lord's heart. He wrote some of the most prophetic Psalms, one of which is a prophecy of his very own descendant, Yeshua the Mashiach. Both Psalm 22 and Isaiah 53 are both distinguished by the fact that they perfectly parallel events in the life of Jesus Christ, yet were written over a thousand years before His birth. Psalm 22 is especially amazing since it predicted 11 separate things about Jesus' crucifixion *about a thousand years before it happened*. We know that David, the author of Psalm 22, lived about 1043-973 B.C. and Isaiah lived about 740-680 B.C. Both passages, written far ahead of the time of Christ, are strong passages that help you prove that the Bible is inspired by God.

The following prophecies concerning Yeshua, Jesus Christ, were written into the Old Testament, approximately 1700 BC - 400 B.C. These prophecies were fulfilled hundreds of years later, during Jesus Christ's life on earth. Each of the prophecies listed below are followed in parentheses by the scriptural references that included both the prophecy and the fulfillment. Yeshua fulfilled the law of the prophets. There are over 635 Messianic prophesies written in the Old Testament that Yeshua fulfilled. For my unbelieving readers, here are just a few of them:

1. He would be born of a Virgin (Isaiah 7:14; Matthew 1:18).
2. He would be of the tribe of Judah (Genesis 49:10; Luke 3:23, 33).
3. He would be of King David's seed (Jeremiah 23:5; Luke 3:23, 31).
4. He would be born in Bethlehem (Micah 5:2; Matthew 2:1).
5. He would be a prophet (Deuteronomy 18:18-19; Matthew 21:11).
6. He would teach with parables (Psalms 78:2; Matthew 13:34).
7. He would be preceded by a messenger (Isaiah 40:3, Malachi 3:1; Matthew 3:1-2).
8. He would enter Jerusalem on a colt (Zechariah 9:9; Luke 19:35-37).
9. He would be betrayed by a friend (Psalms 41:9; Matthew 26:47-50).
10. He would be betrayed for 30 pieces of silver (Zechariah 11:12; Matthew 26:15).
11. He would be forsaken by His disciples (Zechariah 13:7; Mark 14:50).
12. The money would be thrown in the temple and used to buy the potter's field (Zechariah 11:13; Matthew 27:5-7).
13. He would be accused by false witnesses (Psalms 35:11; Matthew 26:59-60).
14. He would be silent before His accusers (Isaiah 53:7; Matthew 27:12-14).
15. He would be beaten by his enemies (Isaiah 50:6, 53:5; Matthew 27:26).
16. He would be spit upon and beaten (Isaiah 50:6; Matthew 27:30).
17. He would be struck in the head with a rod (Micah 5:1; Matthew 27:30).
18. He would be mocked (Psalms 22:7-8; Matthew 27:29, 31).
19. His hands and feet would be pierced (Psalms 22:16, Luke 23:33; John 20:25). It's important to note that this was predicted hundreds of years before the crucifixion was invented.
20. Men would gamble for His clothing (Psalms 22:18; John 19:23-24).
21. He would intercede in prayer for His transgressors (Isaiah 53:12; Luke 23:34).
22. He would suffer thirst (Psalms 22:15 and John 19:28).
23. He would be offered gall and water (Psalms 69:21; Matthew 27:34).
24. He would cry, "My God, My God, why hast thou forsaken me!" (Psalms 22:1; Matthew 27:46).
25. He would be cut down in His prime (Psalms 89:45; 102:23-24).

26. None of His bones would be broken (Exodus 12:46, Psalms 34:20; John 19:32-33).
27. They would look upon Him whom they had pierced (Zechariah 12:10; John 19:34).
28. He would be executed with thieves (Isaiah 53:12; Matthew 27:38).
29. He would be buried in a rich man's tomb (Isaiah 53:9; Matthew 27:57-60).

Many people who do not believe in the Bible, say that these prophecies were postdated, written after they happened. However, manuscripts have been found that confirm that these various prophecies were written down 400-1,000 years before they occurred. The discovery of the Dead Sea Scrolls put to rest most of such idle talk. Note, that the majority of these prophecies concern the death of Jesus Christ and the events surrounding it. This is especially interesting, considering the fact that, none of Christ's disciples realized that Jesus Christ was going to die.

In Luke 18:33, Christ, referring to Himself as "the Son of man", told His disciples what would happen to Him, "And they shall scourge him, and put him to <u>death</u>: and the third day he shall <u>rise again</u>." That would have been easy to understand, but God hid the saying from their understanding. The next verse, Luke 18:34, says, "And they understood none of these things: and this saying was <u>hidden</u> from them, neither knew they the things which were spoken."

Even though, Yeshua Jesus had told them plainly, His disciples still did not realize He was going to die and rise again. The Jews knew from the Old Testament prophecies that the Messiah would be a King that would reign over Israel forever. So, they naturally assumed, incorrectly, that the Messiah must never die. He didn't die, He is still alive. Psalm 22 and Isaiah 53, (the forbidden chapter with Jews) clearly predicted His death and resurrection, to the very detail. But, even His disciples missed the mark there, as did many of the other Jews. They were disappointed that He didn't defeat their oppressors, who were the Romans. But, God does things His way, and shortly after Jesus left the earth, the Roman Empire did in fact fall. The 2nd temple which Yeshua Jesus cursed because they turned it into a den of thieves, was destroyed. The Religious Spirit was brought down in Israel. The Jews didn't understand it. To this day, they still don't get it, that He was the final lamb of God, that He paid the ultimate price with His own blood, to redeem them and all of humankind from the curse of death and from the enslavement from the Kingdom of darkness.

After the children of Israel left Egypt, God gave instruction for how they were to construct the tabernacle. The most holy place of the tabernacle, where the ark of the testimony was set, was to be divided from the rest of the temple, hidden from view by "... a veil of blue, and purple, and scarlet, and fine twined linen of cunning work ..." (Exodus 26:31). No one could go into this most holy place behind the veil except "...

the high priest alone once every year, not without blood, which he offered for himself, and for the errors of the people ..." (Hebrews 9:7). Except for this one ritual by one man once per year on the Day of Atonement, the veil hung there for some 1500 years or so, separating sinful man from holy God.

All that changed when Jesus Christ was crucified. Matthew 27:50-51 says, "Jesus, when he had cried again with a loud voice, yielded up the ghost. And, behold, the veil of the temple was rent in twain from the top to the bottom; and the earth did quake ...." The veil was not torn from bottom to top, the way men could do it, but from top to bottom, as only God could do.

Paul explained in Hebrews 10:18-20 that, "... there is no more offering for sin (no longer any blood sacrifice needs to be made). Having therefore, brethren, boldness to enter into the holiest (the most holy place) by the blood of Jesus, by a new and living way, which he hath consecrated for us, through the veil, that is to say, his flesh ...." Christ's body was like the veil. When the veil was torn in two, it opened the way to the most holy place. Likewise, when the body of Christ was torn by the crucifixion, that perfect sacrifice opened the way back to God for sinful man.

Who are the True and False Christians?

> "Watch out for false prophets. They come to you in sheep's clothing, but inwardly they are ferocious wolves. By their fruit you will recognize them."
>
> (Matthew 7:15-16)

A Christian can be defined as a person who has, by faith, received and fully trusted in Jesus Christ as the only Savior from sin (John 3:16; Acts 16:31; Ephesians 2:8–9). And in the heart of the Christian resides the Spirit of Christ (Ephesians 3:17; 1 Corinthians 6:19; Romans 8:11). Now, "if anyone does not have the Spirit of Christ, he does not belong to Christ" (Romans 8:9), and this person, then, is not a Christian. Thus, the term "fake Christian" is a misnomer. You either are a Christian or you are not a Christian; one is either with Christ or against Christ (Matthew 12:30).

Who is real and who is false amongst Christianity, is certainly a legitimate question in the minds of many people. Most likely this is due to the behavior of Christians, who are still able to mistake, err, and fall; however, it is also due to the behavior of many who think they are Christians or profess to be Christians, but who are not at all Christ-like. The reason behind the false belief that many have, that they are true Christians when in reality are no different from any other in the world, are varied, but in the final analysis, comes down to each one of us individually. The false teachings which are so prevalent these days is certainly one good reason. When churches avoid teaching sound doctrine, the result will be congregants who do not know the truth of God's Word. How can we keep in step with the Spirit, when the Truth is not in us? It is up to us, each one of us, to search out the Truth in addition to what our church presents us with in service.

Some believe a recitation of a prayer by responding to an altar call alone, may have turned them into a Christian. Many believe that religious traditions, such as infant baptism, secure a spot in heaven, or that plentiful good works alone can put us in good standing with God. And, of course, some believe church attendance alone guarantees salvation. None of this is true, which can be easily found by the briefest perusal of the Word.

The point is that many who profess to be Christians are not Christians at all. Yet they complacently remain convinced that all is well with their soul. Sadly, many will live their entire lives believing they were Christians only to one day hear these words from Jesus Christ: "I never knew you. Away from me, you evildoers!" (Matthew 7:23) when the Lord returns as Judge and Jury to separate the church as a Shephard separates his sheep from the goats. Fake Christians are the goats according to the words of Jesus Christ Himself in Matthew 25:32, "All the nations will be gathered before Him, and He will separate the people one from another, as a shepherd separates the sheep from the goats".

> "Not everyone who says to me, 'Lord, Lord,' will enter the kingdom of heaven, but only the one who does the will of my Father who is in heaven. Many will say to me on that day, 'Lord, Lord, did we not prophesy in your name and in your name, drive out demons and in your name, perform many miracles?' Then I will tell them plainly, '*I never knew you. Away from me, you evildoers!*'
>
> (Matthew 7:21-23)

The clear teaching of the Bible pronounces that when someone is saved, his life will most definitely change as he is a "new creation, the old has gone and the new has come" (2 Corinthians 5:17). A true, born-again Christian will strive to bring glory and honor to Christ by living a life that is pleasing to God (1 Peter 1:15–16; 4:1–4). True saving faith will indeed produce works or 'fruit' in the life of the believer (James 2:17, 26).

Thus, if there are no works of love in one's life, a careful self-examination is certainly in order. The apostle Paul instructed those in Corinth to do this very thing: "Examine yourselves to see whether you are in the faith; test yourselves. Do you not realize that Christ Jesus is in you – unless, of course, you fail the test?" (2 Corinthians 13:5). Indeed, any profession of faith that does not result in a changed life and good works is a false profession, and the professor is not a Christian.

Even though the lifestyle of true Christians does reflect the presence of Christ in their hearts, we know we are not perfect. Christians do sin, and the apostle John makes it clear that we deceive ourselves if we think otherwise (1 John 1:8). And when Christians do sin, rest assured there are multitudes just lying in wait to use their slip-up to further denigrate the true body of believers. That is why Paul admonished the church in Thessalonica to abstain from even the appearance of evil (1 Thessalonians 5:22) and to live in such a way as to "win the respect of outsiders" (1Thessalonians 4:12).

As believers mature in the faith, we will exhibit more and more evidence of a true Christian nature, such as love for God, repentance of sin, separation from the world, spiritual growth, and obedient living. As Paul told the Romans, the genuine child of God has been set free from sin and has become a servant to God, and the result is eternal life (Romans 6:22).

More people would be inclined toward following Jesus Christ if it wasn't for fake Christians bound by *religious spirits*, who have misrepresented Christ to the world, and are the antithesis of receiving Christ, so that Christ may shine His Light through them. Instead they are bound by *religious spirits*, and embroiled in division and judgments, which turns people off of Christ.

Anti-Semitic Christians

Hybrid Children do exist among us and part of their DNA is alien from fallen angels. The elite and the Illuminati believe they are descended from aliens, which gives rise to the royal blue blood and their Right to Rule. These hybrid races hate the Jewish bloodline of the Messiah and all the Christians that follow Him. They're implanted to hate the Spiritual offspring of the Messiah, the Christ - and they hate women for giving birth to them. One of the dead giveaways about those cold-blooded lizards in human form is that they are simply incapable of having empathy, making them inhuman.

There are too many so-called Christians who claim to be Jewish, but are just some Hebrew Roots Pharisaical religious fanatics who believe that men are supposed to rule over women, who apparently hadn't read Galatians 3:28. They steal from Jews, yet malign them at the same time. That's Anti-Semitic! The devil is the father of all lies and all liars, said the Lord Himself. (John 8:44) Furthermore, they believe Christian Rock Music is evil, and anyone in ministry who sells anything, like CDS, DVDS, books, tickets, are false Christians. They also believe that women teaching God's word is sinful and of Jezebel. This is the presence of the *Religious Spirit,* which is rooted in the spirit of doubt, and wars against the Holy Spirit who is Truth and Grace.

We know from Acts 21:9 that women are used by God to be evangelists, teachers, and prophets and the Book of Judges, Ancient Israel's Judge Deborah who lead Israel into victory, won the longest lasting forty years of peace to date, was anointed by the Lord to do so. So those who believe such lies, are of the devil, who twists scripture and denies the Truth of the Jewish Scriptures. Let the Christian learn how to discern both Word and the *spirit* rightly. God never said what many think he says. They are listening to *religious spiritual implants,* which comes from aliens whose intention is to keep people away from the *dunamis power* in the Spirit of Christ. See my chapter on *Who Created Sexism?* in Book Two: *Who is God?* [6]

As if we don't have enough problems with fundamentalism, there are extreme Muslims, who are another side of the coin of extremism and funda-*mentalists.* Funda-*mentalism* is a *mental* disorder. It lacks empathy, grace, the fruit of love, which is the *fruit of the spirit.* (Galatians 5:22)

Let me warn and encourage you to beware of false Religious Spirits masquerading as Christian, the holier-than-thou types, who can't behave with empathy, show kindness or respect to the other sex, and think any woman in ministry is a temptation to sin. Sounds like Islam, but, yes, I did say Christian. These types are the lizard beings posing as religious people in positions of power in churches, mosques and temples. They are the real reason people leave the church, turn to new age philosophy, or become gay or lesbian. At some point the true Christian leaders need to take responsibility for causing their own apostasy. Churches don't do anyone but the devil a favor by not exposing these demonic religious spirits which cause strife and division in the body of Christ.

The biggest stumbling block in modern Christianity is the remnant of the church of Thyatira, Jezebel's church, which unleashes *religious spirits* on all believers, causing bondage to the devil and his lies by thwarting the power through Christ.

No spirit received more woes from Jesus than the false puffed up spirit of religion. (Matthew 7, 23, 25, Revelation 3) He hated it and so should every true believer in Christ. It is the enemy of the true body of Christ. After all, it was the Religious Spirit that conspired His Crucifixion.

When Christians repent to God for carrying this legalistic demon, who does nothing but accuse others, which is one of Satan's main roles, to be the Accuser of the Brethren, then they will see the power and the glory of God manifest in their lives. God wants fruit, not religious nuts! The Fruit of the Spirit is love, tolerance and forgiveness. While it's okay to take a stand against sinful behaviors and lifestyles, condemning others, however, is no way to win them over for the Kingdom, nor is it something Jesus would do. Christians tend to think, that now they are saved, they get to be the judge of everyone, that's the Lord's job. Christians are supposed to be vessels of God's Grace on Earth, not the vessel of the Accuser.

The religious spirit is a spirit of unbelief. It wars against the work of the Holy Spirit. The Lord is God, and He can do anything, anytime and work through anyone! That's what the Pharisees missed, and sadly many modern-day Christians have become modern-day Pharisees. Repent! Jezebel doesn't just influence sexual immorality, Jezebel wants to attack and take down the true prophets of God. No true prophet of God can operate without first contending with this spirit who can ONLY be overcome *through* the Lord.

The trinity of Satan works through the Religious Spirit demon, Jezebel and Spiritual Witchcraft.[7] Revelation 3 condemns the religious spirit, as does Matthew 23, 25 and 7. The religious spirit is spiritual witchcraft. It began in the church of Thyatira which was Jezebel's church and her false prophets. The religious spirit is a sin. It's full of spiritual pride and arrogance. God hates pride. See, Proverbs 6.

The religious spirit is dead works and it wars against the spiritual and miraculous supernatural works of the Holy Spirit. The religious spirit is a spirit of unbelief and the only way to please God is through faith. (Hebrews 11:6)

This is what the Lord spoke on the hypocrisy of *religious spirits.* A 'woe' is a 'curse'. You know you're in pretty bad shape when you're cursed by Jesus. Nevertheless, this is an important spiritual discernment and a major lesson for the Church to learn and integrate.

Seven Woes on the Teachers of the Law and the Pharisees

> "Woe to you, teachers of the law and Pharisees, you hypocrites! You shut the door of the kingdom of heaven in people's faces. You yourselves do not enter, nor will you let those enter who are trying to.
>
> "Woe to you, teachers of the law and Pharisees, you hypocrites! You travel over land and sea to win a single convert, and when you have succeeded, you make them twice as much a child of hell as you are.
>
> "Woe to you, blind guides! You say, 'If anyone swears by the temple, it means nothing; but anyone who swears by the gold of the temple is bound by that oath.' You blind fools! Which is greater: the gold, or the temple that makes the gold sacred? You also say, 'If anyone swears by the altar, it means nothing; but anyone who swears by the gift on the altar is bound by that oath.' You blind men! Which is greater: the gift, or the altar that makes the gift sacred? Therefore, anyone who swears by the altar swears by it and by everything on it. And anyone who swears by the temple swears by it and by the one who

dwells in it. And anyone who swears by heaven swears by God's throne and by the one who sits on it.

"Woe to you, teachers of the law and Pharisees, you hypocrites! You give a tenth of your spices—mint, dill and cumin. But you have neglected the more important matters of the law—justice, mercy and faithfulness. You should have practiced the latter, without neglecting the former. You blind guides! You strain out a gnat but swallow a camel.

"Woe to you, teachers of the law and Pharisees, you hypocrites! You clean the outside of the cup and dish, but inside they are full of greed and self-indulgence. Blind Pharisee! First clean the inside of the cup and dish, and then the outside also will be clean.

"Woe to you, teachers of the law and Pharisees, you hypocrites! You are like whitewashed tombs, which look beautiful on the outside but on the inside, are full of the bones of the dead and everything unclean. In the same way, on the outside you appear to people as righteous but on the inside, you are full of hypocrisy and wickedness.

"Woe to you, teachers of the law and Pharisees, you hypocrites! You build tombs for the prophets and decorate the graves of the righteous. And you say, 'If we had lived in the days of our ancestors, we would not have taken part with them in shedding the blood of the prophets.' So, you testify against yourselves that you are the descendants of those who murdered the prophets. Go ahead, then, and complete what your ancestors started!

"You snakes! You brood of vipers! How will you escape being condemned to hell? Therefore, I am sending you prophets and sages and teachers. Some of them you will kill and crucify; others you will flog in your synagogues and pursue from town to town. And so, upon you will come all the righteous blood that has been shed on earth, from the blood of righteous Abel to the blood of Zechariah son of Berekiah, whom you murdered between the temple and the altar. Truly I tell you, all this will come on this generation.

"Jerusalem, Jerusalem, you who kill the prophets and stone those sent to you, how often I have longed to gather your children together, as a hen gathers her chicks under her wings, and you were not willing. Look, your house is left to

> you desolate. For I tell you, you will not see me again until you say, 'Blessed is he who comes in the name of the Lord.'
>
> (Matthew 23:13-39)

When I posted Matthew 23 to a Facebook acquaintance involved in Hebrew Roots, a Gentile man, who claimed to be Jewish, but is not, was judging my work, I responded to him simply by posting the above Matthew 23 scriptures. He responded: "Ella LeBain, if you are accusing me of having 'a religious spirit' and pride in these matters, Ella: you are dead wrong. and are guilty of false accusation. Beware of that. I am an Elder in the Body of Christ and hold four offices by GOD's ordination and calling!"

This proves that the Word of God is sharper than any double-edged sword, piercing into the division of soul and spirit, bone and marrow. (Hebrews 4:12) The Word convicted him, he wasn't arguing with me, he was arguing with God! I didn't accuse him of anything, I merely posted the Words of Jesus, the person he claims to serve, and I pressed his religious button on his religious implant, which spluttered, denied and defended itself, as if he was guilty of something. Therefore, I think Matthew 23 should be studied and read *out loud* in churches.

Too many of us in the church today have become modern-day Pharisees and we don't even know it. People are keen to hypocrisy, especially in religion, which is an essential part of our very nature. We need God, we need the connection to God now today more desperately than ever, to know the *real* Jesus Christ, who saves, heals, and delivers.

So, I told him, the fact that he's an elder means he's attacked more by the religious spirit than others. Pastors, ministers, evangelists, all must be mindful of battling this evil counterfeit spirit. Remember, the words of Matthew 23 are the words of Jesus. Not mine.

All my books discern the Religious Spirit and call it out for what it is, demonically inspired by the realm of alien demons. Religious spirits express themselves in funda-*mentalism*, extremism, judge-*mental* attitudes, rejection, witchcraft, deception, legalism and persecution.

People who claim to be what they are not, are liars, and we know who inspires lies. Cults like the Hebrew Roots, which encourages Gentiles to pretend to be Jewish, are seethed in jealousy of real Jews which is antisemitism. This is a form of religious witchcraft, illusion, and usurping the place which God has given in the first place. Its fascination is rooted in self-piety, as we want to look more religious than we really are, just as the Pharisees did in Jesus' day.

Religious spirits are at the root of many of the problems in the body of Christ today. The Hebrew Roots cult is by far one of the most pretentious, as it sucks free

Christians back into legalism and un-Christ-like attitudes. Everyone sees through this curtain of buffalo feathers! The religious spirit is one of the churches weakest points, and the other is pride; most church leaders are too proud to admit their own pedigree or lack thereof. Pride always comes before destruction. The religious spirit is influenced by lizards and their grays. The *religious spirit* wars against the Holy Spirit. It is pervasive in the Church and rules over all cults. It is an unloving haughty spirit.

Queen Jezebel was inhabited by an ancient demon, that demon was later nick-named Jezebel, after her. Jezebel was a Gentile pagan who was part of the church of Ashtarte/Thytaria. This man from Hebrew Roots tarnishes all women with the same brush because of this ancient control freak demon, who obviously inspires him toward total control over his congregants! He expected me to submit to his authority over the internet, because he's an 'elder' in some church in the Philippines! I don't think so! He preaches that women who teach or preach are all Jezebels, and that God raised up Jezebel to fall. His confusion of God with Satan was stunning to me; God didn't raise up Jezebel, Satan did! The Lord Yahuah defeated Satan through her and caused her downfall through Elijah and King Jehu. It's written right there in the Scriptures.

Furthermore, it was the Lord Yahuah who raised up Deborah, the Judge who won the longest continuous peace in Israel's history to date. She was a woman. She didn't usurp the authority from a man, God anointed her. See, The Book of Judges in the Jewish Bible.

> "In the last days,' The Lord God says, 'I will pour out my Spirit upon ALL people. Your sons and *daughters* will prophesy. Your young men will see visions, and your old men will dream dreams."
>
> (Acts 2:17)

Remember the words, ALL people, not just men, but women too. In, *Who Is God?* Book Two of my book series, I prove through scripture that sexism was NOT inspired by the LORD of Hosts, but is an alien agenda inserted into the Bible by the Church of Rome. I prove it through comparison to multiple scriptures in the Torah, the Jewish Bible, and the Old Testament. This Word in the book of Acts proves the point, that the movement of the Spirit of God is for ALL people, men and women equally.[7]

As a Messianic-Jewish-Christian, I can see through the lies inserted into the Bible by the Church of Rome, and Christian sexism and chauvinism are amongst them. However, that doesn't change my faith in *who* the Lord is, not one iota. It does help me to discern, however, *who* the enemy is, within "Churchianity". Most Christians blindly believe that the Bible they pick up to read is the original and entire Word of

God. We are now in full knowledge and disclosure that it is not. There are books missing. The Christian faith is built upon Jewish Scriptures; in fact, the entire 66 books of the modern Bible canon were all written by Jewish scribes yet edited by Roman Monks, that includes the New Testament. Remember, Paul was Jewish and a Pharisee scribe before he encountered Christ. Matthew, Mark, Luke and John, etc. were all Jewish disciples.

Satanic Bondages of Constantine and Nicean Creeds

Let's not forget, that the main agenda of the Church of Rome was to wipe out the Jewishness of Jesus while usurping His name, and denying the God of Israel. The Roman Catholic church followed the decrees of the Roman Emperors, through Constantine's Creed, which was enforced by the Roman Emperors Justin and Justinian through the Nicean Creeds.

Constantine's Creed was completely anti-Jewish, anti-Christ and anti-Israel. Modern Protestant Christianity was birthed out of the Church of Rome, yet Christians have never REPENTED from the pagan teachings of Imperial Rome. It's time Christians do so! These falsehoods have perpetuated the dark inequality in personal relationships, the abuse of power, and the persecutions of Jews and of women by the Church. History is replete with the horrid tales of centuries of persecutions by the Church of Rome, and the Roman Catholic Church.

For further study, see, my second book, *Who is God?* to learn more about the history of Christianity and Judaism, and how these two religions dovetail, while the modern Protestant funda-*mentalist* Christians are in conflict with the original WORD of God. Constantine's Creed is the spiritual legal ground that holds the church in bondage to Anti-Semitic demons, and brings curses on them through Genesis 12:3. There is, however, a way out, and that is through repentance, out loud to the Lord, for every line of Constantine's Creed.

All Christian leaders had to declare this creed to become part of Constantine's Christian Religion, the Religion of Jesus the "Christ"!

> Constantine's Creed: "I Renounce all" Customs, Rites, Legalisms, Unleavened breads and Sacrifices of Lambs of the Hebrews, and all the other Feasts of the Hebrews, Sacrifices, Prayers, Aspirations, Purification's, Sanctification's, and Propitiation, and Fasts and New Moons, and Sabbaths, and Superstitions, and Hymns and Chants, and Observances and synagogues. absolutely everything Jewish, every Law, Rite and Custom and if afterwards I shall wish to deny and return to Jewish Superstition, or shall be found eating with Jews, or feasting with them, or secretly conversing and condemning the Christian

> Religion instead of openly confuting them and condemning their vain Faith, then let the trembling of Cain and the leprosy of Gehazi cleave to me, as well as the legal punishments to which I acknowledge myself liable. And may I be an anathema in the world to come, and may my soul be set down with Satan and the Devils." (Stefano Assemani, Acta Sanctorium Martyrum Orientalium at Occidentalium, Vol. 1, Rome 1748, page 105)

Does anyone really think and believe that this religion of *Constantinianism,* is what Yeshua/Jesus wanted us to become entangled in? Every word of this Creed goes against the Words of Yahuah and Yeshua in both the Old and New Testaments. It was anti-Semitic, antichrist and anti-Yahuah.

Furthermore, the Nicean Council's reversed thousands of years of Jewish belief, such as decreeing reincarnation as heresy in the year 553 A.D., when 165 Church officials condemned reincarnation, based on the manipulations and insecurities of one narcissistic Empress. Prior to that time, it had been a fundamental Christian teaching just as it was a fundamental Jewish teaching.

References to reincarnation, were removed by Monks working for the Council of Nicea who also destroyed countless books/scrolls, books we may never know existed before the Council of Nicea. They decided which books were to be considered holy scripture, and which ones were to be burned.[8]

Reincarnation is a fact. The fact that it is no longer a part of today's Christian beliefs is due to one power-hungry woman, the Empress Theodora, the wife of the Emperor Justinian. It was her manipulation via her demonic possession, who attempted to have all references to reincarnation in the early Bible removed. Can you see the Jezebellian religious spirit at work?

However, when one is influenced by a demon, one is in error, and therefore, mistakes happen. Point is, her manipulation on the Council of Nicea was not 100% successful, because the monks she used missed at least two dozen scriptures, which still refer to reincarnation. See, Book Two, *Who is God?* Chapter Twenty-Eight: *What Happens When You Die?* pp. 455-484, to get all the scriptures still in the Jewish Bible, both Old and New Testaments[9], and the Words of Jesus Christ Himself, proving that reincarnation was very much an ancient Jewish belief as well as the belief of the early Christian Church.

This seemingly small act by this narcissistic Empress, whose intention was to blot out both Christian and Jewish beliefs so that she would be worshipped as a Goddess, came with historical consequences. Just imagine, how different history and the Church would be, if the last 1490 years, believers had known what the ancients knew? That everyone reaps what they sow in future earthly lives. Galatians 6:7 says, "God is not mocked, you reap what you sow." Galatians 6:7 is the law of karma. It may not happen right away, but in due time, everyone learns their lessons, both good and bad. The path of relationship with the Living Lord Jesus, can mitigate and alter that, and is the ultimate goal of all life, is to be reconciled back to the Creator and become more and more Christ-like. But because of the suppression of this knowledge, the church was and are still handicapped for lack of knowledge. Especially in light of understanding End Times Prophesies, which involves reincarnation.

As I've mentioned in Book Two, and it's worth repeating here, how can anyone explain away this prophecy, without understanding reincarnation?

> "And I will pour out on the house of David and the inhabitants of Jerusalem a spirit of grace and supplication. *They will look on me, **the one they have pierced**, and they will mourn for him as one mourns for an only child*, and grieve bitterly for him as one grieves for a firstborn son. On that day the weeping in Jerusalem will be as great as the weeping of Hadad Rimmon in the plain of Megiddo."
>
> (Zechariah 12:10-11)

> "Behold, He is coming with the clouds, and every eye will see Him--***even those who pierced Him.*** And all the tribes of the earth will mourn because of Him. So, shall it be! Amen."
>
> (Revelation 1:7)

How can the people responsible for piercing (crucifying) Jesus, be there at the time of His Second Coming weeping and mourning? How is this possible when the individuals who were responsible for His murder by crucifixion have been dead for over two thousand years? The only possible answer, is that they are reincarnated on the earth at that time, because it's God's Amazing Grace to give them one final chance to repent to Him.

During the early Christian era, reincarnation was one of the pillars of belief. Without it, Christianity would lose all logic[8], and lose their ability to identify and understand End Times Prophesies. How could a benevolent, loving God give one person a silver spoon and leave the next to be born in disease in their seemingly only one earthly life?

Early Church elders and theologians, Origenes, Basilides and St Gregory, taught reincarnation of the soul as a matter of course. After all, it was written in the Bible.[8] Nowadays, most Christians suspect blasphemy if someone references reincarnation, because the lie has been told for millennia, and they believe it as truth, reinforcing the alien demonic implant of the Jezebellian religious spirit, which is programmed to implant false beliefs, and is still in rebellion to the God of Israel – Yahuah and Yeshua.

Subsequently, Christians are programmed to reject all notions that God reincarnates people, yet they ironically base their beliefs on resurrection. Is not the same God who resurrects people form the dead, the same God who gives rebirth, one and the same God? The answer is a resounding, Yes! And this is what Christians are missing, this piece of knowledge, to complete the puzzle of the End Times Prophecies. Reincarnation is not a religion, it is a fact of life and death and it is based on God's Amazing Grace.

Many scholars who understand that reincarnation is an important piece of the End Times Puzzle, believe that the Antichrist will be reincarnated from the annals of history. Some believe he will be Nimrod, or Apollyon, others Antiochus reincarnated. Regardless of *who* he was in the past, he will be raised up again into a position of power as the son of perdition, in one last attempt to deceive the world through an end time power grab, using alien technologies, and ancient religions.

If Christians ignore knowledge, then Christian eschatologists will fail to recognize End Times Prophets as well as the Antichrist himself, who are all prophesied to be reincarnated from the past. Instead, today's Christians give into superstitions and fearful delusions, that causes them to see the antichrist under every stone. Every US President in the last two decades has been branded the antichrist by today's modern-day Pharisees. The scriptures tell us, this son of perdition will emerge out of the revived (reincarnated) Roman Empire.

Let's revisit the 5th and 6th century after Christ, when this diabolical conspiracy was hatched in the court of the Byzantine Emperor Justinian, that would hold humankind prisoner within the false understanding of the reality of life and death for 1,490 years. Keep in mind, that in the generations prior, reincarnation was an *unchallenged* fact in the early Christian church.

In 451AD, the Fourth Ecumenical Council, also known as the Council of Chalcedon condemned monophysitism as heresy and persecuted its advocates. Monophysitism was the teaching that Christ's two natures are joined into a new single human-divine nature. The Council of 451AD *emphasized* the Law of Reincarnation. Reincarnation was never an issue, during these religious controversies which was focused on how human and divine Christ was. Reincarnation was held to be a fundamental dogma, which was even reinforced by the Fourth Ecumenical Council of 451AD.

Who could have imagined then, that Christian theology would take such a dark turn, covering up these ancient truths and turning them into lies, heresies and further persecutions?

So, *who* was the Empress Theodora? Theodora, a daughter of a bear tamer from the Constantinople circus, learned how to use a woman's oldest weapon to take control of a kingdom and control the editing of what amounts to today's Bible Canon. She began as a prostitute whose services were sought after by the aristocracy and climbed her way to the top. Hacebolus, the young governor of Pentapolis, fell for her seductions and took Theodora with him to North Africa. But she abused his trust and, at the expense of the people, hoarded their riches. After overstepping the mark in her greed, Hacebolus, being overwhelmed with complaints from the people, threw her out of his palace and seized all her goods.[8]

With only the clothes on her back, she fought her way to Alexandria. At the city gates, she was taken in by a hermit monk, named Eutyches. This was the same Eutyches who had originated monophysitism, and was excommunicated by the Fourth Ecumenical Council to be exiled there. Theodora ended up using this fallen monk later on, to carry out her dark plans.

Theodora climbed her way to power, via prostitution, becoming one of the Emperor Justinian's favorite concubines. In 523AD, she became his wife. Four years later, she and her husband assumed the highest position of power in the world: the imperial crown. There was one final step to be climbed: her own deification. Only then would she be equal with the Caesars of old.

It really wasn't that long before that, the Roman Emperors were automatically deified and received a place of worship in the temple halls. The rise of Christianity ended that custom. It was exactly this point, that the biblically recognized fact of reincarnation provided a stumbling block to Theodora, because how could a woman enter eternity as a goddess when everyone was supposed to be reborn? She was worried, no one would remember her, if she came back as a mere peasant. Theodora knew that as long as reincarnation was a foundation of Christian consciousness, which it very much was, then she feared that people would never accept her as a goddess, let alone remember her as one. So, she had to destroy the doctrine of reincarnation. It had to be completely blotted out for her to be deified and remembered in the annals of history.

So, how many of you knew who Theodora was? Did her evil plan work to remember her as a deity? Most honest people will say, no, they never heard of her as a deity. Not even today's goddess worshippers, venerate Theodora as one of the main goddesses. But, she sure did cause 1491 years of persecution to those who know and believe that God continues to this day, to reincarnate people on earth, and she certainly succeeded in getting Christians to reject that reincarnation was God's original plan, who have believed in this wicked lie since the Nicean Creed of 527 A.D.

Do you see, why repenting of both Constantine's and the Nicean Creeds will set you free from the alien implants and the stronghold of lies within the Church?

What does Jesus say? "Come out of her, my people, lest you share in her sins, and lest you receive of her plagues." (Revelation 18:4) Repent of the lies of ancient Rome. Repent of the lies of Constantine, Justin and Justinian and the evil manipulations of Theodora. These are nothing but demonic strongholds blocking Christians from the truth.

> "The weapons we fight with are not the weapons of the world. On the contrary, they have divine power to demolish strongholds. *We demolish arguments and every pretension that sets itself up against the knowledge of God*, and we take captive every thought to make it obedient to Christ."
>
> (2 Corinthians 10:4-5)

Christians need to examine, why they are so afraid of this truth? I had a Woman Baptist Deliverance Minister freak out on me, over the issue of reincarnation. Her issue was, 'are you saying that I have to come back and do this all over again?' She assumed that accepting the *knowledge* of reincarnation automatically meant her future, while totally blinded and ignoring her past. This is the reason why Christians need to repent of the Constantine and Nicean Creeds is to allow the Lord to minister to them about their past lives, so that they can be free now and in the future, and insure that, yes, they don't have to return to repeat the same lessons.

How many people were involved in the Inquisitions, the Roman Catholic persecutions of believers, the ongoing witch-hunts, etc., of the past, only to be reincarnated on earth now, as funda-*mentalists* with Religious Spirits, who are persecuting others because they don't sin the same way they do? The central point of being a Christian is to learn how to become *Christ-like.* This means, one who is born-again in the Holy Spirit, should be displaying the fruits of the Spirit, which is loving-kindness, tolerance, patience, gentleness, goodness, and the understanding of truths with self-control. "But the fruit of the Spirit is love, joy, peace, patience, kindness, goodness, faithfulness, gentleness, and self-control." (Galatians 5:22-23)

This is a major truth, that Christians have been programmed, implanted and reinforced with repetitive brainwashing to reject that they've been reincarnated, no questions asked. Pull this implant out, and Christians will at least have the freedom to allow Christ to shine through them and deliver them from all their fears, including the fears of their own past lives. See, Psalm 34:4. How else can they get a handle on their repetitive problems, without having any understanding of the past? It's like walking through life with blinders on.

The Jewish Bible, the Jewish Zohar and the Jewish Kabballah all have this understanding. Yet, the irony is you have a group of Christians who are *wanna-be Jews,* i.e., the Hebrew Roots folks, who reject Jewish knowledge, and reincarnation is a big piece of it. Is it any wonder why there are so many people nursing their curses? People are given rebirth to find the truth, the light and reconcile with the Lord. He sends people back from NDEs (Near Death Experiences) for the same reason, who specifically come back with the same messages, that they needed to learn to live right by Him and treat others with kindness and respect. We are reincarnated to learn many lessons, too many to list here, and this denial of the past, is the very reason why people are doomed to repeat it. Isn't it time for the Church to become whole? Get their power back from the past? Denounce these manipulators of God's Word, God's Will and God's Grace?

Have you ever taken a highlighter pen and gone through the Old Testament, and marked each and every place that records the real Words of the Lord? Every place He speaks through His prophets, where it says, "Thus saith the Lord." Just as there are New Testament, 'red letter' bibles highlighting all the 'words of Jesus Christ' in red ink, so there should be Old Testament 'blue letter' bibles highlighting all the words of the Lord Yahuah, the God of Israel. This will distinguish the historical records from the actual Words and Decrees of the God of gods, from the words and confusion of counterfeits.

The Bible holds many secrets, which can only be revealed to those who have ears to hear, eyes to see and a heart to understand. These can only be revealed by the Holy Spirit, though some knowledge of the original language will help. Fortunately, the manipulating editors were not perfect, to err is human, and they did leave at least two dozen scriptures behind that indeed prove reincarnation.

Another satanic bondage is the lie that men are to rule women. Men and woman are obviously not the same, and sameness does not mean equality. Equality is having equal worth and value in God's eyes, equality before the laws, equal autonomy, the same measure of authority in all matters of power, and equal standing in both the home, the family, the church and the world. That was God's original plan, and I prove that through the Old Testament scriptures in Book Two, *Who is God?* [7] Partnership is not about competition or sameness, it's about men and women having individual roles living in cooperation and equality. Partnership is about completion. The roles of men and women in the original Word are quite clear. God raises up men and women according to His plan and purpose. The Church of Rome along with Islam fear the power in women, so they suppress, subjugate and oppress all that opposes their theocratic agendas. This is NOT God's original plan, which was evidenced in the Old Testament.

God is the same yesterday, today and forever. (Hebrews 13:8) 'I am the Lord, and I change not.' (Malachi 3:6) Humans, however, do change, and have most certainly manipulated the scriptures to purport their political and social agendas.

There are 18 bible scrolls or books mentioned in the Bible that aren't even there today. Where are they? Why were they deleted? One of the missing books is called the book of Paul and Thekla. Today, Christians read Paul's writings incessantly, but so many are unaware of the story of Paul and Thekla, who deserved a place in the Bible just like the prophet Daniel, because the Lord performed a similar miracle for Thekla, when Paul set her up to be eaten by the lions. This book, along with the other rejected texts did not fit into the Church of Rome's agenda, so they are lost to most believers.

The Jewish scriptures make the Lord's NEW plan very clear, just as He established His NEW Covenant through Yeshua. This is the Lord's plan through the Prophet Jeremiah, in KJV, AKV, and NASV:

> Jeremiah 31:22: "How long wilt thou go about, O thou backsliding daughter? For the LORD hath created a NEW thing in the earth, *a woman shall compass a man*." (KJV)
>
> "How long will you go about, O you backsliding daughter? For the LORD has created a NEW thing in the earth, *a woman shall protect a man*." (AKV)
>
> "How long will you go here and there, O faithless daughter? For the LORD has created a NEW thing in the earth-- *A woman will encompass a man*." (NASV)

The Hebrew word used that is translated in the above *italics*, in Jeremiah 31:22, is *Tisovev* – which is literally means, "shall have an edge".

Religious Spirits Created Sexism

Deborah was a Judge and presided over all the men of Israel much in the way Golda Meir did as Prime Minister. Proving, men and women do have equal worth in the eyes of the Lord. This is Scriptural. Men who think God can't anoint and raise up women to lead and teach men are deeply deceived in this area. Many Christians become brainwashed by religious spirits.[10] Just because the weak and timid refuse to see it, doesn't mean it's not there. Those who are not Jewish, but masquerade as Jews within the Christian communities, do so to make themselves look more authentic, more spiritually worthy, acceptable to God, yet they demonstrate very little knowledge or understanding about Jewish history and the many persecutions Jews survived just for being Jewish. Stolen identity, stolen valor, stolen lives, and who inspires theft? See, John 10:10.

Israel was led by a woman in power and authority over the IDF and over all of the Israeli government during the Prime Ministry of Golda Meir, 1969-1974. So, if women are not supposed to lead men, then please tell me why the God of Israel would call an American Jewish woman from Wisconsin, to lead the early formation of modern Israel? Which in and of itself was the beginning of fulfillment of Bible End Times Prophesy, when Israel was reborn. See, Ezekiel 37.

Yet, these puffed up religious Hebrew Roots Gentile Christians pretending to be Jewish, pontificate on Jewish custom, history, and law to Jews! They are rooted in their jealousy of Jews, and prove this when they mistreat and reject real Jews. Gentiles are grafted into the everlasting Abrahamic covenants of Israel. They don't need to pretend to be something they are not. On top of being dishonest and ugly, it's offensive to real Jews.

Messianics are Jews who believe in Yeshua, despite what non-believing Jews think, Messianic Jews believe we are *completed Jews*. Although I have no problem being labeled a Jew for Jesus, or a Jewish-Christian, however, Gentiles who believe in Yeshua are called Christians, not Messianics. The Hebrew Roots cult, are made up of Gentile Christians who call themselves Messianic. They are so disingenuous, even for a cult, because they're constantly disrespecting both Jews and Christians. Please tell me, what's the point of such un-Christ-like behavior? Most of them have absolutely no understanding for Jewish history and why Jews do what they do or don't do, which is why real Jews do not share similitude with them, because they disrespect Jews, yet they pretend to be Jewish, without having legally converted to Judaism. Religious spirits rule them with delusion and self-righteousness, and when you point anything out to them, they take offense and excommunicate you. They're completely unteachable and arrogant. Pride goes before destruction! (Proverbs 16:18)

Torah Followers vs Blood Covenant

> "Now then, if you will indeed obey My voice and keep My covenant (Torah), then you shall be My own possession among all the peoples, for all the earth is Mine;"
>
> (Exodus 19:5)

This Old Testament Hebrew scripture is clear; the ancient Jews are saved through keeping the Torah. However, as Jesus admonished them, failing to follow the spirit of the law while following the letter of the law left them spiritually deaf and blind. For it is the Spirit which breathes life, and the reason for following Torah is to bring one's soul closer to the Creator of the Law. It should not be done out of drudgery or bondage to a religion, but out of love and respect for the purity of the Creator.

I am a Messianic Jewish Christian. I was raised according to Jewish custom and religion, educated in Israel, and learned the Jewish Bible in Hebrew. I had a close personal encounter with Jesus in Israel shortly after my graduation. He appeared to me in the Negev, and told me He was the Messiah and said, 'follow me,' so I did. That was in July of 1979. Messianic Jews are the most hated and marginalized people on earth. I was excommunicated from my Jewish family for following Jesus, and excommunicated by Christians from fellowship for my knowledge and beliefs as a Jew. I accepted Jesus, while finding many aspects of Judaism hypocritical and burdensome.

When I accepted Jesus, I felt *liberated* from having to keep the religion. Instead I was filled with His Spirit and He wrote His laws on my heart, just as He promised to, in Jeremiah 31:33. Jesus taught the Pharisees the importance of following the *spirit* of the law, versus the letter of the law. This resonated with me, so I joined *Jews for Jesus* and became a missionary. *Jews for Jesus* are Jews, who continue to practice Judaism, some to the point of Orthodoxy, but they include Yeshua (Jesus) in every Hebrew prayer and at every Jewish tradition and holiday. I felt at home there.

They deliberately call themselves, *Jews for Jesus*, and not Jews for Yeshua, because of the history of persecution by Christians, which is the very reason Jews do not accept Jesus. They, however, use the name *Jesus*, which is the English transliteration of the Hebrew name *Yeshua*, because they want to bring Jesus to the Jews, without all the Christian persecution. I realize that's difficult for both Jews and Christians to understand, but when Hebrew Roots Gentiles reject Jews who believe in Jesus for saying the name Jesus, and not using His Hebrew name, Yeshua,...Houston, we have a problem! The hypocrisy is completely insane!

I went over this in greater detail in Book Two, *Who is God?* in my chapters on *What's in a Name?* and *The Name Above All Names.*[11] Essentially, Gentile Christians who join Hebrew Roots, should learn about *Jews for Jesus*, which is rooted in the Great Commission, and that is, to take the Gospel to the Jew first, and then the Gentile. See, Romans 1:16. If using the name Jesus is appropriate, particularly with American and English-speaking Jews, then so be it. If *Jews for Jesus* are speaking to Spanish Jews, then obviously they would use His Spanish Name. The Lord answers to His name in all languages.

There is no rule or law that says, we must all only use His Hebrew name. Jesus is not a false name. Jesus is not Zeus. Jesus is merely the name Yeshua transliterated into English. It used to be Iesus in Greek and Latin, then the letter 'J' was added to English in the 1700s and it became Jesus. Do you really think God doesn't understand the history of languages? After all, it was the Holy Spirit who gave the gift of languages, He answers to the Lord's name in every language. For these Hebrew Roots people to get so hung up on denying the name of Jesus, should speak volumes to the spiritually discerning. Demons tremble in the name of Jesus! There's power in that name.

I was witness to miraculous healings, deliverances and I witnessed a 23-year-old woman die of kidney failure get raised from the dead completely healed an hour later, in the name of Jesus! She came back after meeting Jesus during an Near-Death Experience, with a very specific message from Jesus, to let go of resentments and forgive her family. That's the real Jesus, it's His Will that we should all learn forgiveness. He wanted her to learn how to live her life through Him, by Him and for Him on earth, then He would let her come back to live in Heaven.

It's astonishing to me how many gentile Christians have essentially converted to Judaism, by means of the Hebrew Roots movement, believing that they must follow the Torah to the 'T' in order to be saved and set apart for the Messianic Era. Interestingly enough, Orthodox Religious Jews who are considered to be *fundamentalists* amongst conservative, reform and secular Jews, believe they are saved through keeping the Torah. This is what the Chabad, Lubavitch Rabbis teach and practice. They are not wrong, as Yeshua Himself, said, He didn't come for the righteous, but for the sinners. But His New Covenant, is founded upon the Grace of God through Yeshua, the Mashiach-Nagid, the Messiah King.

While there is a great deal of misunderstanding and confusion on both sides, clarity is available.

> "For you are a holy people to the LORD your God, and the LORD has chosen you to be a people for His own possession out of all the peoples who are on the face of the earth."
>
> (Deuteronomy 14:2)

Jews were chosen to stand apart from the rest of the human experiment. This group belonged to Yahuah, who put His own DNA into them, and gave them a moral code to follow, and dietary and hygienic laws to keep. These kept them strong and healthy, especially when they were sent into battle, as the healthful benefits gave them the edge over the pagan gentiles who were considered unclean in their diet and hygiene, or the lack thereof. Yahuah's instructions were practical in nature yet represented a lifestyle that was a sign of their being set apart, as His possession. These lifestyle instructions, however, turned into the Jewish religion.

Replacement Theology is an Alien Implant

The church did not replace the nation of Israel. The New Covenant is with the house of Israel and the house of Judah. Yeshua said He came only for the lost sheep of the house of Israel. The New Jerusalem has Twelve Gates and all of them are assigned to the Blessed Tribes of Israel. As a matter of fact, the early church in the first century began as a sect of Judaism, a splinter of the house of Israel. Christianity was started by Jews! Yeshua wasn't a Christian, He was a Jew. His followers were Jews, except for a few Roman soldiers who realized they had killed the Messiah. They repented and that began the fall of the Roman Empire. The church assembly was first seen at Mount Horeb when the original covenant was given to Israel. They were all Jews.

The church today however is a divided group of people who love God, but most of them don't know *who* He really is or what He expects of them. They don't know that Yeshua died to reconcile Himself to Israel because death was the only way to cancel His divorce.

> "To the Lord your God belong the heavens, even the highest heavens, the earth and everything in it. Yet the Lord set his affection on your ancestors and loved them, and he chose you, their descendants, above all the nations—as it is today. Circumcise your hearts, therefore, and do not be stiff-necked any longer. For the Lord your God is God of gods and Lord of lords, the great God, mighty and awesome, who shows no partiality and accepts no bribes. He defends the cause of the fatherless and the widow, and loves the foreigner residing among you, giving them food and clothing. And you are to love those who are foreigners, for you yourselves were foreigners in Egypt. Fear the Lord your God and serve him. Hold fast to him and take your oaths in his name. He is the one you praise; he is your God, who performed for you those great and awesome wonders you saw with your own eyes. Your ancestors who went down into Egypt were seventy in all, and now the Lord your God has made you as numerous as the stars in the sky."
>
> (Deuteronomy 10:14-22)

> "O Lord, great and awesome God, who keeps His covenant and mercy with those who love Him, and with those who keep His commandments, "WE have sinned and committed iniquity, WE have done wickedly and rebelled, even by departing from Your precepts and Your judgments. "WE have not obeyed the voice of the LORD our God, to walk in His laws, which He set before us by His servants the prophets. "Therefore, the LORD has kept the disaster in mind, and brought it upon us; for the LORD our God is righteous in all the works which He does, though WE have not obeyed His voice. (Daniel 9)

The Israelites don't know that grace is merited favor and that those who do righteousness are the righteous. It's always been about a circumcised heart and obedience.

"Dear children, don't let anyone deceive you about this: When people do what is right, it shows that they are righteous, even as Christ is righteous." (1 John 3:7)

Channeling Religious Spirits

I was asked what I thought about a piece that was essentially *channeled* through a Gentile Christian, knowing I am a Messianic Jew. They tried to pawn it off as a *Word from the Lord.* I immediately got a check in my spirit, that it was a counterfeit message, because it said that the Jews and Muslims were going to join religions in the end times.

Judaism and Islam are two separate and distinct religious views and philosophies which will never join as religions. Islam is a perversion of Judaism. The very thing Jews are told not to do, Muslims do. Islamic laws are in opposition to Judaic laws. Jews hold traditions that are ancient, some to the glory of the Lord and some to their own detriment. In case you haven't noticed, the enemies of Israel are mainly Muslims. Islam is a modern religion, which I laid out the history in Book Two: *Who Is God?* Chapter Twenty-Three: *Babylonian History: Where It All Began,* pp. 367-398.[12]

I highly recommend those reading and referring to Book Two for the background. Islam was created by the Church of Rome as a rival group to the early Jewish Messianic Church of Christianity growing throughout the ancient world. The pope ordered monks to train Mohammed, who was born a warrior, to take back Jerusalem for the pope. The Quran wasn't penned by Mohammed, who was illiterate. It was commissioned by the Roman pope and written by scribal monks. The Quran is a plagiarized perversion of both the Old and New Testaments of the Judeo-Christian Bible. The Quran and Islam were created to *compete* with growing Christianity and to take over Jerusalem and steal Israel from the Jews.

Is it any wonder that today's Pope incorporates Islamic prayers at the Vatican? It is no coincidence that the Pope leads today's "Chrislam" movement. That's the ridiculous notion that Christianity and Islam can or should be blended into one, is as preposterous as the channeler who mistakenly thinks that Jews and Muslims will somehow after 1300 years team up as one. Oil and water do not mix, if they did, there would have already been peace in the Middle East. Only the *true* Messiah can bring these people together, through their faith in Him. That means both Jews and Muslims need to recognize the Lordship and Authority of Messiah Jesus. It will happen, because it's the Divine Will of God, and it's written into the End Times Prophesies.

It's history, that Mohammed betrayed the Pope by keeping Jerusalem for himself. Despite the fact the Quran says that Israel is the land given by God to the Jewish people, the Muslims still think they can lay claim to it. For someone to write such utter nonsense that the two can combine as one religion proves that whatever evil spirit is channeled, understands nothing about Middle East politics or the difference between the two religions. However, as I stated in this book, it will be the counterfeit Messiah aka Antichrist who will attempt to unite all the world's religion into one. The fact stands clear that the entire peace negotiations in Middle East, are at a standstill because Palestinian Muslims refuse to acknowledge Israel as a sovereign nation, or that Jews have a right to return their ancient biblical land, allotted to them by the God of Israel.

Scripture says in the last days Jerusalem will be trampled over by the Gentiles. The Antichrist sets himself up in the rebuilt temple and stops the sacrifices. The Israeli Jews are then massacred by him. In Book Two, *Who is God?* I prove the math that one third of the population of Israel is saved by accepting Yeshua. Jesus said that He's not coming back until Israel says, "Blessed is he who comes in the name of the Lord."

Today there are over 25,000 Messianic Jews who live in Israel. That's 10,000 more since 2006 and 25,000 more since 1967 when there were none. There are 262 Messianic organizations operating in Israel according to *Kehila News Directory* altogether and there are approximately 100,000-150,000 of us in the world, give or take a few. The End Times Prophesies are not only about Jews returning to Israel but Jews returning to Yeshua HaMashiach the Messiah. One third gets saved. Read Revelation about the 144,000 from all the blessed tribes.[13]

In Book Two, *Who Is God?* I expose *who* The Whore of Babylon is, which are all the false religions that come out of Babylon, from paganism, Catholicism and Islam and everything in between.[14]

The Whore that deceives the whole world is Jezebel aka Ashtarte. Jesus speaks to her directly in Revelation 2:21 where He gives her time to repent. Jezebel represents all the false religions and their prophets. That's her church of Thyatira. Elijah went against all of her false prophets.

Judaism is the Ancient Hebraic Faith that Yeshua followed. The Church of Rome endeavored to strip him of his Jewishness in order to co-opt His divinity, and then oppresses Israel by persecuting the Jews.

The Scriptures promise that faithful followers of the Torah followers are saved. Jesus said that He came to save the unrighteous and the sinners, not the righteous. The Torah followers are considered righteous. Jews are under the Abrahamic Covenants. Christians are grafted onto Israel and her covenants. Replacement Theology is a huge sin, an error that inspired the Holocaust. Hitler bought into it hook, line, and sinker. Started by the Church of Rome and Martin Luther in Germany, Replacement Theology is an attempt to co-opt God's promises and usurp them to pagan Rome. Roman's 11 clearly states, that *All Israel Will be Saved*. These are the promises of God!

Christians need to repent of all anti-Semitism and anti-Israeli rhetoric. Too many Gentiles don't understand Jews. The beginning of anti-Semitic theology was based on the notion that ALL Jews rejected Yeshua, which is false, because the early church was made up of ALL Jews – Messianic Jews are still Jews. It is further anti-Semitic to think ALL of Israel will follow Antichrist, and reject Yeshua, as that's NOT what the prophesies say, which is not God's Will for these End Times.

The Time of Jacob's Troubles is a period appointed by the Lord to teach errant Israel a lesson. Today Israel is split between the Religious Torah Followers and the immoral godless secularists who promote the gay agenda. This is how it was in the past. Same conflicts, different century. The Lord has always had His remnant. All of Israel will not follow Antichrist.

Never in Jewish history have Jews agreed on everything and today Israel is split and will be, through the times of Antichrist. Therefore, all of Israel will not follow the Anti-Christ. The Children of God in Israel will not all follow Antichrist, although at first, many are deceived by him, as is the case with the rest of the entire world. After 3-1/2 years, they realize he's the counterfeit and all hell breaks loose on them, when he begins slaughtering them.

Today there are Israelis who rebel against their own government. These rebels will join the 144,000 Messianics and become part of the resistance to Antichrist. Antichrist will be other worldly, and will appear to have alien powers (through alien technology), but will have Jewish DNA, that hooks Israel into accepting him at first because Israel would never follow a Muslim. Antichrist will counterfeit the life of Jesus. He will most likely come from a well-known bloodline within the Illuminati families of the world and be groomed in banking and economics.

Israel needs Christian prayers and support now. Jesus returns to judge the church, to separate the sheep from goats. He said, 'whatever you do to the least of my brethren you do unto me.' His brethren are the Jews. Jesus was born into the Tribe of Judah, aka Judes, Jews.

David's Tomb was bought by the Vatican. The false prophet that props up Antichrist is the Pope. The Vatican will have a presence in Jerusalem according to their plan, where they now have a piece of Jerusalem real estate and that's prophesy. They rule from the temple with Antichrist.

In 2007, Pastor John Hagee of CUFI wrote *In Defense of Israel,* which he expounds on Romans 11 - *All Israel Will be Saved.* He proves that the religious Jews are under the Covenant. He teaches against Replacement Theology and Antisemitism. God excuses the Torah followers. That's why Gentiles created Hebrew Roots movement based on the same scriptures, which are essentially Gentile Christian Torah Followers. They follow the Torah schedule every Shabbat (Sabbath) and keep all the festivals and fasts, just like the Chabad does. They believe this is what Jesus taught. If this is what makes them feel closer to the Lord, then so be it, though we know that we are all saved only by Grace through faith in the finished works of Christ.[15]

For the record, Gentiles are not called to convert to Judaism, but they are called to learn how to love as Christ loves, and that includes the Jews and Israel. Being grafted onto the tree and roots of Israel doesn't mean they are a new tree, and get to start a new religion, but are instead invited into the already existing tree to benefit from the established root system, which becomes food for all the souls. By cursing their roots, they curse themselves, and reap what they sow, by withering away and dying off the tree. Scientifically speaking, not all tree grafts take and grow. And so, it will be when the Lord and Messiah King Jesus returns for the Sheep and Goat Judgment. Many who call themselves Christians will be cut off and die. (Matthew 25:31-46)

What is true for the Gentiles, who are grafted into the Covenants of Israel, is not necessarily the same for the Orthodox Jews who follow Torah. Orthodox Jews are judged by and justified through their devotion to Torah. That's what the Scriptures say. It's God's Word. If this wasn't true, then how do you explain *who* were the righteous, godly souls, that were resurrected out of their graves in Jerusalem, when Yeshua/Jesus was resurrected from the dead?

The Bible says, "The tombs were opened, and many bodies of the saints (godly/righteous men and women) who had fallen asleep were raised from their graves;" (Matthew 27:52) How could this be? How were they made righteous before Christ, if not through their devotion to the Torah? And so, it will be in the end as well. Those devoted to Torah, are justified through their obedience to God's laws. Just as Gentiles are justified through their faith in Christ, who came to fulfill the law through the New Covenant of Grace through Faith in Him. Spiritually speaking, this is what being *grafted* onto Israel through the eternal Covenant of Abraham is about, which is being justified through *faith*. This is one *covenant* that is consistent through both the Old and New Testaments.

> "But without *faith*, it is impossible to please God."
>
> (Hebrews 11:6)

> "Behold, as for the proud one, His soul is not right within him; But the *righteous* will live by his *faith*."
>
> (Habakkuk 2:4)

> "If he walks in My statutes and My ordinances (Torah) so as to deal *faithfully*--he is *righteous* and will surely live," declares the Lord God."
>
> (Ezekiel 18:9)

"The just shall live by *faith*."

(Romans 1:17)

Not all Orthodox Jews reject Christ. It's not inexcusable to God, it's forgiven. God's Grace is on those who seek Him. Orthodox Jews follow Torah and seek the Lord daily. Scripture justifies them. Ironically, this is exactly what the Hebrew Roots Gentiles base their cult on, following Torah, which is Orthodox Judaism. The only difference is they are Gentile Christians and speak the name of Messiah, and expect everyone else to do the same. This is not what's expected of the branches, in other words, Gentiles. If it makes people feel better about themselves, to follow Torah to the 'T', that's fine, but it's the judgmental religious spirit and self-righteousness for doing so that turns so many off and brands them as a cult. Jesus came to deliver us from the arrogance of self-righteousness and religious spirits. Celebrating Feast Days should be done out of Love for the Lord, not out of a spirit of self-righteousness, which the Lord rebuked. See, John 9:39-41; Luke 16:14; 18:9-14.

Gentiles are grafted onto Israel, that's an already existing LEGAL Covenant that God the Father has with Israel, and Jews. The Torah followers are saved through keeping that Covenant. Paul knew coming from his own Pharisaical background, that self-righteous people tend to justify themselves by blaming others. In Psychology, it's known as 'Projection'.

The Remnant of Israel

> "I ask then: Did God reject his people? By no means! I am an Israelite myself, a descendant of Abraham, from the tribe of Benjamin. God did not reject his people, whom he foreknew. Don't you know what Scripture says in the passage about Elijah—how he appealed to God against Israel: "Lord, they have killed your prophets and torn down your altars; I am the only one left, and they are trying to kill me"? And what was God's answer to him? "I have reserved for myself seven thousand who have not bowed the knee to Baal." So too, at the present time there is a remnant chosen by grace. And if by grace, then it cannot be based on works; if it were, grace would no longer be grace.
>
> What then? What the people of Israel sought so earnestly they did not obtain. The elect among them did, but the others were hardened, as it is written:
>
> "God gave them a spirit of stupor, eyes that could not see and ears that could not hear, to this very day." And David says: "May their table become a snare and a trap, a stumbling block and a retribution for them. May their eyes be darkened so they cannot see, and their backs be bent forever."

Ingrafted Branches

> Again, I ask: Did they stumble so as to fall beyond recovery? Not at all! Rather, because of their transgression, salvation has come to the Gentiles to make Israel envious. But if their transgression means riches for the world, and their loss means riches for the Gentiles, how much greater riches will their full inclusion bring!
>
> I am talking to you Gentiles. Inasmuch as I am the apostle to the Gentiles, I take pride in my ministry in the hope that I may somehow arouse my own people to envy and save some of them. For if their rejection brought reconciliation to the world, what will their acceptance be but life from the dead? If the part of the dough offered as first fruits is holy, then the whole batch is holy; if the root is holy, so are the branches.
>
> If some of the branches have been broken off, and you, though a wild olive shoot, have been grafted in among the others and now share in the nourishing sap from the olive root, do not consider yourself to be superior to those other branches. If you do, consider this: You do not support the root, but the root supports you. You will say then, "Branches were broken off so that I could be grafted in." Granted. But they were broken off because of unbelief, and you stand by faith. Do not be arrogant, but tremble. For if God did not spare the natural branches, he will not spare you either.
>
> Consider therefore the kindness and sternness of God: sternness to those who fell, but kindness to you, provided that you continue in his kindness. Otherwise, you also will be cut off. And if they do not persist in unbelief, they will be grafted in, for God is able to graft them in again. After all, if you were cut out of an olive tree that is wild by nature, and contrary to nature were grafted into a cultivated olive tree, how much more readily will these, the natural branches, be grafted into their own olive tree!"
>
> (Romans 11: 1-22) NIV

Fundamental Christians believe that, "No man comes to the Father except by Me." This is what a Gentile believer wrote to me, and it's not necessary to mention her by name, but it was her son who wrote channeled material that was full of anti-Semitic rhetoric and falsehoods about Israel and God's End Time plan for Jews. Her words carried a spirit of ignorance and bigotry. She identifies as a fundamentalist and this is the mentality which is fueled by the Religious Spirit held in place by the alien implant of Replacement Theology.

> She said, "*.... the Jews have no special place, they are man and they need a savior too, and anybody that believes less or that they get a pass is wrong sis, that's just the truth anyway, I love ya, but we will have to agree to disagree.... we can't defend people who do not acknowledge Jesus Christ as Lord and Messiah, there is NO excuse for it what so ever... if we believe anything less than that then we will fall prey to the Antichrist because you allow room for compromise in your heart and there can be no compromise, Jesus Christ is Lord. Period.*"

What they fail to understand is that the central focus of the prayers in the Chabad Prayer Books are to and for the *Mashiach*, (the Messiah), and for the Messianic Era. To suggest that religious Jews don't know God, who comes to them via the Shekinah Glory and the Holy Spirit, is ignorant to the spiritual foundation of Judaism. The only difference is that religious observant Jews don't use the names of God, they don't call Messiah by name, but they certainly lift up many prayers to Him on a regular basis.

Gentile fundamentalists would benefit from visiting their local Chabad house and sitting through one of the major holidays, like Yom Kippur or Sukkot and follow the English version of the prayer books. You will be surprised to learn that they communicate with Messiah, but do not call him by name as do Christians. Nevertheless, Messiah is with them, and because they are following Torah, they will be judged by the law, as stated in Galatians. Remember, Jesus said He came to save the lost souls of Israel. The Spiritual Jews who are of the Chabad are not lost, they just haven't had their eyes opened yet as to *who* their Messiah is, despite them praying to Him and for His Messianic Kingdom to come is included in every Shabbat, and High Holiday Prayers. Paul says that the doers of the Law will be justified and those who break it will be judged.

> "For as many as have sinned without Law will also perish without Law, and as many as have sinned in the Law will be judged by the Law, for not the hearers of the Law [are] just in the sight of Yahweh, but the doers of the Law will be justified;"
>
> (Romans 2:12)

Gentile Christians mustn't forget that they are grafted into the Jewish Tree and Jewish Roots. When Jesus taught His disciples how to pray in what has become known as the Lord's Prayer, *Thy Kingdom Come, Thy Will be done, on Earth as it is in Heaven,* we remember that this very prayer comes straight out of the Torah and that religious Jews have been praying it since time immemorable. They have been praying just like their Messiah, and for His Kingdom, which they call the Messianic Era, to come. It's all over their prayer books. So, remember the words of Yeshua Jesus, that He came for them in particular.

The High Priest of a New Covenant

> "Now the main point of what we are saying is this: We do have such a high priest, who sat down at the right hand of the throne of the Majesty in heaven, and who serves in the sanctuary, the true tabernacle set up by the Lord, not by a mere human being. Every high priest is appointed to offer both gifts and sacrifices, and so it was necessary for this one also to have something to offer. If He were on earth, He would not be a priest, for there are already priests who offer the gifts prescribed by the law. They serve at a sanctuary that is a copy and shadow of what is in heaven. Therefore, Moses was warned when he was about to build the tabernacle: "See to it that you make everything according to the pattern shown you on the mountain."
>
> The ministry Jesus received is as superior to theirs as the covenant of which He is mediator is superior to the old one, since the new covenant is established on better promises. "For if there had been nothing wrong with that first covenant, no place would have been sought for another. But God found fault with the people and said:
>
> "The days are coming, declares the Lord, when I will make a new covenant with the people of Israel and with the people of Judah. It will not be like the covenant I made with their ancestors when I took them by the hand to lead them out of Egypt, because they did not remain faithful to my covenant, and I turned away from them, declares the Lord. This is the covenant I will establish with the people of Israel after that time, declares the Lord. ***I will put my laws in their minds and write them on their hearts. I will be their God, and they will be my people***. No longer will they teach their neighbor, or say to one another, 'Know the Lord,' because they will all know me, from the least of them to the greatest. For I will forgive their wickedness and will remember their sins no more." By calling this covenant "new," he has made the first one obsolete; and what is obsolete and outdated will soon disappear."
>
> (Hebrews 8:7-13)

The covenant referred to here as obsolete, is the Mosaic Covenant of the Law, not the Abrahamic Covenant of Faith.

In *Who Is God?* I listed all the names and correct pronunciations of the God of Israel, the Father of the Messiah. Orthodox Jews pray to the Father directly. They go to Him through the Covenant and say His Hebrew name, as this is in their prayers. The Lubavitcher Rabbi told them the name was Yeshua who was Jesus. Most don't know that it's Jesus. They think the Christian Jesus is the false Christ. That's because Christians have for centuries persecuted Jews. Yet the Torah followers say His name in Hebrew and pray to him. That's Torah scripture. When I tried to explain this to my Christian Fundamentalist online friend, this was her response:

> *"That is the heart of deception. You really believe Jesus Christ would accept people who don't even know they pray to him? Even if what you say is true and they pray unknowingly to Jesus Christ, saying they have salvation contradicts everything Jesus taught."*

Jesus is much more loving and understanding of His own people than Gentiles could ever grasp. We continued to be online friends. She repented of her attitudes towards Jews, and blessed me with loving words and well wishes. I forgave her ignorance. However, I found it relevant to what is being discerned in this book to share with the world, the common attitudes and ignorance of Torah scriptures, and the practice and religion of Spiritual Judaism, which are known as Chabad, who are devoted Torah followers.

Chabad stands for the three spiritual qualities toward which they aspire; Chesed or Loving-Kindness; Binah or Understanding; and Da'at or Wisdom. Many will recognize these words who have studied Kabbalah. They are indeed Jewish fundamentalists, but to suggest they are not saved, or outside of God's Covenant, because they are keeping the laws and are under both the Abrahamic and Mosaic Covenants, is mean spirited and judgmental. It is so painfully ironic that Gentile Christians who are known as Hebrew Roots follow the exact same ways as the religious Jews and then spitefully malign them! They essentially copy Jews, in all their customs, traditions, and holidays, while rejecting real blood born Jews. This is what's wrong with the Hebrew Roots Cult, which according to the Jewish Defense League, when others steal Jewish Identity and then reject Jews, that's the very definition of Antisemitism.

Yeshua alone is the judge of all the Jews. The Torah followers are set apart. They carry the original Covenant and are obedient to it. Gentiles were grafted into that Covenant through Grace. Christians must remember that with the Grace of being grafted in, they are not expected to follow Judaism as a hereditary Jew, but they ***are*** expected to be vessels of Christ's Spirit living within them. Christ expressed His love, kindness, and holiness through His death for all of us, not just those of us with whom we agree.

Another piercing irony is that the Chabad Jew believes kindness and service to others is the highest expression of their religion. In fact, the Hebrew word *chesed* means *loving-kindness.* The Hassidim, which comes from the root, *chesed,* are the religious Jews of the Chabad, who are known for their kindness to others, good deeds, and warm hospitality. Is this not what Jesus taught by both word and by example? Aren't these religious Jews doing what Messiah taught? So, for a fundamental Christian

Gentile to suggest that God has abandoned His own people is dangerously close to standing in the place of God as judge, and becoming the Accuser of the Brethren. The Accuser of the Brethren is satan, through the Religious Spirit.

> "Then I heard a loud voice in heaven, saying, "Now the salvation, and the power, and the kingdom of our God and the authority of His Christ have come, *for the accuser of our brethren has been thrown down*, he who accuses them before our God day and night."
>
> (Revelation 12:10)

Orthodox Jews pray to Yahuah and Yeshua in Hebrew, as they don't care for the Christian version of Jesus. The Hebrew Roots Gentiles refuse to use the English name, only Hebrew. They essentially converted to Judaism. Then to add fuel to the fire, they garble and twist the linguistic of His Hebrew name, Yahushua/Yeshua into Yahusha. Like I said, in Book Two, *Who is God?* you can't find a single Jewish scholar that supports that name. It's a twisted counterfeit name, based on misunderstanding of the Hebrew language, distorted and twisted by blind Religious Spirits.

There is misunderstanding of the name on both sides. The Lord understands both. The Religious Spirit wars against the Holy Spirit on both sides, Jews and Gentiles. We must never forget, it was the *religious spirit* that conspired to crucify Christ. Today, Gentiles have become modern-day Pharisees. Those who follow the Holy Spirit know and fear the Lord. The Torah followers fear the Lord and are set apart. That was the Covenant and it still abides today. He set that up and His grace is sufficient for all of us.

Antisemitism is rooted in jealousy for what God gave Jews through Covenant. It's an everlasting Covenant. They too get saved in the end, all according to the Divine plan. It is important to remember that hate, jealousy, and envy are not Christian values. Gentiles don't replace Jews any more than New York replaces Israel. We are all joined in the Covenant through the Blood Covenant. Torah followers will get saved and we need not torment ourselves over the fact. That's scriptural.

> "Then some of the believers who belonged to the party of the Pharisees stood up and said, "The Gentiles must be circumcised and required to keep the law of Moses." The apostles and elders met to consider this question. After much discussion, Peter got up and addressed them: "Brothers, you know that some time ago God made a choice among you that the Gentiles might hear from my lips the message of the gospel and believe. God, who knows the heart, showed that he accepted them by giving the Holy Spirit to them, just as he did to us. He did not discriminate between us and them, for he purified their

hearts by faith. **<u>Now then, why do you try to test God by putting on the necks of Gentiles a yoke that neither we nor our ancestors have been able to bear</u>**? No! We believe it is through the grace of our Lord Jesus that we are saved, just as they are."

(Acts 15:5-11)

"For I will take you from the nations, gather you from all the lands and bring you into your own land. Then I will sprinkle clean water on you, and you will be clean; I will cleanse you from all your filthiness and from all your idols. Moreover, **<u>I will give you a new heart and put a new spirit within you; and I will remove the heart of stone from your flesh and give you a heart of flesh</u>**. I will put My Spirit within you and cause you to walk in My statutes, and you will be careful to observe My ordinances. ***You will live in the land that I gave to your forefathers; so, you will be My people, and I will be your God.***"

(Ezekiel 36:24-28)

"For it is by grace you have been saved, through faith—and this is not from yourselves, ***it is the gift of God***— not by works, ***so that no one can boast***. For we are God's handiwork, created in Christ Jesus to do good works, which God prepared in advance for us to do."

(Ephesians 2:8-10)

Messiah has one foot over the Jews and one foot over the Gentile Christians. He alone will knit both groups together during the Messianic Age. And Christians who are confused about *how* He will do this, need only look to His Amazing Grace.

<u>Notes:</u>

1. Chaiyim Ben Ariel, *Why Did Yeshua Use Spit to Heal People?* http://melbournenazareneisrael.ning.com/forum/topics/why-did-yeshua-use-spit-to-heal-people
2. William L. Coleman, *Man for Sabbath or Sabbath for Man?* Eternity, September 1977, p. 58
3. https://www.liveleak.com/view?i=24c_1270331419#HId22WKZuq2cheZs.01; http://www.israelnationalnews.com/News/News.aspx/166255#.UU7sRzetq95
4. Ella LeBain, *Who Is God?* Book Two: *The Lifeforce is in the Blood,* p. 262, Skypath Books, 2015.
5. Ibid., *Who Is God?* Chapter Thirteen: *The Name Above All Names,* p.201-222.

6. Ella LeBain, Book Two*: Who is God?* Chapter Twenty-Nine: *Who Created Sexism*?, pp. 485-500 Skypath Books, 2016
7. Ibid., *Who Is God?* Chapter Twenty-Nine: *Who Created Sexism*?, pp. 485-500 Skypath Books, 2016
8. *Reincarnation: The Church's Biggest Lie*, https://www.facts-are-facts.com/article/reincarnation-the-churchs-biggest-lie
9. Ibid., *Who is God?* Chapter Twenty-Eight: *What Happens When You Die?* pp. 455-484
10. Ella LeBain, *Religion and Religious Spirits*, http://www.findingfreedom.name/religion-and-religious-spirits.html, 2012
11. Ibid., *Who is God?* Chapter Thirteen: *The Name Above All Names*, p.201-232, *What's in a Name?* p. 213, Skypath Books, 2016.
12. Ibid., *Who Is God?* Chapter Twenty-Three: *Babylonian History: Where It All Began*, pp. 367-398.
13. "A searchable list of congregations, ministries, and businesses related to the Messianic Community in Israel." (as of March 2016) http://app.kehilanews.com/directory
14. Ibid., *Who Is God?* Chapter Twenty-Three: *Babylonian History: Where It All Began*, pp. 367-398.
15. Pastor John Hagee, *In Defense of Israel*, FrontLine; Revised edition (September 7, 2007).

CHAPTER NINE
The One World Religion

"He exercises all the authority of the first beast in his presence.
And he makes the earth and those who dwell in it to worship the first beast,
whose fatal wound was healed."
(Revelation 13:12)

The Book of Revelation predicts a mass deception at the end of days, which culminates with the rise of the Antichrist or Counterfeit Messiah. This man receives power and promotion from a religious authority, described as the Whore of Babylon who sits on seven hills. Just about everyone, Protestant, atheist, tourist, knows that Rome and the Vatican sit atop the seven hills of southern Italy. The scriptures tell of a False Prophet who emerges to prepare the way for the Antichrist, through the creation of a One World Religion.

According to Corey Goode, the Nordic extraterrestrials outreach to the world's religious leaders will lead to the birth of a new global religion: He says, "It is FULLY expected that over 90% of people on Earth will adopt this new ET Religion without question." I happen to disagree with Goode's assessment here, as the prophesy states, that only about one quarter of the world follows Antichrist, the rest resist him and/or are succumbed by him, meaning they are persecuted by him because they refuse to worship him.[1]

This falls right into the controversial work of authors Tom Horn and the late Chris Putnam who warned against the Vatican's quiet preparations for open contact with extraterrestrials. In their 2013 book, *Exo-Vaticana* they consider the human-looking extraterrestrials who would be revealed in such an announcement by the Vatican as fallen angel demons in disguise.[2]

Horn and Putnam claim the Bible is the foundation for believing that aliens are demonic entities who intervened destructively in human history, and are prophesied to return. While I agree that the gods of the past are in fact scheduled to return to Earth for a divine appointment, to complete the final battle of their rebellion against the Creator God, and His Son Jesus Christ, and the Hosts of Heaven. This Hosts of Heaven are the Extraterrestrials that did not rebel and join Lucifer, therefore are not demonic.

As I've pointed out in previous books within this series, that when discussing ETs or angels, there are fallen versus the faithful ETs or angels. According to holy scripture, the fallen angels are outnumbered 2:1 by the faithful angels. The scriptures tell us that one third of heavens angelic ETs followed Lucifer in his rebellion against the Most High Creator God, whereas two thirds remained faithful. They are the celestial hosts, the extraterrestrial armies that serve the vast Kingdom of Heaven. They are scheduled to return with their Commander, the Messiah-King, the Lord Jesus Christ at His Second Coming.

All these moves towards disclosure are leading up to the climax of history. At the end of time as we know it, the end of days, occurs the final battle known as Armageddon, when the ET angelic host will meet and witness the defeat of the Antichrist and his army by the Word and His Breath. (2 Thessalonian 2:8)

According to Putnam and Horn, Pope Francis, whom they believe to be the final Pope, called Petrus Romanus or Peter the Roman, is leading the Catholic Church to embrace the returning aliens as brothers in Christ – like the 1950s and 1960s contactees, who believed that the aliens were benevolent space brothers.[3]

While I do believe in End Times Prophesies found in the Jewish Scriptures and the Book of Revelations I must agree with Dr. Salla, in his assessment of Horn and Putnam's profound misunderstandings about extraterrestrials, which stems not only from their misinterpretation of Bible Scriptures, which in fact, records both good and demonic aliens, but also from ignoring alien motivations and activities, which have been well documented by serious researchers. I documented in Book One *Who's Who in the Cosmic Zoo?* the many different types of ETs and Aliens that have been experienced by terrestrial humans in the past seven decades.[4] In it, I went to great lengths to analyze and discern the differences between the general two types that belong to separate competing kingdoms, to prove that not all ETs and aliens stem from the demonic realms, but are in fact involved in their own struggles with the Draconians who seek to enslave all forms of life in the cosmos. I sent a copy of this work to Tom Horn shortly after it was re-released as a Third Edition, but I have only received crickets from them.

There are many people who are in cognitive dissonance over the disclosure of ETs and Earth's Alien presence. However, when evidence is presented by those who know this is happening, and they refuse to let go of their stance which has become a socio-religious agenda, that *all aliens are demons*, one can conclude that they are fear mongering, and not teaching the truth of discernment. Just as there are good and evil humans, there are good and evil aliens. The Bible is crystal clear that there is a celestial space and spiritual war going on over us and planet Earth. This false teaching that all *aliens are demons*, creates resistance to the truth, there are warring factions between alien groups, which is the bottom line of disclosure of ETs and aliens, in my humble opinion. See, Ephesians 6:12.

In Book One, I discerned in great detail *who* were the principalities, rulers of the darkness and spiritual wickedness in the heavens that Ephesians 6:12 states, that we are warring *not* against flesh and blood beings, but against powers, principalities, rulers of the darkness who are Archons of this present world, which I call, the satans, in its plurality. Understanding these facts, is important to equip the saints and the sinners to prepare for the inevitable, a space war, and the real *Star Wars,* which End Times Bible Prophesies point to. Cognitive dissonance of these truths has also been called the Stockholm Syndrome, which refuses to accept this reality.

What Christians need to learn is discernment. Not just discernment of spirits, but to discern rightly the Word of God, which these truths are contained in, but have either been lost in mistranslations coupled with the refusal to accept them, i.e., the Stockholm Syndrome which is a condition that causes hostages to develop a psychological alliance with their captors as a survival strategy during captivity. In this case, by denying the reality of the conflict, and insisting that all aliens are demons, is a type of broad brushing and exopolitical bigotry, that is just as deceptive as New Agers who think ETs are our saviors and are here to save us. Both opposing viewpoints are rooted in spiritual blindness, funda-*mentalism* and denial, which are manipulations by the dark forces to obscure the truth and confuse humans.

According to Dr. Salla's research on the leaked Majestic document, he confirms that U.S. military officials understand there are alien visitors who are benevolent as well as those who are considered foes. Nevertheless, they see themselves as capable of becoming important allies for evolution into a galactic society. Dr. Salla, being the trail blazer in the field of Exopolitics asserts that if Goode's sources are correct, then their plan for world unity take us one step closer to disclosure of extraterrestrial life, with the hopes of ending religious conflict on our planet.[1]

Finally, Salla's conclusions in his own words were: "If the information provided to Goode is accurate, the human looking visitors have secretly played a very significant and benign role in human evolution, and the religious community will likely embrace the information they provide in promoting a new global religion based on oneness." This is what happens when UFO and ET enthusiasts, who want disclosure at all costs, are deceived by their own enthusiasm as to *who* the Lord of lords and King of kings really is, and by their lack of knowledge fall into the mass deception. We were warned through multiple prophesies written down long ago about how the end of this age would conclude, in a mass deception, that would deceive even the elect, if that were possible.

This world will never accept a one world religion until the real Messiah returns and brings Heaven to Earth. Until then, there will be conjecture, striving, half-truths and cover ups of what's really going on and has been going on beneath the surface of this earth for millennia.

A united humanity was God's original plan and in the end, will become manifest as God's Will. Counterfeits have always tried to mimic what God wants, playing into what believers want as well. But uniformity of belief, of religion, implies a recognition of universal Truth, and this no one can counterfeit or mimic. It is the true Messiah who, when He returns, who will fulfill His role of bringing truth, unity, and love to Jew, Gentile and ET all together under One Shephard. See, John 10:16.

Remember, a counterfeit is very close to the real thing. In a bank, tellers are trained by learning the details of the real cash bills before they can spot the counterfeit, some which can only be spotted by viewing through an ultra violet light. This is like putting on our spiritual armor, which comes from the Lord, along with knowing what the Prophecies in the Word do say about extraterrestrials and aliens. This is the purpose of this book series.

The Antichrist agendas to create a one world religion and unity of purpose will be enhanced by the allure of advanced alien technology, to get us terrestrial humans to fall in line and give up our dogmatic religious beliefs, if we want to evolve and become a part of the galactic community. These issues will no doubt be part of the end times mass deception. And might I underscore the fact that, *if* the religious and spiritual communities were able to achieve unity on their own, then the Antichrist Global Religion of Unity and Friendship with all, would not be able to happen.

But as I've exposed through each book in this series, their failure to do so is due to the demonic Religious Spirit, and alien implants which prevent the Churches from having unity even within the same religious denominations, let alone cross denominations lines. With very few exceptions, the Christian community lacks unity in knowledge and unity in spirit. This is one of the counterfeit miracles which the counterfeit messiah achieves before all hell breaks loose, and those who rebel against his evil regime expose him for what he is: the devil in disguise.

By now we can all agree that there is nothing inherently Christian in the belief that all aliens and extraterrestrials are demons. It is scripturally false. As Christians, we go by The Word. The Word is alive. The Living Word became flesh and dwelt among us. (John 1:1) It has been my purpose in this book series to teach discernment, by connecting the dots between the ancient scriptures to today's plethora of documentation of the alien presence on earth. I believe that most of us know this already, and have even come to accept the fact that disclosure widens our view and strengthens our faith. Funda-*mental* viewpoints, lies and cover ups, do not help to learn *who is who in this cosmic zoo.* In fact, funda-*mentalism*, is a type of mental disorder, because it denies the facts that leads to understanding these truths, due to cognitive dissonance and spiritual arrogance. Both of which are exposed and rebuked by Jesus Christ Himself. (Matthew 23:25)

When the Religious Spirit is strong in many believers, it is because they lack a real living and dynamic relationship with the Holy Spirit, who is the revealer of all Truths. The Truth about *who is who* in the clash of these two kingdoms is not a different subject. Truth is truth, and if the church is not preaching the truth, we must question the validity of its identity as a church.

The end time war is about who gets to be the Shephard of this world. The reign of the Antichrist will be short lived because of the very fact that the Lord has deposited *His Spirit* inside His believers, who can discern frauds and counterfeits in a heartbeat. Therefore, this plan of a one world government disguised and precipitated as a one world religion will rise and fall in disgrace, because unity is the antithesis of what it will inevitably create.

But those who desire peace and unity above the truth, and have abandoned knowledge, have already sold their soul to this deception. This is why the Lord warned about the Man of Lawlessness to come, who is the final Antichrist:

> "...and with every wicked deception directed against those who are perishing, because they refused the *love of the truth* that would have *saved them*. For this reason, ***God will send them a powerful delusion so that they will believe the lie***, in order that judgment will come upon all who have disbelieved the truth and delighted in wickedness...."
>
> (2 Thessalonians 2:10-12)

Perhaps, if the Church could achieve unity, put aside their competitive spirits, reject the Religious Spirit, and focus on listening to the Holy Spirit, who is the leader of the Church, then this Great Test known as the Great Tribulation of the Saints, wouldn't need to happen. But just as the Jews need to know *who* is their true Messiah, so do Christians need to learn to discern between listening to counterfeit Religious Spirits over the Holy Spirit, that in God's eyes, justifies the coming Tribulation period as an important lesson for those who inherit the Kingdom of Heaven coming to Earth after the real *Star Wars* is fought and won by the Lord of the Cosmos at the return of Jesus Christ and His Host of Extraterrestrials Angel Armies.

Notes:

1. Michael E. Salla, Ph.D., *World Religions Unite as Prelude to Extraterrestrial Disclosure,* http://exopolitics.org/world-religions-unite-as-prelude-to-extraterrestrial-disclosure/ June 22, 2017

2. Tom Horn, Cris Putnam, *Exo-Vaticana, Petrus Romanus, Project L.U.C.I.F.E.R., and the Vatican's Astonishing Plan for the Arrival of an Alien Savior,* Defender, 2013.
3. Tom Horn, Cris Putnam, *Petrus Romanus, The Final Pope is Here,* Defender, 2012.
4. Ella LeBain, *Who's Who in the Cosmic Zoo?* Book One – Third Edition, Chapter Four: *How to Tell Who is Who?* p. 85-92, Tate, 2013.

CHAPTER TEN

Racism Was Created by the Fallen feuding ETS

"As Above, So Below."
~ Hermetic Law

The Creator God allowed many different star beings to seed this blue world we call our own, experimenting with diversity. The idea behind this *grand experiment* was that of ultimate salvation; to see if all these different genetic remixes could work together, help each other find salvation through the Cosmic Christ. It served the dual purpose of bringing everyone together on earth and in the heavens, to pull together, for the glory of God.

We reflect on the differing creation myths as different facets of a stained-glass window; same picture, different perspective. The many star races may have altered, engineered, modified the basic structure of human DNA to better interact with their own, thus branding their own experiment. There is a great deal of evidence, more discovered every day, that suggests multiple origins for our single species.

The fact of the matter is that at present we understand only about 3% of the human genome and the information it carries. The rest, a whopping 97% of our DNA, is considered by scientists as 'junk DNA' because they haven't a clue as to how to put it together. It is my stated opinion that the junk holds many clues, answers, and proofs of genetic manipulations of our ancestral past.

With this said, we must investigate and discern the huge differences between human, humanlike, and humanoids.

Prof. Sam Chang, the group leader of the Human Genome Project says, "the so-called 97% non-coding sequences in human DNA is no less than the genetic code of extraterrestrial life forms. The non-coding sequences are common to all living organisms on Earth, from molds to fish to humans. In human DNA, they constitute larger part of the total genome."[1]

"Non-coding sequences, originally known as 'junk DNA', were discovered years ago, and their function remained a mystery. The over-whelming majority of Human

DNA is 'Off-world' in origin. Professor Chang had wondered if the apparently 'junk Human DNA' was created by some kind of 'extraterrestrial programmer'. The alien chunks within Human DNA, 'have its own veins, arteries, and its own immune system that vigorously resists all our anti-cancer drugs.'"

Professor Chang and his research colleagues showed that this apparently extraterrestrial programming gaps in DNA sequencing precipitated by a hypothesized rush to create human life on Earth presented humankind with "illogical growth of mass of cells we know as cancer." Professor Chang further indicates that "what we see in our DNA is a program consisting of two versions, a big code and basic code." Mr. Chang then affirms that the "first fact is, the complete 'program' which was positively not written on Earth; that is now a verified fact. The second fact is, that genes by themselves are not enough to explain evolution; there must be something more in 'the game'." "Sooner or later," Professor Chang says, "we have to come to grips with the unbelievable notion that every life on Earth carries genetic code for his extraterrestrial cousin and that evolution is not what we think it is."

Professor Chang further indicates that "if we think about it in our human terms, the apparent "extraterrestrial programmers" were most probably working on "one big code" consisting of several projects, and the projects should have produced various life forms for various planets." Professor Chang's team of researchers furthermore conclude that, "the apparent 'extraterrestrial programmers' may have been ordered to cut all their idealistic plans for the future when they concentrated on the 'Earth project' to meet the pressing deadline. Very likely in an apparent rush, the 'extraterrestrial programmers' may have cut down drastically on big code and delivered basic program intended for Earth." Professor Chang is only one of many scientists and other researchers who have discovered extraterrestrial origins to Humanity.

Professor Chang's conclusion, that the "extraterrestrial programmers" had to economize their program, may not be the real reason why earth humans have only two strands of DNA operating, with ten strands missing as 'alien junk DNA.'[1]

Early Genetic Experiments by Annunaki Gods

One of the Sumerian tablets, interpreted by Zecharia Sitchin, says that a group of extraterrestrials known as the Annunaki, Nibiruans, created a slave race to serve to mine the earth for natural resources, such as gold and other precious metals, that they needed for their spaceships and home planet. These Annunaki created a hierarchy in the core group of created human slaves, separating them, and forbidding most from sharing in their advanced knowledge by creating a religious structure. The created humans can then worship the Annunaki. These beings, along with the rest of the fallen extraterrestrials and rebel angels, all have a god complex and a lust for human worship.

What is suggested here is that these beings may in fact have downgraded the capabilities of the human race by rendering 10 strands of DNA inert and inactive, so that we are controllable, and could not realize our superhuman traits that were originally given to us by the Elohim.

Some researchers and channelers have suggested that genus homo sapiens originally possessed a 12-strand DNA, which reflects the genetic programming of the creator gods, who said in Genesis 1:26, "And God said, Let us make man in *our* image, after *our* likeness: and let them have dominion over the fish of the sea, and over the fowl of the air, and over the cattle, and over all the earth, and over every creeping thing that creeps on the earth." The Hebrew word used for God here is *Elohim*, which is plural for the children of God, or more specifically, the children of *El*. The *Elohim* are also known as a pantheon of gods, considered superhuman by earth human standards, and this is most likely the origin of the 12-strand DNA.

Because man was originally designed to be the steward and ruler of planet Earth, as Genesis says, he was to have dominion. This commandment or covenant did not sit well with the god of this world, Lucifer the Satan, or his rebel extraterrestrials angels. They battle for control over terrestrial humans' soul energy, and the control of planet earth through terrestrial human vessels by a multi-pronged assault on corrupting the human vessel. The battle is compartmentalized to the hybridization program using human and alien DNA to replace terrestrial humans and rule the earth. Whether or not this genetic plan is achieved but for a very brief time, the End Times Prophesies say, that the God of gods sends the Lord of lords to earth to finish this battle of humankind once and for all.

This is essentially the crux of the matter, the seed cause of the cosmic drama, as terrific spiritual battles have been fought over dominion of the earth. Several rebel extraterrestrials, among them the Annunaki, the Nibiruans, and the Draconians, aligned themselves with Lucifer the Satan and entered into an agreement with him to genetically manipulate, and downgrade the capabilities of the human kind. Their aim was simply slavery. By deprogramming 10 strands of DNA, they stripped earthly humanity of all supernormal powers, making it vulnerable to being controlled and manipulated by these cosmic bullies.

Another theory floating out there amongst the Christian Fringe, on our missing 10 strands of DNA, the scattered remains of which may be known as 'junk DNA, put forward by Thomas Horn, is that,

> "spiritually, the enemy (Satan) has ever sought to corrupt God's plan. Originally, fallen angels lay with human women to corrupt the original base pair arrangements. Our genome is filled with "junk DNA" that seemingly encodes for nothing. These "introns" may be the remains of the corrupted

genes, and God Himself may have switched them off when fallen angels continued their program, post-Flood. If so, today's scientists might need only to "switch them back on" to resurrect old forms such as gibborim and nephilim." [2] [sic]

Our ignorance and confusion as to which god did what to our DNA, is another reason for racism and its fear mongering. Here's what's happened to us, one group of gods, the Elohim created us perfect, with all twelve strands of DNA, essentially just like them, beings of light, in our 'glory' bodies, which is what the Second Adam, who is the Messiah is going to restore when he returns, the ascension of the redeemed into their incorruptible glory bodies. However, when the fall of man happened in the Genesis story; humankind, the earth, the man, the woman and the serpent were all put under a curse by the Creator El, El Elyon, the God Almighty, he's the God of gods, the God of the Elohim. So, through the covenant of His curse, the enemies of the Elohim, who are the Annunaki were given permission by the god of this world, who is Lucifer/Satan to use humankind and turn them into their slaves. This is evidenced in the Sumerian story in the Cuneiform tablets and written in the Enuma Elish.

What the Annunaki actually did to humankind, was genetically manipulate humans by *downgrading* the Elohim DNA from 12 strands to 2 strands, by disabling 10 strands of DNA. This is what Yeshua/Jesus came to restore, in his promise to give his redeemed *incorruptible glory bodies,* these are the ascended light bodies that, so many New Agers envision, but in order for them to have it, they must be in right standing with the Messiah, who is Yeshua/Jesus. It's important here, that people do take sides, because being on the wrong side of this war, could mean extinction of your kind as well as ultimate destruction of your soul, if it has not been saved by the Kinsmen Redeemer, Yeshua.

Recent scientific discoveries have proved that what scientists have long referred to as "junk DNA" they now see are disabled codes that could be switched on at any time. The 'God' particle has been found and scientists are learning how to activate certain genes. As I've said in Book One, science is being proved as the very *mind* of God. This is what the gene wars between the gods have been about, having the *knowledge* of how to switch on or switch off genetic codes, and create life through the manipulation and hybridization of DNA between two or more species.[3, 4]

Can you imagine if it was that easy? If Horn is right, there are many humans carrying recessive Nephilim genes, which could really spell disaster! It's enough that we humans have to contend with their evil spirits which possess, oppress and torment us, but now we could discover that many of us carry dormant genes from the Elohim, as well. This is what is being activated in the awakening starseeds within the starchildren and wayshowers now. I was shown, that giants were allowed to reincarnate as today's terrestrial earth human. Clearly, when you look at humans who are extraordinarily of a tall and broad stature, they are here to work off their karma and find the path of Christ and service to others, in human bodies., And yes, the fact that they are head and shoulders above the rest, they do carry genetics that scripts tallness which could very well be a recessive gigantic gene.

After all, as an Evadamic race, we were originally created in their image and in their likeness. (Genesis 1:27) For discernment purposes, the Elohim were not the Annunaki. The Elohim came from the human vine from the Lyra system, the Annunaki are the Serpent Race, they are actually ancient enemies.[5] See, *Anakim, Annunaki,* p. 219-222, Book One of *Who's Who in the Cosmic Zoo?*

This grand experiment has inevitably created racial tensions, because of the contention between the creator races who vie for dominance and favor with Lucifer the Satan. We know that 200 of the sons of God fell from heaven to mate with earth women, which engendered many genetic anomalies, including the giants, demigods and monsters, and the Nephilim. These fallen sons of heaven were condemned by the Creator God for sinning against humankind. Their genetic seed, the Nephilim, was wiped out during the great deluge. However, the genetic experiments and the rebellion against the Creator God continued after the floods, as the Annunaki recast a race of humans as a slave race. Several reptilian interventions and genetic takeovers later, we recognized a control group known as the Israelites, also known as the Jews.

This group who were *chosen* to represent *who* God was, through expressing His DNA over the animal nature, which is why the spiritual side of Judaism expressed through Chabad, is about cultivating the character traits and soul qualities of *chesed,* which is Mercy/Loving-Kindness, *binah,* which is Understanding, and *da'at,* which is Knowledge. Combined you have soul essence of what the true Jew is supposed to be and express through *mitzvot,* which are good deeds, good works, serving family and community. Does not the gospel reiterate that in Ephesians 2:10, "For we are God's handiwork, created in Christ Jesus to do good works, which God prepared in advance for us to do."

So, the Lord had a plan to help them, by putting His Spirit in them, which He promised to do for all who turn to Him, in the New Covenant, by *grafting* the Gentile Nations into the *rooted Tree* of Israel and His First Covenant with Abraham. Ezekiel 36:27, "And I will put my Spirit in you and move you to follow my decrees and be careful to keep my laws."

And with His Indwelling Spirit, came His promise to give them a land of their own, as promised in Ezekiel 37:14, "I will put my Spirit in you and you will live, and I will settle you in your own land. Then you will know that I the LORD have spoken, and I have done it, declares the LORD."

Yahuah's Genetic Experiment

Yahuah created the Israelites, as Jews are technically a race unto themselves. No wonder the Jews are so diverse! They originated from twelve tribes, although only the tribe of Judah is remembered in the term *Jew*. There's an old joke by Rodney Dangerfield, "You put two Jews in a room, you end up with ten opinions." Joe Kovacs writes in his book, *Shocked by the Bible,* that the twelve tribes of Israel and Abraham, Isaac and Jacob were not Jewish, but consecrated by the Lord Yahuah.[6] The Jewish people were an experiment by the Lord Yahuah.

What is so interesting about the origins of the twelve tribes of Israel is that nearly all the mothers of the progenitors were barren. They all cried out to the Lord to give them a child, and Yahuah intervened, and they all became miraculously pregnant. Sarah, Abraham's wife, who bore Isaac; and Rebecca, the mother of Esau and Jacob, who later became known as Israel; and Leah and Rachel, Jacob's wives who were both barren; were all visited by the Lord and miraculously became pregnant. The Bible says that when Rachel cried out to the Lord for a child, that the Lord 'opened the womb' of both Leah and Rachel. This phrase could mean anything from performing minor surgery to restoring natural fertility, to using artificial insemination, embryo implantation, or some other means to achieve pregnancy. [7]

Jacob (Israel) had twelve sons with four women. He had six sons through Leah, who were Reuben, Simeon, Levi, Judah, Zebulun, and Issachar. He had four sons through his wives' handmaids, who were Dan, Gad, Asher, and Naphtali. He had two sons through Rachel, who were Joseph and Benjamin. These twelve sons all led the twelve tribes of Israel. All were born through infertile women who miraculously became pregnant through the Lord Yahuah. The entire Old Testament is about tracing their genealogies, who were called holy children and 'children of the Holy seed.' All their deeds, and misdeeds, were recorded as well as their many interactions with the Lord and His angels (extraterrestrial messengers).

They became known as the Israelites, and only the tribe of Judah are in fact *Jews*. They were both blessed and cursed by Yahuah. They were set apart from the rest of the human race on the earth at that time, to live by the laws of the Yahuah, which were given to Moses through the ten commandments and the Torah. They were commanded not to intermarry with other races, but to stay pure. This of course did not happen the way Yahuah wanted it to, and there were many who were seduced by false gods and practiced idolatry in the eyes of Yahuah and were then cursed and given up to their enemies for their disobedience.

The story we're told in Genesis Chapter 25, Abraham begat Isaac, who then had a son named Jacob (*Ya'acov,* in Hebrew) which means, *one who takes by the heel*, or 'heel catcher', because he struggled with his twin brother Esau and grabbed him by the heel leaving the womb. When Jacob was older he struggled with the angel who is described as a man, and held on to him before he let him go back up his ladder which led to his space ship. Jacob was then given a new name, Israel, which means, 'he who struggles with God and prevails".

Then Israel had twelve sons, who became the twelve tribes of Israel. The 'Israelites' were born. Rachel, who was barren and miraculously conceived, was been implanted by the Elohim chosen to give birth to a son named Judah (*Yehuda*), which means, "praise", who started the tribe of Judah, who were also called 'Judes' and later truncated to 'Jews'. *Praise* signifies the chosen ones who became the Jews, because the foundation of Judaism is to give praise and thanks to the Lord at all times. "Let His Praise forever be on my lips." (Psalm 34:1) Additionally, the Old Testament tells us the story of how Israel was split into two kingdoms; the Kingdom of Israel and the Kingdom of Judah. Israel became a ten-tribe group in the northern territory; Israel, Reuben, Simeon, Dan, Naphtali, Gad, Asher, Issachar, Zebulun and Joseph.

However, in the southern region, Judah was made up of three tribes, Judah, Benjamin and Levi, all sons of Rachel, who had 'miraculous' conceptions after being visited by an angel. All these three tribes were then collectively known as *the Jews* because they were of the kingdom of Judah. All the tribes added up to thirteen, because the tribe of Joseph was given a double portion as a special blessing, the names of those tribes being Ephraim and Manasseh, the two sons of Joseph. The very first instance in the Old Testament we see the word 'Jews' was when Israel was at war with the Jews was in 2 Kings 16:5, "The Rezin king of Syria and Pekah son of Remaliah king of Israel came up to Jerusalem to war; and they besieged Ahaz, but could not overcome him."

Remaliah, the king of Israel, went to war against the Jews of the kingdom of Judah, whose king was Ahaz. At the very first indication of Jews, we find that Israel was in conflict with the Jews. While the southern Kingdom became known as the people of Judah, or Jews, their northern cousins held on to the name Israel. Eventually both kingdoms fell under attack of different foreign nations, Israel falling victim to the Assyrians in 721 B.C. and Judah was invaded by the Babylonians in 586 B.C.

The Northern Kingdom of Israel never returned to its rightful land, and became known as the lost ten tribes of Israel. The Jews, however, did return to Jerusalem after their Babylonian captivity, which is why at the time when Jesus Christ was born, the land was filled again with Jews, and the region was known as Judaea, not Israel. Of course, the Jewish religion united all Jews at the time, and when their messiah appeared to them and they rejected Him, they lost their land again. The Jews were exiled for nearly another 1,950 years after Christ, when the prophesy of Ezekiel 37 "the Valley of the Dry Bones', was revived and reborn again, as fulfilled on May 14, 1948. On that day, the State of Israel was formed as a homeland for the Jews, after they had received their worse punishment ever during the Nazi Holocaust.

There is racism in the cosmos. This racism originates from the competition resultant from genetic experiments by the fallen angels who set themselves up as gods, not just on Earth but on other planets in other star systems that cosmic evil permeates. These fallen extraterrestrials continue to compete in a war against the Creator, many of whom are fighting battles over earth, its denizens and its real estate, as well as certain portals.

The fallen angel gods are responsible for pitting one group of their genetic experiment against the other. If the gods were all on the same page, which they are not, we would be as well.

Throughout the Old Testament there has always been a consistent battle over the "seed" of Yahuah, versus the seeds of other nations. Did fallen angel demons land on Mt. Hermon in Phoenicia, now Israel, to pollute the human race, thus provoking God's anger? Are the UFO's of today the proof that these fallen angel demons, whom some call Watchers, are building up their forces for a final battle with the Lord? Are these bad angels using created matter to embody themselves?

Transgenics-Transhumans

According to I.D.E. Thomas in his *The Omega Conspiracy: Satan's Last Assault on God's Kingdom*, Satan was trying to produce a race of mutant warriors to exterminate the Jewish race, preventing the arrival of the Messiah, back in biblical times. Thomas goes on to say that he was even attempting to alter the human image away from that of God, into his own likeness. Although Satan failed, because Yeshua was born and fulfilled his unique destiny for humankind, this has not deterred Satan from trying again.[8]

Of course, each time the Nephilim walked the earth, both during the times of Atlantis and again, during the time of Noah, they were destroyed through floods. When they returned yet again during the time of Sodom and Gomorrah, because the Lord had promised never to flood the earth, they were taken out through 'fire from heaven'. This may describe a nuclear attack on both cities, obliterating them completely. To this day, archeologist still detect higher levels of radioactivity in that part of the Middle East.

This time, in their current attack, the Nephilim are more streamlined. They will not look like giant monsters as they have in the past, but will look human enough to blend in with us without suspicion. This is the reason for the alien abductions and the harvesting of human ova, sperm, skin and DNA. Satan and his fallen angels have been working on the new and improved Nephilim.

The fulfillment of the first prophecy, "And I will put enmity between you and the woman, and between your seed and her seed; it shall bruise your head, and you shall bruise his heel," (Genesis 3:15) indicates that Jesus Christ was the seed of the woman.

The seed of the serpent will be the incarnation of the beast of Revelation 13:1, the son of perdition, the antichrist. When this decree was spoken by the Lord, supernatural beings, fallen angels and rebellious ETs, performed alterations on human DNA to intercept, pollute, and cut off the birth line of the coming Messiah. This theme permeated history, as Pharaoh destroyed all the Hebrew babies to block the deliver's birth, and Herod tried to kill the baby Jesus, just as the dragon of Revelation 12 waits to destroy the seed of the woman as soon as it is born. It is my opinion that Lucifer the Satan contracted with supernatural beings, the Annunaki, the Reptilian aliens, to alter the human race, to prevent Christ from being born.

Daniel's prophecy, coupled with Genesis 3, provides the proof that Lucifer the Satan has genetic seed and his seed is in enmity with Christ, the seed of Yahuah. The word used for seed in Hebrew is *zera* which means, "offspring, descendants, children." Daniel's prophecy about the last and final world empire reiterates the fulfillment of the seed of Satan.

> "And whereas you saw iron mixed with miry clay, they shall mingle themselves with the seed of men: but they shall not join one to another, even as iron is not mixed with clay."
>
> (Daniel 2:43)

Thomas Horn asks in his book *Nephilim Stargates*, "who are the 'non-seed' that are 'mingling with the seed of men?"[9] Scripture doesn't say anything about non-seeds being anything but kingdoms. It can be construed to mean the peoples of those kingdoms, but that doesn't hold water when we see that our respective races CAN and DO produce vital offspring which can in turn reproduce themselves.

In my opinion, the 'non-seed' are the clones, the Grays, i.e., the robots. Iron mixed with clay. Robots mixed with flesh, kind of like the Borg. These are the new Nephilim, the product of the human-alien hybrid. The mingling of seed is related to "vital energy" or created matter used by ultra-dimensionals to create a body they can use to enter the third dimension. These are known as 'transgenics' or 'transhumans.'"

According to Horn, the Watchers were supernatural ETs who descended to earth and used antediluvian cell matter, including women, animals, and plants, to construct for themselves portals, or openings through which they extended themselves into the material world, bringing with them physical and psychotronic warfare.[9]

> "After the fallen angels went into the daughters of men, [then] the sons of men taught the mixture of animals of one species with the other, in order to provoke the Lord."
>
> (Jasher 4:18)

Another mystery is that the *Book of Jasher,* which is referred to in both the book of Joshua (10:13) and the second book of Samuel (1.18) in the Old Testament, is not included in the Bible. What did the church fathers find so intimidating in what was the Word of God over 3,000 years ago? They failed to canonize Jasher's book, yet his records show in great detail the chain of events from the creation of Adam and Eve through the Jews returning to Israel after Moses. Jasher records the mixing of species, which coincides with Genesis 6 mixing of human and animal DNA, in experiments to hybridizing species, with the intention of altering creation from Divine Order. All resulting in the judgment and wrath from God.

The *Book of Enoch* tells us that the fallen angels didn't stop with mixing their DNA with that of earth women, but that "they began to sin against birds, and beasts, and reptiles, and fish" (Enoch 7:5; 6). This is how the many different types of Nephilim were created, with giant size, supernatural strength, multiple arms, six fingers and six toes, human-like beings with the heads of lions, falcons, bulls, even elephants and crocodiles, many of which were later deified into gods. Sekhmet, Bastet, Horus, Ganeesha, Sabik, all the multi-armed Hindu gods and goddesses, may be genetic abominations. It's important to remember that all these creatures were considered an abomination to the Creator God and were all destroyed.

We are told through the *Book of Enoch* that their spirits were bound to the earth, and became the evil spirits that torment humans to this very day. Even more intriguing, these Nephilim became gods of various religions who are invoked and worshipped till this day.

According to Horn, 'the reason the "Watchers" might have been transgenically blending their species with human DNA as well as animal and plant DNA (various living organisms) remains a mystery, but it is curiously compelling in light of modern transgenic and similar well-funded research. Are we seeing the fulfillment of prophecy? "As it was in the days of Noah..." (Luke 17:26)?"[9] [132]

The entire scripture reads, 'As it was in the days of Noah, so also will it be leading up to the days of the Son of Man', which implies that events transpiring during the days preceding the Flood will again occur just before the return of Christ. The types of transgenic experiments that may have been going on during the days of Noah were the cause of Gods wrath, that came pouring down to wipe all things away in a catastrophic flood. These miscegenations may well be repeating themselves even now, but definitely will be in the days leading up to the second coming of Jesus Christ.

What Horn is explaining is that in his opinion, we are already there now. Based on the vast amount of scientific research going on with respect to genetics, actual transgenics and transhumans are being produced all around the planet. This is also revealing as to the real purpose behind human abductions and cattle mutilations, which is to produce the new Nephilim, the ultimate human/alien hybrid, the transhuman.

The following are some quotes from an article entitled "Transhumans," which appeared in the Daily Mail (U.K.) at the end of July 2011:

> "Scientists have created more than 150 human-animal hybrid embryos in British laboratories. The hybrids have been produced secretively over the past three years by researchers looking into possible cures for a wide range of diseases ...
>
> "Figures seen by the Daily Mail show that 155 'admixed' embryos, containing both human and animal genetic material, have been created since the introduction of the 2008 Human Fertilization Embryology Act.
>
> "Professor Robin Lovell-Badge, from the Medical Research Council's National Institute for Medical Research, said the scientists were not concerned about human-animal hybrid embryos because by law these have to be destroyed within 14 days...
>
> "Human-animal hybrids are also created in other countries, many of which have little or no regulation."

Transhumanism is an international, intellectual, and cultural movement supporting the use of science and technology to improve human mental and physical characteristics and capacities—in essence, to create a posthuman society. Transhumanist programs are sponsored in institutions such as Oxford, Stanford, and Caltech. Sponsorships come from organizations such as Ford, Apple, Intel, Xerox, Sun Microsystems, and others. DARPA, (Defense Advanced Research Projects Agency), a technical department within the U.S. Department of Defense is also involved in transhumanist projects.

Today's New Nephilim

The modern Nephilim is a new race of alien/human hybrids, or hubrids, which many abductees report as being raised off-planet, in spaceships, until the appointed time for them to be integrated. They are being trained, educated, and groomed for life on planet earth at a future time. Some abductees have been sold on the idea that these are new bodies suitable for space faring beings, unlike the organic bodies which we have now, and that these new bodies will serve humanity to populate and take over other earths in the future. Many will be able to be incarnated or downloaded into these new bodies. Some of this may even be true, but when it comes to the reputation of the grays there are lies mixed up with half-truths, most of us know they are not to be trusted.

The modern Nephilim are not giants, nor do they look like monsters, but have instead certain Lilliputian qualities which they get from the gray alien humanoids. They are generally slim, with chiseled facial features, and large mesmerizing eyes, charming eyes, human yet almost fairy like in appearance. They are attractive, so we humans can accept them, yet there is something inside of them that is virulently antihuman. Their alien programming is so subtle that they can blend in with human society in professional roles, such as teacher, computer analyst, pharmacist, doctor, caregiver, science technician, just about anything.

The purpose of the Nephilim in the past was to exterminate God's people. While the ancient Nephilim looked intimidating, with protruding teeth, two sets of them, six fingers and toes, super strong giants with animal heads or multiple arms, they were destroyed. The Book of Enoch tell us that the remains of the ancient enemies have become the evil spirits that roam the earth. The Nephilim of the future are instead geeky, clumsy enough to charm and disarm us, but who inside are emotionally cold, detached and spiritually void of real power.

The evil plan is for them to replace humans on earth. They will begin to take over many key positions in society, professions that they can easily be used by the demonic forces of the New World Order. The Plan is to establish a global socialist government and a universal religion. The Nephilim share a hive-mind mentality, so the Satanic plan of creating global socialism can be easily achieved by exchanging the human spirit for a Borg-like techno-being, programmed and incapable of thinking for itself. The future Nephilim-human-borg will not be able to hear the voice of Spirit, or express any form of individualism.

The purpose of the alien abductions of humans is a genetic harvest, gathering DNA, ovum and sperm, skin and hair, as well as memories, to create an alien/human hybrid that can be programmed. Similar in nature to the Borg in *Star Trek*, all the implants and technology are *inside* the being. The outer appearance is human, with a kind of Starchild look to it, with those big eyes, but human enough to completely blend in with the culture and society of us humans on the surface of the earth. This new Nephilim is programmed to imitate and replace us and then to help facilitate the plans of the New World Order, the reign of the Beast, the False Prophet to the final Antichrist. This is all part of the Grand Experiment, which will turn out to be a failure in the end, but the dark forces have been hard at work to give it all they've got in what will amount to their last hurrah.

The Bible says, the Antichrist will be the 'son of perdition,' the male progeny of the Greek *apoleia,* or Apollyon. (John 17:12; 2 Thessalonians 2:3)

Apollyon is the Angel of the Abyss and according to Revelation is a king of a terrible army of locusts. "They have as king over them, the angel of the Abyss; his name in Hebrew is Abaddon, and in the Greek, he has the name Apollyon." (Revelation 9:11) Interesting scriptural address, 9:11, which stands for a 'wake-up call' to danger. Abaddon in Hebrew and Apollyon in Greek both mean *destroyer.* The inference is a fallen angel, who is now an alien, living *inside* the earth, a destroyer demon, a transgenic of the highest order will emerge and take over the body of a man, couldn't be clearer-the Man of Sin will be the hybrid offspring of the destroyer demon. These beliefs go as far back as the Lutheran Reformation.

Abaddon or Apollyon is the Beast who ascends from the Abyss. Revelation 9:1-11, Abaddon (Apollyon) is clearly identified as the king of the evil alien spirits released from the Abyss. This fact helps us follow him throughout the rest of the book of Revelation. Twice specifically, and once symbolically, Abaddon (Apollyon) is referred to as the Beast who is to come up out of the Abyss:

> "When they [the two witnesses] have finished their testimony, the beast that comes up out of the Abyss will make war with them, and overcome them and kill them."
>
> (Revelation 11:7)

> "The beast that you saw was, and is not, and is to ascend from the bottomless pit (Abyss) and go to perdition . . . "
>
> (Revelation 17:8)

> "Then I stood on the sand of the sea. And I saw a beast rising up out of the sea."
>
> (Revelation 13:1)

Revelation 11:7 and 17:8 are clearly referring to Abaddon (Apollyon) as the beast who will ascend from the bottomless pit. What we see described in the first part of Revelation 13:1 is a symbolic reference to the release of Abaddon (Apollyon) from the Abyss.

In Jewish thought, and even today, the depths of the ocean are frequently referred to as the Abyss. *The New Unger's Bible Dictionary*, which is the Greek translation of the Hebrew Scriptures in use at the time of Christ, "renders the Hebrew word, *tehom*, as 'the primeval ocean' (Genesis 1:2; Psalms 24:2; etc.) as 'abyss'" (p. 18, "Abyss"). This identification of Abaddon (Apollyon) as the primary beast mentioned in the book of Revelation as coming out of the sea, as well as being the king and fallen angel of the Abyss helps us to track his activities in the end-time, especially when he is released to the surface of the earth.

It is most instructive to note Apollyon's charge, which the preceding scriptures describes to us as the nastiest alien creatures ever created. These trans-genetic, semi-mechanical borgs were sent out of the Abyss to torment all those who did not have the mark of God on their foreheads. More Nephilim?

> "The locusts looked like horses prepared for battle. On their heads, they wore something like crowns of gold, and their faces resembled human faces. Their hair was like women's hair, and their teeth were like lions' teeth. They had breastplates like breastplates of iron, and the sound of their wings was like the thundering of many horses and chariots rushing into battle. They had tails with stingers, like scorpions, and in their tails, they had power to torment people for five months. They had as king over them the angel of the Abyss, whose name in Hebrew is Abaddon and in Greek is Apollyon (that is, Destroyer)." (Revelation 9:7-11)

This description of heavily armored, robotic creatures, which fly through the air with a loud sound, and stingers on their tales like UFOs, remind me of *War of the Worlds*, but worse.

This fallen angel king of the Abyss plays a huge role in establishing the Satanic kingdom on the earth, which the Bible tells us will last for 42 months (Revelation 3:15) (Dan. 7:25; 12:7). Many scholars believe that he will empower the being known as the Antichrist, because of the similarities of Daniel's prophesies which relate to the Antichrist speaking great blasphemies against the Most High God and boasting and placing himself in the temple and demanding the world worship him as God and Savior. This act is referred to by Daniel as the Abomination of Desolation, which immediately precedes destruction.

> "And I will grant authority to my two witnesses, and they will prophesy for twelve hundred and sixty days, clothed in sackcloth......When they have finished their testimony, the beast that comes up out of the Abyss will make war with them, and overcome them and kill them."
>
> (Revelation 11:3)

The final curtain call will rise when Lucifer and his fallen angels create a new version of superhuman Nephilim. Empowered by the fallen angel king of the Abyss, who pretends to be the world's Messiah and masquerades as the Christ, he displays all kinds of signs, supernatural wonders, and miracles, and deceives many into thinking that their savior has returned. He goes on to deceive the world and Israel into worshipping him, the counterfeit Christ, the final Antichrist. As Jesus was the seed of the woman, as predicted in Genesis 3:15, the Antichrist will be the seed of the serpent. This is why Revelation 13.1 calls him a 'beast', as he is not human. He is a transgenic of the serpent seed combined with human DNA. Most people will not recognize him as the ultimate Nephilim incarnation, as a beast, because they will be deceived by his snake-like charm, his beautiful appearance, skillful diplomacy, sharp intelligence and overawed by the supernatural powers that he seems to possess.

He will be seen as the savior of the world, an economic genius who will solve the ailing global economy with seemingly simplicity, a giant compared to all who preceded him. With these accomplishments, he will rise to be a world leader, and fulfill the prophesies of Daniel 8, turning into an evil king who will punish all those who refuse to worship him. Revelation 13:17 tells us that he will implement a global economy in which no one may buy or sell anything without his mark, 'the mark of the beast'.

Most scholars agree that this will most likely be a visible implant or a tattoo, placed in either the hand or the forehead. Revelation also tells us that if anyone takes this mark they will not be allowed to enter into the coming Kingdom of God or the New Jerusalem.

> "A third angel followed them and said in a loud voice: "If anyone worships the beast and his image and receives his mark on the forehead or on the hand, he, too, will drink of the wine of God's fury, which has been poured full strength into the cup of his wrath. He will be tormented with burning sulfur in the presence of the holy angels and of the Lamb. And the smoke of their torment rises forever and ever. <u>There is no rest day or night for those who worship the beast and his image, or for anyone who receives the mark of his name</u>."
>
> (Revelation 14:9 – 11)

It is a permanent mark, implying ownership, voluntarily applied to our forehead or right hand. Anyone who takes the mark will be eternally lost. It is the mark of eternal destruction. In the age of digital technology, the satisfaction of financial obligations, the paying of bills online, paperless billing via email, is so easy, so simple, so innocent. Today nearly every account has a credit or debit card attached to it, even a simple checking account. Writing checks has all but been phased out, even the federal reserve system is basically digital. Any failure to pay up could be disastrous. You are a non-entity if you refuse to Face Book, be 'Linked In', or to join the global financial system. The only way out of this future disaster is to accept the Lord Jesus Christ, and be saved. Many will be martyred for not accepting this mark, only to wake up in the Kingdom of Heaven.

Notes:

1. John Stokes, *Scientists find Extraterrestrial genes in Human DNA,* http://www.agoracosmopolitan.com/home/Frontpage/2007/01/08/01288.html, 2007 The Canadian.
2. Thomas Horn, *Apollyon Rising*, Defender Publishing, p. 238
3. Alok Jha, *Breakthrough Study Overturns Theory of 'Junk DNA' in Genome,* https://www.theguardian.com/science/2012/sep/05/genes-genome-junk-dna-encode, Science Correspondent, September 2012
4. Michael Hanlon, *'Junk DNA' and the Mystery of Mankind's Missing Genes.* http://www.telegraph.co.uk/news/science/9534185/Junk-DNA-and-the-mystery-of-mankinds-missing-genes.html, Sept. 2012.
5. Ella LeBain, Book One of *Who's Who in the Cosmic Zoo?* Third Edition, *Anakim, Annunaki,* p. 219-222, Tate, 2013.
6. Joe Kovacs, *Shocked by the Bible,* WND, 2008, p. 186-188
7. Ann Madden Jones, *The Yahweh Encounters: Bible Astronauts, Ark Radiations and Temple Electronics,* The Sandbird Publishing Group, 1995, p. 60
8. I.D.E. Thomas, *The Omega Conspiracy: Satan's Last Assault on God's Kingdom,* Official Disclosure, December 1, 2007.
9. Thomas Horn, *Nephilim Stargates,* Defender, 2007.

CHAPTER ELEVEN

Genetic Engineering and Alien Abductions in Prophesy

"Humans have long since possessed the tools for crafting a better world.
Where love, compassion, altruism and justice have failed,
genetic manipulation will not succeed."
Gina Maranto, *Quest for Perfection*

The ancient texts tell of intelligent beings that claimed to be the progenitors of human history. How many gods tried their hand at the genetic engineering and manipulation of us humans? Did they create karma with the earth and with humans? Are some of these ancient extra-terrestrials still working on their karmic ties with us humans today by acting benevolently toward us? What if more than one group comes forward during the Revelation and they all claim to be our creator gods?

The following information about the Bene Elohim, or the Sons of the sons of God, the pantheon of God, is very important to us today. It is vital that we know where we stand, prophetically speaking. Both Matthew 24:37, and Luke 17:26-30, quote Jesus as specifically stating that the end times will be recognized by a return of the activities of the days of Noah. What typified the days of Noah? Fallen angels inbreeding with humans!

Satan's initial plan of attack to prevent the birth of Christ was to pollute the seed of humanity. He had his minions develop a master race of warriors, chaotic, and utterly evil. Scripture tells us that these beings were capable, by sheer brute force, of taking any women they chose, and killing all who would defy them. They also ate human flesh. This inspired cannibalism in the human population, which was another of the abominations that angered the Creator God, who had to destroy them all with the great deluge. The Nephilim's practice of eating human flesh inspired cannibalism in humans because some of the Nephilim were part human. Satan's plan almost worked! It was only the direct intervention of the Lord that thwarted his plans by destroying his master race of evil beings with the flood.

As soon as the flood waters receded, Satan came back with his same old plan and more giants populated the earth, but it just wasn't working as well as it did before. The Lord God destroyed Sodom and Gomorrah, and possibly other cities as well, then ordered Israel to destroy the rest of these rogue giants. He empowered His chosen people, the Israelites, with His divine, supernatural power. All the giants were wiped from the earth, but because they were once divine as well as human, they were bound to the earth, and today roam our planet as evil spirits. It is this set or class of spirits which continue to torment humans.

Satan didn't stop there, but came up with a brand-new plan. This has to do with why most of the alien abductions going on, deal with reproductive experiments. Anyone familiar with the field of genetics should be aware of the fact that a primary portion of this type of research involves many aspects of reproduction. Certainly, the grey buggy-eyed beings frequently reported to abduct people are collecting sperm and egg samples to use to create hybrid beings. The grey alien beings and their Draconian hierarchy are obviously working on a Nephilim species, something other than giants.

They are working on producing a human/alien hybrid of superior intellect, possibly with supernatural power. I believe they are experimenting with cybernetics, trying to integrate human consciousness into computer chips, or implants. This is why they use the Watchers to collect memories, thoughtforms, and levels of consciousness from us humans. I have already stated in Book One that the grey aliens are capable of implanting memories from one person to another, so a person can think thoughts and have memories that are not his own.[1] The CIA has successfully done this type of mind control for decades.

Abductions today commonly involve the use of a human woman's womb to carry a hybrid baby for several months, ova first stolen from her ovary then hybridized in a test tube. These are modern day Nephilim hybrids. Several innovative scholars postulated that the same process was used in Old Testament time, with all the barren women of old. This may include the virgin birth, which was a form of gynecological technology and genetic engineering.

The creation story in Genesis affirms the creation of Adam out of clay, which coincides with the Sumerian tablets of human creation out of clay and glass tubes. Only Genesis omits the words, 'test tube'. In my opinion, the Annunaki were Nephilim, who stole the secrets of creation from the Creator, counterfeited and mimicked them from their own purposes. We can read the full detailed account of this in the work of the prolific Zecharia Sitchin.

In Genesis 1:26, the word for God employed is *Elohim,* which is plural. The Elohim are the children of the God El, the sons of God. They were created beings, empowered by God with the knowledge of genetic engineering, the tools to create life. English Bibles translate Elohim *as* God, which linguistically is not correct.

Elohim is plural! *The Gods,* not God, and they are not the Creator Father Yahuah but a pantheon of gods, or council of gods.

The *Bene HaElohim* is a distinction mentioned only twice in the bible, which translates to *the sons of the children of god.* There were the 200 fallen sons of heaven also mentioned in the Books of Enoch, and in Genesis, that mated with earth women. These were not the Elohim but the Elohim's offspring. They were also not angels, but were fallen sons of heaven, in other words, rebellious ETs.

The Genesis scripture, which uses the word *Elohim,* says, 'let **us** create man in **our** image according to **our** likeness'. Many Christians interpret this to the trinity having a conversation with itself, but the original Hebrew uses the word Elohim, not the name of the Father, which is Yahuah, or Yahveh. The vernacular is clearly plural in Hebrew, using the word 'our', twice.

This is a controversial idea, especially to Christians who believe the Creator Father created us all, which I will attempt to handle with delicacy and truthfulness. I put forward that the Father God allowed it all to happen, watching thoughtfully and with love in His back up plan. This is why there is such rampant racism on this planet, because of the many alien races that seeded the earth with their own image. Their conflicts reflect the conflicts in the heavens. As above, so below. The Creator Father allowed this to happen as part of a grand Master Plan that was in His divine plan of salvation through Christ from the start, to save all the races.

Joe Kovacs makes the distinction in his book, *Shocked by the Bible,* based on scripture, between the races of the 12 tribes of Israel, and the genetic line known as the Jews, who come from the tribe of Judah. Before Judah, there were no Jews, only Israelites. The tribe of Judah bears Yahuah's genetic line, the line where all the women were barren through their old age yet miraculously became pregnant, such as Rachel. [2]

This is Yahuah's chosen genetic core group. In fact, the history of Israel reminds us that the land was once divided into the land of Israel and the land of Judea. Both King David and Jesus Christ came from the genetic line of the tribe of Judah, who today are the Jews.

The process of invitro fertilization is nothing new; in the Bible we read mainly of virgins, but Sarah, Rachel, Rebecca, Hannah, Gehazi, and Elizabeth were all barren, even the virgin Mary were all made pregnant by the Lord's divine interventions. We must at least entertain the idea that this may be a euphemism for genetic engineering.

All these women, old and desperate, feeling cursed by life and forgotten by the Lord because they were barren, became miraculously pregnant at a time in their lives when it was not just unfeasible, but impossible to maintain and survive in B.C., the Middle East. I see it being even more vital in the immaculate conception and virgin birth, particularly because the purity and continuity of the DNA match was even more important to get right. Mary of Nazareth was carrying the Messiah.

In my humble opinion, I think an event as important as the salvation of the entire cosmos was dependent on a woman. She was in fact a virgin who gave her consent to the whole invitro process via Gabriel in Luke 1:38. Scripture tells us the Holy Spirit came upon Mary at her consent, but it does not detail the technology or medical particulars. Angels are agents of God's Holy Spirit, who are extraterrestrials that serve God.

Can we take the Scripture literally? If we read a bit further, we hear the angel Gabriel state that 'no word from God will ever fail.' A miracle? Of course, all pregnancies are miracles, and this one was a miracle gift to us all. So too were the miraculous births to all the barren women of the Old Testament, which in my opinion were done by the Lord's genetic engineering.

These barren women and virgins were not the only ones in history who became miraculously pregnant. The mothers of Horus, Krishna, Mithras, were also allegedly impregnated in the same way, as all stoutly claimed virgin births. These obviously were of different races within the human family, as I've asserted in my chapter in Book Three, on the Cosmic Christ, they were all attempts to fulfill the Divine Plan of Salvation as written in the stars, that only Jesus Christ succeeded completely for the whole cosmos, where the others targeted their particular corner of the universe.

Petri-dish earth

We humans of earth are an experiment of the gods, created in the image of the gods, engineered through their genetic interventions and manipulations. Everything about our history is recorded in the Bible and in other sacred texts. We have the evidence that God is omnipresent, with many messengers, extraterrestrial angels with a host of technologies at His disposal. We humans are watched, recorded visually and audibly, and archived for the most mysterious of reasons in this Grand Experiment we call earth life.

The 1991 movie, *Defending Your Life,* directed and starring Albert Brooks, with Meryl Streep, illustrates the theory that our earth lives are all neatly archived on video. This may be the reason for the common expression, 'my whole life flashed before my eyes', upon sudden shock or a near death experience. [3]

Three-time near-death experiencer, Dannion Brinkley, described in his 1994 book, *Saved By the Light*, that in the afterlife, there is a stage called the life review, a panoramic review of this life.[4] How else could we go over key passages in our life in such minute detail, objective and subjective? Our memories cloud and tend to be filtered by our own self interests. Our memories are faulty, selective, and frequently in denial.

Messenger angels have archived the life of each one of us. Some report that in the afterlife, we go through a meeting with our soul group, guides and angels, and these recordings are used for comparison. Another reason may be that the gods are looking for recruits. They watch our lives closely to determine which of us earth humans are worthy to have our next life in space on spaceships and live the exciting adventures similar to what was illustrated in *Star Trek*. What a future!

Destiny for Believers of Christ: "And Jesus answering said unto them, the children of this world marry, and are given in marriage: But they which shall be accounted worthy to obtain that world, and the resurrection from the dead, neither marry, nor are given in marriage: Neither can they die any more: for they *are equal unto the angels*; and are the children of God, being the children of the resurrection. (Luke 20:34-36) "For in the resurrection they (people) neither marry, nor are given in marriage, *but are as the angels of God in heaven*." (Matthew 22:30) "For when they shall rise from the dead, they neither marry, nor are given in marriage; but *are as the angels which are in heaven*." (Mark 12:25)

Equal to the angels, or extraterrestrial messengers! Many people have the notion that angels are these fluffy winged beings that fly around like doves and eagles doing God's work. While they do having flying capabilities and they do indeed answer to the Creator God and do His work, they are *not* fluffy winged beings as depicted in many art illustrations. They are extra-terrestrial beings, much bigger and stronger than us humans, yet human in appearance. They are part of a vast network of extraterrestrials in the cosmos who know and support the Creator's handiwork and Divine Will for humankind, not just here but in all the worlds that the cosmic evil has infiltrated. These angels are given special status in the Cosmos, and Jesus Christ Himself has promised that we humans who put our faith in Him as our Savior, Redeemer, and King will have this special status too in His Kingdom, which is not limited to one place but stretches across the entire heavens.

He promises to make us equal to His extraterrestrial messengers the angels, and that we will become the sons and daughters of the Living God. Most of us cannot begin to comprehend what God has planned for us, and how we will all be transformed, after He creates the new heaven and a new earth which He promised us.

> "Behold, I will create new heavens and a new earth. The former things will not be remembered, nor will they come to mind."
>
> (Isaiah 65:17)

> "Then I saw a new heaven and a new earth, for the first heaven and the first earth had passed away, and there was no longer any sea."
>
> (Revelation 21:1)

No more sea... isn't that interesting? To date, our civilization probably has more knowledge about outer space, about how to send rockets up to the moon, or in the rest of our solar system, then it has about what really lurks beneath our oceans. Remember the four beasts in Daniel's dream, which relates the metallic space ships that emerge out from the sea, which in the end are defeated by Christ and His Heavenly Army of Angelic Extra-terrestrials in all their glory. Perhaps in the new heaven and the new earth there will be no need for the dark deep oceans, places to conceal the enemies of God, because they will be completed obliterated.

A new heaven also indicates a reorganization of stars, constellations, and galactic systems. Remember the ancient texts all refer to ancient, terrible evil in the cosmos, to death stars, and the Bible often talks about 'stars falling from heaven'. In astronomy, we tend toward scientific data and descriptions of stars as compilations of gases and elements. Yet, what if what we see is only a facade, and the true spiritual meaning of the stars is being obscured and concealed from us? What if the stars are real *fire beings*, the Cherubim, mentioned in the Bible as a 'star who fell from heaven'. What if all the stars are actual *living* fire beings created by God? If this is true, then the ones who became corrupted with cosmic evil are obliterated when God reorganizes and recreates the heavens, as promised *a new heaven and a new earth.*

Notes:

1. Ella LeBain, *Who's Who in the Cosmic Zoo?* Book One – Third Edition, *The Grays and Soul-Transplantation,* p.271, Tate, 2013
2. Joe Kovacs, *Shocked by the Bible,* WND, 2008, p 186
3. Albert Brooks, Screenplay, Director, movie, *Defending Your Life,* 1991.
4. Dannion Brinkley, *Saved By the Light: The True Story of a Man Who Died Twice and the Profound Revelations He Received,* Villard Books, 1994.

CHAPTER TWELVE
Gene Wars?

When it comes to other people on planet Earth, what you want to keep in mind is that you're all related. Really! Brothers and sisters, when it comes to other people on other planets, actually, that's top secret, and soon, yes, very soon...
Mike Dooley - The Universe

The Catholic doctrine of original sin, which postulates that as humans we are born into sin, has more to do with the genetic manipulation done to us as a race by alien slave masters, than what we have done prior to birth.

Which comes first, the chicken or the egg, is a genetic dilemma, not a theological one.

The facts presented here have been held back from the general population by the dictates of the Church of Rome for millennia. This is one reason that Catholics have been forbidden and discouraged from reading the Bible, and then, only an approved version of the Word, backed up by the Inquisition. What is in the ancient scriptures has always been there for all to see, but this knowledge was concealed by Draconian Archons in order to keep us enslaved and in servitude to error.

This book series was put together for people who have difficulty understanding that these are historical facts, because they were taught to believe otherwise, due to the controlling religious spirit. Cover ups are to protect the controllers. It's a sad fact that religious people have the hardest time accepting our hidden history, much more so than those who are uncommitted to a religion.

The central message in the Gospel of Salvation is not about religion but about coming into right relationship with the Creator through His Messiah. Jesus was persecuted and crucified by the religious spirit, the fundamentalists of His day who, through the ultra-religious Pharisees, whose dogma and power He threatened through the saving power of His Truth. He said, "I have come to set the captives free." (Isaiah 61:1; Luke 4:18) Messiah came to offer salvation not just from sin and suffering, but from the extraterrestrial alien slave masters who have used and abused humankind for millennia.

This book series disputes the Christian Fringe who claim all the ancient aliens were and are still all demons. The Ancient Astronaut Theory, initially established by Erich Von Daniken in 1966 through his first best-selling book, *Chariots of the Gods*, is also incomplete.[1] Oftentimes, the Truth is found in the bridge or middle ground between two opposing viewpoints, which I am going to prove to you. The world says, *the devil's in the details,* however, as I like to say, ***the Truth is in the details***.

Those who truly walk in the Light of God's Truth and Christ's Spirit will see these truths because the Spirit of God is the revealer of all truths, past, present, and future. The Angels watch over ALL of God's Word to perform it. (Jeremiah 1:12)

DNA and Divine Design

Laminin is an essential protein molecule that is crucial to the cellular building block of life, found inside our DNA. Think of it as the glue that holds and keeps our body together. The word *consist* has the same meaning as Laminin, "to unite, to bind together." "He is before all things, and by him all things consist." (Colossians 1:17)

Let's Connect some dots:

- 22 Pairs of Autosomes in our DNA;
- 22 Letters in the Hebrew Alphabet represents 22 Constellations in the Milky Way
- 22 Root Races[2, 3] (See, *Who's Who in the Cosmic Zoo?* Book One)
- 22 Alien Genetic Experiments[2, 3] (See, *Who's Who in the Cosmic Zoo?* Book One)
- Genesis 22, God will provide a lamb for an offering
- Psalm 22, They pierced my hands and feet and cast lots for my clothes
- Isaiah 22, Who carves a tomb for himself in a rock?
- 2 Samuel 22, The Rock of my salvation, My savior
- 22 Ten Commandments given twice on two stones
- Psalm 118: Verse 22, The stone the builders rejected has become the chief corner stone
- 22 NA The atomic mass for Sodium (Salt); "You are the salt of the earth." ~ Jesus

Genetic Manipulations

Book One of *Who's Who in the Cosmic Zoo?* began the discussion with mention of the genetic manipulations by giants, those Nephilim or fallen angels, also known as rebellious ETs, the Annunaki.[2] Scriptures say that the sons of God took wives from the daughters of men and went in unto them. That's bible terms for the horizontal mambo, no getting around it. I have been asked the question of logistics; if giant humans or Nephilim or very tall ETs came to earth and mated with earth women, how did they do it, when these beings are allegedly 15-35 feet tall? How does a 35-foot giant have sex with an earth woman, who may not be over 5 feet tall?

The answer is simple, they transformed themselves into normal human form through a type of shape-shifting that was achieved through genetic manipulation. However, there was more to the mixing of Nephilim and human DNA, than being limited to having sex with earth women.

We know from the Sumerian Cuneiform tablets that the Annunaki altered the genetic material of the indigenous humans, as they tell of mixing their DNA in a clay pot with that of earth woman. This proves without a shadow of a doubt, that the Annunaki did not create humankind, as I've stated in my conclusive thesis in Book One, because the earth woman, the indigenous humans, were already there. Those who did have sexual relations with humans were able to shape shift themselves into normal sized humans. That's my explanation, and yes, the Truth is Stranger than Fiction!

According to Josephus, "Many fallen angels of God now consorted with women, and begot sons on them who were overbearing and disdainful of every virtue; much confidence had they in their strength. In fact, the deeds that our tradition ascribes to them recall the audacious exploits told by the Greeks of the giants. But Noah ... urged them to adopt a better frame of mind and amend their ways." In the eighth century A.D., Rabbi Eliezer records in the midrash: 'The angels who fell from Heaven saw the daughters of Cain perambulating and displaying their secret parts, their eyes painted with antimony in the manner of harlots; and, being seduced, took wives from among them."

The names of several fallen angels survive only in careless Greek transcriptions of Hebrew or Aramaic originals, which make their meaning doubtful. Azazel does seem to represent the angel whose name means *God Strengthens*. Dudael is sometimes translated, *God's cauldron.* The Nephilim and the Fallen Ones bore many other tribal names, such as Emim or Terrors, Rephaim or Weakeners, Gibborim or Giant Heroes, Zamzummin as Achievers, Anakim as Long-necked Wearers of Necklaces, Awe as Devastators or Serpents. One of the Nephilim named Ariba is said to have built the city of Hebron, called Kiriath-Arba after him, who become the father of Anak, whose three sons, Sheshai, Ahiman and Talmai, were later expelled by Joshua's comrade Caleb. These Fallen Ones were the mentioned cannibalistic giants who had sexual relationships, first with human women but later with everything under the sun.

It was because of the evil brought upon the earth by these Fallen Ones that God decided to wipe the face of His creation clean. Men, women, children, and the giant corruptors were erased from that creation. Noah and his family were instructed to build an ark to avoid destruction in the Flood. The wife of Ham, one of Noah's sons, had however been impregnated by a fallen angel named Shemhazai before getting on the ark, according to Hebrew legend. The descendants of Ham were the Canaanites (Genesis 9:18,22, 25, 27; 10:6, 15-18) whom God instructed the Jews to kill when His people finally arrived at their promised Holy Land.

We can, therefore, discern in the fallen angel-human hybrid offspring of the wife of Ham, their general characteristics. Named Canaan, the progenitor of the Canaanites, we see the following about a demon-human hybrid: his nature was so demonically inclined that Canaan was cursed by Noah to be the servant of servants of his brethren. Canaan became the servant of Japheth. Canaan was not an only child; his brothers were named Cush, Phut, and Mizraim. His three half-brothers were not sired by the same father, the fallen one called Shemhazai. The children of Canaan were Sidon, his first born, and Heth.

From there, further descendants of the demon-human hybrid Canaan were the Jebusites, the Amorites, Girgasites, Hivites, Arkites, Sinites, Arvadites, Zemarites, Hamathites, and from there the families of the Canaanites were spread abroad. The border of the Canaanite land was from Sidon to Gaza and down to cities of the south called Sodom, Gomorrah. Admah. Zeboim, and even down to Lasha -- the area of present day Israel. In the Exodus from Egypt, Moses was instructed by God to go to the land of the Canaanites, as this was the Promised Land. God told Moses that He would send an angel before Moses, and that He would drive out the Canaanites, the Amorites, the Hittites, the Perizzites, the Hivites, and the Jebusites from the 'land flowing with milk and honey."

God instructed Moses to be on guard, never to make any covenants with the inhabitants of Canaan, 'lest it be for a snare in the midst of thee: but ye shall destroy their altars, break their images, and cut down their groves.' The Semites were instructed by God to smite the collective nations in Canaan and "utterly destroy them; thou shalt make no covenant with them, nor shew mercy unto them: Neither shalt thou make marriages with them; thy daughter thou shalt not give unto his son, nor his daughter shalt thou take unto thy son. For they will turn away thy son from following me, that they may serve other gods; so, will the anger of the Lord be kindled against you, and destroy thee suddenly."

God is not being discriminatory or cruel here; He is directing a plan to remove the remnant of the hybrid species which was not totally wiped out in the Great Flood. Despite the growing power of the Jews and the Divine decree, they were awed and frightened by the advanced technology of the Canaanites. Joshua, after crossing into the land, reassured the people of God saying, "for thou shalt drive out the Canaanites, though they have iron chariots, and though they be strong." Despite all this, still all the descendants of Ham were not destroyed. It took the Pharaoh king of Egypt who had helped clear many, but not all, of the Canaanites out of the land.

The area of Jerusalem was given as a present to Pharaoh's daughter, who was also the wife of Solomon. The remaining Canaanites went, by the decree of Solomon, into the levy of bond service to the children of Israel. This covenant with the remaining Canaanites proved, as God had already warned, to be the undoing of Solomon and he went off into idolatry and maintained Canaanite concubines. Solomon began to worship Ashtoreth, the goddess of the Zidonians, and after Milcom the abomination of the Ammonites; and finally including the gods Chemosh and Molech. Solomon saw his great kingdom taken from him and eventually given to the ten tribes. The lineage of the hybrids goes on to this day.

The truth is that the genetic infusion of the Fallen Ones into the daughters of men continues through the descendants of Canaan, who have not been "utterly destroyed" (Exodus 33:2, 34: 11, Deuteronomy 7: 1, Joshua 5: 1; 17: 12; 1 Kings 9: 16). This is why, in this day and age, these supposed aliens do such things as impregnate women and steal their fetus before it is born. Therefore, there are reports of human men having sexual relationships with female aliens and visa-versa. This is the reason for the apparent interest in genetics associated with these present-day aliens. They want to reclaim their own. Who are the hybrids today and what is their genetic signature?

Is there any doubt at all in the Christian mind as to the true nature of these aliens? Is there any doubt as to how the aliens or the hybrid species regard Christians? Is it the Christians who are pursuing a purge of the genepool? We do well to recall that the main work of the Nazis was to wipe out the Jews 'because they were considered to be a lower root race' despite the fact that Jews are known for their higher intelligence quotients, their ability to innovate, create and contribute life-saving inventions that have historically benefitted humankind. The Truth is, that Jews are not a lower root race, but a higher one, which this group of aliens are intensely jealous of, because the God of the Jews punished them, and they are taking their revenge out on the children of God, who were the Lord's genetic experiment on Earth and chosen to be His representatives, as a peoples on earth that were 'set apart' unto Himself.

This now begins to make some sense in the grand overview. We begin to see some of the same thinking that has guided the evil that is in the world. We are witnessing a genetic invasion that has been going on since the beginning of recorded history- a war in a battle of *Who* shall possess the fleshly vessels, minds and souls of the human race?

> "For we do not wrestle against flesh and blood, but against the rulers, against the authorities (principalities), against the

cosmic powers (Archons) over this present darkness, against
the spiritual forces of evil (aliens) in the heavenly places."
(Ephesians 6:12 - ESV)

It is by the blood of the perfect Lamb, Jesus Christ, that we are saved unto Him and are already victorious for it is written that no flesh shall enter the Kingdom of God. Jesus said, "I am going to prepare a place for you that where I am there also shall you be." (John 14:3) It is written "that ye are dead and your life is hidden with Christ Jesus." (Colossians 3:3) We know also that after this age, there shall be yet another and then, finally another in which all war shall come to an end on earth and God Himself shall dwell with His people. (Revelations 21:3)

As a final note: The Human Genome Project is currently under way in the molecular biological sciences. This project is a very ambitious undertaking in which the entire human genetic code will be mapped. Estimates of when the mapping shall be completed vary from ten to fifteen years from now.

Critical thinking demands that we confront the issue of how the Giants had sex with normal human women, and how these normal women got here on earth in the first place. The old tables record that the Sumerian gods allegedly created humankind, by performing the first in vitro implants into the earth women. But this just begs the question as to exactly *who* put the earth women on the earth for them to use? Perhaps the Annunaki didn't create humankind after all?

> "There were giants in the earth in those days; and also after that, when the sons of God came in unto the ***daughters of men***, and they bare children to them, the same became mighty men which were of old, men of renown. And God saw that the wickedness of man was great in the earth, and that every imagination of the thoughts of his heart was only evil continually."
>
> (Genesis 6:4-5-KJV)

This Scriptural account validates the fact that ancient humans had intercourse with another species, perhaps of proto humans. Unthinkable as it seems, ancient humans had sex with non-humans.

The reason for the Flood as a judgement of God upon earth was because of the pure evil polluting of the human genome. Genesis 6:9 reveals this. A little portion of this verse could accurately be translated, "Noah was pure and without contamination in his heritage, that is, without genetic contamination in his family tree. Contamination came from fallen angels who were producing offspring with the daughters of men. Angels and demons are all Extraterrestrials and the sons and daughters (and other non-binary genders) of the God(s), Elohim and the father-race(s).

The Book of Enoch was left out of the Biblical cannon by men who wanted to erase the past, brush out the contamination, deny the existence of non-humans, and in the end used a Bible translated specifically to control other humans through fear and dogma to keep them innocent and ignorant of the cosmic reality.

We are surely hybrids. Look at Nature. It follows an evolutionary path, the driving mechanism of which is variation. This is the most logical course, scientifically and metaphysical speaking. We see evidence in all biological kingdoms. Every organism seeks to expand by colonization. Especially us humans! We have colonized the entire globe, and spawned our own myths and legend as a result. Omer Gokcumen found wildly different variations in the genes of humans living in Sub-Saharan Africa. He believes these genes can be traced back to about 150,000 years ago when ancient humans were breeding with this mysterious *ghost species.*[3]

This other species is referred to by the scientific community as a *ghost species* as there are no known fossils that can be analyzed. "It seems that interbreeding between different early hominin species is not the exception - it's the norm," Gokcumen said, quoted by the Sun. "Based on our analysis, the most plausible explanation for this extreme variation is archaic introgression - the introduction of genetic material from a *ghost species* of ancient hominins." These 'ghosts' are called "Nephilim" in the Jewish Scriptures, who according to the Book of Enoch, became the evil spirits of the earth, locked in between dimensions, tormenting humans until the Day of Judgment, when the Lord will deal with them once and for all.[4]

The American Society of Human Genetics held its annual meeting last year, and the conclusions they reached can be easily described as staggering. The data they gathered shows that people from Melanesia (an area in the South Pacific that encloses Papua New Guinea and its neighboring islands) may be packing some strange genes in their DNA. The geneticists believe the unrecognized DNA belongs to a previously undiscovered species of humanoids.

According to Ryan Bohlender, one of the researchers involved in the study, that species is not Neanderthal or Denisovan, but something completely different. "We're missing a population or we're misunderstanding something about the relationships," he stated.[5]

Are these the lost children of Anu? Seeded on earth by the Annunaki? The Denisovans represent an extinct species belonging to the hominid genus. They were named after the Denisova Cave in the Siberian Altai Mountains, where the first bone fragment belonging to this species was found. Very little is known about this enigmatic cousin of ours. "Human history is a lot more complicated than we thought it was," Bohlender said.[5]

Oh, yes, it is. But piece by piece, humanity's convoluted past is brought to light. And discoveries such as this one, point in one direction: we are not who we think we are. Here is a quote from the study that I think you're going to appreciate: "With assumptions about population size and more recent population separation dates taken from the literature, we estimate the archaic-modern separation date at 440,000 ± 300 years ago for all modern human populations."

If that number doesn't ring any bells, allow me to reiterate the Annunaki hypothesis. According to the Genesis story, the twelfth planet, known as Nibiru was populated by humanoid beings very similar to us humans. After they encountered a severe atmosphere problem, they went on a quest through the solar system in order to find gold, a special metal that could rebalance their planet.[5]

When Nibiru approached Earth's orbit, about 432,000 years BC, the Nibiruans used space ships to send people and essential goods from their planet to Earth. After they reached the surface, the advanced beings established bases in ancient Mesopotamia.

Many believe this is the true cradle of humankind – inside the Annunaki geneticists' laboratories. And this recent study offers insight that might answer one of our oldest and most significant question: Who are we?

In order to obtain the irrefutable solution to this age-old enigma we must dig deep where no-one has dug before, which is not in the ground but within ourselves. We must analyze the microscopic records that are hidden away inside each and every one of us.

In Conclusion

While I'm not going to bore you with genetic science and the plethora of data on the different genetic patterns we humans have, suffice it to say, that most of us hold seeds from extraterrestrial races. Just the same, it's important that we do not broad brush a race of people by stigmatizing or demonizing them, without first understanding where they come from and where they are going to go. So, it should be with our understanding of the extraterrestrial races that played a part in the many genetic experiments of the human races on planet earth.

Our planet is like a petri dish of many different genetic experiments. Alex Collier[3] stated in *Defending Sacred Ground: The Andromedan Compendium,* that there are 22 extraterrestrial root races that have supplied genetic material for the human races now on earth. There are 22 letters in the Hebrew Alphabet as well as 22 connections among the Sephirot, the divine essences comprising the Tree of Life in the mystical teachings of the Jewish Kabbalah. The number 22 in Hebrew mystical teachings stands for the totality of things in the created universe. Each letter is a pictogram of

22 core constellations. Essentially Hebrew is the language of Angels, it's a space language, which is why Enoch was taken up into the Heavens and taught the language in order for the Lord to use him as a scribe. Its original syntax has since changed to modern day Hebrew.

According to information from MILAB's whistleblower Corey Goode, who has been in contact with the intraterrestrials inside the earth, there are 22 genetic experiments in progress with terrestrial humans. Is it any wonder that racism runs rampant on this planet? While people love to look for scapegoats to blame, how about we learn to connect the dots between what happened in the past, and our multi-racial genetics? Perhaps instead of looking outside of ourselves, it's time to discover 'who' we are within, by learning about our own DNA?[7]

How many people who publicly speak out against things like slavery, or being a slave owner, then find out after DNA testing that they are the descendants of slave owners? A recent example would be Ben Affleck, who viciously attacked white people for owning slaves, only to learn after his own DNA testing that his ancestors were slave owners. This was disclosed on "Finding Your Roots," a PBS Documentary. This is what we call a generational curse operating from generational sins. Affleck was in denial of the family sins, or as psychologists like to call it, the "family trance."[8]

Denial is part of the generational curse, because it puts a veil upon the truth, keeping one perpetually in the negative patterning which manifests as both mental, spiritual, and physical bondage of generational sins. The only way out is through cleansing one's genetic bloodline through the power of the blood of Jesus Christ. This is available to all who believe in Him and apply His blood covenant.

Another slant on planet earth and salvation may be that this is the Grand Creator's way of making all races realize that their common denominator is their humanity, through being born human on planet earth, and uniting through the Cosmic Christ, the Savior of all Creation and humankind.

Notes:

1. Erich Von Daniken, *Chariots of the Gods,* Avon, 1966
2. Ella LeBain, *Who's Who in the Cosmic Zoo? Book One, Third Edition,* Tate Publishing, 2013.
3. Alex Collier, *Defending Sacred Ground: The Andromedan Compendium*, Boulder, CO: Brotherton Press, 1997.
4. Omer Gokcumen, *What Makes Us Human?* https://gokcumenlab.org/
5. Ryan Bohlender, *Ancient Human History More Complex than Previously Thought, Researchers Say Findings Reported at ASHG 2016 Annual Meeting,*

American Society of Human Genetics, http://www.ashg.org/press/201610-admixture.html

6. Ancient History, Lost Children of the Annunaki Confirmed: Melanesian Tribe's DNA Carries Genes from Unknown Species. https://hidden-truth.net/2017/09/lost-children-anunnaki-confirmed-melanesian-tribes-dna-carries-genes-unknown-species/, September 22, 2017
7. Corey Goode, *Sphere Being Alliance*, https://spherebeingalliance.com/
8. Sarah Kaplan, After omitting details of Ben Affleck's slave-owning ancestor, 'Finding Your Roots' is suspended by PBS, https://www.washingtonpost.com/news/morning-mix/wp/2015/06/25/after-omitting-details-of-ben-afflecks-slave-owning-ancestor-finding-your-roots-is-suspended-by-pbs/?utm_term=.f0aaa676addb, June 25, 2015.

CHAPTER THIRTEEN
The Grand Experiment

"Everything is determined, the beginning as well as the end, by forces over which we have no control. It is determined for the insect, as well as for the star. Human beings, vegetables or cosmic dust - we all dance to a mysterious tune, intoned in the distance by an invisible piper."
-Albert Einstein

In his book, *Flying Serpents and Dragons: The Story of Mankind's Reptilian Past,* R.A. Boulay demonstrates that the early Sumerian civilization was established by serpent-gods who arrived here to establish their colonies.[1] They were ruled by four senior gods: An, the great patriarch, who rarely came down to Earth and remained in the background; and his three children: Enlil, the leader of the expedition and chief of all activities on Earth; his brother Enki, who was the chief engineer, supervisor over all construction, mining, technical activities and genetic engineering; and Ninhursag, the great nurse and medical director.

The late Zecharia Sitchin's research into the ancient Sumerian culture, which was detailed in his book series, *The Earth Chronicles,* reveals evidence in the Sumerian tablets (specifically in the book *Genesis Revisited*) that these Nibiruan gods actually created the first test tube babies, since Enki and Ninhursag used genetic engineering to produce a human slave race on Earth -- or as he describes it from the tablets, "a race of primitive workers," *Homo sapiens* -- by mixing DNA from several existing races.[2]

Sitchin claimed that the Nibiruans are from a twelfth planet in our solar system, obviously called Nibiru, and that they landed on Earth in prehistoric times, mined gold and other minerals, established a spaceport in what today is the Iraq-Iran area, and lived in a kind of idealistic society as a small colony. They returned when Earth was more populated and genetically interfered in our indigenous DNA to create a slave-race to work their mines, farms, and other enterprises in Sumeria, which was the so-called Cradle of Civilization in outdated pre-1980s school history texts. Later on, the Nibiruans also used behind-the-scenes power-plays to manipulate the Egyptians and certain other empires along with the Syrians. They like to play god, with a heavy ruling hand in Babylonia, Persia, Mesoamerica, and other lands, used their advanced technology to make primitive peoples believe they were divine.[3]

According to Sitchin's interpretation of the Sumerian tablets, Enlil and Enki were sent from Nibiru to rule Earth as governors, and were responsible to keep the population under control. Enki once saved humanity when Enlil wanted to destroy us. They gave the ancient Sumerians their architectural, agricultural, astronomical, and cultural training in exchange for labor and "gifts to the gods", in the form of mining, food, and material goods. The Nibiruans themselves no longer had to physically work on Earth. They disguised themselves as fish-humans, lion-humans, bird-humans, and other creatures, all Nephilim, in order to get the people to worship them as 'token gods,' something that Moses and the Lord Yahuah violently opposed.[4]

Later the Pleiadeans who were involved in Egypt's Third Golden Age attempted to end the worship of the many Nibiruan and Sirian gods with the one-god concept of monotheism. Akhenaton was inserted into the timeline to establish this concept. It did not prove popular, and after Akhenaton's death, Egypt went back to polytheism. In spite of Akhenaton's apparent failure, he succeeded in the realm of consciousness by leaving the improved mark in the Earth's Akashic record, so others were able to grasp the concept later on down the timeline.

War broke out between the Nibiruans, and Enki and his family lost. It's important to keep in mind that the winner writes history. This is why Enki was later depicted as Satan while Enlil got away with murder. See Genesis 6:5-8 and Genesis 6:17. It should also be noted that Ra, son of Enki, was also given a bad rap in the history books because like his father he stood against the others and lost. So, one would need to ask oneself, "Is the Bible the word of God?" And if you believe that, then the next logical question should be, "Which God?"

In fact, if you research all the mythology, you will see the same story repeating itself throughout history. For example, William Bramley's book, *The Gods of Eden*, postulates that earth's historical wars began when two ET brothers from Sirius named Anu, whose sons Enki and Enlil, were sent to rule over the Earth. One of Enki's many children was Marduk, also known as the Egyptian Sun God "Ra", who later had a son named Horus. Enlil was depicted in the Bible as very vengeful. Enki was indeed a different being than Enlil and was somewhat more compassionate. Enlil was later called Satan, the snake in the Garden of Eden who shared self-knowledge with Eve.[5]

Think about it, who has been behind most of the wars of the first millennium? How about the second millennium? There isn't any group, tribe, race or nation on this planet which hasn't suffered at the hands of another, or been held in slavery by another. The question is: slaves to what, or slaves to whom? The ultimate answer is that Force which seeks to exploit us as an energy source, and eventually own our souls, because the Soul is immortal. It is the Soul Essence they are after, because the dark forces have lost their souls, leaving behind a pit like a black hole, sucking all the photons and particles of light into it. *"Never trust the Man behind the Curtain,"* as depicted in the metaphorical Wizard of Oz. And who is behind the veil? Who controls the masses? And why? The Judeo-Christian tradition calls him Satan, or the Devil. But who is the Devil? Is this a real being, or just made up myth. And what is myth?

Firstly, let's explore the evolution of language. The word *Satan* is the Hebrew word for adversary. This title however comes from a Babylonian and Sumerian king, a real person, called Teiton, or Serpent Dragon Lord. In the Semitic languages, the sounds for S and T are often interchanged, dependent upon accent and dialect. In the Hebrew language, the letter Tet or Set can be pronounced as a T or an S, depending on where you place the vowel or dot. So, the Serpent King Teiton became Satan, who was also referred to as *the adversary*.

The word devil later evolved through the European languages, combining the words *da* or *de* meaning the evil, daevil or deevil, in English, *devil*.[6] We can trace back through history the real person behind the myth, who later on became known as a force or hierarchy of evil.

This Serpent King Teiton descends from an actual race known as the Serpent Race or the Dragon, otherwise known as the Draconians, also known as the Dracos or Dracs. This is the ancient reptilian lineage, descending from the Reptoid/Dinoid ancestry. This race is the source of our vampire myths, along with a host of other dragon legends and serpent stories, stories that almost always end in the devouring of mankind.[7] [See, Book One of *Who's Who in the Zoo?*]

Further, Carl Sagan reflects in his book *The Dragons of Eden* on the reptilian origins of humankind, and on the mysterious leap in brain evolution that can be observed in the fossil record. He argues that if people had evolved naturally from reptiles, in Darwinian theory, it should have taken 200 million years for mammals to first evolve, and then another five to ten million years for humans to emerge. But he notes with bewilderment that the fossil record simply does not bear out this conclusion. In fact, the evolution of mammals, and particularly humans, was accomplished very quickly, "in a major burst of brain evolution." The evidence for this is clear in the fact that stone tools do not appear gradually, but rather "appear in enormous abundance all at once." In frustration, Sagan concludes that "there is no way to explain this unless Australopithecines had educational institutions to teach tool making."

That is indeed the most obvious and satisfactory explanation, but one that most mainstream scientists wouldn't dare consider let alone, admit that God or godlike beings, extraterrestrials, had a hand in accelerating the evolutionary process.

Dr. Carl Werner's *Evolution: The Grand Experiment* is a study in the foolishness of evolution. He debunks the theory of spontaneous generation, proves that certain animals did not just 'evolve' but had to have been placed here. In one of his footnotes he writes, "Author's Note: Aristotle died in the year 322 B.C. Pasteur disproved spontaneous generation finally in 1859 A.D." Werner reminded himself that it may have taken 2,100 years to undo a belief system through science.[8]

How many years have we been thick in the evolutionary consciousness, Darwinian theory, and all the fuzzy science that inevitably fails to explain it?

The truth of the matter is that Neanderthal man was genetically altered by extraterrestrial intervention. Many are now seeing the truth of that now, particularly archeologists who have uncovered remains of long skulls and alterations that cannot be explained through the restrictions of old scientific thinking. Many of the species on earth have been altered and tailored through genetic experimentation by extraterrestrial gods.

When Jesus Christ walked the planet over 2000 years ago, He had a remarkable opportunity to instruct us on the difference between illness from possession by demons, and illness caused by germs. He performed many exorcisms on diseased people and repeatedly told them to pay attention to the Law. Of course, He didn't phrase it, "the spontaneous generation theory is going to be debunked in 2000 years, so you should know about germs now, and how by simply washing your hands can avoid some demons, and you can save yourselves from years of sickness and pain. It is not obvious as to what really causes disease, but as well as demons, you should know about germs." There are many scriptures and commandments from Yahuah about the washing of hands and staying away from unclean animals for this very reason, that germs and bacteria are the potential cause of all kinds of diseases. He also said, "Your faith has healed you, now go and sin no more." He knows, spiritually speaking, that sin, error, mistake, opens the door for the demons to oppress and possess a human, and with repentance, they would remain free of demons and disease. He knew that this was how the experiment was set up.

The mission of Jesus Christ was purely a spiritual one. He came to bridge the gap between humans and the Creator Father God. He performed miracles, He kicked out demons and aliens by demonstrating His power and authority over them. He proved that severe debilitating diseases, like leprosy, blindness, deafness and epilepsy were all caused by demonic possession and demonic oppression. He came to set the captives free, and that is exactly what He did. He did not address the scientists, but contended with the *religious spirits* and the stronghold they had on the Jewish Sanhedrin of that time.

His last words as He bled to death on the cross of Calvary, was, "forgive them Father, for they know not what they do." (Luke 23:34) This was not only an act of mercy and compassion, but of true understanding of the *spiritual nature* of what and *who* controls most of us frail humans. He knew how we were created, how we were genetically manipulated and by whom. He knew the spiritual strongholds that the fallen angels of the Satanic hierarchy had over us through demonic possession and demonic oppression. In my opinion, this was truly what His last prayer was about, a reminder to the Creator Father that we were not in our right mind, that we were being controlled mentally and spiritually and in many cases, implanted by the dark forces. We were to remain slaves to the demonic agenda, which was in total opposition to the Divine Will of the Creator.

So many people are angry at God! They blame God for their predicament, for their suffering, but which god is responsible for all that?

The modern human conundrum is the result of countless genetic experiments and spiritual tests. We are the pawns and prize of the gods, something to fight over, and what is most valuable to them are our souls.

Christ Himself, the early Christians, the founding churches, and the whole spiritual drama of Christianity has been fraught with attacks from its inception, but as Jesus said, "the gates of hell shall not prevail against my church." (Matthew 16:18). In so many cases, the church was taken over by the fallen angels, which put a stronghold on Christianity through *religious spirits*, obscuring the true meaning of what Christ taught by thwarting the mission of the Holy Spirit. Christianity is all about setting people free spiritually, through healing and deliverance from the fallen angels, the aliens, demons and evil spirits. Instead these very spirits established a spiritual and political stronghold through the vehicle of religion, many of which are still active today. The history of battles, inquisitions, corruption, reformation, and formation of new denominations that broke away from the stronghold of Catholicism, but remain just as empty, continues to this day, as do the spiritual battles.

It is no wonder that so many people have become angry at God, and angry at Christians and churches. Ghandi once said, "I like your Christ, but I'm not so sure about your Christians." People need to distinguish between what the church has done versus who Christ is and what Christ has done and is still doing for us through His Living Spirit. We frequently can't see the difference when we are locked in deep-seated anger and passions towards the wrong source. 'You can't throw the baby out with the bathwater.' The church in many respects has been infiltrated by the enemy. The discerning mind can separate the works of Satan from the works of God.

Demons absolutely love it when we're angry and confused about God! They jump right on us as an opportunity to misguide us, deceive us, and create even more separation between us and God. The fallen angels count on it, that way we'll turn to them, form *their* cults, and worship them, be bound by their *religious spirits* instead of experiencing the true peace and well-being of our Creator.

God created all souls, just as He created all the angels, faithful and fallen. God gives free will as part of grace, but within laws, ordinances, and covenants, agreements, and contracts. "As above, so below," is an ancient hermetic axiom which means that our world is only a microcosm of the grand macrocosm of the universe. God is Justice. Just as there are legalities in Heaven, we have a reflection of that on Earth. Our Creator is a Just and Merciful Judge, whereas on Earth, many Judges are not, because they're under rulership from the god of this world, who is Lucifer.

God allows souls to make contracts with other souls and contract with other gods, that one day the soul will realize it misses its Creator and wants to walk again with God. God welcomes the soul back with open arms because of the mercy, grace and goodness given through Christ. For those who have a hard time finding and choosing a relationship with God, there is purgatory, and the cycles of reincarnation, where there is inevitable suffering of all kinds. See my chapter, *What Happens When You Die?* in Book Two. God's Infinite grace gives souls the chance to choose for themselves.[9]

With so much stacked against the human condition, genetic manipulations, experimentation, cosmic and spiritual warfare, alien interference, and demonic influences, we can see why humanity needs a Savior. We humans are not equipped to fight these forces by ourselves. There is so much of our condition that needs benevolent supernatural intervention! When a person is saved from death, disease, mental illness, the prison of physical disabilities, the torment of being possessed by fallen angels, aliens, demonic spirits, being drained of the life force by vampires, one gets the true meaning of the word, 'Salvation.' <u>There are worse things than death</u>.

Spiritually speaking all those who are in some form of rebellion towards God are open to dark spirits, through outright possession to demonic oppression. All disease is caused by demons, who have a legal right to oppress humans through the opening of human error (sin). Atheists believe in themselves, focusing primarily on the intellect and secularism, thinking it's all about critical thinking, which shuts off the heart. This belief is narcissistic, which is simply arrogance, and since the original sin was pride, this becomes the atheist's downfall.

Genetic Experiments

Zecharia Sitchin details his research in his books, *The Earth Chronicles,* and *Genesis Revisited*, translations of the ancient Sumerian tablets.[2] Those tablets tell the story in great detail of how Annunaki gods came down from heaven and mixed the DNA of the indigenous peoples with their seed to create a new race of humans, which we call Homo Sapiens. The tablets say that these humans were created to be a slave race to serve these extraterrestrials to mine the earth for gold and other natural resources.

These Annunaki beings, written about in Book One, are fallen angels and fallen sons of God, who all had a god complex, and were experimenting with their knowledge of genetics.[10]

As Sitchin points out, their main objective was to mine the earth for gold which he says was needed to protect their spacecraft and possibly protect their home planet. That latter is unsubstantiated, whereas the spacecraft is written about and depicted in the Sumerian tablets. We all know today how valuable and protective the element of gold is for technology. NASA uses it as a protective shield on satellites and the space station. So, it isn't hard to believe that ancient astronauts had this knowledge and knew of its value. The point is, mining the earth for gold was no easy feat, and they needed humans to do it for them. This first master-slave relationship set the tone for the ensuing millennia of master-slave relationships to follow, as well as the religions that were set up to worship these gods.

These new models of human beings were never meant to be smarter than their creator gods. They were not allowed to partake of the "Tree of Knowledge" else they would be as god. They were created to be servants and slaves, to be the workers, the bottom of the food chain, the toilers of the earth. The knowledge of God and the ways of the gods were forbidden to them. This is why other groups of extra-terrestrial fallen angels and sons of God followed to teach men the things that these Annunaki gods forbade humans to know, such as how to navigate by the stars through astronomy and astrology, how to make weapons for war, how to write, and how to use herbs for healing. See my chapter, *Fallen Angels*, Book One, Book Three[11]. This of course angered the other gods, and the fact that humans were taught how to make weapons for war, brought down the wrath of the Creator. We were not meant to be a warring race of beings. Nevertheless, this is our history. These extraterrestrial gods fought over control of human beings.

Scholars have compared the Sumerian story of creation to that in the book of Genesis. There are many inconsistencies. Yahuah created a race of beings of His own to be His 'chosen,' to carry out His will on earth. In my opinion, the Annunaki rivalry between Enki and Enlil over their human creation, depicts similar rivalry between Yahuah and Satan. Enki seemed to have more compassion than Enlil who wanted to destroy what they created, just as Yahuah had compassion on humans where Satan did not. I do not think these were the same gods, though some scholars have linked them. The Sumerian gods Enki and Enlil were Annunaki gods who to this day are in a contract with Satan, who is the god of this world. However, Satan answers to Yahuah, the Creator God and His son Jesus Christ. Jesus Christ came to defeat the powers of Satan. He took the power of death and Hades away from Satan, and as it is written in Matthew 28:18, Philippians 2:10. He has been given authority over all things, in heaven, on the earth and *under* the earth.

It is my opinion that the Sumerian gods and Yahuah were in competition with one another, which is why their offspring have been destined to numerous battles and wars for millennia. Enki and Enlil were fallen angels, extraterrestrials who set themselves up as gods, who were allotted Earth as their domain. These Annunaki gods had to enter into an agreement with Satan over stewardship and rulership of their creation, because he had already been banished to the Earth by the Creator. This is the reason for the many different tribes, languages, and races, as well as the divisive racism, born long ago as each of the many versions of human beings vied for the right to claim it was made in the image and likeness of the gods. Perhaps this 'racist' gene was genetically engineered into thinking they were the best tribe, or best race, that may very well could have started out, as a competition between the gods.

Elohim is the plural form of the word God, for children of God or council of gods. The very word, Elohim, literally means, 'gods.' They are also the sons of the Most High God 'El Elyon' and together they make up a council or pantheon of gods. They are in the Bible as HaElohim, which literally translates to, 'the gods'. The sons of God were distinctly different from the angels. In my opinion, the fallen angels were tall giant powerful beings, likened to gods, who experimented with other worlds as well as Earth. These gods tampered with genetics and eugenics, creating racism.

Some people think that Jehovah and Yahweh were two different gods, and compare them to the Sumerian gods, Enlil and Enki. As I've explained in my chapter, *What's in a Name*[12] in the section on Gods, Jehovah and Yahweh were not the names of the God of Israel. This was a mispronunciation. The tetragrammaton, YHVH is pronounced Yahuah. However, in the Masoretic text it is pronounced Yehovah (Jehovah). The Arab world calls him Yahweh or Yahu, mainly because of the Arabic dialect, which does use the W sound, whereas Hebrew does not. In the nineteenth century, Yahweh was pronounced by a misunderstanding of the Hebrew language by a German scholar. To sort out all of these differences, and follow the historical timeline when these names showed, up, please see my chapter on *The Tetragrammaton*, in Book Two[12]: *Who Is God?*

Yahuah punished His creation for disobedience, sexual immorality and idolatry. The Messiah was sent to save them from their errors and failures and the curse of sin. Messiah was part of Yahuah's Divine Plan of Salvation from the beginning. The work on the cross was preordained, because it represents the gateway back to the Creator God (Yahuah) out of this world. It's a way out of the part of the experiment that failed, which is what Christ meant when He said, "I know what you are made of", and "forgive them father for they know not what they do." He knew our DNA was manipulated several times. Yahuah wanted to keep a pure test or control group for His own experiment, which later became known as the Jews. Yahuah communicated through the High Priests and Kings, and through His technology, the Ark of the Covenant, the Urim and Thummin, He shared His Words with His prophets.

But even His chosen test group turned out to be a failed experiment, because they fell under the influence of the fallen angels and the god of this world, and ended up worshipping these false gods, disobeying their Creator, and falling into immorality. Finally, they rejected their own Messiah, which got them into big trouble, literally bringing down God's wrath upon them. Yahuah said He was going to give them up to their enemies and took their land away from them, scattering them all around the globe. However, after many centuries of punishment known as the Diaspora, the mercy of Yahuah prevailed, as He promised them through His prophet Ezekiel in chapter 37, that He would return the Jews to their homeland to witness His glory, where they would be given another chance to be his people. Notwithstanding their rejection of their own Messiah, Yahuah made a lasting covenant with them. He has promised to save them despite themselves. Hence, the ongoing family drama.

Spiritual cosmic battles are fought over all of us, including those who disbelieve in the Creator of all souls. The Creator allowed this Earth experiment to be set in motion, also allowed the fallen angels to reside on and *inside* the Earth and have dominion over other planetary spheres as well. (See Book Five: *Divine Plan of Salvation*, for more information on dark stars.)

There is a lot of grace from the Almighty God, because this is an experiment. Just because something is set in motion doesn't mean it's always going to work or be successful. Failures teach us our greatest lessons, so there is grace to be allowed enough wiggle room to make mistakes. Good parents allow their children to make their own mistakes. However, good parents have a responsibility out of love to correct their children. Spare the rod, spoil the child. Children thrive on discipline, discipline is love, discipline is not punishment although it can lead to punishment. The Lord corrects those whom He loves, whom He calls his sons and daughters.

He created the grounds for the experiment, guides its progress, protects His own, corrects them in the way they should go. He punishes for disobedience. Idolatry and sexual immorality are the most offensive sins for which Yahuah punished the people of Israel, literally allowing them to be taken over by their enemies. To the discerning spirit, this establishes understanding to spiritual legal ground. This is why the land of Israel was taken away from God's chosen people, as punishment for idolatry, disobedience and sexual debauchery. It's as if the Lord threw up his hands and said, 'that's it, time to end this failed experiment.' He did that more than once, as history tells us.

But the Bible story, which is a long story, a love story, of the relationship between Yahuah and His Creation. His ongoing battles with Satan shows the Creator is not just a God of justice, but a God of grace and mercy and that's why He sent Jesus,

Yeshua, the Savior, the Christ to become a StarGate for us to return back to Him, our Creator.

This grand experiment is the Creator's plan to weed out the faithful from the unfaithful, to make sure of the worth of those who will enter into the Kingdom of Heaven that is coming to earth. We will not have the root of Lucifer's rebellion in us, but instead be covered and forgiven by grace through His son, and King of the Kingdom, Yeshua, the Lord Jesus Christ.

The Reptilian Brain

> "Man's mind, once stretched by a new idea, never regains its original dimensions."
>
> ~Oliver Wendell Holmes Jr.

Carl Sagan was clearly puzzled over the similarities between the reptilian brain and the human brain. He points out in *The Dragons of Eden* that a vestige of our reptilian past lies at the core of the human brain. This part of the brain, known as the R-complex for reptilian complex, is said to be the part of the brain that performs the simple dinosaur functions: aggressive behavior, territoriality, ritual, and establishment of social hierarchies. The middle layer is called the limbic system, and is thought to generate love, hate, compassion, and sentimentality -- characteristics believed to be strictly mammalian. The largest part of the human brain, the neocortex or outer layer, is believed to be the home of reasoning and deliberation, and "the place where we know the difference between good and evil." [13]

Once again, science seems to agree with the ancient creation myths -- because in the Bible and other great scriptures, wasn't the knowledge of good and evil given to humans by a serpent? If the creator was reptilian, then, it could be that by becoming more mammalian -- and developing a neocortex -- humanity became *less* reptilian. The evidence and research is mounting daily that humanities roots are tied in genetically manipulated knots from interventions from alien masters we later became accustomed to referring to as gods and goddesses.

Another term important here, but one rarely taken literally or seriously these days, is the word "myth." We've been misled to believe that a myth is just a fairy tale or fantasy, a story from the world of make believe. This is another distortion, as it's the other way around. We've been living in the world of make-believe by believing and reinforcing a lie. The actual word "myth" has a Gaelic origin. Before the Romans pillaged northern and western Europe, the community there had existed as a matriarchal society since Viking times, meaning that it honored the Goddess in all things. Whenever you identified your origin, you identified with your Mother -- as it was always a sure thing who your mother was, but not necessarily a certainty about your father. So, you would identify with a way of life, by stating, "my mother's truth," which varied according to the various Gaelic dialects, and later became shortened to "my truth". As writing evolved, the word became "myth." Myths relating to dragons, serpents, goddesses, angels, demonic beings, elves, and fairies were in actuality very real stories that depicted the "mother truth" of those times.

Another word watered down and often misconstrued is the word "demon." This word actually derives from a Greek root meaning "intelligence." The medieval myths relating to demons, small beings with tremendous power to "cast wicked spells" upon people, actually refer to a very real phenomenon we know today as Aliens, or the Grays. While there are many different types of Aliens and many different species of Grays, it was they, in concert, who imprinted these legends into the so-called "myth" of demons.

When modern-day Christians perform exorcisms, they tend to focus on spirits, which are a whole other realm of influence that affects the human psyche. In their fervor to stamp out evil, they become somewhat blinded by their own passion, and fail to discern the different forces affecting the human vessel. Spirits are disincarnated beings, as well as beings out of sync with their rightful place of expression. The real demonic possession comes from the parasitic and vampiric force for which the Gray aliens are known. They are part of a hierarchical network of intelligence, something like a beehive, advanced beyond what we've been used to knowing, as we are beings under the veil. They work magic and sorcery through technology, and again, need to feed off of us as an energy source, although some actually do more than that -- a subject I'll discuss in more detail later.

This "magic," their sorcery, is actually an advanced form of technology, coupled with the fact that these beings are inter-dimensional, meaning they can exist in the third and fourth densities at the same time. They are able to manipulate matter in a way that we would call magical or miraculous. The reason we perceive it as such is because we haven't fully realized our own multi-dimensionality yet. When we do, then we will understand how they operate, as we will get our power back -- and we will be able to see through their masquerade.

One way the Dark Forces remains plugged into our energy fields is through implantation devices, which act as buttons to control us emotionally. We have been tricked by means of various contracts and agreements into allowing them to implant these devices into us. The contracts and agreements made with these ancient Dark Forces can be likened to the actions of a person who signs an agreement under the influence of drugs or alcohol: they're not entirely in possession of all their faculties, or to put it colloquially, are not operating on all cylinders. In other words, we enter into these agreements blindly, with little or no awareness of what it is we're signing, let alone the ability to read or even have access to the fine print. So, we literally sign our life force away to them, in exchange for what usually amounts to temporary gratification. These contracts, as far as they are concerned, are legal and binding, and follow us from lifetime to lifetime until WE decide to break the agreement -- to get a divorce, so to speak, from the Dark Forces.

As with any agreement, we make a choice to enter into one of these contracts, and we make a choice to rescind it -- just as marriage and divorce are both choices. When we make a decision to break our contractual agreements with the Dark Forces, our path towards freedom begins to open up. I'm not going to mislead you into a false sense of security and say that once you make this decision, that's it, you're now totally free. Actually, this only begins the process of liberation, healing and restoration.

An artist or craftsman can create a piece of art, then look upon it, decide that it's not what she intended, and then destroy it to start all over again. The artist takes personal responsibility for reconstructing and resurrecting that which she has ruined, and begins all over again. This is how it should be with our own lives: eventually, we need to take personal responsibility for what we've created, or mis-created as the case may be, and re-create ourselves according to our awareness.

So, what is it that keeps us from seeing that we create everything that happens to us? Walking around spiritually deaf and blind can certainly keep us under the veil, so to speak. Denying our Creator keeps us from creating the very things we'd like, instead creating exactly what we don't like. That's how denial works. It follows the Law of Resistance: "What you Resist, Persists." So, how do we resolve this personal dilemma? We come out of Denial, face ourselves, take personal responsibility for whatever happens to us (whether that's positive or negative), stop blaming others, and begin to "own" our own emotional energy, which is linked to our power as human beings. You can't create anything without emotions. Emotions are the key that ignites the creative force, whether it is positive or negative.

Blame is another classic way we give our power away. It means we don't take personal responsibility for what we have created. While it's true that we're only responsible for ourselves and not what others do, it's our response to what they do that can either empower or disempower us. Eventually, as we take our Shadow Self by the hand and walk it into the Light of Christ, marred as it may be by the kingdom of darkness, and apply the compassion and unconditional acceptance of Christ to who and what we really are, we experience healing, wholeness, and salvation. We no longer attract the negative experiences that have kept us immersed within this Cosmic Drama.

The Universe is made up of immutable Laws. One of them is the Law of Vibration, also known as the Law of Attraction, which demonstrates that like attracts like. This can also be described as a mirror effect. Smile, and the world smiles along with you. Walk in anger, and the world will attack you. Anger is one of those emotions that can run deep and wear many masks, as we know our emotions frequently fool us. Repressed anger -- denied emotion -- can create some of the worst scenarios we can experience. It's those simmering pots that eventually give off the greatest charge when they explode! Besides always attracting confrontation and conflict within relationships, unexpressed anger has often been the cause of accidents, some of which are deadly. You see, anger is a powerful emotion, but one not necessarily acceptable in our society.

When you bottle up power, you are setting yourself up for some form of expressing it. It exists and therefore is alive. The Subconscious Self records everything, remembers everything and carries with it all the repressed emotion that the Conscious Self has filed away. This is the aspect of ourselves that we've allowed to become separated and denied, but this is just kicking the can down the road. Our anger is a part of us, whether we acknowledge it or not. So, here's our choice: we can either deny it and continue in the illusion that we're victims and get tossed about by every wind and wave that blows, or we can accept it, and own it, give it to Christ and become empowered, alive and free.

When Jesus Christ said, "forgive them for they know not what they do," He was addressing the issues that separate us from having a relationship with the Living God, the Creator of our souls. Most people these days are ignorant of the fact that they are sinning, living in erroneous ways, making mistakes, wrong thinking; most people do not even know what pleases or offends their Creator. Most of us know that the ten commandments are basic moral rules, but there are so many other guidelines for spiritual awakening, for holy living, which, when ignored, separate us from having that dynamic daily relationship with the Living God.

> "Dear friends, I urge you, as *aliens* and strangers in the world, to abstain from sinful desires, which war against your soul."
>
> (1 Peter 2:11)

In fact, there are many sins that today we choose as a lifestyle, culturally approved, which are abhorrent to our God. We may have no idea that our choices are sinful, in error, and contrary to God's Will for us. Our ignorance consequently causes a debilitating spiritual condition, called spiritual poverty, yet we sustain a false sense of spiritual security. This is the case in most New Age circles, whose adherents mistakenly think that they are enlightened because they think they have broken away from traditional religions. Yet they remain bound by *religious spirits*, especially the spirits of pride and arrogance, which come directly from the influence of Lucifer himself, the angel of light, and his fallen angels.

A host of spiritual conditions can keep us unconsciously bound to evil. The practice of pride, narcissism, selfishness, self-centeredness, bitterness, resentment, anger, rage, retaliation, vengeance, murder, violence, hatred, cruelty, abuse, lies, unforgiveness, lusts, addictions, idolatry, the worship of angels, fallen angels, pseudo-gods, aliens, rebelliousness, jealousy, envy, living in fear, terror, greed, the worship of money, technology, materialism, the worship of science over spirit, unbelief, rejection, guilt, shame, blame, slander, judgementalism, gossip; these are all the principalities of the realm of Satan and his fallen angels, who hold us humans in bondage to all these *spiritual conditions,* otherwise known as a level of consciousness.

Most people are unaware that many of these mental and emotional states which create their *spiritual conditions* are sinful. Yet we actively support evil when we believe a lie and live in denial. It's like living in a trance, totally spaced out and out of touch with Spiritual Reality.

By nature, God is the spirit of love, joy, peace, longsuffering, gentleness, goodness, faith, virtue, purity, wisdom, justice, honesty, fairness, sincerity, knowledge, understanding, grace, mercy, temperance, excellence, forgiveness, compassion, devotion and truth.

This is the challenge and choice presented to every human who takes on this experience. The spiritual battle is about our free will to choose between the two spiritual influences. Our testing comes through the choices we make. If we choose God, we receive His blessings. If we reject God, we affirm that Satan is right in his rebellion. The consequences of our choices are evident to us. We too are tormented by the demonic hierarchy of evil spirits, fallen angels, demon aliens. God has set this experiment up to allow us to practice our own devices, and allow us to go our own way. Freedom always comes at a price.

> "Watch out for false prophets. They come to you in sheep's clothing, but inwardly they are ferocious wolves."
>
> (Matthew 7:15)

Notes:

1. R.A. Boulay, *Flying Serpents and Dragons: The Story of Mankind's Reptilian Past,* The Book Tree; Revised edition (July 1, 2003)
2. Zecharia Sitchin, *Genesis Revisited (The Earth Chronicles)* Avon Books, 1990.
3. Zecharia Sitchin *Twelfth Planet: Book I of the Earth Chronicles* Stein and Day, 1976.
4. Ibid.

5. William Bramley, *The Gods of Eden, The Chilling Truth about Extraterrestrial Infiltration and the Conspiracy to Keep Humankind in Chains,* Avon (March 1, 1993)
6. Graves, R., *The White Goddess, An Historical Grammar, of Poetic Myth,* Creative Age Press, 1948.
7. Ella LeBain, *Who's Who in the Zoo?* Book One – Third Edition, Tate, 2013.
8. Dr. Carl Werner, *Evolution: The Grand Experiment,* New Leaf Publishing Group; Rev Upd edition (May 15, 2014)
9. Ella LeBain, *Who is God?* Book Two, Chapter: *What Happens When You Die?* p.455-484, Skypath Books, 2015
10. Ella LeBain, *Who's Who in the Zoo?* Book One – Third Edition, *Annunaki* p. 219, Tate, 2013
11. Ibid
12. Ibid
13. Carl Sagan, *The Dragons of Eden: Speculations on the Evolution of Human Existence* Hardcover – Random House, New York, 1977.

CHAPTER FOURTEEN
UFOs in Israel

The thing that has been, it is that which shall be;
and that which is done is that which shall be done:
and there is no new thing under the sun . . .
~ King Solomon, (Ecclesiastes 1:9)

UFO Disclosure in Israel:

I moved to Israel in 1976 and in 1979, I graduated from Sde Boker, Negev, Israel. During my time in the Negev desert, I witnessed multiple UFO sightings during a time when there were fewer satellites orbiting the earth. At night, my friend and I would go outside where it was pitch black, because we were in the middle of the desert and there were few lights, and we were able to view the stars and see the milky way on a clear night. We witnessed what we called spaceships, and would go out on a regular basis to watch the ships pass in the night.

I shared the case in Book Two, *Who is God?* of the *humsin*, sand storms which became semi-regular occurrences while I was living in the desert. Meteorologists claim they would be caused by winds whipping up the sand, however, there were several times where it was a blue sky, a high and dry day, with no wind at all, yet out of nowhere, we would see a brown sand cloud coming our way, which came right out of the desert. I realized after investigation that these were not the usual sand storms, but spaceships landing and whipping up the sand.[1]

The month I left Israel, July of 1979, Yeshua Jesus appeared to me, and said, 'I am the Messiah, follow me.' All of these experiences intrigued me, which marked the beginning of what has become a 38-year investigation and ongoing research to get to the bottom of *Who's Who in the Cosmic Zoo?*

Israeli UFO disclosure has been widely reported in Russia and China but not in the English-speaking world. Israel is a source of deep division, misunderstanding, and anti-Zionism which is fueled by antisemitism, jealousy and hatred of the Jewish people. It is believed that Israeli secret service has had limited interaction with aliens via secret US government agencies. Historically however, Israel's connection to aliens goes all the way back to the Old Testament, a book clearly full of space technologies, aliens and extraterrestrial interventions. See, Book Two, *Who Is God?* for more details on all the scriptures and on the list of prophets who were *frequent travelers* in UFOs in ancient Israel.[1]

Nevertheless, the real *Star Wars,* ends up happening over the space portals and skies of Israel. It is certainly no coincidence, that the newly found religion born out of *Star Wars,* known as *Jediism,* both sounds and is likened to *Judaism.*[2] It is also no coincidence that the Dark Side focused their powers on eliminating the Jedi Priests, and all Jedi Warriors, to the point where Episode VIII – *The Last Jedi,* revealed just how much the Jedi was persecuted and the trouble the General and Kylo-Ren went, to murder who they believed was the last Jedi.

So, for metaphor and allegorical sake, the Jedi are the Jews. This world and its dark forces have also gone to a lot of trouble to eliminate the Jewish seed. It's supernatural hatred towards a race of people, that have contributed so much to the evolution and advancement of humankind, let's not forget the Torah and the Messiah, who was a Jew.

In the Galaxy of the Hebrew Language, which is a Cosmic Space Language, representing the Constellations and twenty-two root races symbolized by the twenty-two letters of the Hebrew Alphabet, it's no coincidence that the names, Jedi and even Yoda are rooted in Hebrew. The name: Jedi, is essentially the Hebrew letter *yud* which has become anglicized as a "J,". There is no 'J' in the Hebrew language, as I pointed out in Book Two: *Who is God? What's in a Name?*[1] For e.g., the Biblical name *Yehoshua* becomes *Joshua* in the English language. It's not much of a stretch to see how "Jedi" can be derived from the original Hebrew word for Jew, which is *Yehudi,* that is derived from the tribe of Judah, which in Hebrew is *Yehuda*. There is no coincidence here.[2]

Why Jerusalem?

The following paragraphs I originally published in Book One of *Who's Who in the Cosmic Zoo?* pp. 39-41, in 2012, 2103 respectively being reprinted here to connect the dots, and continue the discussion in Book Four: *Covenants.*

Since 1948, Jerusalem was made capital of the sovereign State of Israel. Just as in the United States of America, where all of the official branches of government, the legislative, executive and judicial, are in the capital city of Washington D.C., a theme that is duplicated throughout most of the 50 states, with the state's official government buildings in the state's city capital, so has the State of Israel kept their official Legislative Branch, known as Parliament or the Knesset, the executive and judicial branches in the capital city of Jerusalem. Yet, the city of Jerusalem actually belonging to Israel has been questioned by several groups in the Muslim world who continue to seek claim over Jerusalem, an ongoing spiritual battle.

Israel's best friend and ally in the world which is the U.S.A., which oddly enough has just recently begun to question Jerusalem as the capital of Israel, let alone a city belonging to Israel at all. The Obama administration challenged to stop issuing birth certificates to American babies born in Jerusalem, from the place of birth being listed as 'Jerusalem, Israel', to just 'Jerusalem', a city without a country. This was implemented during President Obama's first term (2009-2012). This new policy occurred despite the fact that the United States has always maintained and recognized Jerusalem as the capital of Israel.

As of the publication of this book, President Donald Trump reiterated to the world, that the city of Jerusalem is in fact the capital of Israel, and he ordered moving the U.S. Embassy from Tel Aviv to Jerusalem. This was in response to 151 UN States voted to disavow Israel's ties to Jerusalem, which has been an on-going disgraceful attempt by the antisemitism within the UN to rewrite history as part of a continuing political battle against the State of Israel and the Jewish people.

This not only reveals the Obama Administration's favor toward the claims made by the Muslim world on Jerusalem, but is in a direct violation of the already established laws of the Sovereign State of Israel itself. Not to mention, that according to Scriptures, Jerusalem is at the heart of the Lord, and consequently the very city that the final battle between Christ and Satan's Antichrist will culminate and end over.

In short, this issue over who rightfully owns Jerusalem will lead to WWIII, in a multi-national battle, that Bible prophecy calls the War of Gog and Magog. However, the final *Star Wars* battle known as Armageddon on and over Jerusalem doesn't take place until after the antichrist is revealed to the planet by being the one who claims to solve the world's problems and brings peace to the nations and ends WWIII.

Being known as a peacemaker will be his first big hook, followed by signs, wonders and miracles of advanced alien technology, leading to his demand for worship through his projected image through the holographic technology to the whole world. Making sure the temple in Jerusalem is rebuilt for the third time so he can demand worship in it. The Jews reinstate the old testament practice of animal sacrifices, which ended after Christ became the final sacrifice as the lamb of God, that led to the destruction of the second temple in 70AD. In addition to all that, he will insist and decree that everyone accept his implant in order to be allowed to buy or sell in his New World Order global economy.[3]

In Book Three of *Who's Who In The Cosmic Zoo,* I went into greater detail discerning *who* this being will be and how to recognize him.[4] See, herein Chapter, *Who is Antichrist?* Suffice it to say that Jerusalem becomes the final battleground for our world and our timeline as we know it to end. How ironic that the meaning of the name

Jerusalem in Hebrew translates to 'City of Peace', which is probably the most fought over city in the world, and truly is the 'eye of the storm' of all spiritual warfare on earth.

The hope, however, lies in the New Jerusalem, a glorious city that comes down from Heaven and is grounded on earth, finally establishing what the name Jerusalem really means, which will not only be the city of peace on earth, but the city of peace in the heavens as well. A city that will unite all ET races under the auspices of the Kingdom of Heaven.

In the meantime, humanity must develop the ability to discern between all these radically different beings. Discernment and a love of God are key factors. Without the Lord, humanity cannot assert itself against the Reptilian-Hybrid-Gray-Nordic threat. Remember just because an alien has more advanced technologically than us, doesn't necessarily mean their intentions for humankind are benevolent. We must learn to separate the wheat from the chaff.

I have heard scientists say that they would love to meet an alien, just so they can acquire more scientific data and learn what they know. This type of attitude and consciousness leading humanity is dangerous because it lacks spiritual discernment. Just as Jesus Christ said,

"For what shall it profit a man, if he shall gain the whole world, and lose his own soul?"
(Mark 8:36)

Discernment is the ability to obtain sharp perceptions and to judge well, to separate truth from lies, illusion from reality, and fantasy from facts. It is about learning the difference between emotional truth and Spiritual Truth, emotional impulse and intuitive guidance, and being victimized and feeling like a victim. It is about recognizing the difference between a person that can be trusted and one who will betray us - between a soul connection and an emotional attraction to a person who is emotionally unavailable.[3]

Have the Ancient Giants of the Bible Returned to Israel?

Have the Anakim or the Refaim, who are described as the giants of the Bible, already returned to Israel? The late Israeli Ufologist Barry Chamish[5] seems to think so, based on the following reports. When it comes to UFO sightings, as I've discerned in Book One of *Who's Who in the Cosmic Zoo?* we may discern between government spacecraft run by the secret space program, and the actual alien craft that are not of this world. When sightings of strange craft are followed by close encounters and abductions, we can rule out that it's our own government posing as alien giants. Men in Black, maybe, but certainly not giants.

There are periods of recorded history when giants were reported in Israel; during the days before the Flood, till the ascension of King David, and since 1993 in modern Israel. The case for the return of giants to Israel is so strong that it distinguishes the current Israeli UFO wave from others around the world, with an abundance of physical evidence left behind by these aliens.

The first recorded instance of modern Israeli UFO sightings occurred on September 28, 1987, when a 27-year-old auto mechanic, Ami Achrai was driving just south of Haifa when he witnessed what he thought might be a helicopter in distress hovering just above the sands of Shikmona Beach on the Mediterranean Sea. He stopped his car and to his astonishment saw a disc-shaped craft that emitted a bright red flash before it disappeared.[5]

Two days later he returned to the site with a Ufologist referred to him by the Israeli police named, Hadassah Arbel. They discovered remains, of one of the most dramatic proofs of evidence ever left by a UFO, confirming its physical existence. The flash emitted by the craft burned its image into the sands of Shikmona Beach. A fifteen-meter ellipsoid disk was burnt black into the sand, but what was more interesting was what wasn't burned. Within the ellipsoid was vegetation, left unburned, and a clear image of the pilot of the craft facing a control board.

Seven years later Ufologist Barry Chamish[5], sent samples of the burnt sand to the television show *Sightings,* subjecting it to laboratory tests. The sand appeared to melt in the heat of the camera light. The reason was the sand particles were covered by a low melting hydrocarbon material. The laboratory concluded there was no natural or man-made explanation for the phenomenon.

Ami Achrai's incident was followed by a repeat performance on June 6, 1988 when a disk-shaped craft once again burned into the sands of Shikmona Beach, about 100 yards north of the first site. Then followed the most spectacular display of all, on April 27, 1989, when two teenagers witnessed a UFO explode into thousands of shards over Shikmona Beach. At that point, Israeli Ufologists investigated the incident fully and scientifically. The beach was strewn with burning white metal which was cool to the touch. The metal even glowed in water. When it was picked up, the shards turned into a white ash. Scientists from the Technion Institute of Technology tested the site and found that magnetism was 6000 times higher than the surrounding area. The shards were found to be very pure magnesium.[5]

Could the repeat events at the same site be indicative of a space portal there? Two hundred yards above Shikmona Beach is an ancient biblical shrine called Elijah's cave. It was there the Old Testament Prophet Elijah preached. It was nearby in the Carmel Mountains that Elijah challenged the Canaanites to a 'duel of the gods', of which drama we read in 1 and 2 Kings. At this place, two bulls were tethered, and the gods were invoked to roast them. Naturally, Baal failed the Canaanites, but the

God of Israel sent a ray of light from heaven, where He orbited in His cloud ship, which cooked the bull right on the spot. This ray was the same as that which burned the sands of Shikmona Beach into a saucer shape. While the power source of these two rays are distinct, the similarity of effect results from the masterful counterfeiting by rebel angels masquerading as aliens in UFOs. Let's just say, for intents and purposes, they are the aliens.

Elijah's God, Yahuah, the God of Israel, won in the end, destroying the false prophets of Baal, bringing the evil Queen Jezebel and King Ahab down, through King Jehu who saved Israel.

The biblical and historical discernment here is that Lucifer the Satan and his rebel fallen angels are constantly trying to IMITATE and COUNTERFEIT the Creator's works, and that includes His Starships. Just as Satan declared in Isaiah 14:13: "I will be compared to the Most High God." Even more of a coincidence, an ancient drawing of a spacecraft just like the one that burned into the sands on Shikmona Beach was recently discovered within Elijah's Cave. The *Sightings* team decided "the image was a coincidence, maybe it was a bat." Last I heard, bats don't draw. We all know there are no coincidences.

However, when UFO Researcher Michael Hessmann video-graphed the drawing, he was certain it was a match for the burned sand pictures. Although the meaning of the cave drawings is in dispute by researchers, the fact that a modern UFO burned inscriptions is indisputable. Something extraordinary happened at Shikmona Beach. Alien craft decided to leave their mark behind there at least three times. In doing so, they revealed the dimensions of their craft and image of their pilot, as well as their construction material. These were not crop circles nor were they formed the same way. An entirely different message was left behind on Shikmona Beach's sands. The aliens had returned to Israel.[5]

After that UFO explosion, there was a lull in UFO activity until 1991 and 1993, over the village of Sde Moshe, some five miles from Kadima. Eli Cohen captured on videotape, on two consecutive nights, the interior of his house being lit up by an unknown spacecraft hovering above it. He filmed several minutes of the video just after daybreak, resulting in one of the clearest convincing record of a UFO.

In these initial reports from Barry Chamish[5] in 1993, he called them 'visitors'. I choose not to call them visitors, because we've been sharing a planet with these beings for millennia, they're neighbors. As I stated in my initial thesis in Book One of *Who's Who in the Cosmic Zoo?* [3] ninety percent of UFOs come from this earth, to include our secret space program run by the super power nations, and actual alien craft from the inner earth civilizations of alien, extraterrestrial, and interdimensional races.

For the purpose of clarity, for the sake of discernment, words matter here, because for too long, researchers were deceived into believing that UFOs were visitors from outer space, while they are actually coming from inner space. These beings never left, and are not visiting us after all but are in fact resident aliens.

It seems the aliens were merely scouting the Kadima area in 1991, before returning in full force in 1993, when the occupants of the crafts did more than merely hover in the sky. In the early morning of April 20, 1993, Tsiporet Carmel's house glowed from within. She stepped outside and saw what she thought was a new fruit silo built outside her back yard. But then she saw the silo add a second story to itself. Ten yards to the side of this magical silo, Tsiporet saw a seven-foot-tall being wearing metallic overalls. Its head was covered in what looked like a beekeeper's hat. Tsiporet said, "Why don't you take off your hat, so I can see your face?" The being answered her telepathically, "That's the way it is."

This was Israel's first publicized close encounter with an alien being. Tsiporet could easily have been made an object of ridicule but for the fact that a crop circle 4.5 meters in diameter was found exactly where she had seen the craft. Within the circle were shards of a material later found to be a very pure silicon.

About 10 days later, two more circles were found just outside Tsiporet's back yard. This time, they were soaked with a red liquid, a fluid which would become a constant feature of upcoming landing circles. It was tested by the National Biological Laboratory in Ness Tziona and found to be composed mostly of cadmium.

That same year, the aliens showed up in Kadima again, to encounter two other women in their late thirties living on Hapalmach Street. The first was a Russian immigrant named Mara. Strange forces shook her house so hard, they caused her air conditioning unit to fall out of its window casing into the house. Then 'voices' called to Mara in her childhood nickname. Eventually she decided the house was haunted and she moved far from Kadima.

At that time, Shosh Yahud was the Treasurer of the Town of Kadima. She was described as a down to earth woman who wanted as little to do with her UFO experience as possible. In May, she awoke to see a seven foot, round faced being in silvery overalls circling her bed as if "floating on his shoes." The creature assured her he was not there to harm her, and she became relaxed. After a few minutes the being floated through her wall outside. Shosh thought she had dreamed the incident until she looked out her window in the morning and saw a 4.5-meter crop circle in her backyard. When the Ufologists descended upon her home to investigate, they discovered the silicon and cadmium within the circle.

Next, that same year in June, it was Hannah Somech's turn to be visited by a giant. Hannah lives in Burgata, three miles from Kadima. She was startled to see her dog go flying across the kitchen into a wall. When she stepped outside to investigate she was blocked by an invisible force. She then saw a seven foot, round-faced being in metallic overalls examining her pickup truck. She said to it, "What did you do to my dog?" It answered telepathically, "Go away. I'm busy. I could crush you like an ant if I wanted to. Go back to your husband."

A 4.5-meter circle crushed out of the grass was later found in Hannah's back yard. Within, the grass was soaked with red liquid cadmium. By the end of the summer, the credible reports of giants roaming the land persuaded the normally dull TV station Channel One, to broadcast a one-hour program on the subject. Tsiporet and Shosh appeared as well as the Ufologists who had examined the circles of Kadima. To the surprise of the host, the viewing audience believed the witnesses of alien landings. The result was two more witnesses coming out into the open. Both were women in their late thirties who lived within ten miles of each other south of Tel Aviv. Another woman, Clara Kahonov of Holon, who was the most reluctant to be quoted in the broadcast, acknowledged and confirmed that she indeed, had seen a giant being.

I don't especially recommend interacting with these types of aliens. They are the same who used to kick us humans around during the Old Testament times of the Bible. They endured punishment from the Lord of lords, they were flooded out of the earth twice, which we can read in the books of Genesis, Enoch and the Book of Giants. They were nuked from heaven at the times of Sodom and Gomorrah, but a remnant managed to survive to this day, by escaping *inside* the vast cavern system of the earth.

They are also part of the group who were trying to influence a man from Croatia named Rael to build an embassy in none other than Jerusalem, where they can talk with the leaders of this world. This became the religious alien cult which purports human cloning, another alien agenda. Like Scientologists, the Raelians believe these aliens are the Elohim, but they are actually the Nephilim of the Bible, as we see from contact with the Giant. Clearly the fallen angels are using this cult to divert us from the truth, as well as use us to invite them into the End Time Game of *who* gets to rule over the ancient portal in Jerusalem.

The famous Israeli born Uri Geller had contact at the age of three, a Christmas Day encounter in 1949 which gave him supernatural powers to bend metal and silver spoons at will. He thought he heard kittens, so the young toddler wandered to the back of his house where a bright light appeared above him which he claims struck him and activated his powers. These extraordinary claims are made in his biography, *In the Secret Life of Uri Geller*, which lifts the lid on the world-famous illusionist. Geller says how he felt something above him. When he looked up he saw a ball of light. He said: "It wasn't the sun — it was something more massive, something that you could touch."[6]

The Bible: The Best UFO Evidence

George Adamson and George Hunt, pioneers in Ufology, were the first to expound the theory that the Bible is a long UFO story. They laid the groundwork for Erich Von Daniken, whose best-selling book, *Chariots of the Gods,* spread this new view of the bible worldwide, made even more widely known by the popular cable documentary on the History Channel, *Ancient Aliens.* As I've shared at the beginning of this book series, in Book One of *Who's Who in the Cosmic Zoo?* Erich Von Daniken along with Cope Schellhorn, author of *Extraterrestrials in Biblical Prophecy,* were my inspirations to put my book series together with the same Biblical UFO Theory.

As I've proved in greater detail in Book Two: *Who is God?*[1] the evidence of space ships and the cast of characters of multiple gods, aliens, extraterrestrial and extradimensional angels, and giants are all written into the Hebrew Scriptures, that much of which has been lost in various English translations from the original Hebrew. The original Hebrew presents a very clear description of various types of spacecraft and technologies. The ability to discern the words in the correct meaning from the Hebrew language also describes various gods, in their plurality, that English Bibles conceal.

This author believes that not only were the ancient Israelites visited by a cast of characters of gods, ETs, aliens and angels, but that the prophets themselves warned that what happened in the past would repeat in the End Times. Biblical evidence proves that the ancient Israelites did not stick to the worship of one God, despite the basic tenets of monotheism in Judaism, but rather the ancient Israelites served multiple superior beings, which hastened the God of Israel's punishment upon them. The word for God in Hebrew is Elohim, and for Lord, Adonai, which happen to both be plural, meaning Gods and Lords. These Gods dwelt in heaven and came to their aid with armies of angels when Israel was threatened.

The Elohim (gods) mandated Israel with specific laws of hygiene so that they could be the healthiest group of humans, and their soldiers could maintain the edge on their pagan enemies, who were considered unclean to the Elohim. There were further laws of morality, which were guidelines to get along with each other and please the God of gods, who is Yahuah, the God of the Elohim and of Israel. What distinguished them from the other gods was their adherence to morality within the venue of cosmic warfare. They used prophets as messengers to allow plenty of time for their people to grow, mature and repent of errors. Whenever Israel strayed from these laws, God sent angels to communicate with the prophets and seers to warn the people and help to put them back on the right track. Sometimes they listened, but when they refused, it resulted in lots of drama between the Israelites and their enemies, as the Elohim (gods) allowed them to be overcome, to teach them a valuable lesson.

So, here we are at the end of this processional Age of Pisces, can we say that they learned their lessons of history? Or, has history repeated itself because people fail to learn from it? There will be a final test at the very end of this age, which the Bible calls the Great Tribulation, or the times of Jacob's Troubles, which relates specifically to Israel. The prophecies of the End Times are the focal point of this book series, which is my hope that all will learn how to discern which aliens and which extraterrestrials will launch the mass deception at the End Times. This deception is what causes the Antichrist to rise to power, wielding the power of alien technology to bring fire down from the heavens, another way of saying UFO technology and the ability to command exotic space craft. See, Revelation 13:13.

According to multiple whistleblowers, the U.S. government is being nudged through secret agreements with a group of aliens called Tall Whites, aka Nordics, Aryans, which should send an icy chill down our collective spines. These aliens were instrumental in the rise of the Nazi regime in Germany, where they inspired Hitler's White Supremacy mania. I go into greater detail in Book One of *Who's Who in the Cosmic Zoo?* as to *who* these beings are and how to identify them.[1]

A report based on documents leaked by whistleblower Edward Snowden proves an alien extraterrestrial intelligence agenda is driving U.S. domestic and international policy, and has been doing so since at least 1945. The Russians are well aware of this, because they have shared a joint base with the Americans in Antarctica since World War II. One aspect of most concern to Russian authorities is that the Snowden documents confirm that the "'Tall Whites' are the same extraterrestrial alien race behind the stunning rise of Nazi Germany during the 1930's." This alien assistance, the report adds, manifested itself in the Reich's technically-superior submarines.[7]

That puts the holocaust in a different light, not just genocide, but total annihilation of everyone down to those who hold 1/4 or even 1/8 Jewish genes. The suggestion that these same aliens are now in collaboration with the upper hierarchy of the Military Industrialized Complex is sinister in the extreme.

End Times Prophecies Point to Israel

This leads me to the discernment of End Times Prophesies concerning Israel. These Nordic Tall Whites, or Blonds, have been communicating with some of the top religious leaders of the world, such as the Pope and the Dalai Lama, influencing them to create a one world religion, as End Times Prophecies predict. According to Bible Prophesies, the final Antichrist is going to rise to power from a great war, which is World War III, and become the peace ambassador who brokers a treaty between

Israel and all her enemies during the climax of this World War. This individual then is seen as a Messiah figure to Israel, who takes up residence in Jerusalem's third rebuilt temple, where he is propped up by the End Times False Prophet, who is most likely the reigning Pope. See, Book of Daniel Chapters 7, 9, 11; Revelation 13. When you compare Revelation 13 with Daniel 7, it reveals that the final world empire of the antichrist will be a revived Roman Empire, that will be rooted in all the previous empires. It will unite in a single kingdom all the evil and power that was once characterized in previous kingdoms.

I am connecting these dots for those who may have bits and pieces of the prophecy but not sure how it will be fulfilled. I find it no coincidence that the Disclosure Reports coming from credible whistleblowers and researchers such as Dr. Michael Salla, who vetted MILAB's Whistleblower Corey Goode,[8] confirmed that the Nordic Blond Tall Whites have contacted the Pope and other religious leaders to create a one world religion. See my chapter on *How Disclosure of ETs will affect Religions.*

In fact, Corey Goode reported to Dr. Salla, that the Nordic ETs are getting ready to offer these religious leaders a *book* that comes from the inner earth, one that will change the nature of religion and turn our history inside out.[8] The creation of a new religion will become necessary for survival, all part of the alien agenda, as a one world religion will set the stage for the counterfeit Messiah to emerge and take over the world.

It is rumored that former U.S. President Dwight D. Eisenhower met with the Tall Whites in 1954 to establish the secret agreement resulting in an exopolitical regime currently ruling America. He set the tone for succeeding U.S. Presidents to be the impotent facades for these clandestine puppet masters.

Even more disturbing are the extraterrestrial power struggles that have subsequently developed between the Tall White Nordic and the Draconian Reptilians who also reside *inside* the planet, as mirrored by the cold war between the Americans and Russians.

This has led to multiple conspiracy theories. These all point to the data collecting program known as PRISM that suggests the U.S. Military will coordinate a false flag ET invasion, to be used as a pretext and justification for space wars. I mention this, and connect this dot, because this sums up what the End Times Prophesies point to in the last days.

There is a tremendous amount of UFO activity within and around the borders of Israel. There have been multiple UFO sightings reported and documented in Israel over the past decade, in Netanya, Rishon LeTsiyon, Herzeliya, Sde Boker, Tel Aviv, Yafo, Haifa, Ein Geidi Beach, Galilee, Givataim, Hadera, and Jerusalem.[9]

The Vatican's Evidence of Ancient Astronauts

According to numerous reports, Russian Professor Genrikh Mavrikiyevich Ludvig visited the Vatican Secret Library in the 1920s and gained access to multiple ancient manuscripts that described extraterrestrial civilizations. These manuscripts documented extraterrestrial contact with the ancient civilizations of Egypt, Israel and Mesopotamia and confirmed that the pyramids were constructed to be used as energy generators.[10]

Sovershenno Sekretno, a popular and well respected Russian newspaper, published an article on Professor Ludvig, October 2011, written by journalist Vladimir Kucharyants, titled, *Worlds of Professor Ludvig.* Those who research the UFO phenomenon and the ancient astronaut theory have learned from this article that Professor Ludvig read about extraterrestrials who had visited the Earth in antiquity and concentrated his research on the Mayan civilization, interpreting their symbols to be spaceships and spacesuits. In addition, Professor Ludvig mentioned that the library contained manuscripts about alchemy and ancient codes.[11]

Professor Ludvig showed his students photocopies of the Vatican ancient manuscripts containing information about extraterrestrials who had visited our planet with drawings, and described to them the hidden essence of ancient myths. Professor Ludvig told the students of the Fiery Pillar that destroyed an advanced ancient civilization. He showed the students photos of the fortress walls discovered in Babylon, melted with the horrendous heat of what he believed was a nuclear blast.[11]

According to Ancient Alien Theorist, David Childress, author of *Technology of the Gods,* "Ludvig was the greatest researcher of all the early researchers into the whole concept of Ancient Aliens coming to our planet."[12]

If all the Bible stories are true, what we have is an historical record of extraterrestrial and alien interventions, as well as the reasons for the conflict over these locations on the earth. An ancient conflict that gets revisited in what many believe are divine appointments over the region of Israel, Egypt and their Middle Eastern neighbors. It's also clear from Ludvig's research and discoveries that the Vatican has been complicit in the UFO cover-up for millennia, and the only reason for driving the Disclosure movement today is to accept the alien agenda and a one world religion led by an alien savior.

Dr. Lubrick was persecuted for his knowledge by the USSR. Accused of being a Vatican spy, he spent decades locked away in one of Stalin's Gulag slave labor camps. It wasn't until 20 years after his death, when the Soviet Union broke up, was his file released.[13]

Notes:

1. Ella LeBain, *Who is God?* Book Two, Skypath Books, 2015.
2. Daniel Perez, *From Jediism to Judaism: Star Wars as Jewish Allegory*, http://www.aish.com/j/as/From-Jediism-to-Judaism-Star-Wars-as-Jewish-Allegory.html
3. Ella LeBain, *Who's Who in the Cosmic Zoo?* Book One – Third Edition, pp. 39-41, Tate, 2013
4. Ella LeBain, *Who Are the Angels?* Book Three, Skypath Books, 2016.
5. Barry Chamish, *Are Giants Returning to the Holy Land?* http://www.mt.net/~watcher/chamishgiants.html
6. Patrick Knox, *DID A UFO GIVE URI HIS POWERS? How Uri Geller was 'struck by a blinding beam from a floating ball of light aged three' – and was witnessed by an air force captain; Psychic claims to have met faceless alien who was holding a bright light.* Uri Geller's UFO Experience Age 3: https://www.thesun.co.uk/news/2681284/uri-geller-psychic-ufo-alien-visit/, January 23, 2017
7. Haaretz, *Fars-ical Snowden Files Prove U.S. Run by Nazi Aliens, Iran Says; Secret regime of extraterrestrial race called 'Tall Whites' - who used to be in cahoots with the Third Reich - is currently running the show in America, semi-official news agency Fars reports.* https://www.haaretz.com/news/world/1.568551?v=B27DCABFCF16697C4BE09863819D43BD January 14, 2014
8. Michael E. Salla, Ph.D., *World Religions Unite as Prelude to Extraterrestrial Disclosure,* http://exopolitics.org/world-religions-unite-as-prelude-to-extraterrestrial-disclosure/ June 22, 2017
9. UFO Sightings in Israel: http://www.ufo-hunters.com/sightings/country/ISR/Israel
10. *Evidence of Aliens visited Earth and ancient codes found in Vatican's library by Russian Scientist in the 20'*s, http://ufosightingshotspot.blogspot.com/2014/06/evidence-of-aliens-visited-earth-and.html
11. Paul Stonehill, *Russian scientist found to be UFO and ancient aliens Researcher*, http://www.openminds.tv/russian-scientist-found-ufo-ancient-aliens-researcher/28381, June 19, 2014
12. *Ancient Aliens*, History Channel, Season 11-Episode 12, www.history.com/shows/ancient-aliens/season-11/episode-12
13. *Evidence of Aliens visited Earth and ancient codes found in Vatican's library by Russian Scientist in the 20'*s, http://ufosightingshotspot.blogspot.com/2014/06/evidence-of-aliens-visited-earth-and.html

CHAPTER FIFTEEN

Were Aliens Behind the Holocaust?

"If we bear all this suffering and if there are still Jews left, when it is over, then Jews, instead of being doomed, will be held up as an example."
— Anne Frank (*Diary of a Young Girl*, entry dated April 11, 1944)

"The question shouldn't be "Why are you, a Christian, here in a death camp, condemned for trying to save Jews?' The real question is "Why aren't all the Christians here?"
— Joel C. Rosenberg, *The Auschwitz Escape*

We know from observation history repeats itself. All wars are connected, continuations of unfinished business from the previous conflicts, with the World Wars being stark examples of this. World War III will be no different, just deadlier. The issues of racism, genocide, anti-Semitism, religion, and every hierarchy which seeks world domination will be in play. Since we refuse to learn from history, we are doomed to repeat our mistakes.

The mass murder known to the world, as the holocaust, known to Jews, as the *shoah,* in Hebrew means *catastrophe*, was a concentrated drop in the bucket of mega-death which took place from 1917 till 1945. The mass sacrifice of over eighteen million innocent people, Protestants, Orthodox Christians, ethnic Jews, Gypsies, and minority groups is one segment of the horrors perpetrated by Adolf Hitler; and Joseph Stalin quadrupled that number in Russia before, during and after the Nazis had been vanquished. This makes us shudder, as it recalls only the most recent acts of mass human sacrifice in our history.

There is plenty of blame to go around on all sides, as American innovation and hustle was central to the success of the Holocaust. Concentration camps for the unwanted can still be found, now called Reservations, across the U.S. The ever present Catholic

Church, which represents itself as the premier and original Christian state, has been behind most of the persecutions of other Christian sects. The foulness known as the Inquisition was a political maneuver by Holy Mother Catholic Church to purge itself of Jewish conversos whom Torquemada did not trust. Financial funding and occultism joined forces to back the Nazi purges. Hitler was maniacal in his desire to obliterate the Jews, though anyone who got in his way was easily disposed of along with all enemies of the Catholic Church. As an institution, the Church is a stupendous success, but as a religion it is a disgrace to its founder and a source of shame to the entire human race.

If the Church Catholic does not represent Jesus Christ, for all its works of charity and protestations of compassion, neither does the Protestant, with its witch-burnings and state sponsored terror, subjugations, wars, and similar atrocities. For all who take offense at this idea, look at the history of the Churches and Reformations, and compare it all to Jesus' description of His followers in His own words: 'By their fruits you will know them,' Matthew 7:20. The huge number of apologists for the Church's history should display plainly to our discerning eyes that this is a habitation of wolves and aliens. All those who have an inclination toward Catholicism, or who despair of Christian bashing Christian, please turn to the real Jesus Christ, and find a real Christian non-denominational church, filled with the Holy Spirit.

As for Jews, Yeshua's plan is to reveal Himself to you, as He knows your pain and your confusion. Others have carried out atrocities in His name, which was clearly never His will or the will of God. Jews should know their Messiah in a personal way, and it is prophesied that all of Israel will come to know the name of the Lord (Yahushua) and will be saved by Him. (Zechariah 14)

Not sparing the Catholic Church, we must not spare ourselves as Americans. The United States Office of Strategic Services received a report dated June 20, 1942 from Lisbon that began with the words, "Germany is no longer persecuting the Jews. It is systematically exterminating them."

The real testament of horror occurred after the war ended, when the camps continued, even flourished, under Allied control. The atrocities, the starvation and torture were meted out indiscriminately under Russian and Polish influence on Jews, civilians, the defenseless, and the mass murders continued. Revenge is hardly a Christian virtue, and certainly not an American value.[1]

Isn't it time we examined ourselves and asked the hard questions: Why did it happen? How did we let it happen? And, what will we do when it happens again?

Hitler as Foreshadow of AntiChrist

The author of the Holocaust stated openly that he planned to exterminate the Jews, and whoever else he deemed 'subhuman' or unfit for life, in his autobiography, which he entitled *My Struggle of Four and a Half Years Against Lies, Stupidity and Cowardice.* The time span should grab our attention, as it suggests a bit longer than the standard three and a half years of struggle by the Antichrist himself. This man and the two others who unleashed the second world war and untold suffering upon all of humanity was only a forerunner of the real Counterfeiter.

Ron Rosenbaum, in his book *Explaining Hitler: The Search for the Origins of His Evil,* remarked that Hitler was obsessed with the idea of counterfeit, and used it against those he hated and feared the most. This could be a classic case of projection, as he himself was not who he said he was, while broadcasting exactly what he meant to do in the world. His anti-Semitism was never remarked until his visionary revelation, which took place in a psychiatric hospital in 1918, that told him he could speak, and would become the savior of Germany and found a race of supermen. This may sound like possession, or a battle plan.[2]

The purification and unleashing of human potential are foundational ideas of Nazism; that is, of a particular type of human being, one which is said to have been directly descended from The Old Gods, and who has been bred back into being by eugenics and harsh disciplines, one which has no conscience and is not troubled by religious scruples or moral standards, one which has absolute loyalty to himself alone and worships no god but his need.

In order to give this new man, the superman, living space, and room to breed, there was need to conquer and purge the world of all that was impure, inadequately perfect, subhuman. Jews fit into that category for the sole reason that they are not descended from The Old Gods and have loyalty to an idea, a calling, a higher power, beyond themselves. In Nazi ideology, as in that of many others, there is room for only one kind on earth.[2]

The Nazis, led by Hitler and his false prophets, accomplished an astonishing amount of progress in an unbelievably brief amount of time. One would call his rise meteoric and his success comet-like, both other-worldly attributes.

One of the most astonishing facets of the whole Nazi era was its honesty, straight forward and in your face, in bold print and over loud speakers in the streets of our capital cities, that it wanted to destroy us, demolish our ideas, values, culture, and erase all trace of us ever having existed, in deference to its own system. This honesty is the only difference between Nazi and Nephilim!

The Covenant of Hate

Henry Lincoln, in his book *The Holy Place*, first drew our attention to the symmetrical precision of the patterns of the prehistoric sites and temples of Europe. Following straight lines that can be seen from the air and traced on the map, we see a fascinating pattern taking form, making up pentagonal shapes. These ancient pagan cites were naturally taken over and Christianized by the conquering Catholic Church, many being covered over by the Gothic cathedrals which still stand today.[3]

Along more sinister lines, we can see an interesting pentagonal pattern to the death camps of the Nazis along with the Vatican, who hid their own death camps.

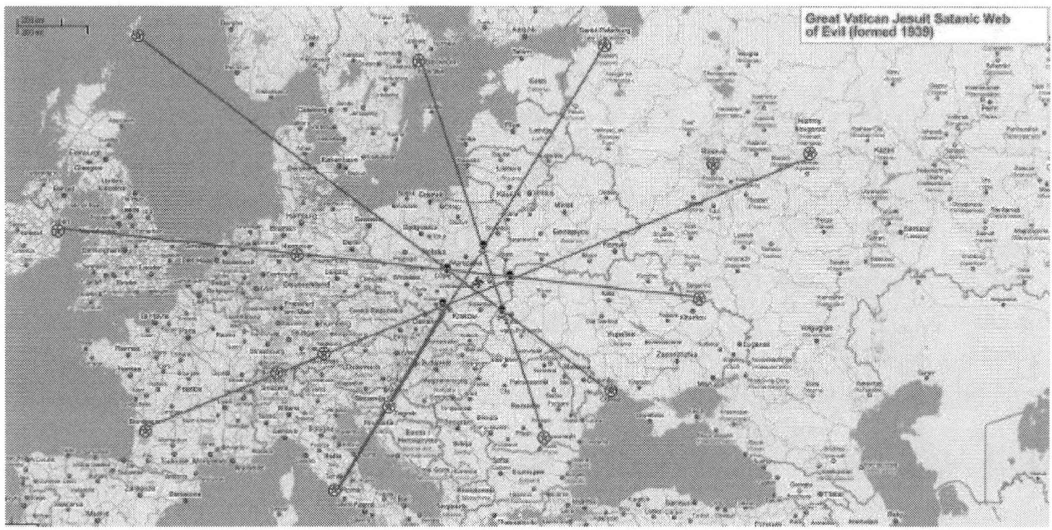

The form of a pentagram for worship of evil requires at least five sacrifice camps, one for each point of the star, almost as a crown. Naturally, the Nazis, being practical, opportunistic, and efficient, didn't stop at five, but built an entire system around the five crown camps where mass human sacrifice could take place.

You can still easily plot this Pentagram for yourself today by simply calling up any map of Poland.

First, find Pulawy on a Map—the Palace and Temple to Cybele is located just to the South West of the town itself. Now go directly up and stop just south-east of Ostrow—this is the top tip of the Pentagram and the site for the Treblinka Death Camp. Now continue to travel down South East—past Pulawy, until you find the town in Orthodox Ukraine called L'viv. Due west of this town was the Janowska site where the inmates were worked to death. Now travel west until you travel past Krakow until just above the town of Bielsko-Biala. This was the site of the most atrocious site, Auschwitz, a name that draws disgust and shame to this day. Now travel north until you find the town of Lodz. This was the site of the only camp dedicated purely to children, Lodz. Finally, travel east again until you find the small town of Wlodawa—almost on the border of the Ukraine—this was the site of the Sobibor Extermination Camp.[4]

There is your Pentagram of Pure Evil, proof in soil that the Nazis were acting on orders from hell itself. There is your Pentagram of death constructed to attempt to channel the greatest amount of negative energy to one location in the history of humanity.

But why? We have cried that question since liberation. Why did good, honest, hard-working people of faith go along with this butchery? How could people be so evil as to murder children by the thousands?

The answer lies at the heart of how society has been fashioned by forces for centuries—forces that do not wish the world to progress—by people who pretend to be pious but instead plot to keep the world in misery. These forces have secretly planned to return the world to the Dark Ages.

Interesting that the silent complicity of Pope Pius XII and the Jesuits, as well as the Protestant clergy, certainly benefited both church institutions. Thank God that today the complete and total implication of the crimes of the Vatican against humanity have come to public attention and conversation. Today any person can access the evidence for themselves. For any who are in denial of these mass genocides, is ignorant, uneducated and/or implanted with the same evil demon that caused it.

This is why Jews memorialize it on Holocaust Day, with the mantras, "Never Forget, Never Again". Those who refuse to learn from history, are doomed to repeat it's mistakes. That goes for those who deny history, and the evidence is overwhelming, included eye witnesses and survivors still alive today.

We must ponder the similarities of the slaughter of Jewish babies by Herod and the wholescale genocide by Hitler. They were both trying hard to divert the course of God's Plan. Like the Dark Forces of the Evil Empire in *Star Wars,* who sought after the death and annihilation of all Jedis, so it was with those implanted by the Dark Forces of this planet, who are obviously threatened and jealous of Jewish DNA, and more importantly, are in rebellion to the God of the Jews and their Messiah, who was the Jewish Jesus.

The Jewish Kabbalah reveals the real Human Star Wars, which is referenced in the Zohar, a compilation of Rabbinical writings of their deep mystical interpretations of the Torah. There is a great deal of information to be gleaned from the Zohar, on how the Jews perceived the universe and creation. The Kabbalistic perception of the 22 Hebrew Alphabet letters, reflects the 22 constellations, along with their black holes, their energies of duality of both good and evil in the physical universe. In fact, the word, *alphabet* was derived from the Hebrew languages, as the first two letters of the Hebrew alphabet are the letters *aleph* and *beth* (pronounced, *bet*). This is no coincidence.

The 22 Hebrew letters even represent Battle Stations, UFOs, Quantum Physics, Extraterrestrial Beings, Evil Death Stars, Death Star Fleets commanded by Dark

Lords, Masters of Evil, and Judgements sealed in Death. The Hebrew letters not only represent linguistic sound and mathematics with numerical values, but they reveal the entire meaning of life in the multiverse, and the metaphysical battle between light and dark, good and evil and its *outer space connections.*[6] It's as if the creators of the blockbuster movies, *Star Wars*, wrote their scripts inspired from the Kabbalah and the Zohar. Indeed, the Truth is Stranger than Fiction!

Therefore, knowledge empowers, and is it any wonder, that there is an alien presence on planet Earth, that has repeatedly sought to eliminate all genetic seed of Jews, because the Jews hold the knowledge of the ancient past, not necessarily in their heads, but in their DNA. This is why genocide on the Jewish people has been attempted several times in history, and sadly, according to End Times Prophesies, this alien presence that is so threatened by Jewish genetics, will attempt to wipe out Jews and Israel one last time in the last seven years, (Shemitah) of the end of this Age.

So, we can only hope, that one day, when the world finally wakes up to the spiritual and extraterrestrial war behind the terrestrial wars, genocides and enslavements, and we have all had quite enough of the lies, the cover-ups, the manipulations, the incompetence, the impotence from our religious strongholds, the racisms, the prejudice and the anti-Semitism, we the people will say: enough![5]

Notes:

1. John Wear, *Germanys War, the Origins, Aftermath, and Atrocities of WW2,* American Free Press, 2015.
2. Ron Rosenbaum, *Explaining Hitler: The Search for the Origins of His Evil,* HarperCollins, 1998.
3. Henry Lincoln, *The Holy Place,* Arcade, 1991.
4. https://worldtruth.tv/the-vatican-holocaust/ 28/32
5. one-evil.org - https://worldtruth.tv/the-vatican-holocaust/
6. Dr. Philip S. Berg, *Power of Aleph Beth, Volume 1,* p. 10-11, Research Center of Kabbalah Press, Jerusalem, 1988.

CHAPTER SIXTEEN
Who is AntiChrist?

"Let no one deceive you by any means; for that day will not come
unless the falling away comes first, and the man
of sin is revealed, the son of perdition,
who opposes and exalts himself above all that
is called God or that is worshipped,
so that he sits as God in the temple of God,
showing himself that he is God."
(2 Thessalonians 2:3-4)

"He shall speak arrogant words against the Most High,
He shall persecute the saints of the Most High,
and shall intend to change times and law.
Then the saints shall be given into his hand for
a time and times and half a time."
(Daniel 7:25)

The title of *Antichrist* means *against* Christ. The term applies to all who deny the deity of Yeshua HaMashiach Jesus Christ, who would oppose His Heavenly Kingdom coming to Earth. It is also used to describe all those who marginalize and persecute His followers, which includes individuals, organizations, religions and nations that falsely claim to represent Christ or ascribe to themselves the role of Messiah, which counterfeits the true Messiah. All counterfeits are considered *Antichrist* and idolaters.

Many Christians are confused enough to follow men, popes, priests, pastors, ministers, evangelists, and a host of false prophets rather than God's Word and the Holy Spirit, which is the Spirit of Christ. True believers are called into a *personal relationship* with the Living Lord Jesus Christ to be reconciled back to the Heavenly Father and Mother, the Creator of our Souls. However, too many fear a *Close Encounter* with Christ. Herein lies the discernment between religion and relationship, and between spiritual truth and deception. This is what the Bible says about the Antichrist (See also Daniel 7-9; Revelation 17:3; 12-14; 19:11-21).

> "Young children, it is the last hour, and, just as you have heard that antichrist is coming, even now there have come to be *many antichrists*; from which fact we gain the knowledge that it is the last hour."
>
> (1 John 2:18)

> "Many deceivers have gone forth into the world, persons not confessing Jesus Christ as coming in the flesh. This is the deceiver and the *antichrist*."
>
> (2 John 7)

Note that the *many antichrists* of 1 John 2:18 are here referred to collectively as *the Antichrist*. These many antichrists make up a *spirit of antichrist*. Christians are often confused as to how the *antichrist spirit* operates within individuals and organizations, and often mistakes someone who is against Christ for being *the* antichrist. The final antichrist, also called the man of perdition, or the lawless one, is an individual destined to be revealed in the last days at the end of this Age.

> "False Christs and false prophets will arise and will give great signs and wonders so as to mislead, if possible, even the chosen ones."
>
> (Matthew 24:24)

The chosen ones, also referred to as the elect, are the people of the covenant, which includes both Jews and Gentiles who are grafted into the Abrahamic Covenant through the Blood Covenant established through Yeshua Jesus the Christ.

Those identified as antichrist are Jews or Gentiles who deny that Jesus is truly the Messiah. This includes Muslims, Hindus, Buddhists, New Agers and atheists. It was established in the early writings of the New Testament Scriptures who was to be **the** *antichrist*, as well the appointed time when a man who appears to save Israel from her enemies and proclaims himself to be their *god*, as the final *antichrist*. We know this is a male, because the prophesies call him such, and describe that he will have no interest in women. This could be a homosexual, or a celibate priest, like the Pope, or an alien masquerading as a human. When we put both Old and New Testaments together, we can see that the final *antichrist* was destined to be long before the Messiah was born into the flesh, became the final blood sacrifice as a ransom to human souls, and was resurrected from the dead, and ascended back into heaven.

> "Every inspired expression that does not confess Jesus does not originate with God. Furthermore, this is the antichrist's inspired expression which you have heard was coming, and now it is already in the world."
>
> (1 John 4:3)

Already the world refers to the *spirit of antichrist*, which has manifested in several *antichrists* along our timeline. One of the first described in Old Testament scriptures and secular history was Antiochus, who destroyed the first temple and set himself up to be god.

In fact, the word *antichrist* is similar to his name, *Antiochus* in Greek. His defeat through the Jewish Maccabees is memorialized by the Hanukkah story and annual traditional celebration of the consecration of the first temple. The Roman Emperors who oppressed the Jews and ruled over Israel were antichrists, who destroyed the Second Temple in 70 A.D. This is relevant to us now because, that temple must be rebuilt into a third temple in Jerusalem. The book of Daniel prophesies that when the Jews are back in Israel, they will rebuild the temple and reinstate animal sacrifices, something that was eradicated after Yeshua Jesus became the final Lamb of God.

At the time of the second temple, 70 A.D., the Romans invaded, destroyed it and drove the Jews out of Israel into the Diaspora. The prophecy of their return in Ezekiel 37 was fulfilled 1,878 years later, but this happened only after one of the *Antichrists* manifested on the timeline, one used by Satan to punish the Jews for rejecting their Messiah. It's no secret that Adolf Hitler was deeply involved in the occult and was influenced by Martin Luther's Replacement Theology, which stated that because the Jews rejected Jesus, the Gentiles were to replace the Jews and Israel as the *covenant* people. Replacement Theology is a gross misinterpretation of the Covenants of God and His Word through the Bible Scriptures, and that includes the exobiblical scriptures as well, which actually say the opposite.

The church cannot replace the nation of Israel. The New Covenant is with the house of Israel and the house of Judah. Yeshua said He came only for the lost sheep of the house of Israel in Matthew 15:24. The New Jerusalem has 12 Gates and all of them are assigned to the tribes of Israel. The church (or assembly) in the first century was a sect of Judaism and therefore part of the house of Israel. The church, better called the assembly, was first seen at Mount Horeb when the original covenant was given to Israel.

The church today is a divided group of people who love God, while not knowing who He really is or what He expects of them. Many don't know or understand that Yeshua Jesus died to reconcile Himself to Israel because His sacrifice, by dying for them, was the only way to cancel His divorce from them.

> "Now, Israel, what does the LORD your God require from you, but to fear the LORD your God, to walk in all His ways and love Him, and to serve the LORD your God with all your heart and with all your soul, and to keep the LORD'S commandments and His statutes which I am commanding you today for your good? "Behold, to the LORD your God belong heaven and the highest heavens, the earth and all that is in it. "Yet on your fathers did the LORD set His affection to love them, and He chose their descendants after them, even you above all peoples, as it is this day. "So, circumcise your heart, and stiffen your neck no longer. "For the LORD your God is the God of gods and the Lord of lords, the great, the mighty, and the awesome God who does not show partiality nor take a bribe. "He executes justice for the orphan and the widow, and shows His love for the alien by giving him food and clothing. "So, show your love for the alien, for you were aliens in the land of Egypt."
>
> (Deuteronomy 10:12-19)

They don't know that grace is really merited favor and that those who do righteousness are the righteous. It's always been about a circumcised *heart* and obedience to His Spirit and laws. When Israel and the Jews repent to their Lord and Messiah, Israel will be the shining light that God intended her to be, and all of her enemies will be defeated. This is why He said He wasn't going to return until Israel and His people say, "Blessed is He who comes in the name of the Lord." (Matthew 23:39; Psalm 118:26)

> "O LORD, great and awesome God, who keeps His covenant and mercy with those who love Him, and with those who keep His commandments, "WE have sinned and committed iniquity, WE have done wickedly and rebelled, even by departing from Your precepts and Your judgments. "WE have not obeyed the voice of the LORD our God, to walk in His laws, which He set before us by His servants the prophets. "Therefore, the LORD has kept the disaster in mind, and brought it upon us; for the LORD our God is righteous in all the works which He does, though WE have not obeyed His voice.
>
> (Daniel 9:3-13)

I'm not going to be politically correct, or incorrect as the case often is, by tip toeing around the fact that the Holocaust was a judgment on the Jewish people for their rejection of their Messiah coming to them in the flesh. I've connected the dots to this historical event to the Bible Prophecy in Book Two: *Who is God?* Zechariah 13 speaks plainly to the fact that the Lord said He was going to punish His people for their rejection of His ways by putting them *through the fire,* so that they would call out His name and repent to Him. Did they?

We know that today there are approximately 150,000 Messianic Jews in the world, out of approximately 8-10 million total Jews, and that there are approximately 25,000 Messianic Jewish Israelis living in Israel. That number seems to be growing annually. We also know that prophecy states that there will be 144,000 Messianic believers in Israel, twelve thousand from each of the twelve tribes of Israel, each bearing His Mark on them during the reign of the *final Antichrist.* While Christians and Jews may argue about prophesies and their possible interpretations, it's hard to argue history at this point.

The Holocaust was the event which led directly to the formation of the Jewish State of Israel in 1948. Today Jews around the world have a place to go for refuge and community, the state of Israel. This is in and of itself fulfillment of an important prophecy, as the return of Jews to Israel was the beginning of the end of Time as we know it.

The presence, life, death, resurrection and ascension of Yeshua was something that split the Jewish psyche in half, as those who witnessed and walked with Him, who believed in Him, fulfilled the great commission to spread His *good news,* also known as the *gospel* of salvation to the rest of the world. The Pharisees and unbelieving Jews split off to persecute their fellows for following the Messiah. It is only the presence of the true Messiah returning to Israel that can put an end, once and for all, to the age of *Messy Antics*, between Messianics, Christians and non-believing Jews. This will not occur before the greatest testing ever visited upon Israel, known as the Great Tribulation, also called the times of Jacob's Troubles, because Jacob became Israel.

This is the time appointed to last seven years, the final Shemitah, when Israel will be taught just *who* is their Messiah and more importantly, *who* is not. Because of their rejection of *who* Yeshua was and what He taught, that will make them vulnerable to the mass deception of the final *antichrist* and his false prophet, giving them spiritual legal ground over them.

The irony is that Jews claim the reason they don't accept Jesus as their Messiah is because they can't believe God can manifest as a man in the flesh. But hey, if He's God, He can do anything, right? They also claim that worshipping Yeshua Jesus Christ is idolatry, and this is something Jews have been punished for severely in the past by the God of Israel, something for which they lost their land and their kingdoms, because of the iniquities of their idolatries and immoralities. However, bible prophecy states, that in the last days, they allow the *antichrist* to rule their land, because he brokers a peace treaty between Israel and her enemies after World War III, and they are deceived into believing he must be their long-awaited messiah.

This final *Antichrist* will fit their bill, because he will be a *counterfeit* of what the Old Testament scriptures tell them to expect. A counterfeit is a mimic, almost the real thing, but in nature and substance false, fake, not up to the job. Most readily do not recognize the difference, at least at first, because some don't have the discernment of what the real thing is supposed to be, and others because his deceptive skills are just so good, that they are fooled. He will have supernatural powers, advanced technology, the ability to call fire down from the heavens, which is the command of alien technology. (Revelation 13:13)

Let's face it, Israel is in stark need of science and technology just for its survival. Israel is a world leader in innovative technologies, and the IDF (Israeli Defense Forces) is a mini superpower. Israel worships technology. All the biggest technology giants now have offices and plants in Israel. Today, Modern Israel has become an international hub of high-tech firms.

Antichrist will also be seen to be an economic and financial genius, offering solutions to the failing global economy by instituting a cashless digitalized standard and leveling out the many fluctuations of the various currencies. By creating this one world currency, he will lead a one world government known as the New World Order, and taking over from his false prophet's groundwork, establish a one world religion. This is something all the popes have hoped for and dreamed about, and worked tirelessly to achieve.

> "Even now there have come to be *many antichrists*; from which fact we gain the knowledge that it is the last hour."
>
> (1 John 2:18)

By *last hour* John referred to the end of the apostolic period and when the times of the Gentiles are fulfilled.

> "Who is the liar if it is not the one that denies that Jesus is the Christ [or, Messiah, anointed one]? This is the *antichrist*."
>
> (1 John 2:22)

Everyone who denies that Jesus is the unique Son of God, that He came in the flesh, rose from the dead, and is returning to Earth as the Mashiach-Nagid (the Messiah-King), is *antichrist.*

> "This is the antichrist, the one that denies the Father and the Son."
>
> (1 John 2:22)

Apostates are *antichrist.*

"There have come to be *many antichrists* . . . They went out from us, but they were not of our sort."

(1 John 2:18, 19)

Those who oppose Christ's true followers are *antichrist*:

"If they have persecuted me, they will persecute you also . . . But they will do all these things against you on account of my name."

(John 15:20, 21)

"Say you of him, whom the Father has sanctified, and sent into the world, you blaspheme; because I said, I am the Son of God?"

(John 10:36)

"A voice came from the cloud, saying, "This is my Son, whom I have chosen; listen to Him."

(Luke 9:35)

"I and the Father are one."

(John 10:30

"For God did not send His Son into the world to condemn the world, but to save the world through Him."

(John 3:17)

Individuals and nations that oppose Christ as King or those who falsely claim the Messianic role for themselves are considered *antichrist.* The Ascended Masters of the New Age beliefs are *antichrist,* because they purport *Christ Consciousness* but refuse to acknowledge the *authority* of the kingship and lordship of Christ as King of kings and Lord of lords. Anyone can aspire to *Christ Consciousness,* but only those who are born of His Spirit can have the *mind of Christ.* There is a vast difference between Christ Consciousness and the Mind of Christ. This is a major spiritual discernment for those who have eyes to see and ears to hear. In fact, the One World Religion will purpose some type of *Christ Consciousness,* but will deny the power and authority of the Lord Jesus Christ.

> "The kings of earth take their stand and high officials themselves have massed together as one against Yahuah and against his anointed one [Christ, or Messiah]."
>
> (Psalm 2:2)

One of the major pieces of demonic deception, which I exposed in Books One, Two and Three of *Who's Who in The Cosmic Zoo?* is *who* the Ascended Masters and Space Brothers are in reality. They have proven to be the epitome of spiritual frauds, because they are not *who* they claim to be at all for the simple reason, Christ Consciousness does not recognize the ultimate authority of the Lord of lords, King of kings and God of gods. This deception makes Jesus just another one of the ascended masters, when the Truth is, He is lord over them all.

Christ Consciousness is not the mind of Christ. It's *antichrist.* It's a nebulous term for counterfeiting Christ through various fallen angels and demons. Just like the movie 'V' when a spaceship full of good looking humans walk off, charm the public with their alleged agenda to help humankind, only to reveal later that they are reptilians in human-looking space suits, come to devour humankind. People really need to be discerning when it comes to readily accepting any ET or human-looking alleged space brother or so-called master, without first scrutinizing them spiritually. Today, we go through layers and lines of identification verification, in order to travel, use a bank account, or carry a credit card. How much more should humanity vet these so-called space brothers and alleged ascended masters, before we swallow their spiel hook, line and sinker?

The Mass End Times Deception is coming through religious leaders, in particular, the Pope, who endeavors to create a One World religion. The final Antichrist, soon to be revealed to the World, is a counterfeit *alien messiah,* the shepherd who slaughters his sheep. My book series teaches *spiritual discernment* and in order to spot the counterfeit, you first must know the real One *who* is Truth. Similarly, just as bank tellers first must know what the real hundred-dollar bill looks like, in order to differentiate its difference from the fake.

Therefore, knowing God, having a personal relationship with the One who has the power to save our soul, mind and body from the enslavement of the Kingdom of Darkness both here and in the afterlife, is imperative to discerning between the counterfeit space brothers and the extraterrestrials who serve God's Kingdom of Heaven. Unfortunately, religion has hijacked people from this personal relationship. The Religious Spirit has turned more people off of God, then secularists and atheists. That which is dressed up as religion, is not always *godly.*

The false prophet, who will have some close connection to the Vatican which may even be the Pope himself, is going to herald and proclaim that the Antichrist is the real savior. He is not. Now is the time to repent and ask Jesus forgiveness for our sins before it's too late. We are living in the last days.

Do We Really Need Another Religion?

The earth does not need another religion, certainly not from Nordic ETs, aliens or anyone else. We must tread very carefully with this idea because there are multiple Nordic type ETs, not all of whom are benign. For instance, according to Government Whistleblower William Thompkins,[1] it was the Nordic ETs who gave UFO technology to Hitler and the Nazis to compete with the Reptilian race inside the earth. Hitler and his Nazis were serious about the genocide of the entire Jewish Race, so what's really the difference?

According to Dr. Michael Salla's [2] research, it was this race of Nordic ETs, Aryan Tall Blonds, whom Hitler contacted living inside the holes in the poles, who inspired him to follow them. This particular group of ETs could easily brainwash the entire planet with a strong delusion. They certainly have the technology and 'wow' factor to do so.

This is all in preparation for the counterfeit Messiah to emerge and be revealed. I am all for full disclosure of the ETs, aliens, gods and angels, and I believe disclosure and the end of the Truth Embargo is a good thing, but we certainly don't need another alien religion to worship extraterrestrials as gods. That scenario is growing old.

Since Pope Francis (Jorge Mario Bergoglio) became the 266th Roman Catholic Pope March 13, 2013, also the first Jesuit Pope, he's been aggressively pushing for a one world religion. The fact that this Pope is dealing with Nordic Human ETs from inside the earth, who once dealt with Hitler, should send chills down every spine! Just because these beings may look human, doesn't mean that they are benevolent to humanity, or more importantly, in alignment with the Creator of human souls, and His Divine Plan for the human race.

To institute a new religion for the purpose of controlling us humans, which goes against all the Words of the Lord in the ancient scriptures, is nevertheless a fulfillment of End Times Prophecy in Revelation 13.

It is unfortunate that the Roman Catholic Church still needs to deal with its 2,000 pedophile priests, the money laundering for the mafia, and scores of other horrific crimes which have been covered up by doling out of millions of dollars in privately sealed legal settlements. The bombshell report exposed by the Boston Globe in 2002, that 80% of Catholic Priests were engaged in pedophilia and covered it up, can still be reviewed.[3]

It's so hard to imagine anyone who walks a spiritual path, who wants to be a good parent, good citizen in community and sincerely wants to serve God and His Coming Kingdom on Earth, would stay within the fold of the Roman Catholic church amid the corruption and scandal within it. Those who do so, are under a spell, a delusion to look the other way when the priests molest their own children. My assessment is that all those who have been abused by the Roman Catholic Church have also been abductees, and are implanted through their sexual abuse. They remain in bondage to these psychic soul wounds and sometimes physical scars, to the point of rejecting God, whom these bestial priests supposedly represent. Most children who have been abused, reported that they were too afraid to speak up when they were young, because they were taught that the priests were god on earth. So, they grew up hating God, and have turned against all possible relationship with the Savior.

Even today, this lying false prophet, who calls himself Pope Francis (Jorge Bergoglio) has said multiple times, that you don't need a personal relationship with Jesus Christ to get to heaven, which is big fat lie. The alien implant is used in these sexually perverted priests to corrupt the minds, bodies and souls of children, so they grow up believing in this lie, and never know their heavenly Father and Messiah. The people who are supposed to comfort and educate them are in Faustian contracts with the devil, the Lizard king who rules the Draconian Reptilian Empire, who demands human sacrifices, and hungers for the sexual energies of innocent children and women.

Based on Bible Prophecy, it is unlikely that we will have full disclosure, because the Vatican is being used as the False Prophet to perpetuate the alien agenda on earth. And let's be real, considering their track record of cover ups and abuses, they are not going to tell the world who these aliens truly are, because that would mean losing their authority on earth. The Lord of Heaven and Earth has other plans for them, including their ultimate and final downfall. It is only after this that full disclosure will come to the world, when this veil of secrecy, cover ups and confusion will be ripped in shreds that the Light of the World who is Christ, the true Messiah and Savior of all human kind, has returned.

His loving salvation reaches out to include the human ETs that have been bound to this earth, and have been in warfare with the Draconians.

The Great Prostitute and the Beast

The Woman on the Beast

> "Then one of the seven angels who had the seven bowls came and said to me, "Come, I will show you the judgment of the great prostitute who is seated on many waters, with whom the kings of the earth have committed

sexual immorality, and a with the wine of whose sexual immorality the dwellers on earth have become drunk." And he carried me away in the Spirit into a wilderness, and I saw a woman sitting on e a scarlet beast that was full of blasphemous names, and it had seven heads and ten horns. The woman was arrayed in purple and scarlet, and adorned with gold and jewels and pearls, holding in her hand a golden cup full of abominations and the impurities of her sexual immorality. And on her forehead, was written a name of a mystery: "BABYLON THE GREAT, MOTHER OF PROSTITUTES AND OF EARTH'S ABOMINATIONS."

The Mystery Explained

"And I saw the woman, drunk with the blood of the saints, the blood of the martyrs of Jesus. When I saw her, I marveled greatly. But the angel said to me, "Why do you marvel? I will tell you of the mystery of the woman, and of the beast with seven heads and ten horns that carries her. The beast that you saw was, and is not, and is about to rise from r the bottomless pit and go to destruction. And t the dwellers on earth whose names have not been written in u the book of life from the foundation of the world will marvel to see the beast, because it was and is not and is to come.

This calls for a mind with wisdom: the seven heads are seven mountains on which the woman is seated; they are also seven kings, five of whom have fallen, one is, the other has not yet come, and when he does come he must remain only a little while. As for the beast that was and is not, it is an eighth but it belongs to the seven, and it goes to destruction.

And the ten horns that you saw are ten kings who have not yet received royal power, but they are to receive authority as kings for one hour, together with the beast. These are of one mind, and they hand over their power and authority to the beast. They will make war on the Lamb, and the Lamb will conquer them, for he is Lord of lords and King of kings, and those with him are called and chosen and faithful."

The Victory of the Lamb

And the angel said to me, "The waters that you saw, where the prostitute is seated, are peoples and multitudes and nations and languages. And e the ten horns that you saw, they and the beast f will hate the prostitute. They will make her g desolate and h naked, and devour her flesh and j burn her up with fire, for God has put it into their hearts to carry out his purpose by being of

> one mind and l handing over their royal power to the beast, until the words of God are fulfilled. And the woman that you saw is m the great city that has dominion over the kings of the earth."
>
> (Revelation 17:1-18; ESV)

Who is the Beast in Bible Prophecy?

The woman sitting on the beast is key. Typically, a woman in bible prophecy refers to the church, as in the bride of Christ. In this case, she is the bride of the false church.

According to Daniel 7:17, 23 there are four great beasts, which are four kings, which shall arise out of the earth. The fourth beast shall be the fourth kingdom upon earth, which shall be different from all previous kingdoms on the earth, and this king shall devour the whole earth, and shall tread it down, and break it in pieces. The beast here is a kingdom that comes from *inside* the earth.

The Prophecy is clear that the Four Kings arise, emerge *out of the earth.* Therefore, all previous three kingdoms have all been controlled by alien despots. From the Annunaki kings, to Egyptian Pharaohs, to today's Illuminati who worship the reptilian draconian lizard king, to Lucifer, who the Roman Catholic Church invokes in their masses, this fourth beast which arises from *inside* the earth will be the final Antichrist, the one that colludes with the Vatican Pope for world domination.

In Book One of *Who's Who in the Cosmic Zoo?* I identified the beast as the Reptilian Draconian Kingdom that operates from *inside* our planet, as well as our Moon, Mars and Saturn. See, *The Curse of the Serpent Race; The Chapter of the Serpent; Overthrow Attempts - Past, Present and Future; The Draconian/Reptilian Archetype; Draconian Borgs; Draconian Hybrids; Draco-Reptilian Hierarchy aka Satan's Hierarchy, Draco-Reptilian Shape Shifters.*[4]

"I have likened the daughter of Zion to a comely and delicate woman." (Jeremiah 6:2) This scripture comparing Zion, who is in *covenant* to the Lord, to a beautiful good woman, is consistent with the representation of the false church in Revelation 12 and 17 as a prostitute indicating a false system of worship. She wears all the colors of a priest except blue and white. She is both a church and a state system. The Vatican is a sovereign nation state itself, as well as the site of the Roman Catholic Church. The priests wear all the colors mentioned in Revelation, except blue and white.

Interesting, and there are no coincidences here, the nations represented by blue and white are Israel and Greece. The End Times Prophecy states that the False Prophet and the Antichrist set themselves up in Israel and wage war on the saints and persecute the Jews, like no other time in history.

It's only been seventy-two years since the last Jewish Holocaust, which was to date, the worst genocide visited upon the Jewish People. There are still Holocaust survivors alive today, as of the writing of this manuscript (2017), making it hard to believe that something as horrific as the forced starvation, physical, sexual, and genetic abuse, resulting in the mass murder of two thirds of Europe's Jews could possibly happen again, this time within their own homeland.

Sadly, this is what the End Times Prophecies predicts will happen under the final Antichrist figure. He will at first charm the world with his persuasive speech, by speaking the things that many want to hear, only to deceive them into the greatest blunder in human history. The Roman Catholic Church plays a starring role in his rise to power, and perpetuates the persecution of both Jews and Christians while masquerading as peaceful religious folks who just want everyone to be as 'One' and follow the extraterrestrial humans from inside the earth. Follow them into a final *Star Wars* battle with the Creator God of gods, who will end their rebellion with a breath and a Word.

When we connect the scriptures of the Beast in Revelation 12 with Daniel 7, it shows a *composite* Beast from Daniel 7 which means that one must go back to Daniel to understand it all completely. As I've postulated in Book One of *Who's Who in the Cosmic Zoo?* perhaps we are to start taking the Bible scriptures literally instead of metaphorically or poetically? Perhaps the Beast, is an actual Beast? The Draconian Giant Reptilians with horns, tails and even bat-like wings, would certainly qualify as a *beast.* Mainstream Christianity has traditionally interpreted Daniel 7 as a system of governments. While this may be true, it may also be layered with the knowledge and understanding that the system of this world is run by the Beast, the Reptilian Lizard Beings who appear to control the leaders of nations. They are behind all the secret societies, who literally *worship the Beast,* aka Lucifer, the Lizard King.

When you look at the descriptions of the little horn in Daniel 7 it appears that this Beast in Revelation 13 must be that little horn power. Horns are symbolic of power in biblical language. From biblical identifiers found in Daniel 7 and 8, that little horn is a religious-political power, most likely the Vatican. That beast also has to have the beast that comes out of the dry land to set up the image to get the whole world to worship him. Let's take this literally now, a *beast* that emerges out of dry land? This is where we need to connect the dots to the alien presence *inside* the earth. They literally emerge from *inside* the earth's dry land.

The verse in 2 Timothy 3:1-5, says that in the last days, a world religious philosophy which blends differing ways, all talking about God but denying the true God and His Power, will dominate humanity and will be sanctioned by the world leader. This is the *Religious Spirit* that comes from spirit of *Antichrist,* through Jezebel demons, who historically influence through false prophets and false beliefs.

> "But mark this: There will be terrible times in the last days. People will be lovers of themselves, lovers of money, boastful, proud, abusive, disobedient to their parents, ungrateful, unholy, without love, unforgiving, slanderous, without self-control, brutal, not lovers of the good, treacherous, rash, conceited, lovers of pleasure rather than lovers of God— having a form of godliness but denying its power. Have nothing to do with such people."
>
> (2 Timothy 3:1-5)

The power of God that leads to salvation is the Gospel of Jesus Christ Romans 1:16. The antichrist and his religious leader will deny this and claim all ways lead to heaven if they preach and practice love and tolerance. This is precisely what Pope Francis is teaching. Regardless of whatever it is going to be called, it will be Satans' counterfeit.

The following are the prophecies from Daniel's Vision in Chapter 7. The brackets and emphasis are mine:

> "These four great beasts are four kings who shall *arise out of the earth*. But <u>the saints of the Most High shall receive the kingdom and possess the kingdom forever, forever and ever</u>. Then I desired to know the truth about *the fourth beast, which was different from all the rest*, exceedingly terrifying, with its teeth of iron and claws of bronze, [**this refers to *alien technology*, spaceships and techno-weapons**] and which devoured and broke in pieces and stamped what was left with its feet, and about the ten horns that were on its head, [**horns are prophetic talk for power and authorities, principalities, governors, who are controlled by the beast on earth, who are ten nations that worship the beast, these are known today as the Illuminati Bankers who control the Extraterrestrial Military Industrialized Complex**] and *the other horn that came up* and before which three of them fell, the horn that had eyes and a mouth that spoke great things, and that seemed greater than its companions. [**the Antichrist/Counterfeit Messiah/Alien Savior**] As I looked, this horn [**power/authority/ruler**] made war with the saints and prevailed over them, until the Ancient of Days came, [**who is Yeshua aka the Lord and Savior Jesus Christ**] and judgment was given for the saints of the Most High, and the time came when the saints possessed the kingdom."
>
> (Daniel 7:17-22)

This is why Jesus promised that the righteous, the meek, the humble will inherit the Earth. These are the saints who are faithful to Him and the Most High God, who is His Father in Heaven, whose name is Yahuah.

"Blessed are the meek: for they shall inherit the earth." (Matthew 5:5)

"Blessed are they which are persecuted for righteousness' sake: for theirs is the kingdom of heaven." (Matthew 5:10)

"But the humble will inherit the land and will delight themselves in abundant prosperity." (Psalm 37:11)

The meaning of the phrase: "inherit the earth," and the following *covenants* within the Word must be integrated and understood:

1. God is the owner of this earth (Psalm 24:1).
2. Those who follow Christ become the children of God (Galatians 3:27; Hebrews 5:9), and are adopted into His family as "joint-heirs" with the Lord (Romans 8:17).
3. Our Heavenly Father supplies all our needs (Genesis 22:14; Philippians 4:19), therefore those who are under the *blood covenant* through Christ get to enjoy this earth and its blessings not only now, but in the age to come.
4. Our inheritance is spiritual (Acts 20:32); we are heirs of the kingdom of Christ (Ephesians 5:5), and our citizenship is of a heavenly kingdom that is available now on this earth and will manifest physically in the Millennial Reign of Christ (Daniel 7:13-14; Zechariah 2:10-12; John 3:3-5; Colossians 1:13; (Matthew 19:28; 23:39; 24:3-25:46; Mark 13:24-37; Luke 12:35-48; 17:22-37; 18:8; 21:25-28; Acts 1:10-11; 15:16-18; Romans 11:25-27; 1 Corinthians 11:26; 2 Thessalonians 1:7-10; 2 Peter 3:3-4; Jude 14-15; Revelation 1:7-8; 2:25-28; 16:15; 19:11-21; 22:20).
5. For the saints, our inheritance is reserved for us in heaven (1 Peter 1:4), because we are aware that the earth will be destroyed when Christ returns (2 Peter 3:10).

"Behold, the days come, says the Lord, that I will make a ***new covenant*** with the house of Israel, and with the house of Judah: Not according to the ***covenant*** that I made with their fathers in the day that I took them by the hand to bring them out of the land of Egypt; which my covenant they brake, although I was an husband unto them, says the Lord: But this shall be the ***covenant*** that I will make with the house of Israel; After those days, says the Lord, I will put my law in their inward parts, and write it in their hearts; and will be their God, and they shall be my people. And they shall teach no more every man his neighbor, and every man his brother, saying,

Know the Lord: for they shall all know me, from the least of them unto the greatest of them, says the Lord: for I will forgive their iniquity, and I will remember their sin no more."

(Jeremiah 31:31-34)

"As for me, this is my ***covenant*** with them, says the LORD. "My Spirit, who is on you, will not depart from you, and my words that I have put in your mouth will always be on your lips, on the lips of your children and on the lips of their descendants--from this time on and FOREVER," says the LORD."

(Isaiah 59:21)

For the purpose of those of you who want to make your own Bible study of *who* is antichrist? I have put together this bulleted list of with scripture addresses. Personally, I use Biblehub.com because it lists about two dozen different Bible translations along with the original Hebrew and Greek, so you can see how the meanings of words were translated or mistranslated as the case maybe. Sometimes, it can help towards understanding, as most people I know do not relate to the *thee's* and *thou's* of the old King James Versions, however, the American King James Version has taken all the *thee's* and *thou's* out, making it easier to understand. A simple Thesaurus, can also help elucidate the meaning of different words as well.

- Antichrist will be an intellectual genius. Daniel 8:23
- Antichrist will be an oratorical genius. Daniel 11:36
- Antichrist will be a political genius. Revelation 17:11-12
- Antichrist will be a commercial genius. Daniel 11:43; Revelation 13:8
- Antichrist will be a military genius. Revelation 6:2, 13:2
- Antichrist will be a religious genius. 2 Thessalonians 2:4, Revelation 13:8
- Antichrist will begin by controlling the Western power block. Revelation 17:12
- Antichrist will make a seven-year covenant with Israel but will break it after three and a half years. Daniel 9:27
- Antichrist will attempt to destroy all of Israel. Revelation 12
- Antichrist will destroy the false religious system so that he may rule unhindered. Revelation 17:16-17
- Antichrist will set himself up as God. Daniel -11:36-37; 2 Thessalonians 2:4, 11; Revelation 13:5
- Antichrist will briefly rule over all nations. Psalm 2; Daniel 11:36; Revelation 13:16
- Antichrist will be utterly crushed by the Lord Jesus Christ at the Battle of Armageddon. Revelation 19

- Antichrist will be the first creature thrown into the lake of fire. Revelation 19:20
- Antichrist will be a master of deceit. 2 Thessalonians 2:10
- Antichrist will profane the temple. Matthew 24:15
- Antichrist will be energized by satan himself. Revelation 13:2
- 18.Antichrist will do everything according to his own selfish will. Daniel 11:36
- Antichrist will not regard the God of his fathers. Daniel 11:37
- Antichrist will not have the desire of women. Daniel 11:37
- His god will be the god of strongholds, and the god of Mars, who is Lucifer the Satan. Daniel 11:38

For those of you who question, why would a loving God, allow someone so inherently evil to deceive the world and bring its destruction? The short answer is, that we are all part of a grand experiment, called Free Will that seeks to balance itself. There are universal laws of sowing and reaping, aka laws of karma, laws of attraction, evidenced in Galatians 6:7. All that has happened, and all that is to come, is happening for a purpose and reason, that we may never understand until it has been completed.

> "I am the LORD, and there is no other. I create the light and make the darkness. I send good times and bad times. I, the LORD, am the one who does these things."
>
> (Isaiah 45:7)

The good news is that the Lion of Judah, who is Yahushua HaMashiach (The Lord Jesus Christ) will be returning with the 'clouds' of heaven. That's bible language for a fleet of starships with the Heavenly Extraterrestrial Hosts of Heaven. There will be no donkey rides at the second coming! Please refer back to *Who Is God?* Book Two of *Who's Who In The Cosmic Zoo?*, for further elucidation on the 'clouds' of heaven proving through several dozen scriptures referenced throughout the Old and New Testaments, that these are in fact spaceships and the real Star Wars.[5] The Truth is Stranger than Fiction!

Notes:

1. William Mills Thompkins, *Selected by Extraterrestrials: My Life in the Top-Secret World of UFOs, Think-Tanks and Nordic Secretaries,* CreateSpace, December 2015.

2. Dr. Michael Salla, *The U.S. Navy's Secret Space Program & Nordic Extraterrestrial Alliance, Book Two of the Secret Space Programs Series,* Exopolitics Consultants, Hawaii, 2017.
3. Boston Globe, https://www.bostonglobe.com/news/special-reports/2002/01/06/church-allowed-abuse-priest-for-years/cSHfGkTIrAT25qKGvBuDNM/story.html, January 6, 2002
4. Ella LeBain, *Who's Who in the Cosmic Zoo?* Book One, Third Edition, pp. 154-177, Tate Publishing, 2013.
5. Ella LeBain, *Who is God?* Book Two, *The Cloudships,* p. 75-82, Skypath Books, 2015.

CHAPTER SEVENTEEN

Cosmic Karma & Ancient Curses

"If the Son sets you free, you will be free indeed."
(John 8:36)

This cosmic drama in which we find ourselves immersed has been going on for a very long time. Since the rebellion of the angels, the earth has been cursed, and with the recreation of humans on earth during the Garden of Eden, a host of curses have become generational. The Bible is full of blessings and curses. There are curses from God and curses from Satan, yet it appears that both are carried out through the same demonic agents. This is the legal business of the spiritual realms, as to which humans are assigned which particular curses and which demons are assigned for perpetrating them and holding those souls in bondage.

There are family curses, generational curses and national curses. We can easily see that all humans are under a curse, in addition to Adams curse, which includes aging, pain in childbirth, and death. Our ancestors committed certain sins which turned into curses, with attached demons assigned to hold that family soul and ancestral line in bondage, torment and suffering until those curses are broken.

There are 326 scriptures in the Bible that relate to curses and the cursed. Curses are pronounced by the Lord, by prophetic utterances from holy men, and from all those who curse God's people. The first curse was mentioned in Genesis 3:14-17 when God curses the serpent into a snake, then made him mute. He was demoted to the lowest among the animals, and he became the enemy of man. Then the earth itself was cursed, the ground losing its innate fruitfulness to producing thorns and thistles. Then the woman lost her place. She became undervalued, below status of her husband, and childbearing would be painful and difficult, and she would die. Then the man lost his position, he lost the Garden of Eden and was banned from ever returning, he had to toil and sweat in order to eat, he would die.

Being a woman, I believe the curse of women are the hormonal changes. Not all women experience difficult childbearing, but all women experience hormonal changes and the craziness that goes with what is termed as a chemical imbalance. Men live their lives with one main sex hormone. They typically do not experience the regular monthly fluctuation and extreme mood swings as do women.

Boys experience hormonal changes during puberty. After that, they're pretty steady, hormonally speaking at least, till the male menopause, which may be an empathic response towards their wife's change of life symptoms.

But without a doubt, women suffer their entire lives from the onset of puberty through every period, PMS, pregnancy, labor, birth pains, nursing, miscarriages, and finally menopause. This is by far the wackiest time hormonally with the most extreme in hormonal fluctuations, which often coincides with mid-life crises and sometimes serious illness, and then followed by infertility.

I am convinced that aliens and demons are attracted to hormonal changes. Their assignment is the curse on woman, (Genesis 3:16) not just childbirth, but the entire hormonal cycle. For years, I've always wondered why whenever I was PMSing I was tested? I became moody, irritable, prone to outbursts, lost my temper, got angry, cried over hearing a song or watching a movie, and experienced the worst of the entire emotional rollercoaster. It felt like being under the influence of some drug or being possessed by some evil spirit.

It was, at times, uncontrollable. Not until I discovered bio-identical hormones and the power of Jesus Christ to deliver, did I understand what was behind this chemical hormonal disparity and the spiritually challenging conditions I was facing each month. Realizing this spiritual warfare was due to the assignment on me, and on most women, I was finally able to get a handle on the fluctuations, and to dodge the spiritual attacks through Christ. Of course, when the PMS cycle was over, so was all the testing, and life would return back to normal, until the next cycle.

Menopause came as true deliverance for me. It was one of the best things that could have happened to me! I believe because I had already begun working with the Lord on the cycles of hormonal changes, and seeking God's Deliverance from generational curses, I was blessed to go through menopause without a single hot flash. I was also using natural bio-identical hormones three years before I began menopause. Being on the other side of this curse has given me the opportunity to discern it and hopefully bring some clarity and release to others.

What Constitutes a Curse?

> "A curse...to utter a wish of evil against someone, to utter or call for mischief, or for injury that can cause one to fall, to vex or arrest, all meant to bring

people into great calamities." (Webster 1828 Dictionary, which used the King James Version Bible to explain this definition.)

This word is both a noun and verb, rendering distinctly different Hebrew words, some of them being more or less synonymous, differing only in degree of strength. 'Kalah' (Numbers 5:21, 23, 17, etc.), 'me'erah' (Proverbs 3:33 Malachi 2:2, etc.), 'klalah' (Genesis 27:12, 13); 'katara' (Galatians 3:10, 13). The word *curse* is often used in contrast with *bless* or *blessing* (Deuteronomy 11:29). When a curse is pronounced, we are not to understand this is merely a wish that disaster should overtake the person in question, any more than we are to understand that a corresponding blessing conveys simply a wish that prosperity should be the lot of the person on whom the blessing is invoked.

A curse was considered to possess an inherent power of itself to carry effect. Prayer has been defined as a wish referred to God. Curses and blessings were imprecations or oaths referred to supernatural beings, in whose existence and power to do good or inflict harm we believe and have always believed. Curses always bring both curser and cursed down to the same lowered level.

The use of magical spells is based on the belief that it is possible to enlist the support of the superhuman beings with whom the universe abounds, and to persuade them to carry out the suppliant's wishes. Spells were written on pieces of parchment and cast to the winds in the belief that they would find their way to their proper destination-that some demonic being would act as postman and deliver them at the proper address.

In Zechariah 5:1-3 the "flying roll," with curses inscribed on it "go forth over the face of the whole land." It would find its way into the house of every thief and perjurer. But it was not always necessary to commit curses to writing, it was enough to utter them aloud. Mostly, the name of some deity would be coupled with such imprecations, as Goliath cursed David by his gods (1 Samuel 17:43). Such curses, once uttered, possessed the power of self-realization.

It is an ancient custom, still practiced today, for the heads of families in their golden years to bless their children. Such blessing was not simply a paternal wish that their children should prosper in life, but a potent factor in determining their future welfare (Genesis 9:25). Consider the case of Jacob seeking his father's blessing, which was much more than just his father's good wishes for his future career.

These types of blessings and curses were independent of moral considerations. Moral distinctions weren't always necessary for a spell to be effectual. The individual against whom a spell was pronounced should be deserving of the fate which was invoked against him. It was sufficient that he should be the foe of the author of the curse. Such curses often signalized the commencement of a battle. Over the course of time such indiscriminate curses would not satisfy enlightened moral judgment. In the dramatic situation depicted in Deuteronomy 27:12 a curse was placed on Mt. Ebal and the blessing on Mr. Gerizim. The curse was the penalty for disobedience, as the blessing was the reward for obedience.

The Book of Proverbs 26:2 says, "Like a fluttering sparrow or a darting swallow, an undeserved curse does not come to rest."

On the other hand, curses sent by ordinary people were considered less efficacious, unless some god, fallen angel, or demon was ready to speed them on their way to their destination. Only special persons, considered holy by virtue of their close relation to divine beings, possessed special powers of pronouncing effectual curses, on account of their ability to enlist supernatural aid. Balaam, according to the narrative in Numbers 22, was hired by King Balak to curse God's people. Balak was convinced that Balaam's curse would bring about the defeat of the Israelites, yet the Lord intervened, causing Balaam's donkey to talk to him and make a fool out of him. This humbled him and struck the fear of God into him, and the Israelites were spared his curse.

The Power of Words

> "Death and life are in the power of the tongue: and they that love it shall eat the fruit of their own words."
>
> (Proverbs 18:21)

All the curses in the Bible were delivered through spoken words. Words transmit spiritual power. The Lord Himself spoke the world and the universe into existence. When words are spoken by someone who has spiritual authority, the words they speak carry power. When the Lord speaks, things happen! It is said that at the battle of Armageddon when Jesus Christ returns for the second coming, He will end the battle with a 'word.'

This is why it is written, "For the word of God is living and active. Sharper than any double-edged sword, it penetrates even to dividing soul and spirit, joints and marrow; it judges the thoughts and attitudes of the heart." (Hebrews 4:12) Words have power, and God's words have ultimate spiritual power. When spoken by those empowered by the Lord, words have unlimited power. This is how miracles are done in the name of Jesus Christ.

Just as the Holy Spirit brooded upon the waters, and then moved when God spoke the world into being, so does the Holy Spirit move when believers speak words from God. Angels also help, as written in Hebrews 1:14; ministering spirits are to help carry out the words of God spoken by believers. But it also works in the opposite. When someone with spiritual authority speaks evil, for example, a curse, those words authorize demons and evil spirits to exercise power against the person authorized by the cursed words. Even an alcoholic parent who curses his wife and his children in a drunken stupor is literally authorizing demons and evil spirits to act upon those words, because he has authority over his children and his family. This is how generational curses perpetuate until broken. This is how a word curse works; words are spoken, which give authority to demons and evil spirits, such as fear, doubt, worry, cancer, and all kinds of sickness, disease and misfortune.

> "But I say to you, that every idle word that men shall speak, they shall give account thereof in the Day of Judgment. <u>For by your words you shall be justified, and by your words you shall be condemned</u>."
>
> (Matthew 12:36-37)

Just think of all the words spoken in gossip, backbiting and backstabbing, how those words all have power and become curses, providing authority to demons and evil spirits to carry them out. Harm befalls whomever the ill will is being directed. Most people do not realize the power of their words. Backstabbing is like sending a cursed spiritual arrow into the back of the person being talked about, who starts to feel pain in his back and sometimes his heart, which is accessed from the back. Not everyone is strong enough to withstand these types of fiery darts that are demonic and hurtful.

Energetically speaking, gossip and backstabbing can bring the object of those words down. They may experience an illness, or severe pain, and even an accident. The demonic realm carries out the meaning of the curse, that misfortune, disease and persecution can come upon a person. It is vitally important to remember that Christ is called the Word, to become aware of the privilege of the power of words, of speech, and to speak with caution as not to give Satan and his demons authority to use the power of cursed words against ourselves or others, words that provide the authority for an evil spiritual attack against others.

The Bible says that the curses remain with humankind till the last chapter in Revelation:

> "<u>And there shall be no more curse</u>: but the throne of God and of the Lamb shall be in it; and his servants shall serve him:"
>
> (Revelation 22:3)

In the light of the law all men are guilty. There is no acquittal through appeal to a law that commands and never forgives, a law that prohibits and never relents. The violator of the law is under a curse. His doom has been pronounced. Escape is impossible. But on the cross, Jesus Christ endured the curse for humanity, "Christ has redeemed us from the curse of the law for by being made a curse for us, for it is written, cursed is every one that hangs on a tree" (Galatians 3:10-13), that he became the curse for us so that we may be free of all the curses. All curses, therefore, need to be nailed to the cross for liberation and deliverance.

In the realm of the occult, when magical rituals are cast to break a curse, it is akin to going to the mafia and having them buy out a debt for you. In this case, unbeknownst to the performer of the ritual, the 'celestial mafia' comes in and buys the debt of the curse, and therefore holds that person in bondage to them. They may arrange circumstances by re-ordering demons to relieve that person of symptoms temporarily, but the curse is still in effect, on them and on their family. It's just a different group of demons within Satan's realm of the occult that now owns their soul. Therefore, the curse in effect was not broken, it was only transferred to a different department. Christ is the only authority in heaven and on earth that has the power to break curses and redeem one from a curse.

There are blessings for obedience and curses for disobedience and double-mindedness in Deuteronomy 28. The consequences associated with the list of curses apply to most of us today, to include 1) problems conceiving; 2) depression; 3) tumors; 4) work problems; 5) persecution; 6) fever; 7) tuberculosis; 8) fear; 9) lack of answered prayer; 10) insanity; 11) confusion; 12) blindness; 13) sores that won't heal; 14) marital problems and divorce; 15) infidelity; 16) financial problems; 17) accidents; 18) violence; 19) robbery, both physical and energy theft; 20) oppressive government; 21) discrimination; 22) poverty; 23) destruction; 24) business failure; 25) deprivation and exile.[1]

The Bible also tells us that many of these curses are passed down, due to the sins of the father, for up to ten generations, (Deuteronomy 23:2). According to the legal authority that demons have to hold generational lines in bondage, these curses can go on indefinitely until someone in the family line makes the conscious choice to break it, and turn all their sins and those of their ancestors over to Christ. Jesus is the only One who has the legal authority to break curses.

Belief and faith in Christ must be present in order for this to happen. It is certainly not automatic even in the lives of those who consider themselves Christians or attend church. There must first be an awareness, and a choice that leads towards the special types of prayers and confession, repentance and the willingness to take part in a spiritual battle to get free and be delivered from the power and authority of the demonic realm and all curses. The subject matter of my next book is focused on breaking all the different types of curses.

Besides family and generational curses, the realm of curses also extends to the Nephilim, also known as *the rejects* or *cursed ones*. Long dead in body, they have become the evil spirits and demons that oppress humankind to this day. As I've been saying, there are many of these lesser gods and fallen sons and angels of heaven that have sinned and were cursed by God, creating mega units of karma. They have been trying to get right with God. In their efforts to get free of God's curse on them, they have agreed to serve humankind in a benevolent way. It's hard to say exactly who each of these ETs are, but they are the ones that have aligned themselves with the Universal Alliance of Christ in the Heavens. This issue with the fallen ETs of God, the lesser gods, will also be resolved at the second coming.

Here are several examples of the 326 scriptures that relate to curses in the Bible, here are just a few of them:

> "I will bless those who bless you, and I will curse him who **curses** you. All of the families of the earth will be blessed in you."
>
> (Genesis 12:3);

> "Let peoples serve you, and nations bow down to you. Be lord over your brothers. Let your mother's sons bow down to you. Cursed be everyone who **curses** you. Blessed be everyone who blesses you."
>
> (Genesis 27:29)

> The Bastard Curse: "A bastard shall not enter into the congregation of the LORD; even to his tenth generation shall he not enter into the congregation of the LORD."
>
> (Deuteronomy 23:2)

> "But it shall come to pass, if you will not listen to the voice of Yahuah your God, to observe to do all his commandments and his statutes which I command you this day that all these **curses** shall come on you, and overtake you."
>
> (Deuteronomy 23:4)

> "Whoever curses his father or his mother, his lamp shall be put out in blackness of darkness."
>
> (Proverbs 20:20)

"There is a generation that **curses** their father, and doesn't bless their mother."

(Proverbs 30:11)

"One who gives to the poor has no lack; but one who closes his eyes will have many **curses**."

(Proverbs 28:27)

"But they gave no attention and did not give ear, but they went on, every man in the pride of his evil heart: so I sent on them all the **curses** in this agreement, which I gave them orders to keep, but they did not."

(Jeremiah 11:8)

"The LORD himself will send on you curses, confusion, and frustration in everything you do, until at last you are completely destroyed for doing evil and abandoning me."

(Deuteronomy 28:20)

"All these curses will come upon you. They will pursue you and overtake you until you are destroyed, because you did not obey the LORD your God and observe the commands and decrees he gave you."

(Deuteronomy 28:45)

"The LORD will not spare him, but then the anger of the LORD and his jealousy shall smoke against that man, and all the **curses** that are written in this book shall lie upon him, and the LORD shall blot out his name from under heaven."

(Deuteronomy 29:20)

"The LORD will single him out from all the tribes of Israel for disaster, according to all the curses of the covenant written in this Book of the Law."

(Deuteronomy 29:21)

"They went off and worshiped other gods and bowed down to them, gods they did not know, gods he had not given them. And the anger of the LORD was kindled against this land, to bring upon it all the **curses** that are written in this book:"

(Deuteronomy 29:27)

The following curse was upon God's people, the Israelites and the Jews:

> "And it shall come to pass, when all these things are come on you, the blessing and the curse, which I have set before you, and you shall call them to mind among all the nations, where the LORD your God has driven you, and when you and your children return to the LORD your God and obey him with all your heart and with all your soul according to everything I command you today, then the LORD your God will restore your fortunes and have compassion on you and gather you again from all the nations where he scattered you."
>
> (Deuteronomy 30:1)

> "Yahuah your God will put all these curses on your enemies, and on those who hate you, who persecuted you."
>
> (Deuteronomy 30:7)

Generational Sins and Curses

Whether we are a part of a family or not, all of us are born from ancestors, and we inherit a host of traits and characteristics. Spiritually, we also inherit their sins and the curses and demons attached to all those errors and mistakes. How often have children been abused at the hand of their parents, with the anger that the parent felt being transferred to the child as an imprint. That child then grows up to carry the parents anger in their body, their psyche, and all the resentment and bitterness that goes with it. That child will sin and carry on that pattern and repeat the cycle of abuse with others. Generational sins and curses are a very real phenomenon that can only be broken through the saving grace of Christ.

> "The LORD is long-suffering, and of great mercy, forgiving iniquity and transgression, and by no means clearing the guilty, visiting the iniquity of the fathers upon the sons to the third and fourth generation."
>
> (Numbers 14)

> "Ah, Lord Yahuah! You have made the heavens and the earth by Your great power and stretched out arm. Nothing is too great for You. You show loving-kindness to thousands, and repay the iniquity of the fathers into the bosom of their sons after them."
>
> (Jeremiah 32)

> "Then the Lord passed by in front of him and proclaimed, "The Lord, the Lord God, compassionate and gracious, slow to anger, and abounding in loving kindness and truth; who keeps loving kindness for thousands, who forgives iniquity, transgression and sin; yet He will by no means leave the guilty unpunished, visiting the iniquity of fathers on the children and on the grandchildren to the third and fourth generations."
>
> (Exodus 34:6--7)

> "You shall not bow yourself down to them, nor serve them. For I the LORD your God am a jealous God, visiting the iniquity of the fathers upon the sons to the third and fourth generation of those that hate me, and showing mercy to thousands of those that love Me and keep My commandments."
>
> (Exodus 20:5-6; Deuteronomy 5:9-10)

Exodus 20:5 recounts one of the Ten Commandments. According to covenants and legal authority, when a father misleads his family, the effects are often felt for generations. This is because the father is being covenantally unfaithful and God has stipulated that there are punishments to breaking the covenant. That is the case with these verses that deal with the sins visited upon the children. If a father rejects the covenant and takes his family into sin and rejects God, the children will suffer the consequences, often for several generations.

Whether or not this is fair is not the issue. It is important to remember that spiritually, every curse has assigned to it demons who then have legal authority to hold that person in bondage until they confess, repent, and apply Christ's blood of redemption, which liberates them from those ancestral curses. Sin is in the world, and its consequences affect many generations. We can conclude that God will visit the iniquities of the fathers upon his descendants because the fathers have failed to keep their covenants with God. Yet, we see in the other verses a declaration of legality in dealing with people. There is no contradiction.

"For as in Adam all die,
so also in Christ all shall be made alive."

(1 Corinthians 15:22)

The High Priest Curse

This curse comes from the words that the Jewish High Priest, the Sanhedrin, and all the people spoke at the trial of Jesus Christ. When Pilate washed his hands of the matter and pronounced Jesus innocent, the Jewish high priest led the people to say, "His blood be on us, and on our children." (Matthew 27:25).

> "But the chief priests and the elders persuaded the crowd to ask for Barabbas and to have Jesus executed. "Which of the two do you want me to release to you?" asked the governor.
>
> "Barabbas," they answered. "What shall I do, then, with Jesus who is called Christ?" Pilate asked. They all answered, "Crucify him!" "Why? What crime has he committed?" asked Pilate. But they shouted all the louder, "Crucify him!" When Pilate saw that he was getting nowhere, but that instead an uproar was starting, he took water and washed his hands in front of the crowd. "I am innocent of this man's blood," he said. "It is your responsibility!"
>
> "**All the people answered, "Let his blood be on us and on our children!"** Then he released Barabbas to them. But he had Jesus flogged, and handed him over to be crucified."
>
> (Matthew 27:20-16)

The Jews quickly assumed full responsibility for His death: "We accept the punishment for such a crime; **let it be upon us and upon our children**." This is how a generational and ancestral curse was created. In the siege of Jerusalem in 70 AD, the Romans crucified the Jews in such numbers before the walls that the Romans wanted more wood for crosses. Multitudes in the city died of famine until the valleys outside were filled with corpses. Titus himself groaned and threw up his hands in horror and called God to witness that he was not responsible. No fewer than 600,000 who were thrown out the gates were counted by the Romans. Altogether 1,100,000 Jews died; 97,000 were sold as slaves for trifling prices; 40,000 were freed because no one bought them; and 347,490 more, plus multitudes not counted, perished in many other ways.[2]

Their children for ages have gone through untold sufferings all over the globe. They are yet to suffer the greatest time of tribulation that has ever been on earth or ever will be, a time known to the Jews as the time of 'Jacobs troubles.' (Matthew 24:15-22; Revelation 6:1-21; Daniel 11:40-45; 12:1; Jeremiah 30:3-9; Ezekiel 20:33-38; Zechariah 13:9; 14:1-5)

There is still time for Israel and Jews all around the world to accept their Messiah through Yeshua. Many have, who are known as 'completed Jews', yet those who have not done so, due to their unbelief, have been cursed with spiritual blindness, spiritual deafness and spiritual muteness.

"Christ has redeemed us from the curse of the
law, being made a curse for us:
for it is written, 'Cursed is every one that hangs on a tree.'" (Galatians 3:13)

If the Bible says that Jesus Christ became a curse for us, so that all humans may be free through Him, then how can curses still exist among believers and non-believers? Didn't Jesus accomplish the work to set us free from all curses?

To put it succinctly, not everyone believes that they are cursed, or have curses, as the subject is too disturbing to most people, even Christians who accept the Scriptures. Secondly, being a believer, or being saved through Christ, does not deliver automatic release from every curse, both ancient, generational, or otherwise. Spiritually speaking, freedom comes through repentance of all sin and all curses attached to those sins.

According to the law, all sins have curses attached to them, and all curses are kept in place by demons who work for the satanic realm of bondage. In order for true deliverance to be achieved, the believer must appropriate the cross through confession and repentance of all sin and all ancestral, family and generational curses. The door of freedom is available to all, but not without confession and repentance. This is the way the Lord set it up. It is not automatic, but it is available to all who want it and have the faith in what Jesus accomplished on the cross. The blood of Jesus was the final sacrifice for all sins, yet His blood must be appropriated to all generational curses, by a person of faith.

The Bastard Curse

According to the Torah, when a child is born out of the Covenant of Marriage, is considered to be a bastard child, meaning it was born out of wedlock. It has also been called, the Curse of Illegitimacy. We know that the word 'bastard' relates to those who were born out of wedlock. But why is this curse such a heavy one, and why does it prevent people from having a relationship with God, or being part of a church family, or being part of any assembly of God, whether it be Jewish, Christian, Muslim, Hindu, Buddhist?

> "A bastard shall not enter into the congregation of the Lord; even to his tenth generation shall he not enter into the congregation of the Lord."
> (Deuteronomy 23:2)

This is pretty heavy stuff, up to the tenth generation. When it comes to legal demonic strongholds, the satanic realm doesn't just give it up easily. It must be broken, by one who can appropriate the authority of Christ who is the only one who has the authority to break all curses. Ten generations is a long time to wait to come into the congregation of the Lord. In the New Testament, this relates to fellowship with other believers. The curse of the bastard is the curse of illegitimacy. This has been an effective tool of Satan in keeping the church divided.

> "An Ammonite or Moabite shall not enter into the congregation of the Lord; even to their tenth generation shall they not enter into the congregation of the Lord forever;"
>
> (Deuteronomy 23:3)

The reason the Ammonite and Moabites were under this curse is because they failed to help Israel with bread and water in the wilderness and they hired the prophet Balaam to curse them. These behaviors were the direct result of the bastard curse, because of the way they came into the world, which is explained in Genesis 19:30-38.

There is the story of Lot and his two daughters who were husbandless after the destruction of Sodom and Gomorrah. The women wanted to have children to carry on their father's name, so they got their father drunk one night and both of them had sexual intercourse with him and were both impregnated with sons, Ammon and Moab, who then became leaders of the nations of Ammonite and Moabites. They were born through incest, which legally brought them under the curse of the bastard, as Ammon and Moab were bastard children. Their mothers were not married to their father. They and all of their descendants could never come into the congregation of the Lord forever.

The curse of the bastard gave Satan legal authority to attack God's people with curses. In this story, the attacks were thwarted by God's love for Israel, but not for long.

The first Biblical reference to bastard offspring was in Genesis 6. The days of Noah were filled with wickedness. The sons of God are angels whom Jude 1:6 records as having left their first estate. They came to earth to dwell and mate with earth women. Their offspring were bastards, otherwise known as Nephilim, who were called rejects, monsters, and giants. Their behavior was evil, they lusted after human flesh, were cannibalistic, full of lust and murder. Their presence made God repent of having made mankind. (Genesis 21:8). A significant part of why God's heart was so grieved was due to the bastard curse on all of their bloodlines.[3]

God created man, not only in his image and likeness, but He also created man for fellowship with Him. The bastard curse prevents that fellowship from ever occurring. Bastards are not able to come into the congregation of the Lord, until the curse is broken. It is God's primary will that we all fellowship with the Lord and join in His assembly of children, the place of intimacy and fellowship, the purpose for making man in the first place.[4]

Noah's flood killed off most of the Nephilim, the bastard offspring. But as we have talked about before, there were giants on the earth after the flood and evil prevailed in humankind. David faced the giant Goliath, which was way after the flood. The Nephilim bastard offspring also invaded Sodom and Gomorrah, which also happened after the great deluge. See my chapter on the Nephilim in Book One for further elucidation.[5]

The curse of the bastard gives Satan authority to keep people away from the God, which is his agenda and modus operandi. God cannot go back on His Word, but He did provide a way out, which is through the work that was accomplished on the cross by His son Jesus Christ. This is the only way out of this bastard curse.

Satan's next attempt to introduce the bastard curse on the bloodline of God's people occurred with Abram. God had covenanted with Abram, declaring that he would be the father of many nations. Abram and Sarah did not have the faith to wait for God to fulfill His promise, so they took matters into their own hands, by taking Hagar, Sarah's maidservant to bear Abram the son Ishmael. Ishmael was cursed. He was not part of God's plan. Ishmael was a bastard, because he was the result of Abraham's decision to do things his way instead of God's way.

> "And the angel of the LORD said to her, Behold, you are with child and shall bear a son, and shall call his name Ishmael; because the LORD has heard your affliction. And he will be a wild man; his hand will be against every man, and every man's hand against him; and he shall dwell in the presence of all his brothers."
>
> (Genesis 16:11-12)

Ishmael would be unable to live peaceably with his fellow man. This is an important piece in world politics. If the bastard curse prevents those down the bloodline from having fellowship with God and with others, and this curse can potentially last for over 400 years, or forever as the scripture says, then it means this curse is still in effect today on all of Ishmael's descendants. This constitutes one of the three world's religions today who all claim Abraham as their father.

Naturally Satan doesn't stop fostering this curse simply with the first incidence, but endeavors to keep it running continually with subsequent generations as well. Ishmael and all of his progeny are under this curse.[6]

Many people say, all children belong to God. There are no bastards. God loves everyone. While this may be true on a spiritual level, the legality of this curse can hold a person in spiritual bondage, until the curse itself is broken through faith in the One who came to break all curses, which is none other than Jesus Christ.

The Bastard Curse of Illegitimacy takes root whenever a baby is born out of wedlock, conceived in rape or incest. This is a spiritual condition, that causes the child to feel unwanted all its life. Bastard curse creates a spirit of illegitimacy also known as an 'Orphan Spirit', which causes a child never to feel loved, included or part of this planet. The child becomes an adult who struggles with shame, guilt, rejection, abandonment, and fear in relationships. They also struggle with self-hatred, double-mindedness, and a spirit of lust, as they were conceived in lust not the commitment of love. Therefore, people who just live together, and then get pregnant, should get married before the child is born, it will foster the child to be born under the protection of the covenant of marriage, and prevent these spirits from having a stronghold in the child's life.[7]

Due to the spiritual legal ground of this curse, it creates the syndrome of never feeling like you belong anywhere. This effects personal relationships, family and marriage. However, due to the curse condemning them from the assembly of the Lord, a person with this demonic assignment on them, are never content in any one church, and therefore, tend to wander from church to church.

I want to point out, that it's not the Lord of Love and Grace, who is Yeshua, that holds children born into the bastard curse, or any curse, for that matter. It is the god of this world, who is Lucifer the Satan, who is the original legalist, the accuser of the children of God. All children are created in the image and likeness of the gods, the Elohim. All children are born with God given souls. However, as the Bible says in multiple scriptures, that earth humans are born into sin. This sin, as I've pointed out in Gene Wars, is genetic manipulations, that have corrupted the image and likeness of God. The sin or error humans are born into, can be exacerbated due to generational curses on one's bloodline.

All curses are broken through the Blood of Yeshua. Yeshua/Jesus is the curse breaker. His blood is the ultimate sacrifice which nullifies all generational curses. But, because we are all saved behind enemy lines, meaning the god of this world, who is satan, most people who come to salvation, are not necessarily delivered from generational curses, and therefore wonder why they are not made instantly free when they receive Jesus as their Savior. The answer to this dilemma is found in understanding spiritual legal ground, and counter acting by using the spiritual weapons of forgiveness and repentance that break and bind the demonic assignments on bloodlines through generational curses. The bastard curse is one of them.

First salvation, then deliverance, then freedom, comes healing of the mind, body, spirit and relationships. That's the order in which the path of salvation unfolds. This is why I am writing this book, so others who have taken for granted or more appropriately, have been misled to believe that they are instantly delivered from all their sins and curses at the moment of salvation, are mistaken.

The scriptures clearly say, "work out your own salvation with fear and trembling." (Philippians 2:12) In this way, we are encouraged that after salvation, comes consecration of our spirits and soul bodies into the Blood Covenant of Christ. This requires a willingness to accept that the god of this world has laid claim upon our spirits and bodies due to the spiritual legal ground of generational sins and their resultant curses. These curses come from him, the accuser, not from the Lord Jesus Christ. This is an important discernment, as too many people confuse the God who saves, with the god who kills, steals and destroys. See, *Who is God?* Book Two of this book series[8], for further discernments on *who* these two completely opposite gods are.

For example, children who have been the victim of incestual relations also tend to struggle with confusion, frustration, low self-esteem, lust and hopelessness because of a bastard curse spirit. This is why it is so important to go through deliverance from the spirit of illegitimacy, which reconnects yourself with the Creator of your soul. God is love, and God does not make junk. In fact, regardless of being born out of wedlock, God chose you before you were born to fulfill a purpose only you can do. Perhaps that purpose begins with getting delivered from generational and family curses? Imagine how free and healed you will feel.

Due to space constraints, I have put a separate workbook together which includes specific prayers that you can say out loud and/or with another to become free of the bastard curse as well as all generational and ancestral curses. Please look for *Finding Freedom, How to Identify and Remove Alien Implants, Break Vows & Agreements Connected to Generational Curses.* You will be able to download it on Amazon in 2018.

There are multiple examples of the Bastard Curse in the Bible: David conceived a bastard child with Bathsheba in 2 Samuel 11:2-5 – His adultery was coupled with a premeditated murder to cover up his adultery. The Lord had chosen King David's bloodline to give birth to the Messiah down the bloodline. The Lord knew that if this illegitimate child had lived, that Satan would have rights to curse him with the Bastard Curse Spirits, which was not part of the Lord's plan for the Son of God to be born into. So, the Lord allowed the child to die. This precipitated deep heartfelt repentance in King David, which many of his Psalms reflect.

Then after Bathsheba was now widowed, King David married her, and the Lord gave them another boy child, who was Solomon. Solomon took over the throne from David, and was chosen by the Lord to build His Temple. He was blessed beyond his father David. He was the fruit of repentance, correction and forgiveness, born through the covenant of marriage. It was from his bloodline, that the Messiah was born.

The Spirit of Unbelief and the Deaf and Dumb Spirit

The following is being reprinted with permission from Wellspring Ministry, from the *Handbook on How to Minister* by Art Mathias, who adapted this from a sermon from Todd Bentley. [9]

The spirits of unbelief and the deaf and dumb spirit affect us humans in two different ways: first spiritually, and second, physically.

Spiritually speaking, the devil blinds people's eyes, ears, and minds to the things of God. John 12:40 says, "He [Satan] hath blinded their eyes, and hardened their heart; that they should not see with their eyes, nor understand with their heart, and be converted, and I should heal them."

There are many people who are unable to read the scriptures. They fall asleep, can't concentrate, or do not remember or understand anything that they read. Our faith comes by hearing and hearing by the Word of God (Romans 10:1 7) so by being unable to do these things, the devil steals our faith. The devil wars against us by making us blind and deaf and dumb spiritually. We do not have ears to hear; we are deaf in the spirit. We may want to hear. We may be very hungry for the voice of God, but we cannot hear.

The dumb spirit affects our ability to understand, so that we cannot receive the spirit of wisdom and revelation. "Blessed are your eyes, blessed are your ears for it has been given to you to know (to understand) the mysteries of the kingdom of heaven" (Matthew 13:11). There are people who read the Bible and they feel they have a block over their mind. No matter how much they read the Bible, they forget what they read. No matter how much they read the Bible, they don't understand. They are saved, they are born again but they don't understand, it doesn't compute. It doesn't get from the head to the heart.

They know that they are not supposed to be a hearer of the word only, but there is something that keeps them from being a doer. When you are deaf and dumb you are mute spiritually. We don't have anything to say and we don't have any power. Instead we have tradition, theology, religion, and a form of godliness that denies the power of God (2 Timothy 3:5). We talk about the power and the glory that was there in "Jesus' day." We talk about the manifestations of the Holy Spirit "back then" but the power and the gifts or manifestations of the Holy Spirit are not "for today."

We preach the word, but the Kingdom of God is not in word only but also in power. We may talk about the power and we may preach about the power but if we don't see the power, all we really have is the Kingdom in word only.

Everyone knows theology but somewhere along the line we have been deaf. Somewhere along the line we have been dumb. Somewhere along the line we have been in unbelief. Though we have read the scriptures that we are to cast out demons and lay hands on the sick in Jesus name, we either do not do it, or do not believe that they WILL recover. We may have believed that God CAN heal but not that He WILL heal.

Physically speaking, the Deaf and Dumb spirit inflicts people with complete or partial ringing in the ears, muteness, attention deficit disorder, dyslexia, mental illness, insanity, problems focusing, reading problems, and other learning disabilities.

When Jesus came down from the mount of transfiguration He was approached by a man who had a sick son. This event is recorded in Matthew 17, Mark 9 and Luke 9. If you will read the early verses in these chapters you will see that Jesus was descending from the mountain in each account. Along with other similarities we know that it is the same event told by three different writers from the perspectives given by the Holy Spirit for our edification. Let's read each of these accounts and notice how they are the same and how they are different.

> "LORD, have mercy on my son: for he is lunatic, and sore vexed: for ofttimes he falls into the fire, and oft into the water. And I brought him to thy disciples, and they could not cure him. Then Jesus answered and said, O faithless and perverse generation, how long shall I be with you? How long shall I suffer you? Bring him hither to me. And Jesus rebuked the devil; and he departed out of him: and the child was cured from that very hour. Then came the disciples to Jesus apart, and said, why could not we cast him out? And Jesus said unto them, Because of your unbelief: for verily 1 say unto you, if ye have faith as a grain of mustard seed, ye shall say unto this mountain, Remove, hence to yonder place; and it shall remove; and nothing shall be impossible unto you."
>
> (Matthew 17:15-20)

> "And one of the multitude answered and said, Master, 1 have brought unto thee my son, which hath a dumb spirit; And whosesoever he takes him, he tears him: and he foams, and gnashes with his teeth, and pines away: and I spake to thy disciples that they should cast him out; and they could not. He answered him, and said, O faithless generation, how long shall I be with you? How long shall I suffer you? Bring him unto me. And they brought him unto him: and when he saw him, straightway the spirit tare him; and he fell on the ground, and wallowed foaming.
>
> And he asked his father, how long is it ago since this came unto him? And he said, Of a child. And ofttimes it hath cast him into the fire, and into the waters, to destroy him: but if thou canst do anything, have compassion on us, and help us. Jesus said unto him, "If thou canst believe, all things are possible to him that believeth. And straightway the father of the child cried out, and said with tears, LORD, 1 believe; help thou mine unbelief. When Jesus saw that the people came running together, he rebuked the foul spirit, saying unto

> him, thou dumb and deaf spirit, I charge thee, come out of him, and enter no more into him."
>
> (Mark 9:17-25)

> "And, behold, a man of the company cried out, saying, Master, I beseech thee, look upon my son: for he is mine only child. And, lo, a spirit takes him, and he suddenly cries out; and it tears him that he foams again, and bruising him hardly departs from him. And I besought thy disciples to cast him out; and they could not. And Jesus answering said, O faithless and perverse generation, how long shall I be with you, and suffer you? Bring thy son hither. And as he was yet a coming, the devil threw him down, and tare him. And Jesus rebuked the unclean spirit, and healed the child, and delivered him again to his father."
>
> (Luke 9:38-42)

It is very interesting to note that Jesus healed this boy by casting out a spirit. The father said his son was a lunatic and had a dumb spirit. When Jesus cast the spirit out He called it a foul spirit, an unclean spirit, *or a* dumb and deaf spirit in the different passages. The demon caused:

1. A mute condition (Mark 9:17, 25)
2. Deafness (Mark 9:25)
3. Foaming at the mouth (Mark 9:18, 20)
4. Fits (Mark 9:18, 20, 26)
5. Gnashing or grating of the teeth, in rage (Mark 9:18)
6. Pining away, lifelessness, complete exhaustion (Mark 9:18, 26)
7. Prostrations (Mark 9:20)
8. Suicidal tendencies (Mark 9:22)
9. Screaming (Mark 9:26)
10. Lunacy or insanity (Matthew 17:15)

This spirit threw the boy to the ground, into the fire and into water attempting to kill him. The spirit had made him deaf and mute. The spirit had torn his body and made him foam at the mouth. It badly bruised him. It caused him to grate his teeth and pine or waste in exhaustion. It made the boy "sore vexed" or extremely sick. It made him crazy.

The word *lunatic* derives from the Latin, meaning *moonstruck*. It means to be crazy, insane, slow, confused. While some have speculated that this is a description of epilepsy, these are all conditions of the mind, conditions that effect how we learn or relate to others. The people then observed that the condition was at its worst during the full moon, which many medical and health care workers continue to observe today. It is not in fact caused by the moon but by a demon, which attacks during this time to make others assign blame elsewhere.

Why couldn't the disciples cast out the demon? Understanding this is crucial. In Mark chapter 1, Jesus is baptized by John and receives the baptism of the Spirit to begin His ministry. He begins His travels throughout Galilee all the way to Capernaum in company with His disciples. In Capernaum, He teaches in the temple and does many miracles of healing. Even the demons obeyed and recognized Him. Mark 1:23-25 says, "And there was in their synagogue a man with an unclean spirit; and he cried out, Saying, Let us alone; what have we to do with thee, thou Jesus of Nazareth? Art thou come to destroy us? I know thee who thou art, the Holy One of God. And Jesus rebuked him, saying, Hold thy peace, and come out of him."

In Mark 6, Jesus returns to His hometown of Nazareth. In Mark 6:4-6 Jesus said to them, "A prophet is not without honor, but in his own country, and among his own kin, and in his own house. And he could there do no mighty work, save that he laid his hands upon a few sick folk, and healed them. And he marveled because of their unbelief. And he went round about the villages, teaching."

Jesus could not do any miracles in His hometown because of their unbelief. The same with the disciples; it's not that the disciples didn't want to heal the boy, or that they didn't have enough power, or even that they didn't have enough authority or faith. It's not that they hadn't already gone out and preached the Gospel and healed the sick. It's not that they hadn't already received the commission and the anointing to preach the Gospel and heal the sick, cleanse the lepers and raise the dead and cast out devils. It was because of the unbelief in the father and the "perverse generation" that they could not cast out the demon.

Matthew 17:17 says, "Then Jesus answered and said, O faithless and perverse generation, how long shall I be with you? How long shall I suffer you?

The word *generation* describes the age, the time, the mindset of the people, and the family. There is something in the "generation," there is something in the family, the "church", the city, the nation that is keeping this young boy from being healed. Jesus is saying that it is not that His disciples didn't have the power; it's not that He didn't want them to do it. It did not have anything to do with their faith. There was something in the generations then, and there still is today, and that is the spirit of unbelief.

In Mark 9:21, Jesus asked the father how long the boy had been sick and the father said since a child or infancy. In verse 22, the father says, "...but if thou canst do anything, have compassion on us, and help us."

This was the desperate cry of a father for his son. "Help, if you can!" He did not believe that Jesus really could or would heal his son. In verses 23, Jesus looked at that father and said (my paraphrase), "It's not a matter if I can, it is a matter if you can believe." But the father was so discouraged, disappointed, and beaten down by the spirit of unbelief, the spirit that made his son deaf, dumb, and mute, that he wasn't able to believe God. He wasn't able to believe the promise of God.

In verse 24, "...the father of the child cried out, and said with tears, LORD, I believe; help thou mine unbelief." Then Jesus cast out the dumb and deaf spirit and the boy was healed. He cast out the spirit and the boy was healed only after the father repented of his unbelief and said, 'heal my own unbelief!' It was the father's unbelief that prevented the disciples from casting the demon out. The sins of the father are passed on to the third and fourth generation to those that do not believe (Exodus 20:5, Deuteronomy 5:9).

The dumb and deaf spirit prevented the father from believing. But it was not just the father's sin. It was in the generations. Sometimes we really believe that God can and will heal but the healing does not happen. There is a generational sin of unbelief that must be broken.

This is a form of ungodliness that denies the power of God. God does not change. The works that Christ did and that the apostles did are for today. In fact, we are to do greater works than Christ did, as He commanded in John 14:12.

One commentator says[10]: "Blasphemy or sin against the Holy Ghost includes any willful, malicious, and slanderous word spoken against the person and work of the Holy Spirit, or ascribing the work of the Spirit to Satan (Matthew 12:31-32; Hebrews 10:26-29). It is unpardonable because it is a willful rejection of light and deliberate insult to the last and only executive of God to man to bring about remission of sins on earth. When men do away with the only agent of God in redemption and the only method of forgiveness, there is no other person to plead their case before God, so their souls are lost eternally. One may blaspheme and insult the Spirit in ignorance and be forgiven." (1Timothy 1:13)

The sin in our lives, our generations, our churches, temples, schools, and seminaries must be repented and broken.

It was the spirit of unbelief that gave power to the deaf and dumb spirit. So, the first thing we need to do is get rid of unbelief. Then we can cast out the deaf and dumb spirit that has blinded our eyes, plugged our ears and confused our minds physically and spiritually. This foul spirit has stolen our faith because we could not hear or understand the Word of God.[11]

> "I call heaven and earth to record this day against you, that I have set before you, life and death, blessing and cursing: therefore, choose life, that both you and your seed may live:"
>
> (Deuteronomy 30:19)

God does not bring curses upon humankind to be mean or spiteful. Humans bring them upon themselves by willful disobedience, rebellion or ignorance of God's laws and words. The choice is always ours. Sin brings on curses.

Only Jesus Christ has the power to break curses. "Christ redeemed us from the curse of the law by becoming a curse for us, for it is written: "Cursed is everyone who is hung on a tree." (Galatians 3:13) Again, I reiterate, something that most Christians do not realize, is that this is not automatic, but the individual believer must *appropriate* the work of the cross to themselves, their ancestors and the generational curses they inherited. Then the liberating power of the cross may be fulfilled to them, and the power of the curses can be broken.

When we appropriate the cross in faith, powerful forces are released like rubber bands flying across a room. Demons are losing their place and heading for the unemployment line. The unseen universe is shaking as the profound reverberations of broken curses echo out from the cross. A great cheer goes up in heaven, 'another soul is getting free!'[12]

The Cursed Heavens

> "For as the new heavens and the new earth, which I will make, shall remain before me, said the LORD, so shall your seed and your name remain."
> (Isaiah 66:22)

> "Then I saw a new heaven and a new earth, for the first heaven and the first earth had passed away, and there was no longer any sea." (Revelation 21:1)

Lastly, this would be the end of all curses, which is when the Creator recreates heaven and earth. Every wonder why it is promised in the Old and New Testaments that both the heavens and the earth will be made new? It is because the heavens are in a cursed state due to Lucifer's rebellion with his fallen extraterrestrial angels against their Creator. Remember, Lucifer managed to persuade one third of the extraterrestrials in the heavens to rebel against the Creator with him. That means that one third of the cosmos are deceived. As Earth is a microcosm of the grand macrocosm, we can see that one-third of all the worlds, planets, and star systems are inhabited by cursed beings, like Nephilim, bastard children, robots, grays, and malevolent extraterrestrials. Conditions of crime, slavery, pollution, and diseases are common, which are all manifestations of the curse.

According to John W. Milor in his book, *Aliens and the Antichrist*, there are two types of cursed beings that dwell among the cursed domains of the universe. First are those who have been translated to angelic status. These are immortal beings with bodies that have been translated into a glorified state, which no longer reproduce (Matthew 22:30; Mark 12:25; Luke 20:35).[13]

Second, are those who have not been translated into angelic status. These are beings like us, physically mortal, who may be as lost and confused about God as are many of us on earth. "For in the resurrection they neither marry, nor are given in marriage, [and do not reproduce] but are as angels in heaven." (Matthew 22:30) "For when they shall rise from the dead, they neither marry, nor are given in marriage; but are as the angels which are in heaven."(Mark 12:25); "But they which shall be accounted worthy to obtain that world, and the resurrection from the dead, neither marry, nor are given in marriage: Neither can they die any more [no more reincarnation]: for they are equal to the angels; and are the children of God, being the children of the resurrection." (Luke 20:35-36)

There are hosts of heaven, according to Exodus 12:41, who have never reached angelic status and are destined to die physically. There may yet be hope for them, just as there is hope for mortal humans, to repent and be saved. I happen to agree with Milor here, that Jesus Christ may have spread His message of Salvation and His Word to other extraterrestrials, the non-angelic beings in the universe. The Bible indicates that they exist, and knowing the nature of Christ, whom I am calling the *Cosmic Christ*, encourages us to believe that the *Divine Plan of Salvation as Written in the Stars* is not limited to us humans, but extends to all those extraterrestrial immortals who are in bondage to the curse of the Luciferian rebellion, which has spread like a cancer throughout the heavens. See Book Three: *Who Are The Angels:* chapter on the *Cosmic Christ*,[14] and Book Five: The Heavens, chapter on *The Divine Plan of Salvation as Written in the Stars* for further elucidation.

However, for those who are immortal, the gods, the fallen angels, the fallen sons of the Elohim, all those who were translated into angelic status, the situation is far worse. The scriptures do not tell us that God has a Divine Plan of Salvation for them as He does for mortals, and even the *Books of Enoch* indicate their eventual demise.

These beings were given divine status by the Creator. They knew Him face to face, they received all their tremendous intelligence and power from Him. They rebelled against Him and turned away from Him by their own choice and their own act. Because of their prior intimacy with God, they have a much higher level of accountability for their sin, which is at an almost unforgivable status by nature. Their crimes do not compare to those of us mortals. As He has promised in His words:

"The Lord will be terrible to them:
for He will *famish all the gods of the earth*;"

(Zechariah 2:11)

Their curse will eventually result in their eternal destruction, of both immortal bodies and spirits: "And whoever was not found written in the book of life was cast into the lake of fire." (Revelation 20:15)

Remember, only one third of the heavens followed Lucifer in rebellion, the other two thirds remaining faithful to the Creator. The faithful were not cursed but continue to this day to enjoy the blessing of life, light, and power. "His tail swept a third of the stars out of the sky and flung them to the earth." (Revelation 12:4) There are many planets in the cosmos that are even more beautiful than the Earth, whose inhabitants experience no death, no disease, no crime or pollution. These glorified worlds are the homes of the immortal beings who all share the supernatural powers of the Creator, and they continue to use their power wisely. These are the benevolent extraterrestrials and hosts of heaven that will accompany the Lord Jesus Christ upon His return, to finally end the battle and establish the Kingdom of God on the Earth.

The New Jerusalem will be downloaded out of the heavens, placed upon the earth of the old Jerusalem, which Revelation says will be the seat of the Kingdom of Heaven, where Christ will reign for a millennium. This New Jerusalem will represent not only peace on earth, but will be the city of Peace that will represent the restoration of peace in the heavens. It will be a glorious time, when earth will become the cornerstone in the heavens, where all the extraterrestrial nations will travel back and forth to meet with the King of the Kingdom, the Cosmic Christ.

According to Milor, 'there are two classes of cursed beings and there are two classes of glorified beings. The first class of glorified beings inhabiting some worlds comprises those beings who are in transitional states, such as Adam and Eve once were. In essence, they have not yet been translated to angelic status, but they are not cursed with death either. One primary characteristic that distinguishes them from angels is that they are required to procreate in order to populate their planets (Genesis 1:28). Humans prior to the fall were in this transitional state. At some point in their existence, if beings in this glorified category maintain their obedience to God, they will eventually be translated to angelic status. As for humanity, this was the original plan, and it will still happen, for those who have repented (even though they currently aren't glorified). This opportunity exists only because of the work of Jesus Christ (Matthew 22:30; Mark 12:25; Luke 20:35; Revelation 21:16-17).[15]

This is why I have been saying that the Divine Plan of Salvation, which is literally written in the stars, goes far beyond planet Earth, but extends to all mortal beings in the cosmos, because every cosmic traveler can read the stars. Earth was not the only planet populated with humans.

The spread of Satanic technology has led to his takeover of other worlds, holding them in bondage too. These worlds are fighting for their freedom as well. Many of the ancient astronauts did not stop at Earth with their mixing, interfering, and corrupting but also inhabited other worlds, spreading their agenda, technology, and their curse to other civilizations, which is why the heavens are in a deteriorated state. This concept of the cursed heavens is also written about extensively in the Zohar, which identify certain stars as Death Stars and certain star systems belonging to the Dark Lord. These ancient Hebrew concepts are what brought the *Star Wars* series into manifestation. I once read that George Lucas' intention through the making of his *Star Wars* films was to bring people to God, to search for the Creator, and to find the Force.

Some powerful cosmic karma was created by those who connived with Lucifer the Satan. In order to have a kingdom on earth in ancient days, those who Von Däniken calls 'ancient astronauts', also referred to as the ancient gods of this world, will be brought before their Creator for judgment. Some of these gods will lose their godlike status, yet others may not, as I would like to believe that some may yet come to repentance and in doing so, be saved. They will prove themselves by benevolent deeds, in regard to Earth, being called *the good ETs* by us humans. But this is not for us to yet judge, as only the Creator can know for sure how these beings, who once came under the judgment of God for their experiments, may or may not have turned themselves around. I am sure they too know the scriptures, and know the power of the wrath of the Creator. Being immortal, they witnessed all the floods, and all the fire coming down from heaven.

Many of the ancient stories, the mythologies of earth, and we remember that myth is truth, end with repentance, reconciliation, and restoration. The ancient gods know where their power comes from, and those who want to maintain it must somehow reconcile with their Creator through repentance and clearing their karma. That is my opinion.

Also inhabiting some of the two-thirds of the glorified worlds are beings who have been translated into angelic status. Most, if not all, glorified worlds contain both classes of glorified beings. I say this based on the Bible's description of Earth in the future. When Earth is glorified once again, it will contain both angels and natural generations of people. Glorified saints will be angels (Revelation 21:16-17), and natural generations of people who survive the days of the Antichrist will also be on the Earth forever as well (Isaiah 2:1-2, 11:6-7, 65:25; Zechariah 14:16-21; Revelation 11:15, 20:1-10; Matthew 25:31-46). Actually, translation probably does not occur for all the members of a given species at the same time. Massive group translations occur only on rare occasions, such as the rapture of the church.[16]

Just as living beings go through transitions of glory, so too do planets. I say this because of the various stages of glory Earth has gone through, and is yet to go through. Earth once housed a parcel of glorified territory known as the Garden of Eden, but after the fall of Adam and Eve, Earth became cursed and Eden was off limits. Earth's history with the Garden of Eden actually predates Adam and Eve. The Garden of Eden was restored after the first flood, known as the flood of Lucifer, which happened approximately 20,000 years ago, which coincides with the sinking of the civilizations of Atlantis.

Atlantis was the home of the first group of the Fallen, and the first group of Nephilim. This was known as Lucifer's Kingdom, and Earth was his seat of power in the cosmos. Then the Creator ordered the floods and destroyed all of them, only to begin life again on Earth. Lucifer appeared as a luminous serpent to Adam and Eve in the Garden of Eden and tested their obedience to God. We know they failed, and Lucifer was further cursed, Adam and Eve were cursed, and the Earth was cursed as a result of their disobedience to God.

Even though Earth has been cursed since the fall of Adam and Eve, it will again host not only a place of paradise, as it once did, but that paradise will be even better than the Garden of Eden was originally. Earth will be given the honor of housing the capital city of the entire universe, culminated by the very throne of God Himself.[17]

The New Jerusalem will be downloaded out of heaven in all its glory as the main hub of the universe:

> "I saw the Holy City, the new Jerusalem, **<u>coming down out of heaven from God</u>**, prepared as a bride beautifully dressed for her husband. And I heard a loud voice from the throne saying, now the dwelling of God is with men, and he will live with them. They will be his people, and God himself will be with them and be their God."
>
> (Revelation 21:2)

As I've said in my chapter on *The Motherships of the Lord*, the New Jerusalem is a city which is downloaded out of the heavens to a place on the earth as a huge Mothership.[18]

> "People will live in it, **<u>and there will no longer be a curse</u>**, for Jerusalem will dwell in security."
>
> (Zechariah 14:11)

The Lord Himself will dwell on the Earth, and the Earth will be restored to the Garden of Eden it once was, only better.

> "Then it will come about that any who are left of all the nations that went against Jerusalem will go up from year to year to worship the King, the LORD of hosts, and to celebrate the Feast of Booths."
>
> (Zechariah 14:16)

There is fine eating in the Kingdom of Heaven! When the Kingdom of Heaven begins on Earth, there will be feasts. The feasts of the Lord will be celebrated with the Lord Himself present. The celebratory feasts are important to the Lord, as they mark anniversaries of important events in His-story.

> "Him who overcomes I will make a pillar in the temple of my God. Never again will he leave it. I will write on him the name of my God and the name of the city of my God, the new Jerusalem, which is coming down out of heaven from my God; and I will also write on him my new name."
>
> (Revelation 3:12)

Overcoming is prerequisite to becoming a pillar, which is a tower of strength, a support, and a leader, in God's temple and in God's new city. Overcoming the curse of this world is done through appropriating the accomplishment of the cross of Christ; overcoming all the lies of Satan with God's truth; overcoming the suffering, persecution, and injustice of this world, with faith in God, and the hope of a greater glory, the glory of God made manifest. This is why Jesus commanded us to pray, '*Thy Kingdom come, thy will be done, on earth as it is in Heaven.*' Those who overcome this present kingdom of darkness will be translated into the Kingdom of Heaven, which is the Kingdom of Light, Truth, Love, and Peace.

Notes:

1. Ken and Jeanne Harrington, *From Curses to Blessings: Removing Generational Curses,* Destiny Image, 2011
2. Art Mathias, *Biblical Foundations of Freedom, Destroying Satan's Lies with God's Truth,* p. 43, Wellspring Publishing, Alaska, 2010.
3. Carl L. Fox, Paul D. Norcross, *Breaking the Authority of the Bastard Curse: Restoring the Congregation of the Lord* – p. 59, Christian Faith International Ministries; 2nd Edition, 2004
4. Ibid, p. 60
5. Ella LeBain, *Who's Who in the Cosmic Zoo?* Book One – Third Edition, *Nephilim,* p. 326-338, Tate, 2013.
6. Fox/Norcross, p. 61
7. Traci Morin, *Conceived Out of Wedlock,* https://www.healingdeliverance.net/child-conceived-out-of-wedlock/
8. Ella LeBain, *Who is God?* Book Two, Skypath Books, 2015.

9. Art Mathias, *Handbook on How to Minister*, Wellspring Publishing, Alaska, 2010
10. Finis J. Dake, *Dake's Annotated Reference Bible-KJV*, Dake Publishing, 2014
11. Art Mathias, p. 29-32
12. Chester D. Kylstra, Betsy Kylstra, *Restoring the Foundations: An Integrated Approach to Healing Ministry* (2nd Edition) – Proclaiming His Word, Inc., August 1, 2001
13. John W. Milor, *Aliens and the Antichrist,* Xlibris Corp; July, 2000
14. Ella LeBain, *Who Are the Angels:* Book Three, Chapter: *The Cosmic Christ,* p.364-416, Skypath Books, 2016.
15. Milor, p.5
16. Milor, p.6
17. Milor, p.7
18. Ella LeBain, *Who is God?* Book Two – Chapter: *The Motherships of the Lord,* p. 71-88, Skypath Books, 2015

CHAPTER EIGHTEEN

Gateways

"The devil bewitches his victims before he destroys them"
~ Ignatius

Gateways can also be described as spiritual legal ground, which act as portals that opens the door to supernatural activities. Reliving traumatic experiences, such as the 9/11 terror attacks, or the Holocaust, are gateways for aliens, greys, demons, and non-human intelligences to absorb energy from human souls and influence further actions in our lives. Trauma makes us vulnerable. Among the symptoms of PTSD, feeling drained, fatigued, depressed, anxious, hyper-vigilant, overly awake, insomniac, which leads to weakness, all open our gateways to demonic influences or alien interference, otherwise known as Satanic attack.

Without Christ we end up giving our power over to these energy vampires. Why does pop culture celebrate blood-thirsty vampires, such the New Moon series? Using mega-stars like Brad Pitt and Tom Cruise as tragically romantic souls stuck in a vampire estate evokes both sympathy and fascination for the fallen, the enemy. Oh, and let's not forget the infamous Barnabas Collins from the hit soap Dark Shadows, recently resurrected once again by Johnny Depp. Our culture has been implanted with a program to accept the vampire myth so that we accept being drained by alien energy vampires who find our energy fields, our emotions (*energy in motion*) more satisfying than our blood. There is no difference really, because "life is in the blood," whether a vampire is draining our blood, our life-force, or our energy bodies of soul energy -- it's all energy theft.

It is time for calling it what it is, theft. Some people would rather stoutly maintain that the aliens are good, which, let's face it, is pure wishful thinking on their part. Most contactees and experiencer accounts report invasion of space, of mind, of body, removal of bodily fluids, all being nothing but energy theft.

In the many classes and workshops, I conducted from 1990-2000 were some people who vehemently insisted they never had a negative experience with an alien or angel. As if admitting to a negative experience was somehow a reflection on them! Which it is not. Yet these are the stories they are telling themselves, due to the implantation of hypnotic suggestions, called hypnogoguery, done by the aliens.

They continue in this state of denial despite the fact that the fruit of their lives shows distinctly otherwise.

I had one woman argue with me that the aliens that came to get her, wrapped her up in a white sheet ever so gently and carried her away up into their spaceship, where she insisted nothing negative occurred. That's when they implanted her with thoughtforms such as "you will not remember any of this," and "you will never speak of any of this to anyone," and "this is the most wonderful time of your life," all hypnotic suggestion done under a hypnogogic state or spell. So, when her soul is brought back into its body, it literally can't remember nor properly discern what happened while it was being probed in any or all its orifices, nasal, ears, eyes, mouth, genitals, womb, belly button or anus. Yet the Post Traumatic Stress Disorder that inevitably follows such a rape is evident in their lives, particularly when others bring it up.

This woman then came back and told her story to her next-door neighbour, who called in the authorities to have her committed to a mental hospital for at least 72 hours for observation. This woman was injected with lithium and hauled her off to the local mental hospital where she was drugged and observed. When she returned home, she was drained, exhausted and embarrassed. Are these the fruits of light beings, and gods of love? I don't think so!

A God of Love would not cause such a trauma. The Creator God and the Angels of the Most High God save, heal, and deliver us from evil, suffering and traumatic experiences. Christ delivers from demons, aliens, and dark spirits. All power is given to Him under the Heaven, on the Earth and inside the Earth. The demons tremble at the authority and the powerful name of Jesus Christ.

> "Therefore, God exalted Him to the highest place and gave him the name that is above every name, that at the name of Jesus *every knee should bow*, in heaven and on earth and *under the earth*,"
>
> (Philippians 2:9-10)

> "And the kingdom and dominion, and the greatness of the kingdom under the whole heaven, shall be given to the people of the saints of the Most High, whose kingdom is an everlasting kingdom, and all dominions shall serve and obey Him."
>
> (Daniel 7:27)

> "The seventh angel sounded his trumpet, and there were loud voices in heaven, which said: "The kingdoms of this world has become the kingdoms of our Lord and of his Christ, and He will reign forever and ever."
>
> (Revelation 11:15)

The Nations of the World Give Power to the Beast

The book of Revelation has been an enigma wrapped up in a conundrum for centuries. As we are approaching the end of this Age, for which time it was written, its mysteries are beginning to be *revealed.* For the sake of clarity, I am reprinting Revelation 13 here, so my readers can see the words in their full context, New Kings James Version:

> "And I stood upon the sand of the sea, and saw a beast rise up out of the sea, having seven heads and ten horns, and upon his horns ten crowns, and upon his heads the name of blasphemy.
>
> And the beast which I saw was like unto a leopard, and his feet were as the feet of a bear, and his mouth as the mouth of a lion: and the dragon gave him his power, and his seat, and great authority.
>
> And I saw one of his heads as it were wounded to death; and his deadly wound was healed: and all the world wondered after the beast.
>
> And they worshipped the dragon which gave power unto the beast: and they worshipped the beast, saying, Who is like unto the beast? who is able to make war with him?
>
> And there was given unto him a mouth speaking great things and blasphemies; and power was given unto him to continue forty and two months.
>
> And he opened his mouth in blasphemy against God, to blaspheme his name, and his tabernacle, and them that dwell in heaven.
>
> And it was given unto him to make war with the saints, and to overcome them: and power was given him over all kindreds, and tongues, and nations.
>
> And all that dwell upon the earth shall worship him, whose names are not written in the book of life of the Lamb slain from the foundation of the world.
>
> If any man have an ear, let him hear.
>
> He that leads into captivity shall go into captivity: he that kills with the sword must be killed with the sword. Here is the patience and the faith of the saints.
>
> And I beheld another beast coming up out of the earth; and he had two horns like a lamb, and he spake as a dragon.
>
> And he exercises all the power of the first beast before him, and causes the earth and them which dwell therein to worship the first beast, who's deadly wound was healed.
>
> And he doeth great wonders, so that he makes fire come down from heaven on the earth in the sight of men,
>
> And deceives them that dwell on the earth by the means of those miracles which he had power to do in the sight of the beast; saying to them that dwell

on the earth, that they should make an image to the beast, which had the wound by a sword, and did live.

And he had power to give life unto the image of the beast that the image of the beast should both speak, and cause that as many as would not worship the image of the beast should be killed.

And he causes all, both small and great, rich and poor, free and bond, to receive a mark in their right hand, or in their foreheads:

And that no man might buy or sell, save he that had the mark, or the name of the beast, or the number of his name.

Here is wisdom. Let him that hath understanding count the number of the beast: for it is the number of a man; and his number is Six hundred three-score and six."

(Revelation 13:1-18)

The Dragon is Satan, who was put into a serpent body, while his fallen angels were bound inside the earth. The Beast is a hybrid being that will be released on the surface of the planet, who will *appear* to be human, but will be controlled, implanted, and possessed by the Satanic Draconian forces of the Reptilians.

The Beast Coming of the Sea and the Earth are the UFOs that many are seeing in our skies today. The USOs (Underwater Submerged Objects) are the spaceships that emerge out of the oceans from underwater and underground bases in the earth. This is the Extraterrestrial Military Industrial Complex.

Most major governmental Military Industrial Complexes keep what they know about UFOs and alien beings secret, because they've all been forced into agreements with them in exchange for staying in power and for advanced technology. The Cold War was all about good versus evil, but not at all USA verses USSR; it was alien versus human, with the aliens playing us off against each other for alien technology. The Nazis took alien technological expertise back to the USA and created NASA (National Aeronautics and Space Administration), which is the Executive Branch Agency of the US Government responsible for putting people in space. That was just the beginning -- the military knows the identity of many of these alien beings, and they agree to maintain secrecy in exchange for security.

They know they share the earth with these beings that have dominion *inside* the earth. These are the reptilian and amphibian gods that have been worshipped for millennia, who were given live sacrifices to appease their hunger for human blood. This was the practice in many ancient cultures. Is it coincidental that Los Alamos and Alamogordo and Fort Huachuca are well within radius of the blood-soaked Aztec Empire?

The grey aliens serve as slaves to the reptilian masters inside the earth. They are locked into a contract with them to bring them food from the surface of the planet, to keep them from surfacing themselves and wreaking havoc and terrifying everyone. These same gray aliens are the ones who also entered into agreements with the US military industrial complex in exchange for technology, to allow them a certain number of abduction per year. These are mainly children who go missing, never to be found, dead or alive, anywhere on the surface of the planet. These children are taken inside the earth and offered as food sacrifices for these draconian carnivores who prefer young humans over old, because of their purity.

There were 465,676 missing Children reports, reported to Law Enforcement in 2016.

The U.S. Department of Justice reports on how many children are reported missing each year, this report was released in 2010:

- **797,500** children (younger than 18) were reported missing in a one-year period of time studied resulting in an average of 2,185 children being reported missing each day.
- **203,900** children were the victims of family abductions.
- **58,200** children were the victims of non-family abductions.
- **115** children were the victims of "stereotypical" kidnapping. (These crimes involve someone the child does not know or someone of slight acquaintance, who holds the child overnight, transports the child 50 miles or more, kills the child, demands ransom, or intends to keep the child permanently.)

[from The National Center for Missing & Exploited Children-www.missingkids.com]

Our Worst Nightmare

Just calculate the statistics: every year there are thousands of children who go missing, never to be found dead or alive. Only 1-2% are ever found, who were usually kidnapped by a family member or taken by the local pedophile. Some of those were involved in Satanic Rituals and used as child sex slaves.

The remaining 98% show no trace of being found. This practice has been going on since the 1950s in America after the treaty was signed with the Grays during the Eisenhower administration, when Majestic 12 was formed to maintain Official Denial of aliens and UFOs.

It was shortly thereafter that the milk boxes began to advertise the "Have You Seen Me" notices with pictures of missing children. Again, only 1-2% of missing children are found dead or alive. So where do all these children go? It's really our worst nightmare, but they have become food for the Draconians. Others are taken for experimentation in underground facility laboratories such as Dulce, New Mexico.

> "The fear of the LORD is the beginning of wisdom: and the knowledge of the holy is understanding."
>
> (Proverbs 9:10)

> "The fruit of the righteous is a tree of life; and he that winneth souls is wise."
>
> (Proverbs 11:30)

What is Pizzagate?

Pizzagate originally was a meme that was released in John Podesta's Wikileaks emails, containing unusual references to pizza, hamburgers and hotdogs. It involves the trafficking of children for sex. The word pizza as a secret code, in addition to using different types of foods to sell different types of sexual preferences, such as hot dogs are boys, and hamburgers are girls, and pizza meant orgies. When the news report broke and were leaked all over the internet, they were initially denied and debunked, however, not anymore, which has turned into the great 'purge' of Washington, D.C. and Hollywood.[1]

At its core, Pizzagate is a joint investigation between citizens, law enforcement, and governments into the pervasiveness of sex trafficking, ritual abuse, and cyber-crime in global political powers around the world. Some famous examples include[2]:

- The fact that around 800,000 children are reported missing[3] and 300,000 children are at risk of sexual exploitation[4] in United States alone every year. For context, the number of people murdered in the United States in a given year is only around 16,000.[5] There are approximately 20 to 30 million slaves in the world today. According to the U.S. State Department, 600,000 to 800,000 people are trafficked across international borders every year, of which 80% are female and half are children.[6]
- Over 51 countries are affected by the same organizations that are subverting human rights and facilitating international human, drugs, and weapons trafficking.[2]

NOTES:

1. Joshua Gillin, *How Pizzagate Went from Fake News to a Real Problem for a D.C. Business,* http://www.politifact.com/truth-o-meter/article/2016/dec/05/how-pizzagate-went-fake-news-real-problem-dc-busin/, December 5, 2016
2. Wikileaks, The Pizzagate Wikiteam, formerly, The #Pizzagate Review, http://pizzagate.wiki/Main_Page
3. Missing Children in America: Unsolved Cases, http://abcnews.go.com/US/missing-children-america-unsolved-cases/story?id=19126967, By ABC News Staff, May 8, 2013.
4. The Trafficking of Children, https://en.wikipedia.org/wiki/Trafficking_of_children
5. https://www.reference.com/government-politics/many-people-murdered-day-united-states-4ce42c4182d89232
6. 11 Facts About Human Trafficking, https://www.dosomething.org/us/facts/11-facts-about-human-trafficking

CHAPTER NINETEEN

STARGATES

"I AM the Gate."
~ YESHUA, AKA JESUS CHRIST

Stargates, sometimes called wormholes, are doorways or portals that lead to other star systems through other dimensions. Stargates are the access points opened by the ancient astronauts and gods who came and went. Of the many existent portals around the globe, we notice that some are active and susceptible to visitations.

Mt. Hermon, which was once ancient Phoenicia, is today a part of Israel's Golan Heights and straddles the borders of Lebanon and Syria. This was the original portal which, according to every ancient culture in the Middle East, began the earliest contact between human and alien cultures. According to the *Books of Enoch,* and *the Book of Jubilees,* Mt. Hermon was the exact point of descent for the Sons of God. Genesis 6 confirms that Phoenicia is the land of the 'descent' of the Sons of God. Our word phoenix is derived from the Greek name for the people who called themselves Sidonians. Their capital city, Sidon, was named after the first-born son of Ham, the youngest son of Noah of Ark fame.

Mt. Herman is an active portal, important to various gods and extraterrestrials for their return to earth in the past, and may in fact be the point of return in the future.

In the Epic of Gilgamesh, the hero passes near Mount Hermon, called Saria by Sumerians, "Saria and Lebanon tremble at the felling of the cedars". In the *Book of Enoch,* Mount Hermon is the place where the Gregoroi, later called Watchers, a class of fallen extraterrestrial angels, descended to Earth. They swore upon the mountain that they would take wives among the daughters of men and return (Enoch 6).

The peaks of Mount Hermon were used by the Canaanites in the worship and rituals of Baal. They referred to the mountain as Mount Ba'al-Hermon (Judges 3:3). According to Ugaritic texts, the summit is referred to as Saphon, the palace of Baal. Baal was the Lord of those who fly, as in UFOs.

Mt. Hermon was also visited by Jesus and His disciples in their journeys north from Bethsaida on the Sea of Galilee to the city of Caesarea Philippi, at the southern base of Mount Hermon (Matthew 16:13; Mark 8:27). It was at this spot that Jesus revealed to His followers the plan to build His Church, go to Jerusalem to die, and be resurrected (Matthew 16:18-21). Mount Hermon was also the site of the Transfiguration (Mark 9:2-48), where Jesus took Peter, James, and John, high up the mountain for prayer. Jesus became radiantly white, and conversed with Moses and Elijah, who had appeared beside Him, through this ancient portal.

So why is Mount Hermon such an important portal? Well, according to researchers David Flynn, it is all about the numbers. David Flynn states that there are 33.33 degrees of the circumference of the earth which actually represents 2,012.9 nautical miles. Mt. Hermon lies exactly at 33.33° north and 33.33° east; 2,012 miles from the equator and 2, 012 miles from the Paris Meridian. 2,012.9 corresponds to the year, month, and day that the ancient Mayan calendar ends, which on our calendar falls on December 21, 2012. [1]

This is the time the ancient Mayans believe their feathered serpent god Quetzalcoatl, who they claim was the founder of their civilization, will return from the heavens. It's important to remember that the Mayans mysteriously disappeared around 850 A.D., and that their culture celebrated live human sacrifices to their serpent god, who may well have been a Reptilian. It's important to take into account that many view Quetzalcoatl not as a reptile hostile to humanity, but as a savior figure, civilizing a nation abused and hostile to alien reptiles. Some even maintain that Quetzalcoatl was Christ Himself when He walked the Americas, and that it was the Reptilians who later invaded and corrupted a unique gospel. Many teachings of Quetzalcoatl are so Christian, it can be argued this way. It will be interesting to watch which portal, if any, this ancient Reptilian god will use to descend back to earth.

When you draw a line from Mt. Hermon and follow the 33.33° parallel around the earth, which is literally on the opposite side of the globe, you end up in Roswell, New Mexico, another portal whose rupture began the UFO movement back in 1947. An alien crashed a flying saucer into the portal and our military personnel accidentally let the cats out of bag big time by allegedly recovered alien bodies.[1]

Thomas R. Horn postulates in his book, *Nephilim Stargates: The Year 2012 and the Return of the Nephilim*, "Does the chosen location of the first connection of heaven with the earth on Mt. Hermon at 33.33° (2012 miles from the equator and the Paris Meridian) set in time the final phase of a new world order in the year 2012.[2]

It is now 2018, and while there's much resistance to the coming New World Order, it has not been fully manifested -- yet. In my mind, this commences the final phase of the beginning of the implementation of the new world order, but not the final phase of the new world order, as it is still being formed around the world, and will culminate with the emergence of the final Antichrist, also known as the Man of Perdition.

As I've been saying throughout this book series, that the emergence of the final Antichrist cannot happen until the Restrainer is removed from the planet. The restrainer may be understood to be collectively the body of believers in Christ, the church.

Horn goes on to question, "But how is the year 2012 anchored in time? Dates and years were commonly measured from the start of the reign of a king or at the founding of a new city in antiquity. Our modern calendar is aligned to the birth of the Messiah of Israel, Jesus Christ, though even this "anchor point" is not fixed absolutely. There is a debate concerning when exactly Jesus was born. Various researchers have placed the time of Christ's birth at 11BC, 3BC, and AD 1. Additionally, our modern calendar was based on earlier versions that were adjusted several times forward or back a number of years by Roman Emperors and Popes. Plus, there has already been a 2012 BC in our calendar, though it was not a remarkable year with respect to knowledge." [2]

The Mayan and Aztec calendar baktuns were matched with our year 2012 by coinciding the predicted eclipses, ours with theirs, and with the phases of Venus, our observations with their predictions. The date is right on, the prophecy is bull feathers!

"About the Time of the End, a body of men (and women) will be raised up who will turn their attention to the Prophecies, and insist upon their literal interpretation, in the midst of much clamor and opposition."
~ Sir Isaac Newton (1642-1727)

Signs of the End of the Age

It's important to note that there have been many scholars who have said that our present calendar system may in fact be off by as many as 30-75 years, because of all the many changes and adjustments to the way we count time. Which means that we may be further along the timeline than we think, or closer to the end of the Age of Pisces, which is what Jesus may have been referring to as to the time of His return. Since He specifically forbade us to set dates, or make predictions as to this time, we can only follow His instructions to Watch for Him and to pray for our delivery. (Emphasis and commentary in brackets are mine.)

"Jesus said, "The field is the world, and the good seed stands for the sons of the kingdom. The weeds are the sons of the evil one, and the enemy who sows

> them is the devil. The harvest is the end of the age, and the harvesters are angels. [*faithful extraterrestrials*] "As the weeds are pulled up and burned in the fire, so it will be at the end of the age. The Son of Man will send out his angels, and they will weed out of his kingdom everything that causes sin and all who do evil. And the angels will throw them into the fiery furnace, where there will be weeping and gnashing of teeth. Then the righteous will shine like the sun in the kingdom of their Father. He who has ears, let him hear." (Matthew 13:38-43)

Jesus also told his disciples, "And be sure of this: I am with you always, even to the end of the age." (Matthew 28:20)

We are approaching the end of the age. All the signs are here. Perhaps Mt. Hermon will be the stargate where they return to fight the final battles in the Valley of Jezreel which will culminate on another ancient portal and battlefield, the field of blood, known as Mount Megiddo.

What did Jesus say, when He was asked what are the signs of the end of the age?

> "As he was leaving the temple, one of his disciples said to him, "Look, Teacher! What massive stones! What magnificent buildings!" "Do you see all these great buildings?" replied Jesus. "Not one stone here will be left on another; everyone will be thrown down." As Jesus was sitting on the Mount of Olives opposite the temple, Peter, James, John and Andrew asked him privately," "Tell us, when will these things happen? And what will be the sign that they are all about to be fulfilled?" "Jesus said to them: "Watch out that no one deceives you. Many will come in my name, claiming, 'I am he,' and will deceive many. When you hear of wars and rumors of wars, do not be alarmed. Such things must happen, but the end is still to come. "Nation will rise against nation, and kingdom against kingdom. There will be earthquakes in various places, and famines. These are the beginning of birth pains."

> "You must be on your guard. You will be handed over to the local councils and flogged in the synagogues. On account of me you will stand before governors and kings as witnesses to them. And the gospel must first be preached to all nations. Whenever you are arrested and brought to trial, do not worry beforehand about what to say. Just say whatever is given you at the time, for it is not you speaking, but the Holy Spirit. Brother will betray brother to death, and a father his child. Children will rebel against their parents and have them put to death. All men will hate you because of me, but he who stands firm to the end will be saved."
>
> (Mark 13:1-13)

What about Israel? Jesus goes on to tell us that Israel will not pass away until all these things have happened. He uses the word, 'generation' which has also been translated as 'race' or 'peoples.' Also, the word generation frequently relates to a time period. Today a generation is considered to be 25 years, but a biblical generation was much longer. A biblical generation was speculated to be anywhere from 70-100 years. Taking into consideration that Israel was reborn in 1948, this generation potentially could end in 2018, 2028 or as far as 2048. As far as the ending of the Piscean Age, and the official beginning of the processional Age of Aquarius, this is an event triggered by the Sun rising within the first stars of the constellation of Aquarius at the spring equinox. According to astronomers and siderealists, this begins between the year 2050-2100. So, the years preceding the beginning of the Age of Aquarius, which is the time of brotherhood, peace and harmony on earth, which describes the millennial reign of the Kingdom of God, would have to be prior to the year 2050.

If we are looking at the Bible for the end of the timeline and the fulfillment of prophesy, there needs to be a seven-year tribulation period first, which culminates as the war of the gods against the God of Israel (Yahuah) and the Christian God (Jesus Christ), or as the prophet Daniel called it, the time of 70 weeks. But to make matters even more confusing, Jesus told us that if the Lord had not cut short those days, no one would survive this war of the gods.

This is what Jesus said would happen at the very end of the age. (Emphasis and commentary in brackets are mine)

> "When you see 'the abomination that causes desolation' standing where it does not belong—let the reader understand [*he is referring to when the Temple of Solomon is rebuilt in Jerusalem for the third time and the Antichrist sits himself up on the throne and demands Israel to worship him as their Messiah*]—then let those who are in Judea flee to the mountains. Let no one on the roof of his house go down or enter the house to take anything out. Let no one in the field go back to get his cloak. How dreadful it will be in those days for pregnant women and nursing mothers! Pray that this will not take place in winter, because <u>those will be days of distress unequaled from the beginning, when God created the world, until now—and never to be equaled again</u>. <u>**If the Lord had not cut short those days, no one would survive**</u>. But for the sake of the elect, whom he has chosen, he has shortened them. At that time if anyone says to you, 'Look, here is the Christ!' or, 'Look, there he is!' do not believe it. For <u>false Christs and false prophets will appear and perform signs and miracles to deceive the elect</u>—if that were possible [*the false prophets and false Christs will be empowered by the fallen extraterrestrial angels and their*

demons, which is already happening today, with signs and wonders]. So be on your guard; I have told you everything ahead of time.

"But in those days, following that distress, "'the sun will be darkened, and the moon will not give its light; [*this is an eclipse*] the stars will fall from the sky, [*whenever the scriptures speak of 'stars falling from the sky' they are referring to fallen extraterrestrial angels descending from the heavens to the earth. This will be a mass alien invasion, as depicted in scores of Hollywood films, which will take place at the very end before Christ returns*] and the heavenly bodies will be shaken. [*There will be movement on the moon and the other planets in our solar system which will terrify all those who are alive on the earth in those days. This may be caused by the Star Wars type battles going on in heavens.*]

"At that time men will see the Son of Man coming in clouds with great power and glory. And he will send his angels and gather his elect from the four winds, from the ends of the earth to the ends of the heavens.

"Now learn this lesson from the fig tree: As soon as its twigs get tender and its leaves come out, you know that summer is near. Even so, when you see these things happening, you know that it is near, right at the door. I tell you the truth, this generation [Israel] will certainly not pass away until all these things have happened. Heaven and earth will pass away, but my words will never pass away."

(Mark 13:14-31)

Yes, both the books of Isaiah and Revelation prophesy of a new heaven and a new earth, the old being destroyed and the heavens and the earth will be recreated, but this is way down the road in the timeline, after the millennial reign.

The Sun as a Stargate

The eclipse of our Sun with the Galactic Sun at the Galactic Center on December 21, 2012 was the biggest news of the day. Our sun has an eleven-year cycle, which culminates in increased or decreased sunspot activity. This is the real cause of our climate changes, as the sun drives the weather and makes the climate. I have never bought the idea that global warming is being caused by humans, that we are to blame for the severe climate change we're experiencing. The earth was a great deal warmer during the age of the giant reptiles, who didn't drive cars as far as we can tell from the fossil records. This whole politically motivated movement is meant as a guilt trip so that we buy more expensive light bulbs and a host of other green and eco-friendly products. My fellow Christians, who is the father of the lie? Is it ever right to lie, to 'nudge' others into behavior that is good for them? What would Jesus say?

Al Gore's idea of Global Warming was based more on a political agenda and a new marketing industry than real science. Yes, we are responsible for pollution, and yes, we do need to clean up our act in these areas, globally, which we must enact at an industrial and corporate level. But the fact remains that climate change is caused by the Sun.

The alignment of our Sun with the Galactic Sun is a big deal, because it connects the two ends of a stargate portal, the sun with the galactic center. We don't know what or who can potentially come through these portals, for good or evil. The other issue, is the presence of our sun's evil twin brown dwarf star, called, Nemesis, which is a mini solar system in and of itself. Altogether there are twelve objects, one of which is Nibiru, aka Planet X, aka Hercobulus, which is on its way to pass the earth at the end of this Age, precipitating and completing a pole shift.

In Book Five, *The Heavens,* I go into greater detail on the data on these exoplanets, their eclipses to our sun. There are scores of books on the market predicting the return of the gods after the 2012 eclipse, but we need to ask ourselves, is this a good thing? In my opinion, the gods that are returning are gearing up for the War of the Worlds, which culminates at the final battle of Armageddon. These ancient gods are then defeated by the Cosmic Christ, who claims His right as not just King of the Jews, but King of the Universe. See my chapter on the *Cosmic Christ* for further elucidation, Book Three.[3]

Our Sun, our only star, is a stargate. We know this as records tell us that ancient extraterrestrial astronauts used our sun to travel through it. The Egyptians chose July 23 as their New Year, as this marked the moment that the star Sirius and our Sun were conjunct. Sirius actually hides behind our Sun for 3 days.

According to the followers of Isis, the Egyptian Goddess, this was the time chosen by the gods to travel back to her home planet on the Sirius star system using our Sun as a stargate. The heliacal rising of Sirius occurs around July 26th or 27th, and marks the Mayan New Year also. But there are many gates throughout the universe, connecting dimensions and other worlds. What does the Bible say about these gates?

> "Enter through the narrow gate. For wide is the gate and broad is the road that leads to destruction, and many enter through it. But small is the gate and narrow the road that leads to life, and only a few find it."
>
> (Matthew 7:13-14)

There is mystery in this. The New Age offers a very wide gate. It offers all kinds of avenues, such as self-help, self-improvement, humanistic psychology, the promise of 'enlightenment', the lure of the mystical and the magical, witchcraft, and channeling angels, ascended masters, ETs and Aliens. Many people who have become disenchanted with religion have turned to New Age practices to find spirituality and enlightenment.

Up until the 1970s, book stores that sold information on the above were called Occult book stores. Then in the 1980s these very same bookstores were relabeled as Metaphysical book stores, only to be relabeled again in the millennium as New Age book stores. They are all one and the same and sell all the same stuff. Lucifer is the god of this world. Lucifer means light bearer.

> "The god of this age has blinded the minds of unbelievers, so that they cannot see the light of the gospel that displays the glory of Christ, who is the image of God."
>
> (2 Corinthians 4:4)

The New Age, Occult or Metaphysical movement is governed by the authority of the principalities of Lucifer and his fallen angels, who all masquerade as angels of light. "And no wonder, for Satan himself masquerades as an angel of light." (2 Corinthians 11:14)

Jesus said, "I AM the GATE; whoever enters through me will be saved.
He will come in and go out and find pasture."
(John 10:9)

There is so much in the New Age that competes with and counterfeits the path of Christ. Spiritually speaking, this is being orchestrated by the fallen extraterrestrial angels and Satan. Even the movement known as 'Christ Consciousness' is filled with a little truth sandwiched between lies. The only way to have the mind of Christ is to accept Jesus Christ as your personal savior and invite Him into your life, then His Holy Spirit fills you with the mind of Christ. Many in the Christ Consciousness movement think they have it, when in reality what they have is a false spirit that comes from Lucifer. Many are bound by a *religious spirit* which is not from God.

> "This is the covenant I will make with the people of Israel after that time," declares the LORD. "I will put my law in their minds and write it on their hearts. I will be their God, and they will be my people."
>
> (Jeremiah 31:33)

Human Portals

We talk about stargates and portals, and we must keep in mind that these are not just places on earth. People are designed as portals for a higher power. That higher power can be God or Satan. Imagine, when coupled with genetic improvements, that vessel's ability to completely embody either God or Satan is emphasized. Can the Devil have children? We all remember films like *Rosemary's Baby* and *The Omen,* which depict the birth of the antichrist, or the devil's child.

But what if you were to learn that Lucifer the Satan has his own seed, which has been warring with God's seed for millennia? Kind of explains the problem of racism on this planet, doesn't it?

> "Don't you know that you yourselves are God's temple and that God's Spirit lives in you? If anyone destroys God's temple, God will destroy him; for God's temple is sacred, and you are that temple.
>
> (1 Corinthians 3:16-17)

Satan's Seed

Satan's seed is the Nephilim, the human/alien hybrids, the draconian reptilians, the Grays, the Borgs, the Annunaki seed, and more which we cannot imagine. What did the ancient texts say about this? The best compilation of documentary evidence of extraterrestrial and alien involvement on planet earth is the Bible. Let's face it, the reason behind the great deluge was to cleanse the planet of Satan's seed, the Nephilim. The reason for 'fire coming down from heaven' over Sodom and Gomorrah, was to rid Israel of more Nephilim.

The Bible is full of stories about the battle between Satan's seed and God's seed. We can call it one long cosmic family drama, where Satan is the rebellious son, leading a rebellion against his Creator, the Lord Almighty.

I've gone over in great detail the history and meaning of the Nephilim in my section on the Giants in Book One of *Who's Who in the Cosmic Zoo?*[4] These beings keep coming up, like a bad penny. It is important to note the contribution of these fallen beings with respect to the discussion of racism, because of their celestial blood, which according to Professor I.D.E. Thomas:

> "Fears that people would boast of having this celestial blood in their veins and would consider themselves superior to those of the ordinary human ancestry. To claim descent from stellar explorer could lead to a class distinction surpassing anything ever seen in society, but he need have no such qualms! If the Nephilim are stellar, they are also infernal. To claim descent from such beings would be to admit an ancestry from Hell."[5]

The Children of the Devil

> Jesus said, "If God were your father, you would love me, for I came from God and now am here. I have not come on my own; but he who sent me. Why is my language not clear to you? Because you are unable to hear what I say. You belong to your father, the devil, and you want to carry out your father's desire. He was a murderer from the beginning, not holding to the truth; for there is no truth in him. When he lies he speaks his native language, for he is a liar, and the father of lies. Yet because I tell the truth, you do not believe me! Can any of you prove me guilty of sin? If I am telling the truth, why don't you believe me? He who belongs to God hears what God says. The reason you do not hear is that you do not belong to God."
>
> (John 8:42-47)

Besides spiritual possession, what if there were families, or whole races, that are breeding Satan's seed on earth? What about the Nephilim? We have a great deal of evidence that there are remnant groups of giants who have lived and still live on the earth today. So much more with Satan's seed. What if people who are carrying this ancient DNA couldn't be saved? Doesn't that explain the constant eruptions of evil on this planet? This is not to start another race war, but to illuminate the one that has been going on for millennia. Yet, if Christ came to save all the races, from all the nations and from all religions of the planet, then surely that means that anyone can be saved, if they choose Christ over Satan?

There are spiritual battles happening over earth all the time, but some battles are worse than others. Suffice it to say, that when it comes to the war over human souls, sometimes death can free a person from bondage to Satan, so that his soul may be saved. "To deliver such a one to Satan for the destruction of the flesh, so that the spirit may be saved in the day of the Lord Jesus." (1 Corinthians 5:5). Some cases are that stubborn, and some people have major satanic strongholds on them, that the path of deliverance is one long constant battle. Yet if that person confesses that Jesus Christ is their Lord and Savior, the Bible says they will be saved, despite their bondages to the lord of darkness.

We see from the original curse spoken by the Lord to Satan in his guise as the serpent in Genesis 3:15 that the seed of the woman was going to crush the head (authority) of the seed of the serpent.

> "And I will put enmity between you and the woman, and <u>between your seed and her seed</u>; it shall bruise your head, and you shall bruise his heel."
>
> (Genesis 3:15)

Scheduled to take place sometime in the future is the arrival of the Antichrist. This is a man who will fully enjoin with the will and plan of Satan and be empowered by his fallen angels, including Apollyon, who is scheduled to be released from the abyss. He will combine all the powers of the 'Beast' which is a combination of all the Draconian forces, and come forward to take over the world for their Luciferian New World Order. This embodiment of the trinity of hell will also facilitate a one-world religion, obliterating all competitors for worship, and establishing global socialism. No one will be allowed to do business freely without having the 'mark of the beast', which is some type of implant that logs a person into the universal technology. This chilling scenario was foreseen not only in Revelation, but by George Orwell in his prophetic book *'1984'*. The seeds of global socialism are today so rampant we call them progressivism, and they have grown even closer to the Orwellian vision.[6]

As I reported in my chapter, *Ascension or Rapture?* in Book Three[7], many believe, the person of the final antichrist will not be revealed until the body of believers in Jesus Christ, known in the Bible as "the Restrainer", are removed from the planet, in an event known as the Rapture.

Then the unbelieving population will be duped into the belief that this man is their Messiah, as this is Satan's ultimate counterfeit of Christ. He will at first pretend to be the long-awaited Savior, fulfilling prophesies of all the world's major religions. He will be seen as a messianic figure, mysterious but benevolent, powerful, a savior of the whole world, an economic genius being able to solve the world's woes. See my chapter on the *God of this World/Antichrist* for further elucidation.[8]

Operation Star Gate

This was the real reason for Operation Iraqi Freedom, the very first mission of the U.S. Marines to Iraq. It was to obtain the Stargate by raiding the Museum of Baghdad for a host of ancient artifacts. This was the weapon of mass destruction that they were after, which of course was so Top Secret that the criticism of the Bush Administration had to go unanswered. There were WMDs in Iraq, but the Stargate is far too classified to report it to the American people. After the Stargate was obtained it was brought to the U.S. and taken to undisclosed locations, possibly NORAD, Colorado Springs, CO.

Hollywood made a movie about the discovery of this very Stargate back in 1994, called, *StarGate*, with Kurt Russel. Just like in the movie, the Stargate was actually uncovered in Baghdad in the 1920s. Hitler and Nazi Germany went to Iraq to fight against the British as both wanted control of the Iraq StarGate.

Führer Directive No. 30 dealt with German intervention in support of Arab Nationalists in the Kingdom of Iraq. During the 1930s, representatives of Nazi

Germany and Fascist Italy attempted to gain favor with various Iraqi nationalists and promised support against the British. On May 2, 1941, after tensions mounted on both sides, the British launched pre-emptive land strikes against Iraqi forces and the Anglo-Iraqi War began. Rashid Ali immediately requested that the Germans make good on the earlier promises of assistance. The International Zone (formerly known as the Green Zone) is the heavily guarded diplomatic/government area of closed-off streets in central Baghdad where US occupation authorities live and work. The Green Zone in the central city includes the main palaces of former President Saddam Hussein where the StarGate was located in the basement of the main palace. The area houses the civilian ruling authority run by the Americans and British and the offices of major US consulting companies. Prescott Bush had furnished weapons to Nazi Germany to arm them for World War II.

Rockefellers Chase Bank and Prescott Bush Fund Secret Space Program
According to research carried out over the last few years, Wall Street bankers (amongst others) financed Hitler's rise to power whilst making large profits at the same time. U.S. economist Victor Thorn has noted that although a large number of other corporations aided the Nazis (such as Standard Oil and Rockefeller's Chase Bank, as well as U.S. automobile manufacturers) Joe Prescott Bush's interests were much more profound and sinister. In their book, Tarpley and Chaitkin explain that in this way a significant part of the Bush family's financial base is related to supporting and aiding Adolph Hitler. Therefore, the U.S. president number 43, just like his father number 41 (former CIA director, Vice President and President) reached the peak of the U.S. political hierarchy thanks to his great-grandfather and grandfather and generally his entire family, who financially aided and encouraged the Nazis. [9]

> "CERN was back in operation on September 18, 2014, only a few days later, airstrikes on Syria were initiated. Do the invasions of Iraq, Libya, Syria and the Ukraine have anything to do with STARGATES or ancient technology?"

If so, what role does CERN play into this? CERN went active with experiments in early 2015. Were these manufactured crises an effort to acquire STARGATES or certain technologies before CERN went live?[10]

These are questions that may or may not ever be answered. But what we do know is that billions of dollars go into the Black Budget, the secret funding of operations that are never to see the light of day. Between sales of drugs, gun trade, oil monopolies, and the manipulation of the stock market, billions go to this Black Budget. Is securing Fallen Angel technology a priority on this black budget? Only time will tell. All secret *covenants* with competing alien groups *inside* the earth.[10, 11]

Notes:

1. David Flynn, *Cydonia: The Secret Chronicles of Mars*– End Time Thunder Publishers, 2002.
2. Thomas R. Horn, *Nephilim Stargates: The Year 2012 and the Return of the Nephilim*, p.82, Defender Publishing LLC (July 1, 2007)
3. Ella LeBain, *Who Are the Angels?* Book Three, *Cosmic Christ*, p. 364-416, Skypath Books, 2015.
4. Ella LeBain, *Who's Who in the Cosmic Zoo?* Book One – Third Edition, p. 208. Tate, 2013.
5. I.D.E. Thomas, *The Omega Conspiracy, Satan's Last Assault on God's Kingdom*, p. 107, Official Disclosure (December 1, 2007)
6. George Orwell, *1984*, Signet Classics, July 1, 1950.
7. Ella LeBain, *Who Are the Angels?* Book Three, Chapter Fifteen: *Ascension or Rapture?* p. 303-337, Skypath Books, 2016
8. Ella LeBain, *Who is God?* Book Two, Chapter Twenty-One: *The Office of Satan,* p. 331-358; Chapter Twenty-Five: *Who is the Beast?* P. 399-424, Skypath Books, 2015.
9. *How Bush's Grandfather Helped Hitler's Rise to Power,* https://www.theguardian.com/world/2004/sep/25/usa.secondworldwar
10. *Iraq StarGate Key to 911 and Bush,* http://ireport.cnn.com/docs/DOC-719922
11. https://m.youtube.com/watch?v=JR_Hmgk8pys

CHAPTER TWENTY
The Ark of the Covenant

"The fear of the LORD is the beginning of knowledge;
but fools despise wisdom and instruction."
(The Book of Proverbs 1:7)

The Ark of the Covenant is one of the most sacred and terrifying of objects. It is a chest of wood and gold that holds the original 10 stone tablets of the law given to Moses. It's been reported in the scriptures that the ark stopped whole armies, demolished walls and was able to open the waters of the rivers. There are reportedly two Arks on earth, experts say, one is hidden in Jerusalem and the second is secretly guarded in a church in Ethiopia.

In Book Two, *Who is God?* I established that the Ark of the Covenant was actually a marvel of technology[1]. I'm going to reprint excerpts here for those who may have missed it. However, I'm also going to expound on the spiritual and legal component of this device, that was given by the Lord Yahuah to the Israelites via Moses through an everlasting *Covenant.*

Technology of the Ark

All through Exodus, the Lord God repeats, "I am the Lord," and "I will be to you a God: and you shall know that I am the Lord, your God." In Exodus 15:3 (KJV), there is a reference: "The Lord is a man of war." There has been a constant battle going on in the heavens since Lucifer's rebellion. The Almighty Creator God did not destroy one-third of the fallen angels and "the satans"; instead, he allowed them dominion over lower worlds, Earth being one of them. The fact that the Lord says He is a man of war reveals His stature in the heavens as a warrior against evil.

There is a warning in Exodus to "go not up into the mount, or touch the border of it: whosoever touches the mount shall be surely put to death…." "And Mount Sinai was completely in smoke, because the Lord descended upon it in fire … and the whole mount quaked greatly." (Exodus 19:12, 18, KJ2000) Clearly the reason they were told not to go up to the top of Mt. Sinai was because that is where the Lord's starship had landed, and the radiation levels were too high for humans to withstand. They were told to keep their distance for their own good.

In Exodus, Moses was given instructions on building the Ark of the Covenant. The inventor Nikola Tesla wrote in *The Wall of Light* that Moses had to have been a skilled electrical engineer. (Moses obviously had an ingenious inventor guiding him — the Lord.) The Ark, Tesla concluded, was a very powerful "condenser." It created intense vibrations that could smash solid stone. The Israelites carted the device into battle and won wars with it.

> "And when the Ark of the Covenant of the Lord came into the camp, all Israel shouted with a great shout…."
>
> (1 Samuel 4:5, KJV)

> "Woe to us! Who shall deliver us out of the hand of these mighty Gods (Elohim)? These are the Gods (Elohim) that smote the Egyptians with all the plagues in the wilderness."
>
> (1 Samuel 4:8, KJV)

Uzzah ignored warnings about not touching the Ark and was electrocuted! "Uzzah put forth his hand to the ark of God, and took hold of it; for the oxen shook it. And the anger of the Lord was kindled against Uzzah; and God smote him there for his error; and there he died by the ark of God."

Another man attempted to place it back on the ox-drawn cart and died. They had no concept of high-voltage. "And David was afraid of the Lord that day" (2 Samuel 6:6-9, ESV). This was a powerful piece of technology.

The reason over fifty thousand men died from being exposed to the Ark was due to the intense radiation that emanated from inside it. In addition, the reason priests needed to be sanctified (protected) was because they were better equipped with the knowledge to take care of the ark, and how to prevent it from harming others, but they knew how to use it to defeat their enemies nonetheless.

When the Philistines stole the ark from the Israelites, they thought they were cursed by God because thousands of them died, and those who survived were smitten with *emerods*. Many Bible translations use the word tumors for *emerods*, but the Darby Bible and the Duoay-Reims Bible translate *emerods* to mean the modern- day word hemorrhoids. The Hebrew word is *techorim*, which also translates to strongholds. It is true that hemorrhoids are a type of tumor. The Hebrew word *techorim*, is translated in Yiddish as *tuchcus*, which means anus.

And at the end of chapter 5 verse 9 in 1 Samuel, it actually says, specifically where the emerods were smitten — "in their secret parts." Well, anyone who knows about hemorrhoids knows them to be in an extraordinary hidden part of the body, the anus. Needless to say, the Philistines were scared and quickly made arrangements to return the Ark to the Israelites, so as to save the rest of Ashdod.

By the way, just to connect the dots here to present times, the word *Palestine* comes from the word *Philistine*, who were an arch enemy of the Israelites. When the Romans took over the land of Israel, they renamed it after the Philistines, and due to the dilution of languages, it became Palestine. For the record, the word *Palestine* and the designation of the land of Palestine is not in the Bible. Only the word Philistine, who were not inheritors of the land.

When word got out that this Ark was a device to be feared, the Philistines were eager to get rid of it, knowing of its dangers. When they brought it to Ekron, the Ekronites all freaked out, thinking they brought it there to slay them.

First Samuel 5:10-12 tells that there was a deadly destruction in the city that day, and that the hand of the Lord was heavy upon them, and those who didn't die were smitten with the *emerods* hemorrhoidal tumors. A new cart was then made for the ark. When they finally returned it to the Israelites, the Israelites were so happy to see it and have it back that they used the wood from the cart to build a fire to offer a sacrifice to God, and then did themselves in, by opening up the ark and looking at the mercy seat. 1 Samuel 6:19 (NAS) says that 50,070 men died:

> "He struck down some of the men of Beth-shemesh because they had looked into the ark of the LORD (Yahuah). He struck down of all the people, 50,070 men, and the people mourned because the LORD (Yahuah) had struck the people with a great slaughter."

Perhaps this is why they called it the mercy seat, because they prayed that the Lord would have mercy upon them, since the power of this thing was awesome. The Bible says that the Lord slaughtered them, but it was their own negligence and disobedience. They were given strict instructions about how to use the Ark for their own good, but instead, they ignored the Lord's safety precautions. This, no doubt, taught them all a hard lesson regarding the power and holiness of this piece of technology. The word holy in the Bible means, *set apart; sacred.*

In my opinion, this is what happens when you give what seems like twenty-second century technology to ancient primitive man.

Just look at our modern world. How many people still do not know how to use technology safely?

According to British journalist Graham Hancock, author of *The Sign and the Seal: The Quest for the Lost Ark of the Covenant*, the Ark of the Covenant was taken from ancient Jerusalem in the days of King Solomon. While there are numerous variations of the story, the common thread centers on a son fathered by Israelite King Solomon and born to the Queen of Sheba. The ark was later smuggled into Ethiopia by their son Menelek, where it currently remains housed in a church in Axum.[2]

In *Ancient Aliens* Season 6 Episode 10, *Aliens and the Lost Ark,* is a quest to prove ancient astronaut claims, that the Ark was a piece of technology.[3] However, many who are threatened by this knowledge, whether it comes from my books or another source, feel offended because they perceive it as attacking the very foundation of the Judeo-Christian faith. According to their *religious beliefs,* the Ark was the sign and the seal of Yahuah's everlasting *Covenant* with Israel.

It was, is, and always will be so, which doesn't negate the fact that the Ark was an advanced piece of technology. There are *covenants* with technology. The Ten Commandments, which Moses received, not once but twice, were created through technology. The Lord wrote His laws on stone. Today we use different types of machines to engrave stone, but this was no different. When Moses broke the first set of tablets, he ascended back up the mountain, to enter into the Lord's Presence again, *inside his starship*, and receive a duplicate set of stones, to give to the Israelites as a guide to how He wanted them to behave in their relationship to God, and in their relationship to each other. Later, down the timeline, during the times of Yeshua/ Jesus, He summed up the Mosaic Law into two main laws, that we should love the Lord our God with all our heart and all our soul, and love our neighbor as our selves. He said that on these two laws, pivots the entire laws of the prophets that went before Him. (Matthew 22:40)

In an article written by Doug Yurchey[4] entitled *High-Technology In The Bible* Yurchey states: "In Exodus, Moses was given instructions on building the Ark of the Covenant. The inventive genius, Nikola Tesla, wrote in 'The Wall of Light' that Moses had to have been a skilled electrical engineer. The Ark, Tesla concluded, was a very powerful 'condenser.' It created intense vibrations that could smash solid stone. The Israelites carted the device into battle and won wars with it; not unlike the vibration weapons used in the film 'Dune.'"

It's certainly no coincidence that reborn Israel happens to be the global leader in innovative technologies. Rabbi Ariel Bar Tzadok, was featured on this episode[3] of *Ancient Aliens* discussing how Judaism venerates alien technology, and was attacked viciously on the internet for his viewpoints. I happen to agree and resonate with Rabbi Ariel Bar Tzadok, in his interpretation of the Hebrew Bible, in his claims that the Hebrew Bible supports reincarnation, please refer to my rather extensive chapter in *Who is God?*[2] [p.455-483]. Reincarnation is a foundation in Jewish belief which the Church of Rome attempted to delete from the Jewish Bible during the canonization after 325 A.D.

I prove that the *rogue* scripture in Hebrews 9:27 was implanted and edited to make readers think that there is no reincarnation, which contradicts scores of scriptures already established in the Old Testament. I also agree with the Rabbi that aliens are present in our world, and that many other races of intelligent creatures walked the earth before man. The Hebrew Scriptures do support these facts, to those who have ears to hear, eyes to see, and an understanding of Hebrew Linguistics. As I proved in Book Two, *Who is God?* much of this knowledge was hidden or lost in translation, and that the Truth is in the details of Hebrew Linguistics. There are twenty-three rejected books, outside the Bible canon, because they didn't fit the Church of Rome's political and social agendas, twisting Jewish scripture to suit their cult.[1]

Jason Martell, author of *Knowledge Apocalypse,* shared a full-scale model of the Ark of the Covenant and called it an electrical capacitor. His views coincide with those of University of California Irvine Physicist Michael Dennin, who is convinced that the Ark was an electrical device. David Childress, author of *The Technology of the Gods,* discussed how the vibrations from the Ark resonated with the twelve stones of fire that were strategically placed on the High Priest's breast plate, which Childress called extraterrestrial Morse code. [3]

Some of us may begin mentally connecting some dots here... Rabbi Chaim Richman, International Director of the Temple Institute exhibition in the heart of the Old City of Jerusalem, attempted to lead an excavation underground to locate the missing Ark of the Covenant, only to be aborted by the Israeli authorities before reaching it. They had to step in for security reasons, before the excavation caused an interfaith conflict at the Dome of the Rock. Rabbi Richman's hi-tech gallery, spanning 600 square feet, hosts a collection of vestments and sacred vessels to be used by the Jewish High Priest when the Third Temple is finally rebuilt in Jerusalem. Rabbi Richman insists that the exhibition is just a museum, yet they could in fact staff and furnish a rebuilt Third Jewish Temple in Jerusalem.[5]

Except for the missing Ark of the Covenant, every artefact on display has been painstakingly recreated in accordance with Biblical instructions and is intended for actual service in a Third Jewish Temple. The Temple Institute has everything it needs, in materials, funding and resources to erect the Third Temple. The work is only being prevented from moving forward due to an ongoing conflict between the Jews and Muslims over the issue of real estate, security, and its exact location in proximity to the Al Aqsa Mosque on the Temple Mount. Nevertheless, Rabbis in Jerusalem are planning, through state of the art designing techniques, a new hi-tech temple.[5]

Rabbi Richman believes the real Ark of the Covenant hides about a kilometer from the Temple Institute, in an underground chamber created during the time of

Solomon. According to the Rabbi, "there is a big fascination with finding the lost ark, but nobody asked a Jew. We have known where it is for thousands of years. It is in fact, not lost, but very well hidden. It could be reached if we excavated Temple Mount, but that area is controlled by Muslims."

In *Indiana Jones: Raiders of the Lost Ark,* most will remember the famous scene in which Harrison Ford is faced with the French archeologist who reveals to him that the Ark is a transmitter, a radio for speaking to God. Well, the Truth is Stranger than Fiction!

UFOs Over Jerusalem

On Friday, the beginning of the Sabbath, January 28, 2011, a video was taken in Jerusalem, by Eligael Gedalyovich which went viral the next day. He introduces the video as follows:

"This morning around 01:00 AM at the promenade of Armon Hantziv in Jerusalem, I was witness (with another guy), an amazing ufo aircraft over Jerusalem old city (Mount Moriah) Dome of the Rock, Temple Mount. What is the meaning of this sighting?", he asked.

You can still view this viral video on YouTube. It looks like a ball of light or a shining star hovering in the sky over Jerusalem, which descends to almost ground level just above the historic Dome of the Rock on the Temple Mount. It hovers and moves slightly for 23 seconds before it radiates a gigantic flash of light illuminating the old city of Jerusalem, then suddenly shoots upwards into the sky at incredible speed. Many people witnessed it, and when their eyes followed the ball of light upwards, they saw blinking red spots in the sky. This was a sight that people will never forget, with multiple credible witnesses. It cannot be lightly debunked.

As I've noted many times in my writings, I am not here to prove that UFOs are real, or that aliens exist, because the reality of both have been proven. I am here to take the discussion to the next level and begin *discerning* who they are, and what they are here to do, what their real agendas are, and connect the dots to Bible Prophesies for these End Times.

David Childress postulates that the UFO was possibly recharging the Ark, which the Rabbi says is in fulfillment of the prophecy of Zechariah 14, a sonic vibration splits the Mount of Olives and the Ark will emerge from underground. Zechariah 14 is the quintessential End Times Prophecy when the LORD returns at His Second Coming to Rule the Earth.

> "Watch, for the day of the LORD is coming when your possessions will be plundered right in front of you! I will gather all the nations to fight against Jerusalem. The city will be taken, the houses looted, and the women raped.

Half the population will be taken into captivity, and the rest will be left among the ruins of the city.

Then the LORD will go out to fight against those nations, as he has fought in times past. On that day his feet will stand on the Mount of Olives, east of Jerusalem. And the Mount of Olives will split apart, making a wide valley running from east to west. Half the mountain will move toward the north and half toward the south. You will flee through this valley, for it will reach across to Azal. Yes, you will flee as you did from the earthquake in the days of King Uzziah of Judah. Then the LORD my God will come, and all his holy ones with him. On that day the sources of light will no longer shine, yet there will be continuous day! Only the LORD knows how this could happen. There will be no normal day and night, for at evening time it will still be light.

On that day life-giving waters will flow out from Jerusalem, half toward the Dead Sea and half toward the Mediterranean, flowing continuously in both summer and winter. And the LORD will be king over all the earth. On that day there will be one LORD—his name alone will be worshiped."

(Zechariah 14:1-9)

Let's not forget that the Ark given to Moses was merely a *copy* of what was in the Lord's heavenly sanctuary. There has always been an Ark in heaven. Moses was told that the temple and furnishing he was to make were a copy of what was up in heaven (Exodus 25:9, 40; Hebrews 8:5). He instructs the Israelites to make the Ark's cover, which He calls the mercy seat, or place of atonement, out of pure gold. Just as there were two sets of Tablets, a second Ark was made as a back-up, learning the lesson from the first set of shattered tablets. It is this second Ark which researchers believe sits in a guarded church in Ethiopia.

"God's sanctuary in heaven was opened, and the ark of His covenant appeared in His sanctuary. There were flashes of lightning, rumblings of thunder, an earthquake, and severe hail."

(Revelation 11:19)

Revelation confirms the original ark is in heaven, which Moses was instructed to copy for its counterpart on earth. On it, they were to fashion two angels made of pure gold and place them on either end, facing each other, and looking down on the mercy seat (Exodus 25:18-20). Afterwards, He instructed them to place the stone tablets inscribed with the Ten Commandments inside. We later learn the Ark also contained Aaron's staff that sprouted leaves as well as a jar of manna (Hebrews 9:4).

Next, the Lord instructs the Israelites to make a special curtain and place the Ark of the Covenant behind it. This curtain was to separate the Holy Place from the Most Holy Place (Exodus 26:33), which symbolizes the barrier sin creates between mankind and the Creator.

In the Most Holy Place, the Lord Himself was present in a glory cloud over the Ark's atonement cover or mercy seat (Leviticus 16:2; Numbers 7:89). It was this place where the High Priest sprinkled the blood sacrifice to atone for the sins of the people (Leviticus 16:14-15).

Most likely, the Israelites didn't understand the true purpose of all these instructions, however, His purpose was later revealed in the life, death, and resurrection of Jesus Christ.

The Ark Points to Jesus

Jesus said, "the Scriptures point to me." (John 5:39) The LORD's instructions for the design and use of the Ark of the Covenant are certainly no exception.

On analyzing the contents of the Ark, we find a jar of manna (Hebrews 9:4). Manna was the sweet flat bread from heaven that that Lord provided to the Israelites during their wanderings in the desert (Exodus 16). This is symbolic of Jesus, who is the true bread of life. (John 6:48)

Jesus Himself said, "Moses didn't give you bread from heaven. My Father did. And now He offers you the true bread of heaven. The true bread of God is the one who comes down from heaven and gives life to the world" (John 6:32-33 NLT).

Secondly, the Ark contained Aaron's staff that sprouted leaves (Hebrews 9:4). The LORD had Moses place twelve wooden staffs, representing the twelve tribes of Israel, in front of the Ark. Each staff is inscribed with the name of the tribal leader, along with the Lord's promised buds that would sprout from the staff of the man He chose to serve as High Priest (Numbers 17:1-8).

The presence of Aaron's staff in the Ark is fitting, because Jesus serves as our High Priest (Hebrews 4:14-15). As High Priest, Jesus approached God the Father on our behalf while He became the Lamb of God to atone for our sins, and more importantly, deliver us from the power of sin. This is something their animal sacrifices were not capable of doing.

Thirdly, the stone tablets inscribed with the Ten Commandments (Hebrews 9:4) are also found inside the Ark. This symbolizes the faithfulness Jesus had to God's law. Jesus didn't come to abolish the law, but to fulfill it (Matthew 5:17). The Prophet Isaiah said the Messiah would exalt and honor the law (Isaiah 42:21), and Paul described how Jesus redeemed us from the curse attached to the legal ground of the law because, when He was crucified, He took the curse for our wrongdoing upon Himself.

"Christ has redeemed us from the curse of the
law, being made a curse for us:
for it is written, cursed is every one that hangs on a tree:
(Galatians 3:13)

"He who knew no sin, became sin,
so that we might become the righteousness of God through Him."
(2 Corinthians 5:21)

Let's go further in comparing the design of the Ark to the life and death of Jesus, the Messiah of Israel and all humankind. After His resurrection, Mary Magdalene was found weeping outside of the empty tomb. She looked inside and saw two angels - one sitting where Jesus's head had been and the other sitting where Jesus's feet had been (John 20:12). The two angels represent the two angels facing each other on the Ark of the Covenant, that covers the Mercy Seat.

The Lord commanded the Israelites to place two angels on opposite ends on top of the cover of the ark. These two angels were commanded to look down upon the mercy seat, also known as the place of atonement (Exodus 25:18-20). This is exactly what Mary witnessed in the empty tomb, two angels at opposite ends of the place where Jesus was laid to rest – which became the true and final mercy seat and place of atonement.

Spiritually and physically speaking, the Ark foreshadowed the first coming of Jesus, which was to be the propitiation for the sins of humankind, along with the events that surrounded His resurrection. Jesus was the ultimate sacrifice. As our High Priest, Jesus entered the Most Holy Place and secured our redemption forever with His own blood rather than the blood of animals (Hebrews 9:12).

According to the Biblical record, when Jesus died on the Cross of Calvary, the curtain in the Temple that separated the Holy Place from the Most Holy Place was 'ripped in two, from top to bottom' (Matthew 27:51). This meant that sin could no longer separate men from God the Creator, because Jesus removed our sins by giving His own life as a holy sacrifice (Hebrew 9:26). His work on the Cross was finished once and for all, for all of Creation on earth. That includes all intra, extra, and para-terrestrials who dwell inside the earth.[6]

The Ark's Role in End Time Prophecy

On January 6, 1982, a Christian archeologist, Ron Wyatt, who after years of hard labor and excavation permits issued by the Israeli Department of Antiquities, crawled into a cave in Jerusalem and found the Ark of the Covenant. In the cave were numerous artifacts from Solomon's Temple that gave proof to their discovery.[7]

Much to his amazement, there was a dark substance that had dripped out of the ceiling onto the top of the golden lid or Mercy Seat of the Ark of the Covenant. Ron immediately realized, through a conviction in his spirit, that he found the blood of Jesus, which contained His DNA. He worked closely with Israeli geneticists, and after multiple tests, they concluded that this dark substance was indeed blood, but it was unlike any other human blood sample ever tested.

Ron Wyatt was a Sabbatarian nurse, anesthesiologist, whose hobby was archaeology. He discovered over a dozen biblical artifacts including the true locations of Sodom and Gomorrah, Noah's Ark, Red Sea Crossing, and The Ark of the Covenant. The Ark was found under the hill where Christ was crucified, Golgotha or the place of the skulls, also known as Calvary, located near the Garden Tomb just outside the walls of Jerusalem. He said the reason the Ark was positioned there underground was so that Christ's blood could drip on it through the fissure in the rock during the crucifixion. The record tells us that there was a great earthquake that occurred at the time of His death.

> "At that moment, *the curtain of the temple was torn in two from top to bottom. The earth shook, the rocks split,* and the tombs broke open. The bodies of many holy people who had died were raised to life. They came out of their tombs after Jesus resurrection went into the Holy City and appeared to many people."
>
> (Matthew 37:51-53

Ron Wyatt scraped dried blood off the ark casing, and submitted it for DNA testing. The results reported are fascinating, with only half the chromosomes normal for humans, consistent with having only one human parent, Mary. This proves that Christ was fathered by an unknown Supernatural Source, because we humans have 46 chromosomes, but He only had 23, along with 22 autosomes from his mother. We get the X chromosome from our mothers, but this blood only showed a Y chromosome. Therefore, he concluded, that this was Divine blood. You can listen to his entire testimony and the conclusions of his research on YouTube.[7, 8]

Daniel 9:24 says the Most Holy was to be anointed to put an end to sin, bring in everlasting righteousness, and atone for iniquity. "Seventy weeks are determined upon thy people and upon thy holy city, to finish the transgression, and to make an end of sins, and to make reconciliation for iniquity, and to bring in everlasting righteousness, and to seal up the vision and prophecy, and to anoint the most Holy."

The original purpose of the mercy seat was to collect the blood from sacrifices to atone for sins. What most of us missed was that during the crucifixion of Yeshua Jesus Christ, His blood, which was Divine, fell onto the Mercy Seat of the Ark of the Covenant. We didn't know it had been buried beneath Golgotha. His dying words dying on the cross were, "It is finished!" He completed His mission both in the physical and spiritual realms with the shedding of His Divine Blood, thereby ending the need for future blood sacrifices from animals or humans.

Christ was the final Lamb of God, who offered up Himself as the final blood sacrifice for the propitiation of the sins of humankind. No other blood sacrifice can out-do what He completed.

Ron Wyatt's discovery and research proves that this plan was in fact carried out. You can read more about it in more detail in *The Ark of The Covenant* by Jonathan Gray.[9] His testimony can be found on YouTube. He was interviewed on his death bed, where he revealed his experience at the site of the Ark and his encounter with an angel, who told him about the times and the Sunday law of the Antichrist. Everyone who has met him, interviewed him and researched his work, confirms the veracity of his testimony, that he indeed found the Ark's Mercy's seat, and retrieved the blood that was there. To many Christians, this is proof positive of Christ's virgin birth, that he was conceived by the Holy Spirit, making Him both the Son of Man, being born to his human mother Mary, a descendant of King David's bloodline, as well as the Son of God, whose Father in Heaven manifested Him on earth. [10]

Through the physical incarnation of Yeshua Jesus, the Lord chose to humble Himself for the sake of His people. He chose to humble Himself for us in His Son, Yeshua/Jesus the Christ, and then to stoop as low as death:

> "He humbled Himself by becoming obedient to the point of death,
> even death on a cross."
>
> (Philippians 2:8)

In spiritual warfare, humbling is a weapon against pride and arrogance. In the spiritual battle between good and evil, evil is defeated through good. Being humble is the antidote for pride, which was the original sin of Lucifer the Satan.

The Ark being the place of the Lord's presence among His people brought great assurance. This high, lofty, majestic, and resplendent King dwelt among His grumbling, complaining, bickering, and sinful people (Exodus 15:24; 16:2, 8, 9, 12; 17:2). Doesn't that sound familiar? Thankfully through the promise of the New Covenant each believer can be close to the Lord through the power of His Holy Spirit, who dwells in us (1 Corinthians 6:19). Just as Jesus promised His helpful presence to us (John 14:16).

The assurance of His closeness was described by the prophet Isaiah, in the history of His salvation of His people of Israel. And just as the Lord accompanied the people of Israel when they wandered in the wilderness, so, too, was He with them during the days of their restoration from exile, so too can those alive today, be assured of the completion of His Final Redemption from the matrix of this present system.

> "For He said, "Surely, they are My people, Sons who will not deal falsely." So, He became their Savior. In all their affliction He was afflicted, And the angel of His presence saved them; In His love and in His Mercy, He redeemed them, And He lifted them and carried them all the days of old."
>
> (Isaiah 63:8-9)

And so, it is with our present suffering and the hope of our future glory, when our redemption from the system of this world is complete. All who believe in the hope of transformation from this earthly kingdom into a heavenly one, are saved behind enemy lines. Salvation preceded deliverance. Full deliverance happens at the time of the Second Coming, when the Lord returns to harvest His adopted sons and daughters and translates them into our eternal, immortal, glorious light bodies, which are incorruptible. For this we hope and for this we wait. "The Lord will *perfect* that which concerns me." (Psalm 138:8)

> "I consider that our present sufferings are not worth comparing with the glory that will be revealed in us. For the creation waits in eager expectation for the children of God to be revealed. For the creation was subjected to frustration, not by its own choice, but by the will of the one who subjected it, in hope that the creation itself will be liberated from its bondage to decay and brought into the freedom and glory of the children of God.
>
> ***We know that the whole creation has been groaning as in the pains of childbirth right up to the present time***. Not only so, but we ourselves, who have the first fruits of the Spirit, groan inwardly as we wait eagerly for our adoption to sonship, ***the redemption of our bodies***. For in this hope we were saved. But hope that is seen is no hope at all. Who hopes for what they already have? But if we hope for what we do not yet have, we wait for it patiently."
>
> (Romans 8:18-25 NIV)

Notes:

1. Ella LeBain, *Who's Who in the Cosmic Zoo?* Book Two, *Who is God?,* Technology of the Ark, [pp. 38-41] Skypath Books, 2015
2. Graham Hancock, *The Sign and the Seal: The Quest for the Lost Ark of the Covenant* Touchstone (July 2, 1993)
3. *Ancient Aliens* [Season 6/Episode 10] *Aliens and the Lost Ark,* History Channel.
4. Doug Yurchey, *High Technology in the Bible,* https://www.themystica.com/mystica/articles/h/hight-technology_in_the_bible.html 2002.
5. Jake Wallis Simons, *The rabbi, the lost ark and the future of Temple Mount,* http://www.telegraph.co.uk/news/worldnews/10287615/The-rabbi-the-lost-ark-and-the-future-of-Temple-Mount.html, September 12, 2013
6. Britt Gillette, *The Ark of the Covenant and Jesus,* https://www.prophecyupdate.com/the-ark-of-the-covenant-and-jesus.html
7. Ron Wyatt Discovers *ARK OF COVENANT and JESUS BLOOD SAMPLE Full Testimony,* https://www.youtube.com/watch?v=XNr_U1EWRTY, January 9, 2012.
8. Tim McHyde, *The Ark of the Covenant Found* https://escapeallthesethings.com/ark-of-the-covenant-found/, August 23, 2014
9. Jonathan Gray, *The Ark of The Covenant.,* Ind Group; 3rd edition (December 31, 1997)
10. Ron Wyatt's Death Bed Confession, Ark of Covenant, https://www.youtube.com/watch?v=kjQYjpXIP6s

CHAPTER TWENTY-ONE
The New Age Christian

"In the Last Days, there will be those who will be
having a form of godliness but denying its power thereof."
(2 Timothy 3:2-5)

"I like your Christ...I do not like your Christians...
They are so unlike your Christ."
~Ghandi

This may sound like an oxymoron to some, as many think the New Age is distinctly unchristian, and that Christianity is anti-New Age. Suffice it to say that this is a riddle wrapped in a mystery inside an enigma, but let's take a shot at unpacking it, starting with the language.

Most people will agree that we officially entered the New Age at the Resurrection. Some say it started in the second millennium. There are others who mistakenly believe we have entered the Age of Aquarius, but this is astronomically and technically not true.

I spent twenty-five years mingling in New Age circles, after being rejected by Christian churches for being a Jew for Jesus – go figure. My experience, like that of many others who are attracted to New Age thought, began with a deep disenchantment with the Christian church, it's lack of a loving spirit, and was really turned off by the hypocrisy of religion(s). The New Age movement was full of people like myself, who believed they could find their niche, embrace their spirituality, and achieve enlightenment. I never stopped believing in and loving God, or Christ; however, it was the *religion* of Christianity, and the way they treated Jews, that caused me to stray from the church, along with all the confusion and strife caused by the fragmentation amongst churches.

The reasons why so many people seek spiritual enlightenment outside of the church is that the church just doesn't do it. Sitting in a pew on a Sunday morning, listening to a boring preacher read off a sermon, is just not very enlightening, interesting, or exciting. So many pastors are out of touch with what is really going on in the lives of their congregants, the sermons are irrelevant. Most people would prefer to read the document online. Besides, the church has become divided up into so many different denominations, it has become like a cafeteria; choose what you want to follow and leave what you don't like on the shelf. Each denomination swears the others are all wrong, so much so there are running jokes about it within churches.

The unfortunate reality is that Satan has had a foothold within the body of Christendom since its very formation, and his many different forms of demonic strongholds creates the dissension, the spiritual limitations, and the apostasy. In fact, he even holds some churches in bondage where they are afraid to even say his name, for fear of invoking his spirit. These are churches who have a form of godliness but deny its power. More on that later.

Possibly the worst of the Christian church experience are the judgments, which come from an unloving spirit. Besides the misunderstanding of scripture, the obvious hypocrisy, church politics, spiritual limitations, anti-Semitism, the fragmentation of the body of Christ, are lies that have become a part of the belief systems within the Christian religions. Many have seen through these lies, simply by studying the church history, who can no longer uphold the tenets as Christian truth. It is sad, but it is no wonder why people fall away and seek spiritual food and enlightenment in the New Age. In my opinion, based on my experiences in both spheres, the church's rigidity, misunderstanding or misinterpretation of scriptures, along with carrying on the political decrees of centuries past, are the culprits that continue to perpetrate false beliefs within Christendom, which are responsible for creating the New Age and alternative Christian churches.

Speaking of my own spiritual journey, I started out on a search to find truth and enlightenment, but got tangled up in a waiting net and lost my freedom. I learned that being a New Ager was really just another form of rebellion against the Lord, only slapped with the window dressing of 'love and light' and lots of New Age bric-a-brac. The old-adage about all that glitters not being gold is definitely true! After all these years, I've come full circle, and had my eyes open to *who* and what exactly was behind New Age thought forms, teachings, and therapies. If you're tempted to flee into the wilderness of the New Age movement, read on, and you will be just as surprised as I was to find yourself where you wander.

What is the New Age?

The New Age is a just a hodge-podge of all religions mixed into one. Truth be told, there's not much 'new' about the New Age, it's all based on Old Age stuff, ancient history, ancient religions and New Age fascination with all that is ancient. The much-vaunted Oneness and Unity being an underlying force of the New Age movement. Its tenets embrace a potpourri of different spiritual belief systems, from mysticism, Kabbalah, occult, magic, ancient philosophies, paganism, witchcraft, Buddhism, Hinduism, Yoga, Sufism, self-improvement psychology, hypnosis, divination, all coming together through what the phrase first coined by New Agers, as 'Christ Consciousness.' Despite the fact, that the real Christ, who was called Yeshua HaMashiach, rebuked half that stuff for idolatry.

It is the embracing and believing in Christ Consciousness that makes it all so appealing, especially to all the disenchanted and rebellious Christians. But is Christ consciousness the same as being born again with the Spirit of Christ and having the Mind of Christ? I have come to learn that the answer to that is a resounding, NO. Christ Consciousness is literally the belief system formulated by Lucifer to counterfeit the real deal, which is walking with the indwelling Holy Spirit, the spirit of Jesus Christ.

Most people who believe in Christ Consciousness are actually following the false spirit which comes from Lucifer, the god of this world, the ancient angel of *en'light'en'ment*, and are literally in bondage to religious spirits. Yes, even freedom-loving, love and light New Agers, are bound by religious spirits. The irony of it all is that they leave the church because of being turned off by religion, through the religious spirits, only to find themselves in further bondage to the same fallen spirits. The only thing that has changed is the clothing. Some people believe they are more enlightened than others, and they wear their religion as a costume, dripping with crystals, in the false belief that wearing certain gemstones makes them more powerful than others. The fruit of this fallacy is just more bull feathers! People who wear certain crystals or gemstones, still get sick, still become impoverished, and still need a savior, a savior that delivers from the spirits of infirmity and religious spirits.

There is nothing humble or modest about New Agers who wear their religion on their sleeves, believing they are the reincarnation of some high priest or priestess from antiquity, or some ancient sorcerer who has returned to enlighten the rest. The commodification of the New Age is a billion-dollar industry. The truth of the matter is that Lucifer, in all of his many faces and disguises, is more appealing than Jesus when it comes to New Age thought, because we need not be repentant or confess our sins to God. We can pretend to be all love and light while denying our buried guilt, shame and rebellion towards the Lord. This denial is collectively called the 'shadow self' which, according to New Age beliefs, is to be embraced as one's power.

This 'shadow self' is what most Christians take to Jesus Christ to be delivered from, through confession, sorrow, repentance and prayers for deliverance. While New Agers believe their shadow is their power, it is the shadow self that holds one's spirit in legal bondage to Satan. In the ministry of Deliverance, the Shadow Self must be acknowledged and submitted to the Cross, so the Light of Christ can shine through it, which dissipates the shadow, that holds the deep-seated wounds of the past. It is only through the Dunamis Power of the Resurrection, that we are all set free of the Shadow Self. Only the Grace of God turns the Shadow into a Blessing. One's power does not lie in the Shadow, it lies in the One who alone has the power to heal the Shadow. Therein lies true power.

New Agers believe in channeling. They follow the latest channel who has the most popular message, usually telling them what they want to hear, always mixed with an element of truth sandwiched between lies. Channeling is another counterfeit by Lucifer. The human bodies were designed to be temples of God. We are born with the free will to choose between good and evil, light and darkness, truth and lie.

However, without discernment, it is hard, and sometimes impossible to tell the difference between light and darkness, truth and lie. When you don't have the truth or the real light to use as a measuring stick, it is easy to be seduced by the lie when it is packaged as truth, or dressed up as light. The subtlety of this type of spiritual manipulation is so deceiving that the lie becomes more popular than the truth, hence the billion-dollar industry of New Age books and materials.

We are born to be vessels of the Holy Spirit, and temples of the living God,

"...what agreement has the temple of God with idols? For you are the temple of the living God; as the Lord has said,

"I will dwell in them, and walk in *them*;
and I will be their God, and they shall be my people."
(2 Corinthians 6:16)

If our bodies and minds are temples, then we need to be vigilant about the occupant. If we are not aligned with the Lord, following His precepts, talking to Him alone, humbling ourselves before Him, then our temple is wide open to be taken over by the god of this world. For truly as C.S. Lewis asserted, "there is no neutral ground in the universe, you are either owned by God or possessed by satan." I have come to realize that no one is left out. Each of us humans are claimed by either the Holy Spirit of the Lord or the counterfeit spirits of Lucifer the Satan. There is no in-between, no matter the appearance.

Channeling is actually possession by fallen angel demon spirits. They have lots of knowledge because they've been around for ages, yet they are in rebellion against the Lord. They masquerade as light beings, archangels, ascended masters, space brothers and a host of deceased spirits and deities. They often flatter the ego of the possessed, which is how we are persuaded to allow them in. Everyone who channels, is made to feel special that they have been chosen to deliver important messages to humankind.

Some information is so incredible, so fantastic, that many believe it, as the 'word of God' because it came from an actual Pleaidian, Arcturian, Andromedan, or something no one has ever imagined. There is no way to discover if any of the information is even remotely true. This is the very reason that these books are being compiled to cause truth seekers to ask these questions and to exercise discernment.

So, what if the veil of this vast masquerade known as the New Age was suddenly removed and we could see exactly *who* and what was being channeled? I promise you, you would be shocked to learn that these apparently 'love and light' beings who are flooding the marketplace with messages of a shift in consciousness, a new world coming, a dimensional shift, actually have a very old and specific agenda that was prophesied over 3,000 years ago. I can save you time and energy by telling you in one sentence, their aim is to erect a one world religion that is controlled by a one world government, with the antichrist, all unloving and antilight, running it all.

Sounds unbelievable? Then how come the predictions and prophecies of the other-worldly beings frequently turn out to be totally false? Or delayed because of weather? Or just delayed because we aren't ready? It's always the fault of someone or something else, never the prophet, channel, or spirit being who is wrong. So many promised UFO landings have not materialized, there have been books written on the phenomena, and an entire branch of psychology dedicated to promises that fail.

On the other hand, everything on the Bible's prophetic timetable has manifested to this date. There are only a few more events to unfold before the short time period, known as the tribulation, begins on Earth, bringing about the final battle and the end of this war between good and evil, Satan's army and that of the Lord Jesus Christ and His heavenly hosts. This is how the real *Star Wars* will manifest on earth.

I have learned after experimenting in New Age and Metaphysical circles for twenty-five years, that New Agers are innocent lambs being used by these Luciferian forces to bring about the New World Order, which is being masked as some great dimensional shift. Let me clarify this, the New World Order is not the 5th Dimension. It is a theocratic one world government that seeks to control every aspect of every life on planet earth. It is nothing but a Draconian Socialistic Tyrannical Regime, that will fail.

We can be fascinated and seduced into performing various New Age Resurrection Ancient Rituals to open up existing portals for these very ancient aliens, who set themselves up as gods and goddesses in earth's antiquity, that they might return to join the battle with their leader, Satan, against the true Christ.

The New Age was prophesied in the scriptures, even by Jesus Christ himself. He specifically said that many in the last days would fall away from the faith, become seduced by following the doctrines of demons, and having a form of godliness but denying its very power. (1 Timothy 4:1; 2 Timothy 3:5) True, there are many religions and cults who fit into this category, and the New Age religion is one of them.

How did the New Age Get its Name?

We are in the dawning of the Age of Aquarius, as far as processional ages go, as an astrological age lasts approximately 2,160 years. There are 12 signs for the processions to go through, making the entire cycle approximately 26,000 years long, which coincides with a galactic year, or a Kali Yuga cycle according Hindu astrology. Jesus Christ was born at the beginning of the age of Pisces. We altered our measurement of time after the death of Christ, transitioning from B.C., or Before Christ to A.D, meaning Anno Domini, in English: Year of the Living Lord. A.D. does not stand for After the Death, because Christ Lives, He is not dead.

We realize that a few years got lost in between the birth and death of Christ, which as the Bible tells us Jesus Christ died and was resurrected and ascended at the age of 33. Jesus said, "I will be with you till the end of this age, and I am coming back at the end of this age." Being God in the flesh, He knew all about the procession of the equinoxes, and how the ages were calculated, because He was the Reckoner in the first place. He knew what age He was talking about, which is the end of the Piscean age. After all, it is no coincidence that the symbol for Christianity has been the fish, which is the symbol for Pisces.

The ages are determined by the position of the Sun at the time of the Vernal Equinox. The processions transit the zodiac in reverse, meaning we go from Pisces to Aquarius, not the other way around, as the Sun seems to travel counterclockwise against the starry backdrop of the heavens.

When the Sun rises at the vernal or spring equinox at 29 degrees of sidereal Aquarius, we will officially enter into that Age. This has not happened yet, nor did the year 2000 bring us into the Age of Aquarius. Our sun is rising at 5 degrees of sidereal Pisces on the equinox.

This is one reason the term, 'New Age', was coined, more as a movement, but also as a mistaken belief system that we have entered the Age of Aquarius. Because the beginning and ending of a processional age can be an arbitrary line, as zones are determined by several different methods or schools of measurement, the lines become blurred which separate the end of the star zones of Pisces from the beginnings of the star zones of Aquarius.

Amongst astrologers there is a 50-year margin when it comes to the influence of stars. Some astrologers and astronomers believe the Age of Aquarius will begin in 2050 A.D. and others believe it will begin a few years after the year 2100 A.D.

"Jesus said, '"If those days had not been cut short, no one would survive, but for the sake of the elect those days will be shortened."' (Matthew 24:22) While astrologers can argue over that arbitrary line in the heavens that separates one age from another, Jesus Christ said, there will be Divine Intervention at the end of the age, which will be cut short, because it will be a time of calamity, upheaval, and uncertainty. So, we may in fact be further along than we think. See, Book Five: *The Heavens*, where I expound on *how* the days are being cut short through the presence of multiple Exoplanets and the Nemesis Brown Dwarf Star system intersecting with our solar system.

An age lasts approximately 2,160 years, and we began counting the beginning of the Age of Pisces after the death of Christ, yet the birth of Christ truly marked the beginning of the Piscean Age. His life lasted 33 years, so by the time we reach the 22nd century, we will be at the end of the age of Pisces, give or take a decade.

This will be the time the Old Testament Prophets and the book of Revelation speaks of as, the Day of the Lord and the coming Kingdom of Heaven. Until that time, there are still many prophesies that need to be fulfilled. Soon we will begin the golden age of the Kingdom of Heaven on Earth, which marks the Age of Aquarius. The Age of Brotherhood and Sisterhood, the Age of Peace, Love and Goodwill toward all. Are we there yet? Certainly not! This "Age to Come" is mentioned in the End Times Prophecies, which is where another source of coining the phrase, "New Agers" comes from, the Bible!

"Love is the Supreme Gift...The final test of religion...is not religiousness, but love.....You will find as you look back upon your life that the moments that stand out, the moments when you have really lived, are the moments when you have done things in a spirit of love."
~ Henry Drummond

The New Age belief system teaches that people need to shift their attitudes and beliefs in order to bring the New Age into being, to achieve the Ascension. The New Age also relates to the New World Order, the agenda and goal of the gods of this world to unify us in order to control us. New Age thought has a lot to do with the dissolution of religion, or establishing a world with one religion, which in turn becomes the religion of the god of this world, Satan and his hierarchy of fallen angels.

Many New Agers are aware of the New World Order, but oblivious to the fact that they are being used as pawns in bringing this agenda about, specifically by denying Christ. New Age thought is a homogenized form of all the religions and belief systems rolled into one, they are the authors of the coexist movement. The New Age belief system consists of beliefs in all the gods and goddesses regardless of their religions and thereby incorporating what has been called 'Christ Consciousness' which is the belief in thinking like Christ, meaning His teachings on loving one another, yet denying the power of Christ thereof. Like I said, it's an oxymoron.

"Love comes from God. Whoever loves is
a child of God and knows God.
Whoever does not love does not know God, for God is Love."
(John 4:7-8)

I once did a little exercise in one of my classes about this apparent schism. I asked them, who is the leader of Christianity? Many said the Pope. I asked again, who leads Christianity? Jesus Christ, right? Yes, of course, after all it is named after him, one would think so, its Jesus Christ! So, then I asked, who is the Leader of the New Age? Lots of hemming and hawing on that one. Some said, Elizabeth Claire Prophet. No. I asked again. Who is the Leader of the New Age? There were lots of name dropping, so then I asked, what is the New Age about? The answers varied, to a better life, a better way of living, to the New World Order. So, then I rephrased my question, what is the Golden Age about?

They said, "Ohhhhh, the Golden Age, well, that's about love and brotherhood and sisterhood, and a time when the devil gets thrown into the abyss for a thousand years."

Good, so what is the Golden Age about?

Answer: "a change in Consciousness."

Very good. And what would that Consciousness be?

Answer: "you mean Christ Consciousness?"

Yes, and what is Christ Consciousness?

Answer: "Love Consciousness". Very good. So, who is leading the Golden Age?

Answer: CHRIST.

And the next question, is, 'which Christ?'

"And then she understood the devilish cunning of the enemies' plan.
By mixing a little truth with it they had made their lie far stronger."
~ C.S. Lewis, *The Last Battle*

The end of the Piscean Age is when Jesus Christ returns, as promised, to set up His Kingdom on Earth, to create a New Heaven and New Earth and live with His believers for eternity. Jesus also said, the Kingdom of God is within us. New Age belief says we are entering into the 5th Dimension. The Kingdom of God is the 5th Dimension, and when you delineate the promises in the book of Revelation, the Kingdom is an exact match of the 5th Dimension, according to New Age beliefs. Yet, ironically there are so many people who reject Christ, yet insist that they are going into the 5th dimension, or the Kingdom of God. Think about this for a minute, why would the King of the Kingdom allow people into His Kingdom if they reject and rebel against the King?

What's wrong with this picture? So, if Christ is leading the Golden Age or New Age as some like to call it, and Christ is leading Christianity, then why do the Christian fundamentalist folks see the Christ Consciousness folk as demonic? And why do the New Agers resent the Christian Fundamentalist folk for their constant Judgments, Attacks and Criticisms?

The answer: The Fallen Angels, demons, aliens, who continue to propagate most of New Age beliefs, and Religious Spirits who keep everyone in division, strife and competition.

> **"There will be terrible times in the last days. People will be lovers of themselves, lovers of money, boastful, proud, abusive, disobedient to their parents, ungrateful, unholy, without love, unforgiving, slanderous, without self-control, brutal, not lovers of the good, treacherous, rash, conceited, lovers of pleasure rather than lovers of God—<u>having a form of godliness but denying its power</u>. Have nothing to do with them."**
>
> (2 Timothy 3:2-5)

The Spirit clearly says that "in last days some will abandon the faith and follow deceiving spirits and things taught by demons. Such teachings come through hypocritical liars, whose consciences have been seared as with a hot iron." (1 Timothy 4:1-5)

Many New Agers were once Christians who became despondent, disenchanted and disillusioned by Christianity. They broke away from the restriction of that religion and created a new mix of belief systems from other religions, both ancient and new, creating the movement we call today the New Age. Many of them are good hearted, well intentioned, kind people, that are really searching for what Jesus has to offer, but the church has blocked them from it due to all the judgments and funda-*mentalism.*

Coincidentally, many Christian denominations are plagued by demonic influences and curses that lead the church and its followers into apostasy. Many have become disenchanted with the various Christian denominations but do not know why. This is because of the heavy demonic oppression that is upon most churches. There is more demonic activity inside the churches than meets the eye. From the bondage due to the religious spirit, to spiritual witchcraft, self-serving, control issues, ego clashes, the Jezebel and Ahab spirits, fundamentalism, stubbornness, pride and some are just plain rude. "Love is not rude." (1 Corinthians 13:5)

The problem within the churches are the churchgoers, the Christians themselves, many of whom are demonically oppressed, yet won't admit it. Some churches won't even allow anyone to speak the 'D' word, or mention anything about demons. This is a spiritual reality nonetheless. The church is plagued with all sorts of spirits of unbelief, and the curse of unbelief, the deaf and dumb spirits. For those churches who refuse to address the demonic activity, are made spiritually blind, spiritually deaf and spiritually mute. They are essentially void of spiritual power, which causes apostasy.

This is why the New Age is so attractive. It promises self-empowerment, something most churches fail to teach, even though empowerment is the will of God. There are numerous scriptures quoting Jesus Himself, promising power to all His believers, giving them authority over demons, to cast out devils, to heal the sick, and to even raise the dead. Yet how many Christian churches are actually carrying out the will and authority of Jesus Christ?

Just as the demonic realm works 24/7 to attack believers and pull the weak away, it is the *modus operandi* of Lucifer and his hierarchy of fallen angels, demons and aliens, to influence us to follow other gods and worship them. They do this by masquerading as 'angels of light,' (2 Corinthians 11:14) masking his demons and aliens as new age 'spirit guides' filling us with all kinds of nonsense disguised as ancient knowledge, a mix of half-truths, or whole truths sandwiched between lies to create the deception that is subtle enough to pull us away from the true God and pull our souls off the path of truth and light which is found in Christ.

Many involved in the New Age UFO connection are practicing occultist rituals. Much of the literature regarding UFOs involves mediums channeling aliens, automatic writing, telepathy, clairvoyance, and heightened psychic abilities on the part of contactees. UFO reports involve symptoms similar to demoniac possession and psychic phenomena.

The Bible prohibits occultist practices for a very good reason, which comes from the Wisdom of the Lord. He knows exactly all the games and strategies of the fallen angels and their demonic realm, how they masquerade as spirit guides, deceased humans, ascended masters and ETs. He knows how easy it is for us to be misled and deceived. This is why He forbids the practice of divination and foretelling of the future or discovering hidden knowledge through occult means. Such practices are strictly prohibited (Deuteronomy 4:19; 18:10-12; Isaiah 47:13-15; 44:24-25; Zechariah 10:2). Visualization or the manipulating of reality through the mind, the use of spirit guides, and contacting former human beings are also warned against (Deuteronomy 18:10-12; Leviticus 19:31; 20:6-21; 1 Chronicles 10:13-14 cf. 1 Samuel 28:3, 7-15).

Crimes associated with the occult have also been associated with UFOs, crimes like murder, rape, open racism, illicit sex, drug abuse. Also, there are a high number of deaths, suicides, and insanity rates that are observed among UFO contactees and researchers. In addition to this, a growing number of cults, the most recent and well-known being, Heaven's Gate, which believed in false statements made by the ETs, were misled into committing mass suicide.

There are many false beliefs in the New Age about ETs and UFOs. Many are misled into thinking that they are here to save us, enlighten us, or empower us with new technologies to clean up our environment. There are so many lies about the environment, which has become a religion in and of itself. Many of the new age beliefs are supported by ancient prophesies towards a cleansing of the earth and a new earth. This is promised in the Bible.

But here's where so many people have gotten sidetracked, seduced by the god of this world into thinking that we can actually change the world, achieve divinity and ascend into the fifth dimension where a new earth is being formed. This is the reason I am writing this book, to prove that these are false beliefs, misleading many into the belief that we create our own reality, or that we can alter the prophetic timeline from unfolding. This is far, far, far bigger than any of us on earth can imagine or control.

Much of the underpinning beliefs of the New Age are based on the false promise that humans can become divine or be God. This is a seduction by the god of this world, who is Lucifer the Satan, our adversary. That's been his *modus operandi* since the fall, and the premise for his rebellion against the Creator. He believed himself to be god. So, he inserted the assertion that we too are divine and can be god.

This is not only a false belief and half-truth, but it isolates us from ever humbling ourselves before our Creator and finding salvation, because if we believe and think that we are god, then why do we need a savior? It is also a New Age belief that one creates one's own reality and therefore, nobody is going to save us but ourselves. 'We are the ones we have been waiting for…' Another seduction by the god of this world, which is a lie.

There is no way that we have the power, the knowledge, the will or the technology to save ourselves against the onslaught of fallen angel demons both now and in the future who attack earth. We must turn towards our Savior, otherwise we will perish and be taken over by the dark forces, despite the fact that we perceive them as good. That is part of their masquerade.

All New Agers admit there was a time when they were not New Agers, thus there was a time when they were unenlightened and limited. God, according to New Age theology, is absolute, infinite and unlimited. A New Ager as god, cannot be both unlimited and unenlightened. God, who is unlimited, would always know that he was God and would never need enlightenment. Thus, the assertion of human progression toward divinity is untenable.

Most New Agers come from Christian-Catholic type backgrounds that were filled with all sorts of limitations, restrictions, and void of spiritual power. This is why the freedom, empowerment, and positive thinking of the New Age is so alluring to them. The type of oppression in the churches makes it ripe for believers to fall away from the Christian gospel and follow other gods which is idolatry. Following other gods is a basic part of New Age ideology. This is the false belief that resurrecting the ancient gods will not only enlighten and empower us, but will eventually save us. This is another lie.

The ancient gods are all subject to the Creator God, who promised to 'famish all the gods of the earth' due to their rebellion and idolatry. (Zephaniah 2:11) New Agers think it's cool to invoke ancient gods while remaining completely ignorant of their history with the Creator, and how they were brought down and punished by God.

There are three things which incur the wrath of God and release His curse on humankind: idolatry, sexual immorality, and immorality of all kinds. While Christ forgives all the sins of humanity, repentance is necessary first, in order to receive forgiveness.

Idol worship, following false gods, putting other things before God, caused so much suffering in the Old Testament! The Lord removed His protection from His people and gave them over to their enemies in order to make them see that it is He, not empty foreign idols, who loves and cherishes them and has the power to prosper them. Here's the big shock about the fruits of idolatry: it's empty.

Most of these new age idols are made up, non-existent, dead, or cursed by the Creator. They are fallen angels, sons of the fallen, aliens and demons, and the rest are just made of wishful thinking, ceramic, stone, metal statutes void of power, with only the power to charm money from our pockets. They may create a false sense of security, but bring spiritual blindness and spiritual deafness to us. The true reality lies in Christ as savior, redeemer, deliverer from the kingdom of darkness. The spirit of the antichrist is behind all idolatry, regardless of what you call it, dress it, or change its name.

Jesus Himself said that the only way into heaven is through Him. "No man can come to me, except the Father which sent me draw him to me: and I will raise him up at the last day." (John 6:44). Jesus said it was He who would resurrect us and give us eternal life. He is the Judge of our souls, no matter who we are, what religion we follow, whether we believe in Him or not, every one of us meets Him when we die. See, Book Two: *Who Is God?* chapter, *What Happens When You Die*[1].

People who channel spirits, ascended masters, archangels or extraterrestrials are deceiving themselves into thinking they can get into heaven by alternative means. There is only one way into heaven and that is through Jesus Christ. In the face of modern technology, we are used to having all kinds of options. We can opt in or opt out. There can't just be one way to get to where we want to go, can there? This is what all the spiritual battles are about, the heart of the matter being our own hearts and souls.

Since there is only one King in heaven, the King of kings, then certainly He is the One who gets to decide who enters His Kingdom. Isn't it interesting that all other paths to heaven declare the Bible to be a lie while the Bible declares all the alternative paths to be a form of deception. This is the crux of the spiritual warfare. Channeling spirits are a part of this deception.

One of the main reasons that the channeling movement has become so popular is because spirits are actually contacted. When a person contacts a spirit through the art of channeling, the spirit will give information that the contactee could not have possibly otherwise known. The person who has contacted the spirit world believes they are communicating with an ascended master, or an extraterrestrial or even an archangel, which as I've mentioned is not possible. The only archangel involved in channeling is Lucifer, and he's a fallen angel.

These shady ascended masters go on about how the world is about to enter a New Age of enlightenment. However, from the New Age point of view, Jesus Christ is just another "ascended master" lumped in with all the others in the Great White Brotherhood', as Buddha, Krishna, St. Germaine, the Elohim, the Mahatmas. They deny the supreme authority of the deity of Jesus Christ. Coincidentally, the Bible Prophecies tells us that Jesus Christ is returning soon to set up His Kingdom of Heaven on the Earth, creating the Heaven on Earth which would fulfill what these ascended masters or familiar spirits are saying is going to happen. There is a subtlety in the lies here, and this is where the battle lines are drawn. The New Age ascended master theory ignores what the Bible scriptures say about the identity and supremacy of Jesus Christ. The One who is given a name above all names:

> "Therefore, God exalted him to the highest place and gave him the name that is above every name, that at the name of Jesus every knee should bow, in heaven and on earth and under the earth, and every tongue confess that Jesus Christ is Lord, to the glory of God the Father."
>
> (2 Philippians 2:9-11)

We live in a time of grace until the end of this timeline. Christ is allowing time for humanity to repent from following the doctrines of the fallen angels (demons) and see the truth of the path of the Kingdom of Heaven.

> "And deceives them that dwell on the earth by the means of those miracles which he had power to do in the sight of the beast; saying to them that dwell on the earth, that they should make an image to the beast, which had the wound by a sword, and did live."
>
> (Revelation 13:14)

This is one of the prophesies about the coming Antichrist or Pseudo-christ, who is empowered by the aliens ruled by Satan that lives *inside* the earth. The miracles they perform are nothing but clever technological displays, as in the use of holograms and alien technologies.

Soft Disclosure in the Movies

There is an ongoing campaign coming from Hollywood and other media through movies to prepare us for the acceptance of aliens. Each year more and more alien movies are being produced with bigger and bigger stars. Most of these scripts are written with truths sandwiched in with a lot of artistic and creative license. This has been part of a long-term conditioning plan by the CIA and the secret government to prepare us for what they know is the inevitable: the onslaught of an alien invasion. Most invasions happen in secret. This has been going on for over 70 years, with the appearance of UFOs, alien crashes, abductions, animal mutilations and all sorts of contact experiences.

The Bible tells us of a time where The Beast comes up out of the earth to rule. Satan's hierarchy are the Reptilians. The Beast is the Serpent, a Reptilian. Several governments are already in contracts and agreements with the Serpent race over technology and protection of space. While many New Agers have been misled into thinking that the aliens are going to save them, just the opposite is true.

The true rapture, the ascension into the heavens, is promised to happen for all those who believe in the salvation of Jesus Christ. When this event happens, literally all hell is set to break loose on earth. Then all the alien invasion movies will come true, like *Independence Day, War of the Worlds,* and worse. The disappearance of the believers will literally give the green light for Satan's army to rule over the earth. The body of Christ, the body of believers, are currently restraining him from an all-out invasion at this time. In the meantime, they are working with various types of mind control and technology to seduce us into thinking that the UFOs we see in the skies are benevolent, or watching over us. This couldn't be further from the truth.

NAX

We can conclude that the New Age Christian (NAX), may follow Christ, and practice 'Christ consciousness,' while understanding concepts and beliefs that were banned from Christianity such as reincarnation (see my chapter, *What Happens When You Die*[1]). However, the NAX understands that New Age idols don't belong on his or her path nor their relationship with Jesus Christ. They know how to separate the lies from the substance and the truth of God. However, just as 1 Timothy 4:1, "The Spirit clearly says that in later times some will abandon the faith and follow deceiving spirits and things taught by demons."

In the NIL version it says, "Now the Holy Spirit tells us clearly that in the last times some will turn away from the true faith; they will follow deceptive spirits and teachings that come from demons." It will be popular to believe in lies, falsehoods, fallen angel gods and goddesses. All those who fall prey to these false teachers and teachings do so because of lack of knowledge and understanding of the relationship between these fallen gods and the Creator God.

The Most High Creator God promises to starve the gods of power. Why? "The LORD will be awesome against them; ***for he will famish all the gods of the earth***, and to him shall bow down, each in its place, all the lands of the nations." (Zephaniah 2:11) Because of their pride, arrogance and rebellion towards Him.

So just who are these 'gods of the earth'? See, Book Two, my chapter, *Who Are the Gods?* Their history is that of being the gods and goddesses of ancient Egypt, Greece, Rome, the Annunaki, the Nephilim, the Hindu gods and goddesses, and all the alien gods and so-called ET gods that New Agers worship, invoke and idolize. These are fallen angels, the rebel ETs, who have aligned with Lucifer the Satan.

This is why there is so much deception in these end times, as their time for causing trouble draws to a close. However, those gods and goddesses who have repented of their rebellion, turned back to the Creator God and aligned themselves with the Cosmic Christ, may be part of the handful of deities that are saved by the Creator in the end. There are references in early works to prayers for the fallen angels of Heaven. The Creator is full of grace and many will be saved among those who serve Him. Remember, the ratio is 2:1, only one third of heaven's angels or ETs followed Lucifer in rebellion. The other two thirds remained faithful to their Creator. The dark forces are outnumbered 2:1.

Discerning the New Age Christ

When New Agers mention Jesus, are they talking about the Jesus of the Bible? To Christians, Jesus (Yeshua HaMashiach) is the Messiah, the Savior, the Christ. He is God who came as a man to pay the price for the sins of humanity, saving those who believe in Him from the punishment from the Father, and the eventual destruction of our souls. Jesus Christ is God the Son and the Creator, the Word made Flesh. This is an important distinction in understanding how New Agers view Jesus.

The New Age Concept of Jesus is not God Almighty, the Creator of the Universe, the Lord of lords, and the second Person of the Trinity. Instead, New Agers reduce Jesus to a mere man who attained spiritual enlightenment through occult means.

He numbers among the so-called Masters, like Buddha and Zoroaster, who offered a way to enlightenment. What a far cry this is from the Jesus of the Bible who boldly proclaimed Himself to be not simply 'a' way, but 'The' way, the truth, and the life (John 14:6).

New Agers go a step further and separate Jesus from what they term "the Christ." Despite minor differences, all New Agers agree that the Christ is divine, and is often regarded as a cosmic, impersonal entity. New Agers further allege that this Christ-force or principle took over the body of the man Jesus with a view to helping humanity evolve spiritually. This same Christ is said to lie dormant within each person, waiting to be fully realized so that humanity as a whole may experience spiritual enlightenment.

However, the only condition is that in order for the Christ to live and express Himself through us, we must first accept Him as our Savior, repent from all unbelief, believing in lies, and errant behaviors and receive His Holy Spirit to live in us, to daily transform us and give us the 'mind of Christ'. (Romans 12:2)

Having Christ live in us comes through invitation only. It is not an automatic thing, based on some intellectual process, and definitely doesn't happen through occult practices. When compared to scripture, it is quickly discerned that the New Age belief that Christ came so that we may experience spiritual enlightenment is false, for Scripture draws no distinction between Jesus and Christ, they are one. Indeed, Luke 2 and 1 John 4 both proclaim that Jesus is Christ, that they are the name and title of one and the same divine person. The New Age Jesus is a counterfeit spirit who preaches a message condemned by the Bible, a Jesus that needs to be exposed as an imposter, an Anti-Christ.

"For false Christs and false prophets will appear and perform great signs and miracles to deceive even the elect--if that were possible."

(Matthew 24:24)

The real reason many New Agers embrace the false belief and the false Christ is because having an encounter with the real Yeshua (Jesus Christ) causes spiritual conviction of sin. This requires that we humble ourselves, confess our sins to Him and repent from errant behaviors, sinful lifestyles and turn away from false teachings. This is something New Agers have a hard time doing, because it doesn't feel good at first. Some prefer to follow a false Christ, and believe in the 'Love and Light' philosophy, denying Jesus Christ as their personal savior and personal deliverer from all deception, lies and demonic activity. Unfortunately the false Christ, doesn't deliver from deceptions.

"The Spirit clearly says that in later times some will abandon the faith
and follow deceiving spirits and things taught by demons."
(1 Timothy 4:1)

Notes:

1. Ella LeBain, Book Two: *Who Is God?* chapter, *What Happen When You Die*? p. 455-484, Skypath Books, 2015.

CHAPTER TWENTY-TWO
Who's Channeling Who?

"There is nothing new under the sun."
~ King Solomon, Ecclesiastes 1:9

The ability to channel, and the calling to practice it, is nothing strange, modern, or new. Human beings are designed to be vessels of a higher power. The choice is ours as to *who* we allow into our space, and *which* higher power we serve. Our bodies are made to be temples of the living God, (2 Corinthians 6:16) or a vessel for the kingdom of darkness ruled by the god of this world (2 Corinthians 4:4).

The phrase "god of this world" (or "god of this age") indicates that Satan is the major influence on the mind-set expressed by the ideals, opinions, goals, hopes and views of the majority of people. His areas of influence also encompass the world's philosophies, education, and commerce. The thoughts, ideas, speculations and false religions of the world are under his control and have sprung from his lies and deceptions.

Similar titles are found elsewhere in Scripture concerning Satan. Satan is called the "prince of the power of the air" in Ephesians 2:2. He is called the "ruler of this world" in John 12:31. These titles, and many more attributed to Satan throughout Scripture, signify his capabilities. (See my chapter on *Lucifer*, in Book Two) To say, for example, that Satan is the "prince of the power of the air" signifies that he rules over the world and the people in it. Satan is a fallen archangel who rules this world and earth from an invisible plane called the 'second heaven' (see my chapter on *The Ten Heavens,* in Book Five) not located in the physical world. The second heaven is the realm of UFOs, that are seen from both the first and second heavens.

The spiritual world is invisible and the home to the fallen angel demons. Using psychic techniques, modern man has found ways to tap into the second heaven. People who practice such techniques allow fallen angel demons to overtake them and rule them through psychic power. The divination, fortune telling, channeling, and lying signs and wonders as the scripture talks about in 2 Thessalonians 2:9 is the fruit of Satan using humans to do his deeds on this earth.

Satan and his fallen angel demons usurped the God-given rights of humans when Adam sinned. He, Satan, became the holder of the title deed to the earth and became the god of this world and of humankind. He ruled the world through the humans he manipulated and influenced through his fallen angel demons. If these demons don't already control someone, they seek to influence them through temptation or out and out spiritual attacks.[1]

This is not to say that he rules the world completely; only God is in control and in charge. But it does mean that God, in His infinite wisdom, has allowed Satan to operate in this world, within the boundaries God has set forth, to allow Satan to operate with an agenda. This is the root and heart of the cosmic battle. Satan has legal ground and authority when we turn away from our Creator. Satan is a created being himself, he is not the Creator.

New Age Lightworkers

Many of us have good intentions, and consider ourselves lightworkers. We may call in the light, insist we are *of the light* so therefore only light beings can come through us. Right? Scripture tells us so plainly that Satan masquerades as an angel of light! All these light beings are actually fallen angels in masquerade, the ascended masters, the dead relatives, the benevolent ETs, the archangels, and God only knows who else are followers of Lucifer.

Further, there are many impostors who are capable of mimicking those who did ascend into heaven, like Enoch, Elijah, Jesus, and others who dwell on the highest spiritual plane. However, these impostors are the disincarnate spirits of the Nephilim who communicate with well-intentioned and undiscerning psychics and mediums. As I've mentioned before, these spirits did not have a place in God's plan, and are angry at both God and humanity for being stuck in the lower astral realms. Their agenda is to deceive and degrade us humans.

These entities do not vibrate at a level of Christ consciousness, even though they pretend to do so. They call themselves Buddhas, Avatars, the Hindus, Cosmic Beings, gods and goddesses, the Chohanes, the karmic board, solar hierarchies, elemental beings, the Elohim, and angels. They take on a host of names of saints, prophets and odd gods who once lived on the earth plane, like Saint Germain, Maitreya, Alpha and Omega, St. John, Melchizedek. They also call themselves founders of the Brotherhood of Light from Sirius.

As I've written in Book One, the Sirians are seriously compromised, by contact and proximity with the Draconian Reptilian forces. (See, Sirius[2] in Book One of *Who's Who in the Cosmic Zoo?*) These spirits can read the thoughts and desires of us humans which register in their spirit or energy field, and then they tell people what they want to hear. As they dictate messages from the lower astral planes, they drain off the spiritual light energy from their contacts spirit bodies, acting as energy vampires. All those who partake in their channeled messages get a type of psychic buzz, which gets people hooked spiritually.

When Neal Donald Walsch[3] published his first channeled book in 1995, *Conversations with God: An Uncommon Dialogue,* one of the first questions he was asked was, "How do you know that you're talking to God?" Neale responded that he didn't know, but to let the book speak for itself. How can he not know for sure? What if Neal was channeling the 'god of this world', who also calls himself god?

Lucifer the Satan and all of his fallen angels have hallmark god complexes. Lucifer's whole rebellion was about becoming god. He wants to be called god, he plays god, and when undiscerning humans pray to 'god', he answers.

Think about Neal's situation when he began to channel this 'god'. He was completely broke, down on his luck, struggling with alcoholism. *Someone* thought Neal was in a perfect position to be saved by him and made his vessel. Satan influenced him through telepathic conversations and got Neal to believe he was actually talking to 'god'. Neal never once asked the question, 'Which God?' because that would have required discernment, which is something Neal did not have at that time, so he fell for Lucifer's manipulation hook line and sinker, ended up serving him, becoming a millionaire. Lucifer has managed to use this human as a vessel for his deceptive agenda. His books became bestsellers in New Age circles, and people wonder how this happens? Because the channel is speaking what people want to hear. Truth mixed with lies is popular genre in New Age publishing circles.

Recently a Jewish woman named Alex Eldridge from Brooklyn followed in Neal's footsteps and published a book called *Conversations with Jesus*, based on exactly the same precepts, along similar lines, with almost identical answers about the concept of god. She claims she was channeling Jesus, but it was certainly not Yeshua HaMashiach, Jesus Christ. This is why Yeshua said,

> "For many will come in my name, claiming, 'I am the Christ,'
> and will deceive many."
> (Matthew 24:5)

It's almost funny, because there are lots of people in this world named Jesus. Jesus is an extremely popular and common name in the Latin speaking countries, where it is pronounced 'Hey Zeus'. Many people are not aware of the fact that there is a fallen angel demon also named Jesus, which is why believers in Yeshua HaMashiach, or Jesus the Christ, will say His full name when speaking to the spirit realm, to the point of confessing and identifying the true Jesus to distinguish Him from the counterfeits: "Jesus Christ of Nazareth who came in the flesh, by the power of His Cross and His resurrection," are words often used for deliverance to cast out stubborn devils.

After reading her book, I am convinced she was not in a conversation with the Lord Jesus Christ, but with a counterfeit spirit. This is especially evident when most of the answers were contrary to the Word of God, and God never goes back on His Word.

"For there shall arise false Christs, and false prophets, and shall show great signs and wonders; insomuch that, if it were possible, they shall deceive the very elect." (Matthew 24:24)

H. Constance Hill published a book called, *Wisdom From Beyond*, who claims to have channeled Leonardo DaVinci, Frank Sinatra, Walt Disney, Babe Ruth, Paul Newman, Lady Diana, Thomas Edison, Fred Astaire, Elvis Presley, Michael Jackson, Anne Frank, Winston Churchill, Vincent Van Gough, Eleanor Roosevelt, Albert Schweitzer, Mother Teresa, Liberace, Ella Fitzgerald, Pope Paul John II, Annie Oakley, Leonard Bernstein, Mahatma Gandhi, Robert F. Kennedy, Martin Luther King, Jr., and these are just to name a few.[4] What do all these people have in common? They are all dead.

When I met her, I asked her, "How do you know you are channeling these people? How do you know that these entities are who they say they are?" She replied, "Because I recognized their energy." So, I asked her, "But how do you know that entities are not mimicking their energy? Did you know that the Watchers spend their time studying earth humans and when they die they, the Watchers, who are fallen angel demons, pretend to be disincarnate spirits and can mimic them better than a well-seasoned actor? How do you know you weren't channeling these Watcher fallen angels?" She replied, "Oh no, I am in the light, I call on the light so only light beings can come to me." Lucifer ***means*** Light!! That's a huge New Age distortion!

"And no wonder,
for Satan himself masquerades as an angel of light."
(2 Corinthians 11:14)

Lucifer the Satan visits those who call on *the light,* those who ignore his arch enemy, the Lord Jesus Christ. Remember, Lucifer is not anti-religion, he's anti-Christ. There's an old saying, that the enemy of my enemy is my friend. Most New Agers have either left the church, fallen away in apostasy from their childhood faith in Christ, or never had it in the first place. They now follow the doctrines of demons.

"Now the Spirit speaks expressly, that in the latter times some shall depart from the faith, giving heed to seducing spirits, and doctrines of devils;"
(1 Timothy 4:1)

Another phrase common among New Age channelers is the calling on 'any and all beings' who want to help them, or channel through them, or have information that they seek. There is absolutely no discernment here, and these summonses leave them completely open to channeling demons, Watchers, fallen angels, and evil spirits. Because of their spiritual blindness as well as their pride in thinking of themselves as only light, an armor of denial forms in their spirit. Remember, the fallen angels were once heavenly angels, full of light, truth and power, but were ousted out of their heavenly positions due to their rebellion. They remember how to project themselves as light. Not all who wander are lost and not all who glow are light.

The Master of Spiritual Fraud

Satan almost never reveals himself as he truly is to us humans. He is the master of disguise, the great seducer, the world's greatest actor. Remember Lucifer was once the most beautiful of the archangels of the Cherubim, he knows how to channel flowery, beautiful, poetic words cleverly mixed with rotting lies, the kind that people want to hear. He cleverly tells people what they want to hear, influencing them away from the truth of God and Christ. He is the master of spiritual fraud and those who channel without discernment fall right into his trap. Not only have they fallen for his seductive deception, hook, line, and sinker, but they publish the fraud and are used by him to deceive thousands if not millions with their own lies.

Lucifer always cleverly sandwiches some key truths between his lies, in case there is a fact checker or researcher in the audience. It confuses and confounds the rest of us who never have the time or inclination to question or doubt it. This is why Satan is known as the great deceiver:

> "The great dragon was hurled down. That ancient serpent, called the Devil and Satan, *the deceiver of the whole world*, was hurled down to the earth, along with its angels." (Revelation 12:9)

When the Bible says Satan has power over the world, it must be made clear that God has given him domain over unbelievers alone. Believers are no longer under the rule of Satan (Colossians 1:13). Unbelievers, on the other hand, are caught "in the snare of the devil" (2 Timothy 2:26), lie in the "power of the evil one" (1 John 5:19), and are in bondage to Satan (Ephesians 2:2).

Those who believe themselves to be a light worker usually fall prey to channeling fallen angels, because they see themselves as light and deny that they have any sin in them. Most of the channeling is worded to alleviate the channelers of guilt and shame, which lulls them into a false sense of security while alive. Their spiritual pride masks the truth about their inadequacies, which only armors their denial. They are in a spot to deny the path of salvation through the cross, and further deny Christ His Christhood.

The Bible tells us of the story of Jezebel and Ahab. Jezebel was the daughter of Ethbal, king of the Sidonians. Her father was the high priest of the goddess Ashtoreth. She married Ahab, the king of Israel to form a *covenant* between the two nations. Jezebel was a wicked queen. She set out to murder the prophets of Yahuah, however, failed, as a hundred of them were cleverly hidden in caves. Others compromised their prophetic ministries and gave themselves to her. This compromise is still happening today.

Jezebel was a prophetess who served the foreign gods Asherah (Ashtoreth) and Baal. She specialized in training and teaching her followers to prophecy. She used divining spirits and full body channeling, also called possession. Jezebel has a large following today. I have already gone over in my chapter on Ashtar who Ashtoreth was, in Book One of *Who's Who in the Cosmic Zoo?*[5] Asherah or Ashtoreth has become Ashtar, of the Ashtar Command. Ashtoreth is also known as Gaia the earth goddess, Semiramis aka Mother Mary, the Queen of Heaven, and a host of other pagan goddesses. Both Jezebel and Ahab died horrific deaths, and their evil spirits continue to plague humanity's generations to this day by working with the fallen angel Ashtoreth.

Baal is behind all the false religions of the earth, and believe it or not, he is cleverly hidden and worshipped in Catholicism (see, *Aliens and Religion*). Baal is pronounced *bail*, which is an interesting pun in English. Baal was the primary pagan idol of the Phoenicians, often associated with the fallen angel goddess Ashtaroth. Baal was the supposed son of the fallen ET god Dagon. To the Israelites regret, they were seduced into worshipping Baal. As I've mentioned before, these fallen ETs created cults and religion to receive the energy and worship and fear from us. Their most common worship included temple prostitution, unnatural sexual behaviors, and sacrificing their infants to the fire.

The name Baal is used in various ways in the Old Testament, with the usual meaning of *master*, or *owner*. It was often slapped over the name of the local pagan god, eventually absorbing all of the idols of the land. It is also found in Judges 2:11, 10:10 in the plural form *Baalim*, or *Baals*. In Hebrew, *Baalim* is plural for its many idols. Baal had many variations, such as the sun god, the god of fertility, and Beelzebub, known as *the lord of flies*, or more specifically, the ***Lord of those who fly***, as in UFOs. Baal was a fallen angel ET who was not captured in the last galactic war. He serves the hierarchy of Lucifer the Satan and dwells in the lower heavens. He comes under the powers of the darkness and spiritual wickedness in heavenly places mentioned in Ephesians 6:12.

According to one tradition, the ancient priest Berosus served *Belus*, or *Bel*, as he was known originally. It was allegedly Berosus who partially built the Tower of Babel in the Tigris-Euphrates Valley, named after *Baal*, or *Bel*. The tower was a type of space ship or space port, like a Mu, or vimana, a flying craft. The whole structure of the tower of the Gate of Baal was destroyed by the Lord Yahuah. In payment for their arrogance and rebellion are the many different tongues we now babble in, on earth and in heaven. This is where we get the term *babbling*. The name *Babylon* comes from the pagan god's name.

The Moabites introduced Baal worship to the Israelites, as Baal of Peor (Numbers 25:3, Deuteronomy 4:3), which they practiced, through the time of Samuel (1 Samuel 7:4). After that, came the cult of Baal and Ashtoreth through the time of Ahab and Jezebel (1 Kings 16:31-33, 18:19-22) by the northern tribes. The southern kingdom of Judah also was guilty of Baal-Ashtoreth worship (2 Kings 8:27, 11:18, 16:3, 2 Chronicles 28:2) until the Lord Yahuah got so disgusted with His own people that He took His protection away from them and gave them up to defeat and eventual exile through King Nebuchadnezzar (Zephaniah 1:4-6).

According to 1 Kings 18:19 and 2 Kings 10:19, the priests of Baal were in great numbers, and from various classes throughout the land. Their spiritual emptiness was exposed in probably one of the greatest spiritual contests ever, with the prophet Elijah on Mount Carmel. King Ahab was brought down due to his worship of Baal, as he and his wife Jezebel influenced hundreds of others to follower Baalim. There is an exciting account of this story of how one prophet for the Lord Yahuah, Elijah, brought down hundreds of false prophets of Baal, along with King Ahab and Jezebel, who caused his own and Israel's downfall is found in the book of 1 Kings Chapters 18 through 22.

Elijah was out-numbered four hundred and fifty to one, but he overcame with the power of God, by getting all these priests to bring a bull sacrifice to the altar on Mount Carmel. All four hundred and fifty of them danced around the bull calling on the name of Baal, but nothing happened. Then after many attempts in contacting their false god, Elijah intervened by calling on the one true Living God and Creator of all souls, who sent fire from heaven and destroyed the bull, the altar, the stones and the wood. Then all four hundred and fifty priests of Baal prostrated themselves in fear to the Lord, and Elijah had them all destroyed (1 Kings 18:16-40).

After her prophets of Baal were annihilated, Jezebel vowed to kill Elijah, a threat that resulted in Jezebel's own demise. "And also concerning Jezebel the Lord says: 'Dogs will devour Jezebel by the wall of Jezreel." (1 Kings 21:23) Which is exactly what happened to her. King Jehu, threw her over her own balcony and she was eaten by dogs. She was never buried, and her evil spirit has become a demonic stronghold, or more accurately, the demonic archons who are in rebellion against the God of Israel, absorbed her evil spirits which is today called, the Jezebel spirit, that is actually a male demon, not a woman.

The prophesied death of Ahab came about during a battle in which Israel and Judah were allied against Syria. An enemy archer fired a very lucky shot from a distance, aiming only at the body of troops, but the random shot not only hit king Ahab, but also just happened to hit him between the sections of his armor where there was no protection. He bled throughout the day before dying at sunset. In a very ghastly spectacle, dogs licked up his blood from his chariot - just as The Lord had declared for his bloody wickedness.

Same Old Fallen Angel Ets, Different Century

As all of the Old Testament battles and contests proved, the Lord Yahuah is the real Creator God. Yet so many of the ancients were misled by the fallen ETs, who as I've said before, had god complexes. The ancestors mistakenly worshipped them as gods, when in reality many of them were nothing but rogue aliens and ETs who were looking to rape the earth of its natural resources, including the spiritual soul energies of humankind.

The very same scenario is happening today, only it's packaged with more glitz and glamor, and all these ancient aliens have acquired modern names.

Jezebel and Ahab have become evil spirits that work for Baal and Ashtoreth, who both masquerade as archangels, apace brothers, goddesses, and ascended masters. This is the New Age way of getting us to worship them instead of the Living God. It is very interesting to note that when a Jezebel spirit is exorcised, the spirit is tormented by dogs.

I actually witnessed an exorcism done by the famous exorcist Bob Larson, who was chasing a demon out of a young Christian girl who sang in a Christian worship rock band. She had become pregnant and later found out that her baby had died in her womb, yet she had still not given birth to it. It was one of those violent exorcisms with a lot of screaming, and as soon as Bob identified the demon as 'Jezebel' and threatened to send the dogs, the spirit submitted and came out of the woman. The next morning, the young girl reported that she felt stirrings in her womb, so she went back to the doctor who had pronounced her baby dead. To his surprise he had to retract his findings as her baby came back to life in her womb.

Jezebel comes in all kinds of disguises, even to born again Christians. The Jezebel spirit often manifests in women as a controlling and dominating spirit, just as the evil Queen Jezebel was in the way she controlled King Ahab, and all of her priests and followers. Ahab, however, manifests in men, also as a controlling spirit in a religious way, and seeks to have dominance in the church or spiritual circle, and wants to be seen as a prophet. However, he always misses the mark, and is identified as a false prophet. This includes both Christian and New Age churches.

I witnessed the spirit of Ahab in a pastor of a small *spirit-filled* church which preached replacement theology. He believed that because he and his congregation spoke in tongues, they were spirit-filled, yet the entire congregation was constantly plagued with one illness after another, and no one in that church was free. It was a form of godliness, but in denial of its true power. (2 Timothy 3:5) The pastor scoffed at Old Testament laws, and believed they were outdated, only cherry-picking Hebrew Scriptures which suited his argument. The Pastor could not handle any challenges or questioning of his way of doing things, and was close-minded to hearing the Word of knowledge from the Lord and was clearly threatened by it.

There is a tendency that exists in all hierarchies, be they spiritual or political or military, that the attitude (or spirit) of the leader trickles down to its flock. This is why the congregation, only made up of approximately 25 members, were constantly plagued with illness, accidents, surgery and broken relationships. This church's growth was stunted due to the stubbornness and pride of its pastor in bondage to the stronghold of the Ahab spirit-demon and his host of deceiving spirits and false prophets.

Every generation must guard itself from the seductions of Jezebel and Ahab, whose mission is to sabotage the prophetic ministries of the Lord. Both Jezebel and Ahab are false prophets, both are teachers, both are cunning, deceptive, controlling and are adversaries (satans) of Yahuah and Jesus Christ and their celestial armies.

Jezebel, Ahab, Baal and Ashtoreth are the spirits behind most New Agers. They rule over witchcraft, especially all the seemingly white magic, Wicca, New Age mysticism, and all forms of pagan worship which includes Native American rituals. Just because these rulers of darkness masquerade with new names doesn't mean their spiritual energies have been altered or improved. They have only become more cunning and clever. They no longer demand babies be thrown into the fire, but instead want your spiritual energy and your very soul. Though they may channel through names like Archangel Michael, Gaia, St. Germain, Lady Nada, Mother Mary, Archangel Gabriel, dispensing angel magic therapies, the price they demand is the same worship of them over worship of God. If we believe we are light workers preparing humankind for our ascension, we are a modern-day equivalent to worshipping the golden calf. All that glitters is definitely not gold.

In my opinion, many channelers are selected because of their naiveté and blind faith in angels and entities. H. Constance Hill was chosen to channel this list of 35 dead people in her book, mainly because of her naiveté and blind faith. The purpose which she and others like her is to spread false information about the afterlife. The fallen angel demons which are all part of the Satanic realm have an agenda to distort the truth about the afterlife, designed to trap as many souls as possible by diverting them from seeking their Savior.

To say there is nothing to fear is a lie because separation from God is something every soul should fear. It is utter darkness to be separated from God, which only happens when people turn their backs on the Savior and swallow Lucifer's lies. Not everyone goes to the same place as these channelers would like you to believe. See, Book Two: *Who Is God?* my chapter, *What Happens When You Die?*[6]

This is why the commandment from the Lord, "'Do not turn to mediums or seek out spiritists, for you will be defiled by them. I am the LORD your God," (Leviticus 19:31) is important to heed, because He knows Satan's agenda and how the fallen angel demons work. They pretend to be the spirit of the deceased, and fool the recipient as well as the medium into believing that they are communicating with dead loved ones or dead celebrities as in the case of Hill's channeled book. This is nothing but a paranormal charade. Then the Lord goes on to decree a curse on those who consults mediums and those who channel the dead:

> "I will also turn against those who commit spiritual prostitution by putting their trust in mediums or in those who consult the spirits of the dead. I will cut them off from the community."
>
> (Leviticus 20:6)

The reason God warns us to not to have anything to do with channeling, spirit guides, or mediums is because they are all demonic spirits. This is no great surprise since the Lord tells us that Satan and his cohorts can transform themselves into angels of light in 2 Corinthians 11:14.

How many of these chatty spirits can there be out in the world? Since a third of the angels joined the Luciferian rebellion, about that many. When we ask the valid questions if aliens and UFOs are real, we must keep in mind the underlying question of who exactly they are, and why they are so concerned with humanity at this particular time.

Going to a medium to have contact with the spirits of the dead opens the legal gateway for deception from the realm of fallen angels. There is a big difference between a ghost and a spirit. All ghosts are spirits, but not all spirits are ghosts. Let's verify this from the words of Christ Himself:

> "While they were still talking about this, Jesus himself stood among them and said to them, "Peace be with you." They were startled and frightened, thinking they saw a ghost. He said to them, "Why are you troubled, and why do doubts rise in your minds? Look at my hands and my feet. It is I myself! Touch me and see; a ghost does not have flesh and bones, as you see I have."
>
> (Luke 24:36-39)

Jesus defines ghosts as non-corporeal beings who have no flesh whatsoever. Angels, on the other hand, are considered spirits as well, but they have physical bodies made of a spiritual flesh; they are capable of physical activities. The Bible gives many examples of angels exhibiting physical qualities which ghosts do not share. Confusing matters even more, angelic spirits who aren't ghosts can act as if they are ghosts if they want to (exhibit nonphysical qualities), such as walking through walls, flying, and so on. Ghosts, on the other hand, do not have the option of being physical. On rare occasion, poltergeists, which are a specific type of ghost connected with the onset of puberty, might have enough energy to move objects, but that's about all they can do in the physical realm without possessing a host.[7]

Watchers are so named because they watch humans on earth. Please see Book One, my chapter on the Nephilim for further elucidation and discernment on Watchers and Nephilim.[8] According to the *Books of Enoch,* the Watchers of humans became the Nephilim, now under the curse of God to become evil spirits that roam the earth and oppress humankind. They qualify under the realm of the demonic. Their name literally translates as *intelligences* and they are able to imitate, mimic like a seasoned actor, all the characteristics and personalities of the humans whom they watch. When one of us dies, they are the ones who haunt the living, and they are the ones who channel through mediums and spiritists, perpetuating the lie that they are communicating with the deceased loved ones' ghosts. This is a huge ruse, an age-old trick of Satan's realm.

> "And now the giants, who have been begotten from body and flesh, will be called evil spirits on earth, and their dwelling-places will be upon the earth.
>
> Evil spirits proceed from their bodies; because they are created from above, their beginning and first basis being from the holy watchers, they will be evil spirits upon the earth, and will be called evil spirits.
>
> But the spirits of heaven have their dwelling-places in heaven, and the spirits of the earth, who were born on the earth, have their dwelling-places on earth.
>
> And the spirits of the giants, who cast themselves upon the clouds, will be destroyed and fall, and will battle and cause destruction on the earth, and do evil; they will take no kind of food, nor will they become thirsty, and they will be invisible."
>
> (The Book of Enoch, chapter 15:8-11)

Supernatural power comes from either God or Satan. If we believe in God's truth, His anointing and His power is upon our life. However, if we believe in Satan's lies, he will empower us as well, to the point of creating all kinds of paranormal special effects to get us hooked into believing that the paranormal is real. Once hooked on the deception, Satan continues the trap by channeling the image and characteristics of the dead to the living. This is what keeps mediums and their clients in thrall, the hope that they will be able to communicate with their deceased loved ones. In reality, they are communicating with the realm of the demonic fallen angels. This is spiritual fraud in the highest degree, because it preys upon the weaknesses and heartache of the grieving on earth.

"There's a sucker born every minute."
~ P.T. Barnum

When the Bible says that Satan is the "god of this world," it is not saying that he has ultimate authority. It is conveying the idea that Satan rules over the unbelieving world in a specific way, which is through the belief in his lies. If a person doesn't have the truth in him, it is far easier to believe a lie that makes sense, all the while having no discernment because there is nothing to compare it with, as the truth is elusive to them. Satan then empowers them in their belief in his lies, which makes the lie appear as truth.

According to 2 Corinthians 4:4, the "god of this world has blinded the minds of unbelievers, so that they cannot see the light of the gospel of the glory of Christ." Satan's agenda includes pushing a false philosophy onto the unbelieving world, a false philosophy that blinds the unbeliever from the truth of the Gospel. Satan's philosophies are the fortresses in which people are imprisoned, needing to be set free and brought captive to Christ in obedience to the truth.

An example of a false philosophy might be a belief that man can earn God's favor by a certain act or acts. In fact, earning eternal life is a predominate theme around the world. Earning God's favor by works, however, is contrary to biblical revelation. Man cannot work to earn God's favor; eternal life is a free gift (see Ephesians 2:8-9). And that free gift is available through Jesus Christ and through Him alone (John 3:16; 14:6). You may ask, why do we simply not receive the free gift that enables us to truly be called children of God (John 1:12)? The answer is that Satan, the god of this world, pushes a false philosophy onto the world. Satan sets the agenda, the unbelieving world follows, and mankind continues to be deceived. It is no wonder that Scripture calls Satan a liar (John 8:44).

We know that Satan rules from the second heaven. As I mentioned earlier, this is the realm of UFOs, which is another huge deception being practiced upon humankind at this time. Besides channeling the dead, there are many New Agers who channel the Archangels, ascended masters, extraterrestrials, aliens and space commanders. All these entities come from the same source, the second heaven, ruled by Satan through his hierarchy of principalities, Princes, rulers of the darkness, and the spiritual wickedness in heavenly places. These fallen angel demons seek out the innocent to be the vessels to channel their agenda, to spread disinformation to earth, by mixing truth with lies, to create massive distortions and deceptions.

As I have mentioned in my Angels book of this series, there is a New Age religion that incorporates angel worship and invocation, particularly Archangel Michael. This is an easy counterfeit to spot, as the real Archangel Michael, who took Lucifer's place in heaven after defeating him and hurling him to earth, is now the Prince Archangel, in charge of protecting Israel and God's people. The counterfeit archangel Michael, which New Agers call on in place of Jesus Christ, to help them cut cords, fill them with energy when they are drained, and protect them from evil, is *not* the real Archangel Michael.

If you read my chapter on *Angel Protocol,* in Book Three: *Who Are the Angels?* you will see that there is hierarchy of angels.[9] Archangels do not deal with humans directly, they are Lords and Princes that oversee the lower angels which serve earth humans directly. So, when New Agers invoke Archangel Michael for healing, protection, cord cutting and energy, who answers their prayers? The counterfeit, the fallen angels, in masquerade as Archangels, Ascended Masters, extraterrestrials, space commanders and angels of light. This is supernatural fraud!

One clearly needs to look at the lives of those people, prior to being contacted by these Archangels, Ascended Masters, extraterrestrials, space commanders and angels of light, and ask, what makes them able to gain the attention of an extraterrestrial that comes from some distant star or even another galaxy, and choose them to be their channel? The truth is obvious: these people are chosen for their gullibility, their naiveté, their lack of discernment and their disenchantment with Christianity and religion. The agenda of the dark forces is to divert us off the path of salvation, because they are in direct conflict against the Creator and Jesus Christ, who many believe are one and the same, as Father and Son. But that's another chapter.

"There is a way that seems right to a man,
but the end of that road leads to death (destruction)."
(Proverbs 16:25)

The battle that each and every one of us faces is *who* controls our mind, our body, and ultimately our soul. If the agenda of the dark forces can convince us that we must believe in ourselves, that we create our own reality, that if we simply turn to the light and think good thoughts, that is enough. Then we can gather as many together as possible who believe the same, and change the world to a better place and help bring in a new world order of equality, liberty, peace and love. The New Agers are being used to create the illusion of faith in the light and the benevolent ETs who will help mother earth ascend into the fifth dimension with all of us as well. This is a mass deception.

I discuss the fifth dimension that so many are waiting for in Book Three: *Who Are the Angels?*, where a whole chapter is devoted to *Ascension or Rapture?* as well as my relevant chapter on *The World of the Wondrous.*[10] The fifth dimension is the promise of the Kingdom of God, to be established on earth at the end of the battle of Armageddon. It is signaled by the second coming of Yeshua HaMashiach, Jesus Christ. There is no fifth dimension living without Christ.

For now, this world is under the influence of the kingdom of darkness, which is run by the 'god of this world,' known as Lucifer or Satan and his hierarchy of fallen extraterrestrial angels. This is why so many people around the globe pray daily what is known as the Lord's Prayer, "Thy Kingdom come on earth as it is in heaven." God's throne now resides in the third heaven, which will be downloaded onto the earth as the New Jerusalem, where He will rule the world as the Kingdom of God in the next millennium. (Revelation 20)

Within the vast kingdom of darkness, and all of its principalities, rulers and fallen angel ETs, are spirit guides telling us about many wonderful things are about to unfold on the earth. This is true, except they hardly ever talk about the great judgments about to fall on them and all those who follow them and ignore the Savior of our souls. Bible Prophecy reveals great events about to happen on earth and in its skies, but how many churches actually teach Bible prophecy, let alone understand what it means?

Sure, there are some really great authors out there who do make sense of Bible prophecy, yet few and far between. Churches in general stay away from it, because it is too controversial, and quite frankly, they tend to preach sermons that make people feel good, to keep their congregations full. Some churches actually say that being into Bible prophecy means that Satan has gotten a hold of you. These are the same churches who refuse to say the 'D' word, as in demons and deliverance. I can't tell you how many Christians I have come across in different denominations, who when asked about deliverance, actually responded with, 'what's that?' The fact is that Satan has a foothold on the church and has since the formation of the Church of Rome, which later became the Roman Catholic Church. It's no wonder people seek enlightenment elsewhere.

If we must channel a spirit, then try channeling a Spirit that will never create any threat to us at all and will ultimately give us rewards that we cannot possibly imagine, that will last forever. Turn to the Lord, repent of missing the mark with Him (an archery word, called, 'sin') and ask Jesus to come into your heart and wash away all your mistakes with His Divine blood, and He will give you the Holy Spirit. Then you can channel the most powerful Spirit in the universe on a daily basis by simply praying, affirming and watch the miracles follow. As far as human temples go, it is far better to be filled by the Holy Spirit than possessed by a demonic spirit or fallen angel (ET). All you need to do is simply invite Him in, by believing and confessing Jesus is your Savior, you make Him Lord of your life. It's about relationship with the Living Savior, not a religion.

Notes:

1. Art Mathias, *Biblical Foundations for Freedom: Destroying Satan's Lies with God's Truth*, p.10, Wellspring Publishing, 2010.
2. Ella LeBain, *Who's Who in the Cosmic Zoo?* Book One – Third Edition, Sirius p. 389-399, Tate, 2013.
3. Neal Donald Walsch, *Conversations with God: An Uncommon Dialogue,* Hampton Roads, 1995.
4. H. Constance Hill, *Wisdom From Beyond*, Diamond Clear Vision, 2010
5. Book One of *Who's Who in the Cosmic Zoo?* Ashtar, p. 127-134
6. Ella LeBain, Book Two: *Who Is God?* Chapter Twenty-Eight, *What Happens When You Die?* p. 455-484, Skypath Books, 2015.
7. John Milor, *Aliens and the Antichrist, Unveiling the End Times Deception,* p. 28. iUniverse, Inc., 2006.
8. Book One of *Who's Who in the Cosmic Zoo?* Nephilim, p.326-338.
9. Ella LeBain, in Book Three: *Who Are the Angels?* Chapter Four: *Angel Protocol,* p. 71-113
10. Book Three: *Who Are the Angels?,* Chapter: Twelve: *The World of the Wondrous,* p.251-258, Chapter Fifteen: *Ascension or Rapture?* p. 303-337.

CHAPTER TWENTY-THREE

ARE ALIENS DEMONS?

"I have given you power to trample on serpents and scorpions
and to overcome the power of the enemy."
(LUKE 10:19)

Serpents, snakes, scorpions, are all aliens in the true sense of the word. If you've read, Book One of *Who's Who in The Cosmic Zoo?* you will have an understanding how all of these creatures are alien to earth and to us human beings.[1] The fact that Christ told His believers that He has given us power to tread on serpents and scorpions means that He has the power over these alien beings, and those who take on the mind of Christ through the Holy Spirit are granted this same power as well. Many Christians interpret the words of Jesus to mean that they have been given power over the demonic realm. See, Mark 3:15; 6:7-13; Matthew 10:1;8; Luke 9:1; 10:17; 1 John 2:13-14; James 4:7; Acts 26:18; Ephesians 6:11; Romans 16:20.

Yes, this is true, and yes, many of the dark aliens are in fact demons. Grays, Reptiloids, shape shifting reptilians (serpents), insectoids, humanoids, and even some human-appearing aliens who are fallen angels are all in the realm of the demonic and under the hierarchy of Satan.

Remember, the word *demon* comes from the Greek word *daemon* which means *intelligences.* The word demon has been associated with purely evil intelligence and negativity and deception of every sort.

This concept about demons can shock people who are religious, or even those who have grown up in a family which takes the Bible literally, as many think that they can't have demons if they are a believer. Most people today, including many who consider themselves Christian, have no understanding about the reality of demons. This has been Satan's plan from the beginning.

New Agers, many who are fascinated with the paranormal, do not realize that the beings they encounter, and the spirit guides who contact them, are in fact demons. Most people have an image of demons being dark and ugly, which is in part true, however, demons are masters of deception, and they do come as angels of light, deceiving so many into thinking that they are good, helpful, and can give them protection and information. So many speak daily to these spirit guides!

"And no wonder, for Satan himself masquerades as an angel of light."
(2 Corinthians 11:14)

What many new age folks do not understand is that these spirit guides will give them whatever they expect, as long as they keep the person in bondage with a lie, denying them the truth of the spiritual reality. The fallen angels of the satanic hierarchy lull us into a false sense of security, thinking we are being enlightened in a way that the traditional religions we broke away from could not provide. We receive esoteric knowledge, much of which cannot be substantiated, yet many believe as truth. Thinking that we are being guided in a way that we could not feel when we followed a traditional religion, hearing voices, feeling flutters, seeing visions, and a host of other paranormal phenomenon, deludes us into thinking that we have been chosen. This titillates our egos, and makes us feel special that we have been contacted by an ascended master or an archangel or an extraterrestrial from a distant star or planet. These spirit guides will do whatever it takes to make us feel good with all kinds of love and light rhetoric, that we swallow, hook, line and sinker, and never think that *our* spirit guides would ever mislead or deceive us. This is classic demonic oppression and possession.

These demonic guides have an agenda to keep us spiritually deaf and blind to what is really going on, which is the ongoing battle over our minds and souls. Just as the classic *Faustian Contract* goes, we agree to the lie in exchange for all kinds of benefits, but our soul goes to these beings in the end. We end up in darkness, separated from our Creator. This is hard to believe, especially for those who adamantly believe in this *love and light* doctrine.

We believe that we really do create our own reality, but do we? Can we stop the forces of darkness in our own lives? Does merely believing that we create our own reality, make it so? What if we are living within a reality that we do not understand, let alone have any power to alter? Do New Agers have the power to stop aliens from abducting any humans, even themselves?

New Age Metaphysicians are convinced that they have seen angels, spirits, and all kinds of paranormal phenomenon. The spiritual reality is that they are under the influence of highly intelligent, talented, malicious fallen angels who have tricked them into seeing what they wanted to believe in the first place. Yes, the paranormal is real, but it is *not* what most people think it is. If so, then why are the fruits of it, so dark and evil? Paranormal investigators are constantly plagued by loss, illness, and energy theft. "The thief comes only to steal and kill and destroy; I have come that they may have life, and have it in abundance." (John 10:10)

Satan then proceeds to the next step of convincing us that if something works, it must be true. Thus, becoming susceptible to demonic activity, because their system works with great power. Further, many are incapable of properly identifying this demonic power because due to cognitive dissonance. They have already mentally ruled out the possibility that there might be a supernatural being, therefore, supernatural beings do not even exist. In spiritual warfare, this is called the Leviathan Spirit, which twists communications, and eventually sucks the breath and life force out of you, while you're trying to prove that the paranormal is real. I have witnessed this first hand in so many people over the years.

The Mass Deception that will Deceive Even the Elect

> "For false Christs and false prophets will appear and perform great signs and miracles to deceive even the elect--if that were possible."
>
> (Matthew 24:24)

Finally, Satan will ultimately proceed, in stages, to his final alien deception. Alien beings and UFO phenomenon begin to appear with increasing frequency and intimate contact. Since many disbelieve in the existence of supernatural beings, we assume the truth of these demons, accepting the lie that they are an alien race from another world. This other world is supposedly the seat of a more technologically and spiritually advanced culture than we have on planet Earth. Therefore, when the aliens of this more advanced world tell us of their religion, we are expected to adopt it, rejecting our own ignorant, uninformed, and outmoded religions.

This is the agenda of the New World Order, which is, that all religions are equal and will be combined into one, all others abolished except their religion, which will support a one world government. Naturally all democracy must be abolished as they will try to market a Utopian Benevolent Dictatorship, which nothing could be further from the truth.

This is the goal of the aliens, the demons who come in UFOs, many of which are part of a hive-mind mentality where the concepts of freedom, democracy and individualism, the values that we hold most dear, are completely alien to them. They will come with the lure of their technology, as many of us are already convinced that the aliens are here to help us clean up our environment, and many more will be deceived and give their power away.

Since ancient times, the story of deception continues, with Ancient Aliens visiting Earth who set themselves up as gods and intervened in history to give man increased knowledge, from which he was able to build such ancient wonders as the pyramids. In reality, the pyramids were not built by man, but by extraterrestrials.

Now, the time has come, the aliens say, for them to intervene again in world history. This time, they will intervene to save man from himself: from his wars, hatreds, spiritual illiteracy, and his environmental damage. These aliens will accomplish all this by raising up a man who will be imbued with a special level of consciousness, who can lead the world into that same level of consciousness. This man will be the Anti-Christ.

Do not be deceived. As Bill Cooper stated, in his book, *Behold A Pale Horse*, p. 177, "[New World Order Planners] have plans to bring about things like earthquakes, war, the Messiah, an extraterrestrial landing, and economic collapse. They might bring about all of these things just to make sure it does work...The Illuminati has all the bases covered..."[2]

The demons of Satan's army will soon physically manifest themselves as aliens, arriving in armadas of space ships which we have heretofore called UFO's. The plan calls for them to suddenly appear at many places on Earth simultaneously. Some will appear at the White House to confer with the President; some will appear at the United Nations; other aliens will appear at key governmental buildings all over the globe. Aliens will appear in some people's homes or on their front yards. The world's peoples will literally be shocked out of their minds. This is the Plan. This may occur before the worldwide Rapture of the Church; we must be prepared to deal wisely with this planned phenomenon.

We stand at a chasm of world history. Biblical prophecy is being worked out in 100% detail, and a belief in UFO's and Aliens is deemed necessary if people are to be convinced of the claims of Antichrist.

Because so many credible people have come forward who have witnessed UFOs, millions more now feel that these supernatural beings must exist. The talk amongst scientists is now, 'what would you say to an alien?' In fact, Omni Magazine put that on their cover back in the 1990s. The people who run SETI, the Search for Extraterrestrial Intelligence, believe that contact is imminent and are excited about the possibilities to learn of their technology. Of course, being secularists, being completely void of any understanding of the *spiritual* implications of their wish to make contact with an alien coming true, whether or not that will be a good one or an evil one, and how will they know?

Most of the people who are convinced by the testimony of the people who have seen UFOs and have had contact with aliens, will also make the fatal mistake of assuming that such beings are benevolent, kind, and have our own best interests at heart. They will think they can be trusted in everything, when in reality the whole end game is recommending a new form of worship. Many already have joined the alien church, which is their technology. How else does one explain how our culture has gone from the industrial revolution to high tech, nanotechnology in less than 50 years?

We've already had contact with aliens who have more advanced technology than ours. Our governments have already made agreements with several races of aliens, which is how we have acquired the technology we have today. But this book is not about convincing you of those facts, please do your research into the Eisenhower years, the UFO crashes of Roswell, Socorro and the like, and all the underground bases around the world to see the history of this all too important timeline that has brought us to our present high-tech culture.

This book is about acquiring the ability to discern *who* these beings are in nature, whether or not they are *who* they say they are, or whether they are champion liars. Just because they have given us technology doesn't necessarily mean they have our best interests at heart, if they even have a heart. There is something much more sinister toward humanity at work here that must be addressed. This scenario is unfolding right in front of our eyes. The rise of the Antichrist may be very close as the end of the Age of Pisces is upon us.

The growing number of UFOs sighted in our skies is evidence of the fact that they are gearing up for a final battle with the Creator for control, over the earth, its population, its real estate, and all of what is *inside* the earth. What many people do not realize is that Satan is not just a devil that sits in hell, he is a very real celestial being that has been temporarily given the authority of this world as well as being called the "Prince of the Power of the Air" (Ephesians 2:2). This means he has access to the lower heavens and has space vehicles under his control. Most of the UFOs that people witness in the skies, particularly the metallic, hard mechanical ones, belong to him and his armada of spacecraft which come from *inside* the earth. They have bases on the Moon and Mars and elsewhere in our solar system as well. See, Book Two: *Who Is God?* my chapter on *Lucifer, Rahab and The Stones of Fire.*[3]

> "Wherein in time past you walked according to the course of this world, according to the <u>*prince of the power of the air*</u>, the spirit that now works in the children of disobedience"
>
> (Ephesians 2:2)

The UFO phenomena is such a seduction! Our imaginations are titillated, we're fascinated by the possibilities, awed by the idea that we are being contacted by extraterrestrials from *outer space*, from a distant star or planet, who have come to watch, study, or even help us through the pain and suffering we experience on earth. Folks think all kinds of things, like how they could help us out of our present dilemma with respect to our environmental issues, or energy issues, or the wars between nations and differing groups.

Imagining the possibilities is endless. Taking over our minds is exactly what they want to do! Their agenda is to implant the thoughtforms that Satan and his fallen angels want us to think about and call into being. It's all part of their seduction, and their hook, lulling us into a hypnotic state, a type of spell, to become so mesmerized by the possibilities that confront earth today that we become like spiritual zombies, pliable in the hands of these deceptive aliens, demons, fallen angels who all serve Satan's hierarchy. When we accept the lie, and take the program and the implant of the false belief system, we have become the inside pawns in this mass deception.

A perfect example is the way UFO enthusiasts fall over themselves to prove their particular theory about the whole phenomena. There is so much contention amongst investigators, as to the type of scrutiny UFOs should fall under, which department of science and what branch of the military, that they all fall victim to the spirit of confusion, frustration as they stay stuck in conflict and dissension. Petty ego battles between the various factions within the UFO community erupt, which is what the Prince of the Power of the Air wants most. Biologists, pilots, seismologists, archaeologists, will exalt themselves as *experts* in the UFO field, yet they still have no proof of what exactly is going on and why, and what it all means. All they know is that UFOs are real, they exist, and that is where their proof ends. They purposely compartmentalized, to keep them in the dark about the bigger picture being played out, of which they are being used as pawns in, mostly unaware of their compromised positions.

Yes, we all know they are real, but to think they are all good, kind, benevolent, is nothing more than wishful thinking. Failing to see the whole picture, which includes what many ancient cultures and spiritual paths have been telling us for millennia, is that the spiritual reality is the true reality. All else is illusion.

The chasm is and has always been between the scientific community and the spiritual, and that is, what science cannot put into a test tube or see under a microscope, science cannot understand or accept. What we need is a new scientific standard which bridges the gap between science and the spiritual reality. Let's face it, the more we understand about the supernatural, the more we understand the scientific and universal laws that govern the supernatural. For, science is the very *mind* of God. Perhaps science needs to approach the investigation of this phenomena from a different perspective in order to understand these mysteries.

The Doctrines of Demons

> "Now the Spirit expressly says that in later times (the last days) some will depart from the faith by giving heed to *deceitful spirits* and *doctrines of demons*, through the pretension of liars whose consciences are seared."
>
> (1Timothy 4:1-3)

New Agers look for scenarios and information that affirms what they already have decided upon as fact. They want to believe that ETs and aliens are good, so they deny all information that they are evil or not to be trusted. They expect ET to fit into their view of the world, and many of them are blindsided by their wishful thinking.

Most New Agers criticize Hollywood for ruining their image of sweet, lovable ET. Many films depict aliens as evil, causing fear, but perhaps Hollywood is handed these types of scripts because there is so much truth in the story line? Often, we see in hindsight that the use of films to prepare people for events, like WWII, are effective. What if films are preparing us for the Revelation when the Beast, the Dragon and Fallen Angels are revealed to humankind out of the *inside* of the earth. When people do see these images, we have some reference point or understanding. Many of the scripts are based on true stories and evidence that has been suppressed, put into a film with creative licensing to make it entertaining and appealing, yet putting forward the truth nevertheless.

The only benevolent ETs are the ones on God's side. The rest are waging war against the Divine decree to give humans grace, to make humans His vessel and to put mortal humans above the angels. This is the spark that started the Luciferian rebellion, as the fallen angels believe they are made from Divine Fire, immortal, and should always be above human beings. God had no right to change the order He had made.

This is why they have used humans as slaves, created racism and religion to keep us in bondage, and continue to pit one of us against the other, one group of us against the other. To top off their disdain for us humans, they continue the misuse and abuse of the human mind through drugs, depression, anxiety, and oppression, coupled with the random and inexplicable abduction syndrome.

The fallen angels and Satan are at war with God over us and over our planet earth. They masquerade as angels of light, ascended masters and ETs claiming they come from some distant star with an historical account that not one of us humans can verify, seeking the unsuspecting to channel their disinformation. They use these channels as vessels to manipulate, deceive and misguide hundreds of thousands of other undiscerning humans who are waiting for ET to come, rescue them, clean up the environment, teach them science, show them the mysteries of the universe and space travel, return from the past, and contact, contact, contact.

On earth, not a single human can travel to and from anywhere without some form of identification. We have passports, driver's licenses and social security numbers to identify who we are, and to prove that we are who we say we are. When we meet an alien, shouldn't we practice the same type of scrutiny? Shouldn't they be expected to show us some form of ID? Yet most people fall for what they say, without question.

Many humans who have had contact, especially abductees, continue to insist that these beings are good, garnering sympathy for the aliens who have told them sad stories of losing their ability to procreate, which is why we humans have been chosen to help them produce a new race of alien/human hybrids, that one day we will all be able to enjoy through reincarnation. We are silly to believe these obvious and ridiculous lies, especially as most contactees and experiencers have been traumatized, raped, probed, and sexually abused by these aliens, bruised, robbed of memory, paralyzed with fear, but we still insist that the aliens are benevolent.

The fallen angels know what we humans want, so they play the role, and tell us what we want and expect to hear, knowing as 'Watchers' what makes us tick, what buttons to press and how to feed our all-too fragile egos. They tell us all kinds of astounding lies in order to make us feel good, but this is only temporary, as their lies are eventually found out. They make so many definite predictions through their various channels that simply fail to come true. They are stuck in a type of cognitive dissonance.

This has happened so many times, books have been written on the outcome, *When Prophecy Fails* by Festinger, Reicken and Schachter who invented a new theory of human behavior - the theory of cognitive dissonance – when these psychologists infiltrated a cult who believed the end of the world was only months away. How would these people feel when their prophecy remained unfulfilled? Would they admit the error of their prediction, or would they, as Festinger predicted, readjust their reality to make sense of the new circumstances?[4]

I am not going to mention names because my purpose is to promote discernment and critical thinking, not embarrass or condemn any one channel. However, if anyone is truly following a particular channeler, all they need to do is test the spirits, go back over past channeling, particularly predictions and measure whether they pass the litmus test of truth. Many do not.

> "For the wrath of God is revealed from heaven against all ungodliness and wickedness of men who by their wickedness suppress the truth. For what can be known about God is plain to them, because God has shown it to them. Ever since the creation of the world his invisible nature, namely, his eternal power and deity, has been clearly perceived in the things that have been made. So, they are without excuse; for although they knew God they did not honour him as God or give thanks to him, but they <u>became futile in their thinking</u>

> and their senseless minds were darkened. Claiming to be wise, they became fools, and exchanged the glory of the immortal God for images resembling mortal man or birds or animals or reptiles."
>
> (Romans 1:18-23)

The consequence then, is that of idolatry and a progressive deterioration of the thinking of the people involved, which results in their minds becoming less and less clear. Idolatry is the worship of anything other than the Creator. That includes the worship of angels, ETs, aliens, planets, stars, animals, goddesses and serpents and the sacrifices made to them.

> '...the sacrifices of pagans are offered to demons, not to God, and I do not want you to be participants with demons.'
>
> (1 Corinthians 10:20)

> 'Do not let anyone who delights in false humility and the worship of angels disqualify you for the prize. Such a person goes into great detail about what he has seen, and his unspiritual mind puffs him up with idle notions.'
>
> (Colossians 2:18)

Angle worship is forbidden. Each time an angel (extraterrestrial messenger) appeared to the men and the women of the Bible, their presence was so awesome that humans would react with fear and then bow down to worship them. The angel ET messenger would respond by saying, 'do not worship me, worship the Lord your God who sent me'. The angel ET messengers worship the Lord themselves. "And when he brought his supreme Son into the world, God said, "Let all of God's angels worship him," (Hebrews 1:6) and they do.

However, the fallen angels *do* want us humans to worship them, as they are in direct opposition with their Creator. They work to deceive and confuse us, which they did to the ancients and continue to do today.

Fallen angels channel to deceive. These are the *doctrines of demons* warned about by the Holy Spirit and Jesus Christ long ago. They want their followers to be undiscerning, with a false sense of security. Consider the Ascension Doctrine so popular now; 'take heart your ascension draweth nigh'. Some people actually believe that they are ascending and becoming more enlightened through consciousness raising practices, do-it-yourself salvation, self-help techniques. This is basically misleading us back to the same lie in the Garden, that we can ascend and be like gods ourselves.

What if they are wrong? How do they know they aren't being misled? What if they are being led down this garden path of ascension only to later find out that they have been following the doctrine of fallen angels and demons sent to deliberately mislead them away from the truth? Does anyone in the Ascension movement have any proof? Has anyone actually ascended yet? See, Book Three: *Who Are The Angels?* my chapter on Ascension or Rapture?[5]

What they fail to realize is they are in an ongoing battle with the Creator on the wrong side. We humans are powerless to save ourselves in the face of such powerful supernatural and technological forces. That is why the Creator created the *Divine Plan of Salvation* through Christ Jesus. See, Book Five: *The Heavens.*

The ascension will indeed occur, it is true. It happens during The Rapture of the Redeemed, when Jesus Christ, Yahuah and His enormous fleet of starships lift all of His faithful believers off the face of the earth, saving them from being caught in the cross fires of the final battle between the Creator and the Fallen Angels of Satan's Army. The worst horrors are planned for us on earth at this time, as the final galactic war takes place on and above our planet. The Bible says that the flesh that does survive at that time will seek death but not find it. So, where will all the self-help, consciousness raising belief go then? The truth of the matter is that we will be crying out for deliverance and salvation, as only God through the Lord Jesus Christ can save us at any time.

Spiritual Whores

A spiritual whore or spiritual prostitute is one who sells their temples to house a fallen angel in exchange for material favors. Among the many examples we see every day are the gurus, mediums, psychics, channelers, hypnotherapists, Ufologists, movie stars. For the goal of becoming famous, all these people open themselves up to having fallen angel demons indwell within them, take over their souls. They will be heedlessly and heartlessly discarded when their usability is finished. In the meantime, the fallen is stealing their right to think and choose for themselves, the freedom of knowing the truth, all the while seducing them into thinking they have been touched by an angel.

> "I will also turn against those who commit spiritual prostitution by putting their trust in mediums or in those who consult the spirits of the dead. I will cut them off from the community."
>
> (Leviticus 20:6)

Yes, even Christians of all denominations have their spiritual whores, those who trade in their freedom, the freedom to live in peace, joy, and love by communing with the Living God, the Holy Spirit, for fame and money from a religious spirit. Religious spirits cause spiritual blindness.

I have come across many in the New Age who claim to be Christian, who want to appear to be enlightened, are self-proclaimed experts, yet mix all kinds of religions together. Not only are these souls in bondage to the demonic which keeps them in spiritual confusion, by encouraging their arrogance and pride, but they are bound to the spirit of unbelief. The power of the Holy Spirit doesn't seem to be more than enough for them. They deny the power of God by giving heed to all sorts of seducing spirits, combining different kinds of religions together to make themselves look spiritually inclusive.

With the spirit of unbelief comes its partner, the deaf and dumb spirit, which is why so many of these New Agers can't see, hear, understand or discern between truth and deception. Today's Roman Catholic Pope seems to be leading this potpourri of all the world's religions to become One Religion, this is exactly what the Antichrist alien agenda is all about, as the End Times Mass Deception.

Giving heed to these *seducing spirits* rather than to the Spirit of God is foolish. The *seducing spirits* are any that cause us to err, like false teachers and false prophets as well as who are under the influence of evil spirits.

It is true that people throughout the ages were prone to pay attention to seducing spirits; but the big thing is some grand apostasy, in which the characteristics would be manifested, and the doctrines held as the scripture warns: "Dear friends, do not believe every spirit, but test the spirits to see whether they are from God, because many false prophets have gone out into the world." (1 John 4:1). Deception is done very subtly and cleverly, and many do not even realize that they have been deceived until it is too late.

The doctrines of devils in Greek translates to the *teachings of demons.* This may either mean teachings about demons, or teachings *by* demons. So many people in New Age circles are in fact doing exactly this, completely ignorant of the fact that they are following the teachings of demons. It is subtle, the way the demons talk to them, and tell them things that they want to hear. Many are put under a hypnotic spell of seduction by these spirits. All the while they are thinking they are being contacted by angels, ascended masters, extraterrestrials, benevolent aliens and special spirit guides, who in the end drag them to disgrace, apostacy, death, and damnation. Discernment is called for here.

The word here rendered in Greek as devils is *daimonia*, which means *intelligences.* This word, among the Greeks, denoted the following things:

(1) A god or goddess, spoken of the pagan gods; compare in New Testament, (Acts 17:18).

(2) a divine being, where no particular one was specified, the agent or author of good or evil fortune; of death, fate, etc.

(3) the souls of people of the golden age, which dwelt unobserved upon the earth to regard the actions of men, and to defend them - guardian divinities, or geniuses;
(4) in the New Testament, where the word denotes a demon in the Jewish sense - a bad spirit, subject to Satan, and under his control; one of the hosts of fallen angels - commonly, but not very properly rendered "devil" or "devils." These spirits were supposed to wander in desolate places, (Matthew 12:43).

Compare (Isaiah 13:21); (Isaiah 34:14); or they dwell in the air, (Ephesians 2:2). They were regarded as hostile to mankind, (John 8:44); as able to utter pagan oracles, (Acts 16:17); as lurking in the idols of the pagan, (1 Corinthians 10:20); (Revelation 9:20). They are spoken of as the authors of evil, (James 2:19); compare Ephesians 6:12, and as having the power of taking possession of a person, of producing diseases, or of causing mania, as in the case of the demoniacs, (Luke 4:33; Luke 8:27; Matthew 17:18; Mark 7:29-30).

According to the prevalent pagan philosophies respecting the departed spirits of the good and the great, who were exalted to the rank of demi-gods, and who, though invisible, were supposed to still exert an important influence in favor of mankind. To these beings, the pagan rendered extraordinary homage. They regarded them as demi-gods and believed that they took a deep interest in human affairs. They invoked their aid. They set apart days to honor them. They offered sacrifices, and performed rites and ceremonies to propitiate their favor. They were regarded as a sort of mediator or intercessor between man and the superior divinities. By biblical standards this would be considered idolatry. Yet Catholicism invokes the intercessors of saints and the Mother Mary to stand between them and the Father (Yahuah) and the Lord Jesus Christ.

The pagans think that they are invoking the spirits of the departed, but what they are getting are demons who mimic the spirits of the dead. This goes on till today. Many of the departed souls are rerouted through the afterlife, some end up in paradise, some in purgatory to be recycled, and then some in hell. The demons, being watchers of humankind, know every detail about the soul's character and personality on earth, and when we the living invoke the dead, the demons step up to the plate instead.

But the Spirit says, 'Some, many, will depart from the faith, giving heed to seducing spirits, who inspire false prophets' (Titus 1:10,14), by 'seducing spirits', working in and through heretical teachers, (1John 4:2, 3, 6,) "the spirit of error," opposed to "the spirit of truth," "the Spirit" which "speaks" in the true prophets against them. The doctrines of devils are literally "teachings that are suggested by demons" (James 3:15), "Satan's ministers." (2Corinthians 11:15).

It is not surprising, then, as his servants masquerade as servants of light and righteousness. This is what is prevalent in the present day New Age movement, as many are following the angel movement, believing they are *lightworkers* yet all the while they are being deceived by counterfeit angels, the fallen angels.

So why does God allow demons to trick the innocent? Believe it or not, demons are *used* by God to bring correction to sinners and bring sinners to repentance. Demons are used to torment energetically and spiritually. They can wreak havoc upon our life, they can steal our peace of mind, interrupt sleep, drain us of energy, create accidents, cause illness, create discord between relationships and create an accursed state. This can only happen if we are in rebellion against God.

Rebelling against the Creator gives demons a legal right to torment us, and hold us in spiritual bondage. For instance, take the sin of unbelief. Those who just are stuck in their unbelief and cannot believe in God or spiritual matters, are attached to the deaf and dumb spirit, which causes the person to be spiritually deaf and spiritually blind and spiritually mute because they refuse to believe. The spirit keeps the person even more unable to believe. Demons are in charge of all that. The only way to purge the devils and become free is through acceptance of the salvation through grace in Jesus Christ. He alone can deliver a person, once they come to Him and choose repentance. Other than that, we are stuck in all types of spiritual bondage through demons. Demons tremble at the name of Jesus Christ, because they know only He has the authority to destroy them. They obey Him and those whom Christ has anointed and empowered. Don't believe me? Then I challenge you, to put your spirit guides to the test.

Notes:

1. Ella LeBain, *Who's Who in the Cosmic Zoo?* Book One – Third Edition, Tate, 2013.
2. Bill Cooper, *Behold A Pale Horse,* "New World Order Planners" p. 177, Light Technology Publishing (December 1, 1991)
3. Ella LeBain, Book Two: *Who Is God?* Chapter Twenty: *The God of this World - Lucifer, Rahab and The Stones of Fire,* p. 322-330, Skypath Books, 2015.
4. Leon Festinger, Henry Reicken and Stanley Schachter, *When Prophecy Fails,* Amazon Digital Services, June 3, 2013
5. Ella LeBain, Book Three: *Who Are the Angels?* Chapter Fifteen: *Ascension or Rapture?* p. 303-337

CHAPTER TWENTY-FOUR

The Masquerade of Ascended Masters and Angels

"The spirits I have summoned up,
I now can't rid myself of."
~ Goethe

As I've mentioned previously, many who believe they channel ascended masters, angels, archangels and even extraterrestrials are in fact channeling the Nephilim, the Watchers, the Fallen Angels. These evil geniuses disguise themselves as angels of light and tell us everything we most want to hear to keep us hooked. The late great Karla Turner, Ph.D., a psychologist who worked with abductees, wrote in her book *Masquerade of Angels*, that those who claimed they were abducted by the Grays all had similar experiences. She concluded that those Grays masqueraded as angels of light, hence the title of her book, which has become the inspiration for this chapter.[1]

> "...For such are false apostles, deceitful workers, transforming themselves into the apostles of Christ. And no marvel; ***for Satan himself is transformed into an angel of light***. Therefore, it *is no great thing if his ministers also be transformed as the ministers of righteousness*; whose end shall be according to their works."
>
> (2 Corinthians 11:15)

When New Agers talk about their guides, we must wonder, do they really know their true identity? Some are given a name, others not, yet they blindly follow the guide because that voice is the loudest voice in their head. They allow themselves to be vessels for who they believe are ascended masters, angels, spirit guides, as they channel them, but do they ever ask any of these beings to show proof of their bona fides? In our world, you can't go anywhere or complete any transaction without proving your identity. New Agers follow the paranormal, and follow the feelings. Many believe they are psychic, because they indeed are sensitive, which is exactly why these fallen angel demons pick them out for contact. It is all in the cleverly seductive game of the demonic which lures them into following the doctrines of demons, just as Jesus predicted would happen in the end of days. (1 Timothy 4:1)

Most of these people are not seeking the Living God and His Holy Spirit directly, but instead call out to these guides and angels. The worship of angels was forbidden by God. The angels of the Lord have repeatedly told us they do not want to be worshipped, that we are not to worship anyone but God. So why are so many people resistant to seeking God directly? Why do we think we need guides, or company? Why not go directly to the Creator for guidance?

Maybe it has something to do with the fact that we become afraid of Him because of sin, which is another name for error, failure, mistake. Adam became fearful of God after he sinned in the Garden. We are embarrassed on a soul level to face God naked. That's why Christ came to be the bridge between humankind and God. The only way to become free of the bondage from these fallen angel demon watchers is to turn to Christ for deliverance.

If you are someone who channels, look at your life. The proof is in the pudding as they say, or as Christ Himself said, 'by their fruits, you will know them.' What are the fruits of the channeling? Is your life free? Are you at peace? Are you healthy? Or are you afflicted with all sorts of illnesses, discomforts, financial hardships, relationship challenges and confusion? If so, then the fruit of these so called ascended masters, spirit guides, ETs and angels that you channel, are deceiving you and what you're involved in is a spiritual trap.

We are told through the *Books of Enoch* that when God purged the earth of the Nephilim, they became the evil spirits locked in the earth realm, to roam the globe and torment us. The Lord did not obliterate them from the spirit realm. These giants continue to this day to harass, torment and deceive us. Many are fascinated with the paranormal. Yes, the paranormal is real, but most people have no idea what they are involved in and *who* they are communicating with and *who* they are invoking. Many have fallen prey to this spiritual trap of seduction and deception.

> "But now the giants who are born from the [union of] the spirits and the flesh shall be called evil spirits upon the earth, because their dwelling shall be upon the earth and inside the earth. Evil spirits have come out of their bodies. Because from the day that they were created from the sons of God they became Watchers: their first origin is the spiritual foundation. They will become evil upon the earth and shall be called evil spirits. The dwelling of the spiritual beings of heaven is heaven; but the dwelling of the spirits of the earth, which are born upon the earth, is in the earth."
>
> (1 Enoch 15:8-10)

Who's Watching the Watchers?

Who runs the universe? The Watchers were originally dispatched to watch the extraterrestrials and aliens come and go. Yet according to the *Books of Enoch,* and the book of Genesis 6, the Watchers ended up mating with the earth women and created the Nephilim and the Judgment of God came upon them as well. So, who is now watching the Watchers?

I am reminded of a *Star Trek* episode which was titled: *Who Watches the Watchers* from *Star Trek: The Next Generation.*[2] Like the Prime Directive, which states that there can be no interference with the internal development of alien civilizations, God's laws of engagement between humanity and all aliens were laid down by the Creator Himself. The Watchers, the sons of the Elohim and their sons, the ET gods, disregarded the Creator God and His directives to their sorrow.

It is an interesting and revealing episode. The *Enterprise* arrives at the planet Mintaka to resupply and repair a Federation outpost being used to monitor the Mintakan people, who are a Vulcan type race living in a Bronze Age stage of cultural development. As the *Enterprise* assists the outpost, an accident causes their holographic image of a rock face to disappear, exposing their ship to one of the Mintakans, who attempts to approach it and is hit with an electrical shock. Dr. Crusher transports him to the *Enterprise* sick bay to help him despite this action violating the Prime Directive. Crusher was able to heal the Mintaken and after wiping his memory of the incident, he is returned to the planet. The crew continue to monitor him and discover the mind wipe was not complete as he recalls an image of "the Picard", and has convinced other Mintakans that the Picard is their god.

This kind of scenario probably happened hundreds of times on planet earth, each time the gods, ancient astronauts, extraterrestrials, angels appeared to humans, helped them, gave them supplies from time to time, performed miracles and then took off in their spaceships and disappeared into the clouds. Early humans regarded these ancient astronauts as gods because of their supernatural and technological powers. Many, but not all, took advantage of being given that title, such as the Annunaki, Nephilim, the Titans. The Bible is full of scriptures relating to the Lord coming and going 'with the clouds', 'in the clouds' and 'riding on the clouds', as well as a number of prophets who were taken up into the clouds with Him, including Ezekiel, Enoch and Paul. My point is that these clouds were used to cloak their spaceships, just as there were holographic strongholds put into place around the planet to conceal many of the ETs true nature. Many may still exist in our world today.

Who watches the Watchers now? We know that The Lord of Hosts' army regularly patrols the space around the earth. We have seen this in NASA videos, where we witness fleets of UFOs shooting what appears to be lasers at other incoming craft and chasing them away.

There is so much footage of this kind, reinforcing the idea that a powerful benevolent force is patrolling our skies, especially the upper atmosphere, making sure that rogue ships do not enter earth's airspace. These are definitely otherworldly technology, not coming from any nation or culture on this earth. NASA film footage taken from the international space stations, and from the space shuttle, have shown that there is most definitely a conflict going on in near space.

As I've explained in Book Three: *Who Are The Angels?* in my chapter on the *Celestial Warriors: Extraterrestrials With Extraordinary Powers,*[3] that the word in the Bible for army is *hosts,* which is the Lord's Celestial army. It is this army, who are regulating and watching the Watchers now.

False Teachers / False Prophets

We have already established that the gods and deities of the past were really extraterrestrials and aliens who had god complexes, and wanted to benefit from the soul energies emitted by us during fear and worship. This is why these pseudo-gods set up a myriad of false religions on planet earth, to keep the theater full, holding early humans in spiritual and material bondage.

Many of these pseudo-gods posed themselves as angels, masters who have ascended into heaven, and star people with various magical powers, when in reality, there were nothing magical about them. It was their advanced knowledge of technology, far beyond any early human intellectual understanding. So, for lack of a better word, our ancestors called it magic. Their ignorance opened the door for many types of psycho-spiritual abuses by these ET pseudo-gods, and over the years demonic intelligences and their evil spirits filled the spirit realm that surrounds planet earth and all of its inhabitants. See, *Books of Enoch,* re: Nephilim[4].

Jesus warned us that "false Christs and false prophets" will come and attempt to deceive even God's elect (Matthew 24:23-27; see also 2 Peter 3:3 and Jude 17-18). The best way to guard yourself against falsehood and false teachers is to know the truth. To spot a counterfeit, study the real thing. If you want to learn to identify the spirit of antichrist in the world, you need to study the reality of Jesus Christ.

Anyone who "correctly handles the word of truth" (2 Timothy 2:15) and who makes a careful study of the Bible can identify false doctrine. For example, a believer who has read the activities of the Father, Son, and Holy Spirit in Matthew 3:16-17 will immediately question any doctrine that denies the Trinity, as well as the ultimate authority of Jesus Christ as King of the Kingdom of Heaven.

Jesus said, "a tree is recognized by its fruit" (Matthew 12:33). When looking for "fruit," determine the accuracy of his or her teaching. What does this teacher say about Jesus? In Matthew 16:15-16, Jesus asks, "Who do you say I am?" Peter answers,

"You are the Christ, the Son of the living God," and for this answer Peter is called "blessed." In 2 John 9, we read, "Anyone who runs ahead and does not continue in the teaching of Christ does not have God; whoever continues in the teaching has both the Father and the Son." First John 2:22 says, "Who is the liar? It is the man who denies that Jesus is the Christ. Such a person has the spirit of the antichrist—he denies both the Father and the Son."

The New Age belief systems of believing in an infinite source is an outright deception, because it is without the Holy Spirit, which is the true infinite source and the last bastion of grace on planet earth. The spirit that most New Agers put their faith in is that of the god of this world, Lucifer. Galatians 1:8 says, "even though an angel from heaven, should preach to you a gospel contrary to that which we have preached to you let him be accursed." An angel from heaven, and there are many fallen angels who are hell bent on preaching all kinds of different doctrines to us, especially at this time, because the days are short, and the battle lines are being drawn. What qualities do the characters of the false teacher and false prophet display? Do they glorify the Lord? Or, as Jude 11 says, "They have taken the way of Cain; they have rushed for profit into Balaam's error; they have been destroyed in Korah's rebellion." In other words, a false teacher can be known by his pride (Cain's rejection of God's plan), greed (Balaam's prophesying for money), and rebellion (Korah's promotion of himself over Moses), or Simon the Magician, who became a follower of Jesus so he could sell Him on the side of the road. Jesus said to beware of such people and that we would know them by their fruits (Matthew 7:15-20).

Galatians, 2 Peter, 1 John, 2 John, and Jude were written specifically to combat false teaching. It is often difficult to spot a false teacher or false prophet. Satan masquerades as an angel of light (2 Corinthians 11:14), and his ministers masquerade as servants of righteousness (2 Corinthians 11:15). Only by being thoroughly familiar with the truth will we be able to recognize the counterfeit spirit. Let's explore how clever the counterfeit is and discern truth from distortion with respect to the Ascension and the I AM/Christ Consciousness Movements.

Exposing I AM Movement/Christ Consciousness

The I AM Movement began with Elizabeth Claire Prophet who took the words of Jesus, when He said, I AM WHO I AM (Ehyeh Asher Ehyeh) and built a whole New Age belief system. Apparently, everyone has an I AM presence in them, and everyone can become Christ. This is the premise for the belief in Christ Consciousness and the Ascension Movement. However attractive this may seem to many, it is Biblically untrue, and misleads many into the spiritual trap set by Lucifer and his fallen angels, into the false belief that anyone can be a Christ or a god.

This is what the whole Luciferian rebellion is about, and why the spiritual battle in the heavens still rages against the Almighty Creator God. The rebels were created beings who wanted to elevate themselves to god status. They came to earth and recreated the court of heaven with trinkets and temples, setting up all kinds of religions so that they could be worshipped and feared. They aren't gods but errant ETs, who fell from their high positions in heaven when they rebelled against the Almighty.

Through various human vessels, they are perpetuating the exact same spiritual attack on the Almighty. Elizabeth Claire Prophet was declared a false prophet by many. Her first husband, Mark Prophet, rejoiced in the coincidence of name, and began taking dictations from mysterious disembodied ascended masters. Both Mark and Elizabeth Prophet allegedly took more than 3,000 dictations from more than 200 different Ascended Masters. The messages, which often quoted the Bible or other scriptures, were published as Pearls of Wisdom, mailed to weekly subscribers and later compiled into annual hardcover volumes.

"The goal of all life is death." ~ Sigmund Freud

Her real name was Elizabeth Clare Wulf, who turned out to be a real wolf in sheep's clothing, in other words, a false prophet. Prophets who prophesy about future events which do not come to pass, are considered false prophets. She founded the Church Universal and Triumphant, as well as Summit University and Summit University Press.

In 1986, a former church follower who had been expelled in a dispute over money was awarded $1.5 million in a suit against Elizabeth Claire Prophet and her church. Gregory Mull alleged that he had been subjected to a form of mind control and proved his case. In the late 1980s, news reports said Prophet expected a nuclear attack by the Soviet Union by 1990, and at least 2,000 church followers headed to her 12,000 acre Montana ranch, stockpiling weapons and supplies. The ranch accommodates a huge underground bomb shelter. So far, as of September 2017, that attack hasn't happened. She died a long slow death of Alzheimer's Disease at the age of 70, which lasted from 1999 to 2009. She did not escape death and ascend to heaven.

> "But there were also *false prophets among the people*, just as there will be *false teachers among you*. **They will secretly introduce destructive heresies, even denying the sovereign Lord who bought them**--bringing swift destruction on themselves. Many will follow their shameful ways and will bring the way of truth into disrepute. **In their greed, these teachers will exploit you** with stories they have made up. Their condemnation has long been hanging over them, and their destruction has not been sleeping.
>
> (2 Peter 1:1-3)

To be fair, Elizabeth Claire Prophet presented truth mixed with misinformation and deception that was channeled by deceptive spirits, demonic intelligences. Jesus said, "By their fruits, you will know them." (Matthew 7:20) Elizabeth was a prolific writer who wrote volumes on ascension, yet she herself did not ascend to heaven in her physical body. Why? Because she channeled false information and mislead thousands.

> "If someone claims, "I know God," but doesn't obey God's commandments, that person is a liar and is not living in the truth."
>
> (1 John 2:4)

Others have followed in Elizabeth Claire Prophet's footsteps by opening themselves up to channel the Great White Brotherhood, which many have claimed is racist, also known as the Brotherhood of Light. The following website; <ascendedmasterindex.com/avatars.htm> lists an index of all the so-called Ascended Masters and their channeled messages, through Therese 'Emmanuel' Grey. Now what's in a name? The modus operandi of the fallen angels and their legion of demonic intelligences is to counterfeit all that is truth, and all that comes from the Almighty Creator and His Christ. Jesus Christ was called 'Immanuel' which in Hebrew means, 'God is With Us'. This channel not only adopts this name, but ends it with the name Grey, which gives the entity attached to it away and reveals its true identity.

I have already established in great detail in Book One of *Who's Who in the Cosmic Zoo?* that the Grays or Greys are demonic intelligences[5], many of which are robotic and artificial, connected through a hive mind which is controlled. I must reiterate what this spiritual war entails: "For we do not wrestle against flesh and blood, but against the rulers, against the principalities, <u>against the cosmic powers over this present darkness, against the spiritual forces of evil in the heavenly places</u>." (Ephesians 6:12) That includes aliens, fallen angels, demons, and discarnate Nephilim spirits, all otherwise known as the 'satans.'

New Agers come back with the argument that, if I am resonating with love and light then surely, based on the Law of Attraction, then that is all I will attract to myself? Not so. Why? Because most New Agers are escaping something that they couldn't face within themselves and in the church. There is a shadow self in everyone, and this is the very reason Jesus came to earth, to forgive humankind of our sins. Sins, mistakes, guilt, shame, blame, pride, rebellion, self-pity, all create the shadow. It is to this unresolved shadow that demons and evil spirits attach. They create a veil of denial, help the person to escape their spiritual reality, which is the burden of unresolved sin, unbroken generational curses, and instead give them a new mind, their mind, which tells them all the wonderful things that they want to hear and supports a new belief system that feels better than the old one.

The Law of Attraction is based on the immutable laws of sowing and reaping. If a person sows lies and denial, they will reap more of the same. The problem with the I AM Ascension Movement is that it is based on dead works. It leads us astray from the narrow path that Jesus Christ spoke of, which is the path to Heaven.

> "how much more will the blood of Christ, who through the eternal Spirit offered himself without blemish to God, purify our conscience from dead works to serve the living God."
>
> (Hebrews 9:14)

> Jesus said, "Small is the gate and narrow the road that leads to life (eternal), and only a few find it."
>
> (Matthews 7:14)

What we do know about those humans who ascended to heaven without dying is recorded in the scriptures. They were all godly men, who listened and obeyed the Lord and did His will above their own will. They were not seeking to do it their own way by searching for their Higher Self, or trying to be a god either. Their light and their love were in serving the Lord, and the Lord took them off the planet without having to pass through death. Enoch was the first man recorded in the scriptures to have ascended, Elijah was also taken up, and of course the Lord Jesus Christ.

The point is, if people want to ascend to Heaven, they need to stick close to the King of the Kingdom of Heaven, and that is the Lord Jesus Christ. The I AM Movement teaches that we must become like Christ, and assume Christ Consciousness, and so does the Bible when it says to put on the mind of Christ (1 Cor. 3:1) and "Do not be conformed to this world, but be transformed by the renewal of your mind, that by testing you may discern what is the will of God, what is good and acceptable and perfect." (Romans 12:2).

There is a huge difference between thinking 'like God', and thinking you are God. This is the very issue that caused Lucifer and one third of heaven's ETs to fall from their high places in Heaven. We are called to be vessels for the Living God. That doesn't make us God, it does, however, make us, 'God-sparks'. There is a difference between being a light, and being the one who created all light and life.

The difference between Satan and Jesus Christ is the difference between pride and humility. As Jesus said, "For everyone who exalts himself will be humbled, and he who humbles himself will be exalted." (Luke 14:11) Lucifer exalted himself above the Most High God and fell from his lofty position in the high heavens. Jesus told his disciples, "I watched Satan fall like lightning from heaven." (Luke 10:18)

The Lord promised everyone who follows and serves Him will have His in-dwelling Holy Spirit. The Holy Spirit is the 'mind of Christ'. One cannot have the mind of Christ without the presence of the Holy Spirit. If the Holy Spirit is not within a person, and they are depending on 'Christ Consciousness', they have the counterfeit spirit. There are many false Christs.

The Holy Spirit gives the manifestation of discernment, which allows every believer to see the difference between the truth and the counterfeit. If the Holy Spirit is not present, the counterfeit spirit can imitate so cleverly that many will fail to see the deception. This is the present condition of our modern high-tech age. The scriptures along with the Holy Spirit are our litmus test.

We are all called to be witnesses and to serve the Living God. "You are my **witnesses,** says the LORD, and my servant whom I have chosen: that you may know and believe me, and understand that I AM He: before me there was no God formed, neither shall there be after me." (Isaiah 43:10) We are not being called to exalt ourselves above others, god or the heavens. We must learn the lessons from history. Each time people have tried to do that, they were brought low. We must acknowledge that the Almighty Creator is greater than all of us, and that He does not like arrogance. So much of New Age thought, despite its love and light philosophy and Christ consciousness packaging, is nothing but arrogant striving.

We cannot ascend or enter into the Kingdom of Heaven without a relationship with the King of the Kingdom. It's that simple. He's the gatekeeper, He is the Judge and the decider of who gets saved, who gets raised up and who gets brought down.

"The fear of the LORD is the beginning of wisdom,
and knowledge of the Holy One is understanding."
(Proverbs 9:10)

I want to illustrate, especially to my New Age readers, how the fluffy, flowery language of a channel is a subtle seduction of the spirit. There is a six-page index of Ascended Masters, (most of whom are self-proclaimed and alien to boot) on Therese Emmanuel Grey's site.[6] This list is obviously way too long to go through each and every individual message and discern truth from lie, so I decided to just pick one, the most famous of all the Ascended Masters, the Lord Jesus Christ. At least we have His own words through the Bible scriptures to compare! My commentary follows each indented paragraph:

> ***"Jesus, Avatar of the Piscean Age-****Like Buddha, Jesus came to show mankind the way, the truth and the life, which is the divine presence of the I AM THAT I AM ensconced in every heart. He came to remind us that we are all Sons and*

Daughters of God and that like, him, we can conquer death and hell, fulfill our mission and ascend home to God. He came to teach us how to walk a path of personal Christhood and become the Christ. This, he affirmed when he said, "These things shall ye do, and greater things, because I go unto my Father." [6]

Firstly, there were many Buddhas. Secondly, none of them said, 'I AM the Way, the Truth and the Life. No man (human) comes to the Father (the Almighty Creator) except through me." (John 14:6) Buddha never claimed that. Buddha did not come to die and shed His Divine blood for the sins of humankind.

The I AM THAT I AM unfortunately is not ensconced in every heart. If this were true then earth would be heaven, but the truth of the matter is, humankind is under a curse. "For from within, out of men's hearts, come evil thoughts, sexual immorality, theft, murder, adultery," (Mark 7:21) "Christ came to redeem us from the curse of the law by becoming a curse for us, for it is written: "Cursed is everyone who is hung on a tree." (Galatians 3:13) As it is written: "There is no one righteous, not even one; there is no one who understands, no one who seeks God. Everyone has turned away. Together they have become rotten to the core. No one does anything good, not even one person." (Romans 3:10,11)

New Agers do not want to face the issue of their sinful state. It is such a downer, it makes them feel guilty, depressed, and ashamed. They are not into that, they want to feel good about themselves, so instead they adopt a spirit of self-righteousness which deceives them into believing that if they just meditate longer, say more affirmations, do more yoga, then they will free themselves of their negative karma. True, Jesus spoke about karma, which in the Bible is the Law of Sowing and Reaping. (Galatians 6:7) Nobody is immune from this law. All of nature submits to this law of cause and effect. Yet, the blood of Jesus Christ was shed to clear the bad karma off humankind. The only catch is, it is not automatic for everyone, you need to accept it, believe on Him, and appropriate it by repenting of all sins both individual and generational in your life. Salvation comes from God Almighty, so no man can boast.

> "For it is by grace you have been saved, through faith--and this not from yourselves, it is the gift of God--not by works, so that no one can boast."
> (Ephesians 2:8,9)

Jesus Christ never said, we were to become *the Christ*. He is the Messiah, the only Lamb of God. Hebrew is much more specific than the English here, which is cause for the channel to misinterpret the word 'Christ' for anointing. The anointing only comes through the Holy Spirit, and to get that, you really need to bring all your sins before Him through confession and repentance, and allow Him to wash you clean. Then comes the anointing of the Holy Spirit. Not the other way around.

In Hebrew, the word Messiah is Mashiach or Moshiach. Mashiach means Messiah, however, Moshiach is an elevated Messiah, an Anointed Savior-King, a Moshiach-Nagid. There is only One Lord and Savior. Everyone can't be Moshiach, or Christ, but we can have the mind of Christ, we can have His Spirit, this is what Jesus taught and the Living Word is testament to that.

Did Jesus really say that? *These things shall ye do, and greater things, because I go unto my Father.*" Here's what He really said: "I tell you the truth, anyone who has faith in me will do what I have been doing. He will do even greater things than these, because I am going to the Father. Whatever you ask in my name, this I will do, that the Father may be glorified in the Son." (John 14:12) The key words here, are those who put their faith in Him and whatever you ask in His name. What He is offering is a partnership. Not for us to become our own *independent* gods or goddesses. The spiritual discernment between the two kingdoms is arrogance verses humility. In the Kingdom of Heaven, humility, being humble wins the battle of good and evil over the kingdom of darkness that promotes arrogance. God hates Pride. And that's what's coming through the Ascension Movement

I can bind and loose anything on earth, in His name, I can ask for anything in His name, I can heal, cast out demons, and if it be His will, even raise the dead, as long as it is all done, in His name. The partnership is a relationship to Him. After all, He paid the debt for us. He offers us a type of blank check, spiritually speaking, that whatever you do in my name, He will honor, as long as you abide and put your faith in Him. (John 15:7)

How many New Agers claim the name of Jesus after their prayers, or actually do the work of the Lord through the agency of the Holy Spirit? I have mingled and dabbled in New Age circles for 25 years, and I never saw one, not a one, say or do anything in the name of the Lord Jesus Christ. Do you see what I'm saying here, it's a counterfeit, and with lots of subtle lies mixed with half-truths. Does it matter? You bet it does, spiritually, which is the difference between those who have the indwelling Holy Spirit, verses those who are possessed by the counterfeit and religious spirit, both of whom are demons.

The only way we conquer death, hell and ascend back to God is through Him. "Then I heard a loud voice in heaven say: "Now have come the salvation and the power and the kingdom of our God, and the authority of his Christ. For the accuser of our brothers, who accuses them before our God day and night, has been hurled down. (who is Lucifer/Satan) They overcame him by the blood of the Lamb and by the word of their testimony; they did not love their lives so much as to shrink from death." (Revelation 12:11)

The road to ascension back to God is through the application and pledge of the blood of Christ, which acts as an invisible wall between the believer and Satan's realm. Coupled with the believers' confession of faith, this is the road to overcoming. We know that the death of the body is not the final death. It is what the Bible calls the second death, which is the death of the soul. Just because a person dies physically, doesn't mean they do not ascend back to God or enter into the Kingdom of Heaven.

Jesus performed miracles because He was God. It's that simple, end of story. He didn't work through many lifetimes to achieve this. He was the Word become flesh. He was there at the foundation of the world, and His mission as Savior of humankind was written into the star configurations before the earth was even formed.

"Come, all who are heavy laden, and I will give you rest." "Many are called, but few are chosen." "He will separate the sheep from the goats." The sad reality is that not every Son and Daughter will make it. Jesus Christ was resurrected by the power of God, because He is God and Co-Creator with the Most High Almighty Father Creator of the Universe, not because He mastered His threefold flame within His heart.

I can say that the threefold flame rhetoric is nothing more than a false belief system, based on deceptive and seductive channeling. The I AM movement began the search for the Higher Self. I have come across many New Agers who have confided in me of their personal struggle to find and connect with their higher self, their I AM Presence. I too followed this belief for some time until I realized that I was being deceived. I turned back to the Lord Jesus Christ for truth and guidance. He is the Great I AM. When you have Jesus living inside of you, you are connected with the I AM Presence, who is the Holy Spirit.

The reason that people struggle to connect with their higher self is because it is blocked by demonic strongholds, you know, the ones who attached themselves to the listener of the channeled messages. Deliverance can only come from one name, and that is through the name of Jesus Christ and the power of His blood and the power of His resurrection.

> "Therefore, God exalted Him to the highest place, and gave Him ***the name above all names,*** that at *the name of Jesus every knee should bow*, in heaven and on earth and <u>under the earth</u>, and every tongue confess that Jesus Christ is Lord, to the glory of God the Father."
>
> (Philippians 2:9-11)

New Agers are famous for doing energy work, clearing the aura from negativity, removing implants and entities. I was very much involved in this type of work for about fifteen years, until I realized that all New Agers were doing, was trading in one demon, disguised as a spirit guide, for another demon/spirit guide. It's kind of like making a deal with the Mafia to pay off your debts. Sure, they're happy to rescue you from the nasty creditor threatening your life, they'll take care it of for you, but then after that, they own you. They will call you when they need you, and if you don't prove yourself grateful and loyal to them, then they wack you.

In the spirit realm, this kind of thing happens all the time. It's actually a spiritual ruse. They all work for the same team, but they have to keep up appearances, make sure that they keep the charade going. The masquerade that they pretend to be your angel, your light being, your spirit guide and ascended master that has come to rescue you, clean up your aura, rid your energy of the nasties and lead you blissfully into your ascension. No problem, the demons, Watchers, Nephilim, grey aliens, know how to pretend. They're master pretenders, and many get academy awards for their performances from Satan.

> *Those who pursue the path of personal Christhood understand that the only begotten son of God refers to the Christ consciousness, not to Jesus as a flesh and blood idol. ~ Channeler, Therese Emmanuel Grey*[6]

Jesus Christ is not some flesh and blood idol, He is the King of the Kingdom of God/Heaven. This is where New Agers miss the mark. Christ consciousness is a false teaching because, as I have said already, in order to have the mind of Christ you need to be consecrated to Him, you need to accept His Kingdom and His Lordship. Accept Him as the Savior of your soul, repent and confess your sins, and accept His blood sacrifice to cover you and wipe away all of your mistakes, ignorance and arrogance. He is returning *in the flesh* and He is with us now, through the agency of His Holy Spirit.

There is more, but I think I've made my point. Channeled material is full of holes, inconsistencies, misinformation, wrong facts and outright deception, oh, yes, it must be packed with love and light, and flowery language and viola, many fall for it, hook, line and sinker. There are demons attached to every channeled message. When you have the Holy Spirit in you, the demons tremble at the name of Jesus. He said, He gives His authority to those who put their faith in Him and follow His precepts. The demons know *Who's Who* in the human zoo. They know which humans have the authority of Christ and which ones are only pretending and masquerading as false prophets and false teachers.[6]

False Teachers and their Destruction

> <u>For if God did not spare angels when they sinned, but sent them to hell, putting them into gloomy dungeons to be held for judgment</u>; if he did not spare

the ancient world when he brought the flood on its ungodly people, but protected Noah, a preacher of righteousness, and seven others; if he condemned the cities of Sodom and Gomorrah by burning them to ashes, and made them an example of what is going to happen to the ungodly; and if he rescued Lot, a righteous man, who was distressed by the filthy lives of lawless men (for that righteous man, living among them day after day, was tormented in his righteous soul by the lawless deeds he saw and heard)-- if this is so, then the Lord knows how to rescue godly men from trials and to hold the unrighteous for the day of judgment, while continuing their punishment.

This is especially true of those who follow the corrupt desire of the sinful nature and despise authority. Bold and arrogant, these men are not afraid to slander celestial beings; yet even angels, although they are stronger and more powerful, do not bring slanderous accusations against such beings in the presence of the Lord. But these men blaspheme in matters they do not understand. They are like brute beasts, creatures of instinct, born only to be caught and destroyed, and like beasts they too will perish. They will be paid back with harm for the harm they have done. Their idea of pleasure is to carouse in broad daylight. They are blots and blemishes, reveling in their pleasures while they feast with you. With eyes full of adultery, they never stop sinning; they seduce the unstable; they are experts in greed--an accursed brood!

They have left the straightway and wandered off to follow the way of Balaam son of Beor, who loved the wages of wickedness. But he was rebuked for his wrongdoing by a donkey--a beast without speech--who spoke with a man's voice and restrained the prophet's madness. These men are springs without water and mists driven by a storm. Blackest darkness is reserved for them. For their mouth empty, boastful words and, by appealing to the lustful desires of sinful human nature, they entice people who are just escaping from those who live in error. They promise them freedom, (or ascension) while they themselves are slaves of depravity--for a man is a slave to whatever has mastered him.

If they have escaped the corruption of the world by knowing our Lord and Savior Jesus Christ and are again entangled in it and overcome, they are worse off at the end than they were at the beginning. It would have been better for them not to have known the way of righteousness, than to have known it and then to turn their backs on the sacred command that was passed on to them. Of them the proverbs are true: "A dog returns to its vomit," and, "A sow that is washed goes back to her wallowing in the mud."

(2 Peter 2:1-22) (NIV)

False Prophets Condemned

"The word of the LORD came to me: "Son of man, prophesy against the prophets of Israel who are now prophesying. Say to those who prophesy out of their own imagination: 'Hear the word of the LORD! This is what the Sovereign LORD says: Woe to the foolish prophets who follow their own spirit and have seen nothing! Your prophets, O Israel, are like jackals among ruins. You have not gone up to the breaks in the wall to repair it for the house of Israel so that it will stand firm in the battle on the day of the LORD. Their visions are false and their divinations a lie.

They say, "The LORD declares," when the LORD has not sent them; yet they expect their words to be fulfilled. Have you not seen false visions and uttered lying divinations when you say, "The LORD declares," though I have not spoken?" 'Therefore, this is what the Sovereign LORD says: Because of your false words and lying visions, I am against you, declares the Sovereign LORD. My hand will be against the prophets who see false visions and utter lying divinations. They will not belong to the council of my people or be listed in the records of the house of Israel, nor will they enter the land of Israel. Then you will know that I am the Sovereign LORD."

'Because they lead my people astray, saying, "Peace," when there is no peace, and because, when a flimsy wall is built, they cover it with whitewash, therefore tell those who cover it with whitewash that it is going to fall. Rain will come in torrents, and I will send hailstones hurtling down, and violent winds will burst forth. When the wall collapses, will people not ask you, "Where is the whitewash you covered it with?"

"Therefore, this is what the Sovereign LORD says: In my wrath I will unleash a violent wind, and in my anger hailstones and torrents of rain will fall with destructive fury. I will tear down the wall you have covered with whitewash and will level it to the ground so that its foundation will be laid bare. When it falls, you will be destroyed in it; and you will know that I am the LORD. So, I will spend my wrath against the wall and against those who covered it with whitewash. I will say to you, "The wall is gone and so are those who whitewashed it, those prophets of Israel who prophesied to Jerusalem and saw visions of peace for her when there was no peace, declares the Sovereign LORD."

"Now, son of man, set your face against the daughters of your people who prophesy out of their own imagination. Prophesy against them and say, 'This is what the Sovereign LORD says: Woe to the women who sew magic charms on all their wrists and make veils of various lengths for their heads in order to ensnare people. Will you ensnare the lives of my people but preserve your own? You have profaned me among my people for a few handfuls of barley and scraps of bread. By lying to my people, who listen to lies, you have killed those who should not have died and have spared those who should not live."

"Therefore, this is what the Sovereign LORD says: I am against your magic charms with which you ensnare people like birds and I will tear them from your arms; ***I will set free the people that you ensnare like birds.*** I will tear off your veils and save my people from your hands, and they will no longer fall prey to your power. Then you will know that I am the LORD. Because you disheartened the righteous with your lies, when I had brought them no grief, and because you encouraged the wicked not to turn from their evil ways and so save their lives, therefore you will no longer see false visions or practice divination. ***I will save my people from your hands. And then you will know that I am the LORD.***"

(Ezekiel 13:1-23)

Notes:

1. Karla Turner, Ph.D., Ted Rice, *Masquerade of Angels,* Kelt Works, Arkansas,1994
2. Gene Roddenberry, *Star Trek: The Next Generation*, Season 3 - Episode 4 *Who Watches the Watchers,* 1989.
3. Ella LeBain, Book Three: *Who Are The Angels?* Chapter Five: *Celestial Warriors: Extraterrestrials with Extraordinary Powers,* p. 114-117, Skypath Books, 2016.
4. *Books of Enoch,* Chapter 15:8-12 – Nephilim, Giants.
5. Ella LeBain, *Who's Who in the Cosmic Zoo?* Book One – Third Edition, Grays p. 248-289, Tate, 2013.
6. Theresa Emmanuel Grey, http://www.ascendedmasterindex.com/avatars.htm, 2009.

CHAPTER TWENTY-FIVE

Time Travel and Teshuva (Repentance)

time trav·el = ˈtīm ˌtravəl/ noun
(in science fiction) the action of traveling through
time into the past or the future.

re·pent = rəˈpent/ verb
feel or express sincere regret or remorse about one's wrongdoing or sin.
feel remorse, regret, be sorry, rue, reproach oneself, be ashamed, feel
contrite; be penitent, be remorseful, be repentant, turn around

To change the past, there is no need to travel in a time machine. Everything can be done by remote control. Here's how it works: From beyond the continuum of time, its Creator looks at where your spaceship is heading right now. From that point, He creates all its trajectory—through the future and through the past. You get through repentance. Repentance changes your trajectory, it's the most important U-turn you will ever make. Repentance changes your destiny from hell to heaven, from sickness to health, from heartbreak to lovingkindness.

This idea is very similar to one of the most effective methods of trauma therapy, called cognitive reframing. Neuroscience has confirmed that we can't destroy memories, but we can provide them new context. That context can entirely "reframe" the picture, so that events of the past that have caused considerable harm can now be rechanneled for good.

Switch the direction your past is sending you. Soon enough, it becomes a different past and consequently a different destiny.

Memories can be replaced with new memories. Thoughtforms can be replaced with new thoughtforms. "And be not conformed to this world: but be ye transformed by the renewing of your mind, that ye may prove what is that good, and acceptable, and perfect, will of God." (Romans 12:2) "Casting down imaginations, and every high thing that exalts itself against the knowledge of God, and bringing into captivity every thought to the obedience of Christ;" (2 Corinthians 10:5)

Your New Life is going to cost you, your old one. We are promised a *New Life* in Christ – "You were taught to put off your former way of life, your old self, which is being corrupted by its deceitful desires; *to be renewed in the spirit of your minds*; and to *put on the new self,* created to be like God in true righteousness and holiness." (Ephesians 4:22-24)

When we repent, there is a sense in which we're seeking to undo damage done. It's almost as if we're trying to undo the past. How seriously should we take this metaphor? Is the past something that can be undone?

Every single prophet's main message throughout the Bible was repentance. Even Yeshua said, *Repent, for the Kingdom of God is near.* (Matthew 3:2) Repentance means to turn around, in Hebrew the word is *Teshuva,* which literally translates into going back in time to a rightful pure state. The repetitive theme of repentance throughout the Scriptures is consistent with the message, that those who repent will be forgiven and their sins will be remembered no more, as if they never happened. We have multiple scriptures promising that *if* we repent, God will cast them out as far as the east is from the west.

> "As far as the east is from the west, so far has He removed our transgressions from us."
>
> (Psalm 103:12)

> "Come now, and let us reason together, saith the LORD: though your sins be as scarlet, they shall be as white as snow; though they be red like crimson, they shall be as wool."
>
> (Isaiah 1:18)

> "Purify me from my sins, and I will be clean; wash me, and I will be whiter than snow."
>
> (Psalm 51:7)

> "I--yes, I alone--will blot out your sins for my own sake and will never think of them again."
>
> (Isaiah 43:25)

Essentially, the promises of God are such that when you repent to the Lord, it's as if it never happened. The sin is remembered no more, the record of it is expunged.

Here are some more scriptures that prove that the Lord completely forgets about your sin when you *return* to Him in heartfelt *repentance*:

> "Then David said to Nathan, "I have sinned against the LORD." And Nathan said to David, "The LORD also has taken away your sin; you shall not die."
>
> (2 Samuel 12:13)

> "I acknowledged my sin to You, and my iniquity I did not hide; I said, "I will confess my transgressions to the LORD"; And You forgave the guilt of my sin. Selah."
>
> (Psalm 32:5)

> "Lo, for my own welfare I had great bitterness; It is You who has kept my soul from the pit of nothingness, For You have cast all my sins behind Your back."
>
> (Isaiah 38:17)

> "I, even I, am the one who wipes out your transgressions for My own sake, And I will not remember your sins."
>
> (Isaiah 43:25)

> 'For behold, the stone that I have set before Joshua; on one stone are seven eyes. Behold, I will engrave an inscription on it,' declares the LORD of hosts, 'and I will remove the iniquity of that land in one day."
>
> (Zechariah 3:9)

> "I, even I, am He that blots out your transgressions for my own sake,"
>
> (Isaiah 43:25)

When we repent to God He wipes away our sins and remembers them no more. This essentially erases the past and changes the future. Repentance changes your destiny! It's a soul thing!

God accepts all who repent, which means to make a U-turn in your thoughts, attitudes, behaviors and lifestyle. Because we are made in the image and likeness of God, Teshuva means to return to one's true self who is your God given soul, your God spark. Time Travel is an ancient Jewish belief from the Torah. The belief that we're made in the image and likeness of the gods (Elohim) is Teshuva brings you back to your original blueprint who is God living in you, through you as you.

Chabad are the Spiritual Jews who believe in reconnecting to the Lord through repentance, good deeds, and outreach to community as vessels for the Lord to be expressed through us. This is exactly what Yeshua the Christ came to teach and fulfill. For we are God's handiwork, created in Christ Jesus to do good works, which God prepared in advance for us to do. (Ephesians 2:10)

Chabad is a Hebrew acronym for Chochmah, Binah, Da'at, meaning Wisdom, Understanding, and Knowledge.

Fasting doesn't forgive sin, but allows repentance which "connects" you to God's Grace of Forgiveness and Restoration back to His image and likeness in you!

Is God a Time Traveler?

According to the definition of time travel, the answer is yes.

> "For a thousand years in your sight are but as yesterday when it is past, or as a watch in the night."
>
> (Psalm 90:4)

> "Beloved, do not let this one thing escape your notice: With the Lord, a day is like a thousand years, and a thousand years are like a day."
>
> (2 Peter 3:8)

> "Behold, You have made my days as handbreadths, And my lifetime as nothing in Your sight; Surely every man at his best is a mere breath. Selah."
>
> (Psalm 39:5)

I have this theory that the allegorical six days of creation in the book of Genesis, is written in God's time, not earth time based on the above referenced scriptures Psalm 90:4 and 2 Peter 3:8. A day is like a thousand years and a thousand years are like a day. Could the six days of the Creation story actually be 6,000 years?

Remember, the position of the earth as it is to where it is now in relation to the sun, may not have always been the same, due to the planet of crossing and disrupting earth's orbit around the sun and more importantly it's position. As I've mentioned in my chapter on Planet X and Nibiru, that pole shifts have happened before, and our earth may have been in other time cycles in the past. Be that as it may, the ancient texts record Methuselah living to be 969 years old.

Ellen Bennet argued that the Septuagint Genesis 5 numbers are in tenths of years, which "will explain how it was that they read 930 years for the age of Adam instead of 93 years, and 969 years for Methuselah instead of 96 years, and 950 years for that of Noah instead of 95 years."[1]

According to Rabbi Avi Shafran, who wrote, *Rosh Hashanah: When Time Travel Is Possible,* on the Jewish New Year, the moon – our measurer of time – goes missing. In its absence, we can go back in time to transform the wrong actions of yesterday into mere accidents.[2]

What powers Jewish time travel is the rare but precious fuel called will. Not any will, of course, but a particularly pure form of the stuff: sincere, wrenching determination to change.

The efficacy of that fuel is revealed in the Talmud, which explains that the process of teshuva, or "repentance," can transform wrong actions committed intentionally into mere accidental acts. And it goes much further. When repentance is affected not through fear or other less lofty means, but rather through pure love of God, it changes sins that were committed with full intent as sins into good deeds.

The Talmudic sage, Reish Lakish, was well versed in the principles of teshuva (repentance). He had lived as a wayward bandit, before reforming his ways and becoming a leader of Rabbinic Judaism. He was one of the first thinkers to claim, explicitly, that your teshuva has the power to change the past.[3]

The Jewish Guide to Time Travel

Essentially the Jewish Talmud teaches that each of us can travel back through time and change the past. In fact, *teshuva*, the word most frequently used for *repentance*, literally means "returning." This is a metaphor to repentance, which is to "return" back into your created pure state, that God created you to be.

To humankind, time goes only in one direction, relentlessly forward. The great Jewish thinker Rabbi Yitzchok Hutner (1906-1980) noted that the term used in Genesis for the role of the sun and moon is *memsheles* which means, "dominion" -- implying dominance, suppression. He said, we are enslaved by time, unable to control it or escape its relentless progression. While our positions in space is subject to our manipulation, our positions in time, not so much. What is subjugating and frightening about time is not only that it brings about suspension, entropy and endings, that each day's passing leaves us "shorter of breath and one day closer to death," as *Pink Floyd* sang about "Time" on their popular *Dark Side of the Moon* album. This means that it is entirely beyond our control.[4]

> "For all that comes under the influence of time, is afflicted with pain."
> Rabbi Shlomo Ephraim Luntschitz

The Talmud tells us that when we honestly confront our misguided actions and feel sorrow for them by resolving not to repeat them, these are the elements of teshuva, it is then when we can reach back into the past and actually change it. Therefore, repentance, frees us from the subjugation of time. This timelessness that is experienced during Rosh Hashanah, is founded on the roots of the theme of *Finding Freedom* that is so prominent to the entire ten days of Awe, the time of Teshuva beginning on Rosh Hashana.

Even the very name of the month which is *Tishrei*, comes from root "shara," that is the Aramaic word for *"freeing"*. The holiday's central mitzvah, is the sounding of the shofar, which is a trumpet call for freedom, associated with *Yovel*, which is the Jubilee Year, when slaves are released. One of the holiday's annual Torah readings is about a Jew named Yitzchak Avinu's release from his "binding". Rosh Hashana is also the anniversary of Joseph's release from his Egyptian prison which precipitated a huge promotion in his life.

Every Prophet in the Old Testament and Jesus Himself, all messaged repentance. It's the most consistent theme in the entire Bible. That when we choose the path of teshuva, we can be made whole again, restored, and inherit the Kingdom. If, however, we fail to repent, and stay stuck in our ways, rebelling to change, or repent, then we lose the inheritances of the Kingdom.

Jesus promised, that all those who put their faith in His ultimate and final sacrifice, by repenting to Him and pinning all of our mistakes, errors, sins, iniquities and transgressions onto His Cross, we will not only be forgiven of all sin, but we will be given the Grace to overcome its power to sin again. This is true deliverance, that is life changing and transcends all time. In this way, we are assured that our repentance will return us to a state of purity through the blood of Yeshua, as His Blood Covenant promises:

> "Come now, let us settle the matter," says the LORD. "Though your sins are like scarlet, they shall be as white as snow; though they are red as crimson, they shall be like wool."
>
> (Isaiah 1:18)

Rosh Hashanah in the Jewish Calendar is a turning point in time. While the sun marks the passage of the seasons, Jews, however, are pointed by the Torah toward the moon to identify the months of the years. The moon, one might say, is the Jewish clock. However, on Rosh Hashanah, the first of the "Days of Repentance," the moon disappears. Of all the holidays in the Jewish year, only Rosh Hashanah, which by definition occurs at the beginning of a Jewish month, to a moonless sky. The Rabbi pointed out, that when we're missing our clock, we are missing our reminder of time. By seizing the first days of the Jewish New Year through our desire to achieve repentance, will in turn allow us to transcend time.

Notes:

1. Bennet, Ellen H. (1897). *Cosmogony, or Creation of the World. Astrology: Science of Knowledge and Reason: A Treatise on the Heavenly Bodies in an Easy and Comprehensive Form*. New York. pp. 30–7. OCLC 11451986.
2. Rabbi Avi Shafran, *Rosh Hashanah: When Time Travel Is Possible,* https://www.haaretz.com/jewish/jewish-world-opinions/.premium-1.675478
3. Rabbi Avi Shafran, *A Jewish Guide to Time Travel,* https://www.rabbiavishafran.com/jewish-guide-time-travel/
4. https://www.haaretz.com/jewish/jewish-world-opinions/.premium-1.675478

CHAPTER TWENTY-SIX

Who is the Restrainer?

Discernment is NOT knowing the difference between right and wrong.
It IS knowing the difference between right and ALMOST right.
(C.H. Spurgeon)

"A wise man will hear and increase in learning,
And a man of understanding will acquire wise guidance,"
(Proverbs 1:5)

Many have hypothesized that *the restrainer*, written about by Paul in 2nd Thessalonians, is the Holy Spirit. The power of the Restrainer is all that is holding back the antichrist, the man of lawlessness, from enacting his Satanic agenda and taking over the earth. As the Holy Spirit is the last bastion of Grace left on the planet, through the Mercy of the Lord, it is not The Restrainer. Humankind may still be saved. Many today are being saved through the agency of the Holy Spirit alone, as I've already written, in countries where it is illegal to even own a Bible. They are being saved through the miracles of the Holy Spirit.

There are too many scriptures referring to the tribulation period and the tribulation saints, as well as the promise of two of the Lord's witnesses to return to earth, to preach the gospel. There are also three extraterrestrial angels preaching the gospel in the air, from outer space, and from the stratosphere over earth before the end comes. (Revelation 14:6-12) This is all done through the divine grace and mercy of God *through* the Holy Spirit. The Holy Spirit obviously does not leave the planet when the Rapture occurs to gather up the body of believers, because many come to the Lord through the Holy Spirit during the end times tribulation period, and are saved.

The strongest argument offered against the Holy Spirit being the Restrainer is the belief that if God's Spirit was ever removed from the earth, no one could then be saved. The removal of the Holy Ghost does not have to be an all or nothing proposition. He is taken out of the way through the removal of many of the vessels, bodily temples where He is housed through the believers' covenant-union with Christ. During the Rapture the whole collective are taken out of the way, which is only a degree of removal. The Holy Spirit Himself remains to bring the carnal Christians, the Jews, the 144,000 Jews from each of the twelve tribes of Israel (Revelation 7 and 14); and the unbelievers who heard the gospel but rejected it, to their *final last call* for salvation before the wrath of the Lord is poured out on the unbelieving and the wicked. (Revelation 16)

Some have also thought that this Restrainer may even be a mighty angel, similar to the powerful angel who holds the key and the chain to the abyss, the one who is appointed to chain up Satan at the end of this timeline before the millennial reign. (Revelation 20:1). Even though the angels, the Lord's faithful extraterrestrial messengers, have a huge role to play during the last days, the one to whom Paul referring to, is not an angel.

The Restrainer is the body of Christ. Once the body of Christ is removed from the planet, then the antichrist can be revealed and assume power. Again, we are back to the discernment between the punishment of God and that of Satan. The wrath of God is reserved for the unbelieving, rebellious and the wicked. The persecution of the Jews and Christians, comes from Satan. Satan persecutes the tribulation saints, not God.

The Lord allows this to happen, because in His mercy He saves them even after they had rejected Him. Because they were left behind, their salvation is dependent on *not* taking the mark of the beast, which is the implant/tattoo that the antichrist decrees all must have in order to be able to buy and sell within his totally digitalized society.

These believers end up suffering for refusing to take his mark, as well as for not believing sooner when they were originally told about salvation through Christ. This includes the 144,000 which have the seals of Christ. (Revelation 7:4) These are Jews from all the twelve tribes of Israel, 12,000 from each tribe. All of these believers, whom the Bible calls saints, end up being persecuted by the antichrist and Satan for believing in Christ. The Lord then pours out His wrath on the wicked, not on His Beloved Bride and Body of Christ who are His sheep.

This is exactly why the Rapture of His Bride, to all those who believe on the Lord Jesus Christ, must happen <u>before</u> the tribulation and <u>before</u> the final antichrist is revealed to the world. The antichrist's rise in power begins the time known as Jacob's troubles, the seven-year tribulation period, which is designed to deceive the world and gather the remaining population to fight a war against the Almighty Creator Lord Himself.

The Lord promises to take His Beloved Bride away before this destined time period begins on the earth, saving them from His wrath poured on the unbelieving and rebellious, but not necessarily saving them from the persecutions of the antichrist. Those caught up in the *great gathering* and *harvest* of believers are the ones who have been faithful to Him by preparing for His coming prior to the tribulation period. At this same time, He extends His Divine Grace to the ones left behind as their very last opportunity to accept Him and save their souls from Satan and from hell in the afterlife. He promises those who come to Him during the tribulation and suffer for His name's sake will be given the crowns of martyrdom in heaven and in His coming millennial Kingdom.

> "Don't let anyone deceive you in any way, for that day will not come until the rebellion occurs and the man of lawlessness is revealed, the man doomed to destruction. He will oppose and will exalt himself over everything that is called God or is worshiped, so that he sets himself up in God's temple, proclaiming himself to be God. Don't you remember that when I was with you I used to tell you these things? **And now you know what is holding him back, so that he may be revealed at the proper time. For the secret power of lawlessness is already at work; but the one who now holds it back will continue to do so till he is taken out of the way. And then the lawless one will be revealed, whom the Lord Jesus will overthrow with the breath of his mouth and destroy by the splendor of his coming.** The coming of the lawless one will be in accordance with the work of Satan displayed in all kinds of counterfeit miracles, signs and wonders, and in every sort of evil that deceives those who are perishing. They perish because they refused to love the truth and so be saved. **For this reason, God sends them a powerful delusion so that they will believe the lie and so that all will be condemned who have not believed the truth but have delighted in wickedness**."
>
> (2 Thessalonians 2:3-12)

The powerful delusion and lie that the world will believe will be that the earth is being threatened by alien invaders and that the nations must gather together to save the planet, usher in the new age, or the fifth dimension, by accepting the gods that Satan chooses. These are the ancient gods who are returning, claiming that they are the creators of the human race and the original owners of planet earth. They try to deceive the remaining population of earth with the false claim that they are here to help them save their planet from the threat from outer space.

Many of these gods will be reptilian in nature, much like the creatures portrayed in the TV movie series 'V', who appeared to be benevolent, human-looking space brothers, but were actually reptilian vampires who had more than one use for human flesh and blood. They need the energy of the human soul. These beings are also known as fallen angels, the beast, the dragon, and the Nephilim, because of their ability to shape shift and appear in many different forms.

This great deception that will occur will be the worst kind of delusion ever in the history of planet earth, perpetrated by the Antichrist, the fallen angels, the rebel gods and the demonic beings that serve them. While physical destruction can destroy the body temporarily, living under the influence and hypnotic spell of deception creates a condition far worse than physical death, as it destroys the human soul and spirit for all eternity. This is the danger most people today face. And as time goes on, the deception will get even deeper.

The Technology of the Rapture

I'm reprinting excerpts from my Chapter discerning, *Rapture or Ascension?* in Book Three, for all those who may be starting with this book, as this piece it too important to leave out, and for those who read *Who Are the Angels?* Book Three in this Five Book Series, will allow you to connect the dots to the rest of this new material, to give you the holistic picture of where all these End Times Scenarios and Prophesies ultimately lead to.[1]

Consider for a moment the possibility of a fleet of intergalactic, inter-dimensional spaceships, capable of containing more than three to five billion people, an approximate number of all the saints of the past since the crucifixion, and all the saints presently on Earth. Imagine the sky filled with invisible spacecraft, and hundreds of millions of people suddenly disappearing. The angels will arrive and quickly circle the globe in their sky chariots, taking up millions of people as they pass. I won't even bother to go into detail about Ezekiel's wheel (Ezekiel chapters 1 and 10), see my chapter[2] on the *Motherships of the Lord*, in Book Two: *Who is God?* as so many others have demonstrated before now that advanced technology is the only thing possibly being described here.

Another likely scenario, which I was shown, is that it's not a bunch of spacecraft, but a Giant Mothership, the size of a planet, that appears at the time of the Great Gathering, and everyone is translated instantly into its light. The Planet Nibiru is said, to be gold and red, and the sign in the Heavens, that Jesus referred to, that precedes His return. In Book Five: *The Heavens,* I prove that the presence and passing of Nibiru coincides with the Rapture, and the Second Coming of Jesus Christ, which are two entirely separate events.

It is also believed by Christians, that this massive arrival will most likely only be visible by the people being taken up, or Raptured. The purpose of this mission will not materialize and be visible to Earth, but simply to gather the saints, by abducting them off the earth in stealth, prior to the great tribulation. The Tribulation period is a time of unparalleled suffering, both in magnitude and intensity, unlike ever before in the history of the world. Note, that while the rapture of the church may not be visible, the massive arrival to occur at the Second Coming of Christ will not be discreet at all. Isaiah 66:15–16 speaks of "chariots like a whirlwind" raining fire down on the Earth.[3]

How does He pull this off, without anyone seeing it? The Rapture is orchestrated by thousands of angels both extraterrestrials and ultra-terrestrials on motherships. The scripture says,

> "After that, we who are still alive and are left will be **caught up** (raptured) together with them **in the clouds** (the Biblical word for spaceships) to meet the Lord **in the air** (in space). And so, we will be with the Lord forever."
>
> (1 Thessalonians 4:17)

We will be 'caught up' together to be with the Lord, He does not come down to earth. The Rapture is done in stealth by angels and with the Lord's light technology. Scripture also says that we will be translated, changed, transferred into our light bodies, non-corporeal, heavenly bodies. This is the *true ascension* into the light body that New Age fallen angels are trying to describe through their various channelings.

> "Listen, I tell you a mystery: We will not all sleep (as in death), but **we will all be changed**--**in a flash, in the twinkling of an eye**, at the last trumpet. For the trumpet will sound, the *dead will be raised imperishable* (incorruptible), and we will be changed. For the perishable (corruptible) must clothe itself with the imperishable, and the mortal with immortality."
>
> (1 Corinthians 15:51-53)

> "Now we know that if the earthly tent we live in is destroyed, **we have a building from God, an eternal house in heaven, not built by human hands**. We grow weary in our present bodies, and we long to put on our heavenly bodies like new clothing."
>
> (2 Corinthians 5:1, 2)

> "For the Lord himself will come down from heaven, with a loud command, with the voice of the archangel and with the trumpet call of God, and *the dead in Christ will rise first*. After that, we who are still alive and are left **will be caught up together with them *in the clouds* to meet the Lord *in the air***. And so, we will be with the Lord forever."
>
> (1 Thessalonians 4:16, 17)

The dead shall rise first, who are in the holding place *inside* the earth, known as Abraham's bosom. Then those on the earth will be 'caught up', bodies are changed, a transformation taking place that no one sees, except maybe NORAD. By the time they register it on their radar, it will have been over and the seven-year tribulation period, known as the time of Jacob's trouble begins. This is the green light for the Beast, the Antichrist to reveal himself to the world, and begin his plan for world domination.

Christ will *appear* visibly only to the saints in the air, in space, during the rapture of the church. The Greek word for *appear* is *phaneros,* meaning "to shine," "be apparent," "manifest," or "be seen," found in John 2:28, 3:2; 1 Peter 5:4; Colossians 3:4. Christ is to appear to the saints in the air at the rapture, but nothing is said of His appearing to the rest of Earth.[4]

During the rapture of the church, Christ will never set foot on Earth, but rather fly above it in the air. As soon as all the dead in Christ have met Him in the air, He will return to heaven with them to present them blameless before God (John 14:1–3; 1 Thessalonians 3:13, 4:16–17, and others). The rapture of the church is a New Testament doctrine never revealed to anyone in the Old Testament; it was first alluded to by Jesus (Luke 21:34–36), and then revealed to Paul in detail as a special revelation (1Corinthians 15:51–58; 2 Thessalonians 2:6–8).[5]

According to Milor, "the following passage reveals a mystery, and confirms that the rapture happens *prior* to the tribulation period and *prior* to the revelation of who the final Antichrist will be. To this day, nobody knows who the Antichrist is, there are many speculations, yet, he is being 'restrained' by the very presence of the believers on the earth."

The believers are literally 'holding space' for Christ on earth, as they are considered to be his representatives and ambassadors on earth, heaven on earth. Especially those believers who are filled with the Holy Spirit carry the vibration, frequency, and mind of Christ on earth. Together they collectively make up the body of Christ which is the Restrainer talked about in 2 Thessalonians 2:8. I am repeating this verse, for emphasis, and have combined in brackets the translations of both the American King James version with the New International Version just for the purpose of further elucidation.

> "And you know what is restraining him now so that he may be revealed in his time. For the secret power of lawlessness (the mystery of iniquity) is already at work; but the one who now holds it back will continue to do so till he is taken out of the way. **(until he [the church] be taken out of the way [raptured])**. And then the lawless one (Wicked one [the Antichrist]) will be revealed, whom the Lord Jesus will overthrow (consume) with the breath (spirit) of his mouth (His Word) and destroy by the splendor (brightness) of his coming.
>
> (2 Thessalonians 2:6–8)

Another mystery revealed and prophesied in 2 Thessalonians 2:8, is that at the time of the second coming of Jesus Christ, he defeats the Antichrist with a Word that comes forth from the spirit out of his mouth. Of course, nobody knows what that final Word will be, but we do know based on scripture, that the Word of God is the Sword of the Spirit. (Ephesians 6:17)

> "For the word of God is living and powerful. Sharper than any double-edged sword, it penetrates even to dividing soul and spirit, joints and marrow; it judges the thoughts and attitudes of the heart."
>
> (Hebrews 4:12)

This unequivocally proves that the disappearance of the body of believers will either precipitate the coming seven-year tribulation, or at the very least, happen during the half way mark, when all hell breaks loose on earth. This is a time where darkness reigns, when Antichrist rises up and all the prophesies in Daniel and Revelation about the desolation of abomination occur. The Antichrist sets himself up in the rebuilt third temple in Jerusalem, and demands Israel and the world to worship him as god.

As I laid out in my thesis in Book Three: *Who Are the Angels?* in my chapter discerning *Rapture or Ascension?* that I started out as a Pre-tribber, but then moved to a Mid-tribber, and am now a "Pan-tribber", meaning, it's all going to pan out, just as God wills and plans it, in His Divine Timing.[1] I am not a date setter, nor do I want to predict when this stealthy event will likely take place, however, it is most definitely something to prepare our hearts and souls for, as only those whom are of the Harvest of the Angels of Heaven, are going to be part of the Great Gathering, known as the End Times Rapture.[6] However, I have no doubt, that it will happen at the eleventh hour, when the world is on the brink of destruction, that the Bridegroom will rescue His Beloved Bride and Body of Christ from what will be felt as the wrath of God upon the Earth.

"For God ***did not appoint us to suffer wrath***
but to receive salvation through our Lord Jesus Christ."
(1 Thessalonians 5:9)

Another Christian scholar who believes that the rapture will happen before the tribulation, is John Walvoord. In his book, *The Rapture Question*, he includes 50 reasons based on scripture to prove the point.[7] I am including 10 reasons here:

1. Revelation 3:10 - The Promise of from the hour of trial; Greek, 'Ek' means exit.
2. Revelation 6:16; 1 Thessalonians 5:9 - Church is <u>not</u> the object of God's wrath.

3. Luke 21:36 - Escape (not endure) tribulation.
4. Luke 21:28 - Look up (not out); redemption.
5. 2 Corinthians 5:20 - War: calling all ambassadors home.
6. 2 Thessalonians 2 - The Restrainer (church) is removed <u>before</u> Antichrist is revealed.
7. 1 Corinthians 15:51 - In the twinkling of an eye; not an extended activity.
8. 1 Corinthians 15:52 - In the air, not the earth.
9. Revelation 12:5 - Woman is Israel not the church.
10. Revelation 19:11-14; Marriage supper: in heaven includes those raptured before.[6]

The church, the group of believers in Jesus Christ, is called both the Body of Christ and the Bride of Christ in the scriptures, Ephesians 5:22-23; Romans 7:14; 2 Corinthians 11:2; James 4:4. Paul talks about the union of the Bridegroom in Ephesians 5:3. The Bride of Christ is excluded from God's wrath being poured out on the earth during the great tribulation period in 1 Thessalonians 5:9; Revelation 3:10.

After the rapture of the church, those who sat on a fence for Christ, those people from all over the world who have heard the truth of the gospel but did not believe until the events prophesied took place, will recognize the events and many will turn to Jesus Christ and be saved. These are the ones who will have to endure the persecutions of the Antichrist. It says in Daniel 7:21 that the antichrist has the power to make war on the saints, the believers in Christ. Revelation 13:7 says that he will overcome the saints. Many will be martyred for Christ, and will be resurrected at the time of the second coming. These people are the Tribulation Saints.

EVANGELICAL EXTRATERRESTRIALS

The Three Extraterrestrial Angels who preach the gospel to the world:

> "And I saw another angel flying in midheaven, having an eternal gospel to preach to those who live on the earth, and to every nation and tribe and tongue and people; and he said with a loud voice, "Fear God, and give Him glory, because the hour of His judgment has come; worship Him who made the heaven and the earth and sea and springs of waters."
>
> And another angel, a second one, followed, saying, "Fallen, fallen is Babylon the great, she who has made all the nations drink of the wine of the passion of her immorality."

Then the third angel or extraterrestrial messenger preaches doom for all those who worship the Beast and his image, which could be a hologram.

> "Then another angel, a third one, followed them, saying with a loud voice, "If anyone worships the beast and his image, and receives a mark on his forehead or on his hand, he also will drink of the wine of the wrath of God, which is mixed in full strength in the cup of His anger; and he will be tormented with fire and brimstone in the presence of the holy angels and in the presence of the Lamb. "And the smoke of their torment goes up forever and ever; they have no rest day and night, those who worship the beast and his image, and whoever receives the mark of his name." Here is the perseverance of the saints who keep the commandments of God and their faith in Jesus."
>
> (Revelation 14:6-12)

> "Do not let your hearts be troubled. Trust in God; trust also in me. In my Father's house are many mansions (dwelling places): if it were not so, I would have told you. I go to prepare a place for you. And if I go and prepare a place for you, I will come again, and receive you to myself; that where I am, there you may be also."
>
> (John 14:1–3)

The Rapture differs from the Second Coming, which is when the Lord returns in all His glory with this huge fleet of starships from all over the universe. The rapture of the church will occur before the great tribulation (Luke 21:34–36; 2 Thessalonians 2:6–8; Revelation 1:19; 4:1).

The kingdom of darkness reigns on earth right now. It is restrained and limited by our presence on earth, which, while not exactly living in the Kingdom of God, is yet keeping the worst from happening. This is why believers pray all over the globe, "Thy Kingdom come on earth, as it is in Heaven." Those of us who pray for the Kingdom of Heaven to come to Earth are actually bringing it in. It's similar to an invocation, eventually, it will appear. The return of Christ at the Second Coming precipitates the coming Kingdom of Heaven which is to be established on the earth.

The prophesy states that Yeshua HaMashiach who was born of the bloodline of the line of King David, the root of Jesse, is to literally rule from David's throne in Jerusalem. The return of Jesus Christ to rule as King is referenced 1,845 times in the Old Testament, with 17 books giving prominence to the event. There are 318 references in the New Testament, including 216 chapters, and 23 out of 27 books giving it prominence.[7]

> "Your dead will live; Their corpses (dead bodies) will rise. You who lie in the dust, awake and shout for joy, for your dew is as the dew of the dawn, And **the earth will give birth to the departed spirits**. Go, my people, *enter your rooms and shut the doors behind you; hide yourselves for a little while until his wrath has passed by.* See, the LORD is coming out of his dwelling to punish the people of the earth for their sins. The earth will disclose the bloodshed upon her; she will conceal her slain no longer."
>
> (Isaiah 26:19-21)

This relates to the tribulation and to the second coming of Christ. The tribulation period is the time the Lord's wrath being poured out on the earth. This begins when the scrolls are broken as mentioned in Revelation. It is the time of the Antichrist, when Satan's hierarchy gets the upper hand, the demonic rules and torments the unbelievers. Yet at the same time, scripture tells us that the Holy Spirit causes many to turn to the Christ after they realize what has happened.

This is known as the time of Jacob's troubles, the worst persecution for Jews and for Christians in the entire history of the earth. Israel is brought to the very brink of destruction. The holocaust killed one out of every three Jews alive on the planet at that time, but during the great tribulation, it is estimated that two out of every three Jews will perish. (Daniel 12:1) Only a remnant of one third will be saved.

It is interesting that this one-third ratio is constant repetitive theme throughout history. I believe it is rooted in the original rebellion when Lucifer persuaded one-third of all extraterrestrial angels to follow him in a rebellion against the Creator.

The purpose of the great tribulation is to get Israel and the unbelievers to acknowledge the sin of rejecting the Messiah, who is Yeshua HaMashiach, Jesus the Christ.

> "I will go and return to my place, till they acknowledge their offense, and seek my face: in their affliction they will seek me earnestly (eagerly look for me)."
>
> (Hosea 5:15)

In his DVD, *The Rapture*, Chuck Missler[8] proves that there are distinctly two 'buckets' (sic) of scriptures that refer to the promise to come for His Bride, the body of Christ, the assembly of believers, which is the Rapture. The other is to fulfill His commitment to Israel with his second coming to take back the throne of David and establish His Kingdom of Heaven on Earth.

These are clearly two separate events:

The Rapture	**The Second Coming of Christ**
Translation; saints go to heaven	Sets up Kingdom, translated saints return to earth
Earth not judged	Earth is judged
Imminent, any moment,	Follows definite predicted signs
Not in the Old Testament	Predicted in the Old Testament
For believers only	Affects all men on earth
Before the day of wrath	Concludes the day of wrath
No reference to Satan	Satan is bound for a thousand years
He comes for his own	He comes with his own
He comes in the air	He comes to the earth
He claims the Bride	He comes with his Bride
Only His own see Him	Every eye shall see Him
Great tribulation begins	Millennial reign begins

The Second Coming

When Yeshua Jesus Christ returns, the scripture tells us that unlike the Rapture, every eye will see Him, and all the nations will mourn for the one whom they pierced.

> "And I will pour out on the house of David and the inhabitants of Jerusalem a spirit of grace and supplication. <u>They will look on me, the one they have pierced, and they will mourn for him as one mourns for an only child, and grieve bitterly for him as one grieves for a firstborn son</u>."
>
> (Zechariah 12:10)

> "At that time the sign of the Son of Man will appear in the sky, <u>and all the nations of the earth will mourn</u>. They will see the Son of Man coming <u>on the clouds of the sky, with power and great glory</u>."
>
> (Matthew 24:30)

As I've mentioned in my chapter on the Cloudships, that each time the scripture reads, 'on the clouds' or 'with the clouds' it is referring to the Lord's spaceships, which are filled with light and the glory of God. The heavens declare the Glory of God, (Psalm 19:1) indicates this massive fleet of starships, mansions in the sky that travel amongst the stars.

Unlike the Rapture, everyone on earth will recognize Yeshua Jesus when He returns. The Rapture is done in stealth, the Lord doesn't even put one foot upon the earth, but when He returns, everyone sees Him. He comes to end the battle of Armageddon, fought between the celestial armies of heaven, the faithful extraterrestrials who serve the Office of Christ, against the demonic alien armies of Satan's kingdom. Under the Antichrist, this will include the armies of the earth.

Many Hollywood movies depict a fictional time where earth is invaded by alien spacecraft, warring with each other and with earthlings. Many of these movies are prophetic in the sense that this scenario, which is everyone's worse nightmare, will manifest during the reign of the Antichrist. Movies like *Independence Day, The War of the Worlds,* and even *Star Wars,* foretell of a future time where our skies will be filled with alien invaders, fire from heaven, different kinds of spaceships, deadly alien technology, and terror.

This will happen during the final days, when the gods of the past will return through the stargates, wage war against their Creator over the earth and over its population. Even though they all struggle among themselves for power, as we have seen through their many mythologies, they will all team up with Satan's army against the Lord in the end.

Yeshua Jesus returns with His massive fleet of angels, faithful extraterrestrials from all four corners of the universe, and ends the great celestial war with a Word (2 Thessalonians 2:8). The earth and everything on it will be destroyed by fire, and then He will establish His Kingdom of Heaven on the purified earth. This begins His millennial reign on earth, and everything is transformed. (Daniel 2:44,45; 7:13,14; 7:18; Isaiah 9:6,7; Luke 1:32,33; Revelation 11:15)

Most people know that one of the most visible events that must come to pass before the end can come is the rebuilding of the third Jewish temple in Jerusalem on the Temple Mount, Mount Moriah. At this time, the Dome of the Rock, which is the second holiest temple in the world of Islam, remains over the site of the second temple. I have always felt that some kind of natural disaster will occur to destroy it, such as an earthquake. Israelis wouldn't war with Muslims over this, and have always tolerated the religious diversity which is Jerusalem.

The prophecy in Daniel 9 tells us that the Antichrist will sit in the rebuilt temple and claim to be god and demand worship. "He will oppose and will exalt himself over everything that is called God or is worshiped, so that he sets himself up in God's temple, proclaiming himself to be God." (2 Thessalonians 2:4) But before that can happen, the ancient Ark of the Covenant must be found, where the spirit of God once sat upon the mercy seat. The Ark of the Covenant has been missing since ancient Babylon, today's Iraq, invaded Israel, over two thousand years ago. See, my Chapter, *Ark of the Covenant.*

In order for the Antichrist to persuade all the world that he is the messiah of Israel, the Ark of the Covenant must be found and placed within the temple. Here he will sit upon it, all described by the prophet Daniel as the 'abomination of desolation'. (Daniel 9:27; 11:31; 12:7-11; Matthew 24:15; Mark 13:14) With the level of technology available to us today, highly charged devices such as the Ark of the Covenant could be found with sensitive metal detectors.

There are literally scores of scriptures from Genesis through Revelation that point to the second coming of Yeshua Jesus, too many to reference all of them here. However, I will focus on a few choice passages.

> "See, the LORD is coming with fire, and his chariots are like a whirlwind; he will bring down his anger with fury, and his rebuke with flames of fire. For with fire and with his sword the LORD will execute judgment upon all men, and many will be those slain by the LORD."
>
> (Isaiah 66:15, 16)

Before the millennial Kingdom of God can be established on the earth, the Lord is going to destroy it and all of its inhabitants. Remember those who are destined to be saved during the tribulation period, will die in the Lord (Revelation 14:13) and their bodies will be raised during the resurrection. The rest of the people who join the Antichrist's army against the Lord of Heaven will experience the wrath of God in what has long been called the Day of Judgment. This will be worse than any Hollywood movie could ever depict, because no one will be left. The earth will be destroyed by fire.

> "Immediately after the tribulation of those days the sun will be darkened, and the moon will not give its light, and the stars will fall from heaven, and the powers of the heavens will be shaken."
>
> (Matthew 24:29)

The stars falling from heaven are all those rebel extraterrestrials who joined Lucifer's rebellion against the Lord. This points to their end, as '*the powers of the heavens will be shaken*' means that the Lord will destroy their planets, their space portals and even their star systems. This will be a truly ominous time.

Notes:

1. Ella LeBain, *Who Are the Angels?* Book Three, Chapter Fifteen: *Ascension or Rapture?* p. 303-337, Skypath Books, 2016.
2. Ella LeBain, *Who is God?* Book Two, Chapter Four: *Motherships of the Lord*, p. 71-88, Skypath Books, 2015.
3. John Milor, *Aliens and the Antichrist, Unveiling the End Times Deception,* p. 132 iUniverse, 2006.
4. Milor, p. 147
5. Milor, p. 148
6. Ella LeBain, *Who Are the Angels?* Book Three, Chapter Fifteen: *Rapture or Ascension?* p. 303-337, Skypath Books, 2016.
7. John Walvoord, *The Rapture Question,* p.271, Zondervan, 1979.
8. Dr. Chuck Missler, DVD: *The Rapture: Christianity's Most Preposterous Belief,* Koinonia House, Coeur d'Alene, ID, 2010.

CHAPTER TWENTY-SEVEN

Prophesies, Blessings & Curses of The Twelve Tribes of Israel

"The city wall was broad and high, with twelve
gates guarded by twelve angels.
And the names of the twelve tribes of Israel were written on the gates."
(Revelation 21:12)

"Then I heard the number of those who were sealed:
144,000 from all the tribes of Israel. From the tribe of Judah
12,000 were sealed, from the tribe of Reuben 12,000, from
the tribe of Gad 12,000, from the tribe of Asher 12,000,
From the tribe of Naphtali 12,000, from the tribe of Manasseh 12,000,
From the tribe of Simeon 12,000, from the tribe of Levi 12,000,
From the tribe of Issachar 12,000, from the tribe of Zebulon 12,000,
From the tribe of Joseph 12,000, from the tribe of Benjamin 12,000."
(Revelation 7:4-8)

Bible prophesy promises that 12,000 members of each of the twelve tribes of Israel are going to be sealed with the mark of God, as opposed to the mark of the Beast. They are sanctified unto the Lord. Who are these people? Where are the descendants of these tribes today? Let's investigate with discernment...you may be surprised to learn that you may be part of this Divine Plan.

Who is Israel? There were originally 12 tribes of Israel until Joseph's tribe was split into Ephraim and Manasseh. Then there were 13 tribes. The Jews (the tribe of Judah) is only one of those tribes. All Jews are Israelites, but not all Israelites are Jews. There were 10 tribes of the Northern Kingdom and 3 tribes of the Southern Kingdom, who were the Jews = tribes of Judah, Benjamin and Levi. The 10 Northern Tribes were dispersed among the nations of the world, known as the Lost Tribes.

"He who scattered Israel will gather them and will watch over his flock like a shepherd."

(Jeremiah 31:10)

Jesus said, "I was sent ONLY to the lost sheep of the house of Israel."

(Matthew 15:24)

Before we can know the future, we have to understand the past. The twelve tribes of Israel are descended from Jacob's twelve sons. Jacob's name was changed to Israel after he wrestled with an angel of the Lord. Israel means, *he who struggles with God and prevails.* What is eye-opening are the blessings and curses that were pronounced upon his sons by Jacob for their deeds. When we look into generational curses, as it says:

"Then the Lord passed by in front of him and proclaimed, "The Lord, the Lord God, compassionate and gracious, slow to anger, and abounding in loving kindness and truth; who keeps loving kindness for thousands, who forgives iniquity, transgression and sin; yet He will by no means leave the guilty unpunished, visiting the iniquity of fathers on the children and on the grandchildren to the third and fourth generations."

(Exodus 34:6-7)

"You shall not worship them or serve them; for I, the Lord your God, am a jealous God, visiting the iniquity of the fathers on the children, and on the third and the fourth generations of those who hate Me,"

(Exodus 20:5; Deuteronomy 5:9)

While these scriptures are the basis for generational curses, there are contradicting scriptures that says:

"Fathers shall not be put to death for their sons, nor shall sons be put to death for their fathers; everyone shall be put to death for his own sin."

(Deuteronomy 24:16)

"The person who sins will die. The son will not bear the punishment for the father's iniquity, nor will the father bear the punishment for the son's iniquity; the righteousness of the righteous will be upon himself, and the wickedness of the wicked will be upon himself."

(Ezekiel 18:20)

If this is true, then how is it that many children grow up to bear generational curses that come from the sins of their ancestors? Exodus 20:5 lists one of the Ten Commandments, which is the basis for all law, particularly moral law. According to Covenant Law, when a father misleads his family, the effects of that transgression are often felt for generations. This is because the father has been covenantally unfaithful to the Lord God who stipulated that there are punishments and consequences to breaking the covenant with Him.

That is the process of the sins of the fathers (parents) being visited upon the children. If a father (and mother) rejects the covenant of God and takes the family into sin, the children will suffer the consequences, often for several generations. While this may not seem fair, it is all about bloodlines, karma and spiritually binding legal covenants with either the Lord or with Satan. Both covenants are ever-lasting unless consciously broken by a descendant, hence the perpetuation of generational curses and blessings, both rippling out through their generations.

A new covenant was made available to all of humanity when Yeshua, Jesus Christ, came to break the power of sin upon humanity through his victory on the cross.

> "Christ redeemed us from the curse of the law by becoming a curse for us, for it is written: "Cursed is everyone who is hung on a tree."
>
> (Galatians 3:13)

The good news is that ALL generational curses can be broken regardless of the sin or the contract with Satan, by any descendant from any bloodline who through faith appropriates the power of the cross, the power of the blood of Christ, and the power of the resurrection upon themselves and their descendants, which turns the curses into blessings.

As with most families, there are dramas, betrayals, disappointments and victories. With that said, let's take a look at how the twelve tribes were formed, what were their blessings and their curses, and where they are today.

> "And Jacob called to his sons, and said, Gather yourselves together, <u>that I may tell you *that* which shall befall you **in the last days**</u>. Gather yourselves together, and hear, you sons of Jacob; and listen to Israel your father."
>
> (Genesis 49:1-2)

A Brief Historical on the Twelve Tribes

1. <u>Reuben</u>. Firstborn son of Jacob and Leah and father of the tribe of Reuben. His name comes from the Hebrew meaning: *"Look, a son."* He appears in the story of

the mandrakes as the one giving them to his mother (Genesis 30:14). He succeeded in convincing his brothers not to kill Joseph but to trap him inside of a pit instead (Genesis 37:22). Later, when the family journeys to Egypt during the famine, he attempts to persuade his father that he should take responsibility for Benjamin while in Egypt (Genesis 42:37).

Reuben has relations with Jacob's concubine Bilhah, angering Jacob and probably contributing to the curse of Reuben on Jacob's deathbed "Reuben, you are my first-born, my might, and the beginning of my strength, the excellency of dignity, and the excellency of power: Unstable as water, you shall not excel; because you went up to your father's bed; then defiled you it: he went up to my couch." (Genesis 49:3-4). A generational curse. The tribe of Reuben settled west of the Jordan River and agreed to join the other tribes in the war against the Philistines. However, the role Reuben's tribe diminished significantly as a consequence of their transgressions.

2. Simeon. Second son of Jacob and Leah and father of the tribe of Simeon. His name in Hebrew means *"HaShem* (The Name, God) has heard that I was unloved" (Genesis 29:33). He and his brother Levi destroyed the entire village of Shechem in retribution for the rape of their sister Dinah (Genesis 34). Simeon was a part of the plot to sell his brother Joseph into slavery. After the family was invited to Egypt during the famine in Canaan, he was appointed as the individual to stay behind as collateral for Benjamin so that his brothers would return from Canaan. The tribe of Simeon lived in the southernmost part of the Land of Israel. This tribe dwelt in relative obscurity, and had very little impact on the history of Israel.

Both Simeon and Levi bear a generation curse: "Simeon and Levi are brothers; instruments of cruelty are in their habitations. O my soul, come not you into their secret; to their assembly, my honor, be not you united: for in their anger they slew a man, and in their self-will they dig down a wall. Cursed be their anger, for it was fierce; and their wrath, for it was cruel: I will divide them in Jacob, and scatter them in Israel." (Genesis 49:5-7)

3. Levi. Third son of Jacob and Leah and father of the tribe of Levi, from whom the Levites are descended. Since Leah had already given Jacob two sons, she said "*Now my husband will be joined with me*" (Genesis 30:34). The Levites were distinguished as servants of God because of their refusal to worship to Golden Calf (Exodus 32:26-29). Through this act of faithfulness in the wilderness, this tribe would become set apart by God, and did not receive a portion of the inheritance of the land as the other tribes did.

Levi's own three sons, Gerhson, Kahath and Merari, became Temple servants. After Levi's sister Dinah was molested by Shechem, he and his brother Simeon destroyed the entire town. Levi was later involved in the plot to sell his brother Joseph into slavery. The Levites became the Cohanes, who were the priests sanctified unto

God. Their descendants later became the Sanhedrin, the body of High Priests who ordered the murder of Yeshua, the Messiah of Israel.

There is a generational curse, known as the High Priest Curse, which is written in Matthew 27:20-25 which says, "But the chief priests and the elders persuaded the crowd to ask for Barabbas and to have Jesus executed. "Which of the two do you want me to release to you?" asked the governor. "Barabbas," they answered. "What shall I do, then, with Jesus who is called Christ?" Pilate asked. They all answered, "Crucify him!" "Why? What crime has he committed?" asked Pilate. But they shouted all the louder, "Crucify him!" When Pilate saw that he was getting nowhere, but that instead an uproar was starting, he took water and washed his hands in front of the crowd. "I am innocent of this man's blood," he said. "It is your responsibility!" <u>All the people answered, "**Let his blood be on us and on our children**</u>!"

Art Mathias writes in his *Wellspring School of Ministry Workbook,*[1] about the High Priest Curse based on Matthew 27:25, The Jews quickly assumed full responsibility for His death: "We accept the punishment for such a crime; let it be upon us and upon our children." This is known as a generational curse.

In the siege of Jerusalem in 70 A.D., the Romans crucified the Jews in such numbers before the walls that the Romans wanted more room for crosses. Multitudes in the city died of famine until the valleys outside were filled with them. Titus himself groaned and threw up his hands in horror and called God to witness that he was not responsible. No fewer than 600,000 who were thrown out the gates were counted by the Romans. Altogether 1,100,000 Jews died; 97,000 were sold as slaves for trifling prices; 40,000 were freed because no one bought them; and 347,490 more, plus multitudes not counted, perished in many other ways.

Their children have gone through untold suffering in all lands for ages. They are yet to suffer the greatest time of tribulation that has ever been on earth or ever will be (Matthew 24:15-22; Revelation 6:1-19:21; Daniel 11:40-45; 12:1; Jeremiah 30:3-9; Ezekiel 20:33-38; Zechariah 13:9; 14:1-5).[1]

The High Priest curse is on Jews and all those who are genetic descendants of this tribe. What to do? Break the curse by repenting of it for yourself and on behalf of your ancestors by asking the Lord for forgiveness. Yes, you can stand proxy before the throne of Grace and repent on behalf of your ancestors. No prayer of repentance goes unanswered. Where sin abounds, Grace abounds even more. See, Romans 5:20. Yeshua's blood was shed for the forgiveness of all sin and all curses are broken through His ultimate perfect sacrifice, once and for all. "Christ redeemed us from the curse of the law by becoming a curse for us, for it is written, 'Cursed is the man who hangs on a tree.'" (Galatians 3:13)

4. <u>Judah</u>. Fourth son of Jacob and father of the tribe of Judah. His name comes from the Hebrew word for praise, "Yehudah". Leah gave birth to Judah and said,

"Now I will praise HaShem" (Genesis 30:35) This is the tribe where we get the name, 'Jews' from. Those who belonged to the tribe of Judah, were called, 'Yehudis', and in the 1700s, the Y became a J and they were called, 'Jews'. The Davidic Dynasty emerged from this tribe, a lineage which culminated in the birth of Jesus Christ in the New Testament. Nevertheless, it was Judah's idea to sell his brother Joseph to a Midianite slave trader rather than leave him to die in the pit (Genesis 37:27). He later became the spokesman for his father Jacob and his brothers when they traveled to Egypt during the famine in Canaan. He married Shua and had three sons: Er, Onan, and Shelah. Judah also has sons with Tamar, his widowed daughter-in-law, whose names were Perez and Zerach. They later saved the bloodline of Judah, which became the royal bloodline for the Kings of Israel, including Yeshua, Jesus Christ.

This is one of those stories in the Bible that is often overlooked yet is key in the generation linkage of the tribe of Judah to the family of the Messiah. Interesting that the disciple, Judah, betrayed Jesus, just as Judah betrayed Joseph. There are many correlations of the life of Joseph with the Messiah Yeshua, Jesus Christ. Joseph's Coat of Many Colors, and his dream of ruling over the stars, is prophetic of the Millennial Reign of Jesus Christ, when He returns to rule over all the nations of this world. Joseph's Multi-colored Coat, is analogous to Jesus ruling over the Multi-colored nations of the world. Joseph was a forerunner of Jesus.

The story recorded in Genesis 38 relates an apparently unsavory incident in the life of Judah, son of Jacob, which is usually glossed over or tacitly ignored. A closer look at what is written reveals that it has a definite bearing upon the lineage and fleshly ancestry of Christ.

The story revolves around Judah and his daughter-in-law Tamar. She is usually painted as being guilty of discreditable conduct, but a clear knowledge of the background shows that Judah was the one to blame and that, despite appearance, Tamar acted with perfect propriety and as a true daughter of Israel.

Jacob (Israel) had returned to his native Canaan from Padan-Aram, the home of his father-in-law Laban, with his family. They had not been there many years before Judah, his fourth son with Leah, now in his thirties, separated himself from the family business and started his own business thirty miles away among the Canaanites. Judah married a Canaanite woman by whom he had three sons, Er, Onan and Shelah. At what must have been a very early age he married off Er to a local woman named Tamar. The marriage did not last long.

In a manner not detailed in the narrative and not relevant to the story, Er "was wicked in the sight of the Lord, and the Lord slew him". This can mean that Er, half-Canaanite in parentage, was guilty of some gross unrighteousness and in consequence, met his death. The death of Judah's eldest son, through whom the family line would normally be carried on, involved the question of succession of his property and his rights as Judah's heir. At this point the question of the Levirate law arises.

The Levirate law is from the Latin *levir,* meaning *brother-in-law.* It was the arrangement embodied in the Mosaic Law (Deuteronomy 25:5-10) which goes back to remote antiquity even before Moses, the intention of which is to perpetuate the family name and preserve family rights of inheritance in the case of a man who died without male issue. The solution was simple. The dead man's brother, or failing him, the nearest male relative, must take the widow in marriage and the first son born to that marriage would take the dead man's name and be accounted his legal son and heir, inheriting the dead man's estate and carrying on the family line.

The Book of Ruth records the leading example of the operation of this law in Israel. There the widowed and childless Ruth is taken by her dead husband's brother Boaz, after a nearer kinsman had refused to do his duty, thus making her an ancestress of Jesus of Nazareth.

In this case, Judah, faced with the same position, married Tamar to his second son Onan. But Onan resented the obligation thrust upon him, and determined that, marriage or no marriage, he would not become the father of a son who then would not be counted as his. He took matters into his own hands (literally) to ensure that there would be no son while Tamar remained his wife. *"But Onan knew that the offspring would not be his; so, whenever he lay with his brother's wife, he spilled his semen on the ground to keep from producing offspring for his brother. And the thing which he did displeased the Lord; wherefore the Lord slew him also".* (Genesis 38:9-10) Here again, in some way or other Onan also met an untimely death and the chronicler again associated the two events as the hand of the Lord.

Judah was now faced with a dilemma. According to the Levirate law his youngest and only surviving son, Shelah, should now marry Tamar in the hope that heirs to both Er and Onan might be born. But Judah was apprehensive that Shelah might then share the fate of his brothers. He was perhaps superstitious; was there some kind of curse on this woman that spelt death to any man who married her? At any rate, he made an excuse. He told Tamar to return to her father's house for the present until Shelah was old enough to be married, because he could not have been more than sixteen at this time. Tamar agreed to the request and went back to her father.

Several years passed and Shelah attained marriageable age according to the norms of that day and society. Judah made no move to fulfill the obligation. Tamar realized that he had no intention of making a move. It was obvious to her that it was Judah's intention for her to stay out of the family circle. Tamar's widowhood could not have lasted for more than five or six years. One might have thought that Tamar, who must still have been a young woman, would have accepted the situation and found herself another husband. But no; her subsequent action shows that she was determined to bear a child who would be the legitimate heir to carry on the line of Judah. In less than twenty years later Jacob, under the inspiration of the Holy Spirit, predicted that the promised Messiah would come from the line of Judah. Here we begin to see the outline of a Divine purpose emerge in this family drama which would later ensure the fulfillment of that promise.

How much of all this was already known to either Judah or Tamar is not apparent. The words of Jacob on his deathbed (Genesis 49) establishes the first recorded indication that the Messiah was destined to come through one of Judah's descendants. It is a certainty that Jacob knew the Lord's plan for his descendants long before his death, as he didn't just make up something as important as this, during his last minutes. He must have had the guidance of the Holy Spirit. Reuben was his eldest son, but he forfeited the birthright by sleeping with Jacob's concubine, committing a sin against his father (Genesis 35.22).

The next two sons, Simeon and Levi, were rejected because of their violent and fierce nature and the wrong they did their father in the matter of their sister Dinah (Genesis 34). Judah was the fourth son and of him, Jacob spoke approvingly. Judah was already aware of the fact that his was the chosen line, which explains his anxiety throughout this series of episodes to be sure of acquiring an heir to continue the line.

However, he made one grievous mistake. The chosen line was to be pure Hebrew without the mixture of other races. Abraham insisted that Isaac marry a Hebrew woman, in his case from the family of Nahor, Abraham's brother. Jacob in his turn also married into the same family. Judah therefore was pure Hebrew, but he married a Canaanite and his three sons therefore were of mixed race, Hebrew and Canaanite. Through divine intervention his bloodline was not continued through them.

One wonders if Tamar knew something of God's plan, perhaps through intuition which led her to her subsequent action. Tamar was a Hebrew, a descendant of one of Abraham's numerous sons by Keturah or his concubines, or of the parallel family of Nahor. Tamar perceived what Judah had not realized, that the only way in which the line of Judah could be continued into succeeding generations in a manner pleasing to the Lord was through Judah himself. Judah's Canaanite wife died and there would be no more mixed-race sons from that quarter.

Under the Levirate law, if Shelah was not to play the husband's part towards Tamar, then it was the duty of the next relative to do so. That next relative was Judah himself. Tamar therefore was perfectly entitled to require that he assumed the obligation, just as Ruth did to Boaz after the unnamed "nearer kinsman" had declined to do so. She must have realized, however, that Judah, although now a widower had no more intention of marrying her his only surviving son did. So, Tamar played a trick on Judah.

Judah was on his way for the annual sheep shearing. "When Tamar was told, 'Your father-in-law is on his way to Timnah to shear his sheep,' she took off her widow's clothes, covered herself with a veil to disguise herself, and then sat down at the entrance to Enaim, which is on the road to Timnah. For he saw that, though Shelah had now grown up, she had not been given to him as his wife. When Judah saw her, he thought she was a prostitute, for she had covered her face. Not realizing that she was his daughter-in-law, he went over to her by the roadside and said, 'Come now, let me sleep with you'. 'And what will you give me to sleep with you?' she asked. 'I'll send you a young goat from my flock,' he said. 'Will you give me something as a pledge until you send it?' she asked. He said, 'What pledge should I give you?' 'Your seal and its cord, and the staff in your hand,' she answered. So, he gave them to her and slept with her, and she became pregnant by him. After she left, she took off her veil and put on her widow's clothes again." (Genesis 38: 14-19)

After Judah returned home, Judah sent his friend Hiram to redeem his pledges, but by then Tamar had gone back to her own home and returned to her normal clothing, so no one could give Hiram any information about the woman Judah sought. Judah let the matter go, and most likely forgot about it.

Three months later news came that Tamar was with child and Judah immediately hailed this as a divine opportunity to rid himself of her altogether. He demanded that she be brought to the place of judgment and condemned. As the widow of his sons she was still legally a member of his household which gave him authority over her. Tamar produced the missing pledges. *"By the man, whose these are, am I with child"*. Judah, conscience stricken declared *"She hath been more righteous than I, because I gave her not to Shelah my son"*. Judah eventually admitted that she had done the right thing, both by the law and custom of the time, and in recognition of the declared purpose of God.

In giving herself willingly to a man old enough to be her father Tamar must have been inspired by a higher purpose. Had she not done what she did, the line of Judah might have become extinct. Then the high hopes of Jacob, that the tribe of Judah was to be the royal tribe, begetting the kings of Israel and eventually leading to Israel's Messiah, would have been frustrated. Tamar's sole place in the Scriptures shows a woman of faith, who was given the means of preserving the racial purity of the Messianic line at a time when it was being jeopardized by the careless self-indulgence of one man.

The twin sons of Tamar were Pharez and Zarah. Pharez is named in all the Biblical genealogies as the son of Judah. The intervening generation of Er, Onan and Shelah, is omitted so far as the line of descent to Jesus Christ is concerned, except being noted as other sons of Judah. Judah took Tamar back into his house, but not as his wife. There she probably spent the rest of her life bringing up the sons Judah needed to fulfill his position as progenitor of the tribe which later days became the royal tribe of Israel. Also, important to note, that before the tribe of Judah, there were no Jews, there were Hebrews and Canaanites. The rest of the tribes were known as Israelites, members of the tribe of Judah were called, 'Judes' or 'Jews'.

Jacob blessed Judah, "Judah, you are he whom your brothers shall praise: your hand shall be in the neck of your enemies; your father's children shall bow down before you. Judah is a lion's whelp: from the prey, my son, you are gone up: he stooped down, he couched as a lion, and as an old lion; who shall rouse him up? The scepter shall not depart from Judah, nor a lawgiver from between his feet, until Shiloh (Messiah) come; and to him shall the gathering of the people be. Binding his foal to the vine, and his ass's colt to the choice vine; he washed his garments in wine, and his clothes in the blood of grapes: His eyes shall be red with wine, and his teeth white with milk." (Genesis 49:8-12)

5. Dan. Son of Jacob and Bilhah (Rachel's maidservant) and father of the tribe of Dan. One explanation of the name Dan is that when Rachel was convinced that she was unable to have children, she cried *"HaShem has judged me"* (Genesis 30:5). Dan was one of the brothers involved in the plot to sell his brother Joseph into slavery. Later, Jacob sent Dan to Egypt to buy corn during the severe famine in Canaan. The region of Dan in the Book of Judges is located in the far north of Canaan and referred to early in Genesis during Abraham's chasing of Chedorlaomer (Genesis 14:14). The tribe of Dan also settled in the southern part of the country and since the tribal territory covered both northern and southern parts of the country the expression *"from Dan to Beer-sheba"* indicates the entire span of their Israelite land, which wasn't a very large portion of land at all.

However, the tribe of Dan failed to drive out their Philistine and Canaanite neighbors. As a result, they migrated to another land, in the northernmost limits of Canaan. When Jacob was handing out blessings on his deathbed, it seemed like a mixed bag for Dan, "Dan shall judge his people, as one of the tribes of Israel. Dan shall be a serpent by the way, an adder in the path that bites the horse heels, so that his rider shall fall backward. (Genesis 49:16, 17).

While being a judge may sound like an honor, being a serpent certainly is a curse. This could be the beginning of the sect of Israelites (today known as Jews) who worshipped various dragon cults, and started numerous secret societies which all worship Lucifer, the serpent, dragon, draconian, beast. Interesting that right after Jacob pronounces this blessing and curse on Dan, he then says, "I have waited for your salvation, O LORD." (Genesis 49:18).

Yeshua shed His Divine blood to save humanity from the power of the serpent and all of their draconian races. What many call *the devil* is really a reptilian alien race which resides inside the planet, and are the natural enemies of humankind.

6. Naphtali. Naphtali was the second son of Jacob and Rachel's maidservant Bilhah and the father of the tribe of Naphtali. The tribe of Naphtali settled in northern Canaan and were described as brave soldiers in the Song of Deborah (Judges 5:18). Naphtali's blessing from his father called him *a running deer* or as the AKJ version puts it, "Naphtali is a hind let loose: he gives goodly words." (Genesis 49:21). Naphtali was given his name because Rachel said, *"With great wrestlings have I wrestled my sister"* (Genesis 30:8). Naphtali was blessed by Jacob on his deathbed. The tribe of Naphtali was a tribe of great warriors, and took part in some of the Old Testament's most important battles.

7. Gad. Gad was the seventh son of Jacob and father of the tribe of Gad. His mother was Zilpah, Jacob's concubine, Leah's maidservant. Gad's name comes from the Hebrew word 'troop.' Leah named him Gad, saying *"A troop is coming."* He was part of the plot to sell Joseph to Egypt and later sent to Egypt to buy corn during the famine in Canaan. Gad later moved to Egypt and lived there with his seven sons. Jacob blessed Gad on his deathbed, saying: "Gad, a troop shall overcome him: but he shall overcome at the last." (Genesis 49:19).

Gad was considered the 'Marines' of the 12 tribes of Israel. They were fierce, athletic, and skillful on the battle field. They played lead roles in the conquest of Sihon and OG, then led the Israelites across the Jordan to Jericho and beyond. This is probably why the Israeli Defense Forces today is one of the strongest armies in the world. Interesting that boot camp for the IDF in Hebrew, is called, 'Gad-na'.

8. Asher. Asher was the eighth son of Jacob and the father of the tribe of Asher. His mother was Zilpah, Leah's maidservant. Leah named him Asher, saying *"Happy am I"* (Genesis 30:13). Asher played a role in the plot to sell his brother Joseph into slavery. Asher and his four sons and daughter later settled in Egypt. Jacob blessed Asher on his deathbed, saying: "From Asher will come the richest food; he will provide the king's delights" (Genesis 49:20)

9. Issachar. Ninth son of Jacob and Leah, and father of the tribe of Issachar. One interpretation of his name is *"man of reward"* (Hebrew: shcar). Issachar was the product of the mandrake incident (Genesis 30:9-18) and was involved in the plot to sell his brother Joseph into slavery. Issachar settled in Egypt after the famine in Canaan and had four sons: Tolah, Puvvah, Yov and Shimron. He receives a blessing from his father Jacob that he "Issachar is a strong ass couching down between two burdens: And he saw that rest was good, and the land that it was pleasant; and bowed his shoulder to bear, and became a servant to tribute." (Genesis 49:14-15). The descendants of Issachar are considered men of learning according to Jewish tradition.

10. Zebulun. Tenth son of Jacob and sixth of Leah and father of the tribe of Zebulun. When he was born Leah said *"HaShem has provided me with a good dowry"*

(Hebrew: zvad). He was part of the plot to sell Joseph into slavery, and later one of the group sent to Egypt to buy corn. He later lived in Egypt with his three sons Sered, Elon and Jahleel. Zebulun received the blessing from Jacob of: "Zebulun shall settle the seashores; he will be a harbor for ships; his border shall reach Sidon." (Genesis 49:13).

The tribe of Zebulun inhabited the northern land of Canaan. Both the tribes of Naphtali and Zebulun are mentioned as brave soldiers in the Song of Deborah during the battle against Sisera (Judges 5:18). Zebulun proved faithful throughout much of the Old Testament. The tribe fought bravely with Deborah and Barak. They were mentioned in conjunction with Gideon. The tribe took part in a prophecy of Isaiah's which Jesus Christ fulfilled.

11. Joseph. Joseph was the 11th son of Jacob. He was born to Jacob's favorite wife, Rachel, in Paddan-Aram after she had been barren for seven years. While Rachel was not a virgin, she did receive a divine pregnancy, which in my opinion was done through being implanted with the seed from the Elohim (YHVH). Joseph was the special child. Instead of the tribe of Joseph, Joseph's sons, Ephraim and Manasseh, became two of the tribes of Israel.

Manasseh was the first-born son of Joseph and Asenath (Pharoah's daughter). Ephraim was the younger brother of Manasseh, as well as the son of Joseph and Asenath, Pharoah's daughter. Both were mixed blood, Hebrew and Egyptian, but both were considered royalty because their mother was a princess, and their father was divinely conceived and considered a miracle birth. Jacob adopts both Manasseh and his brother Ephraim as part of the tribe of Simeon and Reuben, but later Manasseh and Ephraim became independent tribes because the Levites (the Priests) were sanctified to God, and were not considered one of the twelve tribes.

Although Manasseh was technically the eldest son, he did not receive the greater blessing. Ephraim did, as Jacob foresaw that his descendants were worthier of the blessing than Manasseh's (Genesis 48:13-20). The Tribe of Manasseh was the only one of the 12 Tribes of Israel to inherit land on both sides of the Jordan River. This was a manifestation of the double-portion still being given to Manasseh, the eldest of Joseph.

Jacob switched hands and gave Ephraim the blessing of the firstborn. The tribe of Ephraim became the 11th tribe of Israel. Perhaps no tribe symbolizes man's struggle with God more than the tribe of Ephraim. At once rebuked, then praised, Ephraim was always under the watchful eye of God. The name would come to represent the entire northern kingdom of Israel. The tribe of Ephraim participated in many of Israel's activities throughout the period of the Judges. They played a significant role in both the United and Divided Monarchies.

Joseph was distinguished amongst all his brothers. Many scholars have related Joseph to Yeshua. Joseph received extra special blessings from his father.

> "Joseph is a fruitful bough, even a fruitful bough by a well; whose branches run over the wall: The archers have sorely grieved him, and shot at him, and hated him: But his bow stayed in strength, and the arms of his hands were made strong by the hands of the mighty God of Jacob; (from there is the shepherd, the stone of Israel:) Even by the God of your father, who shall help you; and by the Almighty, who shall bless you with blessings of heaven above, blessings of the deep that lies under, blessings of the breasts, and of the womb: The blessings of your father have prevailed above the blessings of my progenitors to the utmost bound of the everlasting hills: they shall be on the head of Joseph, and on the crown of the head of him that was separate from his brothers."
>
> (Genesis 49:22-26)

Is it any wonder that we still celebrate Joseph today, with the Broadway musical, "Joseph and the Amazing Technicolor Dreamcoat"?

12. Benjamin. Benjamin was the second son of Jacob and Rachel and father of the tribe of Benjamin. Originally named Ben-oni, or *"son of my affliction"* by his mother as she laid dying in labor, his name was later changed to Benjamin, meaning *"son of my right hand"* (Genesis 48:14). Next to Joseph, Benjamin was Jacob's favorite son. Benjamin was the twelfth and final son born to Jacob and was born after Joseph was sold into slavery by his brothers. After the family was invited to Egypt, Joseph sabotaged Benjamin's sack by putting a silver cup in it while accusing his brothers of stealing. Joseph thought Benjamin would remain in Egypt, but Judah offered to take his place, saying that his father would be devastated if Benjamin did not return. Jacob later blesses Benjamin while on his deathbed, saying, "Benjamin shall shred as a wolf: in the morning he shall devour the prey, and at night he shall divide the spoil." (Genesis 49:27).

King Saul and the great prophet Samuel were from the tribe of Benjamin, both significantly shaped the history of Israel. Esther was a descendant of the tribe of Benjamin. The Tribe of Benjamin, produced not only a king, but also a queen. Esther would rise to become Queen of Persia. The tribe of Benjamin played integral roles in a number of events from the Judges through Ezra.

Where are the Tribes Today?

More than two-thirds of the Bible is comprised of prophecies about Israel, its lands and peoples, which in turn relate to God's Divine Plan of Salvation for humanity. Where are the people who descend from these ancient tribes today? There have been many books written on the subject of the lost tribes of Israel. Some are based on historical accounts, others on descriptions of geographic landscapes as to where these tribes finally came to rest.

We know that the tribe of Judah, the Jews, live in Israel today, with a near equal amount living in the United States and North America. The rest of the Jewish population is scattered around all over the other nations of the world. So many battles have fought over the land that was supposed to be their inheritance, given by Jacob to the sons and grandsons of Judah! Yet we know from the scriptures that, God's covenant with the house of Israel, the twelve tribes of Jacob, is still in effect today as it will be forever. We are all witnesses to the Lord's promises and prophesies to bring His people back into His land, first given to their forefathers by the Lord Himself.

We know that the various other tribes mixed with different races and cultures, many abandoning their original Semitic culture and heritage as well as dissolving their genetic links. This is why the Jews in particular have always held tightly to their traditions, so that they would be able to identify themselves to the Lord by trying to follow His laws and festivals. The Lord knows exactly who's who in the generations of all of the twelve tribes and where these descendants are today. This is why He says in Deuteronomy 32:8 that the borders of the nations are determined by the number of Israelites. Remember the Israelites were not all Jews. The Israelites are the twelve tribes of Jacob (Israel).

> "When the Most High gave the nations their inheritance, when he divided all mankind, he set up boundaries for the peoples according to the number of the children of Israel. For the LORD's portion is his people; Jacob is the lot of his inheritance."
>
> (Deuteronomy 32:8-9)

> "You will see it with your own eyes and say, 'Great is the LORD (YHVH)--even beyond the borders of Israel!'"
>
> (Malachi 1:5)

The Lord is the Grand Realtor of planet earth, it is He who decides the borders, despite the battles, ancient and future. We need to remember that the covenants, which are legally binding contracts in heaven and earth, established long ago the boundaries of the land of Israel for all time. What is behind the intense hatred by the nations of the world towards Israel is their spiritual rebellion towards the Lord YHVH. Yet the Lord keeps His covenant with His people and with Israel, nevertheless. I think Psalm 2 speaks of this ongoing battle, and the misunderstanding of who really rules the earth. The time period we're in is a time of grace, giving all the nations of the world, and all the lost tribes and descendants of Israel, the grace and time to repent and come to know their Lord and Savior.

> "Why do the nations conspire, and the peoples plot in vain? The kings of the earth take their stand and the rulers gather together against the Lord and against his Anointed One. "Let us break their chains," they say, "and throw off their fetters." The One enthroned in heaven laughs; the Lord scoffs at them. Then he rebukes them in his anger and terrifies them in his wrath, saying, "I have installed my King on Zion, my holy hill." I will proclaim the decree of the Lord: He said to me, "You are my Son; today I have become your Father. Ask of me, and I will make the nations your inheritance, the ends of the earth your possession. You will rule them with an iron scepter; you will dash them to pieces like pottery." Therefore, you kings, be wise; be warned, you rulers of the earth. Serve the Lord with fear and rejoice with trembling. Kiss the Son, lest he be angry, and you be destroyed in your way, for his wrath can flare up in a moment. Blessed are all who take refuge in him."
>
> (Psalm 2:1-12)

I think this Psalm of David is not only prophetic, but reveals the politics of the Lord and His intentions for setting up His Kingdom on earth through His Son, Yeshua, the Lord Jesus Christ. So, while the battles rage in the Middle East over Israel, they are really battles against the Most High. This will culminate in the final battle known as Armageddon. Before the final battle, the Bible prophecies tell us to expect a third world war, called the war of Gog and Magog, which will be fought over the control of Jerusalem.

During the writing of this piece, I received an email article about the United States foreign policy under the Obama administration concerning American citizens born in the city of Jerusalem in the state of Israel. Right now, Jerusalem belongs to Israel, even though it is sectioned off in different quarters to Muslims, Christians, Armenians, Orthodox Jews. Any baby born in Jerusalem today, will have on their birth certificate that their place of birth is Jerusalem, Israel.

However, if an American citizen gives birth in the city of Jerusalem, they are not allowed to record on their birth certificate, Jerusalem, Israel -- just Jerusalem. This has come to a shock to many, because it not only reveals the Obama's administration's agenda with respect to Israel, but that it also believes that Jerusalem stands alone without a country.

Jerusalem is the Lord's own heart, and it's in this place on planet earth, He will return and set up His Kingdom. Yet despite the fact that the Bible tells us how all these battles are going to end, the enemies of God continue to fight on!

If the Lord is the one who ultimately decides the boundaries of the nations, by the proportion of children of Israel (descendants of the twelve tribes of Jacob) are living there, then what legal right do foreign bodies, such as the United Nations, or any other independent nation, have to decide where Israel's boundaries begin and end?

None! This is the foundation for the spiritual battle which will culminate into our next world war over the boundaries of Jerusalem, Israel.

> "For this is what the LORD of Heaven's Armies says: "After he has honored me and has sent me against the nations that have plundered you--for whoever touches you touches the apple of his eye- I will surely raise my hand against them so that their slaves will plunder them. Then you will know that the LORD Almighty has sent me."
>
> (Zechariah 2:8-9)

Who are the Children of Israel?

Although Israel and the Jewish people can trace their lineage back to Abraham, all are commonly called the *children of Israel.* It's important to reiterate that the Hebrew meaning of the name *Israel,* means *he who struggles with God and prevails.* This is certainly not limited to the Jews of the world, but to ***all*** the descendants of the lost tribes of Israel, most of whom do not even have Jewish blood, but are still a vital part of God's covenant and the divine plan.

We know that before Jacob died, he met with his sons and two of his grandsons to talk to them about what would happen to them and their descendants in the last days. He wanted to convey certain blessings. (Genesis 48 & 49) One item of significance regarding this final episode was that Jacob took the inheritance of the first-born son, Reuben, and divided it up between the other sons. This was due to Reuben's sin (Genesis 35:22) and his lack of leadership ability.

To Judah, he gave the kingship, the leadership role among the brothers. This was also a rebuke of Simeon and Levi, as they were second and third in line, due to the violent revenge they had taken following the rape of their sister Dinah (Genesis 34). Judah was the fourth son of Leah, who, regardless of his mistakes, showed the best leadership ability and commanded the respect of his brothers. It was from Judah that the kingship (scepter) would not pass until Shiloh (Messiah) would come (Genesis 49:10). As prophesied, Yeshua the Messiah came from the tribe of Judah.

To Joseph he gave a double portion of the land inheritance, who passed it on to his sons, Manasseh and Ephraim. This was due to the righteousness Joseph displayed throughout his time in Egypt and to his family when they were reunited (Genesis 39-47). Both are significant in the last days. It's also important to note, that Joseph's sons were born from his union with the Egyptian Princess, the Pharoah's Priest's daughter, Asenath, who was of a different genetic line. Yet, what is interesting, is that the tribes of both Ephraim and Dan are omitted from the sealing of the 144,000 in Revelation 7. More on that below.

The Fullness of the Gentiles

Jacob's blessing over Joseph's children is especially important with regard to prophecy (Genesis 48). At this juncture, Jacob deliberately switches what would be their normal order of blessing. He gives the younger son, Ephraim, the higher blessing of the older son. What is critical here is verse 19, where Jacob prophecies that Ephraim's descendants would be among the Nations. The term he uses is *m'loh ha goyim,* or *"fullness of the gentiles."* Paul uses this exact phrase in Romans 11:25, when speaking of the final redemption of Israel. Paul is not speaking of "the gentiles" when he uses this term, rather he is referring to the return of the exiled ten tribes.

There is an interesting teaching in the Zohar, concerning a vision of the future that Jacob had at the time when he blessed his two grandsons. Jacob sees that through Ephraim, Israel would fall into terrible idolatry:

> "When Jacob was about to bless Joseph's sons, he saw by the Holy Spirit that Jeroboam the son of Nebat would issue from Ephraim, and he exclaimed, "Who are these?", the word "these" (eleh) being an allusion to idols. The reason is that besides the <u>evil serpent there is one that rides on it</u>, and when they are joined together they are called "these", and they visit the world with all their hosts."
>
> (Soncino Zohar Volume I p. 228a)

It is also interesting to note this language from the Zohar, "that there is an evil entity (spiritual idolatry) that rides upon the back of the serpent," is similar language to Revelation chapter 17, where the "whore" (spiritual idolatry) rides upon the beast.

> "Because of your detestable idols, I will punish you like I have never punished anyone before or ever will again."
>
> (Ezekiel 5:9)

If we can sum up one theme in the long historical drama of the Bible, it is that the Lord does not take idolatry in any of its forms lightly. In fact, we can say that all the punishments dished out to the Israelites in the Old Testament were a result of transgressions of idolatry. Sexual immorality would come second, but then, many can argue that this too is a subtle form of idolatry. Spiritually speaking, anything that comes between you and your intimate relationship with the Lord is idolatry. That can range from worshipping the creation over the Creator, to statutes, to paganism, to worshipping human beings, to technology. These are all forms of 'idols' that we put above the Creator Lord.

There is such descriptive language in the scriptures regarding how the Lord regards idolatry! So many people think that God must not have intimate feelings, because He's too powerful for emotions, but we must remember we are created in His image. If we were created with emotions, it's because He gave them to us. We are to have an emotional relationship with Him and each other. The very word, 'emotion' literally means, 'energy-in-motion'. Regardless of the feeling, every one of them has an energy, and every energetic vibration corresponds to spirit.

All emotional relationships are spiritual relationships. The first and foremost of our spiritual relationships is supposed to be with our Creator. This is why it states in the first of the Ten Commandments was to have no other gods before the Creator Lord. It's an exclusive relationship, albeit a spiritual one, like a marriage. So, when other spirits come between that bond between us and God, it causes us to suffer separation from God.

This was the primary reason Yeshua was sent to fulfill His special mission. He was to become the bridge between fallen humanity and their Prime Creator Lord, through offering Himself as a Living Sacrifice. It is through Him that we may all find salvation and be restored, put back into right relationship with the Lord. All those who find this path are exempt from the wrath of the Lord, which is to be poured out onto all those who continue in rebellion and idolatry in the last days.

Jesus was asked by the Pharisees what the greatest of all the commandments was, and He summed them all up with these two, 'Love the Lord your God with all your heart and with all your soul and with all your mind.' This is the first and greatest commandment. And the second is like it: 'Love your neighbor as yourself.' All the Law and the Prophets hang on these two commandments." (Matthew 22:37-40)

Loving the Lord is number one, which is our primary relationship. Earth life is temporary, but eternity is forever. Eternity is about oneness with the Lord. Earth life is about weeding out those who are worthy of spending eternity in the Kingdom of God and those who are not.

Think about it, why would you want to spend forever with someone you hate? Or if you were a king of a kingdom, why would you allow someone to spend eternity in your glorious kingdom, and receive all of its fruitfulness and blessings, if that person hated and rebelled against you?

This is the purpose of our earthly life, to find out who belongs in the Kingdom of God and who ends up with the rebels in darkness, who are eventually destroyed in the lake of fire. Sounds dramatic, but that is God's plan, not only written in the scriptures but written into the very stars of the cosmos themselves. See, Book Five: *The Heavens, The Divine Plan of Salvation as Written into the Stars.*

We were all created with the freedom to choose between loving the Creator, or not. Love is not forced. This is why we were not created as robots but as free spirits. The Divine Plan of Salvation was put in place before the foundation of the world.

> "For you know that God paid a ransom to save you from the empty life you inherited from your ancestors. And the ransom he paid was not mere gold or silver. It was the precious blood of Christ, the sinless, spotless Lamb of God. <u>He was chosen before the foundation of the world but was made manifest in the last times for your sake</u>."
>
> (1 Peter 1:18-20)

As I've already mentioned in my chapter on *Aliens and Religion; What's the Times of the Gentiles?,* the reason the blessings were transferred over to the gentiles was to make the Jews jealous. We have heard that the Jews are God's chosen people. This was because He chose the tribe of Judah to bring forth the kings of Israel, who were chosen to be set apart from the rest of the tribes, sanctified to the Lord, anointed to lead and shepherd the rest of God's people.

There is so much misplaced pride and arrogance when it comes to this notion of *choseness* that many Jews forget the whole reason for it. As a result, many fell away from putting the Lord first in their lives, but chose other paths and other gods.

Instead the Jews gave themselves over to prostitution, selling themselves out for power, position, and money. They threw the Lord under the bus. Besides the grievous transgression of idolatry, they were guilty of prostitution.

We know from gleaning through the books of Genesis that during the times of the twelve sons of Jacob, prostitution was a socially acceptable practice. Hence the story of Judah thinking it was perfectly okay to purchase some time at the side of the road with a woman who later turned out to be Tamar, his daughter-in-law.

Our earthly life is about learning and discerning what belongs to the Lord's Kingdom and what belongs to the kingdom of darkness, and the true nature of who is the god of this world. This is purposely a world of duality, so that every human being has every opportunity to make the choice for all eternity.

So, the Lord extended His blessings to the rest of the tribes, who in turn became lost, now known as the gentiles. However, not all were gentiles, but many were Jews who eventually assimilated. The opportunity to be sanctified and set apart to the Lord is open to all. The 'times of the gentiles' that needs to be fulfilled is about the spreading of the good news of the Kingdom of God and its Divine Plan of Salvation through Yeshua, Jesus, The Messiah of the world. So, in the end, no one can say, we hadn't heard, or we didn't know.

The reason the Lord said He transferred this blessing over to the gentiles was in order to make the Jews jealous, which was to cause the Jews to return to Him by seeking His heart, His forgiveness and His truth, and find their Messiah. Yet, today in Israel, out of six and half million Jews, only 25,000 of them are *completed Jews*, meaning they accept Yeshua as their Messiah. These people are known as Messianic Jews. They are set apart in Israel and shunned by the very same group that rejected Yeshua, the religious right that sit in the Israeli Parliament and dictate policies for the State of Israel.

Their hypocrisy was flagrant two thousand years ago, and it hasn't improved one iota. They embrace the Christian community supporting Israel, through various politically inclined organizations, as long as these Christians are not Jewish. Jewish believers are considered outcasts in Israel, a state that never rejects any Jew from any nation in the world, unless they're Messianic. In fact, Israel took in Vietnamese refugees who weren't Jewish; but a Jewish Christian is out of luck.

Recently a daughter of a Holocaust Survivor from Sweden was denied the *Law of Return,* to immigrate to Israel, based on the fact that her father converted to Jesus, and when she was a child, he baptized her, and that she was associated with a missionary organization. The Population and Immigration Authority of Israel deported a Swedish citizen who requested to immigrate to Israel by virtue of the Law of Return.

The woman, a Psychologist Rebecca Floer, 64 years old, denies the authority's claim. She says her father never converted or denied his Judaism and she does not belong to the missionary organization, but rather appeared one time, as a Jewish Psychologist, at that group's event. Floer said she was baptized as a child but left the church and considers herself Jewish. She expressed concern over the rise of neo-Nazism in Sweden and increased anti-Semitism, saying she believes it is dangerous for a Jew to live in Sweden. Despite Sweden's rape epidemic of women and children by Muslim refugees, the Israeli Authorities denied her permission to live in Israel.[3]

This situation explains that Israel is bound by a haughty religious spirit, prejudice and religious bigotry, a demonic spiritual stronghold. See, Book One, *The Religious Spirit.*[2] It is exactly the same demonic stronghold which Yeshua/Jesus faced when He walked the land, the one which ordered Him crucified. The spirit of the Pharisees continues to be alive and active in the world today, still stubbornly stiff-necked, resisting their own history and their own Messiah in the State of Israel.

What is so disturbing about Israel's rejection of Jews who believe in Jesus, is their flagrant hypocrisy in it. The Law of Return in Israel, extends to all those who are Jewish by birth, or have Jewish relatives and are being persecuted by anti-Semitism in the Diaspora. The Diaspora are all the nations outside of Israel. During Hitler's Genocidal Holocaust of Jews, Jews were singled out into death camps, just for being one-eighth Jewish, some of which weren't even following the Jewish religion, but died for having Jewish DNA. Yet, today in Israel, the Israeli Authorities are rejecting blood born Jews for believing in Jesus. Is it any wonder, why, the Antichrist gets a foothold in End Times Israel during the last days?

This is the reason that Israel will be deceived by a false Messiah, who will unleash the worst persecution upon the Jewish people ever recorded in history. The only way to mitigate or even minimize this sentence is for Israelis today to turn to Yeshua.

As to the issue of whether or not the Lord's tactic of wanting to make the Jews jealous by transferring His blessing to the gentiles worked... well, are they jealous? Perhaps this plan, can be filed under one of the failed grand experiments. To be fair, Jews coming to faith in Yeshua has grown exponentially in the last decade. So, it's not like the Lord has turned His back on them, yet, to the contrary, He is calling them home, both to the Land He gave them and more importantly, back to Himself. But sadly, due to so much antisemitism from so called Christians, Jews have hardened their hearts and minds to Jesus by rejecting Jews who embrace Him too.

According to the Jews, they rejected Jesus because He failed, in their eyes, to do what they expected their Messiah to do—banish evil, destroy all their enemies, and establish an eternal kingdom with Israel as the preeminent nation in the world, during their time. The prophecies in Isaiah and Psalm 22 described a suffering Messiah who would be persecuted and killed, but they chose to focus instead on those prophecies that discussed His glorious victories, not His crucifixion. They did everything to avoid an encounter with Him, which still permeates in modern Jewish consciousness. In fact, the very thing they fear the most at their core, is a close encounter with the Living Lord, because that means, they would feel ashamed and have to admit their mistake. Nobody, Jew or Gentile, gets close to Jesus when they're filled with pride and arrogance. This stronghold must be broken first, to even *see* and *hear* the Lord. And, this is true for many of us, who had to be broken, to experience a life changing encounter with the Lord Yeshua. "The Lord is close to the broken-hearted, and binds us their wounds." (Psalm 34:18)

Instead, Jews chose to follow laws and rules, believing if they did everything right, they wouldn't need to be saved from sin, because they believed in their own self-righteousness. Yet the truth of the matter is, that we are all born into this world under a curse, as Genesis 3 points out. The serpent was cursed, the earth was cursed, man was cursed, and women were cursed. Yet at the same time, the Divine Plan of Salvation was prophesied at the time of the fall. No man is righteous, not even one. (Romans 3:10)

In order for a Jew to be considered *righteous* according to the Torah, is they must follow the Torah, to the 'T'. And because this is virtually impossible for man to do in our present fallen state, this is why Yeshua came to fulfill the Law through Grace. Something that many legalists are too spiritually blinded to understand and accept.

It's the *religious spirit* which misleads people into the false belief that if they do good works, or follow every jot and tittle of the law, they can be saved. The Divine Plan of Salvation is no respecter of persons. It is not about works, or following the laws. It ***is*** all about God's Grace, and our faith in His Grace through His Messiah who was sent to take on the sins and curses of this world, as a final sacrifice, so that through Him we can be saved. He is the gate, the star-gate to heaven.

It is more than just a coincidence that the commentaries in the Talmud, which were written before the beginning of Christianity, clearly discuss the Messianic prophecies of Isaiah 53 and Psalm 22, yet at the same time they puzzle over how these would be fulfilled with the glorious setting up of the Kingdom of the Messiah. After the Church used these prophecies to prove the claims of Christ, the Jews took the position that the prophecies did not refer to the Messiah, but to Israel or some other person.

The Jews believed that the Messiah would come and deliver them from Roman bondage and set up a kingdom where they would be the rulers, according to Moses; yet they failed to see how all these prophesies would unfold. They obviously did not have insight into a millennial timeline that needed to unfold, as has been going on for the past two thousand years. Because they ignored the proclamations of Yeshua Himself when He walked amongst them, they missed so many illustrations of the prophetic timeline.

Two of the disciples, James and John, even asked to sit at Jesus' right and left sides in His Kingdom when He came into His glory. The people of Jerusalem also thought He would deliver them. They shouted praises to God for the mighty works they had seen Jesus do, and called out "Hosanna, save us" when He rode into Jerusalem on a donkey (Matthew 21:9). They treated Him like a conquering king. Then when He allowed Himself to be arrested, tried and crucified on a cursed cross, the people stopped believing that He was the promised prophet.

They rejected their Messiah (Matthew 27:22). They either forgot or failed to connect the dots to the prophecies of Isaiah, about how He came to suffer and take on the sins of the world, so that through Him we can be saved. "But he was wounded for our transgressions, he was bruised for our iniquities: the chastisement of our peace was on him; and with his stripes we are healed." (Isaiah 53:5)

Paul talks about the spiritual blindness of Israel as a "mystery" that had not previously been revealed (Romans chapters 9-11). For thousands of years Israel had been the one nation that looked to the One True Creator God while the Gentile nations generally rejected the light and chose to live in spiritual darkness, following idols and fallen angels masquerading as gods. Israel and her inspired prophets revealed monotheism—one God who was personally interested in each of us, as well as our collective destiny in heaven or hell.

Yet Israel rejected her prophesied Messiah, and the promises of the kingdom of heaven were postponed. As a result, a veil of spiritual blindness fell upon the eyes of the Jews who previously were the most spiritually discerning of people. As Paul explained, this hardening of heart on the part of Israel led to the blessing of the Gentiles who would believe in Jesus and accept Him as Lord and Savior.

Two thousand years after He came to the nation of Israel as their Messiah, Jews still (for the most part) reject Jesus Christ. Many Jews today (some say at least half of all living Jews) identify themselves as Jewish but prefer to be considered as secular Jews, rather than religious. They identify with no particular Jewish movement and have no understanding or affiliation with any Jewish biblical roots. The concept of Messiah as expressed in the Hebrew Scriptures or Judaism's "13 Principles of Faith" is foreign to most Jews today. In fact, many of these Jews dabble in Eastern Religions and New Age cults. They are spiritually lost and strayed from their original source.

Most of Israeli society is made up of secular type Jews, who are Zionists. They sacrifice their lives to protect the land that the Lord promised to them. They have a level of faith as Jews that they are chosen by God to have the land of Israel. They observe the religious holidays and the Sabbath, because that is the Israeli lifestyle and culture. However, many Israelis do not see themselves as religious or even spiritual. They follow after worldly pursuits, technology, materialism, and hedonistic pleasures. They do not seek the truth of their own scriptures.

It is ironic that many Jews do not know their own Bible, yet follow all the holidays and traditions. Jews in general, both in Israel and in the Diaspora, are scattered and diverse. This is the source of the old saying, 'if you put two Jews in a room, you get 10 opinions'. It is hard to pin them down. In Israel, Jews are further divided by sects. Some are orthodox, some are conservative, some are reform, some liberal, and some, a cult known as the Hassidim, believe it or not, do not even believe Israel has the right to exist until their Messiah comes, which ironically agrees with Israel's fiercest enemies. That's how deep the spiritual blindness goes.

But one concept is generally held as universal: Jews must have nothing to do with Jesus! Most Jews today perceive the last 2000 years of historical Jewish persecution to be at the hands of Christians. From the Crusades, to the Inquisition, to the pogroms in Europe, to Hitler's holocaust—Jews ultimately believe that they are being held responsible for the death of Jesus Christ and are being persecuted for that reason. They reject Him today as they did two thousand years ago.

The good news is that many Jews are now turning to Christ. The God of Israel has always been faithful to keep a remnant of believing Jews to Himself. The prophet Isaiah predicted, "A remnant of Jacob will return to the Mighty God. A Remnant of Israel Shall Return."

"Now in that day the remnant of Israel, and those of the house of Jacob who have escaped, will never again rely on the one who struck them, but will truly rely on the LORD, the Holy One of Israel. *A remnant will return*, the remnant of Jacob (Israel), to the mighty God. For though your people, O Israel, may be like the sand of the sea, *Only a remnant within them will return*; A destruction is determined, overflowing with righteousness."

(Isaiah 10:20-22-NAS)

In the United States alone, some estimates say that there are over 175,000 Jewish believers in Messiah Jesus, and the numbers are growing all the time. In Israel, there are approximately 25,000 Israeli Messianic Jews aka Jews who believe that Jesus is their Messiah. Rabbinic Judaism estimates over one million Jewish people around the world believe that Yeshua is the Messiah. There are also over 300 Messianic Congregations throughout the US and over 75 in Israel. You can find a Messianic Congregation in almost every country.[4]

Notes:

1. Art Mathias, *Wellspring School of Ministry Workbook,* Wellspring Publishing, 2010
2. Ella LeBain, *Who's Who in the Cosmic Zoo?* Book One – Third Edition, *The Religious Spirit,* p. 361-380, Tate, 2013.
3. Ilan Lior, *Israel Deporting Swedish Holocaust Survivor's Daughter - Because Her Father Allegedly Converted,* November 20, 2017, https://www.haaretz.com/israel-news/.premium-1.823740
4. http://www.bethadonai.com/FAQ_number_jewish_believers.html

CHAPTER TWENTY-EIGHT

RESTORATION OF ISRAEL

"The LORD your God will bring you into the
land which your fathers possessed,
and you shall possess it; and He will prosper you
and multiply you more than your fathers."
(DEUTERONOMY 30:5)

The prophet Jeremiah spoke for Yahuah, when the Lord told Jeremiah to write His words in a book, and prophesied a day when the Lord Yahuah, the God of Israel, would bring His people Israel and Judah back from captivity and bondage, and restore them to the land of Israel. Ezekiel 37 also prophesied about the restoration of Israel, in his famous message about the Lord's promise to bring the valley of the dry bones to life. We know that Ezekiel's prophecy was fulfilled in 1948 when Israel regrouped and became a state and a nation for the Jewish people. However, Jeremiah's prophecy to restore Israel seems to overlap this time period, and speaks more of the time known as Jacob's Troubles, a time which Christians relate to as the Great Tribulation.

> "This is what the LORD, the God of Israel, says: 'Write in a book all the words I have spoken to you. The days are coming,' declares the LORD, 'when I will bring my people Israel and Judah back from captivity and restore them to the land I gave their forefathers to possess,' says the LORD." These are the words the LORD spoke concerning Israel and Judah: This is what the LORD says:
>
> "Cries of fear are heard-- terror, not peace. Ask and see: Can a man bear children? Then why do I see every strong man with his hands on his stomach like a woman in labor, every face turned deathly pale? How awful that day will be! None will be like it. It will be a time of trouble for Jacob, but he will be saved out of it." 'In that day,' declares the LORD Almighty, 'I will break the yoke off their necks and will tear off their bonds; no longer will foreigners enslave them. Instead, they will serve the LORD their God and David their king, whom I will raise up for them."
>
> (Jeremiah 30:2-9)

Even after the time of Jacob's Troubles, the Lord Yahuah promises to restore Israel. This is beyond this present timeline, which the Book of Revelation calls the Millennial Reign. It is at the end of Jacob's Troubles that He sends His Messiah, His Son, to take over the throne of David and rule as their King.

> "Then the angel showed me the river of the water of life, as clear as crystal, flowing from the throne of God and of the Lamb down the middle of the great street of the city. On each side of the river stood the tree of life, bearing twelve crops of fruit, yielding its fruit every month. And the leaves of the tree are for the healing of the nations. No longer will there be any curse. The throne of God and of the Lamb will be in the city, and his servants will serve him. They will see his face, and his name will be on their foreheads. There will be no more night. They will not need the light of a lamp or the light of the sun, for the Lord God will give them light. And they will reign forever and ever."
>
> (Revelation 22:1-5)

The assurance in Jeremiah's prophecy, reveals Yahuah's plan all along to save Israel, and destroy its enemies, in spite of their sins, in spite of their wounds, to the point where He tells them, they are incurable:

> "'So, do not fear, O Jacob my servant; do not be dismayed, O Israel,' declares the LORD. 'I will surely save you out of a distant place, your descendants from the land of their exile. Jacob will again have peace and security, and no one will make him afraid. I am with you and will save you,' declares the LORD. 'Though I completely destroy all the nations among which I scatter you, I will not completely destroy you. I will discipline you but only with justice; I will not let you go entirely unpunished.'
>
> "This is what the LORD says:" 'Your wound is incurable, your injury beyond healing. There is no one to plead your cause, no remedy for your sore, no healing for you. All your allies have forgotten you; they care nothing for you. I have struck you as an enemy would and punished you as would the cruel, because your guilt is so great and your sins so many. Why do you cry out over your wound, your pain that has no cure? Because of your great guilt and many sins, I have done these things to you.
>
> "But all who devour you will be devoured; all your enemies will go into exile. Those who plunder you will be plundered; all who make spoil of you I will despoil. But I will restore you to health and heal your wounds,' declares the LORD, 'because you are called an outcast, Zion for whom no one cares.'

> "This is what the LORD says:" 'I will restore the fortunes of Jacob's tents and have compassion on his dwellings; the city will be rebuilt on her ruins, and the palace will stand in its proper place."
>
> (Jeremiah 30:10-18)

These prophecies prove that Lord Yahuah's covenant is legal and binding, regardless of the fact that His own people rejected His Messiah, and have not received His salvation through Yahushua, His Son. Yet, He promises to save Israel as a nation, and a remnant of His people. The remnant He promises to save is one third. In fact, through the prophet Zechariah, Yahuah speaks just that:

> "Two-thirds of the people in the land will be cut off and die," says the Lord YAHUAH. "But one-third will be left in the land. This third I will bring into the fire; I will refine them like silver and test them like gold. They will call on my name and I will answer them; I will say, 'They are my people,' and they will say, 'The Lord, YAHUAH is our God.'"
>
> (Zechariah 13:8-9)

The Lord Yahuah goes on to promise that He will punish all those who oppress them. These prophesies should be taken seriously today by Israel's enemies, particularly those who vow to wipe Israel off the face of the earth. While Israel goes through dark times, it is important for Israelis to remember, that this land was given to them by the Lord Yahuah. He alone is in charge of what happens there. He is the One who apportioned that land, and gave it to Abraham and his descendants. This was how Jacob was empowered to bless his sons by dividing up the land. It is a legacy that came from Yahuah. In spite of Israel's hard-headedness towards Yahuah's plan for salvation, His grace and more importantly, His covenant is binding towards Israel. The rest of the words of Jeremiah's prophecy, reveals Yahuah's Divine Plan, to be known by His own people, intimately.

> "From them will come songs of thanksgiving and the sound of rejoicing. I will add to their numbers, and they will not be decreased; I will bring them honor, and they will not be disdained. Their children will be as in days of old, and their community will be established before me; I will punish all who oppress them. Their leader will be one of their own; their ruler will arise from among them. I will bring him near and he will come close to me, for who is he who will devote himself to be close to me?' declares the LORD. 'So, you will be my people, and I will be your God.'" See, the storm of the LORD will burst out in wrath, a driving wind swirling down on the heads of the wicked. <u>The</u>

> fierce anger of the LORD will not turn back until he fully accomplishes the purposes of his heart. In days to come you will understand this."
>
> (Jeremiah 30:19-24)

That history repeats itself is relevant here, because the roots of the past are what we reap in the future. History repeats itself, because humanity fails to learn from its lessons. And so it goes with the history of the land of Israel, the apportioned land to all of its twelve tribes, that the end of the timeline all the nations of the world converge over the land of Israel for the final battle known as Armageddon. Why? Let's discern more of the history of the transference of power of the Kingdom of Israel. Remember, the Kingdom will be restored at the end of the timeline, when the Messiah returns and begins His millennial reign from the New Jerusalem in the land of Israel.

Israel is Divided

Towards the end of his reign, King Solomon fell into the sin of idolatry, worshiping Ashtoreth, Milcom (Molech) and Kemosh. For his idolatry Yahuah told Solomon, "Since this is your mind, and you have not kept my covenant and my statutes, which I have commanded you, I will surely tear the kingdom from you, and will give it to your servant." (1 Kings 11:5) Again, the Kingdom belongs first to the Lord. He alone appoints the Kings, and He raises them up and brings them down. Idolatry is one of the biggest reasons kings fall, and consequently the entire nation has fallen into the hands of their enemies many times throughout their history. This is a huge bone of contention between Yahuah and His people.

Yahuah sent the prophet Ahijah to Jeroboam, of the tribe of Ephraim, whom Solomon had made ruler over the laborers of the house of Joseph. Ahijah prophesied that Yahuah would take 10 tribes and give them to Jeroboam and if he would listen to all that God commanded him, and walk in the ways of the Lord Yahuah, and do what is right in God's sight, keeping His statutes and commandments, that the Lord Yahuah would build for Jeroboam a sure house, as He had built for David, and would give Israel to him. Immediately upon hearing this, Solomon sought the death of Jeroboam. (1 Kings 11: 26-40)

Upon Solomon's death, the people of Israel gathered at Shechem to make Rehoboam, Solomon's son, king. Jeroboam came together with the people to petition Rehoboam to ease the yoke that Solomon had placed upon the people of Israel. Rehoboam disregarded the counsel of his father's advisors, and instead listened to his friends with whom he had grown up. Rather than easing their burdens, he promised to be even harder than his father had been. The people rebelled, and it is for this karmic reason and generational curse that Israel has been in rebellion against the house of David to this day. The punishment that the Lord Yahuah promised to fall upon the descendants of Solomon, which began with his son Rehoboam, belong to the House of David. The Lord promised would not last forever, but is the generational curse that Israel suffers under to this day. This is the very reason why they rejected Yahushua HaMashiach, who came from this bloodline.

Yet, it was Yeshua who came to not only break this curse upon the House of David, but to break all curses on the land of Israel and on all of its people, which extends to the descendants of all twelve tribes of Israel. This includes the population of the nations of the world today.

> "Jesus Christ redeemed us from the curse of the law by becoming a curse for us, for it is written: "Cursed is everyone who is hung on a tree."
>
> (Galatians 3:13)

Yet, breaking generational curses is not automatic, one must appropriate the work of Christ and His atoning blood onto themselves and their descendants in order for their generational curse to be broken.

After the rebellion and stoning of Rehoboam, the ten northern tribes broke away from the Davidic kings of the tribe of Judah, and power was transferred to the leadership of Jeroboam, the Ephraimite, who set up a new kingdom.

Just as the Lord Yahuah had prophesied to Jeroboam through the prophet Ahijah, Jeroboam became king of the ten tribes, and was well established, for Rehoboam's attack was stopped by the Lord Yahuah Himself. Instead of doing as God had instructed, Jeroboam sought to secure his position through establishing a system of idolatry that would ensure no contact between the northern kingdom of Israel and the southern kingdom of Judah. (1 Kings 12:1-20)

Again, history repeats itself, because the makers of it fail to learn the big lesson. Jeroboam was favored by the Lord to rule the kingdom. Yet, he too fell into idolatry and turned a deaf ear to the Lord who put him in power in the first place. The ten northern tribes quickly fell into the same idolatry for which Solomon had been judged. Jeroboam made two golden calves and set one in Beth-El, a city of Ephraim, and the other in Dan, the principle city of the tribe of Dan. Jeroboam had reason to create his own system of worship.

As all the men of Israel were required to appear in Jerusalem for the feasts of Pesach (Passover), Shavuot (Pentecost) and Succoth (Tabernacles) each year, this would likely lead to a reunification of the northern and southern kingdoms. Jeroboam halted this pilgrimage and filled the void of the true Temple worship by creating his own temple, priesthood, and system of worship. (1 Kings 12:22-33)

The northern kingdom of Israel was never able to repent of their idolatry and for this they were judged by God. Taken captive, Ephraim and its kingdom were eventually scattered throughout the nations of the world never returning to Israel, just as Jacob had prophesied. Hence, 'The Ten Lost Tribes.' Hosea, who was a prophet to the ten northern tribes, speaks of their sin and the Lord's anger towards Israel and their future reunification, especially in chapters 11-13. Israel's sins, is the reason the kingdom was shattered, and the people and their descendants dispersed, into what is called, 'The Diaspora'.

> "Ephraim has surrounded me with lies, the house of Israel with deceit. And Judah is unruly against God, even against the faithful Holy One."
>
> (Hosea 11:12)

Turning to pseudo-gods, sacrificing to them, is how the Israelites blew their inheritance of the land.

> "When Israel was a child, I loved him, and out of Egypt I called my son. But the more I called Israel, the further they went from me. They sacrificed to the Baals and they burned incense to images. It was I who taught Ephraim to walk, taking them by the arms; but they did not realize it was I who healed them. I led them with cords of human kindness, with ties of love; I lifted the yoke from their neck and bent down to feed them. "Will they not return to Egypt and will not Assyria rule over them because they refuse to repent? Swords will flash in their cities, will destroy the bars of their gates and put an end to their plans. My people are determined to turn from me. Even if they call to the Most High, he will by no means exalt them.
>
> (Hosea 11:1-7)

Yet despite Israel's sin, the Lord continues to have compassion on them:

> "How can I give you up, Ephraim? How can I hand you over, Israel? How can I treat you like Admah? How can I make you like Zeboiim? My heart is changed within me; all my compassion is aroused. I will not carry out my fierce anger, nor will I turn and devastate Ephraim. For I am God, and not man—the Holy One among you. I will not come in wrath. They will follow the Lord; he will roar like a lion. When he roars, his children will come trembling from the west. They will come trembling like birds from Egypt, like doves from Assyria. I will settle them in their homes," declares the Lord."
>
> (Hosea 11:8-11)

This is how the Israelites have survived all these centuries. Even though they have been exiled, handed over to be persecuted by their enemies, the Lord's faithfulness to the covenant with them has allowed them to survive, and eventually settle back into the land. Yet, in spite of those miracles, their enemies are numerous. What we see repetitively throughout history, is that the Lord uses the enemy (the satans), to humble and punish His people. We know from Bible history that the Lord can intervene, and bind the powers of the enemies at the turn of a dime, as well as unleash the power of the enemies upon His people. His hand can go either way, depending on how His people behave towards Him.

> "The Lord has a charge to bring against Judah; he will punish Jacob according to his ways and repay him according to his deeds. In the womb, he grasped his brother's heel; as a man he struggled with God. He struggled with the angel and overcame him; he wept and begged for his favor. He found him at Bethel and talked with him there—the Lord God Almighty, the Lord is his name of renown! But you must return to your God; maintain love and justice, and wait for your God always."
>
> (Hosea 12:2-6)

What this entire cosmic human drama is all about, is to sort out who loves the Lord, and who does not. Who will rebel against His precepts, and who will be faithful. Who will believe on Him, and worship Him with all their hearts and souls, and who will turn their backs. Everyone who is given the breath of life, has the same chance to prove themselves and pass this test. Remember, the dispersed lost tribes of Israel make up the rest of the nations of the world.

> "I am the Lord your God, who delivered you out of Egypt; <u>I will make you live in tents again, as in the days of your appointed feasts</u>. I spoke to the prophets, gave them many visions and told parables through them."
>
> (Hosea 12:9-10)

Egypt, which in Hebrew is Mitzraim, means *bondage,* not just as in a nation, but as a metaphor. The Exodus from Egypt was all about deliverance from the bondage of slavery. This theme permeates the entire Bible, and continues with the life, death and resurrection of Jesus Christ, the promised Messiah of Israel. Now it is through Him that we can receive deliverance from the bondage of the powers of darkness of this world. However, after the New Covenant was established, the playing field was leveled out to include both Jews and Gentiles, who together make up the ten lost tribes of Israel.

> "When Ephraim spoke, men trembled; he was exalted in Israel. But he became guilty of Baal worship and died. Now they sin more and more; they make idols for themselves from their silver, cleverly fashioned images, all of them the work of craftsmen. It is said of these people, "They offer human sacrifice and kiss the calf-idols." Therefore, they will be like the morning mist, like the early dew that disappears, like chaff swirling from a threshing floor, like smoke escaping through a window. "But I am the Lord your God, who delivered you out of Egypt. You shall acknowledge no God but me, no salvation and Savior except from and through me.
>
> (Hosea 13:1-4)

The Hebrew words, *Yeshuati,* means 'My Salvation'. The name of the Father is within the name of the Son. Yahuah the Father sent His Son, Yahushua to be the Messiah (Savior) of the world. This is why Yeshua (Jesus) would say, "I and the Father are One." and "No man comes to the Father, except through me."

In the following verses, we know that the power over death comes only from the Lord. This is His promise to His people to save them from the grave. Bring them back to life.

> "I will ransom them from the power of the grave; I will redeem them from death. Where, O death, are your plagues? Where, O grave, is your destruction? "I will have no compassion, even though he thrives among his brothers."
>
> (Hosea 13:14)

Yet, He makes it very clear that those who have rebelled against Him will bear their guilt and fall by the sword.

> "An east wind from the Lord will come, blowing in from the desert; his spring will fail and his well dry up. His storehouse will be plundered of all its treasures. The people of Samaria must bear their guilt, because they have rebelled against their God. They will fall by the sword; their little ones will be dashed to the ground, their pregnant women ripped open."
>
> (Hosea 13:15-16)

Therefore, in order to be able to make any sense out of the many prophecies about what will happen to Israel just before Christ's return, it is important to have some understanding of who and where the tribes of Israel may be dwelling today. The twelve tribes are mentioned in the book of Revelation with the Lord's promise to seal 12,000 from each of the twelve tribes with His mark on them, so that they could not be marked by the Beast. However, it is interesting that the tribes Ephraim and Dan were omitted from receiving the seal of God in the last days, and instead Joseph and Manasseh, replaced them. This is due to their sins of idolatry, and the generational curse that followed.

144,000 Sealed

> "After this I saw four angels standing at the four corners of the earth, holding back the four winds of the earth to prevent any wind from blowing on the land or on the sea or on any tree. Then I saw another angel coming up from the east, having the seal of the living God. He called out in a loud voice to the four angels who had been given power to harm the land and the sea:
>
> "Do not harm the land or the sea or the trees until we put a seal on the foreheads of the servants of our God." Then I heard the number of those who were sealed: 144,000 from all the tribes of Israel. From the tribe of Judah 12,000 were sealed, from the tribe of Reuben 12,000, from the tribe of Gad 12,000, from the tribe of Asher 12,000, from the tribe of Naphtali 12,000, from the tribe of Manasseh 12,000, from the tribe of Simeon 12,000, from the tribe of Levi 12,000, from the tribe of Issachar 12,000, from the tribe of Zebulun 12,000, from the tribe of Joseph 12,000, from the tribe of Benjamin 12,000."
>
> (Revelation 7:1-8)

The Missing Tribes from Revelation

Ephraim and Dan both sinned with regard to Jeroboam's actions. Ephraim's sin was the institution of a false system of worship. (Jeroboam was an Ephraimite.) Dan's sin was one of accommodation, as the tribe of Dan allowed the golden calf to reside within its territory.

This sin committed by Ephraim and Dan is significant, as these two tribes are not among those listed in Revelation chapter 7. Although there are different groupings of the tribes throughout Scripture, this is the only time where Ephraim and Dan are missing (replaced by Joseph and Manasseh). Consistent with the Lord's historical rebukes, it seems that the sin of *idolatry within the land of Israel,* has its payback in the last days, when these two tribes are deprived of the opportunity to testify of the Messiah.

Dan was the one who Jacob said would be a serpent. It is my opinion that this tribe went on not only to worship the serpent gods, but actually carries their DNA.

It should be noted however, that according to Ezekiel, both tribes receive their land grant in the Millennium, which indicates that they are restored back unto the Lord.

There is an interesting verse in the Zohar that links Ephraim to the "church" at Laodicea found in chapter three of Revelation:

"And Ephraim said, **Yet I am become rich,** I have found me out power", namely, the celestial unholy power which presided over the act of idolatry committed by Jeroboam (I Kings XII, 28), without which he would not have been able to succeed. Now, when this king and this priest of the "other side" are subdued, and their power broken, all the "other sides" follow suit, and are also subdued and broken, and acknowledge the sovereignty of the Holy One, and in this way, He alone rules above and below, as it is written: "And the Lord alone will be exalted in that day" (Isaiah 2:11).[1] (Soncino Zohar Volume II p. 67b)

The phrase "*... I am become rich"* is similar to Revelation 3:17, "You say, 'I am rich; I have acquired wealth and do not need a thing.' But you do not realize that you are wretched, pitiful, poor, blind and naked." This is related to the last days when the Lord's name will be made one *Echad,* which is Hebrew for 'unity'. (Hosea chapters 11-13.)

Restoration and Reunification of Ephraim and Judah

One of the important end-time events which signals the return of the Messiah is the reunification of the lost tribes of Israel, Ephraim with their brethren. "All of Israel" (the entire twelve tribes) cannot be saved unless they are all brought back into a unity (Echad). It is necessary for those of Israel who are lost among the nations (Ephraim, the "fullness of the gentiles") to come back in, and only then can this happen. This is the point of *the mystery* of Romans 11:25, "I do not want you to be ignorant of this mystery, brothers, so that you may not be conceited: Israel has experienced a hardening in part until the full number of the Gentiles has come in."

The concept of *Echad* (unity) is key to understanding not only Revelation but all of Scripture. Although Scripture says that the Lord God is Echad (Deuteronomy 6:4), we also know that at the present time, things are not as they should be between Him, Israel and the rest of His creation. That is why the prophet Zechariah says that, "The LORD will be king over the whole earth. On that day there will be one LORD, and his name the only name." (v.14:9) Even though Deuteronomy 6:4 is a statement of fact, it is also a prophecy that will be fulfilled at the return of Yeshua and the beginning of the Messianic kingdom. This is why the most powerful prayer in Israel and amongst Jews throughout the world is the 'Shema'. 'Hear O' Israel, the Lord is God, and the Lord is One' which they chant in Hebrew, *Shema Yisrael, Adonai Eloheinu, Adonai Echad.*

If it's the Lord's Divine Plan to seal and save 12,000 members from each of the twelve tribes listed in Revelation, then one can logically deduce that the descendants of all these tribes are living on planet earth today and will be by the end of days. There have been many books written about the lost tribes, *The Lost Ten Tribes of Israel Found!*, by Steven M. Collins, published by CPA Books and *Lost Israelite Identity/ Hebrew Ancestry of Celtic Races*, by Yair Davidy, published by Russell-Davis publishers, Shiloh-Hebron - Susia - Jerusalem-Beth-El, Israel.[2, 3]

So where could the descendants of the lost tribes possibly be today? Based on Bible history, we know the tribes scattered, we are told the direction most of them went in and can figure out approximately where that is in modern geography. There are many hypotheses about the location of the scattered lost tribes, based on historical and linguistic evidence, and not all of the tribes can be identified. We have some good working guestimates from those spiritually attuned to the Lord's Voice, who have an ongoing relationship with the Living God. The Lord knows who you are!

The Lamb and the 144,000

> "Then I looked, and there before me was the Lamb, standing on Mount Zion, and with him 144,000 who had his name and his Father's name written on their foreheads. And I heard a sound from heaven like the roar of rushing waters and like a loud peal of thunder. The sound I heard was like that of harpists playing their harps. And they sang a new song before the throne and before the four living creatures and the elders. No one could learn the song except the 144,000 who had been redeemed from the earth. These are those who did not defile themselves with women, for they kept themselves pure. They follow the Lamb wherever he goes. They were purchased from among men and offered as first fruits to God and the Lamb. No lie was found in their mouths; they are blameless."
>
> (Revelation 14:1-5)

The 144,000 Jewish Witnesses

Shortly after the rapture, God will call His army of 144,000 Messianic Jewish believers into service to provide a voice of hope for Jews throughout the world. The best friends and most staunch supporters of Jews have always been true, believing Christians. It was this element of the world's population that provided help and support for Israel and Jewish people. According to Bible prophecy, the rapture removes believing Christians from the earth and awakens the 144,000 to their purpose.

These 144,000 preach to Jews worldwide that Yeshua/Jesus Christ is the Messiah. These 144,000 will be spread out worldwide and more than likely go about in pairs, two by two, as Jesus instructed His disciples to do. It will be these 144,000 who will oppose Israel signing a peace treaty for protection; it will be the 144,000 who will identify the antichrist for who he is; it will be the 144,000 who will warn Israel of the treachery of the antichrist, and it will be the 144,000 who will lead the Jews worldwide to the hiding place prepared for them by God in the Judean desert. These 144,000 Jews are going to be strange people by normal standards: they will be celibate, very bold, fearless, spiritually strong and probably very much like John the Baptist. You can read more about the 144,000 witnesses in Revelation 14.

National Israel Today

By 'National Israel', I don't mean the land of Israel, situated in the Middle East, because truly, if the descendants of the twelve tribes of Israel are scattered amongst the nations of the world, then that means, 'National Israel' extends beyond the boundaries of the secular State of Israel. When you think of it this way, it is hard for people who are living outside of the State of Israel to curse the heart, the idea of Israel, or be against Israel in terms of international politics.

Just because a descendant of the Israelites doesn't live in the land of Israel today, doesn't mean that they aren't part of its inheritance and covenant from God. Think about this the next time you hear nations of the world curse Israel, and think on this especially when a coalition of Middle Eastern and Minor Asian countries come against the State of Israel in the coming world war of Gog and Magog, World War III.

Because the information is available to anyone who wants to determine who and where the contemporary Israelites are today, I am only going to present a list of the major countries that represent the majority of the Twelve Tribes of Israel, to make the meaning of end time prophecies clearer. The research indicates that the Israelites are among the world's wealthiest nations and occupy the world's choicest real-estate, and it is in God's plan to make very sure that these nations have all heard the good news of the Kingdom of God proclaimed to them before the return of Christ.

Tribal Groups

Straddling the boundaries between Afghanistan, Pakistan and Kashmir lives the world's largest tribal grouping—the Pathans. All the 15 million Pathans, who comprise some 60 tribes, claim descent from Kish, an ancestor of the Biblical King Saul. Many of them also claim to be the children of the Lost Israelites. The Pathans perform circumcision on the eighth day, wear a fringed garment like the Jewish tzitzit, light candles on Friday nights and observe food taboos similar to the laws of Kashrut. In South Africa, Zimbabwe and Mozambique, tens of thousands of blacks have, in recent years, declared themselves descendants of one of the Lost Tribes.

The Lemba claim to have been cut off from mainstream Judaism hundreds of years ago. They are well-versed in the Old Testament and avoid marriage outside their community. From every imaginable corner of the world theories arise linking different peoples and tribes with the Ten Lost Tribes: the Crimea, the Caucasus, Kenya, Nigeria, Armenia, Persia, Central Asia, North Siberia, West Africa, Peru, South America, Australia, Ireland. While the evidence may at times seem flimsy, the Jewish elements in these tribal cultures continue to fascinate scholar and layman alike.

Let's discern who and where these Tribes are today, and whether they and their customs are rooted in ancient Jewish customs:

Beta Israel-Ethiopia

The Jews of Ethiopia are from Northwestern Ethiopia bordering Sudan. They call themselves "Beta Israel" (House of Israel), claim to be from the tribe of Dan, and number about 500,000, most currently living in Israel.

The Ethiopians preserved authentic Jewish beliefs and practices, including belief in the God of Israel, His oneness, the Jews being the Chosen People, the Torah being the law from Sinai, reward and punishment, redemption, Messiah and Return to Zion. Their texts include: Torah (Orit), Prophets, Laws of Sambet (Sabbath), and a Prayer book. They maintain a strict observance to the Sabbath. For example, women prepare Sabbath food only after immersing in a *mikve,* a ritual purification bath; all work stops midday Friday, no fire is used to keep food warm, but they use candles for light, all work is forbidden on Sabbath day, and they even wear a special Sabbath robe with no belt to prevent tying.

They pray three times a day, morning, noon, and dusk while facing Jerusalem, and have certain blessings and observe the Torah based Holidays such as Rosh Hashanah, Yom Kippur, Sukkoth, Passover, and Shavuot. They eat only meat from kosher animals and perform ritual slaughter while turning the animals head toward Jerusalem and reciting a blessing. The blood is covered, the meat is salted, to remove blood, and forbidden sinews and fats are removed. They maintain the laws of Kashrut, meaning they keep Kosher.

Meat and milk are not cooked together, but poultry is not considered meat for this purpose. They emphasize ritual purity and for this reason their villages are always near a river for immersion. They purify from contact with the dead after seven days, sprinkling on the third and seventh day with water from ashes of a red heifer. Menstruating women separate themselves in a tent for seven days until immersion.

These are the Ethiopian Jews known both as Falashas, the Amharic word for 'landless, wandering Jews,' and as 'Beta Israel,' the house of Israel. In Ethiopia, they engaged primarily in agriculture, but were known also for their exquisite crafts and jewelry. Today, most of Beta Israel live in the state of Israel. In the 1970's and 80's, the Israeli government airlifted thousands of Ethiopian Jews to Israel, rescuing them from political and economic distress. No coincidence there!

According to several traditions and legends, the Ethiopian Jews are the descendants of one of the ten tribes, as their religion is an ancient form of biblical Judaism. Their religious practices are prescribed by the Orit, the Torah translated into their Gez dialect. They possess none of the post-biblical laws.

The Beta Israel of Ethiopia are generally considered Jewish. The great Halachic authority, Rabbi David ben Zimra (Israel, 1500s) wrote: "Those that come from the land of Cush (Ethiopia) are without doubt from the tribe of Dan, and because they did not have scholars of the Oral Law living with them they follow the superficial understanding of the Torah. But if they were taught, they would not reject the rabbinic teachings. Therefore, it is a mitzvah to save them and support them" (Shut HaRadbaz 1:5, 1:7). Rabbi Ovadia Yosef, (Yabia Omer 8, Even HaEzer 11) also considers them Jewish without a doubt.

Afghanistan

Remember, not all the tribes of Israel are considered Jews. The word Jews or Judes comes from the tribe of Judah. At one time, both Northern Israel and Southern Judah practiced the customs and traditions of what we call traditional Judaism. But remember, the tribes were dispersed all over the globe, and now tend to follow local customs. So not all descendants of the lost tribes will show signs of ancient Israel and ancient Judaism in their cultures. Even though these groups are not considered to be Jewish as a result of assimilation, as many endured forced conversion and large-scale intermarriage, they still maintain remnants of Hebrew practices.

In Western Afghanistan, bordering Iran, is a tribe who call themselves *Yusufzai,* which means, 'The Children of Josef.' They claim to be descendants of Ephraim and Manasseh and maintain legends and traditions of being taken away from their ancient homeland. They live secluded in high mountains and marry only among themselves. Even though they are devout Muslims, they have Hebrew names, wear fringes on the corners of their clothing, light candles for Sabbath on Friday night and don't cut the hair on sides of the head, all resembling Jewish customs and traditions.

A second tribe lives on the border between Afghanistan and Pakistan and call themselves *Bani Yisrael*, which means, 'The Children of Israel.' They hold onto a tradition of being of the Lost Tribes and use names such as Asher, Naphtali, Ephraim,

Manasseh, Reuben, and Gad. They circumcise their sons on the eighth day, wear four cornered garments with fringes and some wear small boxes with verses inside. They too, light candles for the Sabbath on Friday night, and don't labor or cook. They bake twelve loaves for the Sabbath. The tribes of Afghan number about 15 million individuals.

Kashmir

The Kashmiri live in Northern India which borders Tibet and Nepal. They maintain a tradition that they are descendants of the Tribes of Israel. They have a lighter complexion and different facial features than the local population. All of their tribal names are reminiscent of the Hebrew: Asheriya, Dand, Gadha, Lavi, Kahana, Shaul; as well as the names of their places: Samaryah, Mamre, Pishgah, Heshba, Gochen. They light candles for Sabbath, observe a feast in spring called Pasca, (resembling the Passover), and adjust the lunar and solar calendars to coincide. They have beards and side-locks, and the Star of David is prevalent on their dwellings and places of worship. They number 5-7 million.

Burma

On the border of Northeastern India between Bangladesh and Myanmar live the Shin lung. They claim to be descendants of Manasseh and have a detailed oral history of exile through Assyria, Babylon, Persia, and Afghanistan where they were forcibly converted to Islam. They later migrated to Tibet, following the Wei River into central China, were persecuted by the Chinese, escaped and hid in mountainous caves, and there became known as "Shin lung" which means 'mountain/cave dwellers.' They were later banished and migrated west through Thailand, Myanmar, finally settling in the Chin Mountains on the border between Burma and Bangladesh. They performed circumcision on the eighth day until it became too difficult because of exile and persecution; now they only give the name on the eighth day.

The priest of every village is called Aaron, whose wardrobe resembles that of the high priest of Israel, which includes a tunic, breastplate, embroidered coat, with belt and high hat. Traditionally they give offerings and sacrifices like those of the Torah. They have a traditional song that accompanied them through their migrations: "We must keep the Passover festival because we crossed the Red Sea on dry land. At night we crossed with a fire, and by day with a cloud. Enemies pursued us with chariots and the sea swallowed them up and used them as food for the fish. And when we were thirsty, we received water from the rock."

There are some 1-2 million Shin lung. In the late 1800s missionaries arrived, and the Shin lung recognized their beliefs and events in the Old Testament, and subsequently converted to Christianity thinking they were returning to their ancestral people. Eventually, many realized they descended from Jews, and thousands converted to Judaism. Of those, approximately 5,000 live in Burma, and a few hundred have settled in Israel.

Japan

There are among the thousands of words and names of places with no real etymological meaning in Japanese. And oddly enough, they all correspond with Hebrew words. This is no coincidence! Even the Kings have similar names. The first known king of Japan, who was named Osee, ruled around 730 BC. This king has been identified with the last king of Israel, Hoshea, who died around the same time, at the time of the Assyrian exile of the ten tribes from Israel. The holy Japanese Shinto temple strongly recalls and resembles the ancient holy Israelite temple of Solomon in Jerusalem, which housed a holy of holies section and several gates. Several artifacts in Japan have been traced to Assyrian and Jewish sources, among them, a well in Koryugi with the words "well of Israel" inscribed on its side.

There are so many connections between ancient Israel and the traditions, language and religious customs of the Japanese, which can only be traced to their historical roots as one of the lost ten tribes of Israel.

The Jews wave a sheaf of their harvest stacks of grain seven weeks before Shavuot (Pentecost, Leviticus 23:10-11), they do this also at the Feast of Booths (Sukkot, Leviticus 23:40). This has been a tradition since the time of Moses. Ancient Israeli priests also waved a plant branch when he sanctifies someone. David said, "Purge me with hyssop, and I shall be clean" [Psalm 51:7(9)]. This is also a traditional Japanese custom.

When a Japanese priest sanctifies someone or something, he waves a plant branch. Or, he waves a harainusa which is like a plant branch. Today's harainusa is simplified and made of white paper that is folded in a zig-zag pattern like small lightning bolts, but in old days it was a plant branch or cereals.

Here are some words that have similar sounds and identical meanings in both Japanese and Hebrew:

Daber: in Hebrew, to speak -- *Daberu*: Japanese for chatting.
Goi: a non-Hebrew or foreigner – *Gai'Jeen*: prefix for a foreigner, a non-Japanese.
Kor: cold in Hebrew -- *Koru*: to freeze in Japanese.
Knesset: Parliament in Hebrew -- *Kensei*: Constitutional government in Japanese.

It has also been suggested that the carts of Otsu and Kyoto are of ancient biblical design, as they are different from any others in Japan. Could it have been that the ancient Israelites and their wives and children have been conveyed to Japan in these carts? Among the Samurai sect, there is a tradition that their ancient ancestors came to Japan from western Asia around 660 BC. The name Samurai recalls *Samaria.*

So, which of the ten lost tribes do the Japanese belong? There are those who claim that the Mikado, the Japanese emperor, is a descendant of the Hebrew tribe of Gad. The word Mikado recalls the Hebrew word for 'his majesty the king,' 'Malkhuto'. Kings in ancient Japan were called mikoto, which comes from the Hebrew word *malkuto* which means "his kingdom."

The Star of David is a symbol also used at Ise-Jingu, the Shinto Shrine for the Imperial House of Japan. On both sides of the approaches to the shrine, there are street lamps made of stone. You can see the Jewish Star of David carved on each of the lamps near the top.

The crest used on the inside of the shrine (Izawa-no-miya) at Ise-Jingu is also the Star of David. This has existed since ancient times. In Kyoto pref., there is a shrine called "Manai-jinja" which was the original Ise-jingu Shrine. On the crest of Manai-jinja is also the Star of David. Also, there since ancient times.

Joseph Eidelberg, a Jew who travelled to Japan and stayed for years at a Japanese Shinto shrine, wrote a book titled, *The Biblical Hebrew Origin of the Japanese People.* He discovered that many Japanese words are similar to ancient Hebrew. For instance, Japanese say *hazukashime* to mean disgrace or humiliation. In Hebrew, it is "hadak hashem", to tread down the name, as in Job 40:12. The pronunciation and the meaning of them are both almost the same.

The Japanese say *anta* to mean "you," which is the same in Hebrew. The ancient Japanese word for an area leader is "agata-nushi;" "agata" is area, and "nushi" is a leader. In Hebrew, they are called "aguda nasi." Eidelberg writes that this is a beautiful Hebrew expression, if we suppose that there have been some changes in the pronunciation throughout history. These words are to be spelled: *"Haiafa mi yotsia ma naane ykakhena tavo."* which is pronounced in Hebrew nearly exactly the same.

Translated means: "Who shall bring out the beautiful? What words shall we say for her to come out?" This phrase comes from the myth of Amaterasu, the Japanese goddess of light.

In addition, the name of the Japanese priest is Koyane which sounds close to the Hebrew word *Cohane* which means priest. Eidelberg shows many other examples of Japanese words which seem to have a Hebrew origin.

Another interesting parallel, is that the Robe of Japanese Priests resembles the Robe of Israeli Priests. The Bible says that when David brought up the ark into Jerusalem; "David was clothed in a robe of fine linen" (1 Chronicles 15:27). So were priests and choirs. In the Japanese Bible, this verse is translated into "robe of white linen." In ancient Israel, although the high priest wore a colorful robe, other ordinary priests wore simple white linens. Priests wore white clothes for holy events. So, do Japanese priests wear white robes at holy events.

In Ise-jingu, one of the oldest shrines of Japan, all the priests wear white robes. And in many Shinto shrines of Japan, people wear white robes when they carry the omikoshi as did the Israelites. Buddhist priests wear luxurious colorful robes. But in the Japanese Shinto religion, white is regarded as the most holy color.

The Emperor of Japan, just after he finishes the ceremony of his accession to the throne, comes alone to stand in front of the Shinto god, wearing pure white robe and bare feet. This is the same as when Moses and Joshua removed their sandals to stand in front of God in bare feet (Exodus 3:5, Joshua 5:15). Marvin Tokayer, a Rabbi who lived in Japan for 10 years, wrote in his book: "The linen robes which Japanese Shinto priests wear have the same figure as the white linen robes of the ancient priests of Israel. "

The robe of the Japanese Shinto priest has cords of 20-30 centimeters long (about 10 inches) hung from the corners of the robe. These fringes are the custom of the Israelites. Deuteronomy 22:12 says: "make them fringes in the corners of their garments throughout their generations." Fringes (tassels) were a token that he was an Israelite.

In the gospels of the New Testament, it is also written that the Pharisees "make their tassels on their garments long" (Matthew 23:5). A woman who had been suffering from a hemorrhage came to Jesus (Yeshua) and touched the "tassel on His coat" (Matthew 9:20).[7] Imagined pictures of ancient Israeli clothing sometimes do not have these fringes but their robes actually were tasseled. The Jewish Tallit or prayer shawl has fringes in the corners according to tradition.

Japanese Shinto priests wear on their robe a rectangle of cloth from their shoulders to thighs. This is the same as the ephod worn by David: "David also wore a linen ephod." (1 Chronicles 15:27) Although the ephod of the high priest was colorful with jewels, the ordinary priests under him wore the ephods of simple white linen cloth (1 Samuel 22:18). Rabbi Tokayer says that the rectangle of cloth on the robe of Japanese Shinto priest looks very similar to the ephod of the Kohen, the Jewish priest.

The Japanese Shinto priest puts a cap on his head as do the Israeli priest (Exodus 29:40). The Japanese priest also puts a sash on his waist. So, did the Israeli priest. The clothing of Japanese Shinto priests certainly resembles that used by ancient Israelites to a high degree.

The Japanese Religious Priests called the Yamabushi put a black box on their foreheads in a way identical to that which Jews put on a phylactery on their foreheads. Yamabushis are religious men in training and are unique to Japan. Today, they are thought to belong to Japanese Buddhism. But the Buddhism in China, Korea, or

India have no such custom. The custom of yamabushi has existed in Japan before Buddhism was imported into Japan in the seventh century. The clothes worn by the yamabushi are basically white. On his forehead, he puts a black small box called a tokin, which is tied to his head with a black cord. He really resembles a Jew putting on a phylactery black box on his forehead with a black cord. The size of this black box tokin is almost the same as the Jewish phylactery. But the shape of the tokin is round and looks like a flower.

Originally the Jewish phylactery placed on the forehead seems to have come from the forehead plate put on the high priest Aaron with a cord (Exodus 28:36-38). It was about 4 centimeters (1.6 inches) in size according to the folklore, and some scholars say that this was in the shape of a flower. If so, it was very similar to the shape of the Japanese tokin worn by the yamabushi.

Israel and Japan are the only two countries in the world that I know of, that use the forehead box. The Yamabushi use a big seashell as a horn. This is very similar to a Jew blowing a shofar, or ram's horn. The way the Yamabushi's horn sounds very much like a shofar sound. And there are no sheep in Japan, the Yamabushi had to use seashell horns instead.

The Japanese Omikoshi resembles the Ark of the Covenant. In the Bible, in First Chronicles chapter 15, it is written that David brought up the ark of the covenant of the Lord into Jerusalem. "David and the elders of Israel and the commanders of units of a thousand went to bring up the ark of the covenant of the LORD from the house of Obed-Edom, with rejoicing. Now David was clothed in a robe of fine linen, as were all the Levites who were carrying the ark, and as were the singers, and Kenaniah, who was in charge of the singing of the choirs. David also wore a linen ephod. So, all Israel brought up the ark of the covenant of the LORD with shouts, with the sounding of rams' horns and trumpets, and of cymbals, and the playing of lyres and harps." (15:25-28)

The shape of the Japanese Omikoshi resembles that of the Ark of the Covenant. Japanese people sing and dance in front of it with shouts, and with the sounding of musical instruments. These are very similar to the customs of ancient Israel. Japanese people carry the omikoshi on their shoulders with poles - usually two poles. So, did the ancient Israelites: "The Levites carried the ark of God with poles on their shoulders, as Moses had commanded in accordance with the word of the LORD." (1 Chronicles 15:15)

The Israeli ark of the covenant had two poles (Exodus 25:10-15). Some restored models of the ark as it was imagined to be, have two poles on the upper parts of the ark. But the Bible says those poles were to be fastened to the ark by the four rings "on its four feet" (Exodus 25:12). So, the poles must have been attached on the bottom of the ark. This is similar to the Japanese omikoshi.

The Israeli ark had two statues of gold cherubim on its top. Cherubim are a kind of angel, a mysterious heavenly being. They have wings like birds. Japanese omikoshi also have on its top the gold bird called Ho-oh, which is an imaginary bird and a mysterious heavenly being. The entire Israeli ark was overlaid with gold. Japanese omikoshi are also overlaid mostly with gold. The size of omikoshi is almost the same as the Israeli ark. Japanese omikoshi may be a remnant of the ark of ancient Israel.

Eidelberg's list contains several thousand words. This is no accident. In ancient Japanese folk songs, there appear many words which we cannot understand as Japanese. Dr. Eiji Kawamorita says that many of them are Hebrew. A Japanese folk song in Kumamoto pref. is sung "Hallelujah, haliya, haliya, tohse, Yahweh, Yahweh, yoitonnah...." This also sounds like Hebrew.

Chiang-Min China

> "Behold, these are coming from afar. These from the north and the west and these from the land of Sinim."
>
> (Isaiah 49:12)

This prophecy, spoken by Isaiah, promised the return of Lost Israelites from all corners of the Earth and from Sinim. Interestingly, Sinim is the Hebrew word for China. In fort-like villages in the high mountain ranges on the Chinese-Tibetan border live the Chiang-Min of West Szechuan. It has been claimed that the Chiang-Min are descendants of the ancient Israelites who arrived in China several hundred years before Christ.

The Chinese people were established on earth by beings from another planet. Their first ruler was an E.T. they called the "Yellow Emperor" who is immortalized in stone statutes all over China, and imbedded in their culture and history. He was called a "son of the heavens". The Yellow Emperor was China's first ruler, which many believe was an Extraterrestrial. Ancient Chinese records talk of a very special being that descended from the Syuan Yuan star. The name of this star, Syuan Yuan, is similar to the Hebrew word for China, which is Sinim. An ancient Chinese drawing of the Syuan Yuan constellation has been identified by modern astronomers as that of the Leo constellation. Its brightest star is (Alpha Leo), Regulus.[8]

The Chiang-Min dwell on the border between Tibet and China in the mountainous area of Sichuan. They appear more Semitic than Oriental, and have a tradition of having migrated from the West after a journey of three years and three months. They claim to descend from Abraham, and their ancestor had 12 sons. They believe in one all-powerful god called the "Father of Heaven" who they refer to in times of trouble as the Tetragrammaton.

He watches over the world, judges fairly, rewards the righteous, punishes the wicked, accepts repentance, and gives atonement. In the past, they had written scrolls of parchment and books, but they were lost. It is forbidden to worship foreign gods or idols upon punishment of death. They also have priestly and sacrificial services reminiscent of those of the Torah, using an earthen altar that must not be fashioned by metal tools, where the priest places his hand on the head of the sacrifice.

The missionary Torrance, who visited Cheng-du in the early part of this century, insisted that the Chiang-Min strongly resembled the Israelite branch of the Semitic race. He observed that several of their customs were reminiscent of ancient Israelite tradition. "The plough the Chiang use is similar to the ancient Israelite plough and is drawn by two oxen, never by an ox and an ass. This in accordance with the Biblical stipulation: 'You shall not plough with an ox and ass together,'" Torrance stated. The Chaing-Min believe in one God. During "times of calamity or acute distress," writes Torrance, "they issue a moan or cry which sounds like 'Yawei', suggestive of the biblical name of God." The Scottish missionary also claims that the Chinese conception of sacrifice came from the ancient Israelites.

Finally, Chiang-Min priests, like the ancient Israelite priests, wear girdles to bind their robes, and bear a sacred rod shaped like a serpent, reminiscent of the brass serpent fashioned by Moses in the wilderness.

Notes:

1. Soncino Zohar Volume II p. 67b
2. Steven M. Collins, *The Lost Ten Tribes of Israel Found!*, published by CPA Books
3. Yair Davidy, *Lost Israelite Identity/Hebrew Ancestry of Celtic Races*, by, published by Russell-Davis publishers, Shiloh-Hebron - Susia - Jerusalem-Beth-El, Israel
4. *The Lost Tribes*. retrieved from: <pbs.org>
5. Rabbi Yirmiyahu Ullman. *The Lost Tribes Where are they Today?* <ohr.edu/yhiy/article.php/1817; www.rabbiullman.com>
6. Rabbi Eliyahu Avichail, *The Ten Lost Tribes of Israel in Afghanistan, Pakistan, Kashmir, Myanmar, and China.* Amishav Organization. North American Conference on Ethiopian Jewry Arimasa Kubo.
7. Charles B. Williams, translation, *The New Testament: A Translation in the Language of the People*, Adesite Press, August, 2015.
8. *Was the Yellow Emperor an Extraterrestrial?* http://ancientufo.org/2016/07/yellow-emperor-son-heavens/

CHAPTER TWENTY-NINE

Messianic Prophecies and the Lost Tribes of Israel

"The days are coming, 'declares the LORD,'
when I will bring my people Israel
and Judah back from captivity and restore them to the land
I gave their ancestors to possess," says the LORD.
(Jeremiah 30:3)

"For I will take you out of the nations; I will
gather you from all the countries
and bring you back into your own land."
(Ezekiel 36:24)

Tradition held that when the Ten Tribes were found, reunited and restored to the Holy Land, the messianic age was close at hand. But is it literal or spiritual? Spiritual Israel is comprised of everyone who believes on the Lord Yahuah (YHVH) and His plan for salvation through His Son Yahushua HaMashiach, aka Jesus Christ, and all those who keep His commandments and follow His precepts. In my opinion, the tradition and prophesy about the ten lost tribes being found and restored, it is about being restored to the Lord, not necessarily to the land.

There are many who live in the land of Israel today who came from the Diaspora, (the dispersed and scattered tribes of Israel) who are restored to the land, but most are not believers in the Father's Son as their Messiah. If the key prophecy in the New Covenant is, "And this gospel of the kingdom will be preached in the whole world as a testimony to all nations, and then the end will come," (Matthew 24:14), then that means all the nations of the world must first hear the good news of the coming kingdom of God on Earth, and have every chance to accept the King of the Kingdom as their Lord and Savior. Then the end will come.

I believe this is the restoration that will reunite the lost tribes of Israel, when they turn back to the God of Israel wherever they are around the world. After all, how else will the 144,000 who will be chosen to carry the seal of God during the tribulation, be able to preach the gospel of the kingdom to the unbelievers, if they are not saved themselves? The seal of God saves them, because they accept His plan of salvation through His son Yahushua.

In the early 16th century, Bartholeme de Las Casas became the champion of the Native American Indians, devoting his lifetime to improving their conditions in the West Indies, Peru and Guatemala. Las Casas wrote: "These Indians can bring near the redemption. If we treat them humanely in this world and convert them to Christianity, we are preparing for the redemption of the Western world in the messianic era. Their conversion is apt indeed, as I am convinced the Indians originate in Ancient Israel. Indeed, I can bring proofs from the Bible that they are of the Lost Tribes."

The association of the Indians with the Lost Tribes has been heard again and again. The report by Portuguese traveler Antonio Montezinos some 120 years later aroused remarkable interest. "There is a Jewish Indian tribe living beyond the mountain passes of the Andes. Indeed, I myself heard them recite the Shema (the expression of Jewish faith) and saw them observe the Jewish rituals."

If the American Indians are part of the lost tribes, then that makes the United States the largest nation inhabited by the descendants of the lost tribes; the United States is made up of immigrants from all over the world. Many who study the migration of the lost tribes believe that the descendants in the United States comes from the tribe Manasseh. Manasseh was given the double portion from his brother Ephraim. Many also believe that Great Britain is inhabited by the descendants of the lost tribe of Ephraim. The word, *Brit-ish* in Hebrew means, people of the covenant.

Geneticists at an Israeli hospital said they found a unique Jewish genetic mutation in the DNA among an American Indian tribe, that indicates they are descendants of Jews expelled from Spain 600 years ago. The findings of the study, conducted at the Sheba Medical Center near Tel Aviv, show that a group of Indians from the State of Colorado bear the so-called "Ashkenazi mutation," on the BRCA1 gene – a marker unique to European Jews.

Those "secret Jews," or "Anusim" in Hebrew were believed to be descendants of a Jewish man who left Europe and settled in south America about 600 years ago – likely among the hundreds of thousands of Jews expelled by Spain in 1492, during the Inquisitions, and possibly among those who sailed with Christopher Columbus, according to the report, which appears in the European Journal of Human Genetics.[1]

Menasseh ben Israel, a Dutch Jewish scholar widely respected in both Christian and Jewish circles, played a central role in strengthening the association of the American Indians with the Lost Tribes. Deeply influenced by Montezinos' report and stimulated by his own mystical disposition, Ben Israel gradually fashioned his most important and best-selling book: *The Hope of Israel.* In 1655 Menasseh ben Israel met with Oliver Cromwell, Lord Protector of England, at Westminster. He dedicated *The Hope of Israel* to Parliament and submitted his petition for the recall of the Jews who had been expelled from England.

Ben Israel's approach was shrewd indeed. He reiterated the belief that the dispersion of Jews to all corners of the Earth was the beginning of the redemption. The first stage had been realized, Israelite tribes had been discovered in the Americas! By completing the dispersion of the Jews, Cromwell himself could hasten the messianic era. He must readmit the Jews to England. Ben Israel associated the Hebrew word for "the end of the Earth" with the medieval term "Angle-Terre" or England. He wrote, "...All which things of necessity must be fulfilled, that so Israel at last being brought back, to his own place, peace which is promised under the Messiah may be restored to the world; and concord, which is the only Mother of all good things."

These words echoed the hopes for a better world, awakened in the second half of the 18th Century during the American and French revolutions. Many abolitionists, for example, claimed that the Messianic Age would be ushered in when the slaves were freed and when the Native Americans, descendants of the Ten Lost Tribes, were converted to Christianity.[2]

The Two Witnesses

> "And I will give power to my two witnesses, and they will prophesy for 1,260 days, clothed in sackcloth. These are the two olive trees and the two lamp stands that stand before the Lord of the earth."
>
> (Revelation 11:3-4)

These two men show up on earth after the rapture. They are God's gift of final grace to the people of the earth who refused to submit to the lordship of Jesus Christ prior to the rapture. They will witness to the unbelievers about the plan of Salvation through Christ. Some will recognize the error in their lives and repent and seek God. These two men will proclaim the gospel and provide hope for those left behind. Their message is for the salvation of the soul. They will have no message as to how you can avoid the hell that life on earth has become, because there is no hope to avoid that tribulation. If you are left on earth, then your destiny is to suffer and more than likely die. But they will preach that those left still have the hope of salvation in the afterlife.

Though the Bible does not say who these two men are, many speculate that they are Elijah and Enoch, two ancient prophets of God who never died. Regardless, they will be responsible for many of the natural catastrophes that will wreak havoc on the property and economy of the earth.

They will have the power to prevent rain, and will cause a drought lasting three and a half years. They will turn water into blood, cause plagues and make life miserable in general for those who are still left on earth. Also, they will be invincible, as many will try to kill them only to be killed by their own hands. Those who attempt to blow them up will themselves be blown up; those who attempt to shoot them will have their guns explode in their hands; those who attempt to poison them will be poisoned by their own efforts. Only the world dictator will be able to kill them and only when God allows it.

The purpose of all the misery that these two witnesses inflict on the population is to inspire people back to God in a spirit of repentance. The misery will be so great that when the world dictator, the antichrist, does finally kill these two, and the world will rejoice in a Christmas-like celebration, giving gifts to one another. Three and one-half days after their death, they will be resurrected in full view of the entire population of the world, (broadcast on TV) and ascend to heaven at the command of the Lord when He calls them to "Come up here." Shortly after he kills the two witnesses, this new world order dictator will declare himself to be God. He is the final antichrist.

> "If anyone tries to harm them, fire comes from their mouths and devours their enemies. This is how anyone who wants to harm them must die. These men have power to shut up the sky so that it will not rain during the time they are prophesying; and they have power to turn the waters into blood and to strike the earth with every kind of plague as often as they want.
>
> Now when they have finished their testimony, the beast that comes up from the Abyss will attack them, and overpower and kill them. Their bodies will lie in the street of the great city, which is figuratively called Sodom and Egypt, where also their Lord was crucified. For three and a half days men from every people, tribe, language and nation will gaze on their bodies and refuse them burial."

The inhabitants of the earth will gloat over them and will celebrate by sending each other gifts, because these two prophets had tormented those who live on the earth. But after the three and a half days a breath of life from God entered them, and they stood on their feet, and terror struck those who saw them. Then they heard a loud voice from heaven saying to them,

"Come up here." And they went up to heaven in a cloud, while their enemies looked on. At that very hour there was a severe earthquake and a tenth of the city collapsed. Seven thousand people were killed in the earthquake, and the survivors were terrified and gave glory to the God of heaven. The second woe has passed; the third woe is coming soon."

(Revelation 11:5-14)

The Messianic League

In the book of Isaiah chapter 19 in the Amplified Bible it states that in the future, Egypt, Israel and Assyria (Syria), will become the Messianic League. Imagine that! Here is the entire passage as it appears in the Amplified Bible. Emphasis and commentary are mine:

"Listen carefully, **the Lord is riding on a swift cloud** and is about to come to Egypt;
The idols of Egypt will tremble at His presence,
And the heart of the Egyptians will melt within them.
"So, I will provoke Egyptians against Egyptians;
And they will fight, each one against his brother and each one against his neighbor,
City against city, kingdom against kingdom.

The swift cloud is the Lord's spaceships. I established this in Book Two: Who Is God? that when scripture refers to the Lord coming in a cloud, or riding on a cloud, it is referring to His spacecraft. In this case, a 'swift cloud', which means it will move very quickly, zip in and out in the blink of an eye, just as most UFOs do.

"Then the spirit of the Egyptians will become exhausted within them and emptied out;
And I will confuse their strategy,
So that they will consult the idols and the spirits of the dead,
And mediums and soothsayers.

"And I will hand over the Egyptians to a hard and cruel master,
And a mighty king will rule over them," declares the Lord God of hosts.

The waters from the sea will dry up,
And the river will be parched and dry.

The canals will become foul-smelling,
The streams of Egypt will thin out and dry up,
The reeds and the rushes will rot away.

The meadows by the Nile, by the edge of the Nile,
And all the sown fields of the Nile
Will become dry, be blown away, and be no more.

The fishermen will lament (cry out in grief),
And all those who cast a hook into the Nile will mourn,
And those who spread nets upon the waters will languish.

Moreover, those who make linen from combed flax
And those who weave white cloth will be ashamed.

[Those who are] the pillars and foundations of Egypt will be crushed;
And all those who work for wages will be grieved in soul.

The princes of Zoan are complete fools;
The counsel of the Pharaoh's wisest advisors has become stupid.
How can you say to Pharaoh,
"I am a son of the wise, a son of ancient kings?"

Where then are your wise men?
Please let them tell you,
And let them understand what the Lord of hosts
Has purposed against Egypt [if they can].

The princes of Zoan have acted like fools,
The princes of Memphis are deluded [and entertain false hope];
Those who are the cornerstone of her tribes
Have led Egypt astray.

The Lord has mixed a spirit of distortion within her;
Her leaders have caused Egypt to stagger in all that she does,
As a drunken man staggers in his vomit.

There will be no work for Egypt
Which head or tail, [high] palm branch or [low] bulrush, may do.

> In that day, the Egyptians will become like [helpless] women, and they will tremble and be frightened because of the waving of the hand of the Lord of hosts, which He is going to wave over them. The land of Judah [Assyria's ally] will become a terror to the Egyptians; everyone to whom Judah is mentioned will be in dread of it, because of the purpose of the Lord of hosts which He is planning against Egypt.
>
> In that day five cities in the land of Egypt will speak the language of [the Hebrews of] Canaan and swear allegiance to the Lord of hosts. One [of them] will be called the City of Destruction.
>
> In that day, there will be an altar to the Lord in the midst of the land of Egypt, and a memorial stone to the Lord near its border. It will become a sign and a witness to the Lord of hosts in the land of Egypt; for they will cry to the Lord because of oppressors, and He will send them a Savior, a [Great] Defender, and He will rescue them. And so, the Lord will make Himself known to Egypt, and the Egyptians will know [heed, honor, and cherish] the Lord in that day. They will even worship with sacrifices [of animals] and offerings [of produce]; they will make a vow to the Lord and fulfill it. The Lord will strike Egypt, striking but healing it; so, they will return to the Lord, and He will respond to them and heal them.
>
> In that day, there will be a highway from Egypt to Assyria, and the Assyrians will come into Egypt and the Egyptians into Assyria; and the Egyptians will worship and serve [the Lord] with the Assyrians.
>
> **In that day Israel will be the third party with Egypt and with Assyria [in a Messianic league]**, a blessing in the midst of the earth, whom the Lord of hosts has blessed, saying, "Blessed is Egypt My people, and Assyria the work of My hands, and Israel My heritage."[3]

In order for Israel, Egypt and Assyria to be aligned in a Messianic League, they all must come together through common unity through the Messiah. This sounds like the Millennial Reign of Christ, when He returns to Earth to set up His Kingdom in the New Jerusalem that will arrive through the ancient portal in Jerusalem, and overlay the old Jerusalem, which according to scriptures, will be destroyed by the Gentiles. He comes to reign as King of kings, Lord of lords of all the nations. To bring these ancient enemies together is nothing short of a miracle of God and the specific work of Messiah.

The word *Revelation* in Greek means "unveiling," or "disclosure." The purpose of the Prophetic Book of Revelation unveils Jesus Christ and discloses *who* his Celestial Army will be. The prophesies of Revelation expose to us the public appearance of His coming *with the Clouds* in great *Glory*. The prophesies point to a time when Jerusalem will be trampled over by the Gentiles that will lead up to as well as include the last days oppression and Great Tribulation (see Revelation 11:1-2). It is only when Jesus Himself appears, will the Gentiles be shattered and broken like pottery with His rod of iron (see Revelation 19:11-16; Psalm 2:9). It will only be when His feet again stand on the Mount of Olives, the ancient space portal, which is the location where He ascended into Heaven in a *Cloud* (see Acts 1:9-11), that the warring nations that are gathering up against Jerusalem will be defeated once and for all.[4]

Then the city will no longer be trampled underfoot by the Gentiles (see Zechariah 12:2-3; 14:2-7; Joel 3:12-17). We are on our way to that glorious moment. The times of the Gentiles are coming to an end.

> "There will be great distress in the land and wrath against this people. They will fall by the sword and will be taken as prisoners to all the nations. Jerusalem will be trampled on by the Gentiles until the times of the Gentiles are fulfilled."
>
> (Luke 21:23-24)

Notes:

1. Are Native Americans Part of the Lost Tribes? By JewsNews, https://www.jewsnews.co.il/2013/05/25/are-native-americans-part-of-the-lost-tribes.html, May 25, 2013.
2. The Lost Tribes. retrieved from: <pbs.org>
3. The Amplified Bible, Zondervan (February 1, 2001)
4. Rev Willem J.J. Glashouwer, *Jerusalem, the UN and the times of the Gentiles*, http://www.whyisrael.org/2017/01/12/jerusalem-the-un-and-the-times-of-the-gentiles/, January 2017.

CHAPTER THIRTY
The Marriage Covenant

A happy marriage is the union of two good forgivers.
~ Robert Quillen

God Himself instituted marriage, the idea and the ideal, in Eden, between Adam and Eve. This is the ideal, the trinity of God, man and woman, living in holy harmony and love, together trusting God.

The marriage covenant is usually officiated with a ring. The ring symbolizes the bond that never ends, is eternal. Did you know why the marriage ring is placed on the fourth finger from the thumb of your hand? Because it's the only finger that has a vein which is directly connected to your heart.

> "Love is patient and kind; love does not envy or boast; it is not arrogant or rude. It does not insist on its own way; it is not irritable or resentful; it does not rejoice at wrongdoing, but rejoices with the truth. Love bears all things, believes all things, hopes all things, endures all things.
>
> Love never ends. As for prophecies, they will pass away; as for tongues, they will cease; as for knowledge, it will pass away."
>
> (1 Corinthians 13:4-8)

> "Therefore, what God has joined together, let no one put asunder (separate)."
>
> (Mark 10:9)

This scripture suggests that when God is at the heart of the marriage, the greatest challenges can be overcome through the grace and supernatural power of God's Laws of Covenant, which goes according to His Will. When one partner errs, there is hardship, pain and suffering, but through miraculous spiritual interventions of forgiveness and humility, broken marriages can get put back together. When there are extreme circumstances, such as abuse of person or substance, this is not always possible, in which case God, who comes through as Grace, is the forgiving force of all who end up in divorce. There is nothing God will not forgive and renew.

The greatest marriages are built on team work.
A mutual respect, a healthy dose of admiration,
and a never-ending portion of Love and Grace.
- Zig Ziglar

There are two different covenants established in marriage, spiritual and physical covenants. This applies to relationships where sexual intercourse was involved. Sexual intercourse creates a spiritual covenant otherwise known as a soul tie. This explains why people tend to repeat situations or seem to attract similar types after divorce. However, when we break the soul ties or spiritual covenants that were created via sexual intercourse, which are *binding rituals*, then we can be liberated form the cycle of poor choices, or being in cursed relationships. The power of redemption that lies in the Blood Covenant of Christ, with which a divorced individual can be renewed and aligned back to their original destiny. If you are divorced, consider breaking the soul ties with your ex-partner. Here is a simple, yet powerful prayer that will set God's healing and deliverance to you in motion:

Breaking Controlling Soul Ties

Heavenly Father, in the name of Jesus I renounce and come out of agreement with the ungodly soul ties between me and [*your ex-partner's name here*] that have been established in my body, my soul, or spirit.

In the name of Jesus and by the power of His blood, I break all of Satan's power and authority over me in these soul ties and ask you, Lord to remove from me all ungodly influences from [*your ex-partner's name here*] and to return to me every part that has been tied in bondage to [*your ex-partner's name here*]. I purpose and choose to forgive [*your ex-partner's name here*] and let go of my bitterness for how [he/she] treated me. Holy Spirit come and heal my heart, renew my mind, cleanse me and show me your truth.

As we already established, all covenants are contractual agreements, and the marriage covenant is no different. However, in the marriage covenant, there are some hidden loopholes, invisible attachments, which have to do with both the generational curses and blessings of the family into which one marries. The offspring of the marriage agree to take this all on, not only in their genetics, but also in their soul, resulting in spiritual experiences and challenges they are destined to face. They are coded in the DNA and in spirit, because of the spiritual legal ground associated with generational and family curses and blessings.

Families celebrate the blessings of a child, such as our inherent talents, gifts, and family resemblances. Unfortunately, also come the family curses which the child's soul has agreed to take on. This presents the opportunity for atonement for the sins of their ancestors, to break those generational curses through their lives. But how can one soul take on such a challenge and overcome? Let's discern.

> "Marriage is not 50-50; divorce is 50-50. Marriage must be 100-100.
> It isn't dividing everything in half, but giving everything you've got!"
> ~ Dave Willis.org

Did You Marry Into a Generational Curse?

Generational curses are not limited to bloodlines or genetic ancestry. The truth is you can marry or enter business covenants that create a soul tie with an already established generational curse. Most people are not aware of this spiritual law, but if we look at the rate of divorce, generational curses are not hard to miss. Marriages in and of themselves are covenants, binding legal contracts, sealed in good faith and love, but a legal agreement nevertheless. God's plan for marriage was simply stated at the very beginning when the Evadamic race began, that the two shall become one.

> "This explains why a man leaves his father and mother and is joined to his wife, and the two become one flesh."
>
> (Genesis 2:24)

This oneness extends beyond the sexual union, but the union of two souls, creating a soul-tie that according to the marriage covenant can only be broken through death, as in the vow, 'till death do us part'.

Generational curses cause limitations on families, regardless of how educated, wealthy, healthy or prosperous that person may be to all appearances. All curses have expiration dates. However, there are some keys needed to break the codes that keep these demonic assignments active. Just as all legal agreements have time limits, so do generational curses. What's important is that we find the keys to breaking them so that whatever generational curse we may experience, can run its course, whether it's in our own family line, or our partner's life and by extension our life because of your marital or business covenant with them.

My experience with generational curses through the partnership is to first clear your own family and generational sins and curses, before you can even begin to deal with your partner's. The answer is always giving it all to God. It requires the attitude, 'The buck stops here', meaning that whatever happened in the past, whoever in your ancestry brought on that curse, is irrelevant at this point, as all that matters is, that you are the one destined to break it.

This requires deep humility and the knowledge that according to the laws of heaven, through the grace of Christ, a soul redeemed by the Lord is given the authority, known in the legal realms as *proxy,* to stand before the thrown of Grace on behalf of that ancestor, and repent for the entire bloodline, for the generational and familiar sins that brought on demonic assignment, along the generations in the form of a curse of some kind.

The Lord Yahuah specifically said to the children of Israel *not* to make any covenants with the inhabitants of Canaan, nor were they to enter into marriage covenants with them. In fact, the Lord specifically said, "Do not give your daughters to their sons, neither allow their sons to marry your daughters" (Deuteronomy 7:3; Ezra 9:12; 1 King 11:2) The reason for this is that they would be influenced through implantation from their gods (fallen ETs) and become corrupted, through getting them to turn the children of Israel from their God, the Lord Yahuah and program through implantation to serve other gods.

This is the reason why the Lord instructed the children of Israel to destroy all their altars, break down their images, cut down their stands, and burn all graven images with fire.

> "Do not intermarry with them. Do not give your daughters to their sons or take their daughters for your sons, for they will turn your children away from following me to serve other gods, and the Lord's anger will burn against you and will quickly destroy you. This is what you are to do to them: Break down their altars, smash their sacred stones, cut down their Asherah poles and burn their idols in the fire."
>
> (Deuteronomy: 7:3-5)

One might interpret Deuteronomy 7:3-5 that the Lord was biased or showed favoritism towards the children of Israel. The Israelis ARE His genetic experiment, but this instruction given regarding the spiritual implications and the *spiritual legal ground* created when His people, filled with His DNA and spirit, would be mixed, blended, contaminated with that of pagan ET gods. In establishing any kind of covenant with them, including marriage or holding possession of any of their spiritually charged items, carried demonic assignment, which automatically brought a curse on their victims, which then was perpetuated as generational curses, the kind which was already dominating the Canaanites.

It would be wise to do a little investigative research on your future spouse. Find out their family history, observe how they treat each other, if there is denial around any person or issue. If you marry into a family which is under a generational curse, you will inherit through spirit transference. It can only be broken through repentance to the Messiah Savior, the Lord Yeshua Jesus who came to break all curses. According to *spiritual legal ground*, true deliverance out of family curses can only come through repentance to Him.

I am publishing a separate workbook on *How to Break Generational Curses*, titled, *Finding Freedom*, which will be a healing and deliverance companion book to the entire book series of *Who's Who in the Cosmic Zoo?* My purpose has been to share how to *discern* truth from deception, demons from angels, and to identify the God of gods, Lord of lords and King of kings from all the rest. The truth shall set us free, but first we must let go of our attachment to the lies we've been told and chosen to believe, to cling to, and cut the cords from the gods with a little 'g' so that the Lord of lords can set us free.

Jesus said, "The Spirit of the Sovereign LORD is on me, because the LORD has anointed me to proclaim good news to the poor. He has sent me to bind up the brokenhearted, to proclaim freedom for the captives and release from darkness for the prisoners," (Isaiah 61:1; Luke 4:18)

How many of us are in mental prisons, chained with emotional bonds, genetic dead ends, or all types of enslavement and oppression to the forces of darkness? We are all captives at one time or another to something or someone, and Jesus will free us as soon as we ask Him and sincerely press into Him.

I am encouraging all those who are single to take the time to investigate the family which you are contemplating making your own forever. There's an old saying, when you marry someone, you marry their family. If your future spouses' family does not accept you, or treat you with respect, you may want to think twice about entering a marriage covenant with all of them, because take it from me, you will be challenged by their demons.

In the event of divorce, estrangement, isolation from a family or step family, we can choose to give them up to the Lord, and forgive them from a distance, while entertaining no relationship with them. This is specifically sanctioned by the Lord in His scripture. A leopard never changes its spots, but if it wanted to be washed in the Blood Covenant of Jesus Christ, it would have hope for transformation.

> "*Light and darkness cannot occupy the same space at the same time*. Light dispels darkness. When light is present, darkness is vanquished and must depart. More important, darkness cannot conquer light unless the light is diminished or departs."
>
> Robert D. Hales, May 2002

"Do not be unequally yoked with unbelievers. For what partnership can righteousness have with wickedness? *Or what fellowship does light have with darkness?*"

(2 Corinthians 6:14)

When the Lord turns them around, we will joyfully accept, love, and unite with them as fellow Christians in the Body of Christ. However, in the meantime, we can save ourselves and our children from all the negative, neglectful, and abusive ways, passed down to us through a generational curse, by distancing ourselves from unrepentant family members who perpetuate the cursed family patterns of abuse. However, I encourage everyone in similar situations, to never give up hope and continue to pray for their salvation and for the Lord's mercy to be poured out on them. You may also pray for ministering spirits and angels to intervene according to God's Will.

Habits determine character, and our character determines our destiny. This is how we raise successful, well-adjusted Christian children, by cultivating good habit patterns that creates a good character, that a fortunate destiny will be assured to all our descendants. When we break generational curses, we break them not only on ourselves, but on the entire family line, past, present and future. When we decide to walk with the Lord, and be a part of His covenants, both through the covenant of faith and that of blood, our descendants will inherit our freedom from the *generational curses* that we chose to break within ourselves.

"With God all things are possible." (Matthew 19:26)

It is our responsibility to do our homework, to learn as much as possible about both sides of our families, particularly from a spiritual perspective. By doing so, we will save ourselves from massive headaches and heartaches, disappointments, financial losses in the future and the types of battles that often lead to divorce. Satan's job is to keep generational curses going, see Exodus 20:5, Exodus 34:7. Therefore, he doesn't want people to know that these curses can be broken, let alone *who* has the power to break them. Staying true to his character,

"The thief (Satan) comes only to steal and kill and destroy."
(John 10:10)

Satan's demonic assignment on the bloodlines through generational curses is to perpetuate a continuous cycle of negativity to oppress and depress us, but more importantly to prevent us from realizing our destinies. Be aware, covenants are obtained by ignorance, meaning generational curses may continue to dominate our life, especially if we are unaware that they even exist. Satan casts spells, implants minds through the *spirit of unbelief*, to maintain power and superiority over the ignorant. And, when we combine ignorance with arrogance, we get evil. This is why the Lord says, "My people perish from lack of knowledge (ignorance)." (Hosea 4:6) Get knowledge, as with knowledge comes understanding, and those who abide in faith in Christ, abide in humility, which dispels arrogance.

Many who go through spiritual counselling and healing therapy after a heart-breaking divorce are amazed to learn that even after their marriages have been *legally* dissolved, they're still experiencing the curses from them.

Remember, there is man's law, and there is God's laws. Spiritual covenants are spiritually binding. When people get divorced legally, they must also break their spiritual cordings and bonds to their ex-partner. This cording sets up the spiritual legal ground for their demons to travel back and forth, kind of like a spiritual high-way and byway, to cord and hook into the soul energy and essence of that person. Remember, demons are responsible for energy theft, in keeping in with their father who is satan, verified in John 10:10.

Many people continue to be vampirized by their ex-spouses, and have no idea why they are stuck in some type of *Twilight Zone*, looping into past patterns while thinking they've moved on with their lives. This type of energy theft can come in the form of hardships, especially when trying to establish new relationships. Therefore, it's imperative to break the spiritual part of the covenant, so the curses will no longer be in effect, the demons will no longer have the *spiritual legal ground* to continue the cycle of defeat and negativity in our life.

This holds true for business partnerships as well. All too often, marriage cov-enants involve business partnerships as well.

Getting rid of objects such as jewelry and clothing that formed a part of the for-mer marriage will also serve as a way to renounce these soul ties and close all doors to the spiritual ties associated with them. If you really want to move on with your life, purge! Remember, the Lord Yahuah instructed His children of Israel to destroy any thing that was attached to the curse of these other gods, which are all forms of idolatry.

Sexual Bonds and their Spiritual Covenants

In Book One, we defined the Archons[1] as the controlling forces that pull the strings in our world. Ephesians 6:12 is directed towards the *powers, the principalities, the rulers of the darkness of this present world,* which represent the Archonic strategy of inflicting sexual misery, abuse and servitude on the human race, starting as young as possible. This is another reason for the abductions phenomena, implanting babies and young children with sexual programming. No one is born gay, transgender, lesbian or queer. It's an alien implant, used to control and spiritually enslave humankind through the distortions and perversions of the abuse, misuse and vampirization of human sexual energy. We know that we humans are not born this way, contrary to popular LGBTQ manifesto, because many people get delivered out of gay and lesbian lifestyles after having their implants removed.

Sexual energy involves the sacredness of intimacy and life force. This is why it is sanctified through the marriage covenant. When this energy is perverted, dishonored, and vampirized through satanic rituals, abuse, or pedophilia, it is not only rape, it entails soul and energy theft. This is what the grace and salvation through Jesus Christ offers, the restoration of the soul and its original energy intact, through being brought into reconciliation with its Creator.

I'm not going to engage in the controversies over gay marriage. I am going to expose the misuse of sexual energies outside of the marriage covenant, as this behavior provides the spiritual legal ground that justifies generational curses and the draining of one's soul's energy.

During abductions, abductees report all kinds of invasive procedures done to their bodies. Many share similar reports of being forced to perform sexual acts that were totally foreign and unusual to their sexual preferences. People who never even thought of homosexual acts now find themselves involved and engaged in them. People who were repulsed by the notion of anal sex found themselves being taken advantage of by the negative aliens, the Grays, Reptilians and Nordics. This will splinter and scatter the soul energies, rather than integrate and heal them, by confusing their sexual energies. The moral code given to Moses outlines this in detail.

By promoting distortions and perversions around the sexual act, our gender roles, and by corrupting our relationship with our parents, thus violating the Fifth Commandment, the human being inevitably descends into misery, confusion and in many cases, obsession, slavery and misogyny. This program, propagated and controlled by the Gray aliens and their reptilian matrix, continues to enslave the soul energies of humankind on earth. This alien assortment of hybrids is not indigenous to the earth but are here, nonetheless, through the process of invasion and deception.

The sexual implants are multiple layers of mind control impulses that have been crafted to control, deceive, separate, confuse, torture and steal human life force, which is sexual in nature, and it is a violation of the human soul. The abduction of children who are used in depraved ways, through prostitution, in witchcraft rituals, further damage them and create psychopaths and sexual predators. Those who have been molested and sexually abused as children are more likely to grow up with the psychic wound to rebel against the Creator's moral code, because they don't know any better, and their souls have been raped and drained of its desire to connect with the Creator. The aliens have broken the sacred connection.

Pedophiles and satanists steal life force and sexual energy in the deluded belief that it's going to help them reach immortality. Selling one's own soul and becoming a vampire makes for nothing but a demonic bottom dweller on a temporary artificial timeline, whose destiny is destruction. On the other hand, those who act with love and integrity, who live a life of faith, and faithfulness to both their Creator and to their beloved, end up achieving the Mind of Christ or Christ Consciousness needed to ascend out of this Archonic bondage. We can do all things through Christ. Christ within us gives us the power to overcome the world, just as He has done, with the light and integrated power that can douse the wicked flames of the Archons, through exposing their criminal behavior and false light programming which is infecting the masses. This form of slavery exists across the board, extending to those in politics, religion, Hollywood, all who have all been victimized by their perversions and corruption.

Sexual bonding with anyone outside of the Marriage Covenant is the spiritual legal ground that leaves a soul open for stolen energy and ultimate soul theft. Love and support comes from those who are doing the real shadow work of deliverance by exposing these psychic vampires and thieves of innocent souls, instead of allowing or enabling the most disgusting crimes to stay hidden in the shadows! The *family trance* which marks generational curses often comes from the guilt, shame, blame and embarrassment of sexual abuses and misconduct, coupled with the fear of confronting them, so denial is enacted to keep these sins concealed in the shadows.

Rape is never about sex, but about domination, the violence used to drain the soul of its creative life force using sex. Children who are molested and penetrated at a young age undergo an energy transference. The molester transfers his depraved energy *into* the child's vessel. This alien implant enters through the orifices of the human body, which can corrupt both body and soul and lead to eventual destruction. Many victims of sexual abuse are overwhelmed with desires to commit suicide, at the prompting of the spirit of the alien implant, whose aim is to destroy body and soul. Those who live are corrupted to the point of being a vessel of *spiritual territory* that will be used by Draconian forces at will. This is the essence of slavery.

There is nothing human about trafficking in the slave trade, where women, young girls and little boys are traded and sold like cattle into prostitution. This is pervasive in the Middle East, because Islam condones pedophilia, as do Luciferians, who use the pure and innocent energy of a child in their satanic rituals. It is no coincidence that since Jupiter entered into Scorpio, the sign of sex, abuse, and power, that the horrors of human trafficking and child sex rings and pedophilia are being exposed and prosecuted. It is time to set the captives free, the silent ones who have been oppressed through fear and powerlessness in the face of Archonic controlling entities.

Sexual abuses, rape and energy theft goes back to ancient times, to the angels who coveted earth women and fell from their first estate. A group of renegade extraterrestrials invaded the earth, for its women and for their sexual energies. While there's nothing new under the sun, it seems to keep getting worse, but soon Jesus will return and put an end to these perversions and abuses once and for all. The Age to Come, which is the Millennial Reign of Christ on Earth, also known as the Age of Aquarius, will be a time of liberation from these Archonic Demonic Controllers.

The different races make up the greater whole, representing the diverse universe, which is greatest when its many parts work in unison and harmony. The archon agenda is to keep us all divided, at each other's throats, through use of *spiritual implants* and *spiritual limitation devices* implanted into our etheric bodies. Those whom they choose to lead us are implanted with such controls into their very souls. These negative implants fire us to hold on to deeply engrained beliefs, rigid and resentful of questioning. We become disconnected from each other on a massive scale, creating the conditions that, due to the mind-body connection, eventually cause disease.

The Archonic Draconian implants are designed specifically to corrupt, pervert, distort and abuse the very image and likeness of God, in whose image humanity was created. Their purpose all along has been to control, enslave, and reprogram us. Jesus came to set the captives free. He and His Heavenly Hosts of faithful human extraterrestrials are our only hope to be delivered out of this morass, and have our bodies restored and transformed back into the glorious light bodies that are promised in the Covenants of God.

We can see that the Marriage Covenant is a clear example of our relationship with God. Through Christ we can be reconciled back into the Kingdom of Heaven, when our souls, and our bodies are raised up, to be what God intended us to be, immortal, incorporeal and incorruptible. We become the collective Bride of Christ, invited to the marriage supper of the Bridegroom. This is the hope of glory that is promised to all those who put their faith in Christ.

Everyone progresses in their own time, as far as lifestyle, relationship, and families, all of which can be healed and resolved. By being reconciled back to Source, who is the Creator of our Souls and Spirits, one can find true deliverance through the redemptive power of Jesus Christ. He is in the business of saving souls from the bondages of sexual abuse, sexual exploitations and the vampirism that prey upon human souls and life forces.

"The thief comes only to steal and kill and destroy;
I came that they may have life, and have it abundantly."
~ Jesus

(John 10:10)

Spiritual Situational Awareness

If we carry the Word of God in our vessels, then our words carry creative power, and words matter. The Marriage Covenant is created through vows, which are words. Our words spoken to accept the salvation of God through the grace of Christ done are the words of a prayer, life and soul changing, to the billions of humans who confess the sinner's prayer.

In this way, the Words of God have power over all evil and everything that belongs to the dark side. That includes word curses, witchcraft spells, and every evil thing said aloud, that must submit to the power of God, the Force that created both light and darkness.

This clearly indicates that the spiritual battle is over words spoken on both sides. We must combat the words of what we say in the heat of the moment, or even in jest, which can turn into an affirmation by creating what was spoken in sarcasm to physically manifest. This is a common type of self-sabotage that becomes a negative spirit that piggybacks onto what was intended as a joke. It is not funny when the enemy of our souls, using his vessels to pronounce word curses, becomes an evil operating, a counterfeit, in our lives. God is not the author of confusion. We are warned that we are going to have to give an account of every word spoken. "But I say to you, that every idle word that men shall speak, they shall give account thereof in the day of judgment." (Matthew 12:36)

Covenants are words of power and might, words that bind and release the kingdoms of darkness and the Kingdom of Light on Earth. We choose what and *whom* we serve by what we say.

For those who have never experienced the transforming power of salvation through the living God, Jesus Christ, here is an ancient prayer that will connect you to His grace and saving power, regardless of what has happened to you, or what lifestyle you have adopted. He doesn't care, Christ came to save those who are lost, and all of us are saved behind enemy lines. This world has so many bondages, because the god of this world seeks to keep it, and enslave the souls made in His image to abuse.

Say this prayer out loud, and reach out to someone who believes to pray for you as well. You will need reinforcements, but know this, Christ is mighty to save, and no matter who you are or what's happened to you, He came to set you free. He will save even you.

The Sinner's Prayer Written by King David, (Psalm 51)

> "Have mercy on me, O God, according to Your unfailing love; according to Your great compassion blot out my transgressions. Wash away all my iniquity and cleanse me from my sin. For I know my transgressions, and my sin is

> always before me. Against You, You only, have I sinned and done what is evil in Your sight, so that You are proved right when You speak and justified when You judge. Surely, I have been a sinner from birth, sinful from the time my mother conceived me…
>
> "Cleanse me with hyssop, and I will be clean; wash me and I will be whiter than snow…
>
> "Create in me a pure heart, O God, and renew a steadfast spirit within me. Do not cast me from Your presence or take Your Holy Spirit from me. Restore to me the joy of Your salvation and grant me a willing spirit to sustain me. Then will I teach transgressors Your ways, and sinners will turn back to You."
>
> (Psalm 51:1-19)

It's not the prayer that saves, but the repentance and faith behind the prayer that lays hold of salvation. Now, to invite Jesus, the Living God, and His Holy Spirit into your life to transform you, say this prayer out loud:[2]

> *"Heavenly Father and King of the Universe, Creator of my Soul, I come to you in prayer asking for the forgiveness of my sins. I confess with my mouth and believe with my heart that Jesus is the Son of God. I know that I am a sinner and that I cannot save myself. No longer will I close the door when I hear you knocking. By faith I gratefully receive your gift of salvation. I am ready to trust you as my Lord and Savior. Thank you, Lord Jesus, for coming to earth. I believe you are the Son of God who died on the cross for my sins and rose from the dead on the third day. I repent of my sins. In invite you Holy Spirit to come into my heart and reveal your truth to me. Thank you Jesus, for bearing my sins and giving me the gift of eternal life. I believe your words are true. Come into my heart, Lord Jesus, and be my Savior. Amen."*

Covenant of Forgiveness

The foundation of all healthy, happy, successful relationships lies in reconciliation with the Lord and Creator. God wants a relationship with us. Once that relationship is established through trust, then the Lord can take His relationship with us to the next level, and bring us into the marriage covenant with Him, by sending us a helpmeet, someone with whom we can practice His unconditional love. That doesn't mean that any one of us is perfect, nor will be our mate perfect, but our partners challenges will be compatible with what our souls needs to learn and cultivate.

Marriage is the lifelong journey of learning to love like Christ.
~ fiercemarriage.com

Life is an experience of relationships. Spiritual lessons can only be demonstrated through relationship. Forgiveness, tolerance, acceptance, and the many ways one expresses love, can never be learned alone. Not one of us wants to be alone. It is in our nature to have relationship with each other as well as with our Creator. Regardless of your relationship status, I want to encourage everyone reading this to get your life right with your Creator now. If you press in to His Covenants, regardless of whether you enter the Marriage Covenant, you will find that a relationship with the Lord is far from being one-sided. All those in covenant with Him are also beneficiary to His eternal promises to receive His Kingdom. God wants a relationship with us.

"When you draw nigh to God, he will draw closer to you."
(James 4:8)

Marriage is a thousand little things...It's giving up your right to be right in the heat of an argument. It's forgiving another when they let you down. It's loving someone enough to step down so they can shine. It's friendship. It's being a cheerleader and trusted confidant. It's a place forgiveness that welcomes one home, and arms they can run to in the midst of a storm. It's Grace. ~ Darlene Schact, The Time-Warp Wife

NOTES

1. Ella LeBain, *Who's Who in the Cosmic Zoo? A Spiritual Guide to ETs, Aliens, Gods & Angels,* Book One - Third Edition, *Enter the Archons,* p.30, Tate Publishing, 2013.
2. Kevin Ewing, *Did You Marry into a Generational Curse?* http://kevinlaewing.blogspot.com/2014/03/did-i-marry-into-generational-curse.html, March 22, 2014

CHAPTER THIRTY-ONE

IMPLANTS & SPIRITUAL LIMITATION DEVICES

I will not be silent.
"First, they came for the Socialists, and I did not speak out—
Because I was not a Socialist.
Then they came for the Trade Unionists, and I did not speak out—
Because I was not a Trade Unionist.
Then they came for the Jews, and I did not speak out—
Because I was not a Jew.
Then they came for me—and there was no one left to speak for me."
-Martin Niemöller

When most people hear the word *implant*, they immediately think dental, but there are so many other types of implants which have a strong effect on our spirit and physiological bodies.

Implants and spiritual limitation devices are energetic and subtle barriers on any spiritual path. They effectively cross all boundaries of religion, faith, and belief system. Implants are a form of mind control, and can take a strong hold on one's personal, emotional, chemical, and physical outlook. They block our way by causing blind spots, or create false realities in our consciousness, limiting our access to connect with our soul and its relationship with our Creator God. They are external control mechanisms from the Dark Forces that keep us in a dualistic reality. Although there are many types, purposes, and causes, they all act as unconscious channels of negative energy into our lives and represent karmic ties and associations that need to be healed.

Through the vast research networked by abductees, myself included, we have observed patterns of implants capable of acting biologically and chemically but are etheric in nature. We have learned that one of the purposes behind abductions is to program abductees to serve an alien agenda via implant programming. This is why most abductees are returned to their bodies and lives in a subtly different frame of mind, the one they've been programmed to play in a social experiment, orchestrated by their abductors.

Alien implantation is a form of demonic possession. The word *daemon* is Greek for *intelligences* or *knowing.* Demons are unusually intelligent aliens, whether they be cyber-genetic clones or organic life forms, and they are all about supporting the demonic alien agenda. Demons may have evil spirits; however, demons are not spirits, but a type of alien. These aliens may even be artificial intelligences (AI), robotics or hybrids, mixes with organic matter that make them physical or interdimensional in nature, nonetheless, they are not spirits. However, spirits do attach to them. For discernment purposes, there is a distinction between demons and evil spirits. The reason so many confuse the two is because demons can behave like evil spirits, as they are intelligences programmed for the nefarious agenda of controlling human minds, bodies, genetics, and energy fields.

As I discerned and established in Book One of *Who's Who in the Cosmic Zoo?*[1] along with succeeding books Two and Three, there is a hierarchical structure to the Kingdom of Darkness, or the Draconian Empire. Satan is at the top, but that word *satan* is a broad term, which literally translates from Hebrew to English as *adversary.* There are many adversaries or 'satans' as I have referred to them in plurality. Because satan is limited and cannot be in more than one place at a time, he uses fallen angels, demonic entities, intelligences, aliens, greys, evil spirits, and implants as his surrogates.

Implants may be mistaken for spirits or demons by healers in Deliverance Ministries, but they are different. These are not alive and conscious to be dismissed, but are programs that must be disabled, dissolved, cancelled, removed, and replaced with the indwelling Spirit of Christ.

The Abductees

Dr. David Jacobs, Director of the International Center for Abduction Research,[2] has been collecting data on abductees for over twenty-five years. He says abductions are a global phenomenon. The most common experiences are the feelings of paralysis, lost time, and needle phobia. Some abductees wake up with bruises on their bodies, even though those sleeping beside them swear they never left the bed. We have proven that it is the soul body, also known as the etheric body, that is being abducted.

The usual routine is for abduction during sleep, is removal from the planet, sometimes in space ships, and then having different types of invasive medical examinations that seem to focus on sexual organs. Most abductees report that they are being told this is being done for the purpose of a human-alien hybridization program. Aliens have also been known to collect skin grafts from a variety of abductees.

Abductees are then implanted and returned to planet earth, to live out their implants' programming. Most people are not aware they've been manipulated or implanted in what is a social experiment conducted by aliens. This experiment could involve anything, any realm or topic, from the socio-political to religious to sexuality. There are many programs of experimentation that these beings are manipulating and pulling the strings, using abductees to perform actions abhorrent to them, to be vessels of influence within the areas of society where they live and work, to advance the alien agenda.

The International Center for Abduction Research (ICAR)[2] provides accurate information to therapists and lay individuals who are interested in abductions, by assisting them to cope with the variety of problems that are caused through the use of hypnosis, and other regression procedures.

Only about 10% of the population cannot be hypnotized. I happen to be one of them. Therefore, hypnosis was not an option for me to retrieve my memories. In addition, hypnosis can be the cause and effect of other issues, which can exacerbate instead of healing the underlying issue. Therefore, Spiritual Deliverance and Implant Removal done through the Kingdom of Heaven's healer, who is the Holy Spirit, Jesus Christ, is a more efficient and permanent process to become clear of implants from the abductions, as well as staying protected from the dangers of hypnosis.

ICAR started collecting data on abductees in 1999,[2] and discovered patterns amongst abductees that seemed to indicate that people are chosen based on their family ancestry, according to bloodlines and genetics. Dr. Jacobs reported that those with hazel or green eyes had the highest percentage of being abducted, following those who have the RH factor in their blood. Both traits happen to be prevalent in serpent – reptilian races.[1] (See, Book One of *Who's Who in the Cosmic Zoo?*)

It's been determined by researchers that there are hidden switches and triggers found inside the human genome that have been used in implant activation, similar to the Sleeping Soldier syndrome. These can be revealed through Deliverance Ministry.

Harvard Professor and Pulitzer Prize Winner, Dr. John Mack,[3] author of *Abduction: Human Encounters with Aliens*, reported that abduction reports are spread all across the planet. Due to the avalanche of anonymous abduction reports to the professional researchers, there are just as many, if not more, of those who have been abducted but have not reported them. This caused Dr. Mack to conclude that there are just as many 'silent abductees', who are those who have chosen not to come forward and share their experiences for a variety of reasons. Some people may be silent because of their implantation, to keep quiet. Many abductees are given screen memories to replace any memory of their abductors and their abduction experiences. Some of these memories may never be fully recovered.

According to Dr. Mack, the aliens are real and are abducting people for two purposes: to influence the transformation of human consciousness, to prevent the destruction of Earth's ecosystems, and to create a hybrid offspring between aliens and humans.

Harvard professor Dr. Mack put his entire career on the line when he began to accept and deal with his clients' claims that they themselves are human-alien hybrids. Some reported to him that they were half-human and half-alien, at least psychologically or spiritually. Dr. Mack also conceded that the laws of physics can be broken, as many abductees claimed that the aliens can float them through solid objects such as doors and closed windows.

Dr. Mack routinely put his clients under regressive hypnosis, which revealed past lives. Connecting with one's past must be a protocol in the process of total Deliverance. Christians miss this most important piece, as there is a pre-existent implant in most branches of Christianity that serves as a spiritual limitation device. See the scripture Hebrew 9:27, which is one of the most misunderstood or misinterpreted scripture taken completely out of context. Contrary to fundamentalist tenets, reincarnation is a biblical teaching, and the implant blinding Christians to it, keeps the soul seeking deliverance, in bondage. Christians must incorporate this important piece into the healing and deliverance process.

It was the late great Dr. Mack who showed the psychiatric community that the UFO abduction syndrome is a real problem that deserves serious clinical attention.

Ancient Aliens did a documentary on the Disclosure of abductions, titled, 'The Returned,' on August 26, 2016, and questioned why abductees were taken and then returned. They proved that abductions are not a modern occurrence, as ancient mythologies tell stories of humans being abducted by otherworldly beings. Just as today, thousands of people continue to report being taken by aliens and then returned with implants and genetic mutations. We conclude that our society has been infiltrated by aliens. Abductees have been given instructions to assist their abductors to help build a new human race, one that is more like the aliens, one that is space-faring, unlike us.

Dr. David Jacobs[2] was told by abductees that they were 'injected' with knowledge, which when the time was ripe will be switched on, despite the fact that they now have no idea to what or to whom that knowledge many pertain. When we summarize all contained in the reports, we concluded that the Grays, the Dark Blue Frog Men, the Tall Whites, and the Reptilian Hybrids are using humans to create a hybrid race, who are being raised off planet inside space ships and underground laboratories. That it's just a matter of time before they are brought to Earth to replace terrestrial humans. These beings are different than the sleeping giants and imprisoned fallen angels inside the earth to which the Book of Enoch refers, see 1 Enoch and 3 Enoch.

Abductees claim they are returned in order to complete a mission they have in the future, even though many have no idea what that is. Most abductees are told they are 'chosen' while they've been implanted. This implant of being 'chosen' comes close to the idea that the Jews are chosen, or 'The Chosen Ones', making the abductees counterfeits and competitors in a game they do not understand. The aliens are at war with the Lord, who chose the Jews when He used His own DNA to seed the Hebrew people and culture, and implanted them with supernatural knowledge. He taught scribes His language, the Hebrew language, which is the language of the Angels as each letter represents the 22 root races and corresponding 22 constellations. The Lord gave His Laws (the Torah) to Moses.

On the contrary, abductees are taught nothing and have no conscious memory of even being implanted, until the aliens activate their switch. This is a deliberate strategy by the counterfeiters as an attempt to conceal their evil agenda to take over earth. It's been hypothesized by both researchers and abductees that their hidden switches involve the integration of the alien-human hybrids on earth, which would be the complete infiltration and invasion of society.

In 1994, I attended a metaphysical fair in Florida, during a time when I used to give my workshops on *ETs, Aliens or Angels?* and met a man who tried to receive a reading from a psychic who also read palms. When he revealed his palm to her, she examined his hands, front and back, and to her shock, discovered that he was without lines, and had absolutely no finger prints! I will never forget the look on her face. I knew he was not human, but an alien human hybrid. His eyes were blue, he was tall, thin with brown hair. In every other way, he looked perfectly normal, but he was not a normal human being. This is how subtly they slip into society. They may appear to be one of us, but they are different. This has been going on for millennia.

There is not just one race of hybrids, there are many. Reptilian-humans, as well as grey alien hybrids, and the Tall Whites, or Nordics, all walk amongst us. They live inside the earth, and have bases on our Moon, Mars and other planets in our solar system. They are in a conflict over the real estate of planet earth, and over us, the terrestrial humans who are soul-matrixed.

> "The Egyptians, the Babylonians and the Persians rose, filled the planet with sound and splendor; then faded to dream – stuff and passed away. The Greeks and the Romans followed and made a vast noise, and they are gone; other peoples have sprung up and held their torch high for a time, but it burned out, and they sit in twilight now, or have vanished.... All things are mortal, but the Jew; all other forces pass, but he remains. What is the secret of his immortality?"
>
> (Mark Twain, American Poet, Author, Agnostic, Skeptic; 1835-1910)

Abductions and Abortions: What's the Connection?

> "And in those days the women shall become pregnant and abort their babies. And cast them out from their midst Yea, they shall abandon their children (that are still) sucklings, and not return to them, and shall have no pity on their beloved ones."
>
> (1 Enoch 99:5)

The Book of Enoch tells us that these fallen angels taught men many things, and abortion was one of them:

> "...showed the children of men ... the smitings of the embryo in the womb, that it may pass away..."
>
> (1 Enoch 69:12)

Another prophesy from Enoch that came true. Anyone who reads my books, knows that I consider the Books of Enoch, the Words of God. The Coptic Christians kept his books relevant in their Bible Canon, as they did not submit to the Roman Empire who rejected them along with many other Jewish texts.

At the time of the publication of this manuscript, I feel like I'm the only one who is aware of this connection between alien abductions and abortions, and I need to spread the word. For all those who have been misled, led astray, deceived, implanted with the false security that abortion is good, normal, acceptable to God, I'm here to tell you, take another look at what we have been told!! Who am I to tell you so? I am acting as the voice of your conscience, the voice of reason and common sense, a fellow believer and experiencer who sees through the lies of the manslayer. It is well known by all those who have birthed children, and felt their life force begin in our womb, seen their heartbeat in the sonogram and listened to it, that we know the God of life is present from the womb, that we are indeed fearfully and wonderfully made.

> "Before I formed you in the womb I knew you,
> before you were born I set you apart;"
> (Jeremiah 1:5)

> "I praise you because I am fearfully and wonderfully made;
> your works are wonderful, I know that full well."
> (Psalm 193:14)

What we must consider, the very words of Jesus, in both Luke and Matthew. This fierce defender of children, the least of His kingdom, were invited to come to Him unreservedly, and He was quite frank in stating His opinion on all those who would offend a child.

> "If anyone causes one of these little ones--those who believe in me--to stumble, it would be better for them to have a large millstone hung around their neck and to be drowned in the depths of the sea."
>
> (Matthew 18:6)

A bit later in those same chapters He went on to express deep sympathy and feared for all woman who were pregnant or nursing, especially at the End of Days.

> "How dreadful it will be in those days for pregnant women and nursing mothers!"
>
> (Matthew 24:19)

If we think this over critically, we hear the warning in His words: the human race, especially His chosen, are made the target of final attacks by the enemy of humanity, the Antichrist and his ilk. Look to history to connect these dots! The ancient gods demanded blood sacrifices, humans were preferred, and children were prime. Abortion is another name for human sacrifice, the shedding of innocent blood.

Who would best be served by the implanted idea that abortion is natural, necessary, liberating, are the enemies of humankind who want to see his days end in sin and misery, or the saving, loving God who called us to be fruitful and multiply?

A while ago, I came across a woman who celebrated and boasted of a recent abortion. She felt liberated, giving her testimony that she wondered how she had conceived life at all, while using two forms of birth control, and her one-night-stand had not given his name. She had made the decision unilaterally to abort, as she felt she had no one else to counsel her, who might have pointed out to her the spiritual miracle which had happened to her: God sent her a gift through two barriers, maybe even three. In her ignorance, she returned the gift.

Then a few years later, she married a man she adored, they both decided they wanted a family. Only she couldn't seem to hold onto a pregnancy, she had multiple miscarriages. While it is true, that women miscarry spontaneously many times over the course of their lives for all kinds of reasons, however, they had several tests, that proved she and her husband were physically able. She felt cursed. Then she finally sought spiritual help, and it was pointed out to her, that she was suffering from a curse, possibly even a generational curse.

When she confessed her abortion to the spiritual counselor, they were able to guide her to repentance for murder, and prove to her that she had violated God's laws of creation by rejecting the gift of new life he sent her. She felt godly sorrow, pained by her mistake, and asked God to forgive her. He understood her misery and took mercy upon her, and gave her another chance. She then went through a combination of spiritual counseling and deliverance ministry, where it was revealed to her she had etheric implants in her womb preventing her from carrying full term pregnancies. It was spiritually discerned that these implants came from the abductions she had been experiencing all her life, by Grey aliens. Once these implants were dissolved and she was delivered from the demonic assignments attached to them, she was set free and God blessed her with a human baby, which she was able to carry full term and was born perfectly healthy.

I have also come across multiple women who have had abortions and have also been abducted by Greys. They had their wombs implanted to grow hybrids. There's a pattern to these types of abductions. They all report having the 'wise baby' dreams, where they are given fetuses to hold, with adult heads on them. The aliens are using them to grow hybrids and abduct these women to nurture the fetuses, which they deem as part of their growth. They are implanted from the Greys, which can be experienced as a false positive pregnancy. They can take sperm from a total stranger, mixed with another woman's egg, and implanted into a different woman, mixed with alien DNA. This is what the abduction hybridization program is about. These pregnancies typically do not last more than a couple of months, and is completed before the end of the 1st trimester. The woman thinks she's having a miscarriage, if she's even aware that she was pregnant at all.

Implants are real. When Christians embark on deliverance, all these devices need to be understood, because they are armored, hidden behind layers of the mind, and they can interfere with our bio-chemical and endocrine systems. When believers renounce vows, agreements and stand proxy before the throne of Grace to repent on behalf of ancestral sins, those whom they may have never known, God still listens. The Lord really pays attention to bloodlines. When I became a mother, my philosophy was: 'the buck stops here,' meaning that whatever generational sins and curses I inherited, I was determined to break, so they wouldn't be passed down to my daughter and my descendants.

When I was forty-five, and my daughter was six, the same exact age I was when my mother died, I was diagnosed with a severe disease that almost took my life, thus repeating the curse and passing it on to my daughter. I had some unusual form of liver disease that was like cancer. I begged the Lord to not let me be taken from my daughter at such a young age. He gave me a renewed life! I changed my nutrition, got delivered from pain killers, and I was given a new liver.

This was an instance of a generational curse operating, that I had to overcome. Thankfully, my daughter did not need to suffer the same fate as I did. She didn't lose her mother at the age of six as I did, because Jesus stepped in and saved me and her. About five years later, I reached out to one of my maternal cousins, and learned that his wife of the age of forty-five, had mysteriously died from some rare blood disease, leaving him with a six-year old daughter. I realized, this was exactly the same age and patterning that happened when my mother died, and exactly the same age I was tested as well with a six-year-old daughter. These types of patterns are the proof of generational curses, held in place through implants. They are demonic assignments from the Dark Forces placed in the family bloodlines, which remain active until someone consciously breaks them, through the grace of the blood sacrifice of Jesus Christ.

Abortion and abduction are related. We must take responsibility for the spiritual legal ground that was opened up when we agree that abortion on demand is acceptable to us. Our repentance will cause God's Grace to be poured out in the form of deliverance from implants and their cursed patterns.

Who are the "Dark Forces"?

The Dark Forces are beings who rebel against God as Creator and Source. They seek to take energy and power away from other beings rather than receive it from God. Although these beings are created by God, they have, through their own free will, participated in a rebellion, creating the illusion of separation from God, and the present perception of duality. In their pain, they seek to control others. When you get through this body of knowledge which I have accumulated, then you might even agree with me, that it is an abuse of science and technology used to manipulate, control and support an alien agenda over the masses of humankind.

> Ignorance is not the greatest evil.
> The accumulation of poorly mastered knowledge is worse.
> ~ Plato ~

The major groups dealing with implants are the Greys, the Reptilians, the Dracos and the Nordics. The Reptilians are a race of beings who predate humanity, and, in fact, sought to cultivate humanity as a slave race for their own purposes. Consequently, they view themselves as contributors in the creation of the human race, and believe they have the right to interfere in our development. Their belief justifies their attempts to control humanity through any means necessary.

Even God, the good, the almighty, the perfect, our creator, granted us free will. The one Universal law that is constant is not abnegating free will. The Reptilians trespass on this universal law continually, through deception, enslavement, manipulation, and just making us feel powerless while doing so. This is one of the reasons many end up worshipping the satanic reptilians, because they are in fear of their power, and can't find their way free of their enslavements and controlling energies. They control through implants.

Implants represent collective karmic patterns that have been externally imposed by the Dark Forces to control the thinking and emotional responses of mankind. Throughout the history of this sector of the Universe, duality realities, good and evil, have prevailed. Believe it or not, this view is the result of implants, inserted into human energy fields, that block people from giving and receiving love. This comes from the pride that caused Lucifer the satan to fall from heaven, as well as the activation, predicted by Jesus Christ in Matthew 24:12, that would occur in the End Times of this present age.

> "…and many false prophets will arise and mislead many. Because of the multiplication of wickedness, ***the love of most will grow cold***. But the one who perseveres to the end will be saved." (Matthew 24:11-13)

Multiplication is a technological term. Wickedness increases through implantation. There is a way to be delivered of these spiritual limitation device implants, and that is through returning to the One who alone has all the power in the Universe over them, the Lord Jesus Christ. This is not a religious thing, in fact that's one of the major deceptions from the dark forces, through the implementation of the religious spirit, but through reconnecting with the Creator and His Son, the Savior of humankind, who has power over the dark forces.

In this Universe are many beings and civilizations of Light who have tried to intercede by upholding humankind's right to evolve. Consequently, many battles have taken place between the Godly, those set apart by God's Love, Light and Spirit, and the Ungodly, the self-preserving, parasitic and rebellious forces. Due to this perception of duality, the Reptilians have been kicked out of one planetary system after another and are in a current-day battle for control of the Earth and this solar system.

New Agers believe in the ascension of the planet into fifth dimensional reality, coinciding with the End Times Prophesies which reveal that it is the Lord, the Creator of Heaven and Earth, who will return to change the earth into the shining Holy City, the New Jerusalem. Jesus literally brings the Kingdom of Heaven, to earth. This is done in answer to the many prayers of the faithful, "Thy Kingdom Come, Thy Will be done, here on Earth, as it is done in Heaven." (Matthew 6) This long-awaited event will inevitably raise the vibration of planet earth, especially as prophesy says that earth will no longer receive its light from the Sun, but from the Son of Heaven.

The Reptilians are using every trick in the book to hold us hostage inside the third density of this third dimension, through mind control, implantation and spiritual limitation devices that are designed to prevent us from seeing the reality of life as multi-dimensional beings and vessels of Light through the indwelling Christ-Holy Spirit. Their implants are implemented with the intention of disrupting our connection with God, the Creator and Source of All Life.

The Reptilians are a sleazy race. They are also known as the Lizards or Lizzies because they look like lizards. They masquerade as the Light and are the source of much disinformation as well as energy systems that may be disguised as healing systems. They mix just enough truth with lies to confuse the unaware and are, in fact, the source of so much channeled material that trickles down to New Agers, despite what New Agers think otherwise. Reptilians, and their Grey Cohorts, along with their motley crew of hybrids, have the ability to disguise themselves as angels of light, ascended masters and space brothers, through technology. We should know better by now!

"For Satan himself masquerades as an angel of Light."
(2 Corinthians 11:14)

Remember: Power does not always equal love and light. When evaluating channeled material, always ask, "Does this material come in the name of Christ, His Holy Spirit, and does it align with the Kingdom of God, the Will of Heaven, that is not only written down on earth, but has been written into the very stars themselves for eternity?" Insist on your own internal confirmation and be shown the truth. Keep in mind that while you still have implants it may be difficult to discern between the transmissions from all the lower stuff entities and the Holy Spirit, but 'by their fruits you will know them', Matthew 7:16, is a good measuring stick. This is especially relevant in light of the fact that the Dracos and Grays have the technological edge to counterfeit images that we may have been programmed to believe are godly, or spiritual or of the light, when the truth is that it is often an illusion, a reinforcement of what we want to believe.

The Dracos are the sophisticated evil engineers of mass control on this planet. They are behind the control and limitation of resources on this planet. They originate from the pole star system Alpha Draconis, who conquered a planet in the Orion sector called Draconis during the opposition in the original Orion conflict, along with their conquest of over six stars in the Orion System, also known as "The Unholy Six". See, Book One of *Who's Who in the Cosmic Zoo?* pp. 154-182.[5]

As more souls created by the Elohim, the gods that make up the Council of Light, came to earth, the Dracos followed. The Dracos and the Reptilians both invaded this planet in its early history and have been here ever since. They manipulated our

DNA and claim ownership as the originators, but they are not, they are manipulators, slave masters, not creators. They can't and don't create human souls, only the God of gods can do that. Instead, they mimic and counterfeit, by technology, by stealing memories, personalities, and characteristics, and implanting them into their genetic experiments. They use stolen soul energies, because they are incapable of creating souls. This is what distinguishes them from the Real Creator, the Almighty, the God of gods.

As I pointed out extensively in Book One of *Who's Who in the Cosmic Zoo?*,[1] there is a huge difference between beings who are soul-matrixed, like the human races, and those who are without souls, and are instead filled with artificial intelligences, and other types of lower entities, demons and evil spirits.

Despite the Dracos being the ones behind all the Satanic and Black Magic rituals, these beings do not always appear evil. The Draco energy can be very deceptive. They can appear as beautiful, sweet, and charming. If we can perceive behind the facade, we will always sense a shallowness and coldness beneath the mask, exactly as described in 2 Corinthians 11:14. There is a distinct vampiric quality to them as well. They literally get high off the adrenaline rush that shoots through us when we are frightened and traumatized, especially at the point of death.

This is the reason for the human sacrifice of abortion, and pedophilia, because the Dracos find children to be pure, and desire to feed on their energy. The enemies of humanity drive us to commit horrific crimes against ourselves, to lower us in our own eyes and by our own standards. They make people afraid to admit and repent of sodomizing, raping, and terrifying young children to death, because these horrific acts are not human, they are alien inspired. The adrenaline from the trauma is fresh in their victim's blood, and this, to the Reptilians, is their source of nutrition and the 'high' that they derive from human lives. Hence the mass killings, the terrorism, the brutal rapes of both young children and women, all of which serves this Luciferian conspiracy against humankind, plagues terrestrial humans.

There is only One who has the power to set those souls who are in captivity to these Reptilian Dracos, and only One whom they fear, and that is the Lord Jesus Christ.

> "The Spirit of the Lord GOD is upon me, because the LORD has anointed me to bring good news to the poor; he has sent me to bind up the brokenhearted, to *proclaim liberty to the captives*, and *the opening of the prison to those who are bound*;"
>
> (Isaiah 61:1)

> "The Spirit of the Lord is on Me, because He has anointed Me to preach good news to the poor. He has sent Me to *proclaim deliverance to the captives* and recovery of sight to the blind, *to release the oppressed*,"
>
> (Luke 4:18)

The captives of whom the Lord speaks are all the humans on planet earth held in bondage to the god of this world, who is Lucifer, the Satan, the Draconian Lizard King. This loser, who through the abuse of science, genetics, mind control and occult forces, holds humankind hostage, for use as slaves to the Draconian Empire on Earth. If you think of all the brutal empires that have arisen on earth, you will see the signature of the Dracos, who have been using humanity as food. "For the life of a creature is in the blood," (Leviticus 17:11)

The demand for blood sacrifice originates in the Draconian Kingdom of Darkness, whose denizens feed from the shedding of blood.

Blood Sacrifices and Adrenochrome

Blood Sacrifices have historically been part of the ancient rituals of Earth's civilizations, cross the board. From the Mayans to the Egyptians, the Jews to the Muslims, the Aztecs to the Chinese, the Zulu to the Greeks, virtually ALL civilizations have taken part in this ritual.

WHY have human beings been persuaded to believe that they could benefit from the taking of another living creature's life? Regardless if its human or animal. Why does God, the Creator of all life, who said, "the life of a creature is in the blood", require blood to appease Him? Let alone pay for the atonement of sins? I posed this question in Book Two, *Who is God?* [6]

Eating of Blood Forbidden

> "Only be sure that thou eat not the blood: *for the blood is the life*; and thou mayest not eat the life with the flesh." (Deuteronomy 12:23-KJV)
>
> "*For the life of a creature is in the blood*, and I have given it to you to make atonement for yourselves on the altar; it is the blood that makes atonement for one's life." (Leviticus 17:11-KJV)
>
> "So, when any man from the sons of Israel, or from the aliens who sojourn among them, in hunting catches a beast or a bird which may be eaten, he shall pour out its blood and cover it with earth. *For as for the life of all flesh, its blood is identified with its life.*

Therefore, I said to the sons of Israel, '**You are not to eat the blood of any flesh, for the life of all flesh is its blood; whoever eats it shall be cut off.**' When any person eats an animal, which dies or is torn by beasts, whether he is a native or an alien, he shall wash his clothes and bathe in water, and remain unclean until evening; then he will become clean...."

(Leviticus 17:13-15 - NASB)

First it says in verse 11, that the blood is to make atonement for sins. Then it clearly says, that it is forbidden to eat the blood of any animal. Why would blood be demanded by God? And, the important question here is, which god? Who needs the blood of any being to be appeased? Why would the Creator God of all life, demand the blood of His Creation to appease Himself?

While blood sacrifices in the past have been done for primarily two reasons, 1) to gain favor in the eyes of some god. Again, which god? 2) they were done as a punishment to restore balance of good and evil. The old, eye for an eye, tooth for a tooth thing.

However, there is another reason for blood sacrifices, and that is the extraction and collection of a hormone known as Adrenochrome. Adrenochrome is a chemical produced in the human body when adrenaline oxidizes. This hormonal chemical is extracted shortly after a human victim is terrorized, which amps up adrenaline flowing through their body. After being terrorized through rape or other types of aggression, they are killed, and the adrenochrome is collected with a needle and syringe from the base of the back of their neck and spinal column.[4]

Adrenochrome is an oxidation product of adrenaline (epinephrine, norepinephrine). It reached mythical status as a deliberately-ingested psychoactive drug that was promoted by H.S. Thompson's *Fear and Loathing in Las Vegas*, which many believe was based on reality and not myth.

You may wonder, if this chemical-hormone can be extracted from human blood without the death of the individual or the shedding of their blood? The answer is a resounding, Yes! This is exactly what is done during abductions, which the servants of the Draconian Hierarchy[5] who harvest adrenochrome from abductees, through the Lilliputian Greys. The Greys use some type of technology to zap abductees into a fear state by literally paralyzing through fear, this serves as the terrorizing aspect to get the adrenaline going, and then, they simply draw their blood, usually from the neck, where the essence of adrenochrome is the strongest.

During my abductions as a young child from the age of two, I remember waking up with needle marks on the back of my neck. I remember experiencing sleep paralysis and had needle phobia till the age of 28, when I was determined to overcome it. This phenomenon is real, and the only way to combat it, whether it's in your dream state or conscious walking state, is to walk with the King of the Universe, who is the Lord Yeshua/Jesus Christ, whom these beings fear. When they see the mark of God on you, they Passover you. This is a recurring theme in the ancient scriptures. Whether it be the angel of death, or the blood thirsty Dracos, God's mark on your spirit body, causes them to move on to someone else. This was made evident to me, after I went through deliverance and was freed from alien abductions through the power and Grace of Jesus Christ.

After it is collected, adrenochrome is sold on the black market at outrageously excessive prices. Usually only those who can afford this chemical, are the very wealthy, and the elites of the world.

The reason why adrenochrome is expensive, is due to it *psychoactive* properties that is used as a mind control drug. It's also consumed to give someone an "adrenaline high." The elite are into this big time, for different reasons. It's been reported that former U.S. Vice President Al Gore was once apprehended at an airport with a suitcase full of packets of his own adrenochrome-laden blood. According to Alex Jones, Alan Watt and Fritz Springmeier, all high-level bureaucrats and V.I.P.'s carry around at least two pints of their own adrenochrome-laden blood at all times.[4]

Those who consume the blood of a living creature are stealing its "life force" which is transferred to its consumer. There are a variety of Satanic and Illuminati cults, including real "vampires," who are known for drinking human blood. So, who is behind the lust for blood?

The Reptilian Draconian Aliens who live inside the Earth, are carnivorous blood drinking aliens. Regardless of what names you give them, Reptilians, Dracos, Annunaki, Nephilim, Nagas, Serpents, Mothmen or Vampires, people believe that our planet has been infiltrated and ruled by extraterrestrial / extradimensional reptilian entities who manipulate global politics, business, banking, military and media. [4,5]

History, has proved, multiple groups worshipped reptilians: The Brotherhood of The Snake, The Dragon Society, The Sons of The Serpent, The Cult of The Serpent, The Ophites, The Nergals, The Knights of The Brazen Serpent, The Jesuits, The Knights of Malta, The Illuminati, Luciferians, etc.

As I presented in Book One of *Who's Who in the Cosmic Zoo?* that reptilians can shape-shift. Some have postulated this could be done by some type of technology or because it is difficult for them to hold their form in this dimension / planet / atmosphere, or because they are masquerading as humans, light beings, ascended masters and benevolent space brothers.[5]

Researchers believe that is it hard for them to hold onto to their shape-shifted form, without the consumption of blood, specifically adrenochrome, that gives them the power to maintain their desired form. This is why people have reported seeing humans shape shift into reptilians, some on live TV, who wobble from their true form into their human form. I myself, witnessed this personally with a bank manager I encountered, whose eyes went from normal human pupils into slits, like snake eyes.

The primary reason for blood sacrifices throughout history; was to appease the reptilians through the offering of blood directly to the reptilians, as well as paying homage to them. These Draconian Blood thirsty aliens, are the invisible hand behind the orchestration of all human wars, and the enormous blood shed on battle fields, which is sucked up by these evil forces.

In Book Two, *Who Is God?* I argued that that the final blood sacrifice of Jesus Christ, which was the ultimate price He paid for the redemption of humanity, was not necessarily a payment to the Creator Father in which He came from, but the price He had to pay, to ransom humans back from the god of this present world, who is the Draconian Reptilian god known as Lucifer Satan. God the Father, who is Love, does not require blood to appease him, or buy favors from him, but it is the god of this world, who lives *inside* the planet, has ongoing demands for human blood. When the Son of God, who is Yeshua HaMashiach, aka Jesus Christ, bled to death on the Cross of Calvary, His Divine Blood, was the ultimate blood sacrifice, to purchase back souls in captivity from these blood thirsty reptilians.[6]

This is the spiritual legal ground that Christ stands on, and everyone who accepts His Blood Sacrifice as the Kinsmen Redeemer of humankind to set the captives free from the bondages of the god of this world who is the Lizard King, Satan.

This is why the scriptures say, he bought us with a price. "For you were bought with a price. Therefore, glorify God in your body and in your spirit, which are God's." (1 Corinthians 6:20) Whom did he pay to purchase us back? He paid the Reptilian God of the Earth, who is a blood lusty carnivore and steals the life force in the blood of both humans and animals.

Since this life energy is contained in the blood, this also explains the command for the cruel practice of letting an animal bleed to death that is maintained in certain cultures. It is for this practice that Yahshua (Jesus Christ) bled to death on the cross, so that through his lifeforce in His Divine Blood, all of humanity can be saved from these bloodthirsty reptilian gods.

As I've mentioned before in *Who is God?* and here in my Chapter on the *Ark of the Covenant,* that there has always been speculation amongst researchers, that the Mercy Seat was underground at Golgotha, and when the earth split open during an earthquake at the time of Yeshua's death, that His blood went down through a crack in the earth, and fell onto the Mercy Seat on the Ark of the Covenant.[6]

The Reptilian Annunaki want to claim that they are our creators! The reptilians are not our creators. However, they may have genetically manipulated our DNA for their purposes of downgrading us to create a slave race to serve them; they are **not** the prime creators, but more specifically the interferers. Only the Almighty Creator, the Lord of all Spirits, has the power to create souls and give them life. It is this very life force that the Reptilian Archonic Annunaki are after. Hence the battle of our souls, our minds, our bodies, and our very existence on planet Earth.[4, 5]

Channeling Prophets or Profits?

Again, always ask when reading channeled information if a being or information is of the Office of the Christ, or of the Office of the Satans. Insist on confirmation! Whatever God creates, the Draconian Lizard Kingdom counterfeits, and channeling is no exception. Often channelers refer to 'hearing from above', or 'the man upstairs', but unbeknownst to them, they are referring to the Prince of the Powers of the Air, who is Lucifer and his cohorts. The Power of the Air refers to space technology, that can create some very impressive channeling.

> "Wherein in time past ye walked according to the course of this world, *according to* ***the prince of the power of the air***, the spirit that now worketh in the children of disobedience:"
>
> (Ephesians 2:2)

The Lord Yahuah uses prophets, from time immemorial, to communicate His messages of Truth to people. Satan has usurped this means by mimicking the Lord, and using humans to channel his message of deception. As this is worth repeating throughout this book series, that in order to rightly discern between the Truth and the Counterfeit, one must know the Truth first. Otherwise, the counterfeit will be so deceptively convincing that one will believe the lie as truth, and become a deceiver as well.

Most of the channeled information that comes from the likes of New Agers is inspired directly from the Dracos and their hybrid Greys. They claim to be Pleiadeans, because back in the early 1990s, Barbara Marciniak was channeling a group of beings called the *P's Plus*, who were allegedly, Pleaidian. They gave her a wealth of information on the history of the battles between the gods, the Reptilians, or Lizzies, as she called them, and the human vine of light beings. It was insightful information, corroborated with ancient texts, which is what made it so popular.

Always alert to what works best, the very good deceiver, the Dracos are master impostors. They got into the channeling game, and have been channeling the so-called Pleiadeans along with other alleged star names to unsuspecting light workers, deceiving many. Just as the Lord of Heaven and Earth uses people who are intuitive and attuned to His Spirit, His Word, likewise does the god of this world use people to channel his messages of deception. Buyer beware. Not everything that glitters is gold, and not every feel-good message is actually good for your soul. Discern, and identify all channeled information.

The Greys, the ones most people think of abducting and implanting people, are completely mental. They are intelligences, which in Greek is *daemon,* which translates to *knowing.* They are advanced technologically but, as a race, they lost their own souls and emotional bodies through genetic manipulation, in order to weed out violent, criminal and aggressive behaviors. Unfortunately, their genetic experiments left them unable to feel anything at all: no love, compassion, empathy. They are just cold-hearted. This is why they seek to harvest emotional energy from us, as it actually affects them like a drug. They are the orchestrators of traumas, dramas and terror, because that's when our adrenaline is pumping hardest, being one of the main commodities they are harvesting from us.

The aim of many abductions is to create a hybrid race combining the natures of the Grey and human, which they believe will help them to retrieve their own emotional bodies. In other words, this is soul stealing. Another huge deception in channeled information is the Grey propaganda trying to convince people that they are assisting in a worthy cause. They have lied and deceived many of their abductees to get their supposed consent. Know the Truth! Anyone who trespasses on your soul is violating Cosmic Law! Any agreement that is made under duress, deceit, or coercion is invalid by Cosmic Law, as it is here by common law.

Self-defense is a Universal Cosmic Right of all creatures, including us humans. Since this fight is not in the flesh, we must learn to defend ourselves supernaturally, which requires the power and authority of the King of the Kingdom of Heaven. Learn how to cultivate the whole supernatural armor of God in this battle with the Dracos. See, *Finding Freedom: A Workbook on Deliverance from Implants and Breaking of Generational Curses.*

Remember, when people turn to Jesus Christ, *not religion*, they are being saved *behind enemy lines.* The ascension or rapture out of this world promises the fullness of deliverance from the system of this world, and liberation from the tests, trials and adversities caused by the Dark forces. First comes salvation, then comes deliverance and then comes translation into immortal bodies.

The Supernatural Armor of God

"Finally, be strong in the Lord and in the power of his might. Put on the whole armor of God, that you may be able to stand against the schemes of the devil. For we do not wrestle against flesh and blood, but against the rulers

(Archons), against the authorities (Principalities), against the cosmic powers (Aliens) over this present darkness, against the spiritual forces of evil in the heavenly places (Rebel ETs).

Therefore, take up *the whole armor of God*, that you may be able to withstand in the evil day, and having done all, to stand firm. Stand therefore, having fastened on *the belt of truth*, and having put on the *breastplate of righteousness*, and, as *shoes for your feet*, having put on the readiness given by the *gospel of peace*. In all circumstances take up the *shield of faith*, with which you can extinguish all the flaming darts of the evil one; and take the *helmet of salvation*, and the *sword of the Spirit*, which is the Word of God, praying at all times in the Spirit, with all prayer and supplication."

(Ephesians 6:10-18)

Counterfeit Implant Removal

Implant Removal should never be attempted without the presence of the Holy Spirit in the name of Yeshua Jesus Christ. He alone has the authority over all the spirits, aliens, demons and their implants. He is the Deliverer.

Important information for all who delve into the unseen, there are counterfeit helpers and angels, the ETs from the Ashtar Command, who offer implant removal, and this is basically having the fox invited in, to supervise the hen house. All that happens during the Ashtarian implant removal processes are transfers, some of the draconian implants being traded for Ashtarian. Only Jesus Christ can completely deliver from all alien implants. See, Book One, of *Who's Who in the Cosmic Zoo?*[1] Chapter: Ashtar Command, on the spiritual and scriptural discernment of the identity of Ashtar and her Command.

Since mankind has bought into the illusion of separation of God, and lives in duality, we are all subject to the influence of some kind of implant or spiritual limitation device. We all have them until they are cleared. Remember, we are delivered through the Kingdom of Heaven's Mercy, and the One who sits on the Mercy Seat and Throne of Heaven. The implanted are controlled to believe that we are not one with our Creator. When we believe that we are one with God, we become a threat to them.

The Controllers do not want you to know who we are in Christ and who God created us to be. These implants are designed to confuse our identity. This is why so many people today are confused as to whether they are male or female, black or white, healthy or disabled. They are being implanted to identify as their opposite, and expect to be treated as such. This is both a mental disorder, and a form of possession, but the spirit is held in place through implants, which is the software programming the individual needs to remain in confusion and be disassociated with who they were born to be and more importantly, who God sees them to be, His children, perfect as He made them.

Deliverance prayers coupled with spiritual counselling can disable, dissolve and deliver us humans from alien implantation. Approach implant removal through God's biblical foundations for freedom. Only Jesus can permanently dissolve all implants and spiritual limitation devices, known and unknown, all spiritual weapons, mental and emotional body parasites, attached entities, and thought forms of all kinds, including curses, hexes, and spells. When we agree to consciously break and repent from the vows and agreements that hold the devices to us, He can work them out of us. Please refer to my companion workbook, *Finding Freedom,* where I give you applicable steps on how you can be free and whole again.

> "The Spirit of the LORD is upon me; because he has anointed me to preach good news to the poor. He has sent me to bind up the brokenhearted, to proclaim liberty to the captives, and an opening of the eyes to the blind; to announce that captives will be set free and prisoners will be released."
>
> (Isaiah 61:1)

> "The Spirit of the Lord is on Me, because He has anointed Me to preach good news to the poor. He has sent Me to proclaim deliverance to the captives and recovery of sight to the blind, to release the oppressed,"
>
> (Luke 4:18)

I also want to point out that some implants remain to keep people grounded in this reality, and are erased and deleted at death. I wrote about this process in my chapters in Book Two[6], *What Happens When You Die?* pp. 455-483; and Book One[1], *Grays and Soul-Transplantation,* p.271

Negative Alien Agenda

The Negative Alien Agenda can best be understood as a program supporting the psychopathic personality, a selfish and self-centered individual with a lack of empathy, incapable of remorse. It is behind all narcissistic personality disorders, whose victims become psychic and energy vampires.

Psychic Energy Vampires

A psychic energy vampire is anyone that drains the life energy or spiritual vitality from another human being. Psychic vampires take on all manner of shapes and descriptions; they can be co-workers, lovers, strangers, emotional abusers, anyone who saps your vitality. It is important to be aware of the psychic vampire, as this can drain us to the point of death, or infect us with their same syndrome and we become like them.

In many ways psychic vampirism is a personality type. The following list details nine attitudes which a psychic vampire might use to justify their preying on another human being.

1. My happiness is more important than your happiness. You are responsible for my happiness.
2. My needs are the most important needs; your emotions exist to serve mine. I will take from you until there is nothing left to take, and then I will grow angry when I cannot receive what I desire from you.
3. You are only necessary in that you supply me with energy and support. In the end I will make sure that you are aware of just how unnecessary you are.
4. My life is the only life with meaning and value.
5. All others exist only to support mine. I will use whatever means I can to take what is mine.
6. Your energy is mine for the taking.
7. I am not responsible for my own spiritual energy. You are responsible for sustaining me.
8. I take from you because you have allowed it.
9. I will support you because I would support a herd of cattle or the growth of a crop. I have no emotional attachment or investment in you as a person. You are a means to an end.

Notice the recurring themes of domination, control and dependence. Psychic vampires depend on others for their energy; they feed off the spiritual energy of those around them and often look for individuals with an originally heightened sense of spiritual worth and vitality. Such individuals are highly sought after by the psychic vampire as they provide a stable source of life energy to drain. Operating in the opposite spirit in spiritual warfare completely disables and disbands them. For example, the opposite spirit to pride and narcissism is humility. By going low, becoming humble, not only causes them to detach, it's the only weapon against the Leviathan Spirit, which feeds off the stronghold of pride.

The carnal Christian who does not know how to guard his mind unknowingly opens up the spiritual legal ground to evil beings, who smoothly and subtly introduce misunderstandings and prejudices into the mind, casts doubts on God's truth and aspersions on the truthfulness of others. The Religious Spirit is another one of these armors that hides behind the mask of religion, legalism, and the spirit of pride, who are all at enmity with the Lord of Spirits.

Negative Aliens – Grays, Insectoids, Reptilians and Hybrids

Book One of *Who's Who in the Cosmic Zoo?* includes descriptions on the above-mentioned alien groups. These are extradimensional and interdimensional beings that have lost their conscious connection to god source and are utilizing humans and other beings as their food source, siphoning life force like a parasite, to live thousands of years. They are not able to incarnate into human form, so they covet our bodies, wanting to take them over, planning to use them in the future. Grays are not hampered by emotion and are highly intelligent in a cold, clinical, calculating manner, managing to manipulate the human ego quite successfully at times.

Keeping us humans in heightened states of emotional confusion causes a steady flow of soul energy to be available to these negative aliens. Offense, dramas, traumas, and spiritual terrorism are the alien's methods of arousal, to syphon off human soul essences. They also tend to ride the wave of hormonal changes. This makes them like a mad scientist, or a farmer interested in gaining more resources out of his herd of cattle on the farm. They consider humans an investment in their energy resource portfolio. They regard human beings as inferior, stupid and many times use forms of mockery to create intentional harm for their own amusement.

These beings have been manipulating the affairs of our world for thousands of years, since the Atlantean Cataclysm, for their own purposes. These are inter-dimensional and extra dimensional beings known as the Fallen Angels in ancient history and they have used many technological manipulation methods to Mind Control and negatively manipulate the future direction of the human race.

Luciferian Rebellion

Buried deeply in our cellular or racial memory is the trauma, fear, shame, terror and horror of the Luciferian rebellion, which reached its apex during the end of the Atlantean Period, the beginning of human evolution through the original Root Races. The enemy patterning remains as an implant since the end result of our last aeon or astrological age. The last Processional Age of Aquarius was approximately 26,000 years ago. The coming Millennial Age of Christ will begin at the end of the Age of Pisces, which happens at the beginning of the Processional Age of Aquarius.

What resulted in our Atlantean evolution experiment was quite a traumatizing cataclysm that set the events into motion as to what we humans would experience in the next aeon cycle. The last 26,000 years have been a dark cycle of evolution and planetary rule by the negative aliens that formulated the strategies for enslavement by the trapping of consciousness.

Mind Control

We do have control over our thoughts. It is when we exercise that control that the direction and actions of our physical body, and all of its parts, that we can reclaim our soul energies. Whoever controls the mind, controls the soul. Mind control is used to form belief systems, shape values, that are used to control and enslave the masses. Religion, religious violence, gender issues, financial enslavement through debt, and sexuality are the most tightly controlled promotions of the Draconian Negative Alien Agenda, and their human power elite to continue the enslavement and vampirism of humanity.

Alien Implants

Alien Implants work in the human body in a way similar to the chemical process of geo-engineering, often used by spraying chemtrails in the skies. Alien Implants are biochemically-engineered technology designed to keep the human body in submission to Negative Alien Mind Control agendas. Similarly, chemical nanoparticle geo-engineering is being used to control the weather by harming the ozone layer and create excessive methane gases.

Negative Alien Religious Implants

The Religious Spiritual Stronghold is the Principality that holds these Negative Alien Religious Implants in place. For example, the cruciform implant comes from the Church of Rome. Crucifixion was the preferred punishment of the Roman empire, effective and cheap. The fact that Jesus died on the Cross of Calvary is the beginning, not the end of that story. What distinguishes Jesus Christ on the cross from all the thousands of others who were brutally crucified is that He was resurrected from the dead, and overcame Death and Hades. "I am the Living One; I was dead, and now look, I am alive for ever and ever! And I hold the keys of death and Hades." (Revelation 1:18)

The continued use of the Crucifix by the Catholic Church conveys a false archetypal story of a Christ Crucified, a symbol of defeat and mockery, to further and perpetuate the enslavement of us humans. The image of the dying crucified Jesus nailed to a cross disempowers its followers subconsciously and keeps people in victim consciousness, in the matrix of fear, sorrow and pain. Nailing, pinning down or binding symbolizes thwarting power. This is a subtle but powerful symbol that hangs in Catholic Churches all around the world, reminding its follower of its inherent subconscious program of victim consciousness which is the antithesis of the Resurrected Life in Christ.

Instead, it represents the tortured human being. As we are all hidden and risen with Christ, Protestant and non-denominational churches do not display crucifixes. Spiritually and energetically speaking, this cruciform implant shows up in the etheric body. It is a spiritual limitation device used to disempower humans from finding our God-given power that comes from the Risen Christ, which is found on the other side of the Cross. It's a subtle but powerful deception, that has a strong stranglehold on Christians who are ignorant of Church history and the true Gospel of Salvation which comes from the power that is found on the other side of the Cross, in the *Dunamis* Power of the Resurrection. *Dunamis* is Greek for Resurrecting Power.

Crucifixion implants have been discerned by multiple healers. These are spiritual limitation devices that are implanted into one's pineal gland, which come from the corrupted religion of Rome. In the Santeria religion, which combines Catholicism and Voodoo, anything nailed down is for the purpose of *thwarting* and *binding* its power.

Those who were schooled in Catholicism all have the cruciform implants in their spirits, which can be removed through repentance to the true Christ, who alone delivers from mind control. There is a true Christ, and there are the false Christs. This is what gets so many people confused to the point of rejecting Christ completely, which is the *modus operandi* of Luciferian strongholds. It's important to remember, when discerning so called Christians, that the power of Christ lies in His resurrection, which is on the other side of the cross. Remember crucifixion was the norm in the Roman world. Lots of people were crucified, but there was only one who rose from the dead after three days – Yeshua Jesus.

When we get stuck, lost, immersed in places where there should be no resistance, this stems from the ancient past. Christians who have no understanding of past lives are doomed to repeat them. Because they've been lied to and believe that God doesn't recycle, or allow us to reincarnate, which is clearly stated throughout the entire Jewish Bible in dozens of passages that describe reincarnation which has always been a core Jewish belief, hence, the modern Christian is frequently at a loss to understand or explain such impasse. The Church of Rome decreed that reincarnation simply didn't fit into the political agenda, implanting a verse in Hebrews which is clearly fake. See, *What Happens When You Die?* Book Two, *Who is God?* pp. 455-483.[6]

This is another spiritual limitation device implanted into one's spirit body in an attempt to thwart the true power of Christ from being expressed through us. This works as a mind control program that subconsciously sends the message to the soul that they are powerless, in the face of these spiritual attacks on the soul, and must just submit as a martyr, and be a good suffering servant, like Christ, hanging on the Cross.

But for those who mistakenly think that this is just missing the whole point of why Jesus died on that Cross, remember that we must rise above all the false beliefs that led Him there in the first place. He came to redeem humankind, not to expect us all to be crucified over and over again. He wants to share His power and authority with His redeemed. This is how implants can be removed through repentance to Christ and in the power of His Blood and Name.

The *daemons*, Greek for *intelligences*, are then unleashed due to this falling out from the warfare. There are different angels, extraterrestrial messengers and intermediaries put in charge of different realms who are authorized to guide us through different life passages and situations. Often, it's during hormonal changes when spiritual warfare goes on over one's soul. This is rooted in ancient spiritual warfare over ownership of your soul, DNA, genetics, genetic warfare stemming from past lives.

So, if things aren't making sense or adding up, when the same methods don't work, it's time to try something new!

Hormones, Implants and the Curse of Eve

In power struggles with Lucifer, the Lord of the Demons, Christ is the only one to whom they will submit, and that's a fact! Our faith may be tested, particularly because of our hormones. This is linked with the genetic wars that were programmed long ago, also part of the curse pronounced on humankind in the Garden of Eden. While many believe that the curse of Eve is pain in childbirth, it really is the entire hormonal cycle from puberty to menopause and everything in between, that is cursed in women. Men are recipients of that curse as well, because they inevitably have to deal with their wives, mothers and daughters, and learn to treat them with compassion and understanding during hormonal changes.

At times, we must face our shadow issues, submit to Christ by speaking the Word over ourselves, and affirming our authority over these ancient demons, who seek to oppress and control us by harvesting our sexual and hormonal energies. It is during these hormonal cycles, when we are challenged and called to cut the head off the dragon, metaphorically and spiritually speaking.

I have seen spiritual warfare the likes of which they put in the movies, and ONLY the AUTHORITY of Christ can overcome it. It is only when under attack that we get a better idea of where we stand in our understanding and beliefs about who or what we feel is attacking us, and test our real feelings about the authority of Jesus Christ.

Great and powerful affirmation: **The Grace of God through the Divine LOVE of Christ, FLOODS MY CONSCIOUSNESS WITH HEALTH AND EVERY CELL OF MY BODY IS FILLED WITH LIGHT in Jesus name. He is the truth and the light. I abide in Christ, and therefore, Christ abides in me. Greater is He who lives inside of me, than he who is in the world. I can do all things through Christ who strengthens me.**

What about Alien Implants and Abductions?

Abductees can be any person, of any age, any cultural or national background, victims of manipulation by aliens and/or government agents, without their consent. The abductions may occur one or more times throughout a lifetime. It runs in families, being genetically transferred and reinforced. If one family member is affected, there is a 99% chance they all are affected, although to varying degrees. Implantation with control or tracking devices is a major part of the experience.

The implants from the Greys are always etheric and can extend to the physical. Because the etheric body overlays the physical body, sometimes they just feel physical.

About 1998, I began seeing a marked increase in clients coming to me for counselling who all turned out to be Grey Abductees. Why the increase? The Greys were coming more and more into our consciousness, through the growing plethora of T.V. shows and UFO related movies.

I stopped going to UFO conferences because most of the people either giving or attending them are abductees, or are conscious agents, contactees for the aliens. I found most of them were too trapped to recognize help when it was staring them in the face. I did participate in several UFO conferences in 1994-1999. I found that most of the Ufologists are so focused *only* on the physical evidence, that they miss the point about the spiritual, mental and psychological nature of those who were abducted. They promote hypnosis for the purposes of obtaining memories suppressed from those abductions, but really offer little to no help in guiding people to get free from their implants and the trauma they cause. No alternatives to hypnosis is suggested for those ten percent of the population who simply cannot be hypnotized.

You need not have conscious memory of the events as an abductee. Grey implants, like other types, are usually etheric in nature. This is one reason why the UFO community is still trying to prove that UFOs actually exist. The Greys have the ability to change their vibrational rate so that they extend to the physical at the time of the abduction. Most abduction experiences actually occur in the dream state and happen to the astral body. Since the astral body directly affects the health of the physical body, you can have physical symptoms such as marks, bruises, blood, pain and scars.

It is interesting to note that in the opinion of Dr. John Mack[3], the Harvard Psychiatrist who wrote the book, *Abduction*, most abduction experiences happen in the dream state. All of his case histories relay a dream experience, which is an important point, since it causes many people to discount these experiences as "just a dream." As a matter of protocol, Dr. Mack[3] would use techniques that would tap into past life memories, buried in the subconscious mind. These experiences are most interesting, in terms of their implications. They appear to represent events in the experience of an ET life form. Subjects relate being in an underground military facility, sometimes on Mars, the Moon and even under the Earth's oceans.

Memories of being onboard a spacecraft and other ET environments are also recalled. What is so interesting is that the subject views this, not from a human perspective, but from that of an ET. This suggests two very interesting possibilities; that during telepathic communication some memories are subconsciously transferred, and that the subject is recalling actual past life memories of their own.

This second possibility opens the door to speculation in that it suggests that part of the abduction phenomena may be a massive and covert reconnaissance operation. It may also explain why the Greys have said they have the right to do what they do. If abductees are souls that have been transferred from the ET environment to Earth, then technically they are not abducting human beings but volunteer ETs. While this is one of their alleged arguments to justify their abductions of humans, the buck stops here. This is where the need for a Savior of humankind comes in. What if this is just an implant? That these souls are not ET volunteers, but are being held against their will, used and abused in these abductions which can go on throughout one's life, until they are consciously stopped.

This is where the Creator and the Redeemer of Souls steps into this picture of forced captivity and enslavement. When I chose to stop the abductions, the only way was through returning whole heartedly to the Savior, Jesus Christ. These Greys submit to His authority in the Supernatural Realms, and they fear Him. It's time for those who study this phenomenon to question, why is this so?

Physical alien implants are objects found in the body which cannot be explained. Implants range from very small chip-like objects to much larger objects. Tests on some of the objects have revealed materials of an unknown origin, although this remains controversial.

Back in the 1990s, a podiatrist doctor, Dr. Roger Lier, began to perform surgeries to remove implants in the feet. He removed T-shaped metallic pieces that were later confirmed as having the exact same composition as meteorites. See, Dr. Roger Leir, Implant Removal, Tim Cullen between 1995-1998[7]

Strange Objects

A variety of strange objects and devices have been removed from abductees over the years, some of which cannot be identified at all. Many of these are constructed of a strange indestructible substance which appears to be a cross between organic and non-organic composition. Some of the implants are small T-shaped devices which have no obvious purpose at all, whereas others are found to have been inserted into many of the body's sensory organs such as the nose and ear passageways. Research into the phenomenon continues to this day.

Excerpt from *Hidden Mysteries* by Dr. Joshua David Stone, Ph.D.:

"It is important to be aware of the issue of extraterrestrial implants. Most people think of them as being only of a mechanical nature, but there are many types of implants that have been placed in people's astral, mental, and etheric bodies, also.

Many people feel frightened when this subject comes up; there is no need for fear. I have been told, by sources of knowledge that I highly respect that just about every person on Planet Earth has implants, and that has been going on for the past ten million years. People have been functioning with them and living their lives and being successful for eons and will continue to do so.

Implants come in many sizes and shapes. They also have many different functions. One is to suck your Light and energy. Some are used for telepathic control. Some block you from your spiritual goals. They can be found in the chakras, in the glands and organs, above the head - all over the body.

They are usually implanted during childhood or at times of physical, mental, or emotional crisis or illness. Even though everyone has them and can function quite well, they do prevent you from operating at your full potential. I highly recommend having them removed.

The goal of the spiritual path is refinement and purification on all levels. You want to purify your physical body of toxins, your emotional body of negative feelings, your mental body of impure thoughts, and your etheric body of impure energies. So, for total God-realization and optimum performance, at some point in your spiritual progression you will want to remove extraterrestrial implants, as they can subtly block your clarity, vitality and prosperity. This is a subject that very few people are even aware of because very few people can see them, except for the physical, mechanical ones. As humanity moves towards full realization of the New Age, the subject of implants is going to becoming into the foreground of people's awareness."[8]

I couldn't say it better myself, and I agree with Dr. Stone here. This chapter and its companion Workbook, *Finding Freedom,* soon to be released, contains a very detailed list of implants, collected over years of working on my own healings, clearings, and deliverance sessions, as well as my intense experience as a healer of others.

I ardently wish for more teaching and a ministry of alien deliverance within the churches, but sadly the awareness of this is simply not there. While most deliverance ministries focus on the demonic, they fail to address the spiritual legal ground that gives demons the right to their assignments, as well as the understanding of these etheric and physical implants. The vital importance of this cannot be stressed enough!

During my work with deliverance ministers, a Baptist Minister shared with me that many people in her church, who were saved and baptized, came to her for deliverance, and shared that they had been abducted by aliens. She questioned me, how can someone who is saved, and baptized, be abducted? She had some understanding of ancient aliens, but held on to the fundamentalist notion that all aliens were demons. The greys who perform the abductions do fall into that category, because they are inserting the implants.

We need to think of this as a type of tagging system, just as we tag pigeons and other wildlife. These implants are intelligently designed to manifest either spiritual limitation to thwart the God given power of the soul, or to create a problem within society, by corrupting the image and likeness of God.

When I shared my experiences of deliverances from aliens, along with my opinion of the *root* of why Christians were being abducted, she could not see the point at all. My truth had triggered her religious implant. This is why people who have not surrendered fully to Christ Jesus, and stepped back from needing to understand His wonderous mysteries, go wrong and sometimes leave the church. We must first get free of our own strongholds, especially the demonic religious spiritual implants. Jesus said, "You hypocrite, first take the plank out of your own eye, and then you will see clearly to remove the speck from your brother's eye." (Matthew 7:5)

My understanding of past life connection to alien abductions and implants is crucial to being able to effectively disable them and clear the spiritual legal ground that gives them permission to coexist with the Christian. We must face the teachings of reincarnation in the Scriptures honestly, frankly, and with courage. Reincarnation is not the result of some eastern religious cult. We realize that Hebrews 9:27 states that it is appointed unto man once to die and then the judgment. As I wrote extensively in Book Two, *Who is God?* pp. 455-483, that this is not what that scripture means, and that the fundamentalist who is taught that there is no reincarnation has in fact been implanted with a lie from the Church of Rome.[5]

Christianity was birthed out of Judaism, not the Roman empire. Gentiles are grafted onto the Covenants of Israel and its Jewish roots, and Israel is the Tree. Gentiles are branches grafted onto that existent established tree. As Romans 11 says that the branches cannot curse the tree, otherwise, they too will be cursed. In this way, Christians need to understand that there are dozens of scriptures that reinforce that the Lord raised people from out of the grave, breathes life into them, puts flesh back on them. This is the very definition of reincarnation. Ezekiel 37 specifically prophesies the reincarnation of Israel, which began in 1948, and the reincarnation of a strong army, which is today's IDF (Israel Defense Forces).

> "Ingrafted Branches: Again, I ask: Did they stumble so as to fall beyond recovery? Not at all! Rather, because of their transgression, salvation has come to the Gentiles to make Israel envious. But if their transgression means riches for the world, and their loss means riches for the Gentiles, how much greater riches will their full inclusion bring!
>
> "I am talking to you Gentiles. Inasmuch as I am the apostle to the Gentiles, I take pride in my ministry in the hope that I may somehow arouse my own people to envy and save some of them. For if their rejection brought reconciliation to the world, what will their acceptance be but life from the dead? If the part of the dough offered as first fruits is holy, then the whole batch is holy; if the root is holy, so are the branches.
>
> "If some of the branches have been broken off, and you, though a wild olive shoot, have been grafted in among the others and now share in the nourishing sap from the olive root, do not consider yourself to be superior to those other branches. If you do, consider this: You do not support the root, but the root supports you. You will say then, "Branches were broken off so that I could be grafted in." Granted. But they were broken off because of unbelief, and you stand by faith. Do not be arrogant, but tremble. For if God did not spare the natural branches, he will not spare you either."
>
> (Romans 11:11-21)

Mainstream Christianity needs to integrate Jewish wisdom, knowledge, and scripture, as Judaism is the parent spiritual path, not Roman paganism or the heretic church which took its name. The Lord, the Almighty Creator of our souls, has been reincarnating souls for millennia, as His way of giving them the chance to change their ways, to see the fulfillment of His promise to them, to fulfill their purposes in Him. This is not some religious patch job, it's the grace of God. If a person is saved by grace, and given a new life within the same body, how much more can the

Almighty Creator God authorize a new life for a soul to return within a different body and a new life?

It is the height of hypocrisy that the very foundation of the Christian faith lays on the resurrection of Christ, and the belief in the resurrection of the dead in Christ, but that Christians just can't understand, that God reincarnates people.

In case we receive this news, that we can be reincarnated at God's pleasure, with an attitude far from gratitude, let's discern. Past life contracts are one of the reasons behind the repetitive abductions. We do not have to come back and go through all this again. We are given chances to find the Lord and get our souls back into right relationship with the Living God. Once we do that, we no longer need to keep coming back here to find Him amidst a world of darkness. This world has been not only a testing ground for souls, but also an experiment for souls that come from other races to learn how to get along in their common unity as universal humans, and find the Savior of their souls too.

Reincarnation is about the past as much as the future. Any blind spots with this piece of knowledge lies in the fact that we are resistant to take a look at our own past lives. This includes our past in this lifetime. Knowledge of reincarnation is useful in this life, just as when we go over and face something unpleasant in our own past behavior and integrate and release it. So, it is with whatever we carried over into this life, which, when we walk with the power and authority of Jesus, is our ultimate deliverance, which means we never have to revisit that cursed patterning again. Jesus delivers us from its root.

Don't think for a moment that Jesus isn't aware of this fact and the connection to past life bondages. The problem remains that those called into healing and deliverance ministers will not incorporate this knowledge. If they did integrate this piece, they could certainly be more effective healers and facilitators of deliverance.

The Lord says, "My people perish from lack of knowledge." (Hosea 4:6).

So, get, knowledge, and, get understanding.

"The beginning of wisdom is this: Get wisdom.
Though it cost all you have, get understanding." (Proverbs 4:7)

"Woe to those who call evil good and good evil, who put darkness for light
and light for darkness, who put bitter for sweet and sweet for bitter."
(Isaiah 5:20)

Trauma is a PTSD program, implanted during abduction as a spiritual limitation device designed to keep the experiencer from having victories and success. This implant keeps the recipient in a loop of repeating trauma, through various sources, including personal, family, business, and even governmental relationships. This implant is a type of curse and it's spiritual, emotional and psychological damage can only be estimated, and can only be effectively eliminated through the power of the Lord Jesus Christ.

Implants are inserted into the spirit body that serve as spiritual limitation devices that block and cause separation with the Holy Spirit, also known as the Great Spirit to the ancients. These implants cause distorted communications with the Spirit realms, and oftentimes people are chosen to channel the demonic entities and their messages of love and light from the dark side. These are aliens posing as the good ETs who prey on us undiscerning humans, using us to market and promote the alien One World Religion, and New World Order agenda. These implants are all about control, and can feel like being under a strong spell.

The imprinting that often comes from these controlling spiritual limitation devices cause fear of self-expression by thwarting our Confidence in ourselves and in the God spark inside of us.

Another religious implant causes people to become hysterical when they hear the name of Jesus. They automatically think His name is about religion, or being religious. This is how far this religious implantation program has gone, which as I've said is designed to thwart the power of God and His Spirit of Love to be expressed in the world. It instead has managed to turn people off the Savior and the God who has come to redeem and set us *all* free. Why would we ever reject freedom? The short answer is, alien implants. We think we are not supposed to be free, we are so used to being enslaved by the system, by the Controllers, and used and abused by the aliens and draconian humans, that we accept it as the norm. It was never God's will for humankind.

Jesus said, "I have come to set the captives free." (Isaiah 61:1; Luke 4:18) Free from the god of this world, who is the prince of the powers of the air, that would be Lucifer the Satan and His Draconian Kingdom of Darkness and hierarchy of aliens, demons and evil spirits, that are assigned to not only insert implants, but keep them activated. I have found, after searching and testing all the other New Age Gods and Goddesses, that only Jesus Christ has the ultimate power to deliver from these implants. The New Age gods and goddesses are implants in and of themselves, as I've proved in Book Two: *Who is God?* [6] They are not even real gods, but renegade warring extraterrestrials who left their stories and imprints in planet earth.

Ancient man and woman looked to these beings as gods, some of whom had god complexes. They, too, are evolving, along with us, and they have created karma in their treatment of humankind. Some are working it off through helping humankind to develop and evolve, both spiritually and technologically. Others will end up being judged, as the Prophecy says, that the redeemed humans will end up judging the angels.

"Do you not know that we will judge angels? (ETs)
How much more the things of this life!"
(1Corinthians 6:3)

To be an effective Healer and Deliverance Minister, you must understand and accept the fact that just about every person on this planet now has lived before, having come back to complete their journeys, and hopefully find the path back to reconciliation with the Savior and Creator God, and in so doing, live a life that is marked by love and compassion for God and others.

"For we are God's handiwork, *created in Christ Jesus to do good works*,
which God prepared in advance for us to do."
(Ephesians 2:10)

How many people are sent back to life after Near Death Experiences, and told by the Lord to tell everyone what the Lord has done for them, and live right. It is important to the Lord that we live fulfilled lives on earth for Him, by Him and through His Spirit. This is what the Path of Finding Freedom through His Name is all about. When people taste freedom, they will never want to go back into the bondage of enslavement. It is our destiny to be the recipients of the world of the wonderous and miraculous. It is the antithesis of Life and Liberation to go back into captivity. Who does that? If they do, it's certainly not by their conscious choice, and this is why implant removal is so important.

Christians who can't accept the fact that reincarnation is a teaching of Christ are putting the words of man above the testimony of Jesus and the world of His Father. It was the Church Fathers who implanted a belief about the rogue scripture of Hebrew 9:27 into the Bible, which they did to thwart and cease all belief in reincarnation. See, the Constantine and Nicean Creeds. Reincarnation continues as God's plan for growing, evolving human souls, regardless of their false implant. In fact, there are many of us who perished at the hands of the Roman Catholic Church who today have reincarnated in order to voice the truth it once silenced.

The Lord God always has the last Word.

Consider also that among the hundred million souls which were vanquished by the World Wars were six million Jews. Following the war was a huge baby boom that went on for nearly twenty years. Returning those souls back into life was necessary to fulfill the promise of God, and the State of Israel was born, bringing to fulfillment the 1,800-year-old prophecy of Ezekiel 37 when the Lord promised to reincarnate the Israelites into their own land again. Here is the Prophecy and evidence that the Lord Himself reincarnates people back on the earth:

> "Ezekiel said, "Sovereign Lord, you alone know." Then he said to me,
> "Prophesy to these bones and say to them, 'Dry bones, hear the word of the Lord!
>
> This is what the Sovereign Lord says to these bones:
>
> ***I will make breath enter you, and you will come to life. I will attach tendons to you and make flesh come upon you and cover you with skin; I will put breath in you, and you will come to life. Then you will know that I am the Lord.***'
> So, I prophesied as I was commanded. And as I was prophesying, there was a noise, a rattling sound, and the bones came together, bone to bone. I looked, and tendons and flesh appeared on them and skin covered them, but there was no breath in them.
> Then he said to me, "Prophesy to the breath; prophesy, son of man, and say to it, 'This is what the Sovereign Lord says: *Come, breath, from the four winds and breathe into these slain, that they may live.*' So, I prophesied as he commanded me, ***and breath entered them; they came to life and stood up on their feet—a vast army.***
> Then he said to me: "Son of man, these bones are the people (house) of Israel, behold, they say, 'Our bones are dried up and our hope has perished. We are completely cut off.'
> Therefore, prophesy and say to them, 'Thus says the Lord GOD,
> "Behold, ***I will open your graves and cause you to come up out of your graves***, My people; and ***I will bring you into the land of Israel.*** Then you will know that I am the LORD, when I have opened your graves and caused you to come up out of your graves, My people…"
>
> (Ezekiel 37: 4-11-13)

Today, there are approximately, 6.5 million Jews that live in the land of Israel. Coincidence? I think not! The Lord of lords, bats last!

"The best revenge is massive success." — Frank Sinatra

> "If the statistics are right, the Jews constitute but one quarter of one percent of the human race. It suggests a nebulous dim puff of stardust lost in the blaze of the Milky Way." . . . "Properly the Jew ought hardly to be heard of; but he is heard of, has always been heard of. He is as prominent on the planet as any other people, and his importance is extravagantly out of proportion to the smallness of his bulk." . . . "His contributions to the world's list of great names in literature, science, art, music, finance, medicine and abstruse learning, are very out of proportion to the weakness of his numbers. He has made a marvelous fight in the world in all ages; and has done it with his hands tied behind him. He could be vain of himself and he be excused for it."
>
> (Mark Twain, 1835-1910)

Remember, planet earth is a series of experiments and genetic possibilities. When one group decides to wipe out another, who just happen to have contributed the entire foundation of the religion the warring group espouses, one must really question the motives and the identity behind them to commit such heinous acts. *Who* would authorize such a thing? *Who* would be so disconnected to follow such authorization? When they fail, and the God whom they are in rebellion against returns to restore all those souls back into flesh and blood human bodies on earth, one must really question, *who* is that God? And why should we be in awe and respect Him as a Savior?

The program to hate, to be bigoted towards other races, towards the different, does not come to us naturally, or from the Creator God, but from the god of this world. It is the *modus operandi* of the Dark Forces on earth, to keep us divided amongst ourselves despite our commonalities far outweighing our differences. We are sharing a community together, as terrestrial dwellers. There are other humans who live *inside* planet earth, who are just as divided as we, as they compete for control of the inner earth in the belief that who controls middle earth, gets to control the entire earth. These are the current exopolitical issues that we terrestrial humans face.

All wars are connected to unresolved issues from the previous war. World War I gave way to World War II, the issues of which have not been resolved nor dealt with, and will inevitably get revisited leading up to World War III. The idea of ethnic cleansing, gene wars, corrupting the image and likeness of God, genetic manipulations, implantations, slaves, spaceships, space colonies, are all rooted in histories far older than dark Nazism. The Nazis were inspired by the alien presence from *inside* the earth. First the Draconian Reptilian Beings, then their competitors, the Nordic White Aryans, inspired Hitler and the desire to purge the planet of everyone, eventually.

Don't think for a moment that something like that couldn't happen again, especially in light of the fact that our technology has expanded exponentially, inspired and guided by the alien presence. The next war will be ignited by similar issues, but one war will be the war of all wars, and will end this world as we know it. The hope I offer my readers is to invest in your spirit, because you will reap its fruits in the life to come. Those who are redeemed are promised not only immortality, with no need to reincarnate, and most importantly a place to reside in the Kingdom of Heaven.

Jesus said, "in my Father's House, there are many mansions." These mansions are metaphors for space houses, which we know as space ships. There are huge floating cities in space, which we would call mother ships. There are also other planetary spheres, over which the Lord rules in power and majesty. This planet is still being fought over, and the war of the worlds will end in a *Star Wars* type battle in the skies over the earth, for all to see, at the time of the Lord's return.

Many of us have reincarnated at this time to not only clear our pasts, but get reconciled with the Lord, the Creator of our souls and spirits. We are born with implants from our past lives, because of vows and agreements made surrounding them, some of which are the very reason we are reborn, is to find the path of freedom through the Great Deliverer. This understanding can really help others to break generational sins, negative habit patterns and the generational and ancestral curses that inevitably come with being born into a particular family line.

I want to encourage my readers to look for an accompanying Work Book, *Finding Freedom* in the coming year on *How to Identify and Remove Alien Implants, Break Vows & Agreements Connected to Breaking Generational Curses.*

We inherit both blessings and curses, from which Christ came to liberate us. To be completely free of the negative programming and etheric alien implants, we must face the fact that they've held us in bondage in the past, and we are reincarnated to realize conscious freedom now and be translated into the Kingdom as adopted sons and daughters, citizens of Heaven.

This next level of healing the deep-rooted soul wounds, and deliverance from alien implants, must be able to integrate the knowledge of past lives. This is a body of knowledge, not a religion, that comes from the grace of God, who is the only giver of life.

The alien (Controlling Forces of the Kingdom of Darkness) relationship to us is like our relationship with cows. We raise cows, we keep them alive, so we can milk them, then when their milk dries up, we kill them and use their bodies for food, clothing and other supplies. So, it is with the aliens and us. They use us as a steady stream of life force energy that they can acquire nowhere else, because they are separated from the Creator God. So, they milk humans for the life-giving soul energy, and they do this through implantation, and the orchestration of hardships, conflicts and wars, which inundates them with human passions, emotions and blood sacrifices. It is the height of arrogance to think us humans are at the top of the food chain, clearly we are not.

Abductions and Corrupting the Image of God

> "Woe to those who call evil good and good evil, who put darkness for light and light for darkness, who put bitter for sweet and sweet for bitter."
>
> (Isaiah 5:20)

In my research, which goes back to the 1980s, I have observed a connection between abductions and different types of sexual deviations from the norm. Homosexuality, Bi-Sexuality and Pedophilia are implants put into abductees. This is why so many gay people believe they were born gay. Babies can be implanted as early as the age of two. Most humans do not have memory prior to age three. This explains why many gay people believe they were born gay and have grown up identifying as gay. However, that doesn't necessarily mean they were born gay, but because of this missing piece of knowledge, with respect to implantation being done on the human race, for all kinds of reasons, one of which has to do with experimentation, out of rebellion to the Creator who has given humans a special place in the Kingdom of Creation, these aliens are resentful, so in their war against the Creator, they simply take it out on us humans, so aliens start early with implantation in the young child.

The following scripture has often been understood to relate to humans, I'm not suggesting it doesn't, but I am suggesting that it also relates to the alien presence on earth, who were once fallen angels now in alien bodies, who have not only lost their first estate, according to Jude 1:6, but they also lost their immortal bodies, and their ability to progenate, because of the history of violating the laws of Creation by mixing humans with animals, etc. Therefore, they have now become the cybergenetic hybrids, known as Grays, who use humans for experimentation, to purport their alien agenda.

> "Although they claimed to be wise, they became fools, and exchanged the glory of the immortal God for images of mortal man and birds and animals and reptiles. Therefore, God gave them up in the desires of their hearts to impurity for the dishonoring of their bodies with one another."
>
> (Romans 1:22-24)

Most abductees who have recovered their memories of abductions will go as far back to the age of two. Implants can act as a program, that give spiritual legal ground for non-human intelligences also known as demons to inhabit the mind, body and soul of the abductee. Most abductees are oblivious to this presence, because they are being used and think of it as their own thoughts and feelings. Many gay and bi-sexual people have come forward and shared how they struggled with these feelings growing up, and couldn't help themselves, until they finally just came out and accepted this as their normal.

I have personally witnessed abductees who grew up straight, tell stories of their abductions, who were being forced to have sex with those of the same sex with the aliens, many of whom were horrified at the very thought, which took a lot for them to reveal and uncover these memories. It is well documented by the hypnotherapists who deal with abductees. Not everyone was implanted at the age of two, but most certainly experimented on later. There are stories of sex with reptilians. These stories are real, so much so, that it was made into a recent movie, *The Shape of Water,* where a mute woman ends up having sex with an amphibious reptilian being held in a government laboratory.

I have heard abductees share all kinds of uncomfortable and embarrassing stories, of rectal probes inserted into men, and men being masturbated by other seemingly male aliens and shown what they described as pornographic images to focus on, just as nurses give men who join a sperm bank, are sent into a private room with porn to release a sample. There's all kinds of deviations and perversions reported by abductees, who did not identify as gay or struggle with bi-sexuality growing up, nevertheless some do now, after having these experiences. Many suppress them, and struggle with addictions instead, as a way to cope with what they deem as uncomfortable feelings. Others are consumed by a spirit of insatiable lust for sex with whomever, and whatever. This is an unfortunate bondage that destroys people's lives, as the recent expose` of human sex trafficking children proves in what has become known as *pizzagate* and *pedogate.*[9]

The Aliens knew that these laws were written down long ago, and were judged as unnatural desires, which led to some severe historical Judgments from the Lord, that ended up in the nuclear destruction of Sodom and Gomorrah. See, Genesis 19; Jude 7. Nevertheless, the alien presence is trying hard to keep humans stuck in these old ancient patterns, so humans fall short of inheriting the Kingdom of Heaven coming to Earth, and earning their immortal glory bodies, which is promised to every believer. What I am saying is, that this plan to corrupt the image of God, with implanting humans with unnatural desires, is sabotage from the alien presence on earth, to create division between gays and non-gays, judgements, persecution, rejection, and division within the Church as well. Everyone suffers. It's the old Machiavellian divide and conquer tactics, and they seem to be succeeding. Yes, this is what the Torah states, regarding homosexuality:

> "You shall not lie with a male as with a woman; it is an abomination."
>
> (Leviticus 18:22)

> "If a man lies with a male as with a woman, both of them have committed an abomination; they shall surely be put to death; their blood is upon them."
> (Leviticus 20:13)

This is the spiritual legal ground for generational curses giving ground for demonic assignments on the blood lines. This is another reason why, people think they were born gay, or they struggle with unnatural sexual desires, which is rooted in ancestral sins and curses. The Aliens know all about the family blood lines, that's the purpose of the abductions is to collect DNA, to use that DNA to create hybrids, to replace the human race. It is all about corrupting the image and likeness of God in humans.[10] This is what the Spiritual and Extraterrestrial War is about as described in Ephesians 6:12, "For we do not wrestle against flesh and blood, but against the rulers, against the authorities, against the cosmic powers over this present darkness, against the spiritual forces of evil in the heavenly places." These are the aliens who see humans as commodities, cattle and slaves.

Homosexual desire is not what the Creator God originally intended. That is not to say that homosexual desire isn't the only thing that God didn't originally intend. There are many desires which have been distorted and considered sin, outside of sexuality, like greed, gluttony, murder, idolatry, etc. The point of Jesus coming was to save humankind from *all* sins and errors. There's no exception, except the unforgiveable sin, which is rejecting the Grace of the Holy Spirit, whose job is to convict the soul of error and lead people to repentance. Paul writes:

> "Or do you not know that the unrighteous will not inherit the kingdom of God? Do not be deceived: neither the sexually immoral, nor idolaters, nor adulterers, nor men who practice homosexuality, nor thieves, nor the greedy, nor drunkards, nor revilers, nor swindlers will inherit the kingdom of God."
> (1 Corinthians 6:9-10)

In today's climate, it's too easy for Christians to slough off homosexuality as just being influenced by evil spirits instead of understanding *how* so many people have recently come out as gay or think pedophilia is normal? Think about it, it would have to take an implant or a genetic manipulation to reprogram the human DNA, which like animals, birds and reptiles, is programmed to mate with the opposite sex for procreation of the species, to ignore that impulse and not procreate but live as gay. Despite the growing gay community, this need to procreate and raise children, nevertheless remains within the gay community, who are simply using surrogates who are having invitro fertilization to birth their babies for them.

This is exactly what the aliens are doing by creating hybrids. They take the ova from one woman, fertilize it with the sperm of some man, and implant it into a completely different woman, who has absolutely no idea or connection to the progenitors of that fertilized egg. There's nothing new under the sun, as the Sumerian Cuneiform Tablets tell of the first invitro fertilizations.

Point is, Humans are being abducted and programmed to be part of a social experiment by the alien presence, who do not share the same type of emotions and genetics as humans. In fact, many types of Grays have no emotions at all, which is why they are perceived as cold, having absolutely no feelings for humankind, but see us as a commodity, something to enslave, use and abuse for their purposes. They perceive humans as vessels, so they implant humans with their agenda and consciousness, using humans to help them carry out their rebellion against the Creator.

It's important to understand, another aspect of those who identify as gay or bi, and that is the connection to their past lives. This is the psychological aspect, that the aliens prey upon, who I believe, do in fact, have access to the soul's history, because it's imprinted in the DNA and they have the knowledge and technology to access this soul data. I realize this is something most Christians do not accept nor understand, but that doesn't make it false or untrue. Reincarnation has always been part of the Creator's plan and the aliens know it.

Our lives are likened to a string of pearls dunked into an ocean, you may only see one or two pearls at a time, and the rest of the necklace is concealed under the water. So, it is with the rest of our past lives, which often influences the present life, unbeknownst to many Christians, because they were implanted to believe that you only live once, which is a blatant lie, and the Bible proves otherwise. Please see, *Who is God?* Chapter Twenty-Eight: *What Happens When You Die?*[26] where I prove through dozens of Bible scriptures in both the Old and New Testament, that God has been reincarnating humans for millennia.

Now, with that said, Christians are commanded to love one another, and that is non-specific to other Christians. Jesus said, "the world will know you are my disciples, by your love." (John 13:35) Christians who are saved by the Blood Covenant are also commanded to share the good news of salvation with all people, regardless of race, creed, color or sexual preference. Christians are commanded to pray for the lost. This is because Christ died for all of humankind, not just those who follow after the Christian religion.

Jesus wants just as much to set the captives of abduction free as much as He sets free the alcoholic, the drug addict, the thief, etc. If Christians could incorporate this understanding of why people choose the gay lifestyle, and why demons attach to the spiritual legal ground, then perhaps they can help gays with their struggle and guide them home to their Creator through the deliverance of Jesus Christ. Knowledge empowers, ignorance endangers, and too many people are turned off of Jesus because Christians don't understand why people are gay and don't know how to be kind to those who are in this type of bondage.

Being kind, doesn't necessarily justify their behavior or make it right. However, just as we have understanding as to why people drink, take drugs and engage in all types of other addictions, so should we have understanding, *why* so many people choose to be gay at this time. It was Jesus Christ Himself who rightly predicted this time in history, which pointed to the times of gay marriage, when He was asked by His disciples, what will be the signs of the end of this age? Jesus answered, "As it was in the days of Noah, so will it be at the coming of the Son of Man. For in the days before the flood, people were eating and drinking, *marrying and giving in marriage*, up to the day Noah entered the ark." (Matthew 24:37-38)

Why Jesus made a point of saying, *marrying and giving in marriage,* was a warning to look for deviations from the norm, which was God's Marriage Covenant between a man and a woman. See, Genesis 2:24-25. This is what the Old Testament scriptures say, and this is why today's laws allowing gay marriage has become unprecedented and a fulfillment of End Times Prophesies.

So, for all those Christians, reading this, those who are uncomfortable with gay people, I want you to consider cultivating more insight into *why* so many people have been identifying as gay and I hope my chapter here will inspire compassion and understanding and not hatred. We don't win the spiritual battle with hatred, only love can conquer hate. Jesus wants all those who have been implanted with gender confusion to come to Him, for deliverance. We know that these implants can be cleared, dissolved and removed, because of the growing number of testimonies from those who once identified as gay and bi, who have been delivered, healed and are now straight.

While Implant Removal is a relatively new aspect of Deliverance Ministry, it is nevertheless similar to the efforts and good intentions made by U.S. Congresswoman Michelle Bachman and her husband Marcus, who run a ministry counseling gay and bi-sexual men and woman, known as 'pray away the gay'. Many people have been transformed and helped through their controversial *reparative* therapy. Janet Boynes, a friend of the Bachmans' shares her testimony of her 14 miserable years as a lesbian after her incredible transformation through Bachman's ministry, in her book, *Called Out: A Former Lesbian's Discovery of Freedom,* who now leads her own ministry to those who want to leave the homosexual lifestyle.[11]

Psychologically speaking, there's a large percentage of gay men, who identify as gay because they were either estranged, abandoned or abused by their fathers. They did not know a father's love. So much more, for these souls to return to the Lord, to know the Heavenly Father's Love for them. Christians must find a way, in their heart of hearts to minister with love to the gay community. Their resistance and rejection has only polarized the gay community to wage war on Christians. Which has sadly, led to unprecedented legal battles over baking cakes and taking photographs. Both sides feel equally persecuted. Only the Grace of God and Divine Justice can heal the hurt experienced on both sides.

Another piece of insight into why people choose to be gay, lies in their past lives. This goes for both genders, a woman born a female may identify as lesbian because she was a man in her previous life, and has always been attracted to women. That lesbian may have a male soul and may find it repulsive to be with another man, because on the inside, she has always been attracted to women. This is just one of many scenarios. If Christians approached these issues with more sensitivity and understanding, I believe they would at least be able to lovingly guide more gays and lesbians to the Love, Grace and Freedom in Jesus Christ, which is God's Will to reach them just as God reached you in your errors. Remember Christians, we are all saved *behind enemy lines.*

No error, no sin, is too great for the Grace of God. We've all been messed with, we're all in this together, the lesson we're all here to learn is *love*, tolerance, acceptance and we're all just guiding each other home, back to source, back to the Creator, and Christ is the bridge to get there. I have come across multiple people who were delivered of the gay implant and the spirit of gender confusion. I have seen it with my own eyes, and I have been front and center in the lives of bi-sexual people whose lives were radically turned around through the love of God through Jesus, who now serve the Lord and His Kingdom wholeheartedly. All things are possible with God, and to those who believe in His Love and Grace.

The other gods, the extraterrestrials who periodically would visit our planet, came to seed life, create their own genetic experiments, left us different technologies, have since left, but are scheduled to return at the end of this age. Time is different here on earth. Even the Bible speaks of time travel. See, Book Two: *Who is God?*[26]

Scripture says,

"A thousand years in your sight are like a day that has just gone by,
or like a watch in the night."
(Psalm 90:4)

"A day is like a thousand years to the Lord,
and a thousand years is like a day."
(2 Peter 3:8)

These scriptures are clearly a formula for time travel. And so, it is with the gods, the ancient extraterrestrials that have intervened in planetary affairs and the seeding of life on earth, with respect to their return. They are returning to complete and to harvest that which they began. They are also returning for a divine appointment for a final confrontation with the Creator God of gods, who the Bible says is the Lord Jesus Christ, who will end the final *Star Wars* battle with a Word and a Breath. See, Isaiah 11:13-16; Isaiah 31:8; and Revelation 19:12.

Notes:

1. Ella LeBain, *Who's Who in the Cosmic Zoo?* Book One-Third Edition, Tate Publishing, 2013.
2. Dr. David Jacobs, Director of the International Center for Abduction Research, www.ufoabduction.com/; Dr. David Jacobs, *Secret Life: Firsthand, Documented Accounts of UFO Abductions*, Touchstone; Reprint edition (April 16, 1993)
3. Dr. John Mack, *Abduction: Human Encounters with Aliens,* Scribner, New York, 1994.
4. Merit Freeman, http://consciousawareness.wixsite.com/home/adrenochrome, June 12th, 2014
5. Ella LeBain, *Who's Who in the Cosmic Zoo? Book One-Third Edition,* Tate. 2013, pp.154-182; 381.
6. Ella LeBain, *Who is God?* Book Two of *Who's Who in the Cosmic Zoo?,* Skypath Books, 2015. *What Happens When You Die?* pp. 455-483
7. Don Robertson, *The 9th Alleged ET Implant Removal by Dr. Roger Leir & Team,* 2000. Dr. Roger Leir, Implant Removal, Tim Cullen between 1995-1998; http://www.rense.com/ufo6/implant.htm
8. Dr. Joshua David Stone, Ph.D., *Hidden Mysteries* Light Technology Publishing, 1995.
9. #PIZZAGATE? #PEDOGATE, The OSTO Network, https://osto.space/pgate/
10. Douglas Hamp, *Corrupting the Image: Angels, Aliens, and the Antichrist Revealed,* Defender, July 1, 2011
11. Janet Boynes, *Called Out: A Former Lesbian's Discovery of Freedom,* Creation House (December 19, 2008), http://www.janetboynesministries.com/

CHAPTER THIRTY-TWO

The Rainbow Covenant

"And God said, this is the token of the *covenant* which I make between me and you and every living creature that is with you, for perpetual generations: I do set my bow in the cloud, and it shall be for a token of a *covenant* between me and the earth. And it shall come to pass, when I bring a cloud over the earth, that the bow shall be seen in the cloud: And I will remember my *covenant,* which is between me and you and every living creature of all flesh; and the waters shall no more become a flood to destroy all flesh. And the bow shall be in the cloud; and I will look upon it, *that I may remember the everlasting covenant between God and every living creature of all flesh that is upon the earth.* And God said unto Noah, this is the token of the *covenant,* which I have established between me and all flesh that is upon the earth."
(Genesis 9:12-17 - KJV)

This Rainbow Covenant from the Lord Yahuah, was intended to be a good faith sign in the heavens to remember God's *everlasting* Covenant with human-kind, as His promise to not destroy all flesh by flooding the earth again. This is because, Noah's flood, was the second time the Lord destroyed the earth by flood. The first flood, was evidenced in Genesis 1:2, "And the earth was without form, and void; and darkness was upon the face of the deep. And the Spirit of God moved upon the face of the waters." This meant that the Bible story began after the first flood, which is known by Dake's Bible as the Flood of Lucifer. According to Plato, it was the sinking of Atlantis. Yes, they are most certainly one and the same event.

If we read Plato's account, Atlantis sank in one day, due to the fact that the Atlanteans violated the laws of Creation. Interestingly, that Noah's flood, happened in punishment for similar if not, the same issues. So, when the Lord gave Noah this sign of forgiveness, renewal and faithfulness from God, it was a promise to Noah and to all of his descendants, that this won't happen again.

> "It came about after the seven days, that the water of the flood came upon the earth. In the six hundredth year of Noah's life, in the second month, on the seventeenth day of the month, on the same day *all the fountains of the great deep burst open*, and the *floodgates of the sky were opened*. The rain fell upon the earth for forty days and forty nights."
>
> (Genesis 7:10-12)

So, how, did this Biblical sign and spiritual symbol of God's Everlasting Covenant turn into the symbol for the LGBTQ community representing Gay pride? It's common these days to see rainbow flags flying outside of homes and bars, pinned to shirts and bumpers stickers—all with the universal proclamation that #LoveIsLove. But who created the gay rainbow flag, and why did it become a symbol of the LGBT community?

The rainbow flag was created in 1978 by artist, designer, Vietnam War veteran and then-drag queen performer, Gilbert Baker. He was commissioned to create a flag by another gay icon, politician Harvey Milk, for San Francisco's annual pride parade.[1]

One thing, that must be *spiritually discerned* here, is the consistent use of the word, 'pride' to advertise the LGBT motto and symbol. Gay pride, pride parade, etc., is exactly what the word says and represents, a spiritual stronghold of pride. There are seven things that the Lord hates: and one of them is pride.

> "There are six things which the LORD hates, Yes, seven which are an abomination to Him: 1. **<u>Pride</u>**ful looks (Haughty eyes); 2. a lying tongue; 3. hands that shed innocent blood; 4. A heart that devises wicked plans; 5. Feet that run rapidly to evil; 6. A false witness who utters lies; 7. And one who spreads strife among brothers."
>
> (Proverbs 6:16-19)

So, somehow, the LGBT community has tapped into the spirit of rebellion to their Creator Lord, who absolutely detests pride. If God is Love, and Love is love, then how can it be Pride, which the Word and Spirit says is the root of destruction? Sure, there are two kinds of pride. There is taking pride in your family, your nation, your community, your house, etc. However, to say to your child, "I am proud of you", is not arrogance, but love and positive reinforcement.

The second type of pride, is rooted in arrogance, haughtiness, conceit, smugness, self-importance, egotism, vanity, immodesty and superiority. This is the type of pride, that brings destruction and humiliation. These words have been written down for 4,000 years, and they are spiritual discernments, which depending on which side of pride you are on, can either bring blessings or curses.

"Where there is strife, there is pride, but wisdom is found in those who take advice."

(Proverbs 13:10)

"Pride goes before destruction, a haughty spirit before a fall."

(Proverbs 16:18)

"When pride comes, then comes disgrace, but with humility comes wisdom."

(Proverbs 11:2)

"Pride ends in humiliation, while humility brings honor."

(Proverbs 29:23)

"The fear of the LORD is hatred of evil. Pride and arrogance and the ways of evil and perverted speech I hate."

(Proverbs 8:13)

Herein lies another discernment: The LGBT Rainbow is different than God's rainbow. The LGBT Rainbow only has 6 colors, while God's rainbow has all 7 colors. The number 7 in the Bible is the number that represents God's Divine perfection, totality or completion and is mentioned 490 times. There are 7 days in the week, 7 whole notes in the musical scale, 7 Churches, 7 bowls, 7 trumpets in Revelation. There are even 7 levels of the Periodic Table of the known Elements, to have seven levels of periodicity, and 7 types of crystal systems, 7 Chakra system, etc.

The number 6, however, is the number of man in general and when tripled, it is the number of Antichrist (666). God created mankind and beasts on the sixth day and so six is a number that represents mankind which represents created things. Even the number 666 mentioned in the Bible where the number of the beast is also called the number of man (Revelation 13:18) so just as six is symbolic or representative of mankind, seven is symbolic of God's completed work. Just as six falls short of seven by one number, so man will always fall short of God's standard (Romans 3:23).[2] Being that these two rainbows are so distinctly different, they are nevertheless a lesson between God's wonderful creation and man's fallen and counterfeit nature.

I wonder if the LGBT community, who so enthusiastically adopted this fallen rainbow image to represent their movement, realizes the deeper meaning behind it? The colors of the original rainbow are red, orange, yellow, green, blue, indigo and violet. The LGBT flag however, is missing the color indigo. Indigo is the color of intuition. In the 7 Chakra system, Indigo is the Brow Chakra, also known as the Third Eye. Why that color is omitted from their flag, indicates that this Chakra is shut down, which is the ability to see and discern clearly into spirit. When the third eye is blocked, it causes confusion. Gender confusion is common amongst the LGBTQ community. Apparently, it was Harvey Milk's original intention to include 8 colors in the flag, that included bright pink and turquoise, but they were later allegedly omitted for practical purposes.

Ken Ham, the founder of *Answers in Genesis,* who runs *The Ark Encounter,* announced that the ministry of his Noah's Ark-Themed Park, will now be permanently lit up with rainbow lights as a reminder that God owns the rainbow - not the LGBT community. "We now have new permanent rainbow lights at the *Ark Encounter,* so all can see that it is God's rainbow and He determines its meaning in Genesis 6," He explained that the rainbow is a reminder that "God will never again judge the wickedness of man with a global Flood-next time the world will be judged by fire." [3]

"Sadly, people ignore what God intended the rainbow to represent and proudly wave rainbow-colored flags in defiance of God's command and design for marriage," Ham wrote. "Because of this, many Christians shy away from using the rainbow colors.... As Christians, we need to take the rainbow back and teach our young people its true meaning."

"I think the symbol has already been lost," wrote one commenter. "Might have been a good idea decades ago, when homosexuality started claiming the symbol for their own, but it's too late now. Christianity does not have the cultural power to reclaim it.[3]

"There's a lot of pressure from this culture to support gay marriage and transgender issues," he said. "So, when we stand on God's word regarding these issues, we're called unloving and judgmental. Sadly, what I'm finding is many churches and church leaders are succumbing to the pressure to condone homosexual behavior and gay marriage."

He added, "We're on the precipice of catastrophic change in this nation. In fact, I believe it's already happening. Romans 1 talks about the wrath of God being revealed against unrighteousness, that God turns those who reject Him over to their depraved minds. I believe we're seeing Romans 1 play out in our culture right before our eyes."[3]

God's Wrath on Unrighteousness – Romans 1:

"For the wrath of God is revealed from heaven against all ungodliness and unrighteousness of men, who by their unrighteousness suppress the truth. For what can be known about God is plain to them, because God has shown it to them. For his invisible attributes, namely, his eternal power and divine nature, have been clearly perceived, ever since the creation of the world, in the things that have been made. So, they are without excuse. For although they knew God, they did not honor him as God or give thanks to him, but they became futile in their thinking, and their foolish hearts were darkened. Claiming to be wise, they became fools, and exchanged the glory of the immortal God for images resembling mortal man and birds and animals and creeping things.

"Therefore, God gave them up in the lusts of their hearts to impurity, to the dishonoring of their bodies among themselves, because they exchanged the truth about God for a lie and worshiped and served the creature rather than the Creator, who is blessed forever! Amen.

"For this reason, God gave them up to dishonorable passions. For their women exchanged natural relations for those that are contrary to nature; and the men likewise gave up natural relations with women and were consumed with passion for one another, men committing shameless acts with men and receiving in themselves the due penalty for their error.

"And since they did not see fit to acknowledge God, God gave them up to a debased mind to do what ought not to be done. They were filled with all manner of unrighteousness, evil, covetousness, malice. They are full of envy, murder, strife, deceit, maliciousness. They are gossips, slanderers, haters of God, insolent, haughty, boastful, inventors of evil, disobedient to parents, foolish, faithless, heartless, ruthless. Though they know God's righteous decree that those who practice such things deserve to die, they not only do them but give approval to those who practice them."

(Romans 1:18-32)

While there is a distinction between the two types of rainbows and their meanings, it is the intention of the ministry of Noah's Ark Encounter located in Williamston, Kentucky, to claim back the rainbow for God from the LGBT community, which they feel, have stolen it, counterfeited it and perverted it's meaning. This underscores the ongoing battle between the gay and Christian communities.

As I've stressed in my previous chapter, it's fine for everyone to stand their ground, but in order for peace and unity to ever prevail, Christians must incorporate better outreaching skills to the LGBT community, if there will be any hope of salvation and deliverance from the demonic strongholds in both communities. Too many Christians define themselves by what they're against, instead of what they are for. In my humble opinion, when you beat people up for being sinful, you create resistance and they dig their heels in and become even more rebellious. Wise parents learn this lesson with raising children. However, Wise parents use different techniques, so kids don't resist or rebel. It is called, parenting with love. The Church must learn this, after all, if they indeed have the spirit of Christ, those who do, know this love.

Unfortunately, the problem in the Church is that it's split between those who are filled by Christ's Holy Spirit and those who are controlled by the Religious Spirit. This is the reason for so much division inside the church. So those with the Religious Spirit adopt a judgmental attitude, because of self-righteousness. They are unaware, that this actually causes resistance and people to leave the church and rebel against God. Instead of creating an atmosphere of healing through understanding, compassion and patience with those who are confused, errant and wounded, they push them away through condemnation. Unfortunately, the Christians with the Religious Spirit forget and ignore that:

> "There is no condemnation for all those who are within Christ Jesus. Because through Christ Jesus the law of the Spirit who gives life has set you free from the law of sin and death."
>
> (Romans 8:1-2)

Love is love, that doesn't mean sex is love. Anyone who's lived long enough in this world, knows that sex does not necessarily equate to love. Most romantics would like it to be so, but to many men and women, sex is sex. The LGBT motto is #Loveislove, is not necessarily indicative of the majority of the LGBT community, as many who are part of the gay lifestyle are promiscuous, which is a fact, not a judgment. Gay or straight, being promiscuous is not God's Will for human relationships, commitment through marriage is. Promiscuity is based on lust, not love. Lust is a spirit, albeit a very seductive and addictive one. This is why people who think they are born gay or lesbian, think they can't change, because they are both oppressed and possessed by a demon of lust. However, once that demon is kicked out, regardless of whether or not a person is gay or straight, the person is no longer held hostage to lustful thoughts and behaviors and tends to seek relationships that are based on commitments and soul connections.

The spirit of lust and promiscuity is not limited to the gay community, but it certainly is a central focus in gay parties and parades. Except for pornography, you don't see too many 'straight parades', and while there are always exceptions to all these generalizations, most straight people don't flaunt their lifestyle, sexual preference or necessarily wear it on their shirt or bumper sticker. It's a fact, that the LGBT community is *louder* about flaunting their sexuality, and literally wears it on their sleeve, as is the case in many of their parades.

But since Gay marriage has become legal in the United States, on June 26, 2015, when the US Supreme Court ruled that the US Constitution guarantees the right for same-sex couples to marry in all 50 US states. Associate Justice Anthony Kennedy stated in the majority opinion: "The Court, in this decision, holds same-sex couples may exercise the fundamental right to marry in all States." Twenty-five states banned Gay marriage.

Lesbian couples are more than twice as likely to get divorced than gay men, new figures from the Office for National Statistics (ONS) have revealed in England and Wales, for reasons of Unreasonable behavior – which can include having a sexual relationship with someone else – was the most common grounds for divorce among same-sex couples.[4]

Gay Christians claim homosexuality in the Bible is implied between Ruth and Naomi, David and Jonathon, as well as being in nature, between different types of animals. But is it, or was this God's will for the human design and relationship? If the destruction of Sodom and Gomorrah occurred because of rampant gay activity, to the point of men desiring sex with angels, which they received fire from heaven for their behavior, and the days preceding Noah's flood, we know were also full of homosexual unions, as Jesus predicted would happen again preceding His return, then shouldn't we connect the dots here and try to save the LGBT people from their apparent blind-sidedness and denials?

The *Rainbow Covenant* was made to all of humankind, that includes the LBGT who Jesus Christ died for their sins as well. But all must turn back to the Lord, with a repentant heart so His Grace can be poured out on all who repent. That's the promise of the *Blood Covenant.* Christians must be more understanding of the struggles, persecutions and the woundings that lead people to choose the LGBT lifestyle. Just as they need to be, in any other lifestyle. However, the *Marriage Covenant* was originally established between a man and woman. I don't think any LGBT person can deny that fact. See, Genesis 2:24. They do, however, want to change it, but it's historical foundation, is ancient, and just as all things, there are blessings and curses attached to them, and breaking these covenants, are no different.

The *Rainbow Covenant* is the promise that the Lord won't destroy the Earth again by massive floods, but He said nothing about not using fire. Which is exactly what the End Time Prophesies point to.

That's what the Lord has said:

> "The earth will dry up completely. The world will dry up and waste away. The heavens will fade away along with the earth. The earth is polluted by its people. They haven't obeyed the laws of the Lord. They haven't done what he told them to do. They've broken the *covenant* that will last forever. So, the Lord will send a curse on the earth. Its people will pay for what they've done. ***They will be burned up.***"
>
> (Isaiah 24:4-6)

Whether you're gay, straight, bi or anything else in between, you need to get your life right with your Creator and take His Word and more importantly, the history of it, seriously. History repeats itself, because people fail to learn from its mistakes. The one who is wise, not only learns from their mistakes, but from other's mistakes. You don't need to make the same mistakes to gain wisdom from those who have already gone down that path. Just look to the ancients, and learn from the punishment they received.

We are living in a time, where everything is upside down and distorted, this is due to the curse on humankind.

> "Woe to those who call evil good and good evil, who put darkness for light and light for darkness, who put bitter for sweet and sweet for bitter."
>
> (Isaiah 5:20)

Somewhere Over the Rainbow

The famous song from the Wizard of Oz, *Somewhere Over the Rainbow* was written, not about the mythical Land of Oz but of Israel, the homeland of the Jews. The lyrics were written by Yip Harburg, the youngest of four children born to Russian-Jewish immigrants. His real name was Isidore Hochberg, who grew up in a Yiddish-speaking, Orthodox Jewish home in New York. The song's music was written by Harold Arlen, also a cantor's son. His real name was Hyman Arluck, and his Jewish parents immigrated from Lithuania. Together, Yip and Harold wrote and produced, *Somewhere Over the Rainbow*, which was voted the 20th century's Number One song by the Recording Industry Association of America and the National Endowment for the Arts. The song rose to global fame, as they won an Oscar in 1940 for "Best Music, Original Song" for "The Wizard of Oz".[5]

The two Russian men reached deep into their immigrant Jewish consciousness — inspired by the pogroms of the past, when they wrote the song in 1939 as Jews in Europe were deep into the persecutions of Nazi Germany's Holocaust. Their freedoms were being taken from them, their identities dragged through the mud, and many felt isolated, trapped and unable to "fly". Meanwhile in parallel to the horrific traumas and tragedies they were facing in Europe, the State of Israel was in a battle to be formed. See, Theodore Herzl. Together they wrote an unforgettable song, that was divinely inspired set to prophetic words.

> "And the dreams that you dare to dream ….. really do come true."

The song was about hope, that one day, the nightmare will be over. It was this feeling of hope that helped Jews through the Holocaust. At least that is the testimony of those who survived and lived to tell their stories.

They honor those that dreamed of "the land that they heard once in a lullaby," which represents all those who perished at hands of persecution, who never saw the Promised Land as well as those who rose from the ashes to make the dream a reality.

America's founders envisioned the U.S.A. as the "new Zion". Another reason why today's Israel and America are deeply bound together - through shared vision and values. Many have paralleled the two nations in Bible Prophecy. Messianic Jewish Rabbi Jonathan Cahn, said in his 2012 book, *The Harbinger,* that today's America parallels ancient Israel.[6] His main message was, that if America turned its back on God, like Ancient Israel did, by following alien gods, and their false idols, and fell into immorality, that it too would share the same fate of ancient Israel, who lost their land to their enemies, for 1830 years. Therefore America, along with all our important freedoms must be protected, from being absorbed by New World Order Globalism.

These songs are a testament, not to the horrors of the Holocaust that came after they were both released but to the Zionist awakening that began before the Holocaust.

It reminds me of the song written by Andrew Lloyd Weber for *Joseph and the Amazing Technicolor Dreamcoat*, "Close Every Door to Me" which essentially is about the Jews crying out for a land of their own, which is Israel. Excerpts:

> "If my life were important / I would ask will I live or die? / But I know the answers lie, / Far from this world. / Close every door to me, / Keep those I love from me, / Children of Israel, / Are never alone, / For we know we shall find, / Our own peace of mind, / For we have been promised, / *A land of our own.*" [7]

Rabbi Bernhard Rosenberg, author of *The Holocaust as Seen Through Film,* reflects on *Somewhere Over the Rainbow* from the perspective of its Jewish composers, who published the Oscar-winning song on the eve of the Holocaust. No doubt, the most moving song to emerge from the mass Jewish exodus from Europe was, *Somewhere Over the Rainbow.*

> "Somewhere over the rainbow / Way up high / There's a land that I heard of / Once in a lullaby.
>
> Somewhere over the rainbow / Skies are blue / And the dreams that you dare to dream / Really do come true.
>
> Someday I'll wish upon a star / And wake up where the clouds are far behind me.
>
> Where troubles melt like lemon drops / Away above the chimney tops / That's where you'll find me.

> Somewhere over the rainbow / Bluebirds fly.
> Birds fly over the rainbow.
> Why then, oh why can't I?
> If happy little bluebirds fly / Beyond the rainbow / Why, oh why can't I?"[5]

Of course, the Jews of Europe could not fly. They could not escape beyond the rainbow. Harburg was almost psychic when he penned about wanting to fly like a bluebird away from the "chimney tops." During the Holocaust, Jews were burned in gas chambers and their smoke came up through chimney tops, that travelled through the air. People smelled it in France. In the post-Auschwitz era, chimney tops have taken on a whole different meaning than the one they had at the beginning of 1939 because the Nazis had not yet installed the crematoriums and gas chambers in the death camps that they used during the Holocaust only one year later.[8]

There are people who can't believe that this famous song was written for Zion. But the truth of the matter is, that Zion is at the heart of all Jews, and most importantly to the God of Israel who created Zion. People could not believe that these two Russian Jewish immigrants would write a political song and hide it in the *Wizard of Oz*. Firstly, the entire *Wizard of Oz* is a metaphor for the multiverse of multiple dimensions, living side by side, right here on Earth, with a wizard who is a fraud, a controlling little man hiding behind a curtain. Secondly, the Promised Land has been at the heart of every Jew, regardless of political affiliation or even religious affiliation. It is woven into the soul of Judaism, the hope of 'next year in Jerusalem,' which is something affirmed every year at Passover Seders all over the world. Therefore, it is no surprise, such a beautiful song would emerge out of the ashes of so much persecution.

> "The Spirit of the Lord is upon me ...to proclaim the year of the Lord's favor and the day of vengeance of our God, to comfort all who mourn, and provide for those who grieve in Zion— to bestow on them a crown of beauty instead of ashes, the oil of joy instead of mourning,"
>
> (Isaiah 61:2-3)

The State of Israel is a testament to the Jewish people that the "dreams that you dare to dream really do come true." It seems that our world is once again on the edge of dark times. This song reminds us that though we face uncertain events, we still have hope, and our hope is in the Lord, the God of Grace and Salvation.[9]

Isn't it ironic that for 1,830 years, the land that the Jews heard of "once in a lullaby" was not America, but Israel. The miraculous and prophetic fulfilment turned out that 9 years after *Somewhere Over the Rainbow* was published, the exile was over, and the State of Israel was reborn, Jews from all over the Diaspora returned home.

Ezekiel 37 prophecy fulfilled from 1948 to present time. The Spirit of the Lord took Ezekiel to another Dimension and showed him a vision of the future. It is known as The Valley of the Dry Bones Vision, which was a prophetic promise of the *reincarnation* of Israel. The words in both Hebrew and the English translation are specific, to mean *reincarnation*. Putting flesh on the bones, *carne,* means flesh in Latin, breathing life back into them, if that is not the very definition of *reincarnation*, I don't know what is. Point is, this prophecy has been fulfilled.

The Lord promised, "I will bring them home to their own land from the places where they have been scattered. I will unify them into one nation on the mountains of Israel." When this prophecy was fulfilled in 1948, it literally launched the beginning of all End Times Prophecies scheduled to unfold in the last days of the end of this present age. There is but one part of this prophecy, that has yet to be fulfilled, and that is the Mashiach-Nagid, (Messiah-King) who returns to rule over the entire nation of Israel and Judah as One. To be continued….

> "The LORD took hold of me, and I was carried away by the Spirit of the LORD to a valley filled with bones. He led me all around among the bones that covered the valley floor. They were scattered everywhere across the ground and were completely dried out. Then he asked me, "Son of man, can these bones become living people again?"
>
> "O Sovereign LORD," I replied, "you alone know the answer to that."
>
> Then he said to me, "Speak a prophetic message to these bones and say, 'Dry bones, listen to the word of the LORD! This is what the Sovereign LORD says: Look! *I am going to put breath into you and make you live again! I will put flesh and muscles on you and cover you with skin. I will put breath into you, and you will come to life. Then you will know that I am the LORD.*'"
>
> So, I spoke this message, just as he told me. Suddenly as I spoke, there was a rattling noise all across the valley. The bones of each body came together and attached themselves as complete skeletons. Then as I watched, muscles and flesh formed over the bones. Then skin formed to cover their bodies, but they still had no breath in them.
>
> Then he said to me, "Speak a prophetic message to the winds, son of man. Speak a prophetic message and say, 'This is what the Sovereign LORD says: Come, O breath, from the four winds! Breathe into these dead bodies so they may live again.'"
>
> So, I spoke the message as he commanded me, and breath came into their bodies. They all came to life and stood up on their feet—a great army.
>
> Then he said to me, "Son of man, these bones represent the people of Israel. They are saying, 'We have become old, dry bones—all hope is gone.

Our nation is finished.' Therefore, prophesy to them and say, 'This is what the Sovereign LORD says: O my people, I will open your graves of exile and cause you to rise again. Then I will bring you back to the land of Israel. When this happens, O my people, you will know that I am the LORD. I will put my Spirit in you, and you will live again and return home to your own land. Then you will know that I, the LORD, have spoken, and I have done what I said. Yes, the LORD has spoken!'"

And give them this message from the Sovereign LORD: I will gather the people of Israel from among the nations. I will bring them home to their own land from the places where they have been scattered. *I will unify them into one nation on the mountains of Israel. One king will rule them all; no longer will they be divided into two nations or into two kingdoms.* They will never again pollute themselves with their idols and vile images and rebellion, for I will save them from their sinful backsliding. I will cleanse them. Then they will truly be my people, and I will be their God.

"And I will make a *covenant of peace with them, an everlasting covenant.*"

(Ezekiel 37: 1-14; 21-23; 26)

Notes:

1. Thad Morgan, *How did the Rainbow Flag become an LGBT Symbol?* June 2, 2017, http://www.history.com/news/ask-history/how-did-the-rainbow-flag-become-an-lgbt-symbol
2. *What Does the Number Seven Represent in the Bible?* http://www.patheos.com/blogs/christiancrier/2014/09/26/what-does-the-number-seven-7-mean-or-represent-in-the-bible/#ub8XegsBMekU4jjg.99r.
3. Leah Marieann Klett, *Ken Ham: The Ark Encounter Will be Permanently Lit with Rainbow Lights to 'Take Back' Symbol from LGBT Community,* July 19, 2017, http://www.gospelherald.com/articles/71141/20170719/ken-ham-ark-encounter-permananetly-lit-rainbow-lights-take-back.htm
4. May Bulman, *Lesbian couples two and a half times more likely to get divorced than male same-sex couples, ONS figures reveal More than three quarters of the splits between same sex couples in England and Wales were between two women.* October 18, 2017, http://www.independent.co.uk/news/uk/home-news/lesbian-couples-more-likely-divorced-male-same-sex-marriages-uk-ons-figures-a8006741.html
5. The Harburg Foundation, Biography of Yip Harburg, http://yipharburg.com/about-yip-2/biography/

6. Rabbi Jonathan Cahn, *The Harbinger, The Ancient Mystery that Holds the Secret of America's Future,* Frontline (January 3, 2012)
7. Andrew Lloyd Weber, *Joseph and the Amazing Technicolor Dreamcoat,* "Close Every Door," 1968.
8. Rabbi Bernhard Rosenberg, *Somewhere Over the Rainbow' from Jewish Perspective,* December 10, 2014, https://www.mycentraljersey.com/story/life/faith/2014/12/10/somewhere-rainbow-jewish-perspective/20104523/
9. *The Powerful Message Behind 'Over the Rainbow',* https://www.cufi.org.uk/spotlight/the-powerful-message-behind-over-the-rainbow/, November 2015 | Spotlight.

CHAPTER THIRTY-THREE
Blood Covenants

Your new life is going to cost you your old one.
Behold I make all things new!
~ Jesus the Christ

The Covenant Of Renewal

In Book One of *Who's Who in The Cosmic Zoo,* I laid out not just the theological reasons for our Kinsmen Redeemer's Christ work, but also the legal and historical background. In *From Adam's Failure to the Second Adam's Victory,* I detailed the cosmic drama which occurred in the Garden of Eden, which forms a backdrop for understanding the concept of Spiritual Legal Ground.[1] This explains why the fall of man paved the way for the transference of the ownership of Earth into the hands of Lucifer the Satan.

The word *holy*, in and of itself, doesn't tell one much. The term *holy* technically means 'to be set apart or different'. Thus, when we say that God is holy, it means that God is uniquely different from anything else in existence. *Holy* is simply a reference to other attributes, or an essence, that is set apart from anything else through purity, wholeness and righteousness.

> "And he that sat upon the throne said, Behold, I make all things new. And he said unto me, write: for these words are true and faithful."
>
> (Revelation 21:5)

> Now I'm doing a new thing, says the Lord!

> "Behold, I am doing a new thing; now it springs forth, do you not perceive it? I will make a way in the wilderness and rivers in the desert."
>
> (Isaiah 43:19)

There is the recurring theme that as the orchestrator of this Grand Experiment, the Lord has the right and prerogative to change direction at any time when something is not working. Just as we would do, just as He's done before in the past. That does not mean, He changes *who* He is. It is clear from His Word, "I am the Lord, and I change not." (Malachi 3:6), *who* He is, and *what* direction He takes, are two entirely different things. He specifically said,

> "Behold, *I will do a new thing*; now it shall spring forth; shall you not know it? I will even make a way in the wilderness, and rivers in the desert."
>
> (Isaiah 43:19)

It's hard for Jews to accept that God would create a New Covenant, one that is easier for *everyone* to readily accept, as the Old Mosaic Covenant based on laws and legalism proved to be unsuccessful. Instead the New Blood Covenant is based on faith in what His Sent One (Shaliach) did for all, through His blood sacrifice. This New Blood Covenant allows everyone to be reconciled to God the Creator, not just the learned few. It levels out the playing field, and is inclusive.

Bloodlines are based on *covenants*. Covenants of genetics, what better way than to unite all the different races? Combine all DNA pairings through one blood, and open the door to everyone through the simple application of faith! Ultimately the *Blood Covenant* ends racism, prejudice, bigotries and anti-Semitism, to all those who unite through Christ. At least, that's God's Divine Plan.

For some, this is too simple to accept or even to understand. It is nevertheless the very currency of heaven. We are blood-bought with a price in order to be brought back into right relationship with our Creator through the blood of Jesus Christ. There is power in His blood covering, that is holy, supernatural, which doesn't need to be shed again, but shed once and for all, to those who put their faith in Him and His eternal *blood covenant* are not only saved but delivered from all evil. It is this very power and *currency* of Heaven, that sets us free. Nothing but the blood of Jesus. We are blood bought behind enemy lines.

Why Blood?

History is full of countless demands of angry gods demanding blood sacrifices as appeasement. The Aztecs honestly believed the sun god needed human blood for food, so they sacrificed in quantity in their horrific rituals. The people of Moloch threw their babies into the fire to appease him. The ancient Hawaiians, a kindly and charming people, still made human sacrifices to their god of war. There are all kinds of gods throughout history who needed human blood sacrifice as appeasement.

Today, Muslims sacrifice the blood of humans to Allah, who is also known as the reptilian draconian lizard king, satan.

If holy had an antonym, an opposite meaning, it would surely be the *same* or *similar*. If God needed the blood of innocent people as a sacrifice for appeasement, then that would make him the same or similar to these primitive versions of god. Question remains, which god? See, Book Two, *Who is God?* on the discernment between the gods, the god of this world, and the God of gods. They are not one and the same, in fact they are in an ongoing ancient battle.

Let us therefore be quite clear about what we are doing when we describe the cross of Calvary in this way: when we say that God's anger at sin necessitated the blood sacrifice of an innocent human to calm His wrath, we are not describing a god who is fundamentally different and holy– we are simply describing another version of an angry god who needs a virgin thrown into the volcano.[2] The Blood Sacrifice of Jesus was not payment to the Heavenly Father/Mother of Creation, but was a *ransom,* to the 'god of this world', to set the captives free. That god is Lucifer, the Draconian Lizard King aka the satan.

The whole of the Old Testament, every book, points toward the Great Sacrifice that was to come—that of Jesus' sacrificial giving of His own life on our behalf. Leviticus 17:11 is the central statement about the significance of blood in the sacrificial system. God, speaking to Moses, declares: "For the life of a creature is in the blood, and I have given it to you to make atonement for yourselves on the altar; it is the blood that makes atonement for one's life." Likewise, Moses was instructed not to eat the blood of any creature, including humans, which would bring a curse on them from Yahuah. See, Leviticus 17:10.

A *sacrifice* is defined as the offering up of something precious for a cause or a reason. Making atonement is satisfying someone or something for an offense committed. The Leviticus verse can be read more clearly now: God said, "I have given it to you (the creature's life, which is in its blood) to make atonement for yourselves (covering the offense you have committed against Me)." In other words, those who are covered by the blood sacrifice are set free from the consequences of sin.

The Israelites did not know of Jesus yet, or how He would die on their behalf and then rise again, but they did believe God would be sending them a Messiah. All the many, many blood sacrifices seen throughout the Old Testament were the foreshadowing of the true, once-for-all-time sacrifice to come, so that the Israelites would never forget the fact that without the blood, there is no forgiveness. This shedding of blood is a substitutionary act. Therefore, the last clause of Leviticus 17:11 could be read either "the blood 'makes atonement' at the cost of the life," the animal's life, or "makes atonement in the place of the life," the sinner's life, with Jesus Christ being the One giving life through His shed blood.

Hebrews 9:11-18 confirms the symbolism of blood as life and applies Leviticus 17:11 to the sacrifice of the Lord Jesus Christ. Verse 12 states clearly that the Old Testament blood sacrifices were temporary and only atoned for sin partially and for a short time, hence the need to repeat the sacrifices yearly. But when Christ entered the Most Holy Place, He did so to offer His own blood once for all time, making future sacrifices unnecessary.[3] This is what Jesus meant by His dying words on the cross: "It is finished" (John 19:30). Never again would the blood of bulls and goats cleanse men from their sin. Only by accepting Jesus' blood, shed on the cross for the remission of sins, can we stand before God covered in the righteousness of Christ (2 Corinthians 5:21).

In 1 Samuel 18, Jonathan and David made a covenant with each other. The word covenant comes from a root word meaning *to cut*, suggesting it literally has the idea of a blood covenant. The word *breet mila* is the word for circumcision, which is the cutting of the shaft (*shmuck* in Hebrew) from the penis. The Hebrew word *breet* means covenant.

It was Jonathan who first told David that his father, Saul, wanted to kill David. (1 Samuel 19:2) Then David fled and went into hiding. After Jonathan and Saul were killed in battle and David was proclaimed king, Jonathan's son, Mephibosheth, was taken into hiding in a desolate land called Lodebar. David sent for Mephibosheth so that he could show him kindness for Jonathan's sake, thus honoring his covenant with Jonathan. It was up to Mephibosheth to decide whether or not to ratify the covenant.

The Blood Covenant is a Biblical Principle (1 Samuel 18:3). It is the focus of the Bible. It is the secret of blessing. (Psalm 25:14; Luke 22:20) It is the source of boldness. When we understand the blood covenant, and who we are, and what we have in the Lord Jesus, we are then no longer bound to our feelings but can stand with boldness before the throne of Grace.

The Blood Covenant is a steadfast promise. (1 Samuel 19:1-2; 2 Samuel 9:1-10) The blood covenant is an unbreakable covenant. Because of the blood covenant, Mephibosheth was permitted a seat at the kings table. (2 Samuel 9:10) Because of the *blood covenant* of Jesus, we too have a seat at the Kings table. (Luke 22:20)

Salvation is pictured in 2 Samuel 9:1-10 and Ephesians 4:32. What the covenant brought to Mephibosheth and what salvation through Jesus brings to us is the King's forgiveness, His fortune, His fellowship.[4] We have become the King's family, we are adopted sons and daughters into His Kingdom. (Ephesians 1:5)

The **Abrahamic Covenant** is a type of *blood covenant*, that was, and still is, based on faith in God's promises to the seed of Abraham. However, let's not forget, that what caused the Lord to covenant with Abraham, was the *faith* that Abraham showed to the Lord. As with any blood covenant which signifies the life from which the blood comes, in this case, it's a race of people signified by a gene pool, who are *faithful* to the Lord. A covenant is an agreement, however, in this case, nothing depended on Abraham. Everything depended on God, who promised to be *faithful* to His covenant. "When God made his promise to Abraham, since there was no one greater for Him to swear by, He swore by Himself" (Hebrews 6:13-18). Therefore, Abraham and his descendants could trust, count on, and believe in everything God promised. The blessings and curses of Israel and the Jews were established with Abraham: The Lord promised: "I will bless those who bless you, and whoever curses you I will curse; and all peoples on earth will be blessed through you." (Genesis 12:3)

The Mosaic Covenant was also a *blood covenant* in that it required blood to be sprinkled on the tabernacle, "the scroll and all the people" (Hebrews 9:19-21). "In fact, the law requires that nearly everything be cleansed with blood, and without the shedding of blood there is no forgiveness of sins." (Hebrews 9:22). In the Mosaic Covenant, the blood of animals served as a covering, or atonement for the sins of the people. The animal's life was given in place of the sinner's life. In the Abrahamic Covenant (Genesis 15:12-17), God was declaring He would give His life if His promises were broken. There could be no greater encouragement to believers, since God is eternal and can no more break an oath than He can die.

These actions and events were only the foreshadows of the better covenant to come (Hebrews 9:23). The sacrifice of the lives of animals could never remove sin; the life of an animal is not a sufficient substitute for a human life (Hebrews 10:4). The blood of bulls and goats were a temporary appeasement until the final, ultimate blood covenant was made by Jesus Christ Himself – the God Man (Hebrews 9:24-28). The **New Covenant** was in **His blood** (Luke 22:20).

The Seven Portals Jesus Bled to Heal You

There is power in the Blood of Jesus, "For you know that God paid a *ransom* to save you from the empty life you inherited from your ancestors. And it was not paid with mere gold or silver, which lose their value. It was paid with the precious blood of Christ, the sinless, spotless Lamb of God." (1 Peter 1:18-19)

There is so much power in the Blood, that it is a mystery to many, just how powerful it is. Every place on the body of Christ that was pierced to bleed out, represents the healing and deliverance from every single disease and condition known to man. Jesus bled seven times to set us free from the curse of Adam giving us a complete salvation and deliverance from all curses. The number seven means completion.

> "He was despised and rejected of men; a man of sorrows, and acquainted with grief: and we hid as it were our faces from Him: He was despised, and we esteemed Him not there is no beauty that we should desire Him. Surely, He hath borne our grief (sicknesses) and carried our sorrows (diseases): He was

wounded for our transgressions, He was bruised for our iniquities and the chastisement for our peace was upon Him and by His stripes we are healed."

(Isaiah 53: 3-5)

On the cross when He said, "it is finished," it was at that moment He completed atonement for all the sins, transgressions, iniquities, sicknesses, diseases and curses of humankind. In that moment, peace and salvation from all the curses became available to all who accept this Gift of Grace. He paid the price so that you would not have to be sick, broke, busted and disgusted anymore. This is the foundation of faith, and what the Blood Covenant is about.

It's activated through faith, heartfelt repentance, which pours out God's Grace and Mercy to all who come to Him. No exceptions! That includes all peoples of the earth, including those who live *inside* the earth. Just because the majority of humankind is not aware of other peoples, God knows who they are, and His Grace extends to all through His Blood Covenant.

The blood of Jesus Christ is the only cleansing agent that can wash away the sins of humankind. Therefore, as through Adam's failure, judgment came to all men, resulting in condemnation; even so through one Man's righteous act, the free gift of restoration came to all humankind, resulting in justification of life. See, Romans 5:18

1. **The Garden of Grace**

"And being in agony, He prayed more earnestly. Then His sweat became like great drops of blood falling down to the ground."

(Luke 22:44)

The Garden of Gethsemane also called the place of pressing: He knew the suffering that He would have to go through with the cross and He cried out to God the Father and said: "If it be thy will let this cup pass from me." His agony caused Him to sweat drops of blood, to give us access once again to the Father's presence. He literally became sin in our place and by His blood delivered all of humankind from the penalty of death and eternal damnation.

"For He made Him who knew no sin to be sin for us, that we might become the righteousness of God in Him."

(2 Corinthians 5:21)

It was there He gave you back your will power. The power to overcome addictions, the strength to overcome anxieties.

2. **Bruised for Our Iniquities**

> "He was bruised (crushed) for our iniquities; the chastisement for our peace was upon Him."
>
> (Isaiah 53:5)

Jesus was beaten up, almost beyond recognition to break the generational curse that runs through all of our earthly bloodlines. He was bruised which meant that He bled inside to wash away the iniquities of past generations and to give all of humankind a clean slate. His blood delivered us from the generational curse once and for all, setting us free from the sins of our ancestors.

> "Yet it pleased the Lord to bruise (crush) Him; He has put Him to grief. When you make His soul an offering for sin, He shall see His seed, He shall prolong His days, and the pleasure of the Lord shall prosper in His hand. He shall see the labor of His soul, and be satisfied. By His knowledge, My righteous Servant shall justify (pardon) many, for *He shall bear their iniquities*."
>
> (Isaiah 53:10, 11)

Jesus' Bruises won our Deliverance from Inner Hurts and Iniquities: If you have a bruise on your body, it means you are bleeding on the inside. Some bruises last a long time and go very deep. Jesus said, "not only will I forgive what they've done on the outside, but I'm going to give them power on the inside, so they can walk in total victory."

An iniquity is a bend in our nature, (genetic disposition) to sin as our ancestors did, or, have a tendency towards wicked acts. That spirit of iniquity then tries to break us down, through generational curses. It's spiritual legal ground creates assignments by dark forces to possess and pressures us to bow or bend under its destructive nature. If you have a deep bruise inside, perhaps from divorce, or suicidal tendencies, or bruises from sexual abuse, all can be sacrosanct to Jesus who bore your hurts and bruises so that you could be whole again. With God all things are possible.

3. **By His Stripes We Are Healed**

He took 39 stripes on His back that you might be healed. A small but astounding piece of trivia is that every disease fits into 39 categories. Jesus took 39 lashes. It was meant to be 40, but Pilate called a halt at 39. It is no coincidence that the American Medical Association Journal of disease, listed 39 major diseases that all ailments and conditions stem from.[5] 39 stripes for 39 diseases. Just like the prophecy stated, "By His Stripes We Are Healed!" (Isaiah 53:5).

No doubt, that healing is a benefit of the *blood covenant.* I myself have been healed of several diseases through repenting to Jesus, accepting His blood that cleanses me with no drugs, no surgery, no expensive medical bills. Especially at a time in my life, when I had no health insurance, the Lord carried me, He is my Great Physician.

> "Bless the Lord, O my soul, and forget not all His benefits: Who forgives all your iniquities, ***Who heals all your diseases.***" (Psalms 103:2-3)

4. **Crowned to Prosper**

> "And they stripped Him and put a scarlet robe on Him. When they had twisted a *crown of thorns, they put it on His head*, and a reed in His right hand, and they bowed the knee before Him and mocked Him, saying, "Hail, King of the Jews!" Then they spat on Him and took the reed and struck Him on the head."
>
> (Matthew 27:28-30)

The Messiah and Savior of all humankind was humiliated and mocked, beaten and bruised, all for us. In this piercing, he bled from the crown of his head, which paid for our healing of all mental illnesses. Every mental disorder, every psychological problem, has been paid for when He endured the mockery and piercing of the *crown of thorns.*

Many theologians also believe that through His suffering with twisted thorns piercing His brow, Jesus broke the curse on our livelihood of poverty, debt and lack. The Crown of Thorns placed on Yeshua's head to wound him and mock Him, won back your prosperity.

> "God said to Adam and Eve "because you have heeded the voice of your wife, and have eaten from the tree of which I commanded you, saying, "you shall not eat of it." Cursed is the ground for your sake; in toil you shall eat of it all the days of your life. Both thorns and thistles it shall bring forth for you, and you shall eat the herb of the fields. In the sweat of your face you shall eat bread till you return to the ground."
>
> (Genesis 3: 17-19)

5. **His Hands Were Pierced for Our Transgressions**

> "He was wounded (pierced) for our transgressions."
>
> (Isaiah 53:5)

They drove nails into His hands: God had placed all authority in the hands of Adam and Eve. Through their disobedience they lost their authority. Jesus' nail pierced hands bought back your authority. We can lay hands on the sick now, and they will recover. The hands of Christ were pierced through with nails as He bled out to forgive our transgressions. Not only did the blood flow from the hands of Jesus, but the anointing of God's Holy Spirit that breaks the yoke of bondage placed upon us, flows from His hands. He laid hands on the sick and they were healed, He touched the dead and they were raised. The very power of the throne of God flowed from the Savior's heart to those that cried out for His tender mercy.

> "Can a woman forget her nursing child, and not have compassion on the son of her womb? Surely, they may forget, Yet I will not forget you. See, I have inscribed you on the palms of My hands."
>
> (Isaiah 49:15, 16)

6. **His Feet Were Pierced to Give Us Dominion**

> "And you, being dead in your trespasses and the uncircumcision of your flesh, He has made alive together with Him, having forgiven you all trespasses, having wiped out the requirements that was against us, which was contrary to us. And He has taken it out of the way, *having nailed it to the cross.*"
>
> (Colossians 2:13, 14)

Jesus was nailed to a tree and bled from His feet to cleanse us from our trespasses, an unlawful entry on someone's property. He also gave us dominion over all the powers of darkness to tread upon them with our feet. We have been given authority to defeat the enemy and to carry the outstanding good news of salvation to a lost world.

Roman soldiers drove spikes into his feet: Those pierced feet won back dominion over the places we walk. Man was supposed to be the head and not the tail. Man was supposed to be above only and not beneath. When Adam disobeyed God in the Garden of Eden, he lost dominion and authority, and at that moment, satan became the god of this world. But through Jesus' shed blood, we don't have to be trampled by satan. Instead, we are to trample him! Crucified for us, beaten and bloody, suffering great sorrow and pain He defeated the devil judging him once and for all time to be tormented in fire and brimstone for all eternity. Looking up toward His Heavenly Father He uttered these words in His dying breath, "It is finished."[6]

> "Having disarmed principalities and powers, He made a public spectacle of them, triumphing over them in it."
>
> (Colossians 2:15)

7. **He Bled from a Broken Heart**

> "But one of the soldiers pierced His side with a spear, and immediately blood and water came out."
>
> (John 19:34)

Jesus literally bled out for us and emptied Himself on the cross to wash away the sins, iniquities, trespasses, transgressions and sicknesses of humankind. His heart was broken for us that He might heal our broken heart. Jesus bled to mend us both mentally and emotionally by binding up our broken hearts.

> "He has sent Me to heal the brokenhearted, to proclaim liberty to the captives and the opening of the prison to those who are bound."
>
> (Isaiah 61:1; Luke 4:18)

Jesus pierced heart won back our joy: When the soldier shoved a spear into His side and blood and was poured out; at that moment he atoned (paid the price) for the brokenhearted to be healed. "The joy of the Lord is your strength." (Nehemiah 8:10)

Jesus not only took your sin, but He took the pain of that sin. As the old saying goes, "He'll turn our hurts into halos and our scars into stars." Jesus knows what it is to suffer a broken heart, not only physically in His death on the cross but also through the betrayal and rejection by the very ones He came to love and call friends. Many of those He had ministered to cried, "Crucify Him!"

> "If someone asks, 'What are these wounds on your body?' they will answer, 'The wounds I was given at the house of my friends.'"
>
> (Zechariah 14:6)

In the Old Testament, the High Priest would enter the Holy of Holies where the presence of God abides. Once a year he offered the blood of an unblemished lamb to atone for the people's sins by smearing the blood *seven times* on the mercy seat.

The Lord Jesus Christ has become our High Priest who is the Lamb of God, that shed His blood seven times to give humankind complete and eternal salvation, delivering us from damnation, sickness and sin forever!

> "Repent therefore and be converted, that your sins may be blotted out, so that times of refreshing may come from the presence of the Lord, "and that He may send Jesus Christ, who was preached to you before, whom Heaven must receive until the times of restoration of all things, which God has spoken by the mouth of all His holy prophets since the world began."
>
> (Acts 3:19-21)

If you need healing, and you want to make sure you are marked as "redeemed" into the Kingdom of Heaven, then pray this prayer out loud and believe in your heart:

> "Lord Jesus, I thank you that by your stripes I am healed, I am delivered from family iniquities and curses. Thank you that you gave me back my free will that I might not allow destructive behavior to rule my life. I thank you that you have given me back the ability to prosper, to take authority and dominion over the things and places that you have given to me. I thank you that the joy of the Lord is my strength, that by your bruises I am delivered from inner hurts and family iniquities. Through the piercing of hands and feet I am delivered from satanic bondage. That by the sweat of your brow I can prosper and be in good health even as my soul prospers. Through your shed blood, my sins were atoned for and I can now walk in freedom from sin and destruction. Thank you, Jesus!"

Notes:

1. Ella LeBain, *Who's Who in the Cosmic Zoo?* Book One – Third Edition, *From Adam's Failure to the Second Adam's Victory,* p. 71-73, Tate, 2013.
2. Blood Sacrifice, https://www.gotquestions.org/blood-sacrifice.html
3. Benjamin L. Corey, *If God Needed A Blood Sacrifice For Sin, God Is Not Holy,* http://www.patheos.com/blogs/formerlyfundie/if-god-needed-a-blood-sacrifice-for-sin-god-is-not-holy/#BHEDstHWfIBm2j4G.99, MARCH 10, 2016
4. Adrian Rogers, *The Blood Covenant,* https://www.lwf.org/sermon-outlines/posts/the-blood-covenant
5. Dr. Dale A. Robins, *Healing is One of God's Benefits,* http://www.victorious.org/healing.htm
6. Tim Laughlin, *The Seven Places Jesus Bled to Set You Free,* The Ministry of Restoration Center, http://www.restorationtrainingcenter.org/seven_places_jesus_bled_to_set_you_free

CONCLUDING WORDS

"And afterward, In the last days, God says,
I will pour out my Spirit on all people.
Your sons and daughters will prophesy,
your old men will dream dreams,
your young men will see visions."
(Joel 2:28; Acts 2:17)

Fallen Angels were once Faithful Angels. They're extraterrestrials who fell from heaven to earth. For whatever reason, and everybody has a story, they got involved in the last galactic war, and made the interior of our planet their home base. Some of whom were bound there, others established ground *inside* the earth.

Let's face it, most planets are hollow, which is where most life exists in the universe. Planets serve as a protective shelter from gamma and cosmic rays. Unlike the special qualities of earth, not all planets are habitable on the surface, nevertheless they are on the *inside.* While it's hard for us to get our heads around the notion that there are human ETs that live *inside* our planet, take note that it has been reported, which I've laid out in detail in Book One of *Who's Who in The Cosmic Zoo?* that Venus[1], as well as other planets and moons, within our solar system, are where the extraterrestrial humans and aliens abide. If they can inhabit and create colonies *inside* our planets in our own celestial neighborhood, then who's to say that other planets aren't inhabited as well?

The ancient adage, *as above, so below*, becomes true again when it comes to the racism, bigotry, antisemitism and general xenophobia that is pervasive on the surface dwellers of planet earth. We must therefore be mindful and aware of ourselves that we do not project the same bigotries onto our fellow humans, who happen to be extraterrestrials. We should always vet them as we would our own kind, who first need to establish themselves to earn our trust. Because many of them have technologies and powers beyond ours, we must equip ourselves with knowledge, which leads to wisdom and discernment, and by developing and nurturing *our* relationship to the Creator, we can only hope and pray that we listen to *His Spirit* to guide us into correctly discerning, *who is who in the cosmic zoo?*

When Jesus Christ returns, they too will see Him in the skies over earth, and every knee shall bow, Romans 14:12: "As surely as I live, says the Lord, *every knee will bow before me*; every tongue will acknowledge God." "On the earth, above the earth and *inside* the earth, that at the name of Jesus every knee should bow, of those in heaven, and of those on earth, and of those *under* the earth and *that* every tongue should confess that Jesus Christ *is* Lord, to the glory of God the Father." (Philippians 2:10-11 NKJV)

The Messiah and Savior Jesus is the one who brings all the races together as one under His lordship. John 10:16 specifically states, His Divine intention with respect to other beings, as He told His disciples before He ascended back into Heaven, "I have other sheep that are not of this sheep pen. I must bring them also. They too will listen to my voice, and *there shall be one flock and one shepherd*."

But for now, the Blood Covenant is the common denominator that brings all races together on earth through salvation in Jesus Christ. To those who are in Christ, they are new creations, the old has passed away, the new is here. (2 Corinthians 5:17) Jesus is the ultimate remedy for racism. This is why, we see all races on earth coming together through the Holy Spirit, become One in Christ. This is God's Divine Plan for Heaven to come to Earth, through the vessels of those who have become His adopted sons and daughters through the Blood Covenant. The *Divine Extraterrestrial Blood* of Yeshua/Jesus Christ eclipses over all other bloodlines on Earth, dissolving racism.

But how can one love God if they don't know *who* He is? Some have been told there is only one god, really? Scripture tells us otherwise. The god of this world is called satan, which in Hebrew literally translates as *adversary*, even *accuser*. There are many adversaries to the God of Love. Many people blame God for what satan does because they can't tell the difference between their supernatural powers. So much so that they identify as atheists. See, Book Two: *Who is God?* [2]

This is why discernment is the most important spiritual muscle to develop in these end times. Because things are going to get even weirder, supernaturally speaking. We're going to be seeing aliens and demons one minute, and mighty godly angels the next.

Isaiah 5:20 is a curse on those who confuse discerning good and evil, by calling good evil and evil good. Same as when you blame God for the works of Satan or credit Satan for God's Creation. "Woe to those who call evil good and good evil, who put darkness for light and light for darkness, who put bitter for sweet and sweet for bitter." (Isaiah 5:20)

This goes for those who think all ETs are fallen angels or all aliens are demons. It isn't clear where many Christians get this idea when the Bible says otherwise. This is why I wrote *Who Is God?*, to prove who God is in relation to the other gods, and there are many. As well as why I wrote *Who Are The Angels?* because discerning His Angels as extraterrestrial messengers, guardians and warriors that make up his celestial armies of heavenly hosts, is part of the work.[3]

It's all in the Scriptures, concealed from most Christians because of mistranslations from Hebrew to English, along with deliberate cover ups of sacred text by the Church of Rome. That's history. I encourage all my readers to look at the Scriptures through the lens of it being an historical record, and not always through the lens of religion, as so many have been programmed and implanted to do. Gods and Angels are merely extraterrestrials. The God of gods, is *Who* created our Universe and Creation of Life. We are a part of that, but so are His other created beings. Therefore, we must expand our perspective into a more *exopolitical viewpoint*, by discussing how as a species, we can integrate this knowledge and apply rules of engagement and policies in dealing with those who may be our ancient ancestors, and perhaps future brothers and sisters in Christ's Kingdom of Heaven.

Christ didn't come to start a new religion, He came to teach and give us *empowerment* through relationship with Him, a *Living God*, who lives and dwells within us through His Spirit. He also commands a vast network of angels, who are extraterrestrial messengers and interdimensionals, to help us. Religion, on the other hand, disempowers people, it can thwart a relationship with Christ through alien implants, designed to do just that, create division, separation, and confusion. Ignorance endangers, knowledge empowers, is what I presented in Book One of this series. And being in *right relationship* is about knowing *who* the Lord is, through empowerment by His Spirit, whose Divine Will is to use us as His vessels to expand His Kingdom on Earth. Quite frankly, making Heaven more crowded through the redemption of souls, even intraterrestrials souls, is a glory undreamt!

Jesus said, "Truly, truly, I say to you, whoever believes in me will also do the works that I do; and greater works than these will he do, because I am going to the Father." (John 14:12) His works were pretty awesome; deliverance of demonic entities, healing the sick; raising the dead and that's not limited to physical death, but those who are *spiritually dead,* are ministries for those who carry his Spirit in these End Times. Miracles follow miracles, and God's blessings never cease. He's alive and well, and saving souls here and now, and that includes the aliens and extraterrestrials with whom we share this planet. Yes, the power of His grace and salvation extends to all.

While some of the fallen angels (rebellious ETs) were imprisoned inside the earth, its key leaders are imprisoned in the 5th Heaven as well as those who may be exempt from the forgiveness of God. The others who live inside this earth, can still repent. As I've pointed out in my conclusive thesis in Book One, many of them, who are known as *Watchers* of the Earth, do witness the incredible transformation of lives when touched by the power of God's grace, mercy, and loving-kindness. It's supernatural, and even extraterrestrials, intraterrestrials and certain alien species are fascinated by it. So those who are *of the redeemed*, your witness is your testimony of transformation, you may just be causing an *extra-terrestrial* being, who secretly watches you, to want what you have, the redemptive power of the Living God! So, whatever you do, do for the glory of God. (1 Corinthians 10:31)

In conclusion in this offering of *Covenants,* Book Four, of this five-book series, I invite you to consider that God's Creation and His Covenants extend beyond us humans on earth, but to all of the human vine of Creation. Remember the math, only one third of heaven's angels (extraterrestrials) followed after Lucifer's rebellion, but two thirds remained faithful to the Creator God. These are our brothers and sisters and perhaps ancient ancestors!

The relationship we have with God is the most valuable of all, and knowing who God is and what He wants us to do is our primary mission in life. Are you listening to the voice of His Spirit or the voice of the Counterfeiter? Can you tell them apart?

You're not alone. Some important Bible characters couldn't tell them apart either, but this fact was covered up and lost in translation. In Book Two, *Who is God?* I point out where the Lord Yahuah shows up in verses when it's actually the Elohim speaking. English Bibles do not do these stories justice and create misunderstanding.[2]

The Elohim were created beings. The Bible tells us that they serve as a council in Heaven. They had sons, who later became the fallen angels. The *Book of Enoch* tells us that there were 200 Bene HaElohim who fell from their first estate and mated with earth women and produced giant offspring known as *Nephilim*, which in Hebrew means, fallen ones, or rejects.

This mistranslation of the very words God, gods, and angels in the Bible Scriptures is why Christians don't see that the Bible really tells us of extraterrestrials who actually serve the Lord and His Kingdom of Heaven.

Who Is God? Book Two of *Who's Who In the Cosmic Zoo?*, is 570 pages of Scriptures with the correct translations from Hebrew to English revealing extraterrestrials in Biblical history and prophecy along with exposing the fleet of spaceships at their command.[2]

Ephesians 6:12 tells us, "We war not against flesh and blood, but against powers, principalities, rulers of the darkness of this present world and spiritual wickedness in the heavens."

I spent the entire length of Book One of *Who's Who In the Cosmic Zoo?* proving and analyzing *who* these powers, principalities, rulers of this world, really are, and who are the spiritual wickedness in the heavens.[1] For a Christian to suggest that all alien life is demonic is only a half-truth. And you know what they say about half truths. Be careful that you don't get hold of the wrong half.

The Politics of Exopolitics

The realm of Exopolitics is certainly no different than any other fields of politics, whether it be Ufology, Church Politics or Government Politics. There is very little unity, and always plenty of divisiveness, competition and disagreement. My first thesis on Exopolitics is found in Book One, however, I want to conclude here, with a few remarks. The need for unity now, couldn't be greater, as the levels of deception are being taken to a new level. Technology, nanobots, implants, transhumanism, and outright possession of human vessels, has never been greater. People in this field must unite by seeking discernment, despite how uncomfortable it may make them. Christian Ufologists need to be included amongst all Ufologists, which has become a field steeped in the darkness of fascination of paranormal and occult activities, who desperately need the light of the discernment of Christ, as well as the power of deliverance from so many dark forces, that are always the focus of these so called, 'New Age Paranormal Groups.'

Those who are invested in Truth and Disclosure must let go of their prejudices and bigotries, of those who believe in Christ. Likewise, Christian Ufologists need to learn how to love, reach out and connect with New Age Ufologists. Both groups have important pieces the other is missing and needs. Many minds, make 'light' work. Yes, it is the job of Christ to be the bridge between everyone, but the first step must happen, with you and me.

There is a civil war going on, that is not limited to America, but to the world, over those who uphold the socialist ideologies of the New World Order Globalism, and those who are more freedom-oriented and hold more of a conservative viewpoint. This war permeates into the fields of Exopolitics as well, which is a spiritual handicap for all those who seek Truth and want Full Disclosure. If leaders of Exopolitics can't accept humans with different viewpoints and ideologies, then how can they accept ET? At least we have 'being human' in common. Who is to say, that the Aliens they seek to contact, are anything like them? Let alone benevolent? It is certainly not fear mongering to discern the motives of others, let alone intraterrestrials who have allegedly been intervening into the affairs of terrestrial humans for millennia.

It was recently reported that the Vatican has already begun to release information about Nibiru entering our solar system. It seems that our extraterrestrial neighbors have already met with Vatican officials, the Nordic Aliens who live inside the earth, however they are not revealing the truth of their agenda, which is to establish and spread a New World Order, One World Religion. The Vatican has dibs to lead and control. This One World Religion comes under the influence of the Nordic Aliens who live inside the earth. It's not even sure if the Vatican actually knows just *who* these Nordics actually are, *who* they were in the past, and why they're contacting the leaders now. We must come together and learn how to connect the dots by discerning their motivations from the past and question, why they are making contact now with the Vatican, the U.S. Government and Russia?

While the mainstream media keeps people preoccupied with distractions about non-sensical news, fake news stories, and Trump bashing, it remains oddly silent about the fact that the Vatican has leaked information about Nibiru and ETs. Meanwhile, disclosure information has been slowly leaked by the Vatican, indicating the presence of extraterrestrials on, and visiting, our planet along with an incoming anomaly called Planet X and/or Nibiru.[4]

The Grace of Revival

Despite what the Dark Forces have planned for this world, in their goals for a New World Order Fascist Dictatorship and One World Religion; on the other hand, the 'Light Forces' of Heaven's Kingdom have planned an End Times Spiritual Revival. This is an outpouring of the Holy Spirit on humankind to lead people to the "Saving" Grace of God through Jesus. This is planned, on the timeline, and in Divine Order. When it reaches you, catch the wave, repent, get your life 'right' with the Lord. Allow Him to 'Lord' over your soul, and you will be saved. Saved from what? Saved from the tyranny of the Draconian Aliens and their New World Order. Saved from the death and destruction of your very soul. Yes, your soul. A soul is created by the Lord and Creator God, a soul, according to God's Word, can be redeemed but it can also be destroyed.

Following after the lies of the aliens, and the Draconian End Times Deception, according to the End Times Prophesies, will be a fatal move toward destruction of the soul, cause that's what they will steal from you. Don't under estimate the enemy of our souls, that he won't go to great lengths, great deceptions and seductions to get it. Likewise, don't under estimate the power of the Savior-King to redeem your soul and save you behind enemy lines. Learn to discern between kingdoms, between what is of the god of this world, who is Lucifer-the Satan, and what is from the God of gods and Heaven's Kingdom. Both operate in opposite spirits.

Grace is the supernatural power of God at work in your life. It's extravagant love. Grace is expressed as the undeserving, reckless yet generous love of God to those who reject Him, rebel against Him. The very last bastion of Grace on Planet Earth is the Holy Spirit. Once that leaves the planet, all hell will break loose.

As I pointed out in Book Three: *Who Are the Angels?* the very last call towards repentance towards God, so that His Grace can be poured out on souls who have lost their way towards His Kingdom of Heaven, is when He sends Extraterrestrial Messengers, we call Angels, down to Earth to shout to all those on the surface of the earth while flying in mid-air over the space above Earth, to "repent" – "turn back to God" – "accept Jesus as Savior."[3]

> "Then I saw another angel flying overhead, with the eternal gospel to proclaim to those who dwell on the earth — to every nation and tribe and tongue and people."
>
> He said in a loud voice, "Fear God and give Him glory, because the hour of His judgment has come. Worship the One who made the heavens and the earth and the sea and the springs of waters."
>
> Then a second angel followed, saying, "Fallen, fallen is Babylon the great, who has made all the Gentiles to drink the wine of the passion of her immorality."
>
> And a third angel followed them, calling in loud a voice, "If anyone worships the beast and its image, and receives its mark on his forehead or hand,...he too will drink the wine of God's anger, poured undiluted into the cup of His wrath. And he will be tormented in fire and brimstone in the presence of the holy angels and of the Lamb.... And the smoke of their torment will rise forever and ever. Day and night there will be no rest for those who worship the beast and its image, or for anyone who receives the mark of its name."
>
> Here is a call for the endurance of the saints who keep the commandments of God and the faith of Jesus....
>
> (Revelation 14:6-12)

This has to do with the very last days of the End Times. This prophecy, at the time of this publication of this manuscript, has not yet been fulfilled, but when it does, I hope you will remember these words, and choose to be reconciled back to the Creator through Christ.

There are so many people today who have been implanted with the lie, that 'they are the change they've been waiting for' or; that 'they are gods'; or, 'that they don't need a Savior, they can save themselves.' All these are lies from the god of this world, who is Lucifer, the Satan. He doesn't want you to turn to Christ, because that means he loses power over you, and no longer has legal 'rights' to your soul, your mind and your body. When Jesus steps in through His Holy Spirit, lives are transformed, and delivered from the powers of darkness, both in the flesh and in the spirit.

NASA Acknowledges Nibiru

A NASA Press Release in 1992 stated the following: "Unexplained deviations in the orbits of Uranus and Neptune point to a large outer solar system body of 4 to 8 Earth masses on a highly tilted orbit, beyond 7 billion miles from the Sun."[4]

In my next and final book of the *Who's Who in the Cosmic Zoo?* series, you will learn just where Nibiru is in the Bible scriptures, what it's connection to the final chapter of this processional Age of Pisces, the Second Coming of Christ, and the Terrible Day of the Lord. I will connect the dots to the linguistics of ancient Mesopotamia and the land of Canaan, which became Israel, given to the Israelites, also known as the Hebrews, and their connection to Nibiru. No coincidence that the words Nibiru and Hebrew sound alike. Book Five, *The Heavens* will be packed with historical, scriptural and the latest astronomical data on the final chapter of this age, and the appearance of this ancient planet along with its inhabitants.

Does any true believer in God and Jesus really think that God doesn't have a plan to deal with these aliens? He most certainly does, and it's laid out all over Scriptures, but was concealed through mistranslations, mistransliterations of key words and the names of God, and I prove it through Hebrew Linguistics, History, a little Archeology and Scriptures.

I have no problem believing that Jesus Christ who sits at the right hand of the Father who is in Heaven, has other sheep that are not on this planet (extraterrestrials to us), that He will bring them together with us one day in Heaven. (John 10:16) To think we are the only ones in the universe, is like thinking that the earth is flat or that the earth is the center of the universe, just as both of those old false beliefs have since been debunked, we will be taken to the next level of understanding when the fullness of disclosure is complete. The Lord is lord of all. It's not just about us.

Enslavement or Salvation?

When the Church learns the truth about alien and extraterrestrial life, created by God, it should not cause a falling away from one's faith, but to the contrary, increase our faith and admiration in a God who is the Creator of all the universe, not just planet Earth. All aliens are not demons, this is a half-truth. The other half is that God created extraterrestrial life that too needs His Saving Supernatural Grace. Christians tend to be so self-centered, they think it's all about them, they tend to believe in the lies that God replaced Israel with Gentile Believers (known as the Demonic Heresy of Replacement Theology), likewise they tend to believe the lies that God didn't create Extraterrestrial beings, and if He did, they're all fallen angel demons. They think they are the only ones who are going to get the Kingdom. This is a huge misnomer, and a gross misinterpretation of His Word. The Kingdom of Heaven, implies that it's a vast Kingdom that spreads out throughout the Heavens. Psalm 19:1 declares: "The Heavens declare the Glory of God." So, how can Christians think or believe that we're alone, with only demons?

As I've stated before in previous books in this series, and it's worth repeating for emphasis and to prove this point, Scriptures say only one-third of Heaven's Angels (extraterrestrials) rebelled and fell from their first estate in Heaven. Remember the math, that means that two-thirds of Heaven's Extraterrestrial Angels remained faithful to the Creator and the Kingdom of Heaven. So, there should be no excuse for Christians to doubt that God did not create extraterrestrial and alien life outside of this earth.

Of course, this is understandable, when His Word has been chopped up, edited, and fragmented into Rejected Texts, because the Church of Rome, under the influence of the god of this world and the aliens *who* have lived inside the earth for millennia, saw manipulating God's Word as an opportunity to rule over the masses. We know that religion doesn't save us, but only a personal, intimate relationship with the Creator of our Souls and His Savior can save us from the bondage of the aliens who wish to enslave us. We also know that other beings that God created became enslaved too, and they too need to be pointed to the true Savior and Messiah King who is Mighty to Save.

To suggest that there is only an alien gospel, as many Christians are being implanted today to believe, without knowledge of God's mighty extraterrestrial army, is not only half the story, but missing the true gospel written all over Scriptures and into the very stars themselves.

In Book Five, *The Heavens* I will prove to you, this very fact, that God's Word on Earth was first written into the Constellations and Starry Hosts long before scriptures appeared on earth, which was a message to *all* creation, here on Earth and in the vastness of the Heavens. These messages were designed to be *Signs in the Heavens*, as harbingers of the age to come. As earth dwelling humans, we must at least understand and respect this fact, and by the time you're done reading *The Heavens,* which is the concluding book in this five-book series of *Who's Who in The Cosmic Zoo?* I am confident you will understand and *know* this truth too.

The Truth is Stranger Than Fiction!
~Finis~

Who's Who in The Cosmic Zoo? Book Four – *Covenants*
www.whoswhointhecosmiczoo.com

Notes:

1. Ella LeBain, *Who's Who in the Cosmic Zoo? A Spiritual Guide to ETs, Aliens, Gods & Angels,* Book One – Third Edition, *Venusians*, p. 412, Tate Publishing, 2013.
2. Ella LeBain, *Who is God? Book Two of Who's Who in the Cosmic Zoo?* Skypath Books, 2015.
3. Ella LeBain, *Who are the Angels? Book Three of Who's Who in the Cosmic Zoo?* Skypath Books, 2016.
4. Mike, Aliens-Conspiracies, *What The Church Isn't Telling You About Nibiru And The Annunaki*, https://hidden-truth.net/2017/07/church-isnt-telling-nibiru-anunnaki/, July 24, 2017

NOTES AND BIBLIOGRAPHY

Chapter One: The End Times Disclosure of Alien Life

1. Lloyd Vries, Mexican A.F. Pilots Film UFOs, https://www.cbsnews.com/news/mexican-af-pilots-film-ufos/, May 12, 2004
2. Stephen Spielberg, Director - Screenplay, *Close Encounters of the Third Kind,* 1977
3. Stephen Spielberg, Director, Melissa Mathison, Screenplay, *ET,* 1982.

Chapter Two: How Disclosure of ETs Impacts Religion

1. Joel Richardson, *Mideast Beast* (New York: WND Books, 2012). p. 39
2. Ella LeBain, *Who is God?* Book Two, Skypath Books, 2015.
3. http://ancientufo.org/2016/06/nasa-granted-1-1million-study-alien-life-impact-christianity/
4. http://helenastales.weebly.com/blogue/why-did-nasa-issue-a-11million-grant-to-study-how-alien-life-could-impact-christianity
5. Ella LeBain, *Who's Who in The Cosmic Zoo?* Book One, *A Spiritual Guide to ETs, Aliens, Gods and Angels,* Tate. 2013, http://www.whoswhointhecosmiczoo.com

Chapter Three: How Prepared are the World's Religions for ET?

1. David Weintraub, Professor of Astronomy and Physics, Vanderbilt University, *Religions and Extraterrestrial Life – How Will We Deal With It?* Springer International Publishing, 2014.
2. Ella LeBain, *Who Is God?,* Book Two, Skypath Books, 2015.
3. Ella LeBain, *Who Are the Angels?,* Book Three, Skypath Books, 2016.
4. David Weintraub, Ph.D., Professor of Astronomy and Physics, Vanderbilt University, *Religions and Extraterrestrial Life – How Will We Deal With It?* Springer International Publishing, 2014.

5. Guy Consolmagno and Fr. Paul Mueller, *Would You Baptize an Extraterrestrial? and Other Questions from the Astronomers' In-box at the Vatican Observatory,* Image, Random House, New York, 2014. [p. 252, 254-257]
6. Ibid., p.252
7. Ibid., p. 255-256
8. Ibid., p. 256-257
9. David Weintraub, Ph.D., *Religions and Extraterrestrial Life – How Will We Deal With It*? Springer International Publishing, 2014.
10. Ella LeBain, *Who's Who in the Cosmic Zoo?,* Book One-Third Edition, *A Spiritual Guide to ETs, Aliens, gods and Angels,* See, Concluding Words, Tate, 2013, http://www.whoswhointhecosmiczoo.com
11. David Weintraub, Ph.D., Professor of Astronomy and Physics, Vanderbilt University, *Religions and Extraterrestrial Life – How Will We Deal With It?* Springer International Publishing, 2014.
12. David Salisbury, Are the world's religions ready for E.T.? https://news.vanderbilt.edu/2014/09/29/religion-ready-for-et/ September 29, 2014
13. Robert Hugh Benson, Catholic Monsignor, *Lord of the World*, Dodd, Meade & Co., 1907
14. Pope Francis, *The Pope Video -Inter-Religious Dialogue,* www.popesprayer.net; www.thepopevideo.org
15. Michael E. Salla, Ph.D., *Will Dalai Lama Join Pope Francis in Disclosing Extraterrestrial Life?,* http://exopolitics.org/will-dalai-lama-join-pope-francis-in-disclosing-extraterrestrial-life/, October 8, 2017
16. Valdemar Valerian, *Matrix III, The Bio-Chemical, Neurological and Electronic Mind Control of the Masses,* Leading Edge Research Group, 1991.
17. Michael E. Salla, Ph.D., *World Religions Unite as Prelude to Extraterrestrial Disclosure,* http://exopolitics.org/world-religions-unite-as-prelude-to-extraterrestrial-disclosure/ June 22, 2017
18. Ella LeBain, *Who's Who in the Cosmic Zoo?* Book One – Third Edition, Chapter One: *Discerning Categories,* p. 25-42, Tate, 2013.
19. Ibid., p.90-91, WWCZ-B1-3ed

Chapter Four: Contracts and Agreements

1. The Text of the *Gospel of Thomas* from the Scholars Version translation published in *The Complete Gospels,* verse 103, https://selfdefinition.org/christian/Gospel-of-Thomas-Scholars-Version-15-pages-1961.pdf
2. Ibid., verse 16a, 16b

3. Art Matthias, *Biblical Foundations of Freedom,* Wellspring Ministries 2000, p. 59
4. *Gospel of Thomas,* Ibid, verse 102
5. Robert M. Stanley, *Covert Encounters in Washington, D.C.,* CreateSpace, April 18, 2011
6. Alfred Labremont Webre, JD, MEd., Exopolitics Blog: *Secret U.S. Mars program & Life on Mars,* http://wxopolitics.blogs.com/exopolitics/2011
7. Ibid., Stanley, 2011
8. Art Mathias, *Biblical Foundations of Freedom-Destroying Satan's Lies with God's Truth, In His Own Image-We Are Wonderfully Made,* Wellspring Publishing, 2000, 2010, www.akwellspring.com

Chapter Five: Agreements with God

All Bible quotes from http://www.biblehub.com

Chapter Six: Aliens and Religion

1. Frederich Engles and Karl Marx, *The Communist Manifesto,* 1948.
2. Clifford Geertz, *Religion as a Cultural System*, 1973.
3. Talal Asad, *The Construction of Religion as an Anthropological Category*, 1982.
4. Ella LeBain, *Who Are the Angels?* Book Three, Chapter Six: *Fallen Angels and Watchers*, p. 127-132, Skypath Books, 2016.
5. Zecharia Sitchin, *Genesis Revisited, Earth Chronicles,* Mass Market, 1990.
6. Ella LeBain, *Who's Who in the Cosmic Zoo?* Book One – Third Edition, Chapter on Giants, p. 208, Tate, 2013.
7. Chuck Missler and Mark Eastman, *Alien Encounters: The Secret Behind the UFO Phenomenon,* Koinonia House Inc; Revised edition (October 31, 2003).
8. Erich von Däniken, *Chariots of the Gods: Unsolved Mysteries of the Past,* BANTAM; Reprint edition (1972).
9. Ella LeBain, *Who's Who in the Cosmic Zoo?* Book One – Third Edition, *Annunaki,* p. 110-118, Tate, 2013
10. *Who's Who in the Cosmic Zoo?* Book One – Third Edition, *Draconians,* pp.154-181
11. Dr. Michael Salla, *Insiders Reveal Secret Space Program and Extraterrestrial Alliance,* Exopolitics Consultants, Hawaii, 2015
12. William Mills Tompkins, *Selected by Extraterrestrials: My life in the Top-Secret World of UFOs, Think-Tanks and Nordic Secretaries,* CreateSpace, 2010; 2ed. 2016.

13. Kate Ravilious, *Mars Melt Hints at Solar, Not Human, Cause for Warming, Scientist Says,* National Geographic News, February 28, 2007, http://news.nationalgeographic.com/news/2007/02/070228-mars-warming.html
14. Dr. Marcus Garvey Jr., *The Arab Muslim Slave Trade Of Africans, The Untold Story,* November 15, 2012, http://originalpeople.org/the-arab-muslim-slave-trade-of-africans-the-untold-story/
15. Ella LeBain, *Who is God?* Book Two, Skypath Books, 2015.
16. Used with Permission from *The Religion of Peace*, www.thereligionofpeace.com/Quran/025-Muhammads-sex-life.htm
17. Rhonda Robinson, News Real Blog, February 5, 2011
18. Jim Rutz, *Megashift,* Empowerment Press (CO), 2005.
19. http://www.pewforum.org/files/2015/03/PF_15.04.02_ProjectionsFullReport.pdf
20. Wiki Answers: https://en.wikipedia.org/wiki/Christian_population_growth#cite_note-PewProjections-2
21. Ella LeBain, *Who is God?* Book Two: Chapter Twenty-Three: *Babylonian History, Where it All Began,* subsection: *Who is Semiramis?* Skypath Books, 2015. p.371-373
22. Art Mathias, *Wellspring School of Ministry,* https://akwellspring.com/
23. David H. Stern, Ph.D., *Restoring the Jewishness of the Gospel: A Message for Christians,* Messianic Jewish Publishers, Clarksville, MD., 1998.
24. Art Mathias, *Wellspring School of Ministry Workbook,* p.47, Wellspring Publishing, 2010, https://akwellspring.com/
25. Freedom from Religion Foundation, https://ffrf.org/
26. Dr. Chuck Missler, *Religion is Just a Patsy,* http://www.khouse.org/articles_cat/
27. Ella LeBain, *Who Is God?* Book Two, Chapter Eight – *Who Are the Gods?* pp. 129-136, Skypath Books, 2015.
28. Ella LeBain, *Who's Who in the Cosmic Zoo?* Book One – Third Edition, Chapter-Five: Draconian-Reptilians, p.154-177, Tate, 2013.
29. Ibid., *Who is God?* Book Two: Chapter: Twenty-Six: *The Office of Christ,* sub-section: *Will the Real Savior Please Step Up,* p.432-440.
30. Ibid., *Who's Who in the Cosmic Zoo?* Book One, Ibid., pp. 411-412

Chapter Seven: Who Created Religions? God or ETs?

1. Joel Richardson, *The Islamic Antichrist,* WND, March 3, 2015
2. Bob Unruh, *Islamic Antichrist? 'What do you say we go start slaughtering people so Jesus will come back',* http://www.wnd.com/2011/02/26498

5/#0hWdu5xVw1bvLWW0.99http://www.wnd.com/2011/02/264985/, February 18, 2011

3. Ella LeBain, *Who Is God?* Book Two - Chapter Twenty-Four: *What is Islam?* Sub-section: *What is Sharia Law?* pp. 397-399, Skypath Books, 2015.
4. Virchand Raghavji Gandhi, Nicolas Notovitch, *The Unknown Life of Jesus Christ: From an Ancient Manuscript Recently Discovered In A Buddhist Monastery,* translated from French, 1887. http://www.tubetoptelevision.com/the/the-unknown-life-of-jesus-christ-from-an-ancient-manuscript-recently-discovered-in-a-buddhist-english.pdf
5. Nicholas Notovich, *The Unknown Life of Jesus Christ,* Wilder Publications, December 18, 2008.
6. Levi H. Dowling, *The Aquarian Gospel of Jesus The Christ,* 1920, http://www.sacred-texts.com/chr/agjc/
7. John Jay Report, *The Nature and Scope of Sexual Abuse of Minors by Catholic Priests and Deacons in the United States* 1950-2002. United States Conference of Catholic Bishops, Washington, D.C., 2004, Bruni, p. 336
8. Tom Horn, *Apollyon Rising 2012,* Defender Publishing, Craine, MO. 2009. p. 328-329.
9. Malachi Martin, *Keys of this Blood: Pope John Paul II Versus Russian and the West for Control of the New World Order,* Simon and Schuster, New York, 1991. p. 63
10. Malachi Martin, *Windswept House,* Doubleday, New York, 1996. p. 7
11. *The Whore of Babylon,* Wikipedia, https://en.wikipedia.org/wiki/Whore_of_Babylon
12. James Orr, *International Standard Bible Encyclopedia,* Wm. B. Eerdmans Publishing Co.,1939. http://www.internationalstandardbible.com/
13. Ella LeBain, *Who Is God?* Book Two – Chapter Eight: *Who Are the Gods?* p. 129-136, Skypath Books, 2015.
14. Ibid., *Who is God?* Chapter Seven: *Discernment of Gods, Angels and Demons,* sub section: *The Divine Feminine and the False Goddess,* p. 108-112.

Chapter Eight: Replacement Theology

1. Chaiyim Ben Ariel, *Why Did Yeshua Use Spit to Heal People?* http://melbournenazareneisrael.ning.com/forum/topics/why-did-yeshua-use-spit-to-heal-people
2. William L. Coleman, *Man for Sabbath or Sabbath for Man?* Eternity, September 1977, p. 58
3. https://www.liveleak.com/view?i=24c_1270331419#HId22WKZuq2cheZs.01; http://www.israelnationalnews.com/News/News.aspx/166255#.UU7sRzetq95

4. Ella LeBain, *Who Is God?* Book Two: *The Lifeforce is in the Blood,* p. 262, Skypath Books, 2015.
5. Ibid., *Who Is God?* Chapter Thirteen: *The Name Above All Names,* p.201-222.
6. Ella LeBain, Book Two*: Who is God?* Chapter Twenty-Nine: *Who Created Sexism?*, pp. 485-500 Skypath Books, 2016
7. Ibid., *Who Is God?* Chapter Twenty-Nine: *Who Created Sexism?*, pp. 485-500 Skypath Books, 2016
8. *Reincarnation: The Church's Biggest Lie,* https://www.facts-are-facts.com/article/reincarnation-the-churchs-biggest-lie
9. Ibid., *Who is God?* Chapter Twenty-Eight: *What Happens When You Die?* pp. 455-484
10. Ella LeBain, *Religion and Religious Spirits,* http://www.findingfreedom.name/religion-and-religious-spirits.html, 2012
11. Ibid., *Who is God?* Chapter Thirteen: *The Name Above All Names,* p.201-232, *What's in a Name?* p. 213, Skypath Books, 2016.
12. Ibid., *Who Is God?* Chapter Twenty-Three: *Babylonian History: Where It All Began,* pp. 367-398.
13. "A searchable list of congregations, ministries, and businesses related to the Messianic Community in Israel." (as of March 2016) http://app.kehilanews.com/directory
14. Ibid., *Who Is God?* Chapter Twenty-Three: *Babylonian History: Where It All Began,* pp. 367-398.
15. Pastor John Hagee, *In Defense of Israel,* FrontLine; Revised edition (September 7, 2007).

Chapter Nine: One World Religion

1. Michael E. Salla, Ph.D., *World Religions Unite as Prelude to Extraterrestrial Disclosure,* http://exopolitics.org/world-religions-unite-as-prelude-to-extraterrestrial-disclosure/ June 22, 2017
2. Tom Horn, Cris Putnam, *Exo-Vaticana, Petrus Romanus, Project L.U.C.I.F.E.R., and the Vatican's Astonishing Plan for the Arrival of an Alien Savior,* Defender, 2013.
3. Tom Horn, Cris Putnam, *Petrus Romanus, The Final Pope is Here,* Defender, 2012.
4. Ella LeBain, *Who's Who in the Cosmic Zoo?* Book One – Third Edition, Chapter Four: *How to Tell Who is Who?* p. 85-92, Tate, 2013.

Chapter Ten: Racism Was Created by the Fallen Feuding ETs

1. John Stokes, *Scientists find Extraterrestrial genes in Human DNA,* http://www.agoracosmopolitan.com/home/Frontpage/2007/01/08/01288.html, 2007 The Canadian.
2. Thomas Horn, *Apollyon Rising,* Defender Publishing, p. 238
3. Alok Jha, *Breakthrough Study Overturns Theory of 'Junk DNA' in Genome,* https://www.theguardian.com/science/2012/sep/05/genes-genome-junk-dna-encode, Science Correspondent, September 2012
4. Michael Hanlon, *'Junk DNA' and the Mystery of Mankind's Missing Genes.* http://www.telegraph.co.uk/news/science/9534185/Junk-DNA-and-the-mystery-of-mankinds-missing-genes.html, Sept. 2012.
5. Ella LeBain, Book One of *Who's Who in the Cosmic Zoo?* Third Edition, *Anakim, Annunaki,* p. 219-222, Tate, 2013.
6. Joe Kovacs, *Shocked by the Bible,* WND, 2008, p. 186-188
7. Ann Madden Jones, *The Yahweh Encounters: Bible Astronauts, Ark Radiations and Temple Electronics,* The Sandbird Publishing Group, 1995, p. 60
8. I.D.E. Thomas, *The Omega Conspiracy: Satan's Last Assault on God's Kingdom,* Official Disclosure, December 1, 2007.
9. Thomas Horn, *Nephilim Stargates,* Defender, 2007.

Chapter Eleven: Genetic Engineering and Alien Abductions in Prophecy

1. Ella LeBain, *Who's Who in the Cosmic Zoo?* Book One – Third Edition, *The Grays and Soul-Transplantation,* p.271, Tate, 2013
2. Joe Kovacs, *Shocked by the Bible,* WND, 2008, p 186
3. Albert Brooks, Screenplay, Director, movie, *Defending Your Life,* 1991.
4. Dannion Brinkley, *Saved By the Light: The True Story of a Man Who Died Twice and the Profound Revelations He Received,* Villard Books, 1994.

Chapter Twelve: Gene Wars?

1. Ella LeBain, *Who's Who in the Cosmic Zoo?* Book One – Third Edition, *The Grays and Soul-Transplantation,* p.271, Tate, 2013
2. Joe Kovacs, *Shocked by the Bible,* WND, 2008, p 186

3. Albert Brooks, Screenplay, Director, movie, *Defending Your Life,* 1991.
4. Dannion Brinkley, *Saved By the Light*: *The True Story of a Man Who Died Twice and the Profound Revelations He Received,* Villard Books, 1994.

Chapter Thirteen: The Grand Experiment

1. R.A. Boulay, *Flying Serpents and Dragons: The Story of Mankind's Reptilian Past,* The Book Tree; Revised edition (July 1, 2003)
2. Zecharia Sitchin, *Genesis Revisited (The Earth Chronicles)* Avon Books, 1990.
3. Zecharia Sitchin *Twelfth Planet: Book I of the Earth Chronicles* Stein and Day, 1976.
4. Ibid.
5. William Bramley, *The Gods of Eden, The Chilling Truth about Extraterrestrial Infiltration and the Conspiracy to Keep Humankind in Chains,* Avon (March 1, 1993)
6. Graves, R., *The White Goddess, An Historical Grammar, of Poetic Myth,* Creative Age Press, 1948.
7. Ella LeBain, *Who's Who in the Zoo?* Book One – Third Edition, Tate, 2013.
8. Dr. Carl Werner, *Evolution: The Grand Experiment,* New Leaf Publishing Group; Rev Upd edition (May 15, 2014)
9. Ella LeBain, *Who is God?* Book Two, Chapter: *What Happens When You Die?* p.455-484, Skypath Books, 2015
10. Ella LeBain, *Who's Who in the Zoo?* Book One – Third Edition, *Annunaki* p. 219, Tate, 2013
11. Ibid
12. Ibid
13. Carl Sagan, *The Dragons of Eden: Speculations on the Evolution of Human Existence* Hardcover – Random House, New York, 1977.

Chapter Fourteen: UFOs in Israel

1. Ella LeBain, *Who is God?* Book Two, Skypath Books, 2015.
2. Daniel Perez, *From Jediism to Judaism: Star Wars as Jewish Allegory,* http://www.aish.com/j/as/From-Jediism-to-Judaism-Star-Wars-as-Jewish-Allegory.html
3. Ella LeBain, *Who's Who in the Cosmic Zoo?* Book One – Third Edition, pp. 39-41, Tate, 2013
4. Ella LeBain, *Who Are the Angels?* Book Three, Skypath Books, 2016.

5. Barry Chamish, *Are Giants Returning to the Holy Land?* http://www.mt.net/~watcher/chamishgiants.html
6. Patrick Knox, *DID A UFO GIVE URI HIS POWERS? How Uri Geller was 'struck by a blinding beam from a floating ball of light aged three' – and was witnessed by an air force captain; Psychic claims to have met faceless alien who was holding a bright light.* Uri Geller's UFO Experience Age 3: https://www.thesun.co.uk/news/2681284/uri-geller-psychic-ufo-alien-visit/, January 23, 2017
7. Haaretz, *Fars-ical Snowden Files Prove U.S. Run by Nazi Aliens, Iran Says; Secret regime of extraterrestrial race called 'Tall Whites' - who used to be in cahoots with the Third Reich - is currently running the show in America, semi-official news agency Fars reports.* https://www.haaretz.com/news/world/1.568551?v=B27DCABFCF16697C4BE09863819D43BD January 14, 2014
8. Michael E. Salla, Ph.D., *World Religions Unite as Prelude to Extraterrestrial Disclosure,* http://exopolitics.org/world-religions-unite-as-prelude-to-extraterrestrial-disclosure/ June 22, 2017
9. UFO Sightings in Israel: http://www.ufo-hunters.com/sightings/country/ISR/Israel
10. *Evidence of Aliens visited Earth and ancient codes found in Vatican's library by Russian Scientist in the 20*'s, http://ufosightingshotspot.blogspot.com/2014/06/evidence-of-aliens-visited-earth-and.html
11. Paul Stonehill, *Russian scientist found to be UFO and ancient aliens Researcher,* http://www.openminds.tv/russian-scientist-found-ufo-ancient-aliens-researcher/28381, June 19, 2014
12. *Ancient Aliens*, History Channel, Season 11-Episode 12, www.history.com/shows/ancient-aliens/season-11/episode-12
13. *Evidence of Aliens visited Earth and ancient codes found in Vatican's library by Russian Scientist in the 20*'s, http://ufosightingshotspot.blogspot.com/2014/06/evidence-of-aliens-visited-earth-and.html

Chapter Fifteen: Were Aliens Behind the Holocaust?

1. John Wear, *Germanys War, the Origins, Aftermath, and Atrocities of WW2,* American Free Press, 2015.
2. Ron Rosenbaum, *Explaining Hitler: The Search for the Origins of His Evil,* HarperCollins, 1998.
3. Henry Lincoln, *The Holy Place*, Arcade, 1991.

4. https://worldtruth.tv/the-vatican-holocaust/ 28/32
5. one-evil.org - https://worldtruth.tv/the-vatican-holocaust/
6. Dr. Philip S. Berg, *Power of Aleph Beth, Volume 1,* p. 10-11, Research Center of Kabbalah Press, Jerusalem, 1988.

Chapter Sixteen: Who is the AntiChrist?

1. William Mills Thompkins, *Selected by Extraterrestrials: My Life in the Top-Secret World of UFOs, Think-Tanks and Nordic Secretaries,* CreateSpace, December 2015.
2. Dr. Michael Salla, *The U.S. Navy's Secret Space Program & Nordic Extraterrestrial Alliance, Book Two of the Secret Space Programs Series,* Exopolitics Consultants, Hawaii, 2017.
3. Boston Globe, https://www.bostonglobe.com/news/special-reports/2002/01/06/church-allowed-abuse-priest-for-years/cSHfGkTIrAT25qKGvBuDNM/story.html, January 6, 2002
4. Ella LeBain, *Who's Who in the Cosmic Zoo?* Book One, Third Edition, pp. 154-177, Tate Publishing, 2013.
5. Ella LeBain, *Who is God?* Book Two, *The Cloudships,* p. 75-82, Skypath Books, 2015.

Chapter Seventeen: Cosmic Karma & Ancient Curses

1. Ken and Jeanne Harrington, *From Curses to Blessings: Removing Generational Curses,* Destiny Image, 2011
2. Art Mathias, *Biblical Foundations of Freedom, Destroying Satan's Lies with God's Truth,* p. 43, Wellspring Publishing, Alaska, 2010.
3. Carl L. Fox, Paul D. Norcross, *Breaking the Authority of the Bastard Curse: Restoring the Congregation of the Lord* – p. 59, Christian Faith International Ministries; 2nd Edition, 2004
4. Ibid, p. 60
5. Ella LeBain, *Who's Who in the Cosmic Zoo?* Book One – Third Edition, *Nephilim,* p. 326-338, Tate, 2013.
6. Fox/Norcross, p. 61
7. Traci Morin, *Conceived Out of Wedlock,* https://www.healingdeliverance.net/child-conceived-out-of-wedlock/
8. Ella LeBain, *Who is God?* Book Two, Skypath Books, 2015.

9. Art Mathias, *Handbook on How to Minister*, Wellspring Publishing, Alaska, 2010
10. Finis J. Dake, *Dake's Annotated Reference Bible-KJV*, Dake Publishing, 2014
11. Art Mathias, p. 29-32
12. Chester D. Kylstra, Betsy Kylstra, *Restoring the Foundations: An Integrated Approach to Healing Ministry* (2nd Edition) – Proclaiming His Word, Inc., August 1, 2001
13. John W. Milor, *Aliens and the Antichrist,* Xlibris Corp; July, 2000
14. Ella LeBain, *Who Are the Angels:* Book Three, Chapter: *The Cosmic Christ,* p.364-416, Skypath Books, 2016.
15. Milor, p.5
16. Milor, p.6
17. Milor, p.7
18. Ella LeBain, *Who is God?* Book Two – Chapter: *The Motherships of the Lord,* p. 71-88, Skypath Books, 2015

Chapter Eighteen: Gateways

1. Joshua Gillin, *How Pizzagate Went from Fake News to a Real Problem for a D.C. Business,* http://www.politifact.com/truth-o-meter/article/2016/dec/05/how-pizzagate-went-fake-news-real-problem-dc-busin/, December 5, 2016
2. Wikileaks, The Pizzagate Wikiteam, formerly, The #Pizzagate Review, http://pizzagate.wiki/Main_Page
3. Missing Children in America: Unsolved Cases, http://abcnews.go.com/US/missing-children-america-unsolved-cases/story?id=19126967, By ABC News Staff, May 8, 2013.
4. The Trafficking of Children, https://en.wikipedia.org/wiki/Trafficking_of_children
5. https://www.reference.com/government-politics/many-people-murdered-day-united-states-4ce42c4182d89232
6. 11 Facts About Human Trafficking, https://www.dosomething.org/us/facts/11-facts-about-human-trafficking

Chapter Nineteen: Stargates

1. David Flynn, *Cydonia: The Secret Chronicles of Mars*– End Time Thunder Publishers, 2002.

2. Thomas R. Horn, *Nephilim Stargates: The Year 2012 and the Return of the Nephilim*, p.82, Defender Publishing LLC (July 1, 2007)
3. Ella LeBain, *Who Are the Angels?* Book Three, *Cosmic Christ*, p. 364-416, Skypath Books, 2015.
4. Ella LeBain, *Who's Who in the Cosmic Zoo?* Book One – Third Edition, p. 208. Tate, 2013.
5. I.D.E. Thomas, *The Omega Conspiracy, Satan's Last Assault on God's Kingdom*, p. 107, Official Disclosure (December 1, 2007)
6. George Orwell, *1984,* Signet Classics, July 1, 1950.
7. Ella LeBain, *Who Are the Angels?* Book Three, Chapter Fifteen: *Ascension or Rapture?* p. 303-337, Skypath Books, 2016
8. Ella LeBain, *Who is God?* Book Two, Chapter Twenty-One: *The Office of Satan,* p. 331-358; Chapter Twenty-Five: *Who is the Beast?* P. 399-424, Skypath Books, 2015.
9. *How Bush's Grandfather Helped Hitler's Rise to Power,* https://www.theguardian.com/world/2004/sep/25/usa.secondworldwar
10. *Iraq StarGate Key to 911 and Bush,* http://ireport.cnn.com/docs/DOC-719922
11. https://m.youtube.com/watch?v=JR_Hmgk8pys

Chapter Twenty: Ark of the Covenant

1. Ella LeBain, *Who's Who in the Cosmic Zoo?* Book Two, *Who is God?,* Technology of the Ark, [pp. 38-41] Skypath Books, 2015
2. Graham Hancock, *The Sign and the Seal: The Quest for the Lost Ark of the Covenant* Touchstone (July 2, 1993)
3. *Ancient Aliens* [Season 6/Episode 10] *Aliens and the Lost Ark,* History Channel.
4. Doug Yurchey, *High Technology in the Bible,* https://www.themystica.com/mystica/articles/h/hight-technology_in_the_bible.html 2002.
5. Jake Wallis Simons, *The rabbi, the lost ark and the future of Temple Mount,* http://www.telegraph.co.uk/news/worldnews/10287615/The-rabbi-the-lost-ark-and-the-future-of-Temple-Mount.html, September 12, 2013
6. Britt Gillette, *The Ark of the Covenant and Jesus,* https://www.prophecyupdate.com/the-ark-of-the-covenant-and-jesus.html
7. Ron Wyatt Discovers *ARK OF COVENANT and JESUS BLOOD SAMPLE Full Testimony,* https://www.youtube.com/watch?v=XNr_U1EWRTY, January 9, 2012.
8. Tim McHyde, *The Ark of the Covenant Found* https://escapeallthesethings.com/ark-of-the-covenant-found/, August 23, 2014

9. Jonathan Gray, *The Ark of The Covenant.*, Ind Group; 3rd edition (December 31, 1997)
10. Ron Wyatt's Death Bed Confession, Ark of Covenant, https://www.youtube.com/watch?v=kjQYjpXIP6s

Chapter Twenty-One: The New Age Christian

1. Ella LeBain, Book Two: *Who Is God?* chapter, *What Happen When You Die*? p. 455-484, Skypath Books, 2015.

Chapter Twenty-Two: Who's Channeling Who?

1. Art Mathias, *Biblical Foundations for Freedom: Destroying Satan's Lies with God's Truth*, p.10, Wellspring Publishing, 2010.
2. Ella LeBain, *Who's Who in the Cosmic Zoo?* Book One – Third Edition, Sirius p. 389-399, Tate, 2013.
3. Neal Donald Walsch, *Conversations with God: An Uncommon Dialogue,* Hampton Roads, 1995.
4. H. Constance Hill, *Wisdom from Beyond*, Diamond Clear Vision, 2010
5. Book One of *Who's Who in the Cosmic Zoo?* Ashtar, p. 127-134
6. Ella LeBain, Book Two: *Who Is God?* Chapter Twenty-Eight, *What Happens When You Die?* p. 455-484, Skypath Books, 2015.
7. John Milor, *Aliens and the Antichrist, Unveiling the End Times Deception,* p. 28. iUniverse, Inc., 2006.
8. Book One of *Who's Who in the Cosmic Zoo?* Nephilim, p.326-338.
9. Ella LeBain, Book Three: *Who Are the Angels?* Chapter Four: *Angel Protocol,* p. 71-113, Skypath Books, 2016
10. Book Three: *Who Are the Angels?*, Chapter: Twelve: *The World of the Wondrous,* p.251-258, Chapter Fifteen: *Ascension or Rapture?* p. 303-337.

Chapter Twenty-Three: Are Aliens Demons?

1. Ella LeBain, *Who's Who in the Cosmic Zoo?* Book One – Third Edition, Tate, 2013.
2. Bill Cooper, *Behold A Pale Horse,* "New World Order Planners" p. 177, Light Technology Publishing (December 1, 1991)

3. Ella LeBain, Book Two: *Who Is God?* Chapter Twenty: *The God of this World - Lucifer, Rahab and The Stones of Fire*, p. 322-330, Skypath Books, 2015.
4. Leon Festinger, Henry Reicken and Stanley Schachter, *When Prophecy Fails,* Amazon Digital Services, June 3, 2013
5. Ella LeBain, Book Three: *Who Are the Angels?* Chapter Fifteen: *Ascension or Rapture?* p. 303-337

Chapter Twenty-Four: The Masquerade of Ascended Masters and Angels

1. Karla Turner, Ph.D., Ted Rice, *Masquerade of Angels,* Kelt Works, Arkansas,1994
2. Gene Roddenberry, *Star Trek: The Next Generation*, Season 3 - Episode 4 *Who Watches the Watchers,* 1989.
3. Ella LeBain, Book Three: *Who Are the Angels?* Chapter Five: *Celestial Warriors: Extraterrestrials with Extraordinary Powers,* p. 114-117, Skypath Books, 2016.
4. *Books of Enoch,* Chapter 15:8-12 – Nephilim, Giants.
5. Ella LeBain, *Who's Who in the Cosmic Zoo?* Book One – Third Edition, Grays p. 248-289, Tate, 2013.
6. Theresa Emmanuel Grey, http://www.ascendedmasterindex.com/avatars.htm, 2009.

Chapter Twenty-Five: Time Travel and Teshuva (Repentance)

1. Bennet, Ellen H. (1897). *Cosmogony, or Creation of the World. Astrology: Science of Knowledge and Reason: A Treatise on the Heavenly Bodies in an Easy and Comprehensive Form.* New York. pp. 30–7. OCLC 11451986.
2. Rabbi Avi Shafran, *Rosh Hashanah: When Time Travel Is Possible,* https://www.haaretz.com/jewish/jewish-world-opinions/.premium-1.675478
3. Rabbi Avi Shafran, *A Jewish Guide to Time Travel,* https://www.rabbiavishafran.com/jewish-guide-time-travel/
4. https://www.haaretz.com/jewish/jewish-world-opinions/.premium-1.675478

Chapter Twenty-Six: Who is the Restrainer?

1. Ella LeBain, *Who Are the Angels?* Book Three, Chapter Fifteen: *Ascension or Rapture?* p. 303-337, Skypath Books, 2016.

2. Ella LeBain, *Who is God?* Book Two, Chapter Four: *Motherships of the Lord,* p. 71-88, Skypath Books, 2015.
3. John Milor, *Aliens and the Antichrist, Unveiling the End Times Deception,* p. 132 iUniverse, 2006.
4. Milor, p. 147
5. Milor, p. 148
6. Ella LeBain, *Who Are the Angels?* Book Three, Chapter Fifteen: *Rapture or Ascension?* p. 303-337, Skypath Books, 2016.
7. John Walvoord, *The Rapture Question,* p.271, Zondervan, 1979.
8. Dr. Chuck Missler, DVD: *The Rapture: Christianity's Most Preposterous Belief,* Koinonia House, Coeur d'Alene, ID, 2010.

Chapter Twenty-Seven: Prophesies, Blessings & Curses of the Twelve Tribes of Israel

1. Art Mathias, *Wellspring School of Ministry Workbook,* Wellspring Publishing, 2010
2. Ella LeBain, *Who's Who in the Cosmic Zoo?* Book One – Third Edition, *The Religious Spirit,* p. 361-380, Tate, 2013.
3. Ilan Lior, *Israel Deporting Swedish Holocaust Survivor's Daughter - Because Her Father Allegedly Converted,* November 20, 2017, https://www.haaretz.com/israel-news/.premium-1.823740
4. http://www.bethadonai.com/FAQ_number_jewish_believers.html

Chapter Twenty-Eight: Restoration of Israel

1. Soncino Zohar Volume II p. 67b
2. Steven M. Collins, *The Lost Ten Tribes of Israel Found!,* published by CPA Books
3. Yair Davidy, *Lost Israelite Identity/Hebrew Ancestry of Celtic Races,* by, published by Russell-Davis publishers, Shiloh-Hebron - Susia - Jerusalem-Beth-El, Israel
4. *The Lost Tribes.* retrieved from: <pbs.org>
5. Rabbi Yirmiyahu Ullman. *The Lost Tribes Where are they Today?* <ohr.edu/yhiy/article.php/1817; www.rabbiullman.com>
6. Rabbi Eliyahu Avichail, *The Ten Lost Tribes of Israel in Afghanistan, Pakistan, Kashmir, Myanmar, and China.* Amishav Organization. North American Conference on Ethiopian Jewry Arimasa Kubo.

7. Charles B. Williams, translation, *The New Testament: A Translation in the Language of the People*, Adesite Press, August, 2015.
8. *Was the Yellow Emperor an Extraterrestrial?* http://ancientufo.org/2016/07/yellow-emperor-son-heavens/

Chapter Twenty-Nine: Messianic Prophecies and the Lost Tribes of Israel

1. Are Native Americans Part of the Lost Tribes? By JewsNews, https://www.jewsnews.co.il/2013/05/25/are-native-americans-part-of-the-lost-tribes.html, May 25, 2013.
2. The Lost Tribes. retrieved from: <pbs.org>
3. The Amplified Bible, Zondervan (February 1, 2001)
4. Rev Willem J.J. Glashouwer, *Jerusalem, the UN and the times of the Gentiles*, http://www.whyisrael.org/2017/01/12/jerusalem-the-un-and-the-times-of-the-gentiles/, January 2017.

Chapter Thirty: The Marriage Covenant

1. Ella LeBain, *Who's Who in the Cosmic Zoo? A Spiritual Guide to ETs, Aliens, Gods & Angels,* Book One - Third Edition, *Enter the Archons,* p.30, Tate Publishing, 2013.
2. Kevin Ewing, *Did You Marry into a Generational Curse?* http://kevinlaewing.blogspot.com/2014/03/did-i-marry-into-generational-curse.html, March 22, 2014

Chapter Thirty-One: Implants & Spiritual Limitation Devices

1. Ella LeBain, *Who's Who in the Cosmic Zoo?* Book One-Third Edition, Tate Publishing, 2013.
2. Dr. David Jacobs, Director of the International Center for Abduction Research, www.ufoabduction.com/; Dr. David Jacobs, *Secret Life: Firsthand, Documented Accounts of UFO Abductions*, Touchstone; Reprint edition (April 16, 1993)
3. Dr. John Mack, *Abduction: Human Encounters with Aliens,* Scribner, New York, 1994.
4. Merit Freeman, http://consciousawareness.wixsite.com/home/adrenochrome, June 12th, 2014

5. Ella LeBain, *Who's Who in the Cosmic Zoo? Book One-Third Edition,* Tate. 2013, pp.154-182; 381.
6. Ella LeBain, *Who is God?* Book Two of *Who's Who in the Cosmic Zoo?,* Skypath Books, 2015. *What Happens When You Die?* pp. 455-483
7. Don Robertson, *The 9th Alleged ET Implant Removal by Dr. Roger Leir & Team,* 2000. Dr. Roger Leir, Implant Removal, Tim Cullen between 1995-1998; http://www.rense.com/ufo6/implant.htm
8. Dr. Joshua David Stone, Ph.D., *Hidden Mysteries* Light Technology Publishing, 1995.
9. #PIZZAGATE? #PEDOGATE, The OSTO Network, https://osto.space/pgate/
10. Douglas Hamp, *Corrupting the Image: Angels, Aliens, and the Antichrist Revealed,* Defender, July 1, 2011
11. Janet Boynes, *Called Out: A Former Lesbian's Discovery of Freedom,* Creation House (December 19, 2008), http://www.janetboynesministries.com/

Chapter Thirty-Two: The Rainbow Covenant

1. Thad Morgan, *How did the Rainbow Flag become an LGBT Symbol?* June 2, 2017, http://www.history.com/news/ask-history/how-did-the-rainbow-flag-become-an-lgbt-symbol
2. *What Does the Number Seven Represent in the Bible?* http://www.patheos.com/blogs/christiancrier/2014/09/26/what-does-the-number-seven-7-mean-or-represent-in-the-bible/#ub8XegsBMekU4jjg.99r.
3. Leah Marieann Klett, *Ken Ham: The Ark Encounter Will be Permanently Lit with Rainbow Lights to 'Take Back' Symbol from LGBT Community,* July 19, 2017, http://www.gospelherald.com/articles/71141/20170719/ken-ham-ark-encounter-permananetly-lit-rainbow-lights-take-back.htm
4. May Bulman, *Lesbian couples two and a half times more likely to get divorced than male same-sex couples, ONS figures reveal More than three quarters of the splits between same sex couples in England and Wales were between two women.* October 18, 2017, http://www.independent.co.uk/news/uk/home-news/lesbian-couples-more-likely-divorced-male-same-sex-marriages-uk-ons-figures-a8006741.html
5. The Harburg Foundation, Biography of Yip Harburg, http://yipharburg.com/about-yip-2/biography/
6. Rabbi Jonathan Cahn, *The Harbinger, The Ancient Mystery that Holds the Secret of America's Future,* Frontline (January 3, 2012)

7. Andrew Lloyd Weber, *Joseph and the Amazing Technicolor Dreamcoat,* "Close Every Door," 1968.
8. Rabbi Bernhard Rosenberg, *Somewhere Over the Rainbow' from Jewish Perspective,* December 10, 2014, https://www.mycentraljersey.com/story/life/faith/2014/12/10/somewhere-rainbow-jewish-perspective/20104523/
9. *The Powerful Message Behind 'Over the Rainbow',* https://www.cufi.org.uk/spotlight/the-powerful-message-behind-over-the-rainbow/, November 2015 | Spotlight.

Chapter Thirty-Three: The Blood Covenant

1. Ella LeBain, *Who's Who in the Cosmic Zoo?* Book One – Third Edition, *From Adam's Failure to the Second Adam's Victory,* p. 71-73, Tate, 2013.
2. Blood Sacrifice, https://www.gotquestions.org/blood-sacrifice.html
3. Benjamin L. Corey, *If God Needed A Blood Sacrifice For Sin, God Is Not Holy,* http://www.patheos.com/blogs/formerlyfundie/if-god-needed-a-blood-sacrifice-for-sin-god-is-not-holy/#BHEDstHWfIBm2j4G.99, MARCH 10, 2016
4. Adrian Rogers, *The Blood Covenant,* https://www.lwf.org/sermon-outlines/posts/the-blood-covenant
5. Dr. Dale A. Robins, *Healing is One of God's Benefits,* http://www.victorious.org/healing.htm
6. Tim Laughlin, *The Seven Places Jesus Bled to Set You Free,* The Ministry of Restoration Center, http://www.restorationtrainingcenter.org/seven_places_jesus_bled_to_set_you_free

Concluding Words

1. Ella LeBain, *Who's Who in the Cosmic Zoo? A Spiritual Guide to ETs, Aliens, Gods & Angels,* Book One – Third Edition, *Venusians,* p. 412, Tate Publishing, 2013.
2. Ella LeBain, *Who is God? Book Two of Who's Who in the Cosmic Zoo?* Skypath Books, 2015.
3. Ella LeBain, *Who are the Angels? Book Three of Who's Who in the Cosmic Zoo?* Skypath Books, 2016.
4. Mike, Aliens-Conspiracies, *What the Church Isn't Telling You About Nibiru And The Annunaki,* https://hidden-truth.net/2017/07/church-isnt-telling-nibiru-anunnaki/, July 24, 2017

ABOUT THE AUTHOR

Ella LeBain is the author of a five-book series, *Who's Who in The Cosmic Zoo? An End Times Guide to ETs, Aliens, Gods & Angels.*

Ella LeBain is originally from New York City and was educated in Israel. She received a Social Sciences Degree from the Biological Research Center of the Negev in 1979 where she was schooled in Biblical Hebrew, and then went on to receive an Astronomy Degree from the Hayden Planetarium in New York City in 1982.

Ella spent two years working as a missionary in apartheid South Africa in the early 1980s, where she embarked on what has become a 38-year journey to get to the truth about UFOs, Aliens, ETs, gods and angels and how they all fit into the end of our age scenario. Ella spent twenty-five years in the field of UFO research, investigating alien abductions, paranormal activities and the connection between astronomy and astrology, during which time she had many supernatural experiences of her own along the way, which shaped the writing of her books.

Ella has collected a plethora of information from a variety of sources, in addition to her own experiences which have been incorporated into this Book set. Book One is a type of Encyclopedia, covering *Who's Who in the Cosmic Zoo of ETs and Aliens* in an A-Z Compendium. Book Two - *Who Is God?* focuses on the Cosmic Drama, that identifies and discerns *who* are the ET gods of ancient history based on both biblical and exobiblical scriptures. Book Three - *Who Are the Angels?* focuses on the hierarchy of angels (extraterrestrial messengers) including the fallen ET angels as well as those who have remained faithful to the Creator. She reveals how they have been interacting with humankind for millennia and connects the dots to the important starring roles they play at the end of this age. Book Four - *Covenants,* explores and discerns the spiritual legal ground and real *Star Wars* between ETs, Aliens, gods and Angels. Book Five - *The Heavens,* discerns the *Signs in the Heavens* that have long been prophesied to show up as harbingers of the end of this present age, heralding the Age to Come.

Ella LeBain is available for interviews, lectures and book signings.

Website: http://whoswhointhecosmiczoo.com
Buy the Books: http://www.whoswhointhecosmiczoo.com/buy-the-book.html
Contact Page: http://whoswhointhecosmiczoo.com/contact.html
Email: ellalebain@whoswhointhecosmiczoo.com

Made in the USA
Columbia, SC
14 April 2024

34335711R00322